ADVANCE PRAISE FOR

CRIME: Public Policies for Crime Control

*"Public discourse on crime and crime control is often dominated by conventional wisdom and ideological pronouncements. **CRIME: Public Policies for Crime Control** challenges this state of affairs by focusing on data and research to tell us what is known, and equally important, what is still to be learned about crime and its prevention and control. Wilson and Petersilia have engaged some of the best minds in the business, and the result is a comprehensive, sophisticated, and intelligent volume, suitable for a wide audience, including students, policymakers, and researchers. **CRIME** should be on the shelf of everyone who seeks to understand crime and to do something about it."*

— JOHN H. LAUB
Professor of Criminology and Criminal Justice
University of Maryland

"What accounts for recent changes in crime rates? What, if any, gun control, policing, or drug and alcohol strategies work best, and under what conditions? What does the latest empirical research tell us about the efficacy of adult community corrections or youth crime prevention programs? In this timely and well-edited volume, an intellectually and ideologically diverse group of leading experts offers cutting-edge answers to these and many other questions vital to the future of federal, state, and local crime policy in America."

— JOHN J. DIIULIO, JR.
Frederic Fox Leadership Professor, University of Pennsylvania,
and Former Director, White House Office of
Faith-Based and Community Initiatives

"Wilson and Petersilia have done it again and assembled some of the most gifted minds to shed light on one of our most complex social problems. The result is a sophisticated and intelligent book that covers an impressive array of policy-oriented research. This book is particularly timely as the economy slows and the nation searches for ways to keep the crime rate down. For those who study crime or make crime policy, this book is required reading."

— JEREMY TRAVIS
Senior Fellow, The Urban Institute,
former Director, National Institute of Justice

CRIME

CRIME

Public Policies For Crime Control

James Q. Wilson and Joan Petersilia
EDITORS

ICS PRESS

INSTITUTE FOR CONTEMPORARY STUDIES
OAKLAND, CALIFORNIA

© 2002 Institute for Contemporary Studies

Printed in the United States of America. All rights reserved. No part of this book may be used or reproduced in any manner without written permission, except in the case of brief quotations in critical articles and reviews.

This book is a publication of the Institute for Contemporary Studies, a nonpartisan, nonprofit, public policy research organization. The analyses, conclusions, and opinions expressed in ICS Press publications are those of the authors and not necessarily those of the institute or of its officers, its directors, or others associated with, or funding, its work.

Inquiries, book orders, and catalog requests should be addressed to ICS Press, 1611 Telegraph Ave., Suite 406, Oakland, California, 94612. (510) 238-5010. Fax (510) 238-8440. To order, call toll free (800) 326-0263.

Crime was set in Garamond type by Rohani Design, and printed and bound by Phoenix Color.

Library of Congress Cataloging-in-Publication Data

Crime: public policies for crime control / James Q. Wilson and Joan Petersilia, editors.
 p. cm.
Includes bibliographical references and index.
ISBN 1-55815-509-0 (alk. Paper)
 1. Crime prevention—United States. 2. Crime—United States.
3. Crime. 4. Criminology. I. Wilson, James Q. II. Petersilia, Joan

HV9950.C7473155 2001
364.973—dc21   2001024924

3 3131 00077 3568

MONROE COUNTY COMMUNITY COLLEGE LIBRARY
MONROE, MICHIGAN

DEDICATION

To my parents, Ann and Ernie Ramme, for their unconditional love and encouragement. I could not have wished for more.

J.P.

To Richard J. Herrnstein, scholar, colleague, and friend.

J.Q.W.

Contents

Foreword
from the Publisher

I have learned from personal experience that one of the testaments to our experiment in self-governance is service on a jury. It is an experience that every citizen should welcome, because it teaches so much about what is involved in being a citizen and the great responsibilities that we carry.

One of the roles that every juror must perform is to reflect and choose within a community of their peers. This is a concrete example of Alexander Hamilton's presumption, ratified in the constitution, that societies of men and women, through reflection and choice, could choose good government.

When a citizen is called to serve on a jury dealing with a criminal matter, all of the issues raised in this book are implicated in the decisions that will be made in the courtroom, for the court is a key nexus where crime and public policy meet.

Policy makers and judges face even more complex decisions than individual citizens, for within the constraints of our Constitution these policy makers must seek ways to address such issues as how to use police effectively and legally to combat crime, how to sentence convicted criminals, and how to aid communities who are seeking ways to make their streets and homes safer. Just like the jurist, the policy maker must ultimately choose. In good policy processes, this requires arraying alternatives and then marshalling evidence.

For both groups, professionals and individuals, *Crime: Public Policies for Crime Control* provides invaluable information about the capabilities and limitations of potential policies and strategies for addressing issues of crime. This is basically a new book from the 1995 book *Crime: Twenty-eight leading experts look at the most pressing problem of our time*. The editors decided they wanted to provide policy makers as well as students with the latest scientific evidence on the key aspects of crime and what it suggests in terms of policy options.

So how does the student, legislative aide, or police officer use this book? How does one craft public policies or make decisions about crime-related issues using the information in this book? Good public policy processes are based on reflection and choice. Good choices in part are based on alternatives for which evidence regarding their capabilities and limitations to realize the stated goals are specified. Whether it be gun control, community policing, or drug prevention strategies, *Crime: Public Policies for Crime Control* will give you invaluable information on both the capabilities and limitations of alternative policies. It provides the foundation for the reader to begin thinking about complex problems.

It is my bet that if a student will take any given sub-issue of crime, state his or her current policy preference, and then begin to array the evidence from this book, the end result will be different from the starting position. This is one of the great joys of public policy work: the unexpected solutions. The second great joy of public policy work is the puzzling-out of strategies, using ideas and evidence to create a new way of looking at old issues. *Crime: Public Policies for Crime Control* provides the reader with a great opportunity to explore the complex public policy issue of crime in new and unexpected ways.

—Robert B. Hawkins, Jr., President
Institute for Contemporary Studies

Publication of this volume was made possible through the generosity of the Lynde and Harry Bradley Foundation.

1

Introduction

JAMES Q. WILSON AND JOAN PETERSILIA

The essays in this book were written in order to show how social science research might inform our efforts to understand and control crime. We use the word *inform* advisedly. Social science cannot be an unambiguous guide to policy. Though it is a useful source of knowledge, especially about the causes of crime, that knowledge is neither sufficiently comprehensive nor adequately tested to be a reliable source of policy decisions. And even if it were comprehensive and well tested, it would consist chiefly of statements about the general relationship between two or more factors (for example, that between the probability of punishment and the level of crime). Policymakers ought to know these connections, but they cannot be guided simply by what is generally true. They must also make judgments about individuals accused of crime; the particulars of time, place, and circumstance surrounding a crime; the trade-offs between the factors bearing on crime (for example, between the crime-reduction effect of prison and the costs of a large prison population); and the moral and legal bases of crime-control strategies.

This caution is not meant to suggest that social science supplies "the facts" and policymakers supply "the values." Social scientists will supply both facts and values (every author in this book has selected topics and themes that, on value grounds, seemed important to him or her), and policymakers will select their own facts as well as many values (every politician must judge how people feel about crime and respond to many facts that, though important, no one has studied).

To us, one of the most encouraging developments of the last four decades has been the increased cooperation between social scientists and policymakers. Though they obviously play different roles, each now draws upon the other's knowledge in ways that rarely existed before the 1960s. The government spends money on academic research, and many parts of the criminal justice system make use of some of these findings. Many of

1

the ideas that shape crime-control policy—the concept of the career criminal, the desire to maintain public order as well as arrest individual offenders, the effort to develop community-oriented or problem-solving policing, the creation of crime-prevention programs—arose out of academic writings. The gap between "practitioners" and "the ivory tower" has been narrowed, although of course it still exists. After all, practitioners must cope with real-world problems, while the ivory tower worries about many things that may make problem-solving harder, not easier.

Despite this inevitable gap, many people—liberals, conservatives, and libertarians—often make a common mistake when they think about crime. They assume that we already understand the problem and its solution and all we need is action. Most people have at least as much confidence in their view of crime as they have in their views of child-rearing, popular music, and how to improve the local baseball team. "As everyone already knows," they begin, and then urge some course of action.

But in fact, not everyone already knows what ought to be done about crime. They may have strong opinions, but reliable knowledge is much harder to come by. Some people think that crime results from unemployment, inadequate schooling, and the availability of guns. If so, they should read carefully the chapters by Shawn Bushway and Peter Reuter; by Denise C. Gottfredson, David B. Wilson, and Stacy S. Najaka; by Steven D. Levitt; and by Philip J. Cook, Mark H. Moore, and Anthony A. Braga. Some people think that anyone who grows up in a good family will be inoculated against criminality. If so, they should study the chapter by Adrian Raine on how biology predisposes some people to (though certainly does not solely cause) crime. Other people think that putting more police on the streets, imposing longer sentences, and getting rid of useless crime-prevention programs will reduce crime. If so, they should read the chapters by Lawrence W. Sherman, Brian Forst, Alfred Blumstein, and Patrick Tolan. And other people think that legalizing drugs will cut the crime rate. If so, they should ponder the chapter by David A. Boyum and Mark A. R. Kleiman. No author in this book thinks he or she knows of a silver bullet that will end crime, but all of them can tell you a lot of things about what works and what does not.

This edition of *Crime* differs from the last one in several important respects. New chapters have been added on deterring crime, crime prevention, and criminal rehabilitation. New authors have been enlisted to revise and update the chapters on biomedical factors, the family, schools, the labor market, the physical environment, and probation and parole. The chapters on crime rates, juvenile crime, the community, gun control, alcohol and drug abuse, the police, prisons, and prosecution have been revised by the original authors. The final chapter on crime and public policy has been completely rewritten.

As before, in selecting the authors of these chapters, the editors did not look for people with whom they agreed; indeed, the editors are not necessarily in agreement on all matters either. We searched instead for the best available scholars. This book, therefore, does not represent a single point of view, but it does present what we think is the best scholarship on crime and criminal justice. There is no other single volume, we think, that provides as inclusive and as authoritative an account of the research findings on these topics.

We hope that this book will stimulate discussion and clarify issues for policymakers, community leaders, and students of crime and criminal justice. But far more important than the programs to be embraced are the methods to be learned: We want these essays to teach people how to think about crime and the policies that might be used for its reduction. The story of crime is, after all, the story of one side of human nature. Understanding crime is as difficult as understanding the human personality.

2

Crime in International Perspective

James Lynch

For many years conventional wisdom held that the United States was both the most crime-ridden and the most punitive of industrialized nations. More recently, with massive decreases in crime, some argue that our nation's punitiveness has resulted in lower rates of crime than many other industrialized nations. This chapter reexamines both the historic and emerging conventional wisdom and finds them too simple to be useful. The United States continues to have higher levels of lethal violence than other nations, but similar or lower levels of minor violence and property crime than nations normally considered more civil. In terms of prison use, the picture has become much simpler: The United States uses imprisonment for every category of crime more often than other industrialized nations. This is a departure from the past when the use of imprisonment was not radically different from other nations for serious violence; although the propensity to incarcerate and time served has been greater in the United States than in other nations for property and drug offenses.

Cross-national comparisons are often used to inform debates about crime and justice in the United States and elsewhere (Koppel 1992; Maurer 1991; Trebach and Inciardi 1993). Other nations, particularly those similar to the United States in culture and level of development, are used as standards to which the United States should aspire. These comparisons are useful mirrors for evaluating our public policy and searching for ways to improve it. The danger of using cross-national comparisons for these purposes is that they are difficult to do well. The "foreign-ness" of culture, laws, and practices in other nations makes it easy to misrepresent policies and outcomes, and thereby the relative condition of countries. This misinformation distorts rather than informs policy debates by focusing attention on mythical problems or by overstating those that do exist.

While cross-national comparisons should be made, we must be aware of the limitations of such comparisons. In an effort to serve both these ends, this paper examines the conventional wisdom on crime and justice in the United States. Beliefs that the United States is the most crime-ridden and the most punitive of industrialized nations are based upon casual cross-national comparisons of the United States with other countries. More rigorous comparisons are made to illuminate the most common problems with these comparisons, and to see if conventional wisdom can withstand this type of scrutiny.

CHOOSING THE APPROPRIATE OBJECT OF COMPARISON

Most of the issues in cross-national comparisons are unique to the subject being addressed. As we will see in the following sections, the pitfalls common to comparisons of crime are different from those affecting studies of responses to crime. Nonetheless, some issues are common to all cross-national comparisons. Principal among these universal problems is the choice of appropriate nations to compare. Almost any comparison can be enlightening. For the purposes of evaluating or advocating policy, however, comparisons of very similar nations are more useful than comparisons of those very dissimilar (MacCoun et al. 1993). Such comparisons generate both heat and light. They generate the heat necessary for improvement because it is more difficult to attribute observed differences between nations to some fundamental cultural (or equally immutable) difference and thereby dismiss them. Comparisons of similar nations also generate more light in that they suggest that successful policies can be transplanted and may even suggest how or under what conditions.

For purposes of informing criminal justice policy, nations are similar to the extent that their criminal justice systems operate in similar environments. These environments are defined in large part by those institutions of social control that are less formal than the criminal justice system and that employ less coercive force. These less coercive institutions include family, community, schools, and work. The role of the criminal justice system is to intervene when and where these institutions of social control break down (Bittner 1967, 1973). The major burden of social control is carried by these less coercive institutions. Their relative effectiveness will determine the task confronting the criminal justice system in a particular country. Where these institutions are weak or in flux, then intervention by the justice system will be both prevalent and severe.[1]

The second major component of the environment is the political and legal institutions operating in a particular nation. These arrangements shape the types of responses that criminal justice agencies make to the exigencies presented by the relative effectiveness of the less coercive institutions of social control. For example, the response of criminal justice agencies in democratic nations to breakdowns in major institutions of social control will be different from the response in nondemocratic societies. Presumably, agencies in democracies will be less likely to engage in overt, broad-based, and prolonged coercion than will those in nondemocratic nations. In addition, the specific division of labor and the procedures followed on a daily basis within the criminal justice system will also be influenced by the legal culture of the nation. Police in common-law nations, for example, may be more restrained from intruding into the lives of the citizenry than police in civil code countries, but when they do intrude, the police have broader powers to detain than they would in nations with code traditions (Langbien 1979; Lynch 1988).

Nations that are more similar to the United States on these three dimensions will provide much more useful points of comparison than countries that are less similar. Using this schema, nations such as England and Wales, Australia, and Canada would be the best points for comparison because they have similar levels of participation in the major institutions of social control as the United States; they are democracies; and they have common law legal traditions. France, Germany, and the Netherlands would be less similar and therefore less useful because they have somewhat higher rates of participation in the less coercive institutions of social control and do not have common law legal traditions. Switzerland and Sweden, for example, would be even less similar still because of their very high levels of participation in less coercive institutions, very high levels of democracy, and the lack of a common law legal tradition.

CHOOSING THE APPROPRIATE METHOD OF COMPARISON

As with objects of comparison, any method of comparison can be enlightening, but some are more appropriate for policy research than others. Cross-national studies of crime and criminal justice issues have customarily employed two different methodologies—comparative case studies and quantitative models (Farrington and Langan, 1992; Lynch et al. 1994).

The former compare two or several nations on a particular policy or issue.[2] They offer a great deal of descriptive information on the nation and the policy. Comparisons are made qualitatively or on the basis of simple statistics. The latter method employs samples of twenty, thirty, or more nations. Very little descriptive information is provided on policies or practices in the sampled nations. Formal models are used to understand differences in policies or outcomes across nations. These models are tested using very sophisticated multivariate techniques.[3]

These two methods are complementary, and each contributes to our understanding of cross-national differences in policies and outcomes. At this time and for the purposes of informing policy debates, however, comparative case studies hold the most promise and will be emphasized in the discussions that follow. If, as noted above, it is the very foreignness of nations that complicates cross-national studies, then the most important attribute of a study is to "get things right"—that is, policies and outcomes are accurately characterized in and across nations (MacCoun et al. 1993). Comparative case studies have a better chance of doing that than studies employing large samples of nations. This is especially the case with studies of prison populations, for reasons that are presented later in this chapter.[4]

Even when policies and outcomes are understood and accurately characterized across nations, these country-level multivariate models are quite fragile and potentially misleading. First, measures of policies and outcomes are based on highly aggregated data, such as national means or other measures of central tendency. The distribution of crime or sentences in two nations can be very different, but the measures of central tendency can be the same, thereby obscuring the differences. Second, the results of these models are highly dependent upon the group of nations included as well as the variables in the model. Since sample sizes are small (usually ranging from eighteen to thirty-four), including or excluding even a few nations can radically change the results obtained. Similarly, adding or deleting a single variable or employing a different measure for a concept can alter the results. Again, this is aggravated by small samples in that only a few predictors can be included in any model and researchers must choose carefully. Third, usually only simple-direct-effects models can be tested, again because of sample-size limitations. This limits a priori the information that can be gleaned from these studies. These problems affect much of the quantitative modeling in the social sciences, but they are particularly severe in cross-national studies because the level of aggregation is very high and the samples are very small.

Finally, although nation-level quantitative models may contribute to testing theories, they are not as appropriate for informing policy. Theory building requires the identification of principles that hold across all or a specific set of nations. Policymakers are usually more concerned about conditions in their nation or some similar country than they are about general principles that may or may not adhere in their nation. Quantitative models often do not provide the information necessary to determine if the principles pertain to a specific nation. Similarly, it is often sufficient in theory building to identify relationships or principles that are not due to sampling error. The strength of that relationship or its impact on the outcome is less important in formulating policy—the question of how much difference it makes is central. We will see in subsequent sections that many of the "significant" relationships found with quantitative models have little effect on crime rates or other outcomes.

With these two limits on our review, we will now turn to two pieces of common wisdom that have emerged from cross-national comparisons—that the United States is the most crime-ridden nation in the world and that it is also the most punitive of industrialized nations.

CONVENTIONAL WISDOM: THE UNITED STATES IS THE MOST CRIME-RIDDEN OF MODERN INDUSTRIALIZED NATIONS

The basis for this bit of conventional wisdom is not clear. It may be that the country is suffering from its Wild West or gangster movie image. Certainly, there have been spectacular crimes, such as those involving the murder of tourists in Florida, that have attracted a great deal of attention. Also, the extremely high homicide rate in the United States may be a major contributor to the image of the country as the most crime-ridden of developed nations. But homicide is not coincident with crime in general, indeed it is a very rare event even in the United States. Moreover, anecdotes are weak evidence.

There are better sources of evidence available in the form of new and improved statistical systems designed to measure the prevalence of crime cross-nationally. These statistical series have routinized the collection of information on a broad range of crimes in a manner that avoids some of the most common errors in anecdotal observation. While these systems have their limitations (which will be discussed below), they can provide a useful test of the common wisdom, if they are used with an appreciation of their strengths and weaknesses.[5]

Determining the Prevalence of Crime Cross-nationally

There are two major sources of statistical data on crime incidence cross-nationally—police statistics and victimization surveys. Police statistics are compiled internationally by Interpol (Interpol 1988), the United Nations (Kalish 1988), and a number of independent researchers (Gurr 1977; Archer and Gartner 1984; Bennett and Lynch 1990).[6] Victim survey data are routinely collected independently by a number of nations (Kaiser, Kury, and Albrecht 1991), and the International Crime Survey (ICS) has been conducted in as many as thirty-three different jurisdictions (van Dijk, Mayhew, and Killias 1990; Mayhew and van Dijk, 1997). Each of these data sources can tell us something about the relative prevalence (and incidence) of crime across nations. Each also has its own set of distortions that can result in misleading comparisons across nations. It is important to use each source of data for that which it does best.

Cross-national Comparisons: Simple and Complex

From the perspective of police statistics, the United States has much higher rates of serious violence than other industrialized democracies, even those nations most similar in terms of the environment of the criminal justice system.[7] As Table 2.1 shows, the homicide rate in the United States is more than three times that of the next-highest countries—Canada and Scotland—and many times that in other common law countries such as England and Wales. The same is generally true for robbery but the differences are much smaller. The police-reported robbery rate in the United States is only 15 percent higher than in France and 28 percent higher than in England and Wales, but it is 179 percent greater than in Austria and 150 percent higher than in Italy.

With respect to serious property crime, however, the United States is considerably lower than other similar nations. The burglary rate in Australia is 2.7 times that in the United States, in England and Wales it is twice the U.S. rate, and in Canada the police-reported burglary rate is 1.3 times that of the United States. Even the Netherlands, which enjoys the reputation of a low-crime country, has burglary rates 2.45 times greater than the U.S. rate. Among the industrialized democracies we compared, only France has a lower rate of burglary than the United States.[8] The picture is much the same for auto theft. Among the nations most institu-

Table 2.1
Rates of Crime Reported to the Police per 100,000 Population by Nation and Offense, Interpol 1998

	OFFENSE			
NATION	HOMICIDE	ROBBERY	BURGLARY	MVT
Australia	1.537	127.626	2,338.41	706.199
Austria	0.810	59.210	6,008.19	35.788
Canada	1.834	95.551	1,155.69	547.191
England & Wales	1.445	128.506	1,832.69	752.953
France	1.654	144.104	676.855	546.214
Germany	1.200	78.488	1,507.11	137.364
Netherlands	1.195	92.410	3,100.43	238.961
Scotland	1.853	96.699	2,118.73	555.332
Sweden	1.500	70.000	356.00	629.00
United States	6.258	165.235	861.999	459.035

SOURCE: Interpol 1999; Farrington, Langan, and Wikstrom 1994; Wikstrom 2000.
NOTE: MVT = Motor Vehicle Theft

tionally similar to the United States, such as Australia and England and Wales, all have higher rates of auto theft. The nations more dissimilar to the United States are evenly split between those with substantially higher rates (Canada, France, Italy, and Scotland) and those with lower rates (Germany, Austria, and the Netherlands).

The view from victim surveys is similar to that from police statistics in many respects and different in others. United States respondents report high levels of violent crime, but these levels are not significantly different from those in some countries most institutionally similar to the United States, such as Australia, England, and Wales (Table 2.2). In general, however, the rates of violence reported in the victimization survey are approximately 40 percent higher in the United States than in other industrialized democracies.

The differences between the United States and other nations with respect to property crime in the victim surveys are similar to those found in the police statistics. The prevalence of theft is greater in the Netherlands, Australia, and England and Wales than in the United States. The theft rate

Table 2.2

Percent Victimized in the Past Year by Nation and Offense, 1996

NATION	OFFENSE			
	TOTAL VIOLENCE	ROBBERY	TOTAL THEFT	TOTAL BURGLARY
Australia	6.0	1.3	26.1	7.5
Austria	5.2	1.2	23	6.2
Canada	7.3	1.4	25.7	6.4
England & Wales	4.9	1.0	21	4.6
France	5.5	0.8	15.7	3.1
Germany	2.1	1.3	21.4	4.1
Netherlands	4.8	0.6	28.7	5.9
Scotland	5.0	0.8	18.8	4.0
Sweden	5.0	0.5	22.4	2.4
United States	7.0	1.3	22.4	5.6

SOURCE: International Crime Survey 1996; Mayhew and White 1997.

is essentially the same as the U.S. rate in Canada, France, Sweden, and Italy. Of the countries examined, only Germany has a substantially lower prevalence of theft than the United States When we restrict our comparisons to more serious property crime, such as burglary, there are still a number of nations with higher rates of victimization than the United States, and somewhat more nations with lower rates.

In the past these two sources have not always been so consistent. In an earlier version of this chapter that covered a different time period, victim survey data indicated that the United States had higher rates of serious property crime than other nations while the police data suggested the opposite. But these findings can be reconciled if we assume (1) that the police statistics accurately characterize very serious violence and several classes of serious property crime and (2) that the victim surveys better represent lesser violence and most larcenies. This type of interpretation is supported by the fact that when comparisons of violence are restricted to more serious violence such as robbery, the differences between the United States and other nations (even common law nations) using victim statistics begin to resemble those from the police statistics (van Dijk and Mayhew

1993, p. 19). The same is true when we restrict property crime to motor vehicle theft (van Dijk and Mayhew 1993, p. 11). As we will see in the following section, there is a limit to the extent to which data from police statistics can and should be consistent with those from victim surveys (Biderman and Lynch 1991). It is important to demonstrate that the two sources are reasonably consistent where they should be and that anomalies between them are comprehensible. It is equally important to recognize that overall they tap two very different components of the crime problem.

Limitations of Existing Data

One of the major problems in comparing statistics is ensuring that the systems in each country include a large proportion of criminal acts and that the range of crimes is the same in each nation. Given comparable scope, it is important that these statistical systems classify and count crime incidents in a similar fashion. Some systems are sample-based and therefore suffer from sampling error and cannot be easily used to estimate the prevalence of rare crimes, such as rape. Finally, some data systems are highly aggregated and therefore inflexible, so that they cannot be easily used to understand cross-national differences in crime prevalence.

Problems of scope. Both available police statistics and victim surveys focus on a fairly narrow range of common law crimes such as homicide, sexual assault, other types of assault, robbery, and theft. While there is some attention to fraud or drug crimes, most white collar and victimless crimes are excluded from these data systems by design. Hence, there are no compendia of international data on a large component of behavior that many people consider criminal.

Police statistics, of course, exclude crimes that do not come to the attention of the police. In some crime classes—for example, homicide—this omission is trivial (Riedel 1990), while in others—for example, larceny—a substantial proportion of crimes will be excluded.[9] For purposes of cross-national comparisons, however, the absolute number of crimes excluded is of less concern than the constancy of that exclusion across nations. Valid cross-national comparisons of police statistics can be made, if approximately the same proportion of each type of crime is reported to the police in each of the nations compared.

The best evidence we have about differences in reporting to the police across nations suggests that the proportion of crime not reported to the police varies considerably across nations and types of crime. Van Dijk and

Mayhew (1993) indicate that reporting of crimes in the ICS to the police varied from a low of 31 percent in Spain to a high of 62 percent in Scotland.[10] This variability across nations is different for different types of crime. Virtually all of the motor vehicle thefts in the ICS were reported to the police in every country, and the same is true for burglaries involving forcible entry. The cross-national variability of reporting to the police is much greater for theft, vandalism, threats, assaults, and even robbery. This suggests that cross-national comparisons using police statistics are best done for extreme violence, such as homicide, burglary with forcible entry, and motor vehicle theft.

Victimization surveys include crimes that are recognized as such by the respondent whether they are reported to the police or not. They do not include homicide, for obvious reasons. Police statistics include reported crimes against commercial establishments while victimization surveys do not, unless the crimes against commercial establishments involve injuries to employees or theft of an employee's property.[11] Consequently, victimization surveys will also underestimate the total level of crime in a nation. This may not pose a problem if one is interested in the victimization of individuals and not total crime in a society. This could distort comparisons based on police statistics, however, if the volume of commercial enterprises varies considerably across nations. Crime rates that use police statistics in the numerator and population in the denominator will be higher in a nation with a large number of commercial enterprises than in another with fewer commercial establishments, when the risk to private citizens is the same. For some classes of property crime, the effect of commercial crime on cross-national comparisons is not trivial. According to the FBI (1989) the gross burglary rate in the United States was 1,314 per hundred thousand population in 1988. In England and Wales, the rate was 1,628 per hundred thousand (Home Office 1989). When commercial burglaries were excluded, the U.S. rate was 880 and the British rate was 878. Comparing the gross burglary rates, the risk in England and Wales is 24 percent higher than it is in the United States. Risk based on the noncommercial rates is essentially the same. If commercial crimes were uniformly identified in police statistics, commercial and noncommercial rates could be computed and used as appropriate. Unfortunately, this is not the case. Commercial burglaries are identified, but this is not true for most larcenies or motor vehicle thefts.

Problems in classification and counting. The principal classification decision made in these systems is that which places an eligible crime into a subclass, such as homicide. The pertinent rules define the attributes of an event that requires it to be counted in a particular subclass. These rules can vary substantially across nations. In the United States, for example, attempted murder is reported as aggravated assault in the Uniform Crime Reports (UCR), while in England and Australia attempted murder is included with other homicides. The common response to this variability in classification rules is to define classes of crime that are extremely broad and can, thereby, accommodate great differences in classification rules. The disadvantage of this approach is that the resulting crime classes are large and heterogeneous. Two nations can have the same number of thefts, but the type of theft events in the two countries can be quite different. Ninety percent of the thefts in one can involve forcible entry while only 20 percent of the thefts in the second nation are burglaries. Although these nations are radically different in terms of their crime problem, they would appear the same in police statistics.

Even when crime classes are fairly narrow and similarly defined across nations there can be intraclass variations that can distort comparisons. For example, in 1988 the FBI reported 542,968 robberies, of which 33 percent involved firearms (FBI 1989). In the same year, the British Home Office reported 34,137 robberies, of which 8.6 percent involved firearms (Home Office 1989). While all of the events in the two nations may have included the attributes necessary to be classified as robbery-force or threat and theft—the robberies in the United States involved more force, as indicated by the more extensive use of weapons. On this basis one could argue that robberies in England and Wales are not comparable to those in the United States. Given the current state of police statistics, there is not much that can be done about this type of intraclass variation.

The importance of crime classification for cross-national comparisons cannot be overstated. As we will see in a later section, the differences in the mix of crime across nations is much greater than the differences in the level of criminal activity. Crime-specific comparisons across nations will tell us much more than comparisons of total crime. These crime-specific comparisons, however, are predicated on the assumption that crime classification is uniform across nations. Very little of the detailed work necessary to support that assumption has been done.[12]

Since victim survey data are collected on an incident basis rather than as aggregated counts (as most police statistics are), obtaining comparable crime classifications is less problematic than it is with police data. As long as the attributes necessary for crime classification are included in the survey, they can be used to classify crime events. Victimization surveys done under the auspices of individual nations or by individual researchers differ widely with regard to the information included on each crime reported (Kaiser, Kury, and Albrecht 1991; Block 1992). More recently, efforts to standardize the content of crime surveys were undertaken with the International Crime Survey (ICS) (van Dijk, Mayhew, and Killias 1990; del Frate, Alvazzi, van Zvekic, and van Dijk 1993). Given this common core of information, it should be possible to obtain a common crime classification across nations.

Flexibility. Most national police data systems and all international compendia of police data are based on aggregated counts of crime occurring in a jurisdiction. These counts cannot be disaggregated in ways that would help us understand cross-national differences in rates. For example, we may know the gross rate of robbery in the United States and Germany but we cannot compute rates separately for men and women or for racial or ethnic minorities. Victim survey data, on the other hand, are collected on an incident basis, so that crimes can be distinguished by characteristics of the victim, the place of occurrence, and many other characteristics of the event.

Samples and censuses. Victim surveys employ probability samples of the resident population, while most police statistics purport to be censuses of crimes reported to the police.[13] As a result, we must take sampling error into account when comparing victimization data cross-nationally. More important, the small sample sizes in the ICS will limit the extent to which we can use the very detailed information included in the survey. For example, with samples that average about 2,000 per nation, it is impossible to create very detailed crime classes because there will not be enough cases in the class to provide reliable estimates of prevalence. As with police statistics, we are forced to use broad and potentially heterogeneous crime classes that can defeat the purpose of crime-specific comparisons.

Which Data Do I Use When?

We are fortunate to have two reasonably comprehensive sources of data on crime internationally that can be used to establish the position of the United States relative to other countries with regard to crime. Police and victim statistics are complementary in that each measures best a component of the crime problem that the other does not (Biderman and Lynch 1991). Police statistics should be used for comparing those classes of crimes that are known to be well-reported to the police and that are consistently well-reported across nations. This includes homicide, motor vehicle theft, and burglaries involving forcible entry. Victim surveys should be used for comparing classes of crime that are not well-reported to the police. These classes include most larcenies other than motor vehicle theft and more minor forms of violence. In addition, police statistics should be used to assess differences in rare classes of crime such as homicide or rape (if other reporting errors are not too severe) that either cannot be assessed in victim surveys or are seriously affected by sampling error. Victim surveys, on the other hand, can be used to explore the reasons for cross-national differences in crime because they are collected on an incident basis and can be aggregated and disaggregated more than available police data. We should compare and contrast these different sources of data to increase both our understanding of crime and the strengths of these data.

Is There Really More Crime in the United States?

When the various data sources are used with appropriate consideration of their error structure, the picture emerging from international crime statistics both supports and contradicts the common wisdom that the United States is the most crime-ridden of industrialized democracies. The risk of lethally violent crime is much higher in the United States than in other nations, even those most institutionally similar. The risk of minor violence is slightly higher in the United States, but other common law nations (and some code countries such as France) are not far behind. The fact that the police statistics show greater differences in violence rates than the victim surveys may reflect the more extensive weapons use in violent crimes in the United States. In contrast, the United States has lower rates of serious property crime than other similar nations and even lower rates than many countries considered civil or safe. The victim survey and the police data suggest that the prevalence of minor property crime is also lower in the United States than in other common law countries, but greater in the common law countries than in other industrialized democracies.

ILLUMINATING THE NATIONAL DIFFERENCES

Some analyses have been done to explain these differences in cross-national crime rates. These analyses have examined the effects of various factors believed to affect either the motivation or the opportunity to commit crime (Nettler 1978; Cohen and Felson 1979; Clarke and Cornish 1986). Studies that emphasize criminal motivation examine the relative size of crime-prone populations such as the young, persons living in urban areas, or the unemployed. Other studies have examined the effect of the social organization of nations, such as the level of inequality or the depth of social safety nets. Studies emphasizing opportunity have examined the influence of the availability of crime targets or the instruments and situations that permit potential offenders to act on their motives. These have included the volume of property and its portability, the availability of necessary instruments (such as weapons), or appropriate settings—for example, rate of activity out of the home and the prevalence of vulnerable housing structures.

Homicide

There have been a few cross-national comparisons of homicide that have held age and other factors constant (Fingerhut and Kleinman 1990). These studies indicate that the differences between the United States and other nations in the risk of homicide do not disappear when age-specific rather than gross rates are used. The differences between the United States and other nations remain quite large even when comparisons are restricted to the most violence-prone groups—fifteen- to twenty- four-year olds.

Other studies have shown that differentiating homicides into those committed with a firearm and those using other means substantially changes the position of the United States relative to other countries. Fingerhut and Kleinman (1990) find that a much higher percentage of homicides in the United States are committed with firearms than in any other nation, including those nations most institutionally similar to the United States. Sloan et al. (1988) found that the difference between homicide rates in Seattle and Vancouver were due almost entirely to differences in the rate of homicides with firearms. Sproule and Kennett (1990) found that the rate of homicide in the United States is roughly twice that of Canada for homicide by means other than firearms and also for homicides with firearms other than handguns. The U.S. rate of homicides with handguns is 14.6 times that of Canada. The gross homicide rate in the United States for 1988 was 7.4 per hundred thousand population, while the gross rates in England and Wales were 1.31 for the same year. When homicides due to firearms are excluded from the rates, the British rate is 1.22 per hundred thousand and the United States rate is 2.92 per hundred thousand.[14] When gross rates are used, citizens in the United States are 5.6 times more likely to be victims of homicide than citizens of England and Wales. When firearms are excluded, persons in the United States are only

2.4 times as likely to be victims of homicide as persons in England and Wales. The evidence is mounting that firearms and especially handguns are an important determinant of the high homicide rates in the United States relative to other institutionally similar nations, with otherwise comparable levels of violence overall.

The central role of firearms in producing the relatively high rates of homicide in the United States has led to calls for national policies to reduce the availability of guns. These findings cannot be used to support availability reduction policies until there is some evidence that those motivated to kill will not simply choose other weapons to accomplish their ends. Studies of opportunity reduction for suicide (Clarke and Mayhew 1988) suggest that displacement is not great. Killias (1993) and Sproule and Kennett (1990) infer that displacement will not be substantial from the fact that nations with low or reduced availability of firearms do not have high rates of homicides with other weapons. This inference may not be warranted, however, since these same cross-section patterns could be attributed to factors other than gun availability that keep all forms of homicide low in nations with regulation of firearms. Longitudinal data would be more appropriate to make this point. Sproule and Kennett (1989) used longitudinal data to evaluate the effects of handgun restrictions on homicides with handguns in Canada. They observed a slight displacement effect. At this point the preponderance of the evidence seems to suggest that displacement will not be substantial.

Property Crime

Analyses of the ICS have been done to understand observed differences in crime across nations (van Dijk, Mayhew, and Killias 1990; van Dijk and Mayhew 1993). These studies have identified differences in the composition and social organization of nations that are associated with higher rates of criminal victimization both within and across nations. Within nations they have found almost uniformly that

1. The young are at greater risk than the old.
2. Those in large urban areas are more at risk than persons in smaller places.
3. Those with higher income are more at risk than those with lower income.[15]
4. Those who engage in activity out of the home more frequently are more often victimized than those who stay home.

Some regularities have also been observed between nations. These are mostly relationships between opportunity factors and levels of crime. There is a persistent relationship, for example, between car ownership and levels of motor vehicle theft—the higher the ownership the higher the rate of theft. Similar correlations have been observed for the proportion of the population living in detached, semidetached, and terrace houses (attached row houses). The greater the proportion of the population residing in attached housing the greater the risk of burglary (van Dijk, Mayhew, and Killias 1990).

These very interesting data on individual and national factors have not been combined in models or even simple standardizations to determine the effect of individual risk factors on cross-national differences in rates. If, for example, we computed age-specific rates for all nations and then forced the age distribution in each nation to conform to that of the United States, we would be able to determine the effect of differing age distributions on observed differences between the United States and these nations. It is possible that nations will not differ in the distribution of factors related to risk within nations. Consequently, these factors cannot explain cross-national differences. Similarly, correlations observed at the national level may be statistically significant but may explain little of the difference in the level of crime across nations.

The few standardizations that have been done suggest that many of the factors affecting risk within countries, or factors that correlate with differences in the level of crime across nations, have little effect on cross-national differences in property crime rates. Van Dijk, Mayhew, and Killias (1990) report that standardizing motor vehicle rates for vehicle ownership had very little effect on differences in motor vehicle theft. Similar results occurred when burglary rates were adjusted for differences in the distribution of the population across different types of housing. Standardization of property crime rates in the 1988 ICS by age and urban residence also had little impact on cross-national differences.[16]

Standardization by income, however, has a sizable effect on cross-national differences in property crime rates. When income-specific victimization rates in each nation are multiplied by the income distribution found in the United States, the rates of property crime in these other nations become substantially more like that of the United States. The average change in the rate of property crime across the seven nations examined is 19 percent. The property crime rate in England and Wales increased by 27.8 percent, in Germany by 26.8 percent, in France by 26.3 percent, and in Switzerland by 30.8 percent. In almost every case, the difference between the standardized and unstandardized rates was due to the fact that the United States had a greater proportion of the population in higher income groups, and that these groups had higher property victimization rates in each nation. It is interesting to note that the two common law nations that were essentially the same as the United States in terms of the unadjusted property crime rate were not much affected by the income standardization. This provides further support for the importance of income distributions for property crime rates (see Table 2.3).

It is not clear exactly what this effect of income distributions means. One interpretation is that the income distribution reflects the availability of property to steal. The United States, Australia, and Canada have similarly high property crime rates because these nations have more people with more property than other industrialized democracies. Income, and therefore property for taking, is held by a smaller proportion of the population in other nations. More work is required to interpret these initial findings.[17]

Making Better Comparisons

Newly available data on the prevalence of crime cross-nationally and some of the analyses of these data can make cross-national comparisons more useful for informing policy. First, these data indicate that the United States is not the most crime-ridden of industrialized democracies. The fact that the United States does not differ from other common law nations with respect to minor violence and serious property crime casts doubt on global indictments of the United States as having a criminal culture. The United States stands alone, separate from even other common law countries, not in the prevalence of violence but in its lethality. Differences between the United States and other nations are crime-specific, and the search for understanding and remedies should be equally specific. It is unlikely that explanations for such specific differences will operate at the level of culture.

Second, the difference between the relative position of the United States and other nations with respect to homicide when firearm use is held constant clearly indicates that more attention must be given to reducing the availability of firearms. While it may be impossible to eliminate firearms once they are widely available in a nation, it seems that from the standpoint of reducing homicide, it is worth trying.

Third, much more work should be done with the ICS and other victim surveys to inform cross-national differences in property crime rates. Specific attention should be given to elaborating the effects of income distributions on cross-national crime rates.

Table 2.3
Five-Year Prevalence Rates per 100 Population, 1983–1988:
Original and Standardized on U.S. Income Distribution

NATION	PROPERTY CRIME RATES		
	UNADJUSTED	ADJUSTED	PERCENT CHANGE
Australia	37.9	37.6	−0.77
Canada	37.8	38.2	1.00
England & Wales	30.5	38.9	27.8
Germany	39.9	50.6	26.8
France	36.8	46.5	26.3
Netherlands	45.4	54.7	20.4
Switzerland	29.2	38.2	30.9
United States	41.1	41.1	0
Average percentage change			18.9

SOURCE: International Crime Survey 1988.

The work in this area tells us even more clearly that the information that we have on hand to study cross-national differences in crime is not adequate. Incident-level police data on well-reported crimes and especially lethal violence is essential. More information on the offender and the victim would be useful both in police records and in victim surveys. This information should include factors related to the social marginality of victims, such as their race (or ethnicity), participation in the labor force and educational institutions, family structure, and citizenship status. Without these data it is difficult to test many of the arguments concerning the role of heterogeneity in producing the higher violence rates in the United States.

The utility of victim surveys for understanding crimes not well reported to the police would be greatly enhanced if the samples employed in the ICS could be increased. Currently, the samples sizes are too small to take full advantage of the very detailed information that the surveys offer. Our understanding of cross-national differences in minor theft would be increased if more information were gathered in the ICS pertaining to the volume of property in households and to its use and storage. Interpreting the effects of income distributions noted above would be simplified if the surveys included measures of the volume of goods available in households independent of income. It is also important that these surveys include more information about the instrumentation and procedures that they use in each nation. While the ICS is more uniform in its methodology than Interpol or the United Nations, there are differences across nations (e.g., response rates). Since victimization surveys have been shown to be very sensitive to procedural differences (Cantor and Lynch 2000; Fisher and Cullen 2000; Lynch 1996), it is essential that these differences in procedure be taken into account in making cross-national comparisons. Finally, more information on the geographical areas in which crimes occur would be useful in both police and victim survey data.

CONVENTIONAL WISDOM: THE UNITED STATES HAS THE MOST PUNITIVE SENTENCING POLICIES OF ANY INDUSTRIALIZED DEMOCRACY

The common wisdom about the punitiveness of U.S. sentencing policy is based largely on comparisons of incarceration rates across nations. Many studies have shown that the United States has a higher per capita incarceration rate than any nation other than the (then) Soviet Union and South Africa (Doleschal 1977; Waller and Chan 1975; Maurer 1991; Walmsley 1999; Tomasevki 1994). As in the case of cross-national comparisons of crime rates, it is important to characterize accurately the nature of punishment cross-nationally. It is equally important to determine whether the observed differences are the result of more punitive sentencing policies or some other factors. Most cross-national comparisons do neither.

Accurately Characterizing Punishment Cross-nationally

Punishment here refers to sanctions imposed by the state in response to violations of the criminal law. Describing punishment policies cross-nationally is difficult in part because sanctions can be administered at so many points. Police officers can punish by taking you into custody or giving you a warning or a citation. The prosecutor's decision to prosecute or not can be construed as a form of punishment. Judges can punish at sentencing. Prison and parole officials can punish through classification, decisions regarding good time or early release, decisions regarding institutional discipline, and revocation decisions. Few nations document all of these decision points well and in a manner that facilitates cross-national comparison. As a result, comparisons of punishment policies focus on the sentencing decision and beyond. This focus quickly leads to an examination of incarceration, largely because this is generally the most severe form of punishment allowed by the state and because the availability and comparability of data are greater here than at other stages in the postconviction process. Hence, the comparison of punishment policy becomes a comparison of prison use (Young and Brown 1993).

Conceptual Ambiguity

Even with the focus narrowed to incarceration, good comparisons are difficult because the concept remains ill-defined. Incarceration can be defined as taking a person into custody and requiring him or her to reside in a particular secure setting. "Secure" here means that the person is not free to come and go. Certainly, a traditional prison will fall within this definition. It is less clear whether community-based facilities fall in this category or mental hospitals or court-ordered drug treatment facilities or internal exile. Nations differ widely in the mix of facilities used for incarceration, and the decision as to which to include or exclude can be very consequential.[18] It is important, therefore, to establish that the concept of incarceration is equivalently defined across the countries being compared. Young and Brown (1993) maintain that these differences between incarceration and imprisonment do not affect cross-national comparisons substantially. It is likely, however, that offense-specific comparisons can be affected while the import for total rates of imprisonment will not be large.

A second conceptual ambiguity in most comparative studies of prison use is the failure to distinguish the propensity to incarcerate from the length of time served. Both of these decisions are important dimensions of punishment policy, but they can be quite distinct. Nations can have the same incarceration rates—that is, the same number of persons in prison per capita on a given day—yet have very different imprisonment policies. One nation may use incarceration frequently for any given offense but impose very short sentences. Another nation can impose very long prison terms but use that sanction sparingly for any given offense. While comparisons of incarceration rates are useful, it would be much more informative for policy purposes to distinguish the prevalence of incarceration from the length of sentences imposed.

The treatment of pretrial detention is also problematic. While pretrial detention is not a sentence, it is certainly custody and can affect sentencing. Judges can take time served before trial into consideration at sentencing, so that an offender is sentenced to time served pretrial. Absent the pretrial detention, the convicted person would have been sentenced to custody. Since the person is never in custody serving a sentence, he or she will not appear in incarceration rates. To the extent that countries have very different practices regarding the use and duration of pretrial detention, these differences will distort cross-national comparisons. This information is not easily retrievable from correctional data systems cross-nationally. Lynch et al. (1994) found that the proportion of the prison population that was detainees as opposed to prisoners was essentially the same in the United States and England and Wales for 1991. Young and Brown (1993) report levels of detention use similar to those in the United States for England and Wales, West Germany, Scotland, and Norway in 1987. Use of detention in Australia was about 25 percent less than in the United States. This suggests that pretrial detention practices are roughly the same in some of the nations most institutionally similar to the United States and will not confound comparisons based on sentenced populations.

Differences in the age of adult jurisdiction can also influence cross-national comparisons of imprisonment. Most comparisons of imprisonment are based upon the adult prison population. The age of adult jurisdiction can vary both within and across nations. In the United States and Canada, for example, the generally agreed-upon age of adult jurisdiction is eighteen, while in England and Wales it is seventeen. Within the United States, however, some states begin adult jurisdiction at sixteen. Moreover, the increased use of offense-specific waivers further blurs the lower age limit of adult jurisdiction. Young and Brown (1993) maintain that differences in age of jurisdiction do not amount to much. This assessment would seem appropriate for both total and offense-specific comparisons because the age distribution of offenders should not vary much by offense, while the use of mental hospitals will be more pronounced in some offenses than in others.

Finally, the fact that many decision makers have control over the time actually served in prison complicates the determination of length of stay. Most industrialized democracies have some form of sentence reduction after admission—such as good time, or early release—that can substantially alter the sentence imposed by the court. There is some evidence that these practices differ across nations (Farrington and Langan 1992). These decisions must be taken into account in determining length of stay in custody.

DATA AVAILABILITY

Once the concept of incarceration is defined equivalently across nations, those who wish to compare incarceration policies must ensure that the statistics they use include all of the jurisdictions responsible for custody. In a country like England this is a simple matter, since the entire correctional system is administered by the Home Office. It is more complicated in federal systems such as those of the United States and Canada, where responsibility for custody is distributed across federal, state or province, and local levels of government.

In the United States, the federal government has responsibility for persons convicted of violating federal laws. The state has custody of persons convicted of violating state laws and of persons whose sentence generally exceeds one year. Local jails (usually administered at the county level) have responsibility for detainees and sentenced prisoners with sentences of less than one year. State institutions house about two-thirds of the imprisoned population, jails about one-quarter, and federal institutions the remainder. Omitting any jurisdiction will result in an underestimate of the U.S. prison population. Until recently the data available on the state prison population in the United States were more readily available than information on jails. Consequently researchers would include U.S. prison statistics but would fail to include, or would include less precisely, data on jails. This selective inclusion led not only to underestimates of the prevalence of incarceration but also to inaccurate estimates of sentence length. Since persons in jail serve less time in custody by definition than persons in prison, excluding jail populations would result in inappropriately high estimates of time served in custody.

COMPUTATIONAL COMPLEXITY

Even the computation of incarceration rates can introduce distortions into cross-national comparisons. The most common method for computing imprisonment rates is to divide the number of persons in prison by some at-risk population such as the number of adults in the population or the number of arrested persons. This is commonly referred to as a stock rate. This approach is preferred largely because data for prisoners in custody are believed to be most accurate, and they are certainly more readily available than admissions or release data in many countries. However, since the probability of an offender being in prison on a given day is a function of the length of his sentence, stock statistics tend to overrepresent the more serious offenders with longer sentences. Serious offenders with long sentences also accumulate in prison populations, and therefore stock studies overestimate the propensity to incarcerate in those countries with higher rates of serious crime. In contrast, flow studies using annual admissions over some at-risk population, such as adults in the population or arrested persons in that year, are not affected by the accumulation of more serious offenders. This is not to say that length of sentence is not an important dimension of punitiveness but, as I argued earlier, that, for reasons of clarity, it should be treated separately. Flow designs permit the separation of the propensity to incarcerate from the length of sentence served and, thereby provide a clearer picture of both dimensions of punishment.[19]

When flow rates are used to assess the propensity to imprison, other methods must be used to compute the length of time served in custody.[20] The particular choice of computational method can have substantial effects on cross-national comparisons. The usual way of estimating time served in custody for a particular offense involves using the experience of persons released in a given year; that is, exiting cohorts. This can be misleading because these cohorts underrepresent inmates with long sentences (Shryock and Siegel 1973). This can lead to the ironic situation in which a nation that is increasing the length of time served can actually appear to be shortening sentences.[21] Life tables and other techniques, such as ratios of stock to flow rates that take account of long term prisoners, may yield very different estimates of time served.

Standardizing for Factors Other Than Punitiveness

One of the major criticisms of comparisons of imprisonment rates that are used to support statements about relative punitiveness is that they fail to account for differences in the level and nature of crime and criminals in a society. This is crucial because greater punitiveness requires that a more severe sanction be imposed in response to a similar provocation. Unless one is willing to assume that crime and criminals are equally prevalent or similar across nations, comparisons of per capita incarceration rates have little to tell us about the relative punitiveness of sentencing policies. Following this logic, the United States should have higher per capita incarceration rates because it has higher per capita crime rates and more serious crimes. If other nations were confronted with a similar crime problem, they would have the same per capita imprisonment rates.

Accounting for different levels of crime. The best way to inform this debate is to compare incarceration rates for fairly specific types of crime—

for example, homicide—that take account of the differences in the incidence of that crime across nations. Crime-specific comparisons are better than total rates because they increase the comparability of the type of provocation confronted by each sentencing system. Rates based on total incarcerations and total crimes can confound differences in the nature of crime with the relative punitiveness of sentencing policy. Nations with higher levels of homicide, for example, can have higher levels of incarceration without being more punitive. If comparisons are made on the basis of homicides, specifically, then the effect of the mix of crimes in society is reduced.[22] Moreover, if rates are based upon the number of homicides, the number of arrests for homicide, or the number of convictions for homicide, rather than population, then the effect of the volume of crime on incarceration will be held constant.[23]

Accounting for different types of crime. Crime-specific comparisons go a long way toward standardizing the provocation to which the criminal justice system responds. As I noted earlier in this chapter, commonly used crime classes, however, can include very different types of events. Robberies in the United States, for example, involve firearms to a much greater extent than events classified as robbery in England and Wales (see the earlier section "Problems in Classification and Counting"). The United States could imprison convicted robbers at a much higher rate than England and Wales without being more punitive. If firearms use was taken into account as an aggravating circumstance, the two nations may not be different in their response to the crime. This type of intraclass variation in the severity of the crime is not easily accounted for, because most statistical systems classify crime events by charge or crime type without specifying additional aggravating or mitigating circumstances.

Accounting for different types of offenders. The prior criminal history of convicted persons can affect the type of sentences received (see Chapter 18 in this volume). Persons with prior involvement in serious crime receive more severe sentences than those with less prior criminal involvement. If offenders in one nation have more extensive and serious criminal histories than offenders in another nation, then sentences in the first nation can be more severe than those in the other without being more punitive. There is not a great deal of information on the distribution of criminal histories among convicted persons cross-nationally. The available information suggests that in general, fewer prisoners in the United States have prior convictions for criminal offenses than do inmates in England and Wales

(Lynch et al. 1994; Lynch 1993a). Approximately 60 percent of the inmates in both nations claimed to have a prior sentence to custody as an adult, but only 11 percent of the British inmates claim no prior record while 22 percent of the United States prison population have no prior record of juvenile or adult custody (Lynch et al. 1994; Dodd and Hunter 1992).

Comparing the Level and Length of Incarceration

The foregoing discussion describes several of the most prevalent problems encountered in using cross-national comparisons of imprisonment to assess the relative punitiveness of sentencing policies. Some of these problems cannot be easily addressed with available information; others can be. The picture of the relative punitiveness of the United States changes when (1) both the prevalence of incarceration and the time served are evaluated and (2) the extent and nature of crime is taken into account.

The prevalence of incarceration. In 1988 I compared the United States, Canada, England and Wales, and West Germany using both stock and flow incarceration rates for specific offenses, as well as population-based and arrest-based rates (Lynch 1988). This comparison also included both the jail and prison populations in the United States and federal and provincial prisoners in Canada. When arrest-based as opposed to population-based rates are used, the difference between the United States and other nations is reduced substantially.

On the basis of the customary measure of prison use—population-based stock rates—I found that the United States was much more likely to incarcerate for violent offenses than either England or West Germany. In the case of homicide, the United States incarcerated at 7.5 times the rate of Great Britain and 5.3 times that of Germany. The relative propensity to incarcerate was similar for robbery, where the rate for the United States was 8.7 times that of England and 4.7 times that of Germany. Differences in the rates were somewhat less for property crime. For burglary, the English rate was approximately one-half that of the United States. In the larceny/theft category, which combines burglary, larceny, and motor vehicle theft, the incarceration rate for the United States was roughly twice that of Germany and England (see Table 2.4).

When flow rates based upon arrest were used, the probability of incarceration given arrest was roughly the same for violent offenses in the United States, England, and Canada, although England had a somewhat

Table 2.4
Arrest-based Incarceration Rates by Nation and Offense

OFFENSE	NATION			
	UNITED STATES 1982	ENGLAND & WALES 1983	CANADA 1980	GERMANY[a] 1984
Murder	73.8	63.6	na[a]	81.6
Robbery	39.4	38.8	43.5	8.5
Burglary	23.6	21.9	17.5	na[b]
Larceny/Theft	10.7	9.3	11.9	1.9

na = not available
a. Data on admissions to provincial institutions were not readily available on a national basis.
b. Germany does not report data on a class of crime exactly the same as burglary. Burglary is included in the Larceny/Theft class.

lower rate for homicide. Essentially the same was true for burglary and for the more inclusive class of property crime—larceny/theft. With the exception of homicide, the rates for both violent and property crime were still considerably lower in West Germany than they are in other countries.

The rate for robbery was approximately one-fifth of that in the United States, England, and Canada for the larceny/thefts, the incarceration rate in Germany was one-sixth that in the United States and Canada and one-fifth of that in England.

Farrington and Langan (1992) compared the use of incarceration in the United States and England and Wales on the basis of court data. These data avoid some of the problems with incarceration rates, but they do not take into account other problems that were the subject of adjustments in the studies cited above, for example, the effects of plea bargaining. Farrington and Langan's results were different, but consistent with those in Lynch (1988). The probability of incarceration given conviction was not radically different across nations for violent crimes, but it was substantially different for property crimes. The probability of being sentenced to prison or jail for homicide was .86 in England and .98 in the United States, and for robbery it was .87 and .88 respectively. In contrast, a person found guilty of burglary in the United States had a .74 probability of a custodial sentence but only a .40 chance in England and Wales.

Both Lynch's work and that of Farrington and Langan assessed differences in punishment before the massive changes in sentencing practices that occurred in the United States in the early 1990s (Tonry 1999a, 1999b; Ditton and Wilson 1999). To assess the comparability of current practices I compared several nations, using more recent court data on the probability of incarceration given conviction (See Table 2.5). The patterns observed earlier persist. There is little difference across nations in the propensity to incarcerate for very serious violent offenses. In the United States, 96 percent of the persons sentenced for homicide receive a custodial sentence. The comparable figure for Australia is 93 percent, 95 percent in France, 94 percent in Sweden, 89 percent in Germany, and 85 percent in England and Wales. No country seems to take homicide lightly. Sentences for robbery are more variable, with Australia, Austria, and Sweden very similar to the United States, where 78.5 percent of sentenced persons receive custodial sentences. England (63 percent) France (65 percent) and Scotland (65 percent) are somewhat less likely to incarcerate than the United States. Germany uses incarceration much less frequently than the other nations (39 percent), probably because of its well-developed day fine system (Hillsman 1988). In the case of burglary, real differences start to appear. The United States sentences approximately 60 percent of convicted burglars to incarceration, while Australia only employs incarceration in 45 percent of the cases—and Austria in 40 percent, England 38 percent, and Germany 22 percent. The same disparities exist with motor vehicle theft, where the United States is almost twice as likely to incarcerate as other nations. Courts in the United States, then, have been and continue to be much more willing to incarcerate for less serious violence and for property crimes than other industrialized democracies, even those with common law legal traditions.

Time served. I compared the United States, England and Wales, Canada, Australia, and West Germany in terms of the length of imposed sentences and actual length of stay for specific offenses (Lynch 1993a). Again efforts were made to include all components of the custody population in Canada and the United States. I found that the length of sentences imposed for these offenses was much longer in the United States than in the other nations. The mean sentence imposed in the United States was longer than sentences in other countries for similar offenses. The mean sentence imposed for homicide in the United States is 1.12 times that imposed in West Germany. The mean sentence imposed in the United States for robbery is 1.29 times that in West Germany, 1.58 times that in England and Wales, and 2.26 times the sentence imposed in Canada. For burglary, the mean sentence imposed in the United States is 2.17 times the sentence levied in England and Wales, and 3.51 times that imposed in Canada. For the combined larceny/theft category used in West Germany, the mean U.S. sentence is 2.37 times that imposed in England and Wales, 3.1 times that in West Germany, and 3.29 times the sentence levied in Canada.

These differences in the length of imposed sentences persist in comparisons made with more recent data (See Table 2.6). Sentences imposed for homicide in the United States are 1.9 times those in France, three times those of Scotland and Sweden. Only England, with average sentences of 229 months, is similar to the United States. As we move to less serious offenses, the length of sentences imposed in the United States get longer relative to those imposed in other nations. Robbery offenders in the United States receive sentences 2.2 times that imposed in England and Wales and 3.8 times the terms imposed in Sweden. For burglary the length of sentence imposed in the United States is 2.7 times that in England and Wales and 3.9 those of Sweden.

When comparisons were made in the mid-1980s on the basis of the average time actually served, however, the differences between the United States and these other nations were reduced considerably, especially for violence. The mean time served for homicide was greater in Canada (57 months) than it was in the United States (50.5 months without adjusting for the jail population and 42.5 months when jail adjustments are made). The average time served for homicide in England and Wales (43.0 months) was not very different from that served in the United States. The average time served for robbery in the United States and Canada was approximately the same, 20.9 and 23.6 months respectively, when the jail population is included. The mean sentence for robbery is higher in the United States (30 months) than in Canada when only the prison population is used. Time served for robbery is much lower in England and Wales (15.8 months) than in the other countries.[24]

The large differences in time served between the United States and these other countries occur for property crimes—burglary and larceny. The length of time served for burglary in the United States was 16.2 months (for prisons only) or 10.6 months (for combined jail and prison populations), while burglars in Canada served 5.3 months and in England 6.8 months. For larcenies (excluding motor vehicle theft), the average time spent in the United States was between 7.01 months and 12.5 months. In Canada, the average time served was 2.0 months, and in England it was 4.65 months (see Tables 2.7 and 2.8).

Table 2.5
Percent of Convicted Persons Sentenced to Incarceration by Nation and Offense

NATION	OFFENSE			
	HOMICIDE	ROBBERY	BURGLARY	MVT
Australia	93	176	45	
Austria	94	73	40	
England & Wales	85	63	38	38
France	95	65		
Germany	89	39	22	
Scotland	90	65	44	30
Sweden	94	78	57	30
United States	95.8	78.6	59.5	54.9

SOURCE: Farrington, Langan and Wikstrom, 1994.
NOTE: MVT = Motor Vehicle Theft

Table 2.6
Length of Imposed Sentence by Nation and Offense in Months

NATION	OFFENSE			
	HOMICIDE	ROBBERY	BURGLARY	MVT
England & Wales	229.9	40.3	14.9	8.6
France	128	21		
Scotland	77	35	6	
Sweden	76	23	10.5	4.2
United States	244	88.8	41	22

SOURCE: ECCP 2000; Wikstrom 2000; BJS 1998.
NOTE: MVT = Motor Vehicle Theft

These estimates of time served are lower than those obtained by Farrington and Langan (1992) largely because of differing assumptions about the end interval for time served and the treatment of persons receiving life sentences and death sentences. The relative differences between the countries are in the same direction and of approximately the same magnitude.

Table 2.7
Mean Time Served in Custody by Nation and Offense,
Exiting Cohort Method (in months)

NATION	OFFENSE			
	HOMICIDE	ROBBERY	BURGLARY	MVT
Canada	57.2	23.6	5.2	2.0
England &Wales	43.0	15.9	6.7	4.65
U.S. (Prison only)	50.5	30.1	16.1	12.1
U.S. (Prison & Jail)	42.5	20.9	10.6	7.0

Table 2.8
Expected Sentence by Nation and Offense,
Life Table Method (in months)

NATION	OFFENSE	
	HOMICIDE	ROBBERY
England &Wales	80.4	227.3
United States	76.2	44.8
Australia	64.3	23.9

The differences that I observed using exiting cohorts were consistent with those obtained using life tables and stock/flow ratios. There was no appreciable difference in time served for homicide in the United States and England and Wales, but length of stay for homicide was about 14 percent longer in the United States than in Australia.

For robbery, the expected length of stay in the United States is considerably more than that in either Australia or England and Wales. Convicted robbers in England and Wales can expect to spend an average of 27 months in custody and those in Australia will spend 24 months in custody on average. In the United States, convicted robbers can expect to spend approximately 45 months in custody. The stock/flow ratio method allowed for the inclusion of comparisons between England and Wales, the United States, and West Germany. The stock/flow ratio for homicide was some-

Table 2.9
Estimates of Time Served by Nation and Offense,
Stock/Flow Ratio Method

NATION	OFFENSE			
	HOMICIDE	ROBBERY	BURGLARY	THEFT[a]
England & Wales	5.86	1.19	.57	.71
United States	5.06	2.04	.86	.96
West Germany	4.75	3.30	na	1.27

na = not available. Adjustments were made to the jail correction used to estimate the flow rates in Lynch (1988).
a. Theft includes larceny, burglary, and motor vehicle theft.

what higher for England and Wales than for the United States and West Germany, and the U.S. ratio was slightly higher than that of Germany. In the case of robbery, the estimate of time served for England and Wales is only 58 percent of that in the United States and 36 percent of that served in West Germany. Moreover, the estimate of time served for robbery in West Germany is 1.6 times that in the United States. The pattern is similar for the large larceny/theft class. The time served for this crime is lowest in England and Wales, somewhat greater in the United States, and greatest in West Germany. Time served in England and Wales is only 74 percent of that served in the United States, while time in custody in West Germany is 32 percent greater than that served in the United States.

Farrington and Langan (1992) also found that the length of stay for homicide does not differ much between the United States and England and Wales. Time served in the United States, however, is substantially longer for robbery than it is in England, and the difference is even greater for burglary. The ratio of time served in 1987 in the United States to time served in England and Wales is 1.87 for robbery and 2.27 for burglary.

The only more current data available on time served is based upon exiting cohorts and will certainly understate the time served on long sentences that would be imposed for serious offenses (See Table 2.10). These data may be acceptable for comparisons if we can assume that the error would be constant across nations. Given the consistency between the exiting cohort and life table comparisons in the earlier studies, this seems like a reasonable assumption.

Table 2.10
Time Served by Nation and Offense, 1998

	OFFENSE			
NATION	HOMICIDE	ROBBERY	BURGLARY	MVT[a]
England and Wales	99.8	20.5	6.5	3.4
Sweden	na	12.0	6.4	3.0
United States	126.9	42.8	18.0	11.1

na = not available. Adjustments were made to the jail correction used to estimate the flow rates in Lynch (1988).
a. Theft includes larceny, burglary, and motor vehicle theft.

Based on the experience of prisoners leaving prison in 1998, offenders sentenced for homicide in England will only serve 78 percent of the term imposed for the same offense in the United States; in Sweden the time served for homicide would be only one-half that served in the United States. In the case of robbery, these percentages would be 48 percent and 25 percent respectively. For burglary, the time served in England and Sweden would be about one-third that in the United States. Currently, then, the time served by offenders is longer in the United Sates than in the other nations examined for all offenses. Time served in the United States gets longer relative to other nations as the seriousness of the offense decreases. The pattern is consistent with earlier comparisons and a little more pronounced for those nations examined in both time periods.

The special case of drug offenses. In order to maximize coverage within nations and comparability across countries, virtually all of the cross-national studies of prison use have compared nations on their response to serious common law crimes and specifically crimes similar to UCR Index crimes. Many of the most dramatic changes in prison use, however, seem to be occurring in the area of drug offenses. This is certainly true in the United States, where the proportion of the state prison population in custody for drug crimes increased from 8 percent in 1986 to 22 percent in 1991.

Comparisons of prison use for drug offenses are complicated by the breadth and the heterogeneity of drug crime classifications cross-nationally and the ambiguity of the line between treatment and imprisonment in any

Table 2.11

Drugs Crimes Recorded by the Police, by Nation

NATION	DRUG CRIMES KNOWN TO POLICE	PREVALENCE OF ADULT DRUG USE
Australia	451	59.2
Austria	196	na
Canada	235	6.5
England & Wales	261	42.0
France	158	17.9
Germany	264	12.3
Netherlands	48	24.9
Scotland	614	na
Sweden	na	na
United States	576	55.3

SOURCES: AIHW 1998; ECCP 2000; FBI 1999; EMCDDA 1998, 2000; CSSA 2000; SAMHSA 2000.

given nation. These problems are aggravated by the fact that statistical systems that document responses to drug offenses are not as well-established as those for the common law crimes. Nonetheless, some rough comparisons can be made between the response to drug crimes in the United States and in other industrialized democracies.

The issue of punitiveness with respect to drug crimes must start earlier in the criminal justice process than it does for common law crimes such as burglary or robbery. Drug offenses usually do not have a citizen who complains to the police as most other serious crimes do. Drug offenses are usually identified by an arrest or other police-initiated action. This means that the police have a great deal of control over the volume and distribution of drug crimes. If the police choose not to find drug crimes they need not find them. In this sense, the punishment of drug offenses begins at the stage of the police decision to enforce the drug laws.

The rate of drug offenses is much higher in the United States than it is in other industrialized democracies (See Table 2.11). The rate of drug crimes dealt with by the police in the United States is greater than in almost any other industrialized democracy. The U.S. rate of drug enforcement is

1.27 times that of Australia, 2.45 times that of Canada and 2.2 times the rate in England and Wales. The U.S. rates of drug enforcement are even higher when compared to noncommon law countries such as France (3.6 times) and the Netherlands (11.5 times), which has a reputaion for tolerance with respect to drug use.

The high level of drug enforcement activity in the United States could be due to the higher volume of drug use there. Household surveys of drug use suggest that this is indeed the case. A crude prevalence rate was constructed by summing up mentions of the use of any drug across the types of drugs asked about in survey, and assumes that there is no multiple drug use. This will make these "prevalence" estimates too high, but if the volume of multiple drug use is reasonably consistent across nations, then this will give us an indication of the relative level of drug use across nations. With this indicator, about 53 percent of the U.S. adult population has used drugs in the prior 12 months. This is approximately the same as the prevalence of drug use in Australia, but less than that for England and Wales (42 percent), France (18 percent), the Netherlands (25 percent), and Germany (12 percent). In each comparison, the ratio of a nation's enforcement activity to enforcement in the United States is greater than the ratio of the prevalence of use in the respective countries to the prevalence of use in the United States. This suggests that the police in the United States are engaged in more aggressive drug law enforcement than the police in other nations.

More punitive sentencing policies also contribute to the high incarceration rate for drug crimes in the United States (See Table 2.12). The probability of receiving a sentence to prison for a drug offense is higher in the United States than it is in other industrialized nations. Drug offenders in the United States receive custodial sentences at more than 4 times the rate of offenders in England and Wales or Germany. Courts in Austria and France are more likely to incarcerate drug offenders, but even here the United States is almost 2 times as likely to impose custodial sentences for drug offenses. These differences are reduced somewhat when comparisons are restricted to drug trafficking. The probability of a custodial sentence for drug trafficking in the United States is 1.68 times that in England and Wales, 1.25 that in France, and 2 times that in Austria.

Imposed sentences for drug offenses are also longer in the United States than in other nations. For any drug offense, the United States imposes sentences that are 15 to 20 percent higher than those imposed in other industrialized democracies. The average sentence imposed is 21 months in the United States, 17.7 months in England and Wales, 18 months in France, and 16 months in Sweden. For trafficking these differ-

Table 2.12

**Sentences Imposed on Drug Offenders by Nation:
Incarceration and Length of Sentence Imposed**

NATION	PERCENT INCARCERATION		LENGTH OF SENTENCE IMPOSED IN MONTHS	
	TOTAL DRUGS	DRUG TRAFFICKING	TOTAL DRUGS	DRUG TRAFFICKING
Austria	35	35	na	na
England & Wales	17	44	18	26
France	45	59	18	22
Germany	18	na	na	na
Scotland	13	48	na	24
Sweden	21		16	31
United States	73	74	21	38

SOURCE: International Crime Survey 1996; Mayhew and White 1997.

ences are greater. The average imposed sentence for drug trafficking in the United States is 38 months compared with 26 months in England and Wales, 22 months in France and 31 months in Sweden.

The high incarceration rates for drug crimes in the United States, then, are the product of both more prevalent use and more punitive policies. At every stage of the criminal justice process examined here, the United States is more punitive in the enforcement of drug laws than other industrialized democracies. The police are more likely to arrest and the courts are more likely to incarcerate. While the length of imposed sentences are longer in the United States than elsewhere, these differences are not as large as those for arrest and sentencing.

IS THE UNITED STATES
REALLY MORE PUNITIVE?

Although the common wisdom holds that the United States is the most punitive of industrialized democracies, the picture emerging from this discussion is more complex. The United States has the highest per capita rates of incarceration of any industrialized democracy (Walmsley 1999). This is prima facie evidence for punitiveness. When this stock rate is decomposed into the propensity to incarcerate and the length of stay, and when account is taken of the level and type of crime in a nation, however, the relative punitiveness of the United States becomes less clear. The propensity to incarcerate for homicide is not radically different in the United States compared to other institutionally similar countries. The length of sentence imposed and the time served in prison for homicide, however, are longer in the United States than in the other nations examined here. This is probably the result of sentencing reforms introduced in the late 1980s and 1990s, since this was not the case in the early 1980s (Lynch 1995). Indeed, there was some evidence at that time that other nations may require longer terms in custody for homicide than the United States. For violent crimes, as the level of violence decreases, the disparity between the United States and other common law countries increases with respect to time served, but not the propensity to incarcerate.

In the case of property crime, it is clear that the United States incarcerates more and for longer periods than other similar nations. The same appears to be true for drug offenses. The United States, then, is not universally more punitive than other industrialized democracies, but it does seem to be more punitive with respect to property crime and drug offenses. Moreover, the punitiveness of sentencing policies seems to have increased since the early 1980s and this increase seems to have come in the form of longer sentences to incarceration (Farrington and Langan 1992).

If other similar nations are useful standards, then these cross-national comparisons suggest that the United States should reduce both the propensity to use incarceration and the length of time served for lesser property offenses and drugs.[25] The use of incarceration for extreme violence in the United States is not very different from that in other nations and need not change. The length of sentences imposed, however, could be reduced. The relative position of the United States and other similar nations with regard to moderate violence is not clear. The United States seems to impose longer sentences for crimes such as robbery, but this may be due to more extensive use of weapons in the United States. More work must be done in this area.

These findings also have implications for efforts to reduce prison populations. It is clear from these studies that the United States will have larger prison populations than other institutionally similar nations largely because of the relatively high levels of lethal violence. Even if sentencing policies were similar in the United States and England, for example, the high rates of serious violence in the United States would produce higher per capita rates of incarceration. This is a point often missed in studies of prison use that control for total crime in a society. At the same time, reasonably large reductions in the prison population could be achieved by reducing the use of incarceration and the length of time served for property crime (and possibly drug offenses) to the level of nations such as England or Canada.[26]

CONCLUSION

Cross-national comparisons of crime, and responses to it, figure prominently in debates about criminal justice policy. Unfortunately these comparisons are often done without sufficient attention to the complexities involved. This chapter has described some of that complexity. It has also described some of the recently available data that can be used to make appropriately complex comparisons and thereby dispel some of the misinformation created by more casual comparisons. Finally these data have been used to test the common wisdom that the United States is both the most crime-ridden and most punitive of industrialized democracies. I have attempted to show that the differences between the United States and other nations in these areas are less than commonly believed and are more crime-specific. It is hoped that this will help move the policy debate from vague and general prescriptions to more specific suggestions for policy and for research.

3

The Biological Basis of Crime

ADRIAN RAINE

Recognition is increasing that biological processes are at some level implicated in the development of criminal behavior. There is certainly debate about the precise contribution of such factors to crime outcome, and there is considerable debate about the precise mechanisms that these biological factors reflect. Yet few serious scientists in psychology and psychiatry would deny that biological factors are relevant to understanding crime, and public interest in and understanding of this perspective are increasing. The discipline of criminology, on the other hand, has been reluctant to embrace this new body of knowledge. Part of the reason may be interdisciplinary rivalries, part may simply be a lack of understanding, and part may be due to deep-seated historical and moral suspicions of a biological approach to crime causation. For whatever reason, these data have been largely ignored by criminologists and sociologists.

It is hoped that this chapter will go some way to allaying these suspicions. Certainly many reasons exist to take this body of knowledge seriously. Biology is not destiny, and we *can* benignly change many of the biological predispositions that shape the violent offender. One of the reasons why we have been so unsuccessful in preventing adult crime is because interventions to date have systematically ignored the biological side of the biosocial equation that produces crime. If we are to be truly serious about tackling crime and violence in society, we need to give more attention to the biological factors that cause crime.

This chapter will first outline the evidence for a genetic predisposition to crime. If genetic factors are indeed involved, then there has to be some biological basis to crime (although it should also be made clear that environmental factors in addition give rise to biological risk factors for crime). It then turns to a discussion of psychophysiological factors that predispose to crime and how one heritable influence (low physiological arousal) is thought to be the best-replicated biological correlate of antisocial behavior in child and adolescent samples. Technical advances have led to the ability to look directly at the brains of violent and criminal offenders, and the next section reviews the area of brain imaging and findings of prefrontal functional and structural deficits in adult offenders. Other biological processes are then briefly reviewed, including birth complications, minor physical anomalies, nutrition, hormones, neurotransmitters, and molecular genetics.[1] Finally, policy implications of this research will be outlined, covering intervention and prevention programs aimed at reducing the effect of biological risk factors, and also implications of brain imaging research for the criminal justice system.

GENETICS

Twin Studies

The twin method for ascertaining whether a given trait is to any extent heritable makes use of the fact that monozygotic (MZ) or "identical" twins are genetically identical, having 100 percent of their genes in common with one another. Conversely, dizygotic (DZ) or "fraternal" twins are less genetically alike than MZ twins, and are in fact no more alike genetically than non-twin siblings.

When the trait being measured is a dichotomy (for example, criminal/noncriminal), "concordance" rates are calculated for MZ and DZ twins separately. A 70 percent concordance for crime in a set of MZ twins, for example, would mean that if one of the MZ pair is criminal, then the chance of the co-twin being criminal is 70 percent. Similar concordance rates can be calculated for DZ twins. If MZ twins have higher concordance rates for crime than DZ twins, then this constitutes some evidence for the notion that crime has a heritable component. The difference between these correlation coefficients, when doubled, gives an estimate of heritability, or the proportion of variance in criminality that can be attributed to genetic influences (Falconer 1965).

Are identical twins more concordant for criminality than fraternal twins? The answer from many reviews conducted on this expanding field is undoubtedly yes. As one example, a review of all the twin studies of crime conducted up to 1993 showed that although twin studies vary widely in terms of the age, sex, country of origin, sample size, determination of zygosity, and definition of crime, nevertheless all thirteen studies of crime show greater concordance rates for criminality in MZ as opposed to DZ twins (Raine 1993). If one averages concordance rates across all studies (weighting for sample sizes), these thirteen studies result in concordances of 51.5 percent for MZ twins and 20.6 percent for DZ twins. Furthermore, the twin studies that have been conducted since 1993 have confirmed the hypothesis that there is greater concordance for antisocial and aggressive behavior in MZ relative to DZ twins (for example, Slutske et al. 1997; Eley, Lichenstein, and Stevenson 1999).

Twin studies have methodological limitations that restrict the conclusions that can be drawn from individual studies. A very common criticism of twin studies is that MZ twins may share a more common environment than DZ twins. For example, parents may treat MZ twins in a more similar fashion than DZ twins, thus artificially raising concordance rates in MZ twins. If this were true, the greater concordance for crime in MZ twins may be due more to environmental than genetic factors. Some evidence indicates that this may be the case (Allen 1976).

Criticisms such as these tend to lead researchers to discount results from twin studies as showing evidence for heritability, but there is also counterevidence. Grove et al. (1990) studied thirty-two sets of monozygotic twins who were separated and reared apart shortly after birth, and found statistically significant heritabilities for antisocial behavior in both childhood (0.41) and adulthood (0.28). Such evidence for heritability cannot be due to being raised in the same environment. Furthermore, one has to consider the methodological problems with twin studies, which can *decrease* estimates of heritability as opposed to artificially increasing them. For example, there is evidence that some twins make attempts to "de-identify" or be different from one another (Schacter and Stone 1985), while other twin pairs develop opposite (for example, dominant-submissive) role relationships (Moilanen 1987). These effects are expected to be greater in MZ pairs, with the result of artificially *reducing* heritability estimates. Though MZ twins are genetically identical, identical twinning can result in biological differences that can accentuate human differences. For example, there is a greater discrepancy in the birthweights of MZ twins relative to DZ twins, and birth complications have been linked to differences in behavior and cognition. This nongenetic, biological factor will result in an exaggeration of behavioral differences in MZ twins and a reduction in heritability estimates. The methodological problems of twin studies are just as likely to *decrease* heritability estimates as opposed to *inflating* them; in all probability these effects tend to cancel each other out.

Adoption Studies

Adoption studies also overcome the problem with twin studies because they more cleanly separate out genetic and environmental influences. We can examine offspring who have been separated from their criminal, biological parents early in life and sent out to other families. If these offspring grow up to become criminal at greater rates than foster children whose biological parents were not criminal, this would indicate a genetic influence with its origin in the subject's biological parents.

A variation of this type of study is the "cross-fostering" technique that has been used extensively in experimental genetic studies of animals. Applied to humans, the offspring whose biological parents are criminal or noncriminal are raised by parents who themselves are either criminal or noncriminal. This 2 x 2 design capitalizes on what is effectively a natural experiment, and allows for a more systematic exploration of genetic and environmental influences. As will be seen later, this method also allows an assessment of possible interactions between genetic and environmental influences.

A good example of a cross-fostering adoption study is a classic study conducted by Mednick et al. (1984), illustrated in Table 3.1. These researchers based their analyses on 14,427 adoptions that took place in Denmark between 1927 and 1947. Infants were adopted out immediately in 25.3 percent of cases, 50.6 percent within one year, 12.8 percent in the second year, and 11.3 percent after age two. Court records were obtained on 65,516 biological parents, adoptive parents, and adoptees in order to assess which subjects had convictions. When both adoptive and biological parents were noncriminal (neither genetic nor environmental predispositions present), 13.5 percent of the adoptees had a criminal record. This increased to 14.7 percent when adoptive parents only were criminal, meaning that an environmental but not genetic effect was operating. When only the biological parents were criminal, the conviction rate in the adoptees increased to 20.0 percent. When both adoptive and biological parents were criminal (both genetic and environmental predispositions present), the conviction rate increased to 24.5 percent. The effect of an adopted child having a criminal biological parent was associated with a statistically significant increase in the likelihood of the adoptee becoming criminal.

While this is but one example, a review of fifteen other adoption studies conducted in Denmark, Sweden, and the United States shows that all but one find a genetic basis to criminal behavior (Raine 1993). Importantly, evidence for this genetic predisposition has been found by several independent research groups in several different countries. These data, therefore, provide evidence that the basic finding is robust. Interestingly, the three studies that

Table 3.1
Results of Cross-Fostering Analyses (Percentages refer to the proportion of adoptees who had court convictions.)

		ARE BIOLOGICAL PARENTS CRIMINAL?	
		YES	No
ARE ADOPTIVE PARENTS CRIMINAL?	YES	24.5%	14.7%
	No	20.0%	13.5%

SOURCE: Mednick, Gabrielli, and Hutchings (1984).

had a large enough sample size to separate violent from nonviolent, petty property crime found that there is heritability for petty property crimes but not for violent crimes (Bohman et al. 1982; Mednick et al. 1984; Sigvardsson et al. 1982). On the other hand, an adoption study by van den Oord, Boomsma, and Verhulst (1994) found heritability of 70 percent for aggressive behavior compared to 39 percent for delinquency. Consequently, while there is very clear evidence for a genetic basis to adult criminal offending, there is currently some question as to whether adoption studies of violent adult offending in particular show a genetic basis.

One of the key themes of this chapter is the notion that the *interaction* between biological and social factors may be particularly important. This concept is well illustrated in a cross-fostering analysis of petty criminality (Cloninger et al. 1982), results of which are illustrated in Figure 3.1. Swedish adoptees ($N = 862$) were divided into four groups depending on the presence or absence of (1) a congenital predisposition (that is, whether biological parents were criminal) and (2) a postnatal predisposition (how the children were raised by their adoptive parents). When both heredity and environmental predispositional factors were present, 40 percent of the adoptees were criminal compared to 12.1 percent with only genetic factors present, 6.7 percent for those with only a bad family environment, and 2.9 percent when both genetic and environmental factors were absent. The fact that the 40 percent rate for criminality when both biological and environmental factors are present is greater than the 18.8 percent rate given by a combination of "congenital only" and "postnatal only" conditions indicates that genetic and environmental factors are interacting.

Further analyses indicated that the occupational status of both biological and adoptive parents were the main postnatal variables involved in this nonadditive interaction. Cloninger and Gottesman (1987) later analyzed data for females with larger sample sizes. As would be expected, these crime rates in female adoptees are much lower than for males, but the same interactive pattern is present: Crime rates in adoptees are greatest when both heritable and environmental influences are present, with this interaction accounting for twice as much crime as is produced by genetic and environmental influences taken alone.

Evidence for gene x environment interaction is also provided by Cadoret et al. (1983), who presented data from three adoption studies. When both genetic and environmental factors are present, they account for a greater number of antisocial behaviors than either of these two factors acting alone. Crowe (1974) also found some evidence for a gene x environment interaction in his analysis of adopted-away offspring of female prisoners, though this trend was only marginally significant ($p < .10$). Cadoret et al. (1995) in an adoption study of 95 male and 102 female adoptees whose parents had either antisocial personality and/or alcohol abuse showed that parental antisocial personality predicted increased aggression and conduct disorders in the offspring—illustrating evidence for genetic processes. But in addition, adverse adoptive home environment was found to *interact* with adult antisocial personality in predicting increased aggression in the offspring, that is, a gene x environment interaction effect.

A related but different concept is that of gene-environment correlations. An interesting example of this is a study by Ge et al. (1996), who showed that the adopted-away offspring of biological parents who had antisocial personality / substance abuse were more likely to show antisocial and hostile behaviors in childhood. This helps establish genetic transmission of childhood antisocial behavior. In addition, an association was found between antisocial behavior in the biological parent and the parenting behaviors of the adoptive parents. This can be explained by a transmission pathway in which the biological parent contributes a genetic predisposition toward antisocial behavior in the offspring. The antisocial offspring then in turn elicit negative parenting behaviors in the adoptive parents. This study provides direct evidence of an "evocative" gene-environment correlation, and suggests that the association between negative parenting in the adoptive parent and antisocial behavior in the child is mediated by genetic processes. One of the goals of future behavior genetic studies should be to further examine the interplay between genes and environment in this fashion. More generally, there are likely to be future exciting developments with

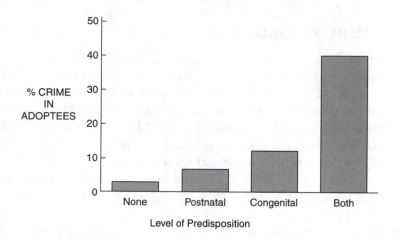

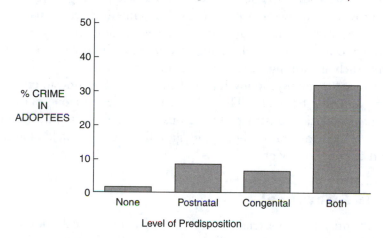

Figure 3.1

Results of a Cross-Fostering Analysis Indicating Evidence for an Interaction between Genetic and Environmental Factors in (a) Males and (b) Females.
SOURCES: Cloninger and Gottesman (1987); Cloninger et al. (1982).

respect to identifying the specific genes which give rise to the risk factors that shape criminal behavior (see section on neurogenetics).

PSYCHOPHYSIOLOGY

Since the 1940s an extensive body of research has been built up on the psychophysiological basis of antisocial, delinquent, criminal, and psychopathic behavior. For example, there have been at least 150 studies on electrodermal (sweat rate) and cardiovascular (heart rate) activity in such populations, and in electroencephalographic (EEG) research alone there have been hundreds of studies on delinquency and crime (Gale 1975). This body of research has received little attention in the broader field of criminology, and is rarely referred to in textbooks on crime. One purpose of this chapter is to bring this body of knowledge to the attention of this more general audience.

Definitions of psychophysiology vary, but one useful perspective outlined by Dawson (1990) is that it is "concerned with understanding the relationships between psychological states and processes on the one hand and physiological measures on the other hand" (p. 243). Psychophysiology is uniquely placed to provide important insights into criminal behavior because it rests at the interface between clinical science, cognitive science, and neuroscience (Dawson 1990). Thus, it is sometimes easier to see the relevance of this research for crime relative to biochemistry research because concepts in psychophysiology are more easily linked to broader concepts such as learning, emotion, arousal, and cognition.

There are many psychophysiological correlates of antisocial, criminal, and psychopathic behavior.[2] The focus here will lie with one particular psychophysiological construct, low arousal, because—as will become clear—it is the strongest psychophysiological finding in the field of antisocial and criminal behavior.

EEG Underarousal

One influential psychophysiological theory of antisocial behavior is that antisocial individuals are chronically underaroused. Traditional psychophysiological measures of arousal include heart rate, skin conductance activity, and electroencephalogram (EEG) measured during a "resting" state. Low heart rate and skin conductance activity, and more excessive slow-wave EEG (delta activity with a frequency of 1–4 cycles per second [cps], 4–7 cps theta activity, and 8–10 cps slow alpha) indicate underarousal, that is, less than average levels of physiological arousal. Most studies tend to employ single measures of arousal, although studies that employ multiple measures are in a stronger position to test an arousal theory of antisocial behavior.

EEG is recorded from scalp electrodes that measure the electrical activity of the brain. Literally hundreds of studies assessing EEG in criminals, delinquents, psychopaths, and violent offenders have been done over the past sixty years, and it is clear that a large number of them implicate EEG abnormalities in violent recidivistic offending. As examples, Bach-y-Rita et al. (1971) and Hill and Pond (1952) examined large samples of violent offenders and observed EEG abnormalities in about 50 percent of the cases, with the most common abnormality being excessive slow-wave EEG (underarousal). These findings have been supported by studies of murderers and other violent offenders (for example, Mark and Ervin 1970; Williams 1969). Fishbein et al. (1989), in a sample of 124 adult male drug abusers, found that aggression was associated with increased slow-wave theta activity and decreased alpha, indicating underarousal. Convit, Czobor, and Volavka (1991) observed the same pattern within a sample of psychiatric inpatients; the number of instances of violence on wards was related to increased levels of delta activity and lower levels of alpha. Drake, Hietter, and Pakalnis (1992) found that, while none of 24 depressed patients and only 1 of 20 headache control patients had abnormal EEGs, 7 of 23 patients with either intermittent explosive disorder or episodic dyscontrol (brief periods where the individual lacks control) had diffuse or focal slowing in EEG. Murderers have more recently been shown to have more EEG deficits in the right than the left hemisphere of the brain, with multiple abnormalities being especially present in the right temporal cortex (Evans and Park 1997). On the other hand, Pillmann et al. (1999) showed greater abnormalities in the *left* temporal region of repeat violent offenders.

Generally speaking, the prevalence of EEG abnormalities in violent individuals in this large literature ranges from 25 percent to 50 percent, with the rate of abnormalities in normals estimated as ranging from 5 percent to 20 percent. The bulk of this research implicated the more frontal regions of the brain, areas that regulate executive functions such as planning and decision making. Similar conclusions are drawn by Volavka (1987) and Milstein (1988) for crime in general and violent crime in particular.

Cardiovascular Underarousal

Data on resting heart rate provides striking support for underarousal in antisocials. Indeed, the findings for heart rate level (HRL) on noninstitutionalized antisocials are believed to represent the strongest and best replicated biological correlate of antisocial behavior. A detailed review of these studies and full theoretical and methodological considerations are given in Raine (1993) and Raine (1996a). Briefly, twenty-four studies of resting heart rate and conduct-disordered, delinquent, and antisocial children and adolescents performed between 1971 and 1996 yielded twenty-nine independent samples of antisocials and a total of thirty-eight effect sizes (a measure of the strength of the effect). Of the thirty-eight effect sizes, thirty-two were significant and positive (that is, low heart rate associated with antisocial behavior), while only one was significant and in the negative direction. This latter, unexpected finding (Zahn and Kruesi 1993) was interpreted by its authors as possibly due to biased referral to the clinic by anxious, easily stressed parents who worried about their child and who may genetically transmit high HRL to their child.

A low resting heart rate is the best-replicated biological marker of antisocial and aggressive behavior in childhood and adolescent community samples. Resting HRL was measured in a wide variety of ways, including polygraphs, pulse meters, and stopwatches. A wide number of definitions of antisocial behavior are used, ranging from legal criminality and delinquency to teacher ratings of antisocial behavior in school, self-report socialization measures, diagnostic criteria for conduct disorder, and genetically inferred law breaking (i.e. offspring of criminals). Subjects were also assessed in a wide variety of settings, including medical interview, study office, school, university laboratory, and hospital. In the light of such variability, it is surprising that consistency in findings have been obtained, attesting to the robustness of the observed effects. Importantly, there has also been good cross-laboratory replication of the finding, and it has also been found in six different countries—England, Germany, New Zealand, the United States, Mauritius, and Canada—illustrating invariance to cultural context.

The link between low heart rate and crime is not the result of such things as height, weight, body bulk, physical development, and muscle tone (Raine, Venables, and Mednick 1997; Raine, Buchsbaum and La Casse 1997; Wadsworth 1976; Farrington 1997); scholastic ability and IQ (Raine, Venables, and Williams 1990; Farrington 1997); excess motor activity and inattention (Raine, Venables, and Mednick 1997; Farrington 1997); drug and alcohol use (Raine, Venables, and Mednick 1997); engagement in physical exercise and sports (Wadsworth 1976; Farrington 1997); or low social class, divorce, family size, teenage pregnancy, and other psychosocial adversity (Raine, Venables, and Williams 1990; Wadsworth 1976; Farrington 1997). Intriguingly, an unusual and important feature of the relationship is its diagnostic specificity. No other psychiatric condition has been linked to low resting heart rate. Other psychiatric conditions, including alcoholism, depression, schizophrenia, and anxiety disorder, have, if anything, been linked to *higher* (not lower) resting heart rate.

Low heart rate has been found to be an independent predictor of violence. Out of forty-eight psychosocial and individual measures, only two risk factors were related to violence independently of all other risk factors in all six analyses: low resting heart rate and poor concentration (Farrington 1997). Indeed, low heart rate was more strongly related to both self-report and teacher measures of violence than having a criminal parent. These findings led Farrington (1997) to conclude that low heart rate may be one of the most important explanatory factors for violence (p. 99). There is also a substantial heritability for resting heart rate, suggesting that it may be a genetic marker for antisocial and criminal behavior (Raine et al. 1990). Furthermore, the offspring of criminal parents have been shown to have low resting heart rate in two separate studies (Farrington 1987; Venables 1987). Low heart rate characterizes female as well as male antisocial individuals. Several studies, including two that are prospective, have now established that, *within* females, low heart rate is linked to antisocial behavior (Raines et al. 1990; Maliphant, Hume, and Furnham 1990; Raine, Venables, and Mednick 1997; Moffitt and Caspi In press).

Prospective Studies of Underarousal

One of the major difficulties in trying to draw conclusions on the psychophysiological basis of criminal behavior is that most studies conducted to date have been nonprospective and have utilized institutionalized populations. In addition, most studies report results from only one of the three most commonly measured psychophysiological response systems (electrodermal, cardiovascular, and cortical). Prospective longitudinal research—that is, research that follows people forward through their lives—allows for much more powerful statements to be made about predispositions for criminal behavior and to elucidate cause and effect relationships; but because prospective research is more difficult to execute, there are few such studies.

Regarding heart rate levels, five prospective studies of heart rate alone have confirmed that low heart rate is predictive of later antisocial behavior, while five additional prospective studies also show significant effects for electrodermal and electrocortical arousal. Wadsworth (1976) found that lower resting heart rate in unselected eleven-year-old schoolboys predicted delinquency measured from ages eight to twenty-one. The very lowest

HRLs were found in those who committed nonsexual violent criminal offenses as adults. Similarly, Farrington (1987) found that resting heart rate measured at age eighteen to nineteen in noninstitutionalized males predicted to violent criminal offending at age twenty-five. With respect to EEG, two separate studies have shown that slow alpha frequency predicts to adult thievery in a sample of 129 Danish thirteen-year-old boys (Mednick et al. 1981) and 571 Swedish one- to fifteen-year-old boys (Petersen et al. 1982). Low heart rate characterizes life-course-persistent antisocial individuals in particular; Moffitt and Caspi (In press) have recently found that low resting heart rate assessed at ages seven, nine, and eleven is particularly characteristic of life-course-persistent offenders, a group who have been hypothesized as having early neurobiological deficits (Moffitt 1993).

As with most other studies, evidence in these prospective studies for prediction to antisocial behavior is based on only one measure of arousal. One nine-year prospective study of crime by Raine, Venables, and Williams (1990) has shown, however, that low resting heart rate, low resting skin conductance activity, and excessive slow-wave theta EEG (indicating underarousal) measured at age fifteen in normal unselected schoolboys predicted criminal behavior at age twenty-four. These three measures correctly classified 74.7 percent of all subjects as criminal/noncriminal, a rate significantly greater than chance (50 percent). In the total population, the three arousal measures were statistically independent; the fact that they all independently predicted to criminal behavior indicates strong support for an arousal theory of criminal and antisocial behavior (although this finding also cautions against the use of a simplistic, unitary arousal concept in explaining crime). Group differences in social class, academic ability, and area of residence were not found to mediate the link between underarousal and antisocial behavior.

Interpretations of Low Arousal: Fearlessness and Stimulation-Seeking Theories

Why should low arousal and low heart rate predispose to antisocial and criminal behavior? There are two main theoretical interpretations. Fearlessness theory indicates that low levels of arousal are markers of low levels of fear (Raine 1993; Raine 1997). For example, particularly fearless individuals such as bomb disposal experts who have been decorated for their bravery have particularly low HRLs and reactivity (Cox et al. 1983; O'Connor, Hallam, and Rachman 1985), as do British paratroopers decorated in the Falklands War (McMillan and Rachman 1987). A fearlessness interpretation of low arousal levels assumes that subjects are not actually at "rest," but that instead the rest periods of psychophysiological testing represent a mildly stressful paradigm and that low arousal during this period indicates lack of anxiety and fear. Lack of fear would predispose to antisocial and violent behavior because such behavior (for example, fights and assaults) requires a degree of fearlessness to execute, while lack of fear, especially in childhood, would help explain poor socialization since low fear of punishment would reduce the effectiveness of conditioning. Fearlessness theory receives support from the fact that autonomic underarousal also provides the underpinning for a fearless or uninhibited temperament in infancy and childhood (Scarpa et al. 1997; Kagan 1994).

A second theory explaining reduced arousal is stimulation-seeking theory (Eysenck 1964; Quay 1965; Raine 1993; Raine, Reynolds, Venables, et al. 1998). This theory argues that low arousal represents an unpleasant physiological state; antisocials seek stimulation in order to increase their arousal levels back to an optimal or normal level. Antisocial behavior is thus viewed as a form of stimulation-seeking, in that committing a burglary, assault, or robbery could be stimulating for some individuals. Before leaving this theory, the possibility has to be considered that fearlessness theory and stimulation-seeking theory may be complementary rather than competing theories. That is, low levels of arousal may predispose to crime because it produces some degree of fearlessness, and also encourages antisocial stimulation-seeking. Indeed, behavioral measures of stimulation-seeking and fearlessness, both taken at age three in a large sample, predict to aggressive behavior at age eleven (Raine, et al. 1998). The combined effect of these two influences may be more important in explaining antisocial behavior than either influence taken alone.

Psychophysiological Protective Factors against Crime Development

Until recently, there had been no research on biological factors that *protect* against crime development, but that is changing. We are discovering that *higher* autonomic activity during adolescence may act as a protective factor against crime development. Raine, Venables, and Williams (1995, 1996) report on a fourteen-year prospective study in which measures of arousal, orienting (sweat rate and heart rate responses to tone stimuli), and classical conditioning (learning through association) were taken in 101 unselected fifteen-year-old males. Of these, seventeen adolescent antisocials who desisted from adult crime (Desistors) were matched on adolescent antisocial behavior and demographic variables with seventeen adolescent antisocials who had become criminal by age twenty-nine (Criminals), and seventeen non-antisocial, noncriminals (Controls). Desistors had significantly higher HRLs as well as higher scores on the other psychophysiological measures than did the Criminals. Findings suggest that boys who are antisocial during adolescence but who do not go on to adult criminal offending may be protected from such an outcome by their high arousal levels.

Findings from a second study on adults provide some support for this initial finding in adolescents. Brennan et al. (1997) report on a study of protective factors in fifty men predisposed to crime by virtue of having a seriously criminal father who had been imprisoned. Of these men, twenty-four developed a criminal record and were imprisoned themselves, while the other twenty-six did not show any criminal offending. Heart rate and skin conductance measures of reactivity to fourteen orienting tones were measured at age thirty-five. The group who desisted from crime was found to have significantly higher levels of physiological orienting relative to those who exhibited criminal behavior, and to a noncriminal control group who had noncriminal fathers. Desistors seem to have a nervous system particularly sensitive to forming associations between signals of punishment and the punishment itself. In a similar fashion, higher resting heart rates in Desistors may be interpreted as indicating higher levels of fearfulness in these individuals.

Overall, the initial profile that is being built up on the psychophysiological characteristics of the Desistor is one of heightened information processing (better orienting), greater responsivity to environmental stimuli in general (fast recovery), greater sensitivity to cues predicting punishment in particular (better classical conditioning), and higher fearfulness (high HRLs). The importance of research on psychophysiological protective factors such as these is that they offer suggestions for possible intervention and prevention strategies.

BRAIN IMAGING

Advances in brain imaging techniques in the past fifteen years have provided the opportunity to gain dramatic new insights into the brain mechanisms that may be dysfunctional in violent, psychopathic offenders. In the past, the idea of peering into the mind of a murderer to gain insights into his or her acts was the province of pulp fiction or space-age movies. Yet now we can literally look at, and into, the brains of murderers using functional and structural imaging techniques that are currently revolutionizing our understanding of the causes of clinical disorders.

Brain imaging studies of violent and psychopathic populations have been reviewed by Raine (1993), Raine and Buchsbaum (1996), and Henry and Moffitt (1997). These reviews (that cover studies up to 1994), while showing variability in findings across studies, concur in indicating that violent offenders have structural and functional deficits to the frontal lobe (behind the forehead) and the temporal lobe (near the ears). Between 1994 and 1997, six more studies support this key finding of anterior brain dysfunction (Goyer et al. 1994; Volkow et al. 1995; Kuruoglu et al. 1996; Seidenwurm et al. 1997; Intrator et al. 1997; Soderstrom et al. 2000). Taken together, these later studies show continued support of the notion that poor functioning of the frontal and temporal regions may predispose to crime. Out of the six more-recent studies, five showed evidence for frontal dysfunction and four showed evidence for temporal lobe dysfunction. Despite some discrepancies, the first generation of brain imaging studies supports earlier contentions from animal and neurological studies implicating the frontal (and to some extent temporal) brain regions in the regulation and expression of aggression.

Prefrontal Dysfunction in Murderers

In the first published brain imaging study of murderers (Raine, Buchsbaum, Stanley et al. 1994), we scanned the brains of twenty-two murderers pleading not guilty by reason of insanity (or otherwise found incompetent to stand trial) and compared them to the brains of twenty-two normal controls who were matched with the murderers on sex and age. The technique we used was positron emission tomography (PET), which allowed us to measure the metabolic activity of many different regions of the brain including the prefrontal cortex, the frontalmost part of the brain. We had subjects perform a task that required them to maintain focused attention and be vigilant for a continuous period of time, and it is the prefrontal region of the brain that in part subserves this vigilance function.

The key finding was that the murderers showed significantly poorer functioning of the prefrontal cortex, that part of the brain lying above the eyes and behind the forehead. It is thought that poorer functioning of the prefrontal cortex predisposes people to violence for a number of reasons. Reduced prefrontal functioning can result in a loss of the ability of this part of the brain to control deeper and more primitive subcortical structures, such as the amygdala, which are thought to give rise to aggressive feelings. Prefrontal damage also encourages risk-taking, irresponsibility, rule breaking, emotional and aggressive outbursts, and argumentative behavior that can also predispose to violent criminal acts. Loss of self-control, immaturity, lack of tact, inability to modify and inhibit behavior appropriately, and poor social judgment could predispose to violence as well. This loss of intellectual flexibility and problem-solving skills, and reduced ability to use information provided by verbal cues can impair social skills essential for formulating nonaggressive solutions to fractious encounters. Poor reasoning ability and divergent thinking that results from prefrontal damage can lead to school failure, unemployment, and economic deprivation, thereby predisposing to a criminal and violent way of life. A further study showed that it was especially the impulsive, emotionally undercontrolled murderers who were especially likely to show prefrontal deficits (Raine, Meloy et al. 1998). Nevertheless, it should be recognized that, while there is an association between poor prefrontal function and impulsive violence, this brain dysfunction may be essentially a predisposition only, requiring other environmental, psychological, and social factors to enhance or diminish this tendency.

Corpus Callosum, Left Angular Gyrus, and the Subcortex

What other brain deficits, apart from prefrontal dysfunction, characterize murderers? We took this imaging research a step further by expanding our sample from twenty-two to forty-one murderers, and also by increasing the size of our control group to forty-one. This increase in sample size gave us more statistical power to detect group differences, and in 1997 we reported our updated findings (Raine, Buchsbaum, and La Casse 1997). The results were interesting for a variety of reasons. First, we confirmed that there was a significant reduction in the activity of the prefrontal region in murderers.

Second, we now found in this larger sample that the left angular gyrus was functioning more poorly in the murderers. The angular gyrus lies at the junction of the temporal (side of head), parietal (top and back of head), and occipital (very back of head) regions of the brain and plays a key role in integrating information from these three lobes. Reductions in activity of the left angular gyrus have been correlated with reduced verbal ability, while damage to this region has been linked to deficits in reading and arithmetic. Such cognitive deficits could predispose to educational and occupational failure which in turn predisposes to crime and violence. The fact that learning deficits have been found to be common in violent offenders lends further support to this interpretation.

Third, we found reductions in the functioning of the corpus callosum, the band of white nerve fibers that provide lines of communication between the left and right hemispheres. Although we can only speculate at the present time, we think that poor connection between the hemispheres may mean that the right hemisphere, which is involved in the generation of negative emotion (Davidson and Fox 1989), may experience less regulation and control by the inhibitory processes of the more dominant left hemisphere, a factor that may contribute to the expression of violence. Furthermore, researchers have commented on the inappropriate nature of emotional expression and the inability to grasp long-term implications of a situation in split-brain patients who have had their corpus callosum surgically severed. This implies that the inappropriate emotional expression of violent offenders and their lack of long-term planning may be partly accounted for by poor functioning of the corpus callosum. Nevertheless, callosal dysfunction by itself is unlikely to cause aggression. Instead, it may only contribute to violence in those who also have other brain abnormalities.

Effect of the Home Environment on Brain-Violence Relationships

How do psychosocial deficits moderate the relationship between prefrontal dysfunction and violence? We addressed this question by dividing our sample of murderers into those who came from relatively good home backgrounds and those who came from relatively bad ones (Raine, Stoddard, et al. 1998). In this study, ratings of psychosocial deprivation took into account early physical and sexual abuse, neglect, extreme poverty, foster home placement, a criminal parent, severe family conflict, and a broken home. The results of the study showed that, while the deprived murderer shows relatively good prefrontal functioning, it is the nondeprived murderer who shows the characteristic lack of prefrontal functioning. In particular, we found that murderers from good homes had a 14.2 percent reduction in the functioning of the right orbitofrontal cortex, a brain area that is of particular interest. Damage to this brain area results in personality and emotional deficits that parallel criminal psychopathic behavior, or what Damasio and colleagues have termed "acquired sociopathy" (Damasio 1994).

These findings are at one level counterintuitive, but from another perspective they make some sense. If a seriously violent offender comes from a bad home environment, then it seems likely that the cause of the offender's violence is due to that bad environment. But if they come from a good home background, then environmental causation seems less likely and instead biological deficits may be a better explanation. Consistent with these brain imaging findings, previous research has shown that poor fear conditioning in schoolchildren is related to antisocial behavior especially in those from a *good* home environment (Raine and Venables 1981). That is, the biological deficit (poor conditioning) is found in those who *lack* a social predisposition to antisocial behavior. Perhaps not surprisingly, it is the right orbitofrontal cortex (situated above the eye orbits) that has been found to play an important role in the development of fear conditioning.

Reduced Prefrontal Gray Matter in Antisocial Personality Disorder

Ranging from single case studies (Damasio et al. 1994) to series of neurological patients (Damasio, Tranel, and Damasio 1990; Stuss and Benson 1986), those who have suffered demonstrable damage to both gray and white matter within the prefrontal region of the brain proceed to acquire an antisocial, psychopathic-like personality. These patients also show autonomic arousal and attention deficits to socially meaningful events (Damasio 1994, Damasio, Tranel, and Damasio 1990), a finding consistent with the role played by the prefrontal cortex in modulating emotion, arousal, and attention (Stuss and Benson 1986; Davidson 1993; Raine, Reynolds, and Sheard 1991).

We recently conducted a structural magnetic resonance imaging (MRI) study on volunteers from the community with Antisocial Personality Disorder and made volumetric assessments of prefrontal gray and white matter (Raine et al. 2000). Skin conductance and heart rate activity during a social stressor was also assessed in addition to psychosocial and demographic risk factors for violence. Subjects were drawn from temporary employment agencies in Los Angeles and consisted of twenty-one males with Antisocial Personality Disorder, a normal control group of thirty-four males, and a psychiatric control group of twenty-seven males with substance dependence. Antisocials had significantly lower prefrontal gray volumes than both Controls and Substance Dependents. In contrast, groups did not differ on white prefrontal volume, indicating specificity of the deficit to gray matter (neurons). Furthermore, Antisocials also showed reduced autonomic reactivity during the social stressor compared to both Controls and Substance Dependents.

When prefrontal gray matter was expressed as a function of whole brain volume, groups were again found to differ significantly, so the results are not due to general difference in brain size but a specific difference in prefrontal size. Further analyses indicated that the three prefrontal and autonomic variables (prefrontal gray/whole brain, heart rate, skin conductance) predicted group membership with an accuracy of 76.9 percent. These prefrontal and autonomic deficits were independent of psychosocial deficits in the Antisocial group. After ten demographic and psychosocial risk factors for antisocial personality were statistically controlled for, the prefrontal and autonomic deficits added substantially to the prediction of Antisocial vs. Control group membership. As such, the brain deficits cannot be easily accounted for by psychosocial factors, and instead appear to reflect a different risk process. When both biological and social measures were used together, they correctly classified to 88.5 percent, indicating the importance of a biosocial perspective that integrates biological and social factors.

Brain Deficits in Violent Offenders with a History of Childhood Abuse

While the relationship between physical child abuse and violence is well established (Lewis et al. 1988; Tarter et al. 1984; Widom 1997), there appears to be little or no research, biological or social, on factors that differentiate abused victims who go on to perpetrate violence from those who refrain from adult violence. We recently conducted a study (Raine, Park, et al. In press) in which we used functional magnetic resonance imaging (fMRI) to address two important gaps in our knowledge of brain functioning and violence: (1) What are the brain correlates of adults in the community who have suffered severe physical abuse early in life and who go on to perpetrate serious violence in adulthood? (2) What characterizes those who experience severe physical abuse but who refrain from serious violence?

We recruited four groups of participants from the community: (1) nonviolent controls who had not suffered abuse; (2) participants with severe physical child abuse only (that is, had suffered severe physical or sexual abuse in the first eleven years, but were not violent); (3) ones with serious violence only (violence that caused either bodily injury or trauma, or that were life-threatening acts); and (4) severely abused, seriously violent offenders. All underwent fMRI while performing a visual/verbal working memory task. Functional magnetic resonance imaging measures blood flow within brain tissue, and thus allows one to assess the functional properties of the brain. In this sense, it is like PET, but unlike PET there is no exposure to radioactivity. Furthermore, it detects activity in brain regions that are as small as 1 millimeter. The task involved subjects holding in short-term memory pictures shown very briefly and pressing a response button any time a picture was repeated, a task known to activate the temporal and frontal regions of the brain.

Violent offenders who had suffered severe child abuse show reduced right hemisphere functioning, particularly in the right temporal cortex. Abused individuals who refrain from serious violence showed relatively lower left, but higher right, activation of the temporal lobe. Abused individuals, irrespective of violence status, showed reduced cortical activation during the working memory task, especially in the left hemisphere. These findings constitute the first fMRI study of brain dysfunction in violent offenders and indicate that initial right hemisphere dysfunction, when combined with the effects of severe early physical abuse, may predispose to serious violence. They also suggest that relatively good right hemisphere functioning *protects* against violence in physically abused children.

OTHER BIOLOGICAL PROCESSES: BIRTH COMPLICATIONS, MINOR PHYSICAL ANOMALIES, NUTRITION, AND NEUROCHEMISTRY

Birth Complications

Several studies have shown that babies who suffer birth complications are more likely to develop conduct disorder, delinquency, and impulsive crime and violence in adulthood (see Raine 1993 for a detailed review). Birth complications such as anoxia (getting too little oxygen), forceps delivery, and preeclampsia (hypertension leading to anoxia) are thought to contribute to brain damage, and this damage in turn may predispose to antisocial and criminal behavior. On the other hand, birth complications may not by themselves predispose to crime, but may require the presence of negative environmental circumstance to trigger later adult crime and violence.

One example of this "biosocial interaction" is a study of birth complications and maternal rejection in all 4,269 live male births that took place in one hospital in Copenhagen, Denmark (Raine, Brennan, and Mednick 1994). Birth complications were assessed by obstetricians and midwives. When the baby was one year old, the mother was interviewed by a social worker and the degree of maternal rejection was assessed by three measures: mother did not want the pregnancy, mother made an attempt to abort the fetus, and the baby was institutionalized for at least four months in the first year of life. Babies were then followed for eighteen years, when their arrests for violent crimes were assessed. A highly significant interaction was found between birth complications and maternal rejection. Babies who only suffered birth complications or who only suffered maternal rejection were no more likely than normal controls to become violent in adulthood. On the other hand, those who had both risk factors were much more likely to become violent. Only 4 percent of the sample had both birth complications and maternal rejection, but this small group accounted for 18 percent of all the violent crimes committed by the entire sample. This finding from Denmark was replicated by Piquero and Tibbetts (1999) in a prospective longitudinal study of 867 males and females from the Philadelphia Collaborative Perinatal Project; those with both prenatal/perinatal disturbances and a disadvantaged familial environment were much more likely to become adult violent offenders.

This sample was studied again when they were age thirty-four (Raine, Brennan, and Mednick 1997). The results indicate that the biosocial interaction previously observed holds for violent but not nonviolent criminal offending. Furthermore, the interaction was found to be specific to more serious forms of violence and not threats of violence. The interaction held for early onset but not late onset violence and was not accounted for by psychiatric illness in the mothers. Rearing in a public care institution in the first year of life and an attempt to abort the fetus were the key aspects of maternal rejection found to interact with birth complications in predisposing to violence.

Minor Physical Anomalies

Minor physical anomalies (MPAs) have been associated with disorders of pregnancy and are thought to reflect maldevelopment of the fetus (including brain maldevelopment) toward the end of the first three months of pregnancy. MPAs are relatively minor physical abnormalities consisting of such features as low seated ears, adherent ear lobes, furrowed tongue, curved fifth finger, single transverse palmar crease, gaps between the first and second toes, unusually long third toes, and fine hair that doesn't easily comb down. They are not stigmatizing as they are not obvious unless a careful physical examination is done. While MPAs may have a genetic basis, they may also be caused by environmental factors of the fetus such as anoxia, bleeding, and infection (Guy et al. 1983).

Minor physical anomalies have also been found to characterize preadult antisocial behavior and temperament. Paulus and Martin (1986) found more MPAs in aggressive and impulsive preschool boys, while

Halverson and Victor (1976) also found higher levels of MPAs in elementary male schoolchildren with problem school behavior. MPAs have even been linked to peer aggression as early as age three (Waldrop et al. 1978). Although MPAs have generally characterized behavior disorders in children drawn from the normal population (see Pomeroy, Sprafkin, and Gadow 1988 for a review), at least one study failed to observe a link between MPAs and conduct disorder within a mixed group of emotionally disturbed children (Pomeroy, Sprafkin, and Gadow 1988).

Mednick and Kandel (1988) assessed MPAs in a sample of 129 twelve-year-old boys examined by an experienced pediatrician. MPAs were found to be related to violent offending as assessed nine years later when the subjects were age twenty-one, though not to property offenses without violence. However, when subjects were divided into those from unstable, nonintact homes versus those from stable homes, a biosocial interaction was observed. MPAs only predicted violence in those individuals raised in unstable home environments. A similar interactive relationship was also observed for birth weight and family stability (Kandel and Mednick, 1991). These findings are quite similar to those on birth complications reported above; in both studies the presence of a negative psychosocial factor is required to "trigger" the biological risk factor, and in both cases the effects are specific to violent offending. In a study confirming specificity to violence, Arseneault et al. (2000) found that MPAs predicted to violent delinquency during adolescence in 170 teenagers, but not to nonviolent delinquency. Furthermore, effects were independent of family adversity.

Nutrition

Although deficiency in nutrition itself has been rarely studied in relation to childhood aggression, several studies have demonstrated the effects of related processes including food additives, hypoglycemia, and more recently cholesterol on human behavior (Rutter, Giller, and Hagell 1998; Raine 1993; Fishbein and Pease 1994). In addition, some studies have shown associations between overaggressive behavior and vitamin and mineral deficiency (Breakey 1997; Werbach 1995). Furthermore, one study (Rosen 1996) claimed that nearly a third of a population of juvenile delinquents (mostly males) showed evidence of iron deficiency. Nevertheless, these findings remain both conflicting and controversial (Rutter, Giller, and Hagell 1998).

One intriguing study illustrates the potentially causal role of malnutrition as early as pregnancy in predisposing to antisocial behavior. Toward the end of World War II when Germany was withdrawing from Holland, they placed a food blockade on the country that led to major food short-ages and near starvation in the cities and towns for several months. Women who were pregnant at this time were exposed to severe malnutrition at dif-ferent stages of pregnancy. The male offspring of these women were followed up into adulthood to ascertain rates of Antisocial Personality Disorder and were compared to controls who were not exposed to malnu-trition. Pregnant women starved during the blockade had 2.5 times the rates of Antisocial Personality Disorder in their adult offspring compared to controls (Neugebauer, Hoek, and Susser 1999).

Initial evidence also shows relationships between both protein and zinc deficiency and aggression in animals (Tikal, Benesova, and Frankova 1976; Halas, Reynolds, and Sanstead, 1977). Recent studies of humans support these animal findings. Protein and zinc deficiency may lead to aggression by negatively impacting brain functioning. There is extensive experimental evi-dence in animals that the offspring of rats fed a diet containing marginal levels of either zinc or protein throughout pregnancy and lactation showed impaired brain development (Oteiza et al. 1990; Bennis-Taleb et al. 1999). In humans, zinc deficiency in pregnancy has been linked to impaired DNA, RNA, and protein synthesis during brain development, and congenital brain abnormalities (Pfeiffer and Braverman 1982). Similarly, protein provides essential amino acids for the rapid growth of fetal tissue. PET studies of vio-lent offenders have revealed deficits to the prefrontal cortex and corpus callosum (Raine, Buchsbaum, and La Casse 1997; Volkow et al. 1995), and it is of interest that the offspring of rats fed a low-protein diet during preg-nancy show a specific impairment to the corpus callosum (Wainwright and Stefanescu 1983) and reduction in DNA concentration in the forebrain (Bennis-Taleb et al. 1999). The amygdala, which also shows abnormal func-tioning in PET imaging of violent offenders (Raine, Buchsbaum, and La Casse 1997; Raine, Meloy, et al. 1998; Davidson, Putnam, and Larson 2000), is densely innervated by zinc-containing neurons (Christensen and Frederickson 1998), and males with a history of assaultive behavior were found to have lower zinc relative to copper ratios in their blood compared to nonassaultive controls (Walsh et al. 1997). Consequently, protein and zinc deficiency may contribute to the brain impairments shown in violent offenders which in turn are thought to predispose to violence.

Environmental Pollutants and Neurotoxicity

It has long been suspected that exposure to pollutants, particularly heavy metals that have neurotoxic effects, can lead to mild degrees of brain impairment which in turn predisposes to antisocial and aggressive behavior. One of the best studies to date is that of Needleman et al. (1996) who assessed lead levels in the bones of 301 eleven-year-old schoolboys. Boys with higher lead levels were found to have significantly higher teacher ratings of delinquent and aggressive behavior, higher parent ratings of delinquent and aggressive behavior, and higher self-report delinquency scores. These findings do not occur in isolation: Similar links between lead levels and antisocial, delinquent behavior and aggression have been found in at least six other studies in several different countries (see Needleman et al. 1996 for a review). Furthermore, experimental exposure to lead during development increases aggressive behavior in hamsters (Delville 1999), thus suggesting a causal link.

Less strong to date, but nevertheless provocative, are findings with respect to manganese. At high levels, manganese has toxic effects on the brain and can damage the brain so much that it can even lead to Parkinson-like symptoms. Furthermore, it reduces levels of serotonin and dopamine, neurotransmitters that play a key role in brain communication (see later "Neurotransmitters" section). One study by Gottschalk et al. (1991) found that three different samples of violent criminals compared to controls had higher levels of manganese in their hair. On the other hand, not all studies have found this association (Schauss 1981). It may be that low levels of calcium intake interact with high manganese in predisposing to violent behavior because animal research indicates that the neurotoxic effect of manganese is particularly strong when the animal is deficient in calcium.

Hormones

Testosterone. Excellent reviews and discussions of the potential role played by testosterone in both animals and man can be found in Olweus (1987), Brain (1990), Archer (1991), and Susman and Ponirakis (1997). Animal research suggests that the steroid hormone testosterone plays an important role in the genesis and maintenance of some forms of aggressive behavior in rodents, and early exposure to testosterone has been found to increase aggression in a wide range of animal species (Brain 1990).

A key question generated by this literature is whether testosterone is involved in aggression and violent crime in man. Studies correlating questionnaire measures of aggression in normals to testosterone levels have generally produced weak or nonsignificant findings (Rubin 1987). Studies of violent incarcerated inmates on the other hand have been more consistent in producing significant effects of moderate to large strength (Rubin 1987). This theme is reiterated by Archer (1991) in a rigorous and critical review of the literature, arguing effects are small or negligible when aggression is measured using personality inventories, but strong and significant when groups high and low on behavioral measures of aggression are compared. Five studies of prisoners reviewed by Archer resulted in substantial effects. Furthermore, female prisoners also show high testosterone levels, and interestingly this effect was found to be specific to females who committed unprovoked assault but not those who reacted violently when physically assaulted (Dabbs et al. 1988).

The critical question in this literature concerns whether testosterone-violence relationships are causal. Little doubt exists that castration decreases aggression in animals and administration of testosterone increases aggression. Few experimental studies have been conducted in humans, but there is nevertheless evidence of a causal relationship. Olweus et al. (1988) assessed their finding of higher testosterone in male adolescents with high levels of self-report aggression using path analysis and concluded that testosterone had causal effects on both provoked and unprovoked aggressive behavior. One study that comes close to such an ideal experiment is that of Wille and Beier (1989), who showed that ninety-nine castrated German sex offenders had a significantly lower recidivism rate eleven years postrelease (3 percent) compared to thirty-five noncastrated sex offenders (46 percent). There is in addition some limited evidence that less drastic methods of reducing testosterone levels such as administration of anti-androgens and progesterone derivatives have some effect in lowering violence and sexual aggression (Rubin 1987; Brain 1990; Archer 1991). One double-blind, crossover hormone replacement study administered testosterone to male adolescents with delayed puberty and found that medium doses increased aggressive behavior twenty-one months later (Susman and Ponirakis, 1997). It could be argued that extreme alterations in testosterone are not a good model for the less severe variability found in the general population, and that moderate changes of this hormone do not significantly influence aggression. On the other hand, Loosen, Purdon, and Pavlou (1994) found that mild reductions in testosterone in men were associated with reductions in outwardly directed anger, thus suggesting that mild changes in testosterone can modulate aggression.

Testosterone levels are in part heritable (Turner et al. 1986), and it is conceivable that the genetic predisposition to crime may in part be expressed through the hormonal system. On the other hand, it is also known that environmental influences such as success in competition, the perception of winning, exposure to erotic films, and social dominance can increase circulating levels of testosterone (Brain 1990; Archer 1991). Clearly, links between testosterone and aggression are complex, and simplistic explanations of this link are probably incorrect. By the same token, it would be equally erroneous to discount the evidence for the role of hormones in influencing aggression merely because hormones are influenced by the environment. In this context, theoretical perspectives should take into account reciprocal influences between behavior and aggression and the roles hormones play in the regulation of arousal (Susman et al. 1996).

Cortisol. Cortisol (also called a glucocorticoid) is a hormone produced by a corticotropin-releasing factor (CRF), a peptide, which is in turn produced by a brain area called the hypothalamus, which regulates autonomic functions (like heart rate and skin conductance) and emotional responses. Individuals who are aroused or stressed show an increase in cortisol. As such, one might expect reduced cortisol levels in antisocials who, as we saw earlier, are thought to be relatively underaroused and fearless.

A number of studies in a wide variety of contexts have now shown that there is indeed a link between low resting cortisol and antisocial, aggressive behavior. McBurnett et al. (1991) found that boys with conduct disorder without comorbid anxiety disorder showed significantly lower concentrations of cortisol than did boys with CD and comorbid anxiety disorder. Cortisol has similarly been reported to be low in habitually violent incarcerated offenders (Virnkunnen 1985), in aggressive schoolchildren (Tennes and Kreye 1985), in adolescents with conduct problems (Susman and Petersen 1992), boys with disruptive behavior (McBurnett et al. 2000), disinhibited children, and boys with oppositional defiant disorder (van Goozen et al. 1998).

Taken together, these studies suggest that resting cortisol may play a nontrivial role in mediating antisocial, violent, and criminal behavior. In this context it supports and extends the findings described earlier for resting heart rate, confirming the finding of autonomic arousal deficits in antisocial populations. On the other hand, the link between antisocial behavior and cortisol *reactivity* to a stressor (that is, the change in cortisol before and after a stressful event) is less clear, with some studies finding decreased reactivity in antisocial children (for example, van Goozen et al. 1998) while other studies find increased reactivity (for example, Susman et al. 1997). Even accepting that there are differences in antisocial children in basal cortisol levels, it must be remembered that, as with many other biological measures, cortisol is part of a dynamic system that is responsive to environmental changes and demands (Susman, Dorn, and Chrousos 1991; Susman and Ponirakis 1997). As such, integration with social and environmental factors must be a primary aim of future studies in this area.

Neurotransmitters

Basic neurotransmitters such as dopamine, norepinephrine, and serotonin form the basis to information processing and communication within the brain, and in this sense underlie all types of behavior, including sensation, perception, learning and memory, eating, drinking and, more controversially, antisocial behavior. Neurotransmitters are chemicals stored in the synaptic vesicles (small globules) of a communicating cell's axon; this axon carries the nerve impulse of the cell body to other cells. During cellular communication, these chemicals are discharged into the synaptic cleft (the space between two neurons) and are taken up by special receptors in the postsynaptic membrane of the recipient cell, initiating what is termed a postsynaptic potential. Thus, neurotransmitters form the basis to the transmission of information throughout the brain.

Paradoxically, the well-known and best-studied neurotransmitters (serotonin, dopamine, norepinephrine) account for only a small proportion of cell firing in the brain. For example, serotonin is thought to be the transmitter substance in fewer than 0.1 percent of brain synapses. Nevertheless, they are thought to be highly important in the context of brain and behavior; for example, serotonin, norepinephrine, and dopamine have been implicated in the etiology of major disorders such as schizophrenia and depression.

A meta-analysis of twenty-nine studies examined the relationship between norepinephrine, dopamine, and serotonin, and antisocial behavior (Raine 1993). Results indicated a relatively large effect size (-0.75) between reduced central serotonin and antisocial behavior, and a medium effect size of -0.41 between reduced norepinephrine and antisocial behavior, with no effect for dopamine. Subanalyses were conducted in an attempt to specify to which subgroups of antisocials these findings pertain. These analyses indicated that serotonin was lowest in antisocials with a history of alcohol abuse, borderline personality disorder, and violence, while cerebrospinal fluid norepinephrine was lowest in those with alcohol abuse, borderline personality disorder, and depression.

Increased impulsivity has been associated with lower serotonin, and there is some evidence that aggressive individuals who are impulsive have particularly lower serotonin. Humans low in social class have also been found to have reduced serotonin, and it is possible that reductions in serotonin produced by a fall in dominance triggers impulsive aggression as a way of raising the individual in the dominance hierarchy. In evolutionary terms this would be adaptive as increased dominance gives greater access to food and sex, thus increasing the individual's ability to reproduce and pass on their genes. Yet again, poor diet may play a role. Diets low in, or otherwise blocking, the uptake of tryptophan or tyrosine (the precursors of serotonin and norepinephrine respectively) have been found to lower the levels of these transmitters in the brain (see Weisman 1986). In addition, even when returned to a normal diet, brain serotonin levels are never fully compensated (Timiras, Hudson, and Segall 1984). Poor nutrition possibly occurring in individuals of lower socioeconomic status (including poor dietary care during pregnancy) could conceivably influence neurotransmitter levels throughout life.

Neurogenetics

As outlined earlier, genetic studies are now beginning to progress from simply demonstrating that there is indeed a genetic basis to crime. A new generation of neurogenetic studies is now beginning to identify specific genes that give rise to abnormally aggressive behavior, often via abnormal functioning of specific neurotransmitters.

Some of the first clues have come from animal research where "knock-out" mice have been genetically engineered to lack individual genes that normally give rise to specific neurotransmitters. One of the neurotransmitter systems implicated to date is nitric oxide. Mice that lack the gene essential for nitric oxide in the brain have been found to become highly aggressive, and furthermore agents which inhibit nitric oxide also lead to very aggressive behavior in normal mice (Demas et al. 1997).

Particularly interesting are findings on the knockout of the gene that codes for monoamine oxidase-A (MAOA), an enzyme that metabolizes brain neurotransmitters including serotonin. Adult mice who are deficient in MAOA are abnormally aggressive to other males and are much rougher and aggressive in their mating behavior with females (Cases et al. 1995; Nelson et al. 1995). These mice also showed very high levels of serotonin. What makes animal MAOA findings such as these more provocative is that they have also been found in humans. Brunner et al. (1993) have shown that a family in the Netherlands with a history of highly aggressive behavior have a mutation in the MAOA gene. They also showed impaired IQs, and like the MAOA mice, had very high levels of serotonin.

Animal findings such as these which are also found in humans are particularly interesting. Nevertheless, such genetic mutations affecting the MAOA gene are rare in humans and therefore it will be difficult to test whether Brunner's findings will be replicated in other samples. Furthermore, deletion of this produces high, not low, serotonin levels, a finding not consistent with the finding of *lower* serotonin in the cerebrospinal fluid of impulsive violent offenders. Nevertheless, it is not unlikely that the field of neurogenetics will produce multiple breakthroughs in the next few years on the molecular genetic basis of crime and violence.

POLICY IMPLICATIONS

One of the biggest and widely held myths in criminology research is that biology is destiny. Instead, the reality is that the biological bases of crime and violence are amenable to change through benign interventions. In the past fifty years, intervention programs have not been as successful in reducing crime and violence as had been hoped, and it is possible that part of their failure has been due to the fact that they have systematically ignored the biological component of the biosocial equation.

Brain damage and poor brain functioning have been shown to predispose to violence, and one possible source of this brain damage could be birth complications (Raine, Brennan, and Mednick 1997). The implication is that providing better pre- and postbirth health care to poor mothers may help reduce birth complications and thus reduce violence. Alternatively, rather than attempting to reduce birth complications, interventions could focus on the psychosocial half of the biosocial equation and attempt to reduce early maternal rejection which intensifies the effect of birth complications (Raine, Brennan, and Mednick 1994; Raine, Brennan, and Mednick 1997). Consideration might be given to multiple efforts across time to reduce maternal rejection by, for example, making parenting skills classes compulsory in high school to the next generation of mothers with unwanted pregnancies; providing more pre-birth visits from nurses to monitor both the pregnancy and the parent's attitude to the unborn baby; and providing home visits from pediatricians specifically to mothers who suffered birth complications to monitor the mother-infant bonding process, assess the physical and cognitive development of the infant, and provide appropriate remediation of cognitive and physical deficits which are known to follow from perinatal complications (Liu and Raine 1999; Raine and Liu 1998).

Another source of brain damage could be poor nutrition; and as has been seen earlier, there is evidence for a link between poor nutrition during pregnancy and later crime. Furthermore, cigarette and alcohol usage during pregnancy have been linked to later antisocial behavior (for example, Brennan, Grekin, and Mednick [1999]). In this context, Olds et al. (1998) in a methodologically strong randomized controlled trial showed that improving the quality of pregnant mothers' prenatal diet (among other factors) reduced offspring criminal and antisocial behavior fifteen years later. The intervention was also shown to improve the quality of the mothers' prenatal diet. Similarly, Lally, Mangione, and Honig (1988) showed that advice to pregnant women on good nutrition, health, and child rearing leads to a reduction in juvenile delinquency at age fifteen. These studies provide more support to the notion that nutrition plays a causal role in the development of childhood aggression, but future prevention trials that focus explicitly on the specific role of nutrition are required to further support the specific role of malnutrition.

It has been shown that low physiological arousal is the best-replicated biological correlate of antisocial behavior in child and adolescent samples. An important question from a prevention perspective concerns whether low arousal is amenable to change using noninvasive procedures. Recent findings from Mauritius suggest that it is. A nutritional, physical exercise, and educational enrichment from ages three to five resulted in increased psychophysiological arousal and orienting at age eleven compared to a matched control group (Raine et al. In press). Furthermore, a longer-term follow-up of these children to age seventeen showed a reduction in conduct disorder ($p < .01$) and motor excess scores ($p < .03$) in the experimental group compared to the control group (Raine et al. 1999). It should be noted, however, that these latter behavioral effects are sleeper effects; no effect of the intervention was noted on age-eleven aggression scores. Some initial reports have shown the possible efficacy of using biofeedback to increase physiological arousal in hyperactive children (Lubar 1989), while more recent pilot work has indicated that this technique shows some short-term behavioral improvement in children with conduct problems. Biofeedback training, as part of a larger multimodal treatment package, could conceivably help to reduce antisocial and violent behavior in adolescents.

The policy implications of biological research on crime also extend to the criminal justice system. One question raised by these and other studies is whether any of us have freedom of will in the strict sense of the term. If brain deficits make it more likely that a person will commit violence, and if the cause of the brain deficits was not under the control of the individual, then the question becomes whether or not that person should be held fully responsible for the crimes. Of course we have to protect society, and unless we can treat this brain dysfunction, we may need to keep violent offenders in secure conditions for the rest of their lives; but do they deserve to be executed given the early constraints on their free will? It could be argued that if an individual possesses risk factors that make him disproportionately more likely to commit violence, then he has to take responsibility for these predispositions. Just like an alcoholic who knows he suffers from the disease of alcoholism, the person at risk for violence needs to recognize his risk factors and take preventive steps to ensure that he does not harm others. These persons have risk factors, but they still have responsibility and they have free will.

This makes good, practical sense, but responsibility and self-reflection are not disembodied, ethereal processes but are rooted firmly in the brain. Patients who have damage to the ventromedial (lower) prefrontal cortex are known to become irresponsible, lack self-discipline, and fail to reflect on the consequences of their actions. The ability to take responsibility for one's actions is damaged in violent offenders. It can be argued that they are no longer able to reflect on their behavior as others do and take responsibility for their predispositions. It is not just that the brain mechanisms subserving responsibility and internal soul-searching are damaged in the violent offender and prevent him from taking action to rectify the causes of his violence.

Brain scan information is increasingly being used in capital cases, most frequently in the punishment stage of a trial as a mitigating circumstance against the death penalty, but it has also been used successfully in the guilt phase of a trial (D'Agincourt 1993). Nevertheless, use of brain imaging data in law courts is hotly debated, with some arguing against their use. Of course, brain scans are not diagnostic in that they do not perfectly predict who is violent and who is not. On the other hand, brain imaging data such as PET and fMRI constitute more direct indexes of brain function than EEG and neuropsychological test data, which have frequently been used in courts. Still, others worry that brain imaging data will be inappropriately used to "excuse" violent crimes.

Yet perhaps brain imaging research on violence is most troubling to some because it challenges the way we conceptualize crime. It questions our treatment of murderers in just the same way that we now look back 200 years and question the way in which the mentally ill were kept in shackles and chains, treated little better than animals. The history of civilization has shown that as time progresses, society becomes wiser and more humane.

Two hundred years from now, we may have reconceptualized recidivistic serious criminal behavior as a clinical disorder with its roots in early social, biological, and genetic forces beyond the individual's control (Raine 1993). Will we look back aghast at our current practices of execution and inhumane treatment of seriously violent offenders? Will we view this execution of prisoners as barbaric and unjustified, as we now view the burning of witches?

Biological research is beginning to give us new insights into what makes a violent criminal offender. It is hoped that these early findings may lead us to rethink our approach to violence and goad us into obtaining new answers to the causes and cures of crime while we continue to protect society.

4

Juvenile Crime and Juvenile Justice

PETER W. GREENWOOD

TRENDS IN JUVENILE CRIME

I s juvenile crime on the rise? Are juvenile crimes becoming more serious? From recent coverage provided by the news media, one could get a strong impression that juveniles have come to represent an increasing threat of criminal violence in many communities. Not only are juveniles perceived as committing more violence, but the popular media also conveys the impression that their violence is becoming more callous and gratuitous. Many juvenile killings appear to take place without any rational cause or purpose. Stories about juveniles killing helpless old ladies or innocent bystanders have become a staple of most big city newspapers. It is this latter characteristic, hardened malice, that has caused many to question the concept of protecting and rehabilitating youth—upon which the juvenile justice system has historically been based. This section will attempt to reconcile the available data with these common perceptions.

SOURCES OF INFORMATION ON JUVENILE CRIME TRENDS

While many media stories may give the impression that both the number and seriousness of juvenile crimes are on the rise, we have only the most rudimentary of measures to tell whether or not this is the case. The most widely cited measure of crime, the FBI's Uniform Crime Reports (UCR), tells us nothing about the level of juvenile crime because it contains no information about the characteristics of offenders. The only indirect sources of information on juvenile crime rates are arrest rates and surveys of victims or high-risk youth.

Arrest rates are probably the best measure for monitoring nationwide trends in juvenile offending, although these data also reflect the shifting priorities of both the public and the police. If the public's consciousness about certain types of crime is raised, as it has been recently for so-called date rapes and child abuse, then the likelihood that any particular offense of that nature will be reported is likely to increase. On the other hand, if police resources become so strained in dealing with violent crimes or drug-selling that they are unable to engage in preventive patrols or to respond to calls about suspicious groups of youth, then the number of youth arrested for minor types of property crimes and antisocial behavior will probably decline, even though the number of crimes has not changed.

Victim surveys are not very useful for tracking juvenile crimes because they rely on victims' perceptions of whether offenders are over or under 18 years of age. These perceptions are often not very reliable and, furthermore, victims can only give age estimates for those crimes where their assailant is seen, not for most property crimes where the offender is unlikely to be observed.

Self-reporting surveys of youth, in theory, could provide a valuable means of assessing changes in delinquent behavior over time, if they were implemented in a systematic fashion. However, the self-reporting surveys that have been conducted to date are so varied in their methods and their geographic and age-group focus that they provide little basis for estimating changes in prevalence and offending rates between age cohorts (Menard and Elliott 1993).

AGE-SPECIFIC ARREST RATES AND CRIMES ATTRIBUTABLE TO JUVENILES

Although crime is still a young man's game, with arrest rates peaking in the mid- to late-teens, there are considerably fewer young men around now than there were just a few years ago. Between 1980 and 1990, the total U.S. population increased by 9.5 percent, while the number of juveniles between the ages of 10 and 17 declined by 10.2 percent. The figures in Table 1 show how the juvenile population and the fraction of arrests they accounted for has declined over the past two decades. In 1980, as shown in Table 4.1, juveniles from the ages of 10 through 17 represented 14 percent of the total U.S. population, but they accounted for 41 percent of all arrests for property crimes included in the FBI's Uniform Crime Reporting Index and 22 percent of all arrests for the four violent crimes included in the Index. By 1990, this age group had shrunk to just 11 percent of the total population, where it remained for the entire decade, and accounted for only 32 percent of all index property crime arrests and just 16 percent of all index violent crime arrests.

During the late 1980s and early 1990s, the rate of juvenile involvement in violent crime, particularly homicide and assault, increased significantly, accounting for 19 percent of all arrests for Part 1 Index violent crimes in 1995. But by 1998 the fraction of violent crime attributable to juveniles had dropped back to the low percentage of the previous decade. Clearly, over the decade, juveniles accounted for a disproportionate but diminishing share of arrests for serious felonies. Furthermore, since juveniles are more likely than adults to commit their crimes in groups, they probably account for an even smaller percentage of actual offenses than they do arrests.

However, the declining proportion of juveniles within the general population hides some very significant changes in their rates of arrest, defined as the number of juveniles arrested divided by their number within the general population. This data is presented in Table 4.2, with the arrests stated in terms of arrests per 100,000 juveniles age 10 through 17. Between 1980 and 1985, while the arrest rate for adults (for all index felonies) was decreasing by 3 percent, the arrest rate for juveniles fell by 14 percent—more than four times as rapidly. Then between 1985 and 1990, while the adult arrest rate for index crimes increased by 15 percent, the juvenile index arrest rate increased by only 9 percent.

Unfortunately, more of the decline in juvenile arrest rates is accounted for by property offenses than by violent offenses. By 1990, the juvenile arrest rate for violent offenses had climbed back up to what it was in 1980, while the arrest rate for property offenses was about 6 percent lower. Further evidence that the involvement of juveniles in violent crimes grew much more rapidly than their involvement in property crimes in the late 1980s is provided by trends in their arrest rates for homicide. In 1980, juveniles accounted for just 10 percent of all arrests for homicide. By 1990, juveniles accounted for 13.6 percent of all homicide arrests. Between 1984 and 1992 the number of juveniles arrested for homicide who were *under the age of 15* increased by 50 percent. Thankfully, as is shown in Table 4.2, by 1998 arrest rates for juveniles had declined sharply, in both the violent and property categories. Arrest rates for juveniles at the end of the decade were at their lowest point in 30 years.

Clearly, the rise in juvenile homicide arrest rates provides significant substantiation for the common perception that juvenile crime is becoming more serious. However, the diminishing number of juveniles and small

Table 4.1
Percentage of Total Population and Index Felony Arrests
Accounted for by Juveniles Age 10 to 17

YEAR	1980	1985	1990	1995	1998
Percentage of Total U.S. population	14	12	11	11	11
Percentage of Violent Index felonies	22	17	16	19	17
Percentage of Property Index felonies	41	34	32	35	33

SOURCE: Calculated from data presented in the FBI Crime in the United States reports, 1980 to 1999 (Washington D.C.: Federal Bureau of Investigation).

Table 4.2
Arrest Rates for Juveniles Age 10 to 17
(per 100,000 youths)

YEAR	1980	1985	1990	1995	1998
Index Violent Felonies	393.6	334.3	392.8	516.5	333.2
Index Property Felonies	2,887.2	2,491.0	2,689.3	2,509.6	1,763.6
All Index Felonies	3,280.8	2,825.3	3,082.1	3,026.1	2,096.8

SOURCE: FBI Crime in the United States reports, 1980 to 1999 (Washington D.C.: Federal Bureau of Investigation).
NOTE: Only some jurisdictions, which make up about half of the total U.S. population, report their arrests to the FBI broken down by age. In calculating age-specific arrest rates from these figures, it has been assumed that the age distribution in other jurisdictions is the same as that for the country as a whole.

percentage of total crime that is attributable to this age group raises the question of why they are being singled out for so much concern. One part of the answer is clearly the attention being given to the subject by the media and elected officials. People are hearing more about gratuitous juvenile violence than they used to, even if they are not experiencing it themselves— especially incidents that involve innocent bystanders, as in the case of some drive-by shootings and the Central Park muggings. Another reason may be that the popular media is often careless in distinguishing juveniles from those over 18 years of age. Since so many young adults and gang members continue to dress and act like teenagers, adult offenders may often be mistaken for juveniles, when in fact they are not. Another reason for the increase in public concern with juveniles may be the fact that our increasingly aged population, which does not have contact with children in the home, is more likely to be frightened or disturbed by the increasingly boisterous and possibly disrespectful behavior of teenagers who hang out in shopping malls and on the street. In other words, youths may appear more threatening and difficult to understand to those who do not have any of their own currently living with them.

POSSIBLE EXPLANATIONS FOR RECENT TRENDS IN JUVENILE VIOLENCE

The decreasing juvenile arrest rates for all types of crime from 1980 through 1985, and then the sharp reversal and increases in arrests for violence through 1993, were mirrored by cohorts of slightly older young adults over the same time period. For both age groups, a number of analyses have shown that the increases in arrest rates were attributable to gun crimes, as opposed to those committed without guns, and fell much more heavily on minority youth in large cities (Cook and Laub 1998).

Many have attributed the sharp rise in juvenile and young adult gun homicides of the latter 1980s to the introduction of crack cocaine in the mid-1980s, the disorganized street markets through which it was sold, and the recruitment of young minority males to do most of the street level selling. They argue that increased involvement in dangerous street-level drug markets led many of these youth to arm themselves, initially for protection, which in turn led many of their peers to also engage in defensive arming. The end result of this process, particularly in large cities, was much more gun-carrying and use by a population not noted for their dispute-resolution or decision-making skills (Blumstein and Rosenfeld 1998). Although the initial motive for most of these youths in carrying guns was to defend themselves, the end result was a much higher rate of homicide and aggravated assault among this very same population.

An increasing involvement in street level drug-selling, the increased availability and lethality of firearms, and the glorification of violence in movies, videos, and rap music are all factors that are consistent with increasing violent crimes, but not property crimes, among the young. Other factors that many believe contribute to higher delinquency rates include diminishing blue-collar employment opportunities in inner cities, the increasing proportion of youth being raised in single-parent households, increasing animosity and tensions between recent immigrants and those with whom they compete for the declining number of low-skill urban jobs and low-income housing, and the decline of the public schools. If these really are primary causal factors, then recent increases in youth violence appear to be due, at least in part, to economic, demographic, and social trends over which individual families and youth have little control.

Counterbalancing their disproportional involvement in committing violent offenses, juveniles are also disproportionately represented as victims. The annual risk of victimization by violent crime peaks at age 16 to 19 for both sexes, and declines substantially with age thereafter (Reiss and Roth 1993). In 1992, there were 2,428 murder victims under the age of 18; 662 of them were under the age of 4. In 1989, it was estimated that at least 1,200 and perhaps as many as 5,000 children died as a result of maltreatment from their guardians, and more than 160,000 children were seriously harmed (U.S. Department of Health and Human Services 1990). Between 1980 and 1988, the number of incidents of child maltreatment reported to authorities increased more than 100 percent, from 1.1 million to 2.4 million. Since victimization surveys show low reporting rates for incidents of child abuse and maltreatment, it is not clear how much of this increase is due to higher reporting rates (as increased sensitivity to the problem and mandatory reporting requirements took effect), as opposed to increases in the true level of maltreatment. Rates of reported abuse, both physical and sexual, are six times higher for children in families with incomes under $15,000 per year than for children from higher income families (Reiss and Roth 1993), although again, some of this difference may be due to differences in reporting rates between income groups, with lower income groups more likely to be affected by mandatory reporting requirements.

THE JUVENILE JUSTICE SYSTEM

The juvenile court was founded at the turn of this century as a specialized institution for dealing with dependent, neglected, and delinquent minors. At that time, American cities were being flooded by poor European immigrants, whose values, behavior, and child-rearing practices were alien and frightening to middle-class moralists. But to the progressives who took the lead in developing the new court, these factors represented a challenge.

The original guiding principle of the juvenile court was *parens patriae*, a medieval English doctrine that allowed the Crown to supplant natural family relations whenever a child's welfare was at stake—in other words, to become a substitute parent. The procedures of the court were purposefully informal, and its intentions were presumed to be benign. Fact-finding focused on the minor's underlying problems and special needs rather than the specific acts that brought him or her before the court. Dispositions were intended to reflect the "best interests" of the child, which were assumed to be the same as the public's.

The new court represented one aspect of a broad progressive movement to accommodate urban institutions to an increasingly industrial-immigrant population, and to incorporate recent discoveries in the behavioral, social, and medical sciences into the rearing of children. The juvenile court was also part of another philosophical movement that has been termed "the revolt against formalism." The new juvenile procedures reflected the ultimate pragmatic philosophy: "It's all right if it works" (Empey 1979).

In juvenile court, children were not charged with specific crimes. The central language of the criminal law—*accusation, proof, guilt, punishment*—was dropped in favor of terms reflecting from the social worker's vocabulary: *needs, treatment, protection, guidance,* and so on. It did not matter whether a child came into the court because of neglect or an act of delinquency. In all cases, the court's intervention, guidance, and supervision were presumed to be required and benevolent.

Juvenile courts have come a long way over the course of this century. Social scientists and juvenile advocates have demonstrated that the "benign" intentions of the court can be just as punitive and onerous as the sanctions inflicted by the criminal courts, often for much less serious behavior. In contrast to the early stance of complete informality, juveniles are now accorded most of the procedural protections available to adults, in theory at least, if not always in practice—the two primary exceptions being the right to a jury trial and bail.

In spite of these reforms, or perhaps encouraged by them, juvenile law activists continue to advocate further expansion of procedural protections, the current objective being the right to a jury trial. In somewhat the same vein, there is a youth advocacy lobby that argues for reducing the amount of juvenile court intervention in delinquents' lives. Diversion, deinstitutionalization, and community treatment are the current battle cries of this group, which argues that formal sanctions and institutionalized treatment only aggravate delinquent tendencies and that youth are better served by returning them to their own communities. In the 1990s, this group added fiscal retrenchment as another reason for reducing the use of training schools and detention centers (Schwartz and Van Vleet 1992).

But the most numerous critics of the juvenile court take it to task for failing to protect the public from predatory juvenile criminals in deference to what is seen as its naive concern for protecting these minors' "best interests." The views of this group are articulated most forcefully by police and prosecutors, who generally support tougher, more adult-like sanctions for serious or repeat juvenile offenders and much longer terms. Reform recommendations from this group range from decreasing the age jurisdiction of juvenile courts (from 18 years of age to 16) to increased waiver of serious juvenile cases to the adult court to mandatory (or at least longer) sentences for violent juvenile offenders.

However, the juvenile court is easier to criticize than to reform. Juvenile justice continues to remain a troublesome public policy issue because of the competing social objectives it involves and because our basic knowledge about how to reform troublesome youths is so deficient. Other obstacles to change include 1) the system's heavy reliance on informal discretionary decision making, 2) the confidentiality that protects its case records from outside scrutiny and the lack of quantitative data on its operations, 3) the unfamiliarity of most state legislators with actual juvenile court practices and policies, and 4) a shortage of community-based programs and services to deal with the problems of delinquency-prone youths.

Are juvenile offenders coddled by the system? Does the juvenile system get in the way of protecting the public? How effective is the juvenile justice system compared with the adult criminal justice system? Are programs run by private providers more effective than those run by public agencies? This section describes the policies, practices, and programs of the juvenile justice system and some of the major reforms that have been proposed by its critics.

THE OPERATION OF THE JUVENILE COURT

In most states, the dividing line between the juvenile and adult systems is the 18th birthday, although a few use the 17th, 16th, or 19th birthday for this purpose. Crimes committed before that birthday fall within the jurisdiction of juvenile courts. Crimes committed after it are subject to criminal penalties and procedures. Almost all states provide for some procedure by which cases involving serious felonies (homicide, rape, aggravated assault, etc.) and older juveniles (typically 16- and 17-year-olds) can be transferred to adult criminal courts. In some jurisdictions, motions for such transfers can be initiated by the prosecutor. In others, they have been made presumptive, with juveniles so waived retaining the right to "fitness hearings," at which their attorney can argue why such a transfer should not be made.

Originally, four basic characteristics distinguished the juvenile court system from the criminal courts: informality in procedures and decorum; a separate detention center for juveniles; contributory delinquency statutes that encouraged the judge to punish adults, primarily parents, who actively contributed to the delinquency of juveniles; and probation.

Today these distinguishing features are considerably blurred. The informality is largely gone. In many jurisdictions juveniles sit through proceedings with their counsel just like any adult defendant in criminal court, unless they have waived that right. Unfortunately, there are jurisdictions in which juveniles routinely waive that right without ever consulting with a lawyer or any other supportive adult (Feld 1989).

Juvenile hearings proceed along much the same lines as criminal trials. The rules of evidence and rights of the parties are about the same, except that juveniles in most states still do not have the right to a jury trial or to bail. Parents are no longer held accountable for the delinquency of their children, and in most states cannot even be compelled to participate in delinquency proceedings. Even the liability of parents for the acts of their children in civil tort litigation has been severely restricted by statute.

The separate detention centers remain. Separateness, in fact, is now the principal distinguishing characteristic of the juvenile system: separate detention, separate records, separate probation officers, separate judges, even separate funding agencies for program development and research.

And finally, probation has seeped over into the adult court. The distinguishing feature about probation in the juvenile court is its role in screening arrests made by the police. Originally, the prosecutor had no role in a juvenile hearing. A delinquency case was handled solely by a probation officer. Then, as the appellate courts became more demanding about due process considerations in juvenile proceedings and granted juveniles the right to counsel, prosecutors were brought into the process to represent the interests of the state. In most states, probation still screens all juvenile arrests and decides in which ones the prosecutor should be asked to file a petition. However, several states have eliminated this function (Washington is one) and many prosecutors would like to see it discarded completely.

CURRENT CRITICISMS

In most states, interest in the juvenile justice system on the part of elected officials and the public is highly sporadic; it is usually prompted by media-supported perceptions that the juvenile crime rate is getting out of hand or that juvenile offenders are being coddled by an antiquated system designed to serve truants and runaways rather than remorseless killers. We are currently in the midst of such a period of renewed attention. The last such period occurred in the late 1970s and early 1980s, when juvenile arrest rates were increasing rapidly and juveniles represented a much larger proportion of total arrests than they do today. The current attention appears to be driven by concerns about increases in the severity of juvenile crime rather than its absolute volume.

Many of the criticisms currently being leveled against the juvenile justice system appear to ignore the fact that the systems in most states are a far cry from the earliest versions. Current juvenile courts have far less power and interest in dealing with the truant- and runaway-status offenders who made up the bulk of juvenile caseloads in earlier times. Just like criminal courts, juvenile courts have had to focus their attention and resources on the most serious offenders, with whom the public is most concerned.

Some criticisms ignore basic differences in the character of juvenile and adult crimes. Victimization data indicates that within any given crime category, crimes committed by juveniles tend to be less serious than those committed by adults. For instance, juveniles involved in robberies are less likely to be armed with a gun or seriously injure their victims (Greenwood et al. 1983). The property losses from crimes committed by juveniles are also likely to be less than in those committed by adults. And, as we have mentioned before, juvenile crimes are more likely to involve multiple offenders than crimes by adults. A comparison of average disposition patterns between juvenile and adult criminal courts ignores the fact that the juvenile court must dispose of a much higher percentage of less serious cases, involving either minor offenses or real first-time offenders. A study that compared case outcomes between samples of older juveniles and young adults revealed that when aggravating factors were present (lengthy prior record, gun use, violent prior, etc.), juveniles were just as likely to be convicted and sentenced to state time as were young adults (Greenwood 1986).

In 1996, 59 percent of all juvenile cases involving crimes against persons were formally petitioned, compared with a petition rate of 52 percent for juvenile cases involving property crimes (U.S. Department of Justice 1999, p. 157). The petition rates for juvenile homicide and robbery cases were 91 and 87 percent respectively. Among those cases where the juvenile was adjudicated delinquent for a violent offense in 1996, the percentage who were sent to residential placements was 31 percent, compared to a 26 percent placement rate for adjudicated property offenders. The placement rates for homicide and robbery offenders were 59 and 46 percent respectively. The residential placement rate for both violent and property offenders declined by 2 percentage points between 1987 and 1996.

RECENT REFORMS

In spite of the evidence cited above that the juvenile justice system does provide fairly severe sanctions for the most serious offenders it deals with, many commentators continue to proclaim that juvenile offenders get off with a "slap on the wrist." A typical example of this type of misleading and inaccurate rhetoric is a *Wall Street Journal* editorial ("Bad Boys," September 28, 1998) that appeared following the arrest of two juveniles for the killing of a British tourist in Florida and the arrest of two 18-year-olds for the killing of Michael Jordan's father. The editorial says, "the current system is essentially a license to kill. No matter how awful the crime, violent youngsters rarely get more than a suspension or year or two in jail."

Aside from the more general calls for increasing toughness or abolishing specialized juvenile courts altogether, the five areas of potential reform that are currently receiving the most attention are: 1) expanding the criteria under which juveniles can be waived to criminal courts, 2) changes in sentencing structure within the juvenile court, 3) greater procedural protections to juveniles, 4) reducing the number of "free rides" or "diversions" received by repeat juvenile offenders before some significant intervention and/or sanction is imposed, and 5) removing some of the confidentiality restrictions on juvenile court records.

Waiver Criteria

In three states (Connecticut, North Carolina, and New York) the jurisdiction of the juvenile court ends after the age of 15, and all 16-year-old offenders are handled in criminal court. In ten states (Georgia, Illinois, Louisiana, Massachusetts, Michigan, Mississippi, New Hampshire, South Carolina, Texas, and Wisconsin) juvenile court jurisdiction applies through the 17th birthday, and in the remaining states and District of Columbia, the jurisdiction of the juvenile court ends on the 18th birthday (Griffin, Torbet, and Szymanski 1998).

Yet all these states have procedures for waiving the juvenile court's jurisdiction over a serious case and transferring the matter into regular criminal courts, and many have expanded the basis for waiver in recent years, primarily by increasing the list of offenses for which waiver applies and/or lowering the age at which juveniles are eligible (Torbet and

Szymanski 1998). The criteria vary from specific offense categories and age ranges to general criteria. The primary mechanisms for transferring jurisdiction from juvenile to criminal courts are judicial waiver, direct filing by prosecutors (with minimal judicial review), and statutory exclusion. In some states, the so-called "fitness" or "waiver" hearings are held in juvenile court. In others, fitness hearings for juveniles who meet specified criteria are held in criminal courts, to determine in which court the proceedings should take place.

Many states are now considering a variety of proposals intended to increase the number of youths waived to the criminal courts. Colorado legislators recently passed a law which provides for 14- to 17-year-olds charged with certain violent felonies to be tried as adults, and if convicted, to serve their time in new intermediate prisons. California voters recently passed a ballot proposition that reduced the minimum age for waiver from the 16th to the 14th birthday.

The use of judicial waivers has been tracked for a number of years and appears to be quite stable at around 1.0 to 1.6 percent of all petitioned cases (Sickmund et al. 1998), but there is no systematic count of cases transferred by prosecutor direct file or statutory exclusion. It is estimated that in 1994 approximately 12,000 persons under the age of 18 were convicted of a felony in a state criminal court through judicial waiver, prosecutor direct file, or statutory exclusion (Brown and Langan 1998).

Analyses of waiver cases consistently show that the primary considerations in waiving a case are current offense seriousness, prior record, and the youth's current age. Studies that have looked at the impact of waiver on sanctions have found mixed results, with some finding waiver resulting in more incarceration and others not (Fagan 1995; Brown and Langan 1998). Studies of the impacts of waiver on juveniles have generally found higher recidivism rates among those waived (Fagan 1995).

Sentencing Structure

A number of states have reduced the dispositional discretion of juvenile court judges by moving to offense-based sentencing, involving guidelines, blended sentences, mandatory minimum sentences, and extended jurisdiction. Blended sentences allow the imposition of combined juvenile and adult correctional sanctions being served in sequence. Extended jurisdiction allows a judge to commit a juvenile to the state's juvenile correctional system beyond the age of the court's jurisdiction for hearing cases. In California, Oregon, and Wisconsin the extended age is 25, and in Colorado,

Connecticut, Hawaii, and New Mexico it extends to the full term of commitment regardless of age.

Increasing Procedural Protections

Some of those who would like to see more juvenile offenders treated like adults are less concerned with their sanctions than their rights. Barry Feld, for one, has criticized the procedures by which many juveniles voluntarily waive their right to counsel without ever consulting a lawyer or supportive adult. He would make such consultations mandatory before the right to counsel could be waived (Feld 1989). Professor Feld also questions the trend of the juvenile court toward increasing punitiveness, based on the seriousness of the charged offense, without also granting juveniles the right to jury trials (Feld 1984).

Decreasing Free Rides and Increasing Accountability

In 1996, about 22 percent of the juveniles taken into custody by police were handled informally and released; the remainder was referred to court. Of the 1.7 million delinquency cases referred to juvenile courts in 1996, 56 percent were formally handled (petitioned) by the court; the remainder was disposed of informally. For the majority of juvenile offenders, who do not repeat after one or two arrests, station house adjustment and informal diversion appear to be wise and prudent actions. For the small percentage who do repeat, time and time again, this lenience appears to be seriously misguided. Simple common sense would suggest that repeated diversions lead determined offenders to believe that they will not be punished.

Some jurisdictions have responded to these concerns by attempting to develop and impose a sequence of sanctions that will ensure that no offenders get off with just a free ride. The state of Washington provides an example of how a state can modify its juvenile laws to bring more accountability to juvenile proceedings and to more explicitly balance the competing interests of public protection and reformation of juvenile offenders. The 1977 revision, which was sponsored by the King County prosecutor, was designed to provide greater due process protection to juveniles and more protection to the community against serious juvenile crime. One key aspect of the revised law is a presumptive sentencing framework that ties dispositions to the seriousness of the current offense and the juvenile's prior criminal history.

The Washington juvenile law eliminates the role of probation officers in screening petitions and places filing decisions completely in the hands of the prosecutor. Legally, sufficient cases must be either filed or diverted, a decision that is based on the seriousness of the current offense and prior record. A diversion agreement involves a written contract between the juvenile and diversionary unit, whereby the juvenile agrees to fulfill certain conditions in lieu of prosecution. In theory, these conditions are supposed to be the same as would be imposed following conviction. The primary advantage of diversion to the juvenile is the avoidance of a formal conviction record. However, if the juvenile is subsequently charged with another offense, prior diversions can be counted a part of his or her prior record.

The code's sentencing scheme is semi-determinate or presumptive in nature. It is based on the concept that accountability for an offense should be determined primarily by the seriousness of the offense, the age of the offender, the offender's prior criminal history, and the recency of that history (Greenwood et al. 1983, pp. 149–50).

"Restorative justice" is another strategy that communities are adopting to increase the accountability of first-time or low-level delinquents, victim reparation, and community healing. Restorative justice programs are well established in Australia, New Zealand, and more than 300 communities in the United States. These programs usually involve some form of community sentencing or accountability board and victim-offender mediation (Braithwaite 1998).

Reducing the Confidentiality of Juvenile Proceedings

Juvenile court records were traditionally sealed and offenders' names kept out of the papers in the beliefs that this confidentiality was required to enhance the court's efforts to identify the antecedents of each juvenile's problems and that disclosure of the juvenile record might unfairly penalize defendants for their youthful indiscretions. However, along with increasing concerns about juvenile crime came concerns about protecting the public from youthful predators and holding the juvenile court more accountable for punishing youth. A number of states have now relaxed their restriction on what can be reported about juvenile cases in the press, and most states have some procedure for ensuring that criminal courts and prosecutors have access to juvenile records, at least for some specified period, lasting for several years after the youth becomes an adult. As of the end of 1997, 30 states permitted or required open juvenile court hearings in cases involving serious offenses or repeat offenders (Torbet and Szymanski 1998). A number of states require notification of a juvenile's school when the youth is found guilty of particular offenses.

Finally, while the "get tough on juveniles" efforts get most of the press, a group of individuals and organizations continue to work for the original goals of the federal Office of Juvenile Justice and Delinquency Prevention (OJJDP): reducing or eliminating the use of large training schools; removing juveniles from adult jails and police lockups, reducing the use of detention through improved screening for risk, and increasing the number and variety of community-based alternatives. With the assistance of these individuals and organizations, a number of states and local jurisdictions have revamped their juvenile justice systems, reducing the use of "unnecessary" confinement and increasing the variety of community-based options. Utah, Pennsylvania, Oklahoma, Florida, Alabama, and Maryland have been among the leaders in instituting such reforms.

THE EFFECTIVENESS OF JUVENILE CORRECTIONS PROGRAMS AND PLACEMENTS

Juvenile courts are granted considerable procedural leeway and provided with a variety of dispositional alternatives in the belief that these concessions allow them to be more effective in rehabilitating and protecting the youths who come before them. Therefore, one primary measure of the juvenile justice system is its effectiveness in protecting those youths and decreasing the likelihood of their committing future crimes. Unfortunately, there is no clear-cut evidence that allows us to compare the effectiveness of juvenile programs with those available for adults. The evidence is even quite limited for comparing different types of juvenile programs against each other. This section summarizes recent reviews and evaluations of specific treatment modalities.

TYPES OF PROGRAMS AND FACILITIES

Since the disposition of juvenile cases in most states is still supposed to be tailored to the individual needs and circumstances of each juvenile, it should come as no surprise that a wide variety of programs have been developed to meet these needs. For those juveniles whose crimes or records are not very serious and whose family is sufficiently supportive that the youth can continue to reside at home, a variety of programs exist, including informal and formal probation, intensive supervision, tracking and in-home supervision by private agencies, mentoring programs, after-school or all-day programs in which a youth reports to the program site for part of the day and then returns home, and community service. Some judges and probation departments have established special programs to seek out and develop unique community services and contacts that might be of help with particular youth and their families.

For those youth who must be placed out of their homes but do not represent such a risk that they must be removed from the community, many jurisdictions provide or contract for a wide variety of group homes, foster care, and other community living situations. Placements in such facilities are typically in the range of 6 to 24 months, depending on the program and seriousness of the youth's offense. For those youth who represent a more serious risk to the community, or who cannot function appropriately in an open setting, most states provide a continuum of increasingly restrictive settings ranging from isolated wilderness camps and ranches to very securely fenced and locked facilities. In some jurisdictions, youths are committed to detention centers for punitive or allegedly protective purposes.

The big issues that divide the field are the extent to which residential placements are necessary, the best settings for such placements, and the most effective way to run them. Up until the early 1970s, the typical residential placement for juvenile delinquents in most states consisted of small community group homes or large congregate training schools. A significant departure from this pattern occurred in 1971, when Jerry Miller, head of the Department of Youth Services (DYS) in Massachusetts, abruptly removed most of the youth who were residing in that state's training schools, and placed them in a variety of small community-based institutions and programs. Those youth who required secure care were placed in a number of small (typically 20-to-30-bed) facilities. To this day, the Massachusetts system continues to operate with only a fraction of the secure beds utilized in many other states and with the majority of its youth in a variety of small, privately operated programs. Over the last decade a number of other states (Utah, Pennsylvania, Maryland, Florida) have adopted similar reforms in their systems.

An evaluation of the Massachusetts reforms, which compared outcomes for samples of youth committed to DYS before and after the reforms occurred, found higher average recidivism rates for the post-reform youth, which were partially explained by a decrease in less serious offenders being committed to DYS. However, in those parts of the state where the new models were most successfully implemented, post-reform recidivism rates appeared to be lower (Coates, Miller, and Ohlin 1982). A more recent attempt to evaluate the Massachusetts model (Krisberg, Austin, and Steele 1991) compared recidivism rates for all youth released by the Massachusetts DYS in 1985 to those reported for several other states (California, Pennsylvania, Utah, Florida, and Wisconsin) and found the Massachusetts rates to be among the lowest, using several different indicators of post-release failure (rearrest, reconviction, reincarceration). The 1985 Massachusetts release cohort also had lower recidivism rates than the groups studied earlier by Coates and his colleagues (1982). However, the significance of these comparisons is obscured by systematic differences in the characteristics of youth committed to state programs, across the states, and differences in the reporting of juvenile police and court contacts.

The primary criticisms leveled against traditional training schools have been that they offer sterile and unimaginative programs, are inappropriate places to run rehabilitative programs, and that they foster abuse and mistreatment of their charges (Bartollas, Miller, and Dinitz 1976; Feld 1977). At this point, the debate still goes on. A number of comparisons that set out to demonstrate that small community-based programs are more effective than traditional training schools failed to do so (Coates, Miller, and Ohlin 1982; Empey and Lubeck 1971; Greenwood and Turner 1993). Yet, several recent meta-analyses purport to demonstrate that particular types of treatment programs, primarily those employing cognitive/behavioral techniques, are more effective when run in community rather than institutional settings (Lipsey 1991).

Many states have used these results as the basis for shifting more of their youth to privately run, community-based programs. National surveys of juveniles in custody (Thornberry et al. 1989) have found that between 1975 and 1986 the number of commitments to private programs increased by 122 percent, while commitments to public programs declined by 7 percent. However, many states, most prominently California, remain steadfast in their reliance on large, secure training schools. California alone accounts for 20 percent of the youth locked up in the entire nation. Institutional populations in the badly overcrowded California Youth Authority range from 700 or 800 in institutions serving younger youth to more than 1,500 in those serving older populations.

It is difficult to tell whether the shift to community programs has resulted in less abuse or mistreatment of confined youth. This is because major efforts to cut down on mistreatment of youth in all types of programs were already under way at the time the deinstitutionalization movement began to have its effects. What is clear is that community programs appear to offer a much wider variety of settings and methods. Part of the reason for this difference may be that community-based programs are more likely to be run by private (usually nonprofit) providers, rather than the county or state. Nationwide, about 40 percent of delinquent youth placed out of their homes are in privately run placements. In some states (Massachusetts, Pennsylvania, Maryland, and Florida), the private sector also runs a variety of secure programs for even the most serious youthful offenders. In addition to offering a greater variety in programming, surveys show that privately run programs offer more treatment services, compared to publicly run programs, and are less likely to be overcrowded (Thornberry et al. 1989).

WHAT WORKS

Although there is still a good deal of debate among academics about what types of treatment, if any, are more effective than simple custody or outright release, there are some clear favorites among the politicians. Juvenile boot camps are definitely in, apparently satisfying the need to be both humanitarian and tough.

Few if any corrections practitioners believe that strict discipline and harsh living conditions on their own will lead to lasting behavioral changes. However, many are prepared to accept that techniques for harnessing peer pressure and group spirit may contribute to rehabilitative goals. Therefore, most boot camp or short-term challenge programs attempt to strike a balance between rigorous exercise and strict discipline on the one hand and behavioral training and skill-building efforts on the other. Many also include long-term aftercare and intensive follow-up supervision when youth are returned to the community (Deschenes, Greenwood, and Adams 1993; MacKenzie 1990), a programming technique that has recently received favorable comment by several experts in the field (Altschuler and Armstrong 1991). However, a recent evaluation of intensive aftercare programs in Detroit and Pittsburgh (Greenwood, Deschenes, and Adams 1993), which failed to find any significant effects of the experimental program on post-release recidivism, drug use, or involvement in school or work, raises serious questions about the value of such supervisory and advocacy efforts without the availability of more structured programming.

Most evaluations focus on a particular program or variations of a particular strategy, such as using college student volunteers to develop and enforce performance contracts with juvenile probationers, compared with the traditional methods that have been used in that site. In reviewing the results of many such evaluations, researchers combine similar methods into broader categories (such as intensive supervision, behavior modification, vocational education, or life-skills training) for the purposes of comparing alternative methods. In the 1970s, a series of reviews concluded that the available evidence was insufficient to support the claim that any one particular form of treatment was more effective than any other, including no treatment at all (Lipton, Martinson, and Wilks 1975; Sechrest, White, and Brown 1979). More recently, a number of critics have argued that these earlier reviews failed to take into account the therapeutic integrity of the experimental treatment or the quality of its implementation. Several recent meta-analyses have attempted to control for these factors.

A meta-analysis of more than 400 juvenile program evaluations by Mark Lipsey (1991) found that behavioral, skill-oriented, and multimodal methods produced the largest effects, and that positive effects were larger in community than in institutional settings. The mean effect of treatment in this study, in comparison to untreated control groups, was to reduce recidivism rates by 5 percentage points—say, from 50 percent to 45 percent.

A more recent meta-analysis that focused on evaluations of programs (N=200) handling more serious juvenile offenders reinforces and expands upon the findings from earlier studies (Lipsey and Wilson 1998). The grand mean effect of treatment in these evaluations, in comparison to the no-treatment control group, was equivalent to a 6 percent reduction in recidivism, from 50 to 44 percent. However, there was a great deal of variation about this mean, depending on the characteristics of the youth and the programs, with the most effective program groupings demonstrating something like a 40 percent reduction in recidivism (from 50 to 30 percent). In this analysis the most effective types of programs for noninstitutionalized serious juvenile offenders were very similar to those found to be effective for general delinquency in Lipsey's earlier (1991) meta-analysis. The most effective approaches involved individual counseling, interpersonal skills, behavioral programs, multiple services, and restitution with probation or parole. Programs that accepted mixed types of offenders (violent, property, and drugs) did better than those with just property offenders. For institutionalized juveniles, the most effective interventions were based on interpersonal skills or the teaching family home model. For all types of programs, the less involved the researcher was in the design and implementation of the program, the smaller the average effect size.

At this point it is difficult to say what, if any, effect program evaluations have on correctional programming. Most state juvenile systems, like those for adults, are struggling with reduced budgets to handle an increasingly more difficult and dangerous population. Community-based interventions for less serious offenders are often sacrificed to meet the custodial needs of those who are seen to represent more of a risk to the community, while here and there a few states continue to experiment with alternative forms of community programming. What can be said is that some changes in correctional programming techniques can produce modest, but still valuable, reductions in recidivism rates for juvenile offenders—but not wholesale changes in the basic pattern of criminal career development and transition from juvenile to adult crime. Remember, in many of the evaluations contained in the meta-analyses described above, recidivism rates for subjects in the experimental programs were compared to control samples that received no treatment at all. The effect sizes that are observed in such comparisons are not what we can expect when we compare two different forms of intervention of approximately the same intensity (Greenwood and Turner 1993). In the next section of this paper we will describe the characteristics and effectiveness of several well-designed prevention programs that have been shown to produce substantial reductions in recidivism.

THE CASE FOR EARLY TARGETED PREVENTION

A common piece of fireside wisdom holds that "an ounce of prevention is worth a pound of cure." Yet, in spite of this common wisdom, in most states the current pattern of funding for juvenile justice activities concentrates most of the available resources on secure residential placements for the most serious and chronic juvenile offenders. Even though some states and the federal government are beginning to increase their funding of delinquency prevention programs, only a small fraction of the at-risk children who could benefit from such programs actually receive them.

Ten years ago the greatest impediment to the funding of delinquency prevention programs was the lack of proven or validated models to meet the needs of different types of youth. However, in recent years a number of carefully designed and rigorously tested program models have proven their ability to produce strong positive effects on youth behavior, in a variety of organizational settings. Furthermore, cost-benefit studies of these programs have shown that many can virtually pay for themselves by way of the savings they produce in future law enforcement and correctional costs.

At this point the greatest impediment most communities face in attempting to build a network of effective delinquency and violence prevention programs is the reluctance of local program providers to adopt and faithfully replicate the small number of models that have proven effective. In the remainder of this section we will review the program models that have been shown to be effective in reducing delinquency and the organizational issues involved in getting these model programs implemented effectively.

PROMISING INTERVENTION STRATEGIES

Given the wide range of risk factors that are believed to predispose youth to serious or chronic offending (see chapters 3 and 6) it should not be surprising to find a wide range of programs designed to address these factors at various stages in the life course development. At the earliest stage are those programs designed to help young mothers cope with their new child-care responsibilities and improve parent-child attachment. Few, if any, of these programs were designed specifically as crime- or delinquency-prevention efforts, but as we will show later, some of them, in pursuing their other objectives, do contribute substantially to reducing later delinquency and violence.

At the other end of the spectrum are those programs designed specifically to deal with youth who have been adjudicated for violent or serious delinquent acts. Many of these programs were designed and serve as a final effort to reestablish delinquent youth on a prosocial development path before they become further enmeshed in the formal juvenile and criminal justice systems. Between these two extremes lies a broad range of programs designed to address particular risk factors and developmental stages.

Some of these programs are universal in that they are applied to the entire population of a classroom, school, or neighborhood. Such programs usually address higher level community risk factors that are indirectly related to violent offending such as drug use, impaired communication skills, or lack of economic opportunity. Targeted or selective programs are designed to identify and intervene with youth who are at higher risk than their peers or who already have demonstrated some level of antisocial behavior. Since universal programs are less likely to label or stigmatize their participants, they are often preferred by community leaders, for political reasons, over those that target specific high-risk individuals and families.

A number of basic intervention methods or techniques have been gradually developed over time, and they provide the basic building blocks from which specific program models are developed. At this stage in our review we will describe those basic strategies that have shown some evidence of success in reducing youth violence and delinquency and some of the programs that have used them. When we have completed this first pass, we will take a more detailed look at a small number of programs that are able to pass much more stringent tests in regard to our confidence in their ability to produce significant violence- and delinquency-reduction effects in a variety of settings.

Since many children come into the world with characteristics or in situations that place them at risk for delinquency and violence, a number of fairly sophisticated strategies have been developed to address these risk factors as soon as possible. Nurse home visitation programs attempt to work with at-risk mothers to improve their prenatal health status, reduce birth complications, and provide guidance and support in caring for the infant. In David Olds' Prenatal/Early Infancy Project, young, poor, first-time mothers received about 20 nurse visits over the first two years of their child's life. A 15-year follow-up showed that the nurse home visits significantly reduced child abuse and neglect in the participating families and arrest rates among the children (Olds et al. 1997). The women who received the program also spent much less time on welfare and, among those who were poor and unmarried, experienced significantly fewer subsequent births. A number of less-expensive and less-structured home visitation models have been tested, using paraprofessionals rather than nurses, but they have not been successful in achieving the same level of success as the Olds program with nurses (Greenwood, 1996).

Early childhood education is another modality that has shown some promise. These preschool programs attempt to advance cognitive and social development so that participants will be better prepared and more successful when they enter regular school. The Perry Preschool Program that operated in Ypsilanti, Michigan (Schweinhart, Barnes, and Weikart 1993), and the Syracuse University Family Development Research Project (Lally, Mangione, and Honig 1988) are two such programs that produced significant reductions in long-term follow-up arrests (although only among boys in the case of Perry), possibly because they combined early childhood, center-based education programs with some home visiting by teachers or health care workers.

Parent training programs have been shown to reduce some of the risks associated with poor family management techniques. Such programs typically provide instruction and practice to parents in setting clear expectations, monitoring behavior, reinforcing positive behavior, and providing consequences for negative behavior (Howell and Hawkins 1998). Two recent experiments suggest that parent training efforts become even more effective when they are combined with problem-solving skills training for the youth. Tremblay and his colleagues in Montreal developed a two-year intervention for disruptive kindergarten boys that combined home-based parent training with school-based social skills training for the boys. By age 12, the experimental youth were 50 percent less likely to have serious school adjustment problems and significantly less likely to have initiated delinquent behaviors (Tremblay et al. 1992).

Kazdin, Siegel, and Bass (1992) tested a similar program for boys and girls age 7 to 13 who were exhibiting antisocial behavior. They found that a combination of parent training and problem-solving skills training significantly reduced self-reported and parent-rated aggressive, antisocial, and delinquent behavior, at one-year follow-up, compared to either parent training or problem-solving training alone.

Several programs that use different strategies to promote school adjustment and improve achievement among students age 6 to 12 have shown positive effects in reducing delinquency-related risk factors. The Success for All program was developed for preschool and kindergarten to third grade students and based on prevention and immediate, intensive intervention. Prevention consists of providing children with the best available classroom programs and engaging their parents in supporting their success. Corrective interventions, including one-on-one tutoring, are applied immediately when learning problems are observed. The program also provides a family support team consisting of social workers, parent liaisons, and counselors. An evaluation of the initial program in Baltimore found that participating students scored significantly higher than nonparticipants on a variety of achievement tests. Successive implementations in Philadelphia, Charleston, Fort Wayne, and other cities have shown similar positive results, particularly among the more disadvantaged students (Slavin et al. 1994).

The Seattle Social Development Project (SSDP) is a multicomponent intervention specifically designed to prevent delinquency and other problem behaviors. It includes parent training, a social competence curriculum for students, and a package of classroom-management and instruction methods in the elementary grades. Long-term follow-up results show greater academic achievement, better teacher-rated behavior, lower rates of delinquency initiation, and lower rates of lifetime violent delinquent behavior (Hawkins et al. 1998).

The Positive Adolescent Choices Training (PACT) program uses a cognitive behavioral group-training curriculum to reduce violent behavior and victimization risks, and was developed specifically for African American middle school or junior high students. Students attended two 50-minute training sessions per week for a full semester. Trained doctoral-level facilitators led the group instruction and practice sessions in such social skill areas as giving positive or negative feedback, resisting peer pressure, problem solving, and so forth. A three year follow-up study found that treated youth were much less likely than control youth to have been referred to juvenile court and less likely to have been charged with a violent offense (Hammond and Yung 1993).

Given the growing concerns about how children are supervised when they are out of school, and the large amounts of funding that are now going into after-school programs, it is surprising that there are not more evaluations of such efforts. The one positive study of a program in this area was conducted in a public housing project in Ottawa (Canada) for children ages 5 to 15. Project staff actively recruited all children in the housing project to participate in a variety of structured after-school courses and activities such as scouting, dance, social skills development, and sports. Using a nonequivalent comparison group design, the evaluators of the program found a substantial and significant decline in juvenile arrests in the experimental projects, compared with an increase in the comparison sites (Jones and Offord 1989). However, the reductions in antisocial behavior did not appear to carry over into home or school settings.

THE UNIVERSITY OF COLORADO'S "BLUEPRINT" PROGRAMS

The promising programs we described above may have been judged to be "promising" on the basis of a single evaluation, or possibly on multiple evaluations of similar but not identical programs. The delinquency-prevention programs that we describe below were identified as "proven" programs by the Blueprints for Violence Prevention Program located in the Center for the Study and Prevention of Violence at the University of Colorado. For inclusion in Blueprints, a program must meet four rather stringent criteria: 1) a strong research design, 2) evidence of significant prevention effects, 3) successful multiple site replication, and 4) sustained impacts past the point of release from the program (Elliot 1998).

The most important factor in the research design is random assignment into treatment and control groups. This type of experimental design ensures that any observed program differences between the two groups can be attributed solely to the program and not to preexisting differences. Other factors associated with a strong research design include low rates of participant attrition, and adequate measurement of process and outcomes.

A proven program must show evidence of significant prevention effects. That is, the program should be able to demonstrate that it effectively reduces the rate of violent offenses among its treatment group. Very few programs, however, have shown reductions in violent behavior. As a result, the Blueprints Project considered programs that effectively deterred correlates of violent behavior, such as delinquency and drug use.

The replication of results in various settings provides important information about whether a program can be generalized and exported to other sites successfully. Replication ensures that the positive results obtained were just not the product of some special circumstance or a charismatic leader. It is important that programs be replicated in sites other than the one where they were developed and that they reliably achieve the same level of impact associated with the original program. This aspect of the Blueprints Project selection criteria is particularly important for the purposes of this report. Policymakers choosing violence-prevention strategies for their communities must be confident that the program and its results can be replicated successfully.

The final criterion for selection as a Blueprints project requires that the program's effects persist for at least one year post-treatment. Many programs show positive impacts on behavior and skills while the youth are still participating in the program. These positive effects, however, can be quick to fade when program participation is terminated and the individual returns to the influence of family, friends, and neighborhood. Results that fade quickly cannot have much impact on the overall level of violence.

Using these four criteria, Blueprints has identified ten programs that it classifies as proven and suitable for replication to other sites. Brief descriptions of the specific programs and their violence prevention effects are presented below.

Proven Programs

Prenatal/Early Infancy Project. David Olds's nurse home visitation program, described earlier, is designed to improve parent and child outcomes. Nurses are sent to the homes of women whose babies are at risk for health and developmental problems. Treatment is initiated during pregnancy and continues through 24 months postpartum. Home visiting provides parent training and support as well as promoting the cognitive and social-emotional development of the child.

The Bullying Prevention Program. This program seeks to reduce bullying among primary and secondary school children by increasing awareness about the problem. The program involves teachers and parents in the setting and enforcement of clear rules against bullying behavior. Bullying incidents decreased by 50 percent in Bergen, Norway, in the two years following implementation of the program. In addition, there were improvements in school climate and reductions in theft, vandalism, and truancy.

Promoting Alternative Thinking Strategies. PATHS is a school-based intervention program. A universal program, it is administered by teachers who have gone through a three-day training workshop. The curriculum is implemented with entire classrooms of children from kindergarten to fifth grade. The major goal is to promote emotional competence. The curriculum includes a feelings unit and an interpersonal cognitive problem-solving unit. There is a strong focus on applying the learned skills to children's everyday lives. Evaluation results reveal reductions in hyperactivity, peer aggression, and conduct problems.

Big Brothers Big Sisters of America. BBBSA is a well-known mentoring program. Local program affiliates carefully match adult volunteers to the youth in the program. Although it is not a requirement of the program, a large portion of youth participants are from disadvantaged single-parent households. The mentor meets with his or her youth partner at least three times per month for three to five hours at a time. The one-to-one relationship promotes the development of a caring relationship between the pair. Studies of the BBBSA have shown that participants are less likely to start using drugs, to hit someone, or to be truant than a control group of youth on a waiting list to enter the program. Improvements in attitudes, school performance, and family relationships were also noted for the treatment group.

The Quantum Opportunities Program. QOP serves a small group of high-risk youth from poor families and neighborhoods. The program provides an opportunity for education, development, and service activities. Students are part of the same group for the four years of high school. This continuity provides a sustained relationship with a peer group and a caring adult leader. All program activities occur outside of regular school hours. The participants receive 250 hours per year of 1) competency-based basic skills training, 2) development opportunities such as cultural enrichment, and 3) service opportunities in their communities. Financial incentives are used to increase participation and completion. The pilot test results indicate that participants are less likely to be arrested during their high school years than a control group of similar high-risk teens. In addition, QOP participants were more likely to complete high school and continue on to college than the control group.

The Midwestern Prevention Project. This comprehensive drug abuse prevention program is aimed at reducing the rates of onset and prevalence of drug use (cigarettes, alcohol, and marijuana) in young adolescents age 10 to 15. Five intervention strategies are used: mass media, school, parent, community organization, and health policy change. This program has been effective in reducing drug use among youth, and the effects have been shown to persist through age 23.

Life Skills Training. This is a drug use prevention program targeted at children in junior high or middle school. In the first year of the program, teachers conduct 15 sessions focusing on general life and social resistance skills training. Booster sessions are provided in years two and three of the program (10 and 5 sessions respectively). The program has been shown to reduce the use of alcohol, cigarettes, and marijuana among participants. The reductions in alcohol and cigarette use are sustained through the end of high school.

Multisystemic Therapy. MST is designed to decrease antisocial behavior among violent and chronic juvenile offenders. The overriding purpose of MST is to help parents deal effectively with their youth's behavior problems, including engagement with deviant peers and poor school performance. To accomplish family empowerment, MST also addresses identified barriers to effective parenting and helps family members to build an indigenous social support network. To increase family collaboration and treatment generalization, MST is typically provided in the home, school, and other community locations. Masters-level counselors provide 50 hours of face-to-face contact over four months. Evaluations of the program demonstrate that the therapy is effective in reducing rearrest rates and out-of-home placements.

Multidimensional Treatment Foster Care. MTFC is a cost-effective alternative to residential treatment for adolescents who have problems with chronic delinquency and antisocial behavior. In keeping with social learning concepts, community families are recruited, trained, and closely supervised to provide MTFC placements, treatment, and supervision to participating adolescents. MTFC parent training emphasizes behavior management methods to provide youth with a structure and therapeutic living environment. After completing a preservice training, MTFC parents attend a weekly group meeting run by a program case manager where ongoing supervision is provided. Supervision and support is also given to MTFC parents during daily telephone calls. Family therapy is also provided for the youth's biological family. The MFTC model has been shown to be effective in reducing arrests among participants.

Functional Family Therapy. FFT targets youth in the 11-to-18 age range who have problems with delinquency, substance abuse, or violence. The program focuses on altering interactions between family members and seeks to improve the functioning of the family unit by increasing family problem-solving skills, enhancing emotional connections between family members, and strengthening parental ability to provide appropriate structure, guidance, and limits to their children. FFT is a relatively short-term program that is delivered by individual therapists, usually in the home setting. The effectiveness of the program has been demonstrated for a wide range of problem youth in numerous trials over the past 25 years, using different types of therapists—from paraprofessionals to trainees—in a variety of social work and counseling professions. The program is well-documented and easily transportable.

COST EFFECTIVENESS OF PROGRAMS

The programs that have been found consistently effective in reducing future violence are not inexpensive. Most are in the range of $1,500 to $5,000 per subject, with some of the early childhood programs exceeding $14,000. Many require the immediate expenditure of these funds to support the operation of the program, and then a wait of up to 15 or 20 years before the benefits of fewer crimes and arrests and lower criminal justice costs are realized. These conditions raise the issue of whether the apparent benefits of these programs are worth the costs, either in absolute terms or in comparison to other investments the government might make to reduce violent crime.

The first attempt to estimate the relative cost effectiveness of different types of intervention in a consistent manner was published by RAND in 1996. That study used a relatively simple model and outcome data (reported in the evaluation literature) to estimate the potential costs and crime reduction benefits that might result from scaling up four different types of interventions and applying them to the appropriate populations in California. The study found three of the four interventions analyzed (parent training, Quantum Opportunities, and community programs for young delinquents) to be more cost effective in reducing serious and violent crime than was increasing sentence severity for the type of offenders eligible for Three Strikes sentencing (Greenwood et al. 1996). Without considering any potential benefits from the interventions, other than reduced crime and criminal justice costs, the least cost effective of the four interventions considered turned out to be a very expensive combination of nurse home visits and preschool education.

This limitation was remedied by another RAND team in a subsequent study of two very well-documented and evaluated early-childhood programs. That study found that all the potential benefits, in terms of reduced government expenditures, resulting from investments in these programs exceeded their costs by at least a factor of two or three. The two programs analyzed were David Olds's Nurse Home Visiting Program and the Perry Preschool Program. Results from evaluations of the Nurse Home Visiting Program show that among the higher risk families (unmarried and low SES mothers) who received the services, there were lower rates of child abuse and neglect, lower levels of criminality for both the mothers and their children, and less time spent on welfare. As a result, in the Nurse Home Visiting Program, reductions in criminal justice costs made up only 20 percent of the total monetary benefits to taxpayers resulting from the program. Reductions in welfare costs accounted for 57 percent of the benefits, and taxes on increased income produced the rest (Karoly et al. 1998).

The High/Scope Perry Preschool Program participants were followed up annually through age 11 and again at ages 14, 15, 19, and 27. The follow-up studies found that program participants showed higher levels of academic achievement (as reflected in test scores, grades, and high school graduation rates), less use of welfare, better employment, and lower rates of criminal activities. When the noncrime effects are considered, only about 40 percent of the total monetary benefits produced by the program came from reductions in criminal justice costs. The remainder of the benefits was derived from reductions in education costs (25 percent), taxes on increased income (26 percent), and reductions in welfare costs (9 percent). The benefits to potential crime victims of not becoming a victim were not included in these calculations.

THE WASHINGTON STATE COST BENEFIT MODEL

Following the two RAND reports, the most recent and comprehensive effort to assess the costs and benefits for a broad range of crime prevention

Table 4.3
Summary of Key Economic Outcomes
Estimated in Washington Analysis

PROGRAM	PROGRAM COST PER PARTICIPANT	CRIMINAL JUSTICE BENEFITS PER PARTICIPANT	CRIMINAL JUSTICE BENEFITS PER DOLLAR OF COST	CRIMINAL JUSTICE AND VICTIM BENEFITS PER PARTICIPANT	CRIMINAL JUSTICE AND VICTIM BENEFITS PER DOLLAR OF COST
Perry Preschool	$13,938	$9,237	$0.66	$20,954	$1.50
Olds Prenatal Infancy Program	$7,403	$6,155	$0.83	$11,369	$1.54
Seattle Social Development Project	$3,017	$2,704	$0.90	$5,399	$1.79
Quantum Opportunities Program	$18,292	$1,582	$0.09	$2,290	$0.13
Big Brothers Big Sisters of America	$1,009	$1,313	$1.30	$2,143	$2.12
Multisystemic Therapy	$4,540	$38,047	$8.38	$61,068	$13.45
Functional Family Therapy	$2,068	$14,167	$6.85	$22,739	$10.99
Multi-dimensional Treatment Foster Care	$1,934	$27,202	$14.07	$43,661	$22.58
Juvenile Intensive Supervision (Probation)	$1,500	$1,347	$0.90	$2,235	$1.49

SOURCE: Aos, S., P. Phipps, R. Barmoski and R. Lieb, 1999.

strategies has been undertaken by the Washington State Institute for Public Policy (Aos et al. 1999) at the direction of the Washington Legislature. Table 4.3 summarizes some of the key findings from their recent work in regard to Blueprints and other promising programs.

The first column in the table shows the actual cost of each intervention program. Column 2 shows the dollar value of the benefits that are expected to result from implementation of the program in terms of savings in future criminal justice costs (for arrests, convictions, incarceration, etc.). The last two columns show the value of the expected benefits and the benefit-cost ratio, respectively, factoring in the additional likely benefits to potential crime victims.

The Washington results highlight a number of important points. First, the most cost-effective programs are not necessarily the least expensive. Second, the Blueprints programs that target juvenile offenders are typically more cost-effective than those that treat a broader population of at-risk youth. Results such as these raise questions regarding how program characteristics affect cost-benefit analyses.

Table 4.4 compares the programs that were evaluated by the Washington group on a number of characteristics that together determine their cost effectiveness, most of which are self-explanatory. Effect Size is a measure of the difference between the experimental and control groups in the fraction of subjects offending; it utilizes the arcsine transformation recommended by Cohen (1988).[5] From this table, we begin to see which program characteristics have the greatest impact on cost effectiveness. For the cost-benefit analysis the most important information in the table is the effect size. In general, effect size measures a program's ability to reduce criminal behavior in the treatment group relative to the control.

The Perry Preschool and Nurse Home Visitation programs both have significant effect sizes, but both are also extremely expensive. Furthermore, children participate in these programs in their early childhood, long before their crime careers would even have begun. Because the analysis discounts crimes, so that crimes prevented immediately are more valuable than crimes prevented years in the future, these programs are likely to be less cost-effective.

The targeting ratio, presented in column eight, is a measure of the type of youth the program seeks to treat. It is calculated as the ratio of the expected number of crimes committed by the target population without the program to the expected number of crimes committed by a similar-size group of average youth. Thus, a high targeting ratio indicates that a program deals with a high-risk population. Multisystemic Therapy and

Table 4.4

Characteristics of Youth Violence Prevention Programs Evaluated by Washington Study

Program	Target Population	Cost	Duration	Effect Size	Control Recidivism Rate
Perry Preschool	Disadvantaged preschool-age children	$13,938	2 years	−0.26	4.6 arrests per person
Olds Prenatal Infancy Program	Low-income, at-risk first-time mothers and their children	$7,403	2 years	−0.44	0.45 self-reported arrests per person
Seattle Social Development Project	High-risk elementary school children	$3,017	6 years	−0.23	6.73 self-reported offenses per person
Quantum Opportunities Program	Disadvantaged high school students	$18,292	4 years	−0.42	0.26 self-reported convictions per person
Big Brothers Big Sisters of America	At-risk youth	$1,009	Varies from several months to years	−0.05	0.26 convictions per person
Multisystemic Therapy	Chronic juvenile offenders, age 12–17	$4,540	60 hours of contact over 4 months	−0.68	1.76 reconvictions per person
Functional Family Therapy	Delinquent youth, age 11–18	$2,068	26 hours	−0.34	1.12 reconvictions per person
Multidimensional Treatment Foster Care	Chronic juvenile offenders	$1,934	6–12 months	−0.63	1.76 reconvictions per person
Juvenile Intensive Supervision (Probation)	Juvenile offenders	$1,500	Varies by jurisdiction	−0.03	1.12 reconvictions per person

Table 4.4
Characteristics of Youth Violence Prevention
Programs Evaluated by Washington Study (cont.)

CRIMES PER ACTIVE OFFENDER	TARGETING RATIO	ESTIMATED ARRESTS PREVENTED PER PARTICIPANT	NON–CRIMINAL JUSTICE BENEFITS PER PARTICIPANT	NUMBER OF REPLICATIONS (STUDIES SHOWN BY WASHINGTON)
6.64	3.85	0.54	Improved test scores, graduation rates; reduction in public assistance	1
Not stated	1.97	0.32	Fewer future pregnancies; reduced substance abuse, child abuse, neglect	1
11.28	0.63	0.05	Less alcohol abuse; more attachment to family, school	1
1.63	0.70	0.23	Fewer teen pregnancies; improved high school completion rates, family/life skills	2
1.95	3.81	0.20	Reduction in drug abuse; improved performance in school, family relations	2
2.93	18.14	5.84	Reduction in drug use, out-of-home placements	5
2.44	11.54	2.18	Reduction in drug use, out-of-home placements	7
2.93	18.14	4.18	Reduction in behavior problems	1
2.44	11.54	0.21	None stated	6

SOURCE: Author

Multidimensional Treatment Foster Care have the highest targeting ratios of all the programs evaluated: 18.14. This means that the target population is expected to commit 18.14 times as many crimes as an average group of youth. This is not surprising since these programs work with chronic, violent, and drug-abusing juvenile offenders. At the other extreme is the Seattle Social Development Project, with a targeting ratio of 0.63. This program treats all youth at selected schools in high-crime neighborhoods.

As shown, programs targeting offenders have significantly higher targeting ratios than the earlier interventions do. Because early and school-based intervention programs target a wider segment of the population, many of the children targeted would not have committed crimes even without the intervention. Juvenile offender programs, on the other hand, target youth who have already begun to offend. As a result, a juvenile offender program is likely to be more cost-effective than programs with lower targeting ratios, even if the programs prevent an equal fraction of the population from offending.

CONCLUSIONS

Following a sharp increase in violent offense rates in the early 1990s, juvenile arrest rates for both property and violent offenses have declined substantially in the latter half of the decade. At this point in time, juveniles are making less of a contribution to our national crime problem than they have in the past 20 years.

Meanwhile, over the past 20 years, the emphasis of the juvenile justice system has been shifting away from rehabilitation and the best interests of the child toward greater accountability and harsher sanctions for serious offending. And this is in spite of the fact that we have much better information about the type of interventions that work in reducing recidivism. Many more youth are being handled in adult courts, and proceedings in juvenile courts are much more open to public inspection. Whether these changes in the juvenile justice system can be given any of the credit for recent declines in juvenile offending is difficult to say. In all likelihood the increase in sanction severity for the more serious offenders, the improved knowledge about effective intervention strategies, and the renewed interest in prevention programs all made their contributions to reducing juvenile crime rates, along with a booming economy and the improvements it brought to the impoverished neighborhoods where many high-risk youth are raised.

5

Crime Prevention: Focus on Youth

Patrick Tolan

Crime prevention is a broad category, encompassing almost all activity undertaken in criminology and criminal justice. Efforts to prevent crime can diverge greatly on the causes of crime and the actions necessary to deter it. Activities as different as conflict management training (Farrell and Meyer 1997), punitive sentencing for crimes (Greenwood et al. 1996), policing philosophy (Moore 1992), and economic policies that encourage business investment in poorer sections of cities (Wilson 1987) all fall under the rubric of preventing crime. The unifying factor in these divergent approaches is the goal of reducing and preventing future crime. Whether preventing a first crime by increasing a youngster's cognitive skills so he or she can better negotiate conflict, or stemming a criminal career through incarceration, the action is valuable because it prevents crime.

However, if prevention encompasses any action taken in relation to crime, then what meaning is there in the concept of prevention? Why dedicate a chapter to prevention? The entire book could, in essence, be about prevention. We argue in this chapter that it is not valuable to include under the category "prevention" any and all activity oriented to understanding and affecting crime. Rather, we apply a public health view of prevention that distinguishes it from remediation (treatment) or harm-minimizing interventions (sanctions and incapacitation) (Mercy and O'Carroll 1988). From this perspective, prevention is limited to actions intended to prevent the onset of criminal activity in individuals or the occurrence of criminal activities within a given location (Moore 1995). Under this definition, most legal procedures and punishment-based actions should not be considered prevention. In essence, prevention works to block the formation of a pattern of delinquent activity among at-risk youth or in high crime locations. Therefore, after a description of prevention principles as they are applied to crime, we focus on promising approaches to preventing crime, particularly youth crime (Loeber and Farrington 1998). The final section provides commentary on the state of knowledge and related policy implications.

A PUBLIC HEALTH VIEW OF PREVENTION

The public health concept of prevention arose from two motivations or sources, practical and etiological (Turnock 1997). The practical motivation stemmed from the recognition that treatment and management of diseases were ultimately futile; resources were used in an unending attempt to cure or minimize harm from each new case that arose while never stemming the tide of new cases (Institute of Medicine 1994). Often the resources were deployed only after irreversible harm had occurred. A second impetus derived from a medical typology of disease. For disease to occur, the coincidence of three components—a pathogen, a susceptible host, and an environment that could sustain the pathogen—was necessary (Dyal 1995). Removing any one of the components could prevent the disease.

Analogous components are evident in crime prevention, with some debate as to which focus is the most useful. These three components are (1) individual and environmental risk factors for criminal involvement, (2) the at-risk youth, and (3) the aspects of the social and political system that permit or promote crime. Thus, prevention is aimed at removing one of the necessary components (Mercy and O'Carroll 1988).

In public health, prevention is differentiated from treatment by the fact that it intervenes prior to the components coinciding, while treatment responds after the components have coincided (Dyal 1995; Tolan, In press a). Intentions also differ between the two. After-the-fact interventions usually focus on ameliorating or minimizing symptoms—the equivalent of appropriate punishment or, at least, incapacitation. Crime prevention alters individual susceptibility, that is, the risk factors that precipitate crime among predisposed youth or the conditions that support criminal activities (for example, opportunities for crime, limited social opportunities for legitimate activity) (Fagan 1995). Also paralleling medical treatment, most punishments and sanctions seek to restore the person to normal social and legal responsibility or minimize the future harm the criminal may impose on others (Tolan and Gorman-Smith 1998). The crime locus is attributed to the individual and the process within the "host."

Determining the cause and related interventions also differ in prevention. The first step in understanding cause is to determine variations in the prevalence of the problem by population and location. Once established, one can compare the variations in prevalence with risk factors and settings (Institute of Medicine 1994). The goal is to identify the necessary risk factors for the problem to occur. By manipulating these risk factors, one can presumably prevent the occurrence of the disorder. Similarly, in crime prevention, if one can lessen susceptibility of at-risk youth, eliminate or modify key risk factors they face, or lessen situations that promote and sustain criminal involvement, then crime can presumably be prevented. Based on this perspective and the ensuing definition, the remaining portions of this chapter will focus on prevention of youth crime involvement, particularly prevention of patterned, persistent involvement of youth.

THREE TYPES OF CRIME PREVENTION

Crime-prevention efforts can be grouped into three strategies: (1) setting or situational; (2) community or environmental; and (3) developmental (Tonry and Farrington 1995). Setting or situational strategies attempt to alter the immediate contextual influences that may precipitate criminal activity among at-risk youth. Included in this category are strategies, for example, that occupy youth during the late afternoon and evening when youth crime is most likely to occur, or that increase teacher patrols in schools to minimize unsupervised areas (Tolan, In press b). Community or environmental prevention strategies seek to alter environmental conditions that might predispose to criminal activity (for example, by cleaning up abandoned houses or limiting areas where youth can gather unmonitored [Wilson 1987]). They also seek to alter environmental conditions that might precipitate serious involvement of at-risk youth (for example, by providing opportunities for academic success in school for at-risk youth [Bry 1982]), or that might encourage early and sustained involvement in criminal activity (for example, by clearing a block of drug houses so youth are not enticed to work for dealers [Fagan 1995]). Developmental strategies focus on altering the developmental trajectories of youth who show delinquent tendencies, such as early aggressive behavior, difficulties with self-control, and early rule breaking (Tolan and Gorman-Smith 1998). The developmental perspective and strategies are much more advanced and extensive than the other two approaches.

Situational Prevention Strategies

Situational prevention is based on the view that crime requires an opportunity for an individual to act (Clarke 1995). This view assumes that crime is substantially a rational choice, which weighs the likelihood of success against the ease of obtaining goods or needs otherwise. By increasing the likelihood of getting caught or by making crime more difficult, this approach reasons that an individual who may otherwise commit a criminal act will not (Barr and Pease 1990). Another important basis for this view is the recognition that criminal activity tends to cluster geographically and in time (Clarke 1995). This suggests there are situational determinants of crime that can be modified, thus eliminating a "carrier" of the criminal intent. The situational contributors can be momentary and very specific (for example, a corner of a store that is hard to monitor, making theft easier, or a time of day when youth are out of school) or very general (for example, living where there is limited opportunity for positive social engagement after school). What differentiates situational strategies from others is the view that individual tendency is less critical than the opportunity and risks the situation presents (Clarke 1995). Some theorists have suggested that the focus on individual proclivity misleads crime-prevention efforts and limits potential effectiveness (Downes and Rock 1982). By altering the situations where crime is more likely to occur, they argue, one can prevent most crime, regardless of the individual predisposition.

Of the three prevention strategies, situational strategies most resemble after-the-fact interventions. For example, a common situational strategy is to increase public scrutiny of known drug-selling areas or to increase police patrols during those times when youth crime is most likely to occur or in areas where gangs gather. "Target hardening," or making it harder for those with criminal intent to carry out the crime, is another frequently used situational strategy (Brantingham and Brantingham 1991; Cohen and Felson 1979). Rearranging store displays to make theft more difficult or making vending machines harder to break open are two examples of target hardening.

Identifying "hot spots," or locations of frequent youth crime, is another situational strategy. With increased scrutiny and quick and complete intervention when crime seems imminent, future crimes are prevented (Sherman, Gartin, and Buerger 1989). More recently, analysis of hot spots suggests that preventive interventions might address the reasons these situations or locations become high-risk crime areas in the first place. For example, it may be that a corner is a hot spot for drug deals because it is easily accessible to a freeway, making it convenient for suburban drug buyers. Making streets one way only, for example, may lower the value of the corner as a crime spot. Another example might be negotiating disputed gang boundaries to ease tensions between gangs (Fagan 1995).

Additional situational crime-prevention efforts include access control (for example, ID badges, fences), deflecting offenders (for example, mounting graffiti boards to channel graffiti), controlling facilitators (for example, safety and identification locks on guns, ID checks to purchase guns, caller ID on phones), screening at entry and exit (for example, metal detectors, guards searching bags), and increasing opportunities for detection (for example, periodic checks of employees for drug use, more streetlights).

Situational strategies are often not clearly preventive. For example, target hardening is often implemented in response to a specific problem; it is meant to ameliorate crime. Also, situational strategies have been criticized for not preventing crime as much as displacing it (Mayhew, Clarke, and Elliott 1989). The actions taken do not lessen the prevalence of crime but merely move it to a different place. For example, if one makes a drug distribution center less useful, the sellers may simply move to the next most valuable location, maintaining their level of sales and the same customers.

Community-Oriented Strategies

Community-oriented strategies are based on the assumption that much of crime or criminal tendency can be linked to macrosocial conditions. Economic disparities, a lack of educational and health resources, a concentration of risk factors for social problems, and racial and ethnic oppression all can be considered macrosocial conditions (Wilson 1987). In addition, this strategy is built on theory and findings that macrosocial forces affect the microsocial relations and structures within communities (Sampson, Raudenbush, and Earls 1997; Tolan, Gorman-Smith, and Henry 2000). For example, Tolan, Gorman-Smith, and Henry (2000) found that the level of ethnic diversity, amount of business investment, and range of household income help predict the level of neighborhood involvement and perceived support from neighbors. These neighborhood processes predict subsequent parenting practices and, ultimately, the likelihood of youth criminal involvement. Sampson, Raudenbush, and Earls (1997) found a similar link at the neighborhood level; neighborhoods with more neighborhood activities and involvement with other residents had less crime, even after controlling for macrosocial factors. Notably, macrosocial factors still had a direct and substantial influence on crime rates.

Community-oriented strategies have frequently been linked to developmental strategies (Shaw and McKay 1942). In their early studies at the Institute for Juvenile Research, Shaw and McKay and others noticed that neighborhood conditions seemed to explain criminal involvement more than ethnic group or individual constitution did. This recognition led to a focus on the overall social setting as a developmental concern, although the immediate application for Shaw was to delinquency. It was thought that by organizing communities to be more responsible for "parenting" youth, crime could be prevented. If the community provided the protection and opportunities youth needed, they would not stray into crime (Tolan, Sherrod, Gorman-Smith, and Henry, In press). This view incorporates the interrelation of risk factors in an "ecology" of risk for crime, but places primary genesis in the social factors that determine the social and economic viability of the community. This viability, in turn, affects the structure and quality of informal social processes, such as pride in neighborhood, supervision of youth in public spaces, and interdependence of neighbors through shared values (Bursik and Grasmick 1993; Sampson 1987). This approach to crime prevention has recently become most focused on the inner city; Wilson's (1987) theories about the dynamics leading to the particular concentration of poverty and social problems in inner-city communities have been most influential. Developmental-ecological perspectives view the interaction of individual and family risk factors with community settings as the critical focus for prevention because it is thought that a multilevel, multiple variable approach is needed to adequately determine risk (Tolan and Lorion 1988; Tolan, Guerra, and Kendall 1995; Tolan, Gorman-Smith, and Henry 2000).

Following this theoretical view, community-oriented strategies tend to either decrease the "underlying" social, economic, and political disparities thought to promote social problems or they create the informal social relations that might mitigate the risk caused by these disparities (Tolan and Guerra 1994). An example of lessening disparities is federal funding intended to encourage business investment in low-employment communities devoid of commerce, ultimately increasing the diversity of income levels in the community and fostering neighborhood pride and involvement (Papke 1994; Rosenbaum 1992). An example of the second strategy—promoting social ties—is found in studies showing that an interdependence among multiple-family groups in managing risk for delinquency can reduce aggression and other behaviors linked to later delinquency in inner-city youth (Metropolitan Area Child Study Research Group 2000; Tolan, Gorman-Smith, and Henry 2000).

Although community-oriented prevention is among the most popular approaches to youth crime prevention, the empirical support is thin. Notably, Sherman and colleagues, in their congressional report on crime prevention, found no single community-level effort that was empirically demonstrated to be effective (Sherman et al. 1997). However, they did not include school, police, and criminal justice interventions under community efforts; many such interventions in effect change informal and formal social control mechanisms within the community, and thus could fall under the rubric of community-level efforts to reduce crime. For example, community policing, which helps to set priorities for police and encourage police integration into the community, has been shown to reduce crime (Skogan 1996). Similarly, use of drug courts to help manage drug-addicted early offenders seems to reduce later criminal activity (Deschenes et al. 1996). Also, there is evidence that building community involvement in schools and managing child exposure to violent media, weapons, and community violence can reduce the likelihood of later criminal activity (Gottfredson 1986; Tolan and Guerra 1994; Tolan, In press b). The widely reported community organization among clergy, law enforcement, social welfare, and criminal justice experts in Boston in the early 1990s to reduce adolescent homicides is an example of a community intervention that combines many promising elements for effective crime prevention (Sherman et al. 1997).

More recent efforts take a pro-social development, or strengths-based, approach, to crime prevention. These programs may use a community agency or center, such as an athletic club, as a base for connecting youth to educational and vocational training, social skills interventions, and auxiliary services to help promote successful development (Tolan et al., In press). They also tend to integrate youth crime prevention with prevention of related social problems. Most of these approaches work to aid youth in attaining conventional goals and to help families manage potential threats to reaching these goals (Tolan and Guerra 1994).

Community-oriented prevention is less well studied for several reasons. The theories of measurement (for example, which critical processes to evaluate) and of risk-crime relations (for example, how the processes relate to the causes of crime) have not been well articulated until recently, and few adequate neighborhood-crime risk-relation studies exist (Sampson 1987). The most impeding factor is the complexity involved in evaluating community-level interventions, particularly when standards devised for individual-level intervention evaluation are applied.

This difficulty is due to several features. The effort required to empirically evaluate community interventions can overwhelm many evaluators and is often beyond typical budgets for intervention evaluation (Tolan and Brown 1998). Sample size is another problem. Conventional experimental designs that rely on random assignment and comparisons of treatment / no treatment groups assume that one can find an adequate sample size of a relatively homogenous group. This is very difficult in community-level interventions and may be impossible to meet. For example, typically one needs at least thirty units (in this case neighborhoods or communities) for random assignment to be plausible and for statistical assumptions to be met. Almost no researcher can command cooperation from thirty neighborhoods or communities, obtain the budgets necessary to support such an evaluation over time, or overcome the variations (the heterogeneity) in the communities included. Thus, if the evaluations occur at all, they will almost certainly fall short of the criteria typically applied for reliably assessing the efforts (Elliott and Tolan 1998; Tolan and Guerra 1994).

This inherent limitation must be considered when judging the effectiveness of community prevention, particularly when compared with efforts that are focused on more controllable situations, such as individual differences or changing conditions that might precipitate crime. This critical difference is not usually mentioned in evaluation reviews and is almost never part of the examination of research trends often used for policy recommendations. Therefore, it is easy to infer that community-oriented prevention is not as valuable, or not as scientifically sound, as developmental or situational approaches. Nevertheless, there is still a need to develop alternative evaluation procedures that can realistically impose needed scientific controls for confident interpretation of results and a better balancing of concern for experimental quality with practical limitations and pertinence of evaluations (Tolan and Brown 1998).

Some important understanding of the value of community efforts can be derived from process evaluations (descriptive assessment of how and for whom interventions are effective). For example, community organizing is a promising approach, but it is unclear how sustainable it is, particularly if there is not a charismatic leader and a recent crisis to generate interest. Process studies suggest that block watches may fail because they monitor what is not easily observed and which occurs infrequently (that is, criminal activity). They also infer real risk of repercussions from the criminals whom the block watch is impeding (Merry 1981). Similarly, evaluations of community policing show that the impact varies substantially depending on how the community relations are built and managed and the extent to which police practices can shift to collaborate more with community members (Skogan 1996).

Developmental Prevention Strategies

Most research on risk and prevention of youth crime has taken a developmental perspective. Initially, efforts tended to focus on risk factors within the individual or the family, and apart from context. High-risk youth were especially targeted for prevention (Loeber and Farrington 1998). The developmental theory was one of accumulating risks springing from individual temperament (for example, readily distracted, impulsive, and reluctant to comply) coupled with poor parenting (for example, poor monitoring of the child, and inconsistent and harsh discipline practices). This, in turn, led to early aggression with peer rejection and academic failures during the elementary years, followed by involvement with deviant peers and alienation from conventional morals and roles during adolescence (Coie and Dodge 1998). Thus, the focus for much of the past twenty years has been on the small portion of youth who seem to start their criminal behavior early and remain involved throughout life (Moffitt 1993). This focus was predicated on the finding that 6–8 percent of youth seemed to commit the majority of and most serious crimes (Moffitt 1993). However, more extensive studies have shown that developmental risk effects are not always straightforward and easily discriminated (Tolan and Gorman-Smith 1998). Although individual differences in risk were still important, evidence began to suggest that developmental risk was not fixed but seemed responsive to the overall social and setting influences on developmental trajectories, including changes in experiences and settings over time (Gorman-Smith, Tolan, and Henry, In press; Henry, Guerra, Huesmann, Tolan, VanAcker, and Eron 2000). This view, the developmental-ecological perspective, as it is called, is an attempt to integrate setting and developmental patterns—in which youth, from which risk factors, and in which settings is serious delinquent involvement likely to emerge and merit intervention (Loeber and Farrington 1998; Conduct Problems Prevention Research Group 1999).

The shift toward these multivariate models, which track development and risk behaviors and test the relative predictive value of various risk factors, has advanced our understanding substantially (Elliott 1996; Farrington 1998). Recently, interest is growing in determining how the social ecology affects risk patterns (Garbarino 1996; Gorman-Smith, Tolan, and Henry, In press) and in examining multiple pathways of risk (Nagin and Tremblay 1999; Gorman-Smith et al., In press). There is also growing emphasis on integrating biological and psychological factors (Perry 1997). Social-cognitive styles and coercive family interactions that promote aggression are prominent components in most risk models (Coie and Dodge 1998; Patterson, Reid, and Dishion 1991). Risk models have also been expanded to include protective factors that might temper risk (Thornberry, Huizinga, and Loeber 1995). These advances have led to a developmental perspective that is multivariate, focuses on multiple developmental pathways, and considers how different clusters of risk factors might explain variation in outcome among youth at risk.

For example, Gorman-Smith, Tolan, and Henry (In press) demonstrated that the protection provided from strong family functioning varied as a function of the neighborhood. Similarly, depending on the extent of exposure to violent peers, the protection accorded from strong family functioning varied, as did the risk tied to poor family functioning (Henry, Tolan, and Gorman-Smith, In press). These developmental-ecological models suggest that different types of prevention efforts may be needed, depending on the delinquent population, the timing of intervention, and the setting in which it occurs (Conduct Problems Prevention Research Group 1999; Metropolitan Area Child Study Research Group 2000). Next we outline several approaches to developmental prevention that have empirical backing.

Determining which developmental prevention approaches work.
Although several extended reviews of crime-prevention efforts for youth have been undertaken (Guerra, Tolan, and Hammond 1994; Lipsey and Wilson 1998; Mulvey, Arthur, and Repucci 1993; Sherman et al. 1997; Tolan and Guerra 1994; Wasserman and Miller 1998), there is limited empirical understanding of what works in preventing youth crime (Sherman et al. 1997; Tolan and Guerra 1994). Of the three strategies for crime prevention, the developmental approach is better documented with empirical risk studies and empirical trials using strict standards. This does not mean that the field is fully developed or that most of the research is sound enough to lead to confident interpretations. The enormous volume of research, the extent of development and refinement of theories, research methods, and practice and policy considerations do, however, allow trends to be culled from the research, which can direct understanding, action, and policy (Elliott and Tolan 1998; Tolan, In press b; Tolan and Guerra 1996).

Two approaches to judging and organizing information about what works from a developmental perspective in crime prevention are helpful. The first identifies specific programs that have been rigorously evaluated and that show significant, positive effects (Elliott and Tolan 1998; Sherman et al. 1997). To be considered, the studies, in most cases, must use random assignment, and longitudinal and reliable measurement; and the results must be able to be generalized to larger populations. A number of such efforts are under way, although the standards applied vary substantially. A major weakness of this approach is the limited diversity of the samples studied and the limited correspondence to the segments of the U.S. population most at risk. However, among the most carefully and fully developed of these approaches is the "Blueprints for Violence Prevention" project of the University of Colorado, Center for Prevention of Violence (Elliott and Tolan 1998). The Blueprints project requires programs to have at least two scientifically sound, published evaluation reports and to have been applied to samples that are diverse. Dissemination is directed by technical assistance from the program developers and Blueprints staff as well as by a guide for program replication. This model attempts to reproduce as closely as possible program conditions and activities of the given Blueprint program. Currently, there are ten programs certified as Blueprints, and another dozen that are "promising" (having at least one published efficacy report with adequate methodology). This approach has the advantage of identifying "packages" that can be applied with confidence and that, presumably, if implemented faithfully, should be beneficial.

A second approach to gaining an understanding of youth crime prevention uses meta-analysis, or a statistical summary of findings across a collection of prevention studies. Meta-analysis can help determine the relative advantage of different approaches and the importance of different characteristics of the intervention, the program delivery, and participants. This approach is exemplified by the work of Lipsey and colleagues (Lipsey and Wilson 1998). It has the advantage of identifying "critical elements" for delinquency prevention, while not being wedded to specific programs. These reviews can indicate what activities and elements of program design and intervention contribute to effectiveness. Presumably, one could develop a program that fits the local social ecology by incorporating the effective elements identified across studies. In combination with descriptive reviews of existing approaches, this method of knowledge accumulation could aid in developing prevention programs that combine different approaches and avoid conforming to a specific program. However, this approach does require the demanding task of developing and organizing intervention activities, materials, and administration that will make for effective crime prevention. Whether a given effort captures the critical elements of a program cannot be known with certainty.

Each approach to assessing what works in developmental prevention can advance knowledge and provide a good foundation for policy. However, the sophistication of knowledge and the diversity of the findings are limited, so both approaches are needed to inform the field. In tandem, these two approaches can help determine the need either for standardization in disseminating exemplary "packages," or for packaging the most promising elements and approaches for a more local fit (Tolan and Brown 1998; Tolan, In press a).

Useful distinctions among the developmentally oriented prevention strategies are those that focus on characteristics of the youth (individual level), those that focus on the two primary interpersonal relationships affecting youth development (families, peers), and those that focus on the contexts of youth development (school, neighborhood). In some cases, the latter are also community oriented; they attempt to modify conditions in settings thought to be conducive to delinquency and crime.

Individual-level approaches. Strategies with empirical support that focus on the individual are those that modify or enhance social-cognitive processes, such as problem-solving skills, moral reasoning, ability to generate alternative solutions, and beliefs about the use of aggression (Guerra and Slaby 1989). In the genre, conflict management techniques show particular promise (Aber et al. 1998; Hawkins, Farrington, and Catalano 1999). However, effects are found only when the individual cognitive training occurs within a larger ecological-change effort, such as changing teacher practices and shifting school behavior-management policies (Tolan and Guerra 1994). Studies also show some indication that anger management programs may benefit youth who are impulsive (Dangel, Deschner, and Rapp 1989). Although recent results from mentoring evaluations are mixed, there is evidence that if the effort is well organized, systematic, and delivered competently, benefits can accrue (Grossman and Tierney 1998). A controlled experiment with 959 youth in eight cities, for example, found that the Big Brothers / Big Sisters program resulted in a 46 percent reduction in drug use, a 32 percent reduction in hitting people, and a 52 percent reduction in truancy (Grossman and Tierney 1998). However, despite the widespread popularity of mentoring, there has been relatively little research on its effects. We also need to better understand the characteristics of successful mentors and successful mentoring relationships, given that some studies have found that approximately half of mentor pairings fail to develop into ongoing relationships (Freedman 1993; Styles and Morrow 1992).

In contrast to these promising programs, supportive or insight-oriented psychotherapy and intensive casework programs have been found to be ineffective in preventing youth crime, and they may even have negative effects (Berleman, Seaberg, and Steinburn 1971; Schwitzgebel and Baer 1967; Moore 1987; Weisz et al. 1990). The evaluations were focused on high-risk youth; therefore, the results may not be generalizable to other segments of the population. Similarly, there is little sound empirical evidence that psychopharmacological treatments are effective in reducing or preventing crime. The exception is one study that points to the benefits of pharmacological approaches with repeatedly violent individuals in a residential setting (Williams et al. 1982). In addition, there is some case evidence of beneficial outcomes for adolescents with histories of psychological neglect and traumas (Grizenko and Vida 1988). This is a rapidly developing area, and it is quite possible that evidence will show that psychopharmacology can lessen youth risk.

Family interventions. The strongest and the most consistent evidence of effectiveness is for programs that focus on family processes, particularly parenting (Henggeler, Melton, et al. 1993; Tolan et al. 1997). Specifically, there is robust data that family-oriented intervention to (1) change parenting style and practices (increase predictability and parental monitoring, and lessen negative parenting methods) and (2) improve intrafamily relations (closeness, positive feedback, communication clarity, and emotional cohesion), or both, can affect risk (Borduin et al. 1995; Metropolitan Area Child Study Research Group 2000). Notably, all of the successful family interventions have combined behavioral parent-training techniques with other intervention components based in family systems theory (for a summary, see Tolan and Mitchell 1989, and Tolan and McKay 1996).

Peer group interventions. Peer group interventions have been a popular approach to crime prevention. They appear to be an efficient method of service delivery and are assumed to encourage more pro-social and conventional methods of relating as well as values about behavior. However, researchers have consistently found no effect and, in some cases, a negative effect of peer group or small group interventions (Dishion et al. 1996; Feldman, Caplinger, and Wodarski 1983). In fact, there is consistent evidence that using group-programming for high-risk adolescent youth has a negative effect. Our own research suggests this effect may extend downward from adolescence into late childhood (Metropolitan Area Child Study Research Group 2000). In contrast, there is some evidence of positive effects with younger children, particularly if the group is a mix of pro-social and high-risk youth (Dumas, Blechman, and Prinz 1992).

Teacher training and school-focused interventions. These interventions have shown some positive effects as primary prevention and, in some cases, as secondary prevention for high-risk youth (Hawkins, Farrington, and Catalano 1999). Evidence also indicates that school-based interventions that shift how high-risk children are managed or that increase parental involvement in school can reduce risk (Bry 1982). However, despite the intuitive appeal of this approach, few empirical studies of interventions have emerged. Many of the existing studies are methodologically inadequate to provide reliable evidence of effects. This is one of the areas most in need of evaluation, given that most programs are school based, often are delivered by teachers, and include teacher behavior management as a presumed contributor to outcomes. It is important to know to what extent teacher training, norms, and behavior affect risk. For example, a recent study demonstrated that when teachers hold norms that do not tolerate aggression and use behavior management that does not support it; and if these norms are also assumed by youth in the class, aggression can be lowered in youth. When only the teacher and not the students adopt the norms, however, aggression is not decreased and may even be increased (Henry et al. 2000).

More evidence amply shows that school organizational changes can affect antisocial behavior related to delinquency risk (Gottfredson, Gottfredson, and Skroban 1996). In a series of studies, Gottfredson and colleagues showed how organizational efforts that increase order, organizational access, and clarity, and that help implement strong, shared values decrease problem behaviors, including drug use. Most of these efforts generally involve increasing parental involvement and implementing team approaches to organizational decisions. However, many of the supporting evaluations used quasi-experimental designs, and the lack of equivalency between schools being compared reduces confidence.

MOVING FORWARD ON CRIME PREVENTION

Suggestions for Further Research

Although there has been much effort in the past twenty years, and the sophistication and diversity of the populations studied have increased greatly in the last decade, much of the research is still generated from a relatively small set of studies that may have limitations. Some studies do not focus on U.S. samples, some were gathered quite some time ago, many were not designed to consider different patterns of delinquency and criminal involvement, and most do not permit much consideration of demographic and social-ecological variations in risk or prevention effects. However, there is a portfolio of mature longitudinal risk and prevention trial studies that have rich data that could be analyzed to help advance understanding and guide policy. In addition, there are evaluation efforts that could be undertaken to provide good policy analyses.

Fundamentally, the field needs continued and expanded evaluation of intervention efforts. Especially in need of good evaluations are community and situational prevention strategies. In addition to fundamental advancements, the field could benefit from further innovations in existing research. First, there is much to be gained by mining existing data sets. Secondary data analyses that cross-validate analyses with multiple samples, particularly analyses that are person- or subgroup-centered, would permit the field to advance from "variance explanation" to explanations of patterns followed by people (Cairns 1987). These analyses would not only offer insight into important subpatterns of development, they would also permit a more user-friendly estimation of the effects of risk factors and their interdependence (Tolan 1998). The field must move beyond identifying laundry lists of statistically significant risk factors and develop profiles of co-occurring risk and protective factors that compose at-risk populations (Gorman-Smith, Tolan, and Henry 1999). With such an approach, we could also gain insight into how different, naturally co-occurring characteristics vary in their relation to risk and prevention effects by setting. As the core risk factors and the most promising intervention targets emerge, the field must identify how they vary systematically with the population, context, and developmental timing of interest. Person- or unit-centered analyses may be the best method for gaining good insight about "what works for whom," that is, how intervention effects vary by ethnic group, social status, and other subgroup differences. This approach may be one of the most effective methods to quickly gain understanding of youth crime prevention.

Second, more research is needed that evaluates how implementation variations affect the outcomes. For example, a recent meta-analysis suggests that program implementation characteristics can overshadow the potential of intervention components (Lipsey & Wilson 1998). Among the findings is that a strong and careful implementation (for example, well-trained staff, consistent delivery of program, full involvement and adherence to completion of the program by service delivery staff) can make an otherwise weak program as effective as a stronger program that has not been implemented carefully or strongly managed. Many empirically supported programs have not been tested in less-controlled conditions, in which inclusion criteria may not be fully specified or implementation as originally tested may not be realistic. Systematic study of implementation in various settings is needed, as is study of how other service delivery constraints affect intervention. Such work is important not only in determining the robustness of program effects, but also in illuminating under what conditions, for what groups, and with what delivery and administrative characteristics preventive benefits occur (Tolan and Brown 1998). A series of such studies can bridge the significant gap between research and practice by showing how findings of controlled studies translate with changing community needs.

The third area of critical research development includes both method and research content. It is commonly thought that primary prevention will necessitate major change in institutions, settings, and communities that affect youth development (Loeber and Farrington 1998). Despite the formidable evaluation requirements, studies that use a large sample to examine change in schools, neighborhoods, or communities are clearly still needed. For example, there is growing evidence that school-level and community-level programs that integrate primary and universal strategies to change the norms and social ecology, along with secondary prevention strategies that target high-risk youth, are most promising. Yet, there is not, to date, a study of adequate scale to test this important hypothesis. A large-scale, random-assignment test of school- and community-level interventions is needed (Tolan and Brown 1998). Also needed are evaluation strategies that maximize objectivity but that are not dependent on sample sizes of thirty or more units per condition or cell, as is a "rule of thumb" for assuming representativeness and randomization (Aber et al. 1998).

The fourth area of innovation is comparing cost-effective and cost-benefit analyses of prevention programs with after-the-fact interventions. Evaluating the relative costs and benefits of crime prevention is a new enterprise, and the standard against which such estimates are measured is often simplistic or misleading. The existing cost-benefit analyses are also often mired in a political agenda either in favor of or against prevention as a crime strategy, which makes objectivity difficult (Aos et al. 1999). Also, the extent of cost-benefit analyses is limited, and often they are applied as post-intervention afterthoughts. However, the picture is changing. The few existing, sound cost-benefit analyses suggest that prevention is more effective and less costly than after-the-fact interventions, including legal sanctioning and incarceration (Greenwood et al. 1996; Tolan and Gorman-Smith 1998). Greenwood et al. (1996) compared three prevention approaches with California's "three strikes" policy (extended and mandatory incarceration for the third felony offense), and found that two out of three preventive interventions were more cost effective. The third intervention was an amalgamation of the two other interventions, and the cost estimates were much higher than those used in other cost-estimate evaluations of the two studies. If more commonly used cost estimates are applied, this program, even though more comprehensive and widely implemented in the model than was originally intended, was still more cost effective (Tolan, In press b). A more thorough and careful comparison of multiple approaches to youth crime prevention by the Washington State Institute for Public Policy finds a return of up to $31 for each $1 invested in prevention (Aos et al. 1999).

Suggestions for Advancing Service Structures

Translate demonstration effects into effective services. In addition to the suggestions for research, more attention is needed in developing the organizational structures that will support, sustain, and evaluate youth crime-prevention efforts (Tolan, In press b). Given the evidence that service delivery methods, support of staff, and other organizational characteristics can greatly affect the impact of interventions, there is need to identify methods to translate these characteristics into valued features of crime-prevention efforts. For example, many prevention efforts are undertaken as demonstration projects without consideration for the important characteristics of most community-based organizations, such as staff development and supervision constraints. Similarly, it is not uncommon for demonstration projects to be substantially transformed when implemented; staff responsibilities might be increased, training may be reduced, and supervision that maintains enthusiasm and fidelity of intervention delivery might be decreased. Also, most demonstrations are not undertaken with a goal of community ownership and sustainability; yet most interventions require that such perceived ownership be incorporated by schools, community groups, and other local agencies. Maintaining fidelity, ensuring consistency in practice while encouraging innovation and personal responsibility, and applying proven approaches while permitting local determination, are all issues of organization maintenance that can affect not only the immediate impact of a given approach, but the impact over time (Tolan and Brown 1998; Weissberg and Greenberg 1997). For example, there may be resistance to crime prevention, but great interest in the same efforts if they are considered to be focused on positive development of youth. Efforts may also be sustainable if undertaken as part of a general approach that emphasizes supporting adolescent social development (Tolan et al., In press). Youth crime prevention is just beginning to address these issues, and they will be central to moving from sound demonstrations to effective efforts.

Youth crime prevention is also affected by the policies and funding mechanisms that frame what is important. The research suggests a need for policy approaches that promote stable service organizations yet permit local innovation, encourage collaboration among local groups, and ensure adequate evaluation of these efforts. Also, the policies must permit a consistent approach over several years. This need conflicts with much of the history of the support in this area, which has been based on dramatic responses to specific incidents and politically expedient oversimplifications (for example, that of the "super predator"; Snyder 1998). The more policy can rely on scientific findings and respect the steady accumulation of information based on empirical evaluation, the greater the likelihood that efforts will make a real difference. It is important to remember that there are many examples of heartfelt intentions to implement "good ideas" that have ultimately been ineffective in preventing crime and, in some cases, have increased risk. This issue leads to two major policy recommendations from the research.

Integrate service funding and delivery for high-risk youth. Youth at risk for future criminal involvement are often identified by many service systems—some through behavior problems at school, some through involvement with the child welfare system, some through early involvement with police, and some through the health care system. These diverse identification systems also operate disjunctively as service systems, particularly for children and families with needs that cross service systems. Strategies to develop service funding, program development, service delivery, and collaborations across systems are critical. The evidence shows that integrated services, particularly if family-focused, can have substantial effects on later incidence of crime (Aos et al. 1999; Henggeler et al. 1996). Initiatives that identify the most effective financial and administrative approaches for promoting and maintaining integrated and sound interventions for these high-risk youth are needed. Models for legislation that are based on both cost management and program quality should be developed.

Implementing, supporting, and maintaining centralized-decentralized responses. Much of the existing research grows out of theoretical interests of academic researchers, while many services grow out of clinical interests of practitioners. From a quality control perspective, centralizing the organization of prevention efforts allows a more efficient dissemination of "what works." However, this "top-down" approach can conflict with recognition that local needs will determine much about what is required and what works. Local issues can easily overwhelm model programs. Thus, there is interest in programs that promote ownership of youth crime prevention. Prevention efforts cannot merely be disseminated across diverse communities and service providers and be "owned" by these communities. Yet, local perspectives and involved community constituencies are not inherently wise and may implement strategies without any likelihood of effectiveness. Tensions arising from these contending perspectives need to be integrated into service development and delivery systems that have a centralized component (for example, technical assistance, standards of care) and a decentralized component (for example, what specific strategies are done and under what organization in a given community). Developing a relation between a centralized source of information and standards and the opportunity for local initiative and ecological fit should be encouraged. One model for such integration of the "top-down *and* bottom-up" program is partnerships between academic institutes with policy or community interests and community collaboratives focused on a given community. In such an organization, the academy provides knowledge about best practices, evaluation methods, and aid in troubleshooting impediments.

The actual program and organization is developed by the community collaborative, incorporating the scientific methods and best practices knowledge of the academic partner. In turn, the community collaborative informs the academic development by bringing into focus issues in implementation, program utility, and management over time. Guidelines for such partnerships, funding streams, and initiatives that support such partnerships as well as identify exemplars would help aid the integration of prevention science with efforts to reach our youth.

These research and service organization recommendations focus on how knowledge and "on the ground" effectiveness can be improved. In addition, there is need for continued exploration of innovative approaches and refined evaluations of situation-oriented and community-focused approaches. If these efforts are approached in a prevention framework, they should provide convincing evidence of the public benefits of greater emphasis on prevention in reducing crime.

6

Families and Crime

DAVID P. FARRINGTON

When people are asked what they think are the main causes of crime, they often nominate poor parental child-rearing methods, and especially poor discipline or control of children. For example, in 1988, the British newspaper *Sunday Mail* reported the results of survey of a quota sample of more than 1,000 adults who were asked what they thought were the main causes of violent crime. The most popular cause (nominated by 53%) was lack of parental discipline, followed by poverty (20%), television violence (19%), lack of school discipline (15%), broken homes (13%), and alcohol or drugs (13%).

Academic research confirms the importance of family factors as predictors of offending. The American psychologists Rolf Loeber and Tom Dishion (1983) extensively reviewed the predictors of male offending. They concluded that the most important predictors were (in order) poor parental child management techniques, childhood antisocial behavior, offending by parents and siblings, low intelligence and educational attainment, and separation from a parent. Later, Rolf Loeber and Magda Stouthamer-Loeber (1986) completed an exhaustive review of family factors as predictors of offending. They found that the best predictors were (in order) poor parental supervision, parental rejection of children, large family size, low parental involvement with children, parental conflict, and antisocial parents.

More recent reviews confirm the importance of family factors. Carolyn Smith and Susan Stern (1997, pp. 383–84) concluded:

We know that children who grow up in homes characterized by lack of warmth and support, whose parents lack behavior-management skills, and whose lives are characterized by conflict or maltreatment will more likely be delinquent, whereas a supportive family can protect children even in a very hostile and damaging external environment . . . Parental monitoring or supervision is the aspect of family management that is most consistently related to delinquency.

Mark Lipsey and Jim Derzon (1998) reviewed the predictors at ages 6 to 11 of serious or violent offending at ages 15 to 25. The best explanatory predictors (i.e., predictors not measuring some aspect of the child's antisocial behavior) were antisocial parents, male gender, low socioeconomic status of the family, and psychological factors (daring, impulsiveness, poor concentration, etc.). Other moderately strong predictors were minority race, poor parent-child relations (poor supervision, poor discipline, low parental involvement, low parental warmth), other family characteristics (parental stress, family size, parental discord), antisocial peers, low intelligence, and low school achievement. In contrast, abusive parents and broken homes were relatively weak predictors. It is clear that some family factors are at least as important in the prediction of offending as are gender and race.

Reviewing these kinds of results reveals the bewildering variety of family constructs that have been studied, as well as the variety of methods used to classify them into categories. In this chapter, family factors are grouped into six categories: (a) criminal and antisocial parents and siblings; (b) other characteristics of parents (young age, substance abuse, stress or depression, working mothers); (c) large family size; (d) child-rearing methods (poor supervision, poor discipline, coldness and rejection, low parental involvement with the child); (e) abuse (physical or sexual) or neglect; (f) parental conflict and disrupted families. It was decided to group parental discipline with child-rearing methods, rather than with physical abuse, and to group delinquent siblings with criminal parents, rather than with large family size. Excluded are such socioeconomic factors as low family income, low social class of the family, living in a poor neighborhood, and residential mobility of the family.

Methodological issues, such as the independent, interactive, sequential, or cumulative effects of family factors, are discussed after the review of evidence, as is family-based crime prevention. However, two methodological issues need to be mentioned here. First, most studies focus on family influences on the child's onset of offending, not on family influences on the later criminal career, such as on the persistence or desistance of offending (for exceptions, see Farrington and Hawkins 1991; Loeber et al. 1991). Similarly, most studies focus on family influences on children in their childhood years, not on later family influences, such as the effects of a person's getting married or becoming separated on the person's own offending (for exceptions, see Sampson and Laub 1993; Farrington and West 1995).

Second, the best method of establishing that a family factor predicts later offending is to carry out a prospective longitudinal survey, and the emphasis in this chapter is on results obtained in such surveys (for a review, see Loeber and Farrington 1997). They avoid retrospective bias (e.g., where the recollections of parents about their child-rearing methods are biased by the knowledge that their child has become a delinquent) and help in establishing causal order. Also, offenders emerge naturally in community surveys, avoiding the problem of how to choose a control group of nonoffenders. Most longitudinal surveys focus on family risk factors, but information about family protective factors is also needed.

CRIME RUNS IN FAMILIES

Criminal and antisocial parents tend to have delinquent and antisocial children, as shown in the classic longitudinal surveys by Joan McCord (1977) in Boston and Lee Robins (1979) in St. Louis. The most extensive research on the concentration of offending in families was carried out in the Cambridge Study of Delinquent Development, which is a prospective longitudinal survey of more than 400 South London males from ages 8 to 46. Having a convicted father, mother, brother, or sister predicted a boy's own convictions, and all four relatives were independently important as predictors (Farrington et al. 1996). For example, 63% of boys with convicted fathers were themselves convicted, compared with 30% of the remainder. Same-sex relationships were stronger than opposite-sex relationships, and older siblings were stronger predictors than younger siblings. Just 6% of the families accounted for half of all the convictions of all family members.

Similar results were obtained in the Pittsburgh Youth Study, which is a prospective longitudinal survey of more than 1,500 Pittsburgh males from ages 7 to 25. Arrests of fathers, mothers, brothers, sisters, uncles, aunts, grandfathers, and grandmothers all predicted the boy's own delinquency (Farrington et al. 2001). The most important relative was the father; arrests of the father predicted the boy's delinquency independently of all other arrested relatives. Just 8% of families accounted for 43% of arrested family members.

In the Cambridge Study, having a convicted parent or a having a delinquent older sibling by the tenth birthday was consistently among the best age 8 to 10 predictors of the boy's later offending and antisocial behavior. Apart from behavioral measures such as troublesomeness and daring, these two were the strongest predictors of juvenile convictions (Farrington 1992a). Having a convicted parent or a having a delinquent older sibling was also among the best predictors, after poor parental supervision, of juvenile self-reported delinquency.

There are several possible explanations (which are not mutually exclusive) of why offending tends to be concentrated in certain families and transmitted from one generation to the next. First, there may be intergenerational continuities in exposure to multiple risk factors. For example, each successive generation may be entrapped in poverty, disrupted families, single and teenage parenting, and the most deprived neighborhoods. Parents who use physical punishment may produce children who use similar punitive methods when they grow up, as indeed Leonard Eron and his colleagues (1991) found in New York State. One of the main conclusions of the Cambridge Study is that a constellation of family background features (including poverty, large family size, parental disharmony, poor child-rearing, and parental criminality) leads to a constellation of antisocial features when children grow up, among which criminality is one element (West and Farrington 1977, p. 161). According to this explanation, the intergenerational transmission of offending is part of a larger cycle of deprivation and antisocial behavior.

A second explanation focuses on assortative mating: female offenders tend to cohabit with or marry male offenders. Children with two criminal parents are disproportionally antisocial (West and Farrington 1977, p. 122). There are two main classes of reasons why similar people tend to marry, cohabit, or become sexual partners (Rowe and Farrington 1997). The first is called *social homogamy.* Convicted people tend to choose each other as mates because of physical and social proximity; they meet each other in the same schools, neighborhoods, clubs, pubs, and so on. The second process is called *phenotypic assortment;* people examine each other's personality and behavior and choose partners who are similar to themselves. In the Dunedin study in New Zealand, which is a longitudinal survey of more than 1,000 children from age 3, Robert Krueger and his colleagues (1998) found that sexual partners tended to be similar in their self-reported antisocial behavior.

The third explanation focuses on direct and mutual influences of family members on each other. For example, perhaps younger male siblings tend to imitate the antisocial behavior of older male siblings or perhaps older siblings encourage younger ones to be antisocial. There is considerable sibling resemblance in delinquency (Lauritsen 1993). In the Cambridge Study, co-offending by brothers was surprisingly common; about 20% of boys who had brothers close to them in age were convicted for a crime committed with their brother (Reiss and Farrington 1991, p. 386). However, intergenerational mutual influences on offending seem less plausible, since co-offending by parents with their children was very uncommon in the Cambridge Study. There was no evidence that parents directly encouraged their children to commit crimes or taught them criminal techniques; on the contrary, a criminal father usually disapproved of his son's offending (West and Farrington 1977, p. 116).

A fourth explanation suggests that the effect of a criminal parent on a child's offending is mediated by environmental mechanisms. In the Pittsburgh Youth Study, it was suggested that arrested fathers tended to have delinquent boys because they tended to impregnate young women, to live in bad neighborhoods, and to use child-rearing methods that did not develop a strong conscience in their children (Farrington et al. 2001). In the Cambridge Study, it was suggested that poor parental supervision was one link in the causal chain between criminal fathers and delinquent sons (West and Farrington 1977, p. 117). In Boston, Robert Sampson and John Laub (1993, p. 92) found that maternal and paternal deviance (criminal or alcoholic) did not predict a boy's delinquency after controlling for family factors such as poor supervision, harsh or erratic discipline, parental rejection, low attachment, and large family size.

A fifth explanation suggests that the effect of a criminal parent on a child's offending is mediated by genetic mechanisms as discussed in chapterc 3. In agreement with this, twin studies show that identical twins are more concordant in their offending than are fraternal twins (Raine 1993). However, an objection to these kinds of twin studies is that the greater behavioral similarity of the identical twins could reflect their greater environmental similarity. Also in agreement with genetic mechanisms, adoption studies show that the offending of adopted children is significantly related to the offending of their biological parents. However, an objection to adoption studies is that some children may have had contact with their biological parents, so again it is difficult to dismiss an environmental explanation of this finding. In a more convincing design that compares the concordance of identical twins reared together and identical twins reared apart, William Grove and his colleagues (1990) found that heritability was 41% for childhood conduct disorder and 28% for adult antisocial personality disorder. This design shows that the intergenerational transmission of offending is partly attributable to genetic factors. An important question is how the genetic potential (genotype) interacts with the environment to produce the offending behavior (phenotype).

A sixth explanation suggests that criminal parents tend to have delinquent children because of official (police and court) bias against known criminal families, who also tend to be known to official agencies because of other social problems. At all levels of self-reported delinquency in the Cambridge Study, boys with convicted fathers were more likely to be convicted themselves than were boys with unconvicted fathers (West and Farrington 1977, p. 118). However, this was not the only explanation for the link between criminal fathers and delinquent sons, because boys with criminal fathers had higher self-reported delinquency scores and higher teacher and peer ratings of bad behavior. It is not clear which of these six explanations is the most important.

OTHER PARENTAL FEATURES

Numerous parental features predict delinquency and antisocial behavior of children. For example, early child-bearing or teenage pregnancy is a risk factor. Merry Morash and Lila Rucker (1989) analyzed results from four surveys in the United States and England (including the Cambridge Study) and found that teenage mothers were associated with low-income families, welfare support, and absent biological fathers; that they used poor child-rearing methods; and that their children were characterized by low school attainment and delinquency. However, the presence of the biological father mitigated many of these adverse factors and generally seemed to have a protective effect. Similarly, a large-scale study in Washington State showed that children of teenage or unmarried mothers had a significantly increased risk of offending (Conseur et al. 1997). Boys born to unmarried mothers age 17 or less had an 11 times greater risk of chronic offending than boys born to married mothers age 20 or over.

In the Cambridge and Pittsburgh studies, the age of the mother at her first birth was only a moderate predictor of the boy's later delinquency (Farrington and Loeber 1999). In the Cambridge Study, for example, 27% of sons of teenage mothers were convicted as juveniles, compared with 18% of the remainder. More detailed analyses in this study showed that teenage mothers who went on to have large numbers of children were especially likely to have convicted children (Nagin et al. 1997). It was concluded that the results were concordant with a diminished-resources theory: the offspring of adolescent mothers were more crime prone because they lacked not only economic resources but also personal resources such as attention and supervision. Of course, it must be remembered that the age of the mother is highly correlated with the age of the father; having a young father may be just as important as having a young mother. Also, since juvenile delinquency predicts causing an early pregnancy (Smith et al. 2000), the link between teenage parents and child delinquency may be one aspect of the link between criminal parents and delinquent children.

Substance use by parents predicts delinquency of children, as found in the Pittsburgh Youth Study (Loeber et al. 1998a). Smoking by the mother during pregnancy is a particularly important risk factor. A large-scale follow-up of a general population cohort in Finland showed that maternal smoking during pregnancy doubled the risk of violent or persistent offending by their sons, after controlling for other biopsychosocial risk factors (Rasanen et al. 1999). When maternal smoking was combined with a teenage mother, a single parent family, and an unwanted pregnancy, risks of offending increased tenfold.

In the Pittsburgh Youth Study, parental stress and parental depression were only moderate predictors of the boy's delinquency (Loeber et al. 1998a). Rand Conger and his colleagues (1995) carried out an interesting study of parental stress (caused by negative life events) and delinquency, based on two surveys in Iowa and Oregon. They concluded that parental stress produced parental depression, which in turn caused poor discipline, which in turn caused childhood antisocial behavior.

In the days when working mothers were statistically uncommon, it was often argued that they caused delinquency, presumably because they were thought likely to supervise their children less well than nonworking mothers. However, in the Cambridge Study, having a working mother was associated with a relatively low risk of delinquency, possibly because full-time working mothers tended to coincide with higher income and smaller families (West and Farrington 1973, p. 27).

LARGE FAMILY SIZE

Large family size (a large number of children in the family) is a relatively strong and highly replicable predictor of delinquency (Fischer 1984; Ellis 1988). It was similarly important in the Cambridge and Pittsburgh studies, even though families were on average smaller in Pittsburgh in the 1990s than in London in the 1960s (Farrington and Loeber 1999). In the Cambridge Study, if a boy had four or more siblings by his tenth birthday, his risk of being convicted as a juvenile doubled (West and Farrington 1973, p. 31). Large family size predicted self-reported delinquency as well as convictions (Farrington 1992a). It was the most important independent predictor of convictions up to age 32 in a logistic regression analysis: 58% of boys from large families had been convicted at age 32 (Farrington 1993).

There are many possible reasons why a large number of siblings might increase the risk of a child's delinquency. Generally, as the number of children in a family increases, the amount of parental attention that can be given to each child decreases. Also, as the number of children increases, the household tends to become more overcrowded, possibly leading to increases in frustration, irritation, and conflict. In the Cambridge Study, large family size did not predict delinquency for boys living in the least crowded conditions, with two or more rooms than there were children (West and Farrington 1973, p. 33). This suggests that household overcrowding might be an important intervening factor between large family size and delinquency.

In a study of delinquent boys and girls in Ottawa, Marshall Jones and his colleagues (1980) proposed that there was male potentiation and female suppression of delinquency by boys. This theory was intended to explain why they found that male delinquents had many more brothers than sisters. However, this result was not obtained in the Cambridge Study, where the number of sisters was just as closely related to a boy's delinquency as the number of brothers (West and Farrington 1973, p. 32).

David Brownfield and Ann Sorenson (1994) reviewed several possible explanations for the link between large families and delinquency, including those focusing on features of the parents (e.g., criminal parents, teenage parents), those focusing on parenting (e.g., poor supervision, disrupted families), and those focusing on economic deprivation or family stress. Another interesting theory suggested that the key factor was birth order: large families include more later-born children, who tend to be more delinquent. Based on an analysis of self-reported delinquency in a Seattle survey, they concluded that the most plausible intervening causal mechanism was exposure to delinquent siblings. Consistent with social learning theory, large families contained more antisocial models.

CHILD-REARING METHODS

Many different types of child-rearing methods predict a child's delinquency. The most important dimensions of child-rearing are supervision or monitoring of children, discipline or parental reinforcement, warmth or coldness of emotional relationships, and parental involvement with children. Unlike family size, these constructs are difficult to measure, and there is some evidence that results differ according to methods of measurement. In their extensive review of parenting methods in relation to childhood antisocial behavior, Fred Rothbaum and John Weisz (1994) concluded that the strength of associations between parent and child measures was greater when parenting was measured by observation or interview than when it was measured using questionnaires.

Parental supervision refers to the degree of monitoring by parents of the child's activities and their degree of watchfulness or vigilance. Of all these child-rearing methods, poor parental supervision is usually the strongest and most replicable predictor of offending (Smith and Stern 1997; Farrington and Loeber 1999). It typically predicts a doubled risk of delinquency. Many studies show that parents who do not know where their children are when they are out and parents who let their children roam the streets unsupervised from an early age tend to have delinquent children. For example, in the classic Cambridge-Somerville study in Boston, poor parental supervision in childhood was the best predictor of both violent and property crimes up to age 45 (McCord 1979).

Parental discipline refers to how parents react to a child's behavior. It is clear that harsh or punitive discipline (involving physical punishment) predicts a child's delinquency, as the review by Jaana Haapasalo and Elina Pokela (1999) showed. In a follow-up study of nearly 700 Nottingham children, John and Elizabeth Newson (1989) found that physical punishment at ages 7 and 11 predicted later convictions; 40% of offenders had been smacked or beaten at age 11, compared with 14% of nonoffenders. Erratic or inconsistent discipline also predicts delinquency (West and Farrington 1973, p. 51). This can involve either erratic discipline by one parent, who sometimes turns a blind eye to bad behavior and sometimes punishes it severely, or inconsistency between two parents, where one parent is tolerant or indulgent and the other is harshly punitive. It is not clear whether unusually lax discipline predicts delinquency. Just as inappropriate methods of responding to bad behavior predict delinquency, low parental reinforcement (not praising) of good behavior is also a predictor (Farrington and Loeber 1999).

Cold, rejecting parents tend to have delinquent children, as Joan McCord (1979) found 20 years ago in the Cambridge-Somerville study. More recently, she concluded that parental warmth could act as a protective factor against the effects of physical punishment (McCord 1997). Whereas 51% of boys with cold, physically punishing mothers were convicted in her study, only 21% of boys with warm, physically punishing mothers were convicted, similar to the 23% of boys with warm, nonpunitive mothers who were convicted. The father's warmth was also a protective factor against the father's physical punishment.

Low parental involvement in the child's activities predicts delinquency, as the Newsons found in their Nottingham survey (Lewis et al. 1982). In the Cambridge Study, having a father who never joined in the boy's leisure activities doubled his risk of conviction (West and Farrington 1973, p. 57), and this was the most important predictor of persistence in offending after age 21, as opposed to desistance (Farrington and Hawkins 1991). Similarly, poor parent-child communication predicted delinquency in the Pittsburgh Youth Study (Farrington and Loeber 1999), and low family cohesiveness was the most important predictor of violence in the Chicago Youth Development Study (Gorman-Smith et al. 1996).

In psychology, there has been a great emphasis on parenting styles rather than parenting practices. Diana Baumrind (1966) originally distinguished three broad styles: authoritarian, authoritative, and permissive. Briefly, authoritarian parents are controlling, punitive, demanding, and rather cold; authoritative parents set firm rules but are also warm and supportive and allow the child some autonomy; and permissive parents are rather lax, nonpunitive, and warm. Authoritative and permissive parents have good communication with their children, negotiating, explaining, and being sensitive to the child's needs. While parenting styles are influential in psychology, largely due to the work of Laurence Steinberg and his colleagues (1992; see also Darling and Steinberg 1993), they have rarely been investigated in criminological research. However, in the Cambridge Study (Farrington 1994), having authoritarian parents was the second most important predictor of convictions for violence (after hyperactivity/poor concentration).

Most explanations of the link between child-rearing methods and delinquency focus on social learning or attachment theories. Social learning theory suggests that children's behavior depends on parental rewards and punishments and on the models of behavior that parents represent (see e.g., Patterson 1995). Children will tend to become delinquent if parents do not respond consistently and contingently to their antisocial behavior and if parents behave in an antisocial manner. Attachment theory was inspired by the work of John Bowlby (discussed later), and suggests that children who are not emotionally attached to warm, loving, law-abiding parents will tend to become delinquent (see e.g., Carlson and Sroufe 1995). The sociological equivalent of attachment theory is social bonding theory, which suggests that delinquency depends on the strength or weakness of a child's bond to society (see e.g., Catalano and Hawkins 1996).

Another possibility is that the link between child-rearing methods and delinquency merely reflects the genetic transmission of offending, as David Rowe (1994) argued. This idea was tested in the Cambridge Study. The specific hypothesis was that child-rearing factors (supervision, discipline, and warmth/coldness) would not predict offending after controlling for parental criminality. This was confirmed in a LISREL analysis but not in a regression analysis (Rowe and Farrington 1997). Thus, genetic factors could explain only part of the link between child-rearing factors and delinquency.

CHILD ABUSE AND NEGLECT

Children who are physically abused or neglected tend to become offenders later in life. The most famous study of this was carried out by Cathy Widom (1989) in Indianapolis. She used court records to identify more than 900 children who had been abused or neglected before age 11, and compared them with a control group matched on age, race, gender, elementary school class, and place of residence. A 20-year follow-up showed that the children who were abused or neglected were more likely to be arrested as juveniles and as adults than were the controls, and they were more likely to be arrested for juvenile violence (Maxfield and Widom 1996). Child sexual abuse and child physical abuse and neglect also predict adult arrests for sex crimes (Widom and Ames 1994).

Similar results have been obtained in other studies. In the Cambridge-Somerville study in Boston, Joan McCord (1983) found that about half of the abused or neglected boys were convicted for serious crimes, became alcoholics or mentally ill, or died before age 35. In the Rochester Youth Development Study, which is a prospective longitudinal survey of about 1,000 children originally aged 12 to 14, Carolyn Smith and Terry Thornberry (1995) showed that recorded child maltreatment before age 12 (physical, sexual, or emotional abuse or neglect) predicted later self-reported and official delinquency. Furthermore, these results held up after controlling for gender, race, socioeconomic status, and family structure.

Numerous theories have been put forward to explain the link between child abuse and later offending. Timothy Brezina (1998) described three of the main ones. Social learning theory suggests that children learn to adopt the abusive behavior patterns of their parents through imitation, modeling, and reinforcement. Attachment or social bonding theory proposes that child maltreatment results in low attachment to parents and hence to low self-control. Strain theory posits that negative treatment by others generates negative emotions such as anger and frustration, which in turn lead to a desire for revenge and increased aggression. Based on the Youth in Transition study, Brezina found limited support for all three theories.

Ronald Symons and his colleagues (1995) tested a fourth theory, that the link between child abuse and offending was one aspect of the intergenerational transmission of antisocial behavior from parents to children. Their findings in Iowa were most concordant with this theory. Lisabeth DiLalla and Irving Gottesman (1991) more specifically suggested that the link reflected the genetic transmission of violent behavior. It is clear that the importance of genetic factors needs to be estimated in future studies of the effects of child abuse.

PARENTAL CONFLICT AND DISRUPTED FAMILIES

John Bowlby (1951) popularized the theory that broken homes cause delinquency. He argued that mother love in infancy and childhood was just as important for mental health as were vitamins and proteins for physical health. He thought it essential that a child experience a warm, loving, and continuous relationship with a mother figure. If a child suffered a prolonged period of maternal deprivation during the first five years of life, this would have irreversible negative effects, including becoming a cold "affectionless character" and a delinquent.

Most studies of broken homes have focused on the loss of the father rather than the mother, because the loss of a father is much more common. In general, it is found that children who are separated from a biological parent are more likely to offend than children from intact families. For example, in a birth cohort study of more than 800 children born in Newcastle-upon-Tyne, Israel Kolvin and his colleagues (1988b) discovered that boys who experienced divorce or separation in their first five years of life had a doubled risk of conviction up to age 32 (53% as opposed to 28%).

Joan McCord (1982) in Boston carried out an interesting study of the relationship between homes broken by loss of the biological father and later serious offending by boys. She found that the prevalence of offending was high for boys from broken homes without affectionate mothers (62%) and for those from unbroken homes characterized by parental conflict (52%), irrespective of whether they had affectionate mothers. The prevalence of offending was low for those from unbroken homes without conflict (26%) and—importantly—equally low for boys from broken homes with affectionate mothers (22%). These results suggest that it might not be the broken home that is criminogenic but the parental conflict which often causes it. They also suggest that a loving mother might in some sense be able to compensate for the loss of a father.

The importance of the cause of the broken home is also shown in the National Survey of Health and Development, a survey of more than 5,000 children born in one week in England, Scotland, and Wales (Wadsworth 1979). Illegitimate children were excluded from this survey, so all the children began life with two married parents. Boys from homes broken by divorce or separation had an increased likelihood of being convicted or officially cautioned up to age 21 (27%) in comparison with those from homes broken by death of the mother (19%) or death of the father (14%) or from unbroken homes (14%). Homes broken when the boy was under age 5 especially predicted delinquency, while homes broken when the boy was between ages 11 and 15 were not particularly criminogenic. Remarriage (which happened more often after divorce or separation than after death) was also associated with an increased risk of delinquency, suggesting a negative effect of step-parents. This negative effect was confirmed in research in Montreal by Linda Pagani and her colleagues (1998). The meta-analysis by Edward Wells and Joseph Rankin (1991) also shows that broken homes are more strongly related to delinquency when they are caused by parental separation or divorce rather than by death.

There is no doubt that parental conflict and interparental violence predict antisocial behavior by a child (see, e.g., Kolbo et al. 1996; Buehler et al. 1997). In the Christchurch Health and Development Study, which is a prospective longitudinal survey of more than 1,200 New Zealand children from birth, children who witnessed violence between their parents were more likely to commit both violence and property offenses according to their self-reports (Fergusson and Horwood 1998). The predictability of witnessing father-initiated violence held up after controlling for other risk factors such as parental criminality, parental substance abuse, parental physical punishment, a young mother, and low family income. Parental conflict also predicted delinquency in both the Cambridge and Pittsburgh studies (Farrington and Loeber 1999).

Much research suggests that frequent changes of parent figures predict offending by children. For example, in a longitudinal survey of a birth cohort of more than 500 Copenhagen males, Birgitte Mednick and her colleagues (1990) found that divorce followed by changes in parent figures predicted the highest rate of offending by children (65%), compared with divorce followed by stability (42%) and no divorce (28%). In the Dunedin study in New Zealand, Bill Henry and his colleagues (1993) reported that both parental conflict and many changes of the child's primary caretaker predicted the child's antisocial behavior up to age 11. However, in the Christchurch study in New Zealand, David Fergusson and his colleagues (1992) showed that parental transitions in the absence of parental conflict did not predict an increased risk of the child offending. Also, in the Oregon Youth Study, Deborah Capaldi and Gerry Patterson (1991) concluded that antisocial mothers caused parental transitions, which in turn caused child antisocial behavior. In the Woodlawn longitudinal study in Chicago, which is a follow-up of more than 1,200 African American children from age 6, the diversity and fluidity of children's living arrangements was remarkable (see, e.g., Kellam et al. 1977; Hunter and Ensminger 1992).

Explanations of the relationship between disrupted families and delinquency fall into three major classes. Trauma theories suggest that the loss of a parent has a damaging effect on a child, most commonly because of the effect on attachment to the parent. Life course theories focus on separation as a sequence of stressful experiences and on the effects of multiple stressors such as parental conflict, parental loss, reduced economic circumstances, changes in parent figures, and poor child-rearing methods. Selection theories argue that disrupted families produce delinquent children because of pre-existing differences from other families in risk factors such as parental conflict, criminal or antisocial parents, low family income, or poor child-rearing methods.

Hypotheses derived from the three theories were tested in the Cambridge Study (Juby and Farrington 2001). While boys from broken homes (permanently disrupted families) were more delinquent than boys from intact homes, they were not more delinquent than boys from intact high-conflict families. Overall, the most important factor was the post-disruption trajectory. Boys who remained with their mother after the separation had the same delinquency rate as boys from intact low-conflict families. Boys who remained with their father, with relatives, or with others (e.g., foster parents) had high delinquency rates. It was concluded that the results favored life course theories rather than trauma or selection theories.

KEY METHODOLOGICAL ISSUES

It is difficult to determine what are the precise causal mechanisms linking family factors—such as parental criminality, young mothers, family size, parental supervision, child abuse, and disrupted families—to the delinquency of children. This is because these factors tend to be related not only to each other but also to other risk factors for delinquency such as low family income, poor housing, impulsiveness, low intelligence, and low school attainment. Just as it is hard to know what are the key underlying family constructs, it is equally hard to know what are the key underlying constructs in other domains of life. It is important to investigate what family factors predict delinquency independently of other family factors, independently of genetic and biological factors, and independently of other factors (e.g., individual, peer, neighborhood, and socioeconomic).

Another important question focuses on the interactions between family and other factors in the prediction of delinquency. There are many examples of interactions between family and biological factors. For example, Adrian Raine and his colleagues (1997, p. 5) found that maternal rejection interacted with birth complications in predicting violence in a large birth cohort of Copenhagen males. The prevalence of violence was only high when both maternal rejection and birth complications were present. Family factors have different effects on children of different ages (Frick et al. 1999). Similarly, family and other risk factors have different effects on offending in different neighborhoods (Wikström and Loeber 2000).

It might be expected that family factors would have different effects on boys and girls, since there are well-documented gender differences in child-rearing experiences. In particular, boys are more likely to receive physical punishment from parents (see, e.g., Lytton and Romney 1991; Smith and Brooks-Gunn 1997). However, in their extensive review of gender differences in antisocial behavior, Terrie Moffitt and her colleagues (2001) concluded that boys were more antisocial essentially because they were exposed to more risk factors or a higher level of risk. Family risk factors did not seem to have different effects on antisocial behavior for boys and girls.

Family factors may have different effects on African American and White children in the United States. It is clear that African American children are more likely to be physically punished, and that physical punishment is more related to antisocial behavior for White children than for African American children (see, e.g., Kelley et al. 1992; Deater-Deckard et al. 1996). In the Pittsburgh Youth Study, 21% of White boys who were physically punished (slapped or spanked) by their mothers were violent, compared with 8% of those not physically punished. In contrast, 32% of African American boys who were physically punished were violent, compared with 28% of those not physically punished (Farrington and Loeber 2001). It was suggested that physical punishment may have a different meaning in African American families. Specifically, in these families it may indicate warmth and concern for the child, whereas in White families it tends to be associated with a cold and rejecting parental attitude. The main difference between London and Pittsburgh in risk factors for delinquency was in physical punishment, which may reflect this racial difference.

While family influences are usually investigated as risk factors for delinquency, it is important also to investigate their effects as protective factors. In the Pittsburgh Youth Study, good supervision (compared with average levels) predicted nondelinquency, just as poor supervision (compared with average levels) predicted delinquency (Stouthamer-Loeber et al. 1993). In the Newcastle-upon-Tyne survey, Israel Kolvin and his colleagues (1988a) studied high-risk boys (from deprived backgrounds) who nevertheless did not become offenders. The most important protective factors included good maternal care and good maternal health for children under age 5 and good parental supervision at ages 11 to 15.

It is important to investigate sequential effects of risk factors on offending. Several researchers have concluded that socioeconomic factors have an effect on offending through their effect on family factors (see e.g., Larzelere and Patterson 1990; Dodge et al. 1994; Stern and Smith 1995; Bor et al. 1997). In the Pittsburgh Youth Study, it was proposed that socioeconomic and neighborhood factors (e.g., poor housing) influenced family factors (e.g., poor supervision), which in turn influenced child factors (e.g., lack of guilt), which in turn influenced offending (Loeber et al. 1998a, p. 10). There may also be sequential effects of some family factors on others (e.g., if young mothers tend to use poor child-rearing methods: see Conger et al. 1995), or of family factors on other risk factors (e.g., if antisocial parents tend to have low income and live in poor neighborhoods).

Just as parental child-rearing methods influence characteristics of children, so child characteristics may influence parenting, as Hugh Lytton (1990) suggested. For example, an antisocial child will provoke more punishment from a parent than a well-behaved child. In a longitudinal survey of nearly 1,000 children living in upper New York State, Pat Cohen and Judith Brook (1995) found that there were reciprocal influences between parental punishment and child behavior disorder. Similarly, several researchers have concluded that there are reciprocal relationships between parental supervision and delinquency (e.g., Paternoster 1988; Jang and Smith 1997).

It is also important to investigate the cumulative effects of family risk factors (and indeed of all risk factors) on delinquency. Rex Forehand and his colleagues (1998) showed how the probability of conduct disorder and delinquency increased with the number of family risk factors. A logical implication of the clustering of risk factors is that boys with multiple risk factors should be studied. Rolf Loeber and his colleagues (1998b) investigated how multiple risk factors were related to multiple types of child problems (including delinquency, substance use, hyperactivity, and depression) in the Pittsburgh Youth Study. Relationships were general rather than specific. Many types of risk factors predicted many types of problems, and the number of risk factors predicted the number of problems.

These results are in agreement with the hypothesis that delinquency is one element of a larger syndrome of antisocial behavior, and hence that predictors of one type of offending (e.g., violence) are similar to predictors of another (e.g., theft). Nevertheless, it is still useful to search for specific relationships between types of family factors and types of antisocial behavior. An important question is how far all the predictive results are essentially generated by a small minority of multiple-risk factor, multiple-problem chronic offenders.

FAMILY-BASED CRIME PREVENTION

To the extent that ineffective methods of child-rearing cause delinquency, it should be possible to prevent delinquency by educating or training parents to use more effective methods (for a review, see Farrington and Welsh 1999). The behavioral parent management training developed by Gerry Patterson (1982) in Oregon is one of the most hopeful approaches. His careful observations of parent-child interaction showed that parents of antisocial children were deficient in their methods of child-rearing. These parents failed to tell their children how they were expected to behave, failed to monitor their behavior to ensure that it was desirable, and failed to enforce rules promptly and unambiguously with appropriate rewards and penalties. The parents of antisocial children used more punishment (such as scolding, shouting, or threatening), but failed to make it contingent on the child's behavior.

Patterson attempted to train these parents in effective child-rearing methods: noticing what a child is doing, monitoring behavior over long periods, clearly stating house rules, making rewards and punishments contingent on behavior, and negotiating disagreements so that conflicts and crises do not escalate. His treatment was shown to be effective in reducing child stealing and antisocial behavior over short periods in small-scale studies (Patterson et al. 1982, 1992; Dishion et al. 1992). Other types of parent training, such as that devised by Carolyn Webster-Stratton in Seattle, are also effective in reducing child antisocial behavior (Webster-Stratton et al. 1988; Webster-Stratton and Hammond 1997; Webster-Stratton 1998).

It is more common to use parent training in conjunction with other prevention techniques. For example, the Montreal longitudinal-experimental study combined child skills training and parent management training.

Richard Tremblay and his colleagues (1995) identified disruptive (aggressive/hyperactive) boys at age 6, and randomly allocated more than 300 of them to experimental or control conditions. Between ages 7 and 9, the experimental group received training designed to foster social skills and self-control. Coaching, peer modeling, role playing, and reinforcement contingencies were used in small-group sessions on such topics as "how to help," "what to do when you are angry," and "how to react to teasing." Also, their parents were trained using Patterson's parent management training techniques.

This prevention program was quite successful. By age 12, the experimental boys committed less burglary and theft, were less likely to get drunk, and were less likely to be involved in fights than the controls (according to self-reports). Also, the experimental boys had higher school achievement. At every age from 10 to 15, the experimental boys had lower self-reported delinquency scores than the control boys. Interestingly, the differences in antisocial behavior between experimental and control boys increased as the follow-up progressed.

As another example of the use of parent training in conjunction with other techniques, David Hawkins and his colleagues (1991) combined parent management training, teacher training, and child skills training. About 500 first grade children (aged 6) in 21 classes in eight schools were randomly assigned to be in experimental or control classes. The children in the experimental classes received special treatment at home and at school which was designed to increase their attachment to their parents and their bonding to the school. Also, they were trained in interpersonal cognitive problem solving. Their parents were trained to notice and reinforce socially desirable behavior in a program called Catch Them Being Good. Their teachers were trained in classroom management, for example, to provide clear instructions and expectations to children, to reward children for participation in desired behavior, and to teach children prosocial (socially desirable) methods of solving problems.

This program had long-term benefits. In the latest follow-up, at age 18, the full intervention group (those who received the intervention from grades 1 to 6) admitted less violence, less alcohol abuse, and fewer sexual partners than the late intervention group (grades 5 and 6 only) or the controls (Hawkins et al. 1999).

General parent education, especially in the context of home visiting programs, is also effective in reducing delinquency. In the most famous intensive home visiting program, David Olds and his colleagues (1986) in Elmira, New York, randomly allocated 400 mothers to receive home visits from nurses during pregnancy, to receive visits both during pregnancy and during the first two years of life, or to a control group who received no visits. Each visit lasted about one-and-a-quarter hours, and the mothers were visited on average every two weeks. The home visitors gave advice about child-rearing, about prenatal and postnatal care of the child, about infant development, and about the importance of proper nutrition and avoidance of smoking and drinking during pregnancy.

The results of this experiment showed that the postnatal home visits caused a decrease in recorded child physical abuse and neglect during the first two years of life, especially by poor, unmarried teenage mothers; 4% of visited versus 19% of nonvisited mothers of this type were guilty of child abuse or neglect (Olds et al. 1986). In a 15-year follow-up, the main focus was on lower-class unmarried mothers. Among these mothers, those who received prenatal and postnatal home visits had fewer arrests than those who received prenatal visits or no visits (Olds et al. 1997). Also, children of these mothers who received prenatal and/or postnatal home visits had less than half as many arrests as children of mothers who received no visits (Olds et al. 1998). Furthermore, several economic analyses show that the financial benefits of this program outweighed its financial costs for the lower-class unmarried mothers (for reviews, see Welsh et al. 2001).

Ideally, the results of prevention experiments should help to draw conclusions about which family factors have causal effects (see e.g., Robins 1992; Farrington 1992b, 2000). However, causal conclusions can only be drawn from experiments that study the effects of targeting each risk factor separately. In practice, experimenters are very concerned to use intervention programs that work. Consequently, they use multiple-component interventions, which tend to be more effective than single-component interventions (Wasserman and Miller 1998). There is a clear tension between maximizing the effectiveness of programs and drawing causal conclusions by disentangling the effects of different components.

CONCLUSIONS

It is clear that many family factors predict offending, but it is less clear what are the key underlying family dimensions that should be measured. The strongest predictor is usually criminal or antisocial parents. Other quite strong and replicable predictors are large family size, poor parental supervision, parental conflict, and disrupted families. In contrast, child abuse and young mothers are relatively weak predictors.

Many theories have been proposed to explain these results. The most popular are selection, social learning, and attachment theories. Selection theories argue that relationships between large family size, poor parental supervision, disrupted families, and so on and delinquency are driven by the fact that antisocial people tend to have large families, poor parental supervision, disrupted families, and so on, as well as antisocial children. An extreme version of this theory suggests that all results reflect the genetic transmission of antisocial behavior from parents to children. Social learning theories argue that children fail to learn law-abiding behavior if their parents provide antisocial models and/or fail to react to their transgressions in an appropriate, consistent, and contingent fashion. Attachment theories argue that low attachment to parents (created, for example, by cold, rejecting parents or by separation from a parent) produces cold, callous children who tend to commit delinquent acts.

In order to advance knowledge about causal effects of family factors on offending, new longitudinal studies are needed. Such studies should aim to estimate genetic influences and should measure a wide range of risk factors (individual, family, peer, school, neighborhood, etc.). They should aim to establish independent, interactive, sequential, and reciprocal effects of family factors on offending. They should study protective factors as well as risk factors, and should investigate family effects on later criminal careers (e.g., on desistance) as well as on the onset of offending. Systematic observation in addition to interviews and questionnaires should be used to measure family factors. Ideally, intervention experiments targeting family factors should be included in longitudinal studies in order to establish causal effects more securely. A new generation of longitudinal studies should go beyond demonstrating that family factors predict offending, and should seek to determine the key causal mechanisms that are involved. This should help greatly in designing family-based prevention programs to reduce crime.

7

The Schools

DENISE C. GOTTFREDSON,
DAVID B. WILSON, AND STACY S. NAJAKA

Schools play an important role in controlling youth crime. Although the most serious forms of interpersonal violent crime are exceedingly rare in schools, a disproportionate amount of crime occurs in or around school buildings. This is of concern not only because people are harmed by these crimes, but also because their occurrence may signal that schools are not exercising their roles as socializing agents and may be providing training grounds for delinquent behavior. Considerable variability in the level of crime exists between schools, and research shows that schools can influence their own level of crime despite the large influence of the community in which the school is embedded.

Aside from schools' potential to reduce crime that occurs in and around their facilities, evidence about the association of school-related factors and crime in general suggests a larger role for schools in preventing crime. Students who are impulsive, are weakly attached to their schools, have little commitment to achieving educational goals, and whose moral beliefs in the validity of conventional rules for behavior are weak are more likely to engage in crime than those who do not possess these characteristics. To the extent that schools can influence these risk factors for criminal activity, they can reduce crime in general.

This chapter summarizes what research has taught us about what schools can do to prevent crime. It begins with a description of youth crime that occurs both in and out of schools, and the characteristics of schools and students that place them at elevated risk for experiencing high levels of crime. It then turns to a meta-analytic summary of the evaluation literature on school-based prevention, including narrative descriptions of the most effective approaches. It concludes with recommendations for future research on and practice of school-based prevention.

YOUTH CRIME
Self-Reports

Arrest data, summarized in the Greenwood chapter in this volume, show that juveniles are only slightly overrepresented among arrests relative to their presence in the population, and that the offenses for which they are most often arrested are generally of a non-serious nature. But arrest statistics underestimate the amount of crime because they count only crimes that have been detected by the police. They are also undesirable as a measure of youth crime because they measure police activity as well as crime. Self-reports of crime are not affected by these biases. Several sources of national self-report data are available. The most recent data on the prevalence of substance use among young persons come from the 1999 Monitoring the Future (MTF) survey (Johnston, O'Malley, and Bachman 1999), an annual school survey of eighth-, tenth-, and twelfth-graders in public and private schools in the coterminous United States whose sample is drawn to be representative of students in the nation. In 1999, 74 percent of twelfth-grade students reported having used alcohol, 42 percent having used illicit drugs, 21 percent having used illicit drugs other than marijuana, 6 percent having used cocaine, and 1 percent having used heroin, all in the past twelve months. The same percentages for eighth-grade students are as follows: 20 percent reported having used alcohol, 25 percent having used illicit drugs, 10 percent having used illicit drugs other than marijuana, 3 percent having used cocaine, and 1 percent having used heroin.

MTF also provides estimates of the level of youth involvement in other criminal activity, but these estimates are available only for twelfth-grade students. The National Study of Delinquency Prevention in Schools (NSDPS) conducted in 1998 provides national estimates of youth criminal activity for secondary school students (G. D. Gottfredson et al. 2000). Data comes from a school survey of students from a nationally representative sample of 1,287 public and private secondary schools (primarily serving grades six through twelve) in the United States. Table 7.1 shows the percentage of youths admitting to engaging in a variety of crimes in the past twelve months. The table shows that males are far more likely to admit criminal involvement than are females. It also shows that relatively minor property crimes are fairly common among students and that more serious property crimes are less common. For example, 12 percent of males and 4 percent of females reported carrying a hidden weapon other than a pocketknife in the past year.

Table 7.1
Self-reported Delinquent Behavior in the Last Twelve Months among Secondary Students, by Gender, 1998

	PERCENT	
BEHAVIOR	BOYS	GIRLS
Hit or threatened to hit other students	44	27
Stolen or tried to steal things worth less than $50	24	15
Purposely damaged or destroyed other property that did not belong to you, not counting family or school property	26	12
Purposely damaged or destroyed property belonging to a school	21	11
Taken a car for a ride (or drive) without the owner's permission	12	8
Sold marijuana or other drugs	13	6
Stolen or tried to steal something worth more than $50	11	5
Carried a hidden weapon other than a pocketknife	12	4
Broken into or tried to break into a building or car to steal something or just to look around	11	4
Been involved in gang fights	10	5
Used force or strong-arm methods to get money or things from a person	9	3
Hit or threatened to hit a teacher or other adult at school	7	3

NOTE: Serious violent crimes include rape, sexual assault, robbery, and aggravated assault. Violent crimes include serious violent crimes and simple assault. "At school" includes going to and from school.
SOURCE: National Crime Victimization Survey 1996, from P. Kaufman, X. Chen, S. P. Choy, K. A. Chandler, C. D. Chapman, M. R. Rand, and C. Ringel. 1998. *Indicators of School Crime and Safety, 1998.* NCES 98-251/NCJ-172215. Washington, D.C.: U.S. Departments of Education and Justice.

The Youth Risk Behavior Surveillance Surveys (YRBSS), a survey conducted biannually in schools in thirty-three states and certain localities, also provides recent statistics regarding violent youth behavior (Kann et al. 1998). This survey yields prevalence rates for physical fighting and weapon use from a national sample of students in grades nine through twelve. The 1999 survey shows that fighting is common among high school students: 36 percent of students (44 percent of males and 27 percent of females) surveyed had been in a physical fight in the last year. Almost a fifth (17 percent) of students had carried a weapon (for example, gun, knife, or club) in the past month, again with males (29 percent) far more likely than females (6 percent) to have done so. Five percent (5 percent) of students had carried a gun in the past month. This estimate is in line with that from another national survey (Sheley and Wright 1998) showing that in 1996 3 percent of tenth- and eleventh-grade males possessed a revolver or automatic or semiautomatic handgun, and that 6 percent had carried a gun outside the home in the past year. Interestingly, half of the males in this study reported that obtaining a gun would be little or no trouble.

Data on the geographic distribution of self-reported crime can be gleaned both from self-reports of crime and self-reports of victimization experiences. The National Crime Victimization Survey (NCVS) is a survey of nationally representative households conducted twice each year by the U.S. Department of Justice's Bureau of Justice Statistics in which household members aged twelve and older are asked to report on their victimization experiences every six months for three years. The 1995 School Crime Supplement (SCS) to the NCVS asked students between the ages of twelve and nineteen in the sampled households to report in more detail about their victimization experiences *at school* (Chandler et al. 1998). Table 7.2 displays victimization rates per 1,000 students aged twelve to eighteen from the 1996 NCVS separately for crimes that occurred at school or away from school. It shows that the most serious forms of violent crime victimizations (rape, sexual assault, robbery, and aggravated assault) are more likely to occur in urban areas and least likely to occur in rural areas. When simple assault is included among violent crimes, the same differences are observed for crimes that occur away from school, but the distinction between urban and suburban in-school victimizations disappears. Theft victimizations are more evenly distributed across geographic areas, although they tend to be somewhat lower in rural areas. Other victimization data sources also show that rates of serious violent crimes against school-aged children vary by geographic region: The rate of

Table 7.2

Number of Nonfatal Crimes against Students Ages 12 through 18 Occurring at and away from School per 1,000 Students, by Type of Crime and Urbanicity, 1996

	URBAN		SUBURBAN		RURAL	
TYPE OF CRIME	AT SCHOOL	AWAY FROM SCHOOL	AT SCHOOL	AWAY FROM SCHOOL	AT SCHOOL	AWAY FROM SCHOOL
Theft	77 (5.8)	84 (4.8)	62 (4.1)	68 (5.5)	72 (6.2)	57 (5.4)
Violent	55 (4.9)	54 (3.8)	52 (3.7)	69 (5.5)	29 (3.8)	43 (4.7)
Serious violent	16 (2.6)	9 (1.4)	23 (2.3)	38 (4.0)	4 (1.4)	17 (2.9)
Total	131 (7.7)	138 (6.2)	114 (5.6)	138 (7.8)	101 (7.3)	99 (7.3)

NOTE: Standard errors appear in parentheses. Serious violent crimes include rape, sexual assault, robbery, and aggravated assault. Violent crimes include serious violent crimes and simple assault. "At school" includes going to and from school.
SOURCE: National Crime Victimization Survey 1996, from P. Kaufman, X. Chen, S. P. Choy, K. A. Chandler, C. D. Chapman, M. R. Rand, and C. Ringel. 1998. *Indicators of School Crime and Safety, 1998.* NCES 98-251/NCJ-172215. Washington, D.C.: U.S. Departments of Education and Justice.

school-associated violent student deaths during the 1992–93 and 1993–94 school years was higher in urban school districts (0.18 per 100,000 students) than in suburban or rural districts (0.09 and 0.02 per 100,000 students; Kaufman et al. 1998). The 1995 SCS showed that students residing in inner cities were more likely than other students both to know a student who brought a gun to school and to have seen a student with a gun at school.

Self-reports of crime tend to focus on the less serious forms of crime that occur with greater regularity among youth. As might be expected, these surveys fail to show a large difference in the prevalence of crime across students attending schools in urban, suburban, and rural areas. G. D. Gottfredson et al. (2000) report the percentage of students participating in delinquent activities as a function of their membership in urban, suburban, and rural schools. These data, shown in Table 7.3, show no meaningful differences in the distribution of crime across urban, suburban, and rural locations. Even with the large sample sizes available, few statistically significant differences are observed by location. The data show a tendency toward lower crime prevalence among youth in suburban schools as opposed to urban or rural schools. Consistent with the victimization data, the behaviors for which slight differences emerge tend to be violent ones as opposed to property crimes. The data also show a tendency for a greater proportion of urban youths to report involvement in the most serious crimes, but this difference is not great. These self-report findings of only minor differences across geographic location are consistent with reports from earlier national studies (Elliott, Huizinga, and Menard 1989), which showed only weak associations between place of residence and prevalence and frequency of delinquent activity. The apparent discrepancy between these youth reports on the one hand and arrest statistics and victimization surveys on the other may come about for a number of reasons. The most likely one is that the geographic differences observed in victimization reports and arrests are due to differences in the location of the crime occurrence, and not so much to the residence of the perpetrator, and that the victimizations and arrests reflect a higher proportion of crimes committed by older persons against younger persons or by school-aged persons who are no longer enrolled in school and are therefore excluded from school surveys.

Student reports suggesting that school crime is fairly uniform across schools in urban, suburban, and rural communities contrast sharply with reports of teachers and principals by location. Teachers in urban schools in the NSDPS reported significantly higher rates of threats, serious and minor attacks, minor and major theft, obscene remarks, and major property damage than teachers in suburban or rural schools. Interestingly, teacher reports of having a weapon pulled on them were similar in urban and rural schools, both of which were higher than suburban schools (G. D. Gottfredson et al. 2000). In a survey conducted with principals from a nationally representative sample of regular public schools during the 1996–97 school year (U.S. Department of Education 1998), principals in city schools were far more likely than principals in towns and rural areas to report having reported one or more serious crimes to the police during the school year. This same discrepancy between reports of adults and students regarding the level of crime in schools was also observed in a national study conducted in the 1960s (Gottfredson and Gottfredson 1985). Several explanations for the discrepant reports of adults and students are possible. Among the likely reasons are that the school crime adults see is

Table 7.3
Self-reported Delinquent Behavior in the Last Twelve Months among Secondary Students by Location, 1998

BEHAVIOR	URBAN		SUBURBAN		RURAL		TOTAL	
	%	95% CI	%	95% CI	%	95% CI	%	95% CI
Hit or threatened to hit other students	34	30.7–38.6	34	30.7–38.6	34	30.7–38.6	34	30.7–38.6
Stolen or tried to steal things worth less than $50	19	17.3–21.2	19	17.3–21.2	19	17.3–21.2	19	17.3–21.2
Purposely damaged or destroyed other property that did not belong to you, not counting family or school property	18	15.1–20.1	18	15.1–20.1	18	15.1–20.1	18	15.1–20.1
Purposely damaged or destroyed property belonging to a school	16	13.3–18.4	16	13.3–18.4	16	13.3–18.4	16	13.3–18.4
Taken a car for a ride (or drive) without the owner's permission	10	8.7–12.1	10	8.7–12.1	10	8.7–12.1	10	8.7–12.1
Sold marijuana or other drugs	10	8.0–12.5	10	8.0–12.5	10	8.0–12.5	10	8.0–12.5
Stolen or tried to steal something worth more than $50	10	8.3–11.0	10	8.3–11.0	10	8.3–11.0	10	8.3–11.0
Carried a hidden weapon other than a pocketknife	8	6.5–10.6	8	6.5–10.6	8	6.5–10.6	8	6.5–10.6
Broken into or tried to break into a building or car to steal something or just to look around	7	5.8–9.1	7	5.8–9.1	7	5.8–9.1	7	5.8–9.1
Been involved in gang fights	8	6.5–10.6	8	6.5–10.6	8	6.5–10.6	8	6.5–10.6
Used force or strong-arm methods to get money or things from a person	6	5.1–7.5	6	5.1–7.5	6	5.1–7.5	6	5.1–7.5
Hit or threatened to hit a teacher or other adult at school	5	4.0–7.0	5	4.0–7.0	5	4.0–7.0	5	4.0–7.0

NOTE: CI = Confidence Internal

perpetrated by nonstudents or intruders to the school setting or that persons in different geographical settings perceive actions differently and that these perceptions influence self-reports.

IN-SCHOOL AND OUT-OF-SCHOOL CRIME

Parents, students, and educators expect their schools to provide "safe havens" from harmful activities as well as environments conducive to learning and social development. Are their expectations met?

The 1995 SCS (described earlier) showed that 15 percent of students aged twelve through nineteen reported criminal victimization at school during the previous six months. Property crime victimizations were more prevalent than violent crime victimizations[1]—12 percent and 4 percent of students reported being victimized by each type of crime. Males were more likely than females, and younger students more likely than older students to report such victimizations.

The SCS data generated low estimates of the extent of school crime by asking only about a few types of criminal victimizations, and by using a shorter reporting time frame than other national surveys. The 1998 NSDPS and MTF surveys, both of which asked about a wider variety of criminal victimizations using a twelve-month reporting time frame, found higher rates of victimization in schools. G. D. Gottfredson et al. (2000) report that nearly half of the secondary school students surveyed reported that somebody at school stole something from them (47 percent for something worth less than $1, and 45 percent for something worth more than $1). Interpersonal crime victimizations were less prevalent: 18 percent reported being threatened with a beating, 13 percent reported being physically attacked, 6 percent reported being robbed of something worth more than $1, and 5 percent reported being threatened with a knife or gun at school. These 1998 figures are strikingly similar to those reported from the 1998 MTF survey. As with self-reports of crime, self-reports of victimizations in school generally showed that males are more likely to be the victims of school crimes than are females, and that differences by place of residence are minor.

But are children safer in school than out of school? Several sources provide partial answers to this question. One is the YRBSS, described earlier, which asks youths to report on their participation in certain dangerous activities both in school and out of school. In 1997, 18 percent of students reported that they had carried a weapon in the last thirty days, and 8 percent reported doing so on school property. Thirty-seven percent reported being in a physical fight in the last year, and 15 percent reported fighting on school property (Kann et al. 1998). The MTF survey provides similar comparisons of in-school victimization experiences with all such experiences. The proportion of twelfth-grade seniors reporting being victimized *at school* in the past twelve months is about three-fourths as large as the proportion being victimized *at all*. For example, 15 percent of twelfth-grade students reported that somebody had injured them on purpose without using a weapon, and 11 percent said that the same had happened to them *at school*. Thirty-two percent said their property had been deliberately damaged, and 25 percent said that had happened to them in school. Interestingly, about the same percentage (4.6 percent vs. 5 percent) reported being injured with a weapon in school and in all locations.

These comparisons of in- and out-of-school delinquency can be better understood by taking into account the relative amounts of time spent in school and in other places by students. Timmer, Eccles, and O'Brien (1985) asked children and adolescents to keep time diaries. Children aged twelve through seventeen reported spending an average of 5.47 hours in school on weekdays and no time on weekends, or about 18 percent of their waking hours. Relative to the amount of time spent in school, the percentages of youths who report carrying guns and fighting in school and who are victimized in school appear high.

Table 7.2 from the 1996 NCVS shows that more crime victimization actually occurs in school than out of school, despite youths spending less time in school than out of school. But the total crime figures are driven largely by theft victimizations, which are far more likely to occur in school than out of school. Serious violent victimizations are more prevalent out of school than in school, although the differences are not as large as one would expect given that students spend only 18 percent of their time in school. Violent victimizations are somewhat more likely to occur out of school than in school, but the confidence intervals overlap for the in-school and out-of-school figures. In all, 52 percent of crimes against students aged twelve to eighteen occurred at school or on the way to and from school. The proportion is highest for theft (56 percent), but also substantial for violent crimes (47 percent). Twenty-eight percent of all serious, violent crimes against twelve- to eighteen-year-olds (for example, those including rape, sexual assault, robbery, or aggravated assault) occur during school or on the way to and from school. Clearly, although serious, violent crimes are not common in schools, schools are by no means "safe havens" against crimes. In fact, youths are at elevated risk for criminal victimization when they are in school or on the way to and from school.

School crime has increased over the past twenty years. The only strictly parallel comparison that can be made over a long period of time is the percentage of secondary students reporting being physically attacked at school in a one-month period in 1976 (from the National Institute of Education's Safe School Study, as reported in Gottfredson and Gottfredson 1985) and 1998 (from the NSDPS, described earlier; G. D. Gottfredson et al. 2000). For big-city schools, the percentage increased from 2.0 percent to 7.6 percent. For rural schools, it increased from 1.6 percent to 6.5 percent. This squares with results from public opinion polls (Gallup Poll 1999) showing that the percentage of parents who feared for their oldest child's physical safety when he or she was at school increased from 24 percent in 1977 to 52 percent in 1999. Trend data over a more recent time period are available from the 1989 and 1995 SCSs. Comparisons of the level of school crime between these years show that although property crime victimizations remained stable, the percentage of students reporting violent victimizations (physical attacks or robbery) in the past six months increased from 3.4 percent to 4.2 percent from 1989 to 1995.

All data sources converge in implying that minor crime is common among young people, that very serious crime is relatively rare, and that males are more far more likely to engage in most forms of crime than females are. The data also converge in implying that the most serious forms of violent crime are more likely to occur in urban areas than in suburban or rural areas, but the minor geographical differences observed in self-reports (summarized earlier) suggest that this disproportionality is most likely not due to student perpetrators. Students are not protected from crime while they are in school. Rather, they are more likely to fall victim to crimes—especially crimes of a less serious nature—while in school or on their way to and from school than at other times. The level of crime in and around school in general has not changed in the recent past, although violent crime has increased somewhat over the past twenty years.

THE ROLE OF SCHOOLS IN CRIME CONTROL AND PREVENTION

Research suggests that the way discipline is handled in schools is related to the level of crime they experience: Schools in which rules about expected behavior are unambiguous, effectively communicated, and consistently enforced, and schools which provide rewards for rule compliance and punishments for rule infractions experience less crime. Schools that excel in general management functions, such as coordination and resource allocation and communication, that articulate clear goals for the organization, that deliver instruction in ways that promote maximal learning, and that encourage a sense of community experience less crime. These schools create an extended network of caring adults who interact regularly with the students and who share norms and expectations about their students. The research implies that when educators succeed at creating "communal social organizations" (Bryk and Driscoll 1988), they increase social control and therefore reduce the likelihood that youths will engage in problem behavior.

Apart from their role in preventing or controlling crime that occurs in school, schools also share with families, churches, and other community organizations the responsibility for socializing youths more generally. Students spend 18 percent of their waking hours in school for approximately twelve years. No other organization has such frequent access to students over such a long duration. Moreover, many of the factors that predict variability in level of criminal involvement are school related or at least in principle manipulable by schools. Although youth involvement in criminal activity during adolescence can often be traced back to early personality dispositions and early parenting practices, schools also have a role in shaping youth behavior. From the day students arrive at school, school officials impose rules and expectations for behavior and set out to teach students self-discipline. Just as schools vary in their capability to teach academic material, so do they vary in their effectiveness as socializing agents. The least effective schools provide inconsistent or conflicting messages about what is expected, role models for negative behaviors, and, often, rewards for misbehavior.

By adolescence, several individual characteristics predict the level of delinquent involvement (Gottfredson et al., 2000). Students are more likely to engage in crime if they are only weakly attached to their schools, have little commitment to achieving educational goals, and have weak moral beliefs in the validity of conventional rules for behavior. Students' academic achievement is also related to their criminal activity, although this association may be spurious due to the reliance of both on early behavior problems. Students who associate with delinquent peers are especially more likely to engage in crime. Surely schools have a role in shaping these precursor attitudes and experiences.

The remainder of the chapter examines the effectiveness of school-based efforts to reduce crime. It casts the net of potential crime-prevention strategies very broadly to encompass efforts to shape youthful dispositions and capabilities that will serve as natural protections against crime involvement, as well as efforts to reduce the level of crime that occurs in the school building. Within each of these two very general approaches is found a wide array of different strategies ranging from parent training to behavior modification, to improving general school management, to installing metal detectors. The effectiveness of these diverse practices and policies for reducing crime is examined using meta-analytic techniques. Because any review of existing research is only as strong as the original research, we begin with a summary of the limitations of the existing research on school-based prevention.

LIMITATIONS OF STUDIES OF SCHOOL-BASED PREVENTION PRACTICES

Existing studies of school-based prevention efforts have several limitations. First, studies of the effects of school-based prevention on crime are rare. Far more common are studies assessing program effects on alcohol, tobacco, or other drug use and other less serious forms of defiant behavior. Of the one hundred studies examined for this review[2], only thirty measured criminal behavior. In comparison, fifty-two studies measured noncriminal forms of antisocial behavior or conduct problems, and fifty-seven studies measured alcohol, tobacco, or other drug use. While this tendency for studies to focus on noncrime outcomes is entirely appropriate given the young ages of many targeted students and the presumed link between less serious problem behaviors and later, more serious crime, it limits the generalizability of program effects to more serious forms of behavior.

A second limitation is weak evaluation design. Few studies use randomized experimental research designs, one of the most effective designs for eliminating competing explanations for observed effects. Even when random assignment is used, the unit of assignment to conditions often differs from the unit of analysis. In other words, researchers often assign whole schools or classes to experimental conditions but later analyze the data as though students within these schools or classrooms had been individually assigned. This practice can result in erroneous conclusions about the statistical significance of effects. Of the 100 studies examined for this review, only 17 percent used random assignment to conditions *and* performed statistical analyses at the same level as the unit of assignment. Studies were also judged as to their overall methodological quality.[3] Each treatment-comparison contrast was rated on a five-point scale with the following anchors: (1) no confidence should be placed in the results of this evaluation because of serious shortcomings in the methodology employed; (3) methodology is rigorous in some respects, weak in others; and (5) methodology is rigorous in almost all respects. Less than 10 percent of the studies contained a treatment-comparison contrast with the highest rating of 5.

A third limitation of existing studies of school-based prevention is their failure to measure long-term program effectiveness. Evaluations often assess program impact immediately following the conclusion of the intervention but lack a follow-up assessment, and are thus unable either to detect effects that may be less immediate or to determine whether immediate effects deteriorate over time. Of the 100 studies reviewed, 40 percent included a posttest assessment only immediately following program implementation. Thirty-two percent included a follow-up occurring between one month and one year following the conclusion of the intervention, while only 28 percent examined program effects for periods longer than one year. Limiting outcome measurement to an immediate post-test provides a high-end estimate of program effects.

A final drawback of existing evaluations of school-based prevention practices is their failure to report on the strength of program implementation. Quality and quantity of implementation are important predictors of program effectiveness (Lipsey 1992; Wright and Dixon 1977). Yet many researchers fail to measure these factors. Before dismissing an intervention program and its underlying program theory, it is necessary to determine whether the proposed intervention actually took place as intended. Doing so requires a careful assessment of the strength and fidelity of program implementation.

META-ANALYSIS OF DELINQUENCY AND SUBSTANCE USE PREVENTION STUDIES

Meta-analysis is a systematic approach to the quantitative review of empirical studies. An essential feature is the analysis of the magnitude and direction of a relationship, such as a program effect, across a collection of studies. Of interest is both the variability of effects across studies and the average effects for studies sharing common features, such as similar prevention strategies. Since its inception in the mid-1970s, meta-analysis has developed a strong statistical foundation and has been widely used to synthesize research throughout the social and medical sciences.

The validity of a meta-analysis is contingent on the thoroughness of the search for relevant studies. A biased selection of studies will lead to biased findings. The identification of potentially eligible studies for this meta-analysis included searches of computer bibliographic databases (for example, PsychLit, ERIC, and Sociological Abstracts) and examination of the references of recent reviews of prevention programs (Botvin 1990; Botvin, Schinke, and Orlandi 1995; Dryfoos 1990; Durlak 1995; Hansen 1992; Hawkins, Arthur, and Catalano 1995; Institute of Medicine 1994; Tobler 1986, 1992; Tremblay and Craig 1995). In some instances, the search of recent reviews resulted in the identification and inclusion of a number of unpublished studies. This list was augmented with additional studies already known to the authors. The identified studies were retrieved and examined for eligibility in the meta-analysis. To be included, a study had to meet the following criteria:

(a) it evaluated an intervention, that is, a distinct program or procedure intended to reduce problem behaviors among children and youth;
(b) the intervention was school-based—that is, the intervention took place in a school building or was implemented by school staff or under the authority of the school administration, such as classroom instruction or other classroom activities, a school-wide environmental change, or modification of teacher or school administrator behaviors and instructional practices;
(c) it used a comparison group evaluation methodology, including non-equivalent comparison group research designs, and the comparison group was a no-treatment or minimal-treatment condition; and
(d) it measured at least one outcome of interest to this review. These included: (1) indicators of crime, delinquency, theft, violence, illegal acts of aggression, as well as measures of antisocial and aggressive problem behaviors[4]; and (2) indicators of alcohol and other drug use, excluding use of cigarettes and smokeless tobacco. Excluded from the synthesis presented below were studies that did not report sufficient statistical information to compute the index of the direction and magnitude of the effect (that is, an effect size) for at least one of the outcomes specified above. A total of 100 studies, representing 135 documents, met these criteria. In this synthesis we have not included studies that only examined school problems, such as truancy (see Gottfredson, Wilson, and Najaka, 2000).

A protocol for coding the studies was developed to extract information regarding the research methodology, intervention, sample characteristics, and outcome data from each study. For purposes of this synthesis, the primary unit of analysis was the treatment-comparison contrast. It was common for studies to report multiple treatment-comparison contrasts, often in the form of several intervention conditions contrasted with a single comparison group. This synthesis included each possible treatment-comparison contrast when the different contrasts represented unique intervention strategies or distinct age groups; otherwise, the data were aggregated into a single treatment-comparison contrast.[5] The index of a program's effect was the *standardized mean difference* (henceforth referred to as an *effect size*). The standardization of program effects allowed for the direct comparison of effects across studies, even though there were differences in the method of measuring the outcome (see D. C. Gottfredson et al., 2000 for more details). Furthermore, this form of the effect size can be computed from a wide range of summary statistics typically found in research reports (Lipsey and Wilson 2001).

Effect sizes were coded such that positive values indicated a positive preventive effect, that is, a lower rate of problem behavior in the treatment condition relative to the comparison condition. Likewise, negative effect size values indicate a negative program impact. Effect sizes were adjusted for pretest differences whenever such data were present. Effect sizes less than 0.20 are generally considered small, although prevention interventions with effects as small as 0.10 may lead to meaningful reductions in delinquent behavior (Lipsey 1992).

An aid to the interpretation of an effect size is its translation into failure rates (see Cohen 1988; Rosenthal and Rubin 1983). The equivalent failure rates for the treatment group relative to a comparison failure rate of 50 for selected effect sizes are shown in Table 7.4 (the failure rate for the comparison condition serves as a benchmark for the effect-size translation, and the specific value chosen is irrelevant; other reasonable values can be

Table 7.4

Translation of Effect Size into Percentage of Youth with a Negative Outcome

	% WITH NEGATIVE OUTCOME	
EFFECT SIZE	TREATMENT	COMPARISON
0.10	46	50
0.25	40	50
0.50	31	50

SOURCE: Author

chosen). As shown in the table, an effect size of 0.50 represents a reduction in the percentage of youth with a negative outcome of 21 percentage points, from 50 percent to 31 percent. This is generally considered a medium-size effect in the social sciences (Cohen 1988). An effect size of 0.10 represents a rather small reduction in problem behavior (that is, from 50 to 46 percent of the youth exhibiting the behavior following the intervention) and represents the lower bound that is likely to have practical significance. An effect size smaller than 0.10 may have practical significance depending on the costs of the program, both in terms of public expenditures and in terms of student time not spent engaged in other potentially beneficial experiences.

Categorization of Prevention Programs

A challenge in a broad meta-analysis such as this one is the categorization of the programs into meaningful groups that represent distinct and relatively homogeneous intervention strategies and activities. The program categories we developed emerged from our knowledge of the studies, and represent a reasonable and meaningful categorization of these interventions. Each treatment program was assessed for the presence or absence of seventeen treatment components or activities (for example, instruction, cognitive-behavioral or behavioral modeling, reorganization of grades) using a classification system developed for use in the National Study of Delinquency Prevention in Schools (G. D. Gottfredson et al. 2000). If a treatment component was present, a judgment was made as to whether it was a major or minor component of that intervention. Each of these seventeen components had sub-elements that detailed the specific activities associated with that intervention. After all studies were coded, the programs were grouped into ten mutually exclusive categories (see figures that follow). These ten intervention categories are further grouped as being either environmentally focused or individually focused. Half of the individually focused categories involve classroom instruction. This large category is further subdivided into instructional programs that do and do not focus primarily on teaching self-control or social competency skills. Most instructional programs do contain this type of content.

Among programs having this type of content, we further distinguish among programs that make use of certain teaching methods thought to be more effective. These "cognitive-behavioral methods" include behavior modification strategies that focus directly on changing behaviors and involve timely tracking of specific behaviors over time, behavioral goals, and feedback (generally positive or negative reinforcement) to change behavior, thus relying on reinforcers external to the student to shape student behavior. Cognitive-behavioral methods involve modeling or demonstrating behaviors and providing rehearsal and coaching in the display of new skills. Students are taught, for example, to recognize the physiological cues experienced in risky situations. They rehearse this skill and practice stopping rather than acting impulsively in such situations. Students are taught and rehearsed in skills such as suggesting alternative activities when friends propose engaging in a risky activity. And they are taught to use prompts or cues to remember to engage in desired behavior. Finally, among instructional programs that teach self-control or social competency skills without using these methods, studies of Drug Abuse Resistance Education (D.A.R.E.) are broken out separately because D.A.R.E. is used by more schools than any other prevention program currently on the market (G. D. Gottfredson et al. 2000). Although other categorizations of these programs are possible, we believe that this categorization is both conceptually meaningful and consistent with the actual practices of school-based prevention programs.

Below we present the findings from a synthesis of the effects of prevention programs within each of these ten program categories. We analyzed the effect sizes for delinquent and other antisocial or aggressive problem behaviors separately from the effect sizes for substance use. Some of the programs examined were designed specifically for the prevention of substance use and therefore may be more effective at reducing or preventing future substance use than other forms of delinquent behavior.

Prevention of Delinquent and Other Antisocial and Aggressive Problem Behaviors

Direct measures of criminal behavior, such as arrest or conviction for a criminal offense, were less common than general measures of problem behaviors that are highly related either to delinquency or to behaviors that could be considered delinquent, such as hitting someone in school. This section presents a meta-analysis of delinquency and other antisocial and problem behavior effects across studies, excluding substance use. The criminal behavior outcomes included measures of serious delinquent behavior, such as arrests for serious offenses, self-reported serious delinquency, and carrying a weapon, as well as less serious forms of delinquency, such as theft in the home, status offenses, and throwing objects at people. The measures of antisocial and aggressive problem behaviors included measures of aggressiveness, conduct problems, school disruption and suspension, disciplinary infractions, and the like.

Effect sizes of delinquency and other problem behaviors could be computed for ninety-one unique treatment-comparison contrasts from sixty-seven studies. If necessary, multiple delinquency and/or problem behavior effect sizes were averaged to create a single effect size for each treatment-comparison contrast. The numbers reported here may differ slightly from those published elsewhere (for example, D. C. Gottfredson et al., 2000), for only those effect sizes that could be computed directly were included, excluding various methods of effect size imputation. The average effect sizes reported below do not represent a simple arithmetic average (the sum of the effect sizes divided by the number of effect sizes); rather they represent averages based on a weighting system that takes into account the precision or confidence that can be placed on each effect size and is the accepted method for synthesizing effects across studies.[6]

Several of the intervention types are designed to change the school environment. Figure 7.1 shows the effect size and 95 percent confidence interval for each study and the overall average effect size and associated confidence interval for each category. The confidence interval is the range over which we believe, based on statistical theory, that the true effect of the program being studied is likely to be. For example, a 95 percent confidence interval from 0.20 to 0.40 indicates that we are 95 percent confident that the true effect of the program may be as low as 0.20 or as high as 0.40. Confidence intervals that extend below zero are statistically nonsignificant at the conventional .05 significance level. Also shown in this figure is the overall method quality rating score discussed in the previous section and the sample size for each study. In all cases, studies rated as a 5 were randomized with no obvious methodological problems that would undermine the validity of drawing a causal inference. Studies rated as either 4 or 3 were randomized designs that were compromised in some fashion (for example, high attrition) or quasi-experimental designs with a treatment and comparison group that appeared roughly equivalent in most important respects.

Examination of Figure 7.1 shows that the majority of studies designed to change aspects of the school environment observed positive program effects on criminal behavior. The average effect size across these seventeen studies was 0.16 (95 percent confidence interval of 0.06 to 0.26), suggesting that environmentally focused approaches are an effective prevention strategy.

More specifically, the five studies evaluating *school and discipline management* had a generally positive overall effect with an average effect size of 0.24 and a confidence interval that did not include zero. Unfortunately,

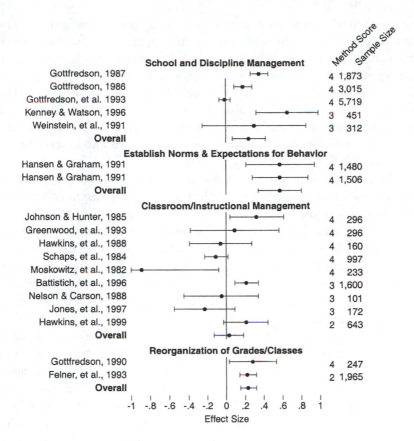

Figure 7.1
Treatment-Comparison Criminal Behavior Effect Sizes for Environmentally Focused Interventions

one of the high quality studies had a near zero effect size (Gottfredson, Gottfredson, and Hybl 1993). In this study, substantial heterogeneity in effects was observed across different schools participating in the study, with positive effects observed only in those schools that implemented the program with most fidelity.

Two treatment-comparison contrasts from a single study (Hansen and Graham 1991) evaluated the effectiveness of alternative strategies for *establishing norms and expectations for behavior*. The overall average for these two comparisons was moderate in size (average effect size = 0.58). To get a sense of the practical meaning of this effect size, we can translate it into a problem behavior rate for the treatment and comparison groups. The effect of programs to establish norms and expectations for behavior is equivalent to a problem behavior rate of 50 percent in the comparison conditions and 35 percent in the intervention condition, or a 30 percent reduction (1–35/50) in problem behavior. Although this finding should be interpreted cautiously in the absence of independent replication, it is encouraging that three additional studies measuring crime or antisocial behavior for which effect sizes could not be computed also observed positive effects (D. C. Gottfredson et al., 2000).

The effect sizes for *classroom and instructional management* approaches range from a modest positive effect (effect size = 0.33, Johnson and Hunter 1985) to a large negative effect (effect size = -0.89, Moskowitz, Schaps, and Malvin 1982). The overall average effect size was near zero (average effect size = 0.02). The inconsistency of effects across studies suggests that some unmeasured feature of these programs (for example, content, methods, quality of implementation) may drive the effect size. Further research is needed to better understand the features contributing to variability in effects in this category.

Only two studies examined the effects of *reorganization of grades and/or classes* on problem behavior. The overall effect for these studies was positive and of a magnitude we believe to be meaningful for a prevention program (average effect size = 0.24). As a general strategy, there are promising effects across the studies evaluating programs that focus on the school environment. However, there are too few studies and too much inconsistency in effects across studies for strong conclusions regarding the effects of these programs on problem behavior. More research attention to this area is clearly warranted.

Figure 7.2 presents the treatment-comparison criminal behavior effect sizes for instructional, individually focused interventions. The figure shows effects for the subcategories of instructional programs described earlier. This figure does not report the individual study-level effects, for the number of studies was too large. Rather, it reports the overall average effect size and the average effect size for the higher (method score of 3, 4, or 5) and lower quality studies (method score of 1 or 2).

The overall average effect size for the four evaluations of the effect of D.A.R.E. on criminal and problem behaviors was near zero (average effect size = 0.02), with the better quality studies observing similar results to the single low quality study. An analysis of the variability in effects across studies showed that the results for these four studies are highly consistent. This evidence suggests that D.A.R.E. is not effective at modifying the delinquent and other problem behavior of school-aged children and youth. Eleven studies evaluated programs which, like D.A.R.E., emphasize self-control or social competency instruction but do not use cognitive-behavioral or behavioral methods. These evaluations lead to the same conclusion as the evaluations of the D.A.R.E. program, with no evidence of effectiveness on this outcome.

Many school-based prevention programs were delivered in an instructional format using the cognitive-behavioral and behavioral methods described earlier to effect individual behavioral change. Shown in Figure 7.2 are twenty-nine effects from such programs, examples of which include Second Step, Responding in Peaceful and Positive Ways, Interpersonal Cognitive Problem-Solving (ICPS), Anger Control Training, PASS (Plan a Safe Strategy), Think First, Fast Track, Alcohol Misuse Prevention Study, and the Montreal Longitudinal Study. The overall effect of this collection of studies was positive (average effect size = 0.24) and of a meaningful magnitude, translating into a problem behavior rate of 41 percent in the program group relative to 50 percent in the comparison group. Analysis of only the higher quality studies reduced this average only slightly (average effect size = 0.22). This evidence suggests that cognitive-behavioral approaches are an effective school-based strategy for reducing problem behavior.

Two instructional prevention programs did not fit into the above categories. These two studies failed to show positive effects on criminal behavior (see Figure 7.2). One of these programs (Stuart 1974) observed a modest negative program effect. These studies reinforce the conclusion that instructional prevention programs that do not rely on cognitive-behavioral or behavioral methods are an ineffective approach to modifying the criminal activities and other problem behaviors of youth.

The final broad category of interventions is non-instructional approaches that focus on the individual. These include *cognitive-behavioral or behavioral interventions, other counseling/therapeutic treatments,* and *mentoring, tutoring, and work-study programs.* The effects of these programs on criminal behavior are shown in Figure 7.3. These studies tend to be much smaller in size and as such have larger confidence intervals (that is, less stability in the findings from a single study). The thirteen studies of cognitive-behavioral or behavioral methods produced a modestly large overall average effect size (0.36). The lower bound of the 95 percent confidence interval is a very small effect that is likely to lack practical significance (0.06). Although a few studies in this category observed negative effects, it is worth noting that four of the five highest quality studies (method score of 5, all randomized designs) observed positive and relatively large effects. Despite some inconsistency across studies, cognitive-behavioral

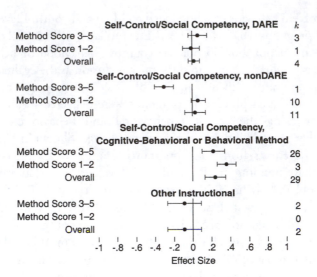

Figure 7.2

Treatment-Comparison Criminal Behavior Effect Sizes for Instructional, Individually Focused Interventions

or behavioral approaches that are not based on classroom instruction models appear to be effective as a broad category. Further investigation is needed to establish the characteristics of the more effective implementations of this approach.

Three of the five treatment-comparison contrasts of the effects for *other counseling/therapeutic* programs were negative, with a confidence interval around the average overall effect that ranges from a modest positive effect (0.26) to a large negative effect (-0.57). Although there is too little evidence for any broad conclusions regarding this mixed category, the evidence suggests that the approaches examined by these studies may not be fruitful avenues to the prevention of delinquent and other problem behaviors.

The effects in the final category on Figure 7.3, *mentoring, tutoring, and work-study* type programs, ranged from modest negative to modest positive effects, with a small overall effect size (average effect size = 0.13). As a rather mixed program category, it is not possible to generalize these null findings to all programs of this type. As with the previous category, the evidence is not encouraging.

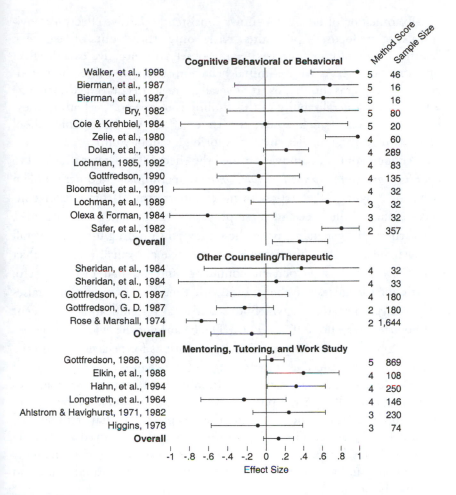

Figure 7.3
Treatment-Comparison Criminal Behavior Effect Sizes for Individually Focused, Noninstructional Interventions

Prevention of Substance Use Behavior

Measures of substance use were far more prevalent in the studies identified for this meta-analysis than measures of criminal behavior. Available for analyses were seventy-eight treatment-comparison effects from fifty-seven studies. As with earlier comparisons, we will present the findings for the environmentally focused programs first, followed by the instructional, individually focused, and non-instructional, individually focused programs.

Examination of Figure 7.4 shows consistently positive effects for environmentally focused programs with only three out of eighteen treatment-comparison contrasts having observed a negative overall effect on substance use. As with criminal behavior, school and discipline management programs show a positive overall average effect (average effect size = 0.24). The generalizability of this finding is uncertain, for both of these effects are from a single study; the larger effect was for middle school youth, whereas the smaller effect was for high school youth.

Although only one study examined the effects of programs designed to *establish norms and expectations for behavior* on criminal and other problem behaviors, eight studies representing eleven treatment-comparison contrasts evaluated the effects of these programs on substance use outcomes. This reflects the general focus of these programs on drug use. The overall average effect size for this category was positive and small (average effect size = 0.10) with a 95 percent confidence interval that included zero. Restricting the analysis to the studies with a method score of 4 or 5 raises the average effect (0.17), which was statistically significant (95 percent confidence interval of 0.07 to 0.26). The balance of the evidence suggests that programs to establish norms and expectations for behavior within the school setting are effective at preventing substance use.

The four studies that examined classroom and instructional management programs all observed positive effects, with an overall average effect of 0.16. The sole study to examine a program that reorganized grades/classes (Project STATUS; Gottfredson 1990) observed a relatively large effect on self-reported drug use. As a broad category, environmentally focused programs appear to be effective at reducing both substance use and criminal behavior.

The number of studies evaluating instructional, individually focused programs was too great to list all of the individual effects for each major category (fifty-five treatment-comparison contrasts across categories). Therefore, only the overall average effect and the average effect for treatment-comparison contrasts rated high (3, 4, or 5) or low (1 and 2) on the method scale are shown in Figure 7.5. Consistent with the effects of these programs on criminal behavior, the evidence suggests that most of these programs are ineffective at modifying substance use behavior.

The overall average effect for the twelve treatment-comparison contrasts evaluating D.A.R.E. was near zero (average effect size = 0.02). Both the higher and lower quality studies present the same impression regarding D.A.R.E.'s effectiveness. The "top" end of the 95 percent confidence interval

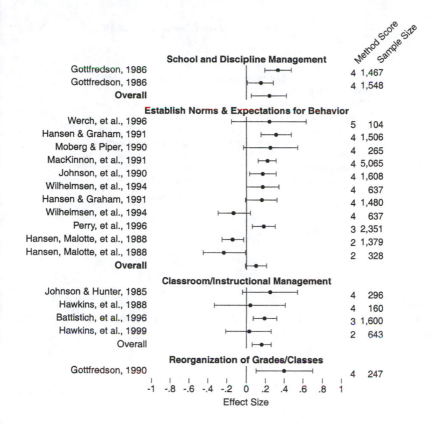

Figure 7.4

Treatment-Comparison Substance Use Effect Sizes for Environmentally Focused Interventions

for the average effect size of these studies was only 0.09, a rather small effect of uncertain practical significance. That is, if we assume that the true effectiveness of the D.A.R.E. program is at the top end of the confidence interval for the overall effect (the best case scenario), the effect is likely to be too small to justify the program costs. As we would expect, the non-D.A.R.E. programs (that is, programs that, like D.A.R.E., emphasize self-control or social competency instruction but do not use cognitive-behavioral or behavioral methods) also had an average effect size near zero (average effect size = 0.06 based on eleven treatment-comparison contrasts) with a 95 percent confidence interval that included zero. The high quality studies in this category had a negative average effect. A test of the difference between the average effect size for the D.A.R.E. and non-D.A.R.E. programs was statistically nonsignificant, that is, the distinction does not

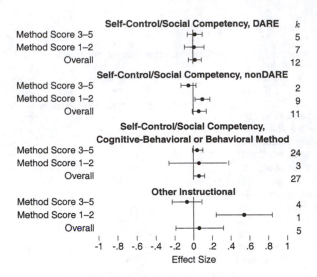

Figure 7.5
Overall Mean Substance Use Effect Sizes for Individually Focused, Instructional
Interventions

explain variability across effect sizes within this category of individually focused, instructional programs.

Many high quality evaluations of instructional programs that teach self-control or social competency skills using cognitive-behavioral and behavioral methods that examined a substance use outcome were examined. The overall average effect and the average effect for these studies were small (0.06) and statistically significant, albeit barely so. It appears that these programs are far more effective at reducing conduct-type problem behaviors, than at reducing substance use. For the "other" category of instructional programs, the overall average effect size was positive, although the average effect for the higher quality studies was negative. These findings for instructional programs reinforce the dismal outlook for programs of this type, particularly those that do not rely on cognitive-behavioral methods.

Only nine effects on substance use were found in examining four different types of noninstructional, individually focused prevention programs (Figure 7.6). Only the category of cognitive-behavioral and behavioral programs had an overall average effect size that was positive (effect size average = 0.23). Once again, the lower statistical power of the studies in the cate-

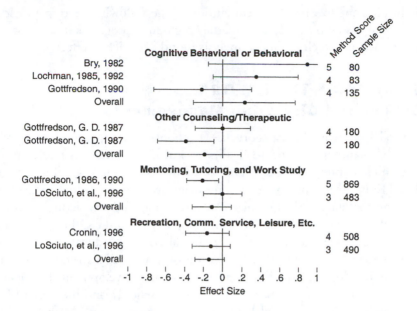

Figure 7.6
Treatment-Comparison Substance Use Effect Sizes for Individually Focused,
Non-instructional Interventions

gory prevents any firm conclusions. Clearly more research is needed of programs relying on these methods. The substance use effects for the remaining categories shown in Figure 7.6 were consistently negative.

The above synthesis of criminal behavior and substance use outcomes across a broad range of school-based prevention programs suggests that the most promising types of intervention strategies are those that are designed to change the school environment, either through school management and consistent discipline or through the establishment of norms and expectations for behavior. Instructional programs that teach self-control or social competency skills using cognitive-behavioral methods are also effective for reducing crime and substance use, although the small magnitude of the average effects on substance use suggest that such programs by themselves will not usually make a noticeable difference in the level of student substance use. The heterogeneity of effects suggests also that certain features of the programs (for example, who delivers them, duration, timing) may moderate their effectiveness. Also, non-instructional, cognitive-behavioral and behavioral programs show promise, although the current research base is insufficient to draw firm conclusions. The following section provides narrative descriptions of a few of the "high-end" programs in each of the categories for which the meta-analysis found evidence of effectiveness.[7]

PROGRAMS THAT WORK
School and Discipline Management

Several studies in this category use a school-team approach and a well-defined planning method to facilitate local involvement in planning for and implementing changes related to school safety and discipline. Project PATHE is an example. It was a comprehensive school improvement intervention that altered the organization and management structures in seven secondary schools between 1981 and 1983 as part of the Office of Juvenile Justice and Delinquency Prevention's alternative education initiative (Gottfredson 1986). District-level administrators used a structured organization development method called Program Development Evaluation (PDE) to develop a general plan for all seven schools, and then used PDE to structure specific school-level planning interventions. Applying PDE (Gottfredson 1984; D. Gottfredson, Rickert, G. Gottfredson, and Advani 1984), researchers and practitioners collaborate to develop and implement programs using specific steps spelled out in the program materials. A spiral of improvement is created as researchers continuously provide data feedback during the implementation phase to the practitioners and work with them to identify and overcome obstacles to strong program implementation.

In PATHE, PDE was used to develop and implement activities in each of the participating schools to increase academic achievement (for example, providing teacher training in instructional methods, carefully aligning the curriculum with the academic goals), improve school climate (for example, reviewing and revising discipline policies and practices, providing teacher training in classroom management), and improve transitions to post-secondary education and careers (for example, providing a career assessment program and apprenticeship experiences in the community). These activities targeted the entire population in each school. Individualized assistance in academics and behavior management was also provided for 100 students in each school identified as at high risk for academic failure or behavior problems.

Many different activities were carried out in each school. The positive effects of the program were most likely due not to any one activity carried out, but rather to the social climate created in the schools as staff and students increased their participation in planning for and implementing school improvement efforts. The planning activities served to provide a clear organizational focus. The changes to discipline policies and practices increased the clarity about expectations for student behavior as they improved the consistency of the enforcement of the rules. All of these changes together promoted a sense of community among students and staff in the schools.

The evaluation of the project compared change on an array of measures from the year prior to the treatment to one year (for four high schools) and two years (for five middle schools) into the intervention. One school at each level was a comparison school selected from among the non-participating schools to match the treatment schools as closely as possible. The students in the participating high schools reported less delinquent behavior and drug use, and fewer school punishments after the first year of the program. Students in the comparison high school did not change on these outcomes. A similar pattern was observed for the middle schools after two years. As serious delinquency increased in the comparison school, it decreased in the program middle schools. Changes in drug use and school punishments also favored the program schools. Several indicators of the school climate directly targeted by the program (for example, safety, staff morale, clarity of school rules, and effectiveness of the school administration) also increased in the program schools.

Establishing Norms and Expectations

Some programs that focus on establishing norms and expectations are instructional in format. Others focus more on school-wide activities to establish norms. Olweus reported on a program of the latter type undertaken in Norway that was designed to limit conflict in schools (Olweus 1991, 1992; Olweus and Alsaker 1991). Olweus noted that certain adolescents, that is, "bullies," repeatedly victimized other adolescents. This harassment was usually ignored by adults who failed to actively intervene and thus provided tacit acceptance of the bullying. A program was devised to alter environmental norms regarding bullying. A communication campaign sought to redefine the behavior as wrong. School personnel received a booklet that defined the problem and spelled out ways to counteract it. Parents were sent a booklet of advice. A video illustrating the problem was made available. Surveys to collect information and register the level of the problem were fielded. Information was fed back to personnel in forty-two schools in Bergen, Norway. Among the recommended strategies to reduce bullying were: establishing clear class rules against bullying; contingent responses (praise and sanctions); regular class meetings to clarify norms against bullying; improved supervision of the playground; and teacher involvement in the development of a positive school climate.

The program was evaluated using data from approximately 2,500 students (aged eleven to fourteen) belonging to 112 classes in 42 primary and secondary schools in Bergen. The results indicated that bullying decreased by 50 percent. Program effects were also observed on self-reports of delinquent behavior, including truancy, vandalism, and theft.

More common are curricular programs that combine a focus on social competency skill development with normative redefinition. Such curricula, often designed to reduce substance use, include portrayals of drug use as socially unacceptable, identification of short-term negative consequences of drug use, presentation of evidence that drug use is less prevalent among peers than children may think, encouragement for children to make public commitments to remain drug free, and the use of peer leaders to teach the curriculum (Institute of Medicine [IOM] 1994, p. 264). These activities are present in 29 percent of drug prevention curricula (Hansen 1992), but always in conjunction with other components such as conveying information about risks related to drug use and resistance skills training. Norm setting and public pledges to remain drug free are usually elements of the most effective drug education curricula, but meta-analyses have not been able to disentangle the effects of the various components. In a randomized study designed to do just that, Hansen and Graham (1991) found that positive effects on marijuana use and alcohol use were attributable more to a normative education than to a resistance skills training component. The normative education program corrected erroneous perceptions of the prevalence and acceptability of alcohol and drug use among peers and established conservative norms regarding substance use, whereas the resistance skills program taught adolescents to identify and resist peer and advertising pressure to use alcohol and other substances.

Instructional Programs

Instructional programs are most effective when they teach self-control or social competency skills and when they are taught using cognitive-behavioral methods, as described earlier. An example of such a program applied to very young children is Shure and Spivack's Interpersonal Cognitive Problem-Solving (ICPS) skills. This program helps children learn to generate alternative solutions to problems, become aware of the steps required to achieve a certain goal, consider consequences of actions, understand how events are causally related, and become more sensitive to interpersonal problems. The program is designed for use with children as young as four years old. More sophisticated skills are taught to children in the early elementary school grades. Using the program, teachers work with small groups of children for about twenty minutes per day, employing scripts prepared for each lesson. The intervention lasts approximately three months.

Shure and Spivack (1979, 1980, 1982) tested the program with 219 inner city, African American nursery school children. Of these subjects, 113 continued with the study through kindergarten. Some children received the training in nursery school only, others in kindergarten only, and others in both years. A fourth group received no training. The investigators measured both the specific interpersonal cognitive problem-solving skills targeted by the program and teachers' ratings of overt behavioral problems. Results showed that (a) students trained in nursery school improved more than controls both on measures of ICPS skills and behavioral adjustment; (b) these improvements were still evident a year following training, even when no additional training was provided; (c) students trained for the first time in kindergarten improved more than controls both on measures of ICPS skills and behavioral adjustment; and (d) students trained for two consecutive years scored higher than any other group on measures of ICPS, but a second year of training made no difference in terms of behavioral ratings (that is, one year of training was sufficient and equally effective either year).

An example of an effective instructional program for older students is Feindler, Marriott, and Iwata's (1984) Anger Control Training program. They delivered this program to junior high school boys who were participating in an existing program for disruptive youths. These students had been suspended for offenses other than smoking or truancy at least twice during the previous year. The program consisted of ten fifty-minute sessions delivered by a trained therapist over a fairly brief (seven-week) period. The sessions taught (in small groups of six youths) both behavioral and cognitive controls. Students were taught to analyze the components of the provocation cycle—the antecedent anger cues, aggressive responses, and consequent events—using self-monitoring and written logs. They learned to impose their own time-out responses and to relax themselves. They learned to replace aggressive responses (for example, threatening gestures, harsh tones) with appropriate assertive verbal and nonverbal responses. They learned specific cognitive behaviors, including self-instructions (for example, thinking, "I'm going to ignore this guy and keep cool"), reinterpretation of potentially aggression-eliciting situations, self-evaluation during conflict situations (for example, thinking, "How did I handle myself?"), and thinking ahead. They also learned a sequence of problem-solving steps to take in difficult situations instead of reacting impulsively. The therapist relied almost entirely on behavioral modeling, role-playing, rehearsal, cues, and other cognitive-behavioral strategies to teach the new skills. Participants also received immediate reinforcers (for example, Coke and snacks, activities) for participation.

The students randomly assigned to receive the anger management training showed greater improvement than the students in the control condition on an interview measure of problem-solving skills and on teacher ratings of self-control. Daily records of "fines" for misbehavior (a measure both of student behavior and the staff's recording practices) were collected for six weeks prior to, seven weeks during, and five weeks following the intervention. They showed a positive treatment effect on the more frequent category of fines for mild verbal and physical misbehaviors such as cursing, arguing, shoving, and throwing small objects. For more serious infractions, the trend favored the anger management students, but the differences were not statistically significant—perhaps due to the relative infrequency of these behaviors, the short duration of the experiment, and the small number of students.

Note that the most effective instructional strategies are often targeted at high-risk populations and delivered in small groups. Universal programs such as Botvin's Life Skills Training (Botvin, Baker, Botvin, et al. 1984; Botvin, Baker, Renick, et al. 1984) and the STAR curriculum used in the Midwestern Prevention Program (Pentz et al. 1989) have also been shown to have positive effects on substance use, but the effects are generally small.

Cognitive-Behavioral and Behavioral Interventions

The highest quality studies in this category are similar in nature to those just described, but they are more often delivered to extremely high-risk youths, often by or with the help of mental health professionals. Walker et al.'s (1998) "First Step to Success" is a good example. The researchers randomly assigned at-risk kindergartners to the program or to a wait-list control group. Students in the intervention group were exposed to three months of school and parent intervention. The school-based intervention is a behavior modification program delivered first by a trained consultant during the classroom period, and then taken over by the regular classroom teacher (who is trained and supported by the consultant). The parent intervention consists of six parent-training lessons designed to assist parents in helping their children adjust to school and perform well. Teacher reports of aggressive and maladaptive behavior declined substantially following the treatment.

Lochman's work (1984, 1992) with highly aggressive boys is another example of the effective application of cognitive-behavioral methods to high-risk boys. His Anger-Coping Intervention targets specific cognitive skills (for example, using self-statements to inhibit impulsive behavior, identifying problems and social perspective taking, generating alternative solutions, and considering the consequences to social problems) and uses behavioral techniques (operant conditioning) to reward compliance with group rules. The program is targeted at boys in grades four through six who are identified as aggressive and disruptive by their teachers. A school counselor and a mental health professional from a Community Guidance Clinic co-lead groups of aggressive boys for twelve to eighteen group sessions, each forty-five minutes to an hour. Importantly, this cognitive training is augmented with teacher consultation in which the mental health professional running the children's group assists the children's regular teachers in classroom management in general and in helping the targeted youths generalize new skills to the regular classroom.

The effectiveness of this "anger coping" intervention was investigated in a series of studies which systematically varied features of the program to learn more about its essential elements. In one study (Lochman et al. 1984), seventy-six boys ranging in age from nine to twelve from eight elementary schools were studied. They were not randomly assigned to experimental conditions, but pretreatment measures showed the groups to be similar on the outcome measures of interest. In comparison to aggressive boys receiving no treatment or minimal treatment, aggressive treatment-group boys reduced their disruptive-aggressive, off-task behavior in school and their aggressive behavior as rated by their parents directly after the intervention. A three-year follow-up study was conducted when these and some boys from other earlier studies were fifteen years old (Lochman 1992). The study found that the intervention affected self-reported alcohol and substance abuse, but the effect on self-reported criminal behavior was not statistically significant. It can be argued that a reduction in delinquency of this magnitude (approximately a five-percentage-point difference in the crime rate between the treatment and control group) in a highly delinquent population has practical meaning. Also, the treatment group in this follow-up study was younger than the comparison group, which worked against finding program effects as younger age was associated with higher rates of delinquency.

SUMMARY OF EFFECTIVENESS OF SCHOOL-BASED CRIME PREVENTION STRATEGIES

The earlier synthesis of criminal behavior and substance use outcomes across a broad range of school-based prevention programs suggests that the most promising types of intervention strategies are those that are designed to change the school environment, either through school management and consistent discipline or through the establishment of norms and expectations for behavior. Gottfredson's (1986) Project PATHE is an example of an effective strategy for improving school and discipline management. Olweus's (1991, 1992; Olweus and Alsaker 1991) bullying prevention program and Hansen and Graham's (1991) normative education program are examples of more effective strategies for establishing norms and expectations for behavior. Instructional programs that teach self-control or social competency skills using cognitive-behavioral methods such as rehearsal, role playing, and feedback are also effective for reducing substance use and crime, although the small size of the average effect of such programs on substance use suggests that, by themselves, such instructional programs will not make a noticeable difference in the level of student substance use. The heterogeneity of effects in this category suggests that certain features of the programs (for example, who delivers them, duration, timing) may moderate their effectiveness. Examples of two of the more effective instructional programs are Shure and Spivack's (1979, 1980, 1982) ICPS program and Fiendler's Anger Control Training (Fiendler, Marriott, and Iwata 1984). Non-instructional, cognitive-behavioral and behavioral programs also show promise, although the current research base is insufficient to draw firm conclusions. Walker's First Step to Success (Walker et al. 1998) and Lochman's (1992) Anger-Coping Intervention are examples of more effective strategies contained in this category.

ARE PREVENTION EFFECTS MEANINGFUL?

It is possible, using effect sizes, to place the findings from prevention research studies into a more policy-relevant context by comparing the typical effect to one that, in theory, would capture the attention of policy makers and the public. Table 7.5 shows the average effect size for the four most promising types of school-based prevention as well as the effect size that would be required to reduce the current prevalence rates for four types of youth criminal activity by 25 percent and 50 percent. The prevalence rates are based on 1998 or 1999 rates shown in the MTF survey for substance use and the NSDPS for other criminal activities. The rates are for males only. Of course, the comparisons are rough at best because the behaviors included in the actual effect sizes do not necessarily include the behaviors that are represented in the prevalence rates, and the populations targeted in the prevention programs represented in the studies do not necessarily correspond to those that form the basis for the prevalence rates: males in certain grades in the nation. If we are willing to accept these imprecise comparisons, they show that certain prevention strategies (for example, school and discipline management, and non-instructional programs using cognitive-behavioral or behavioral methods), by themselves, seem capable of producing noticeable reductions in the rates of crime or substance use. Others (for example, establishing norms and expectations for behavior and instructional self-control/social competency programs using cognitive-behavioral or behavioral methods) seem likely to produce meaningful reductions in crime and antisocial behavior but not in substance use when implemented as stand-alone activities.

The estimates of practical meaningfulness presented above are, we believe, optimistic. This is so because the average effect size estimates come from research studies that are generally conducted under more favorable conditions than is usual in the everyday life of the typical school. More often than not, studies are conducted under idealized conditions, with much more support and attention given to program implementation than would typically be so. Effects found in research studies, usually not large as indicated earlier, may actually overestimate the effects that can be expected in real life. The National Study of Delinquency Prevention in Schools (G. D. Gottfredson et al. 2000) found that the quality of implementation of school-based prevention activity varies a great deal from activity to activity and is typically low. When judged according to standards for quality present in published research studies that had produced positive effects on measures of problem behavior, 47 percent of actual school-based programs received failing grades. This implies that there is plenty of room for improvement in the quality of implementation of the typical school-based prevention activity, and that a matter of high priority should be finding ways for schools not only to select types of prevention activities known to be effective in research, but to implement them in a fashion that might be expected to produce similar results to those shown in research studies.

Table 7.5
Observed Average Effect Sizes for Promising Programs and Effect Size
Needed for a 50% and 25% Reduction in Specific Problem Behaviors

TYPE OF SCHOOL-BASED PREVENTION	OBSERVED AVERAGE EFFECT SIZE AND 95% CONFIDENCE INTERVAL	
	DELINQUENT, ANTISOCIAL, AND AGGRESSIVE BEHAVIOR	SUBSTANCE USE
School/discipline management	0.30 [0.01–0.59]	0.24 [0.05–0.42]
Setting norms and expectations	0.58 [0.34–0.80]	0.10 [0.00–0.21]
Self-control instruction with cognitive-behavioral methods	0.24 [0.13–0.35]	0.06 [0.00–0.12]
Noninstructional cognitive-behavioral methods	0.39 [0.09–0.69]	0.23 [0.30–0.76]

TYPE OF BEHAVIOR	EFFECT SIZES NEEDED FOR 50% AND 25% REDUCTION IN PROBLEM BEHAVIOR
CARRYING A HIDDEN WEAPON . . .	
from 12% to 6%	0.38
from 12% to 9%	0.17
PURPOSELY DAMAGING PROPERTY (OTHER THAN SCHOOL OR FAMILY PROPERTY)	
from 26% to 13%	0.48
from 26% to 19.5%	0.22
HITTING OR THREATENING TO HIT OTHER STUDENTS	
from 44% to 22%	0.62
from 44% to 33%	0.29
ILLICIT DRUG USE	
from 45% to 22.5%	0.63
from 45% to 33.8%	0.29

CONCLUSIONS AND RECOMMENDATIONS

For Policy Makers

More money should be appropriated for school-based prevention activities. An influential report by the RAND Corporation (Greenwood et al. 1996) showed that compared with home visits by childcare professionals, parent training, monitoring and supervising already-delinquent youths, and imprisoning felony offenders at a higher rate (for example, "three strikes" legislation) a prevention intervention targeting high school–aged youths to provide educational and social development was more cost effective. Yet, relative to federal expenditures on control strategies such as policing and prison construction, expenditures on school-based substance abuse and crime prevention efforts are modest. Gottfredson (1997) reported that the U.S. Office of Justice Program's total expenditures on school-based prevention are less than $25 million per year, compared with $1.4 billion for the extra police programs and $617 million for prison construction.

The single largest federal expenditure on school-based prevention in the United States was made by the Department of Education's Safe and Drug-Free Schools and Communities, which in 1999 spread $566 million across most school districts in the nation according to a population-based formula. When spread across so many school districts and schools within districts, these funds amount to a pittance. Silvia and Thorne (1997) estimate that Drug-Free Schools funds for implementing drug prevention programs averaged $6 to $8 per pupil. Additional funding for school-based prevention of crime is needed.

How should the money be spent? We have demonstrated that some prevention activities are unlikely to make a difference in levels of crime or substance use. Others are likely to make a noticeable difference. Clearly, legislation and funding guidelines that have the effect of shifting monies away from approaches with less research support and toward approaches with more research support would help.

Unfortunately, the meager federal expenditures on school-based prevention are not well spent. Safe and Drug-Free Schools and Communities monies administered by the U.S. Department of Education fund a relatively narrow range of intervention strategies, many of which have been shown either not to work (for example, counseling) or to have only small effects (for example, drug instruction programs such as D.A.R.E.). The department's Principles of Effectiveness, put in place in 1997 to guide local expenditures of these funds, call for limiting programs to those for which research and evaluation activities have demonstrated a preventive effect on drug use, violence, or disruptive behavior. This is a step in the right direction. However, state and local interpretations of research and evaluation may be faulty, especially because of the proliferation of technical assistance websites and other publications that apply very different standards for judging effectiveness. The push toward the use of research-based strategies also has the potential to backfire because it will inevitably lead to increased use of the strategies that have been *evaluated* rather than strategies that are effective. As we have seen, instructional programs account for the lion's share of evaluated programs, and they predominate in collections of activities that have received the research stamp of approval. Yet they produce smaller effects than other strategies that have received less research attention.

Also underemphasized in the federal effort to improve prevention practices is attention to the quality of implementation. Because implementation in the typical school is not likely to produce the kind of effects found in research studies, policy makers should require that mechanisms to monitor the quality of implementation of funded activities be established and should encourage systems to provide necessary technical assistance and organization development assistance to improve implementation. The Department of Education's Principles of Effectiveness require that recipients of Safe and Drug-Free Schools and Communities funds evaluate the programs and use the evaluation results to refine, improve, and strengthen the programs. The principle has been implemented in such a way that some form of outcome evaluation (not necessarily involving a control group) is now required after two years for programs that have not already been demonstrated to reduce substance use or violent behavior. If programs have been evaluated and received a stamp of approval, evaluation is not required. We believe that a more fruitful use of evaluation dollars would be to develop implementation standards against which actual implementation quality can be compared and to require all recipients of funds to collect data on the extent to which these standards are met. Mechanisms for providing helpful technical assistance and organization development could then be established to help schools reach these implementation standards. Of course, outcome evaluations should also be conducted, but resources for such evaluations should be concentrated and allocated to high priority areas requiring more evaluation work (such as the environmental strategies described earlier) rather than spread thinly across school districts which have neither the resources nor the expertise to conduct high quality evaluations.

For Schools

The typical school operates fourteen different activities concurrently in an attempt to prevent or reduce problem behavior or improve school safety, and the typical activity is implemented with poor quality (G. D. Gottfredson et al. 2000). Because research on school-based prevention is dominated by certain categories of prevention, little is known about the effectiveness of most of what schools do. But we do know that many of the strategies that schools frequently employ (for example, counseling, recreation, many instructional programs) are not likely to make a difference, and that even among the strategies that in principle work, the compromises made during the implementation process are likely to render the activity ineffective.

We recommend that schools incorporate cognitive-behavioral teaching methods to improve the effectiveness of their instructional prevention programs, but that they not limit their prevention efforts to such curriculum. They should embed instructional approaches within a broader environmental change strategy that attends to clarifying norms for behavior, establishing and maintaining firm and fair discipline management programs, improving general school management, and creating cohesive social environments. They should also make use of intensive behavioral or cognitive-behavioral coaching strategies, such as Lochman's Anger Coping Model, for the most at-risk students.

More than anything else, schools need to attend to the quality of their activities. The National Study of Delinquency Prevention in Schools (G. D. Gottfredson et al. 2000) suggested a number of avenues for improved implementation quality. First, local involvement of school personnel in selecting and planning for their prevention activities is important. Schools that engage in needs assessment activities and that use a variety of sources of information to select programs are more likely to implement high quality programs. However, schools are better off selecting externally developed programs than creating their own, probably because externally developed programs have undergone more extensive development and have benefited more from research. When program materials and methods are more standardized (for example, when they provide implementation manuals), they are better implemented. In addition, better integration of prevention activities into normal school operations is related to higher implementation quality. When programs are isolated or have an auxiliary status, they are less likely to be implemented in a high quality fashion. Finally, greater amounts of organizational support in the form of principal support, high quality training, monitoring, and supervision are related to higher quality implementation. These findings converge in implying that if schools (and school systems) approached the prevention of problem behavior in the same way they do the teaching of academic material, we could expect to see vast improvement in the effectiveness of prevention efforts. This recommendation echoes recent calls in the education and prevention literatures to move prevention "from the fringes into the fabric of school improvement" (Adelman and Taylor 2000) and to empower and enable school personnel to incorporate effective strategies for increasing school safety into their more comprehensive school improvement efforts (Morrison, Furlong, and Morrison 1997).

A final word concerns the increased emphasis schools and school districts have placed on "get tough" crime prevention strategies. In response to the widely publicized school shooting incidents that have occurred since 1997, schools have attempted to tighten security in schools and to impose severe consequences for potentially dangerous student behaviors. A recent report on the nation's response to these incidents notes that rates of school suspension are increasing nationally, and that schools are increasingly developing crisis prevention plans which often involve the use of S.W.A.T. teams on campus, evacuation readiness plans, and helicopters. More schools are hiring school police or security officers, mandating identification badges, and installing metal detectors (Brooks, Schiraldi, and Ziedenberg 2000). The National Study of Delinquency Prevention in Schools (G. D. Gottfredson et al. 2000) showed that 66 percent of middle schools and 57 percent of high schools use at least one form of security or surveillance strategy, including metal detectors; police or security personnel in schools; locker searches; and drug-, gun-, or bomb-sniffing dogs. Most schools (91 percent) automatically or usually suspend or expel students from school for possession of a gun, drugs, alcohol, or a knife. Our meta-analysis of the effectiveness of school-based prevention programs uncovered only one relatively poor quality study of any of these security-oriented strategies.

Evaluations are needed. This is made all the more evident by a growing body of research that suggests that key to a school's ability to produce positive student outcomes (both academic and behavioral) is its ability to maintain a "communal social organization" (Bryk and Driscoll 1988). This type of social organization is characterized by, among other things, meaningful social interactions and strong ties among members of the school community, and a feeling among students that the adults in the school care about them. This type of school climate is related to a number of positive school outcomes, including reduced school misbehavior, presumably through increased *informal* social controls. How does the presence of formal security mechanisms and police in the school affect the social organization of the school? We do not know. Clearly, when students are suspended or expelled from school, they cannot benefit from the instruction that occurs in school and are at elevated risk for dropout and other problem behaviors. In addition, ethnographic studies (Devine 1996) have suggested that increased reliance on formal control strategies changes the role of the teacher in the school and the nature of teacher-student interactions in ways that erode informal social controls. Teachers in security-oriented schools tend to stay in their classrooms and interact with students only around subject matter, and they have tended to delegate their authority to school security guards. The national shift toward heightened security and surveillance may increase rather than decrease school crime. Research is sorely needed to guide national and local policy in this area.

8

Labor Markets and Crime

SHAWN BUSHWAY AND PETER REUTER

The sustained and substantial drop in crime rates in the second half of the 1990s coincided with the longest economic expansion since 1945. This has refocused attention on the exciting possibility that an economic expansion reduces crime by increasing legitimate economic opportunities (Bernstein and Houston 2000). It also reinforces hope that employment-based policy interventions might aid low-income urban areas, where most crime in the United States is concentrated. The federal government currently sponsors several billion dollars worth of employment programs focused on inner city areas based at least partly on the hope of reducing crime. The goal of this chapter is to assess the current state of knowledge on how labor market-oriented programs impact crime prevention in high crime, urban areas.[1]

Although numerous theoretical justifications can be offered for a relationship between labor markets and crime,[2] the one that receives the most attention is individual and economic. In its simplest form, the economic theory of crime hypothesizes that people commit crime when the benefits outweigh the costs. The costs include forgone earnings from legitimate work and the risk of incarceration. The calculation is more than merely the sum of monetary factors and risks; individual attitudes also matter. Tighter labor markets mean more available jobs and / or higher wages, which, other things being equal, should then lower the participation in crime.

By focusing on the individual, this framework inadvertently focuses the attention away from the key policy question—Can changes in the labor market affect the crime rate, especially in places with very high crime rates?—and onto the general relationship between unemployment and crime at the aggregate level. Recent reviews of the unemployment and crime literature (Freeman 1999; Piehl 1998) conclude that while the unemployment rate does have a measurable impact on property crime of approximately 2 percent for every one percentage point change in unemployment at the state or county level, this effect is quite small. For example, a relatively large drop in unemployment from 8 percent to 4 percent (approximately the range from trough to peak in a typical postwar business cycle) will only decrease the crime rate by 8 percent. This conclusion is consistent with the aggregate level research done in Europe (European Committee on Crime Problems 1985, 1994). Piehl and Freeman (1998; 1999) both conclude that aggregate unemployment levels cannot explain the high concentration of crime in poor inner city communities.

This focus on unemployment (and, indirectly, on the economic theory of crime) may understate the importance of labor markets. Many dimensions of the labor market (such as the distribution of jobs by skill and location) in addition to aggregate unemployment may affect crime rates in high crime communities. In this chapter we primarily focus on whether targeted labor market interventions, aimed at high-risk people or locations, can substantially reduce inner city crime.

We start by noting that labor markets, like other markets, have a demand and a supply side. The demand comes from employers seeking workers to fill specific jobs. The supply consists of individuals seeking work. An equilibrium wage and employment level will be reached in this market by interaction between employers and workers.

Because we are particularly interested in the role of labor markets for low-income urban areas characterized by high demographic homogeneity, it seems appropriate to concentrate on a broad classification of low skill labor markets.[3] In what follows, we will look at the relationship between the labor market and crime, focusing on what is known about how crime can impact and be impacted by the supply side (employees) and demand side (employers) of the low skill labor market. It is perhaps counterintuitive, but adopting a focus on labor markets rather than unemployment rates (which ignore the substantial numbers who may choose not to participate in the labor market at all), allows us to consider non-economic theories of crime, including but not limited to control theory and labeling theory. These more criminological theories of crime consider how the behavior of other participants in the labor market can impact the individual's decision to commit crime.

We consider the two components of the labor market separately, first examining demand, then supply. In each section, we begin by presenting evidence from observational data that try to establish the existence of the relationship or pattern in question, followed by evidence from policy interventions that attempt to leverage that relationship. We exclude general macroeconomic policies, (for example, looser monetary policy aimed at lowering interest rates) though these have modest effects on crime; such policies are driven by other factors and are not focused on urban areas in any particular way. We include, however, a range of community and individual programs that do not specifically target crime, but rather target a component of the labor market thought to affect crime in these urban areas. Thus much of this review assesses just how effective such job training and job creation programs are at increasing employment in the targeted community or among the targeted groups, even if the programs do not target criminal justice-involved offenders. The crime consequences are inferred from our review of the relationship between employment and crime at various levels.

We also consider how crime itself may have an impact on the demand for and supply of labor. For policy purposes the reciprocal relationship of crime and employment presents a major challenge. Not only may a criminal history affect an individual's employability, but areas of high crime are unattractive for investment. Both property and personnel are at risk; goods are stolen, premises damaged, employees assaulted, and customers intimidated. Attracting capital requires a reduction in crime so as to allay the legitimate concerns of investors, employers, and customers. On the other hand, crime reduction on a large scale may require the creation of employment opportunities for the large numbers of young adults who are the source of so much of the crime in an area. Unfortunately, many offenders lack the skills needed to obtain and retain attractive jobs, that is, positions that pay enough to avoid poverty (well above the minimum wage for a two-parent, two-child household with only one wage earner) and that offer potential progress and a sense of accomplishment. Thus, improving their workforce skills may be essential even when capital, a prerequisite for new jobs, can be attracted into the community.

DEMAND-SIDE FORCES

Substantial economic and social forces have led to the loss of many jobs in urban areas and to the movement of other jobs to the suburbs (Bluestone and Harrison 1982; Hughes 1993). New technology has led to new manufacturing processes. It is often easier to build new factories at suburban or ex-urban "greenfield" sites than to retrofit old buildings. Global competition in textiles and other industries has led to the mass relocation of manufacturing operations away from "Rust Belt" locations in northeastern U.S. cities with their old factories and heavily unionized workforces to more rural "Sun Belt" locations with cheaper land and labor. In some cases, technological change has even led to the outright elimination of many jobs in a specific industry. Consider, for example, the development of container shipping in the late 1950s. Until the invention of containers that could be carried on trains, trucks, and ships, thousands of well-paid, union-organized longshoremen were needed to unload trains and trucks and reload the material onto ships in inner city ports located in most major coastal cities. Although the unions managed to negotiate contracts that eased the short-term impact of containerization, the long-term impact was the virtual elimination of many attractive low skill jobs in central city urban locations.

Massey and Denton (1993) also argue that the strong desire for racial segregation has been an additional impetus for the exit of jobs from center cities. "White flight" from urban areas has been a well-documented phenomenon in the United States as white middle class families (followed closely by a growing black middle class) have fled to suburbs in pursuit of cheaper, high quality housing, good schools, and safer communities (Cullen and Levitt 1996). Companies, especially those increasingly owned by nonlocal national and international corporations without a commitment to the urban area, often follow their workers and customer base into the suburbs. The result of these structural changes is a national net loss in low-skill, high-paying jobs (primarily in manufacturing) and a general flight of jobs, especially well-paying, low-skill jobs, from the inner cities into suburban and rural locations.[4] The effects are quite substantial. From 1967 to 1987, Chicago, Philadelphia, New York City, and Detroit lost more than 50 percent of their manufacturing jobs, numbers that represent millions of jobs (Wilson 1996). Furthermore, certain demographic groups were hit harder than others. Nationally, the proportion of employed black males age 20 to 29 working in manufacturing jobs fell from 37.5 percent to 20 percent between 1978 and 1987 (Black, Levitt, and Sanders 1998).

The link between job loss and crime is at some level fairly straightforward. The reduced availability of high-paying jobs makes crime more attractive to people who would otherwise be working. This is the standard economic model of crime. But more than a decade ago, William Julius Wilson (1987) proposed a more structural sociological explanation for the effects of employment changes in the inner city. He identified the loss of well-paying manufacturing jobs from the inner city as the key factor in the growing concentration of African-American poverty and social problems, including family dissolution, welfare, low levels of social organization, and crime. More precisely, Sampson and Wilson (1995) hypothesize that the permanent loss of high-paying manufacturing jobs leads to the destruction of the social fabric of the community. It is this loss of the social fabric that ultimately worsens crime (for similar explanations, see White 1999; Gans 1990; Currie 1993).

Rosenbaum (1996) also argues that youths have difficulty finding employment when they live in impoverished neighborhoods because their friends and family are not likely to provide many job connections. Businesses that acted as a key social force by encouraging interaction either moved or closed. The general pattern of detachment from the legal world of work means that children no longer grow up in environments where adults go to work every day, eliminating a key socialization mechanism. This lack of socialization leads to low graduation rates and high attrition in training programs, maintaining the underinvestment in human capital of the previous generation in high poverty neighborhoods. These and other processes lead to a reduced level of social control in the environment, or of what Sampson, Raudenbush, and Earls (1997) refer to as collective efficacy. Crime is both more available and less disapproved in these disorganized environments.

Although the ethnographic evidence supporting this hypothesis is fairly well developed (Sullivan 1989; Anderson 1990; Wilson 1996), the supporting quantitative evidence is mixed. For example, Holzer (1991) finds that the most recent evidence suggests that the spatial mismatch hypothesis can explain some but not all of the black-white employment difference. Other researchers have not been able to link the lower levels of African-American employment to lower levels of marriage in the African-American community (Wood 1995; Lerman 1989). Berry, Portney, and Thomson (1991) show that living in a poor neighborhood has little effect on a person's political attitudes and behavior. Also, Jencks (1991) attempts to show that, while employment definitely declined in the inner cities, the plight of those in the inner cities has not gotten uniformly worse in the 1980s and, as a result, all problems are not inherently interconnected.

Wilson (1991) responds to these findings by claiming, rightly according to Peterson (1991), that much of this research has not focused on the extremely isolated, racially segregated, urban neighborhoods that are at the heart of his theory (and of our interest in this chapter). Other papers that do focus on these urban areas do appear to support parts of Wilson's theory (see, for example, Crane 1991; Mayer 1991). While we do not have the space to further detail the ongoing debate about Wilson's hypothesis, we do agree that the unemployment and crime literature has not focused on the places or on the types of economic dislocation discussed in Wilson's hypothesis. Most tests of the unemployment and crime relationship have not distinguished between transitory economic slowdowns (the business cycle) and permanent loss of high-paying, low skill jobs focused in urban areas. Yet the impact of incentives for job search and educational decisions by individuals are quite different depending on whether one's unemployment is the result of a temporary recession or a permanent structural change in the labor market. Most of the unemployment and crime tests have also focused on higher levels of aggregation (that is, national and state level) rather than the community-level analysis suggested by Wilson's theory (Chiricos 1987).

There seems to be a consensus for the existence of a weak positive relationship between unemployment and property crime at the state and national level (Levitt, Forthcoming). The measured relationship is commensurate with what one would expect due to normal transitory economic changes, that is, the business cycle (Cook and Zarkin 1985). However, Chiricos (1987) has observed that studies which use intracity data (census tract or police precinct) provide stronger evidence for the positive relationship between unemployment (including withdrawal from the labor market, the "discouraged worker effect") and crime, including violent crime. He explains this result by suggesting that

> researchers using more local data are better able to capture what can be termed the "milieu effects" of unemployment on a particular area. That is, high unemployment may have a demoralizing impact on a particular neighborhood or section of a city or county that creates a climate of hopelessness or anomie with criminogenic consequences even for those not directly unemployed (e.g., teenagers or others not in the labor force). (p. 195)

This explanation is consistent with the social control explanation explicated by Sampson and Wilson (1995).

One unpublished study (Black, Levitt, and Sanders 1998) tries to measure this effect directly by looking at the impact of changes in earnings on crime over time (1970–1993) in counties that were heavily dependent on steel manufacturing in 1969. Crime had a much stronger relationship with the changes in employment that were permanent as a result of steel plant closings than with changes that were not correlated with changes in the steel industry. These results are preliminary; similar work is needed to explore what happens to the crime rate when there are large structural changes in the makeup of the local economy. But we believe that there is enough evidence at this point to conclude that the social disorganization story has some merit—permanent losses of low-skill, well-paid jobs may be a major contributor to subsequent social disorder and criminal activity.

Wilson (1996) argues forcefully that government employment-oriented programs can reduce the social problems of these communities. Yet, as we will see in the following section, stimulating economic development in the inner city through tax incentives or direct capital subsidies has proved very difficult.

Enterprise Zones

Community development programs use demand-side policies to help particular neighborhoods. New jobs present more opportunities for legitimate work. Jobs visibly available in an area may also provide motivation for young people to continue their education and to enroll in training programs. The economic activity that new or expanded businesses represent can also lead to increased social interactions among residents and strengthen social institutions (for example, churches, business organizations, schools), which can exert a positive influence on individuals who might otherwise revert to crime.

The enterprise zone is one relatively new policy tool focusing tax incentives at generally narrowly defined, economically depressed geographic areas (Papke 1993; Erickson and Friedman 1991). These programs typically use investment, labor, and financial incentives to encourage job development (Erickson and Friedman 1991). The investment incentives include credits for property taxes, franchise taxes, sales taxes, investment taxes, and other possibly state-idiosyncratic employer taxes (for example, inventory tax credits). The labor incentives include a tax credit for job creation, for hiring a zone resident or some other disadvantaged person, and for training expenditures. Finally, the financial incentives sometimes include an investment fund associated with the program and preferential treatment for federal bond programs. These programs are based on the assumption that employers are sensitive to state and local tax incentives in their location decisions (Bartik 1991).

As of 1995, thirty-four states had a total of 3,091 active enterprise zone programs (median = 16), and the Federal Empowerment Zone and Enterprise Community Program has introduced 106 more zones (Wilder and Rubin 1996). The state zones are limited in the value of the incentives they can offer, precisely because federal taxes (for example, corporate profits tax) are so large and cannot be waived by the state. The median zone population for the state programs is about 4,500 persons, and the median zone size is about 1.8 square miles (Erickson and Friedman 1991). Zone designation is usually based on unemployment rates, population decline, poverty rates, median incomes, the number of welfare recipients, or the amount of property abandonment. The federal government provided direct funding of about $40 million in 1999. Beginning in 2000, the government started providing $1.5 million each year per zone for the next ten years.[5]

All the evaluations consider only the immediate economic outcomes of these programs and do not examine the larger social implications, such as crime reductions; only Bartik and Bingham (1997) show an awareness of this shortcoming. The evaluations also do not attempt to determine the impacts of individual incentives. The incentives are typically used in concert, so that the economic growth in any given zone cannot be attributed to any one incentive; nor is it possible to separate out component effects using econometric techniques.

A New Jersey study (Boarnet and Bogart 1996) found that the zones had no impact on total employment or property values in municipalities with zones,[6] while an Indiana study (Papke 1994) found that the zones led to a long-term 19 percent decline in unemployment rates in municipalities with enterprise zones. More recently, four studies by a group of researchers attempt to go beyond these single state studies to look at variation across states for state enterprise zones (Bondonio and Engberg 2000; Engberg and Greenbaum 1999; Greenbaum and Engberg 1999, 2000). They have generally reported negative or insignificant employment effects. One study even suggested that enterprise zones are actually harmful in the most depressed locations.

In an attempt to peel back the layers of the onion on what may be going on in these enterprise zones, Greenbaum and Engberg (1999) looked at establishment-level employment statistics for enterprise zones in metropolitan areas in six states. They found that enterprise zones increased employment and business activity in new establishments while decreasing employment and business activity in old establishments. The net effect was a small decrease in employment. Essentially, this study finds that, as in England, zones lead to increased churning of business activity without any net gains in employment. In fact, the British government, which pioneered these zones, abandoned its enterprise zone program after researchers found that nearly all jobs in enterprise zones (86 percent) represented relocation from neighboring communities.

This new body of rigorous research on many zones over a number of states raises serious questions about the ability of state enterprise zones to significantly change the business environments in depressed urban areas.

The evaluation of the federal program should shed light on whether this approach with substantially more financial resources is capable of producing more of an impact.

COMMUNITY DEVELOPMENT BLOCK GRANTS

The 1974 Community Development Block Grant (CDBG) Program represents the other major federally funded program aimed directly at revitalizing distressed neighborhoods. Instead of relying on tax credits as incentives, this program provides direct funding to local governments. In 1992, CDBGs provided local jurisdictions with $4.8 billion to be spent on activities that support any one of three objectives: benefiting low- and moderate-income persons, preventing or eliminating slums or blight, and addressing other urgent community needs. The program funding breaks down broadly into five main areas: housing (38 percent), public facilities (22 percent), economic development (12 percent), public services (9 percent), and acquisition and clearance (6 percent). Although there are no outcome evaluations of this program[7], the sheer size of the economic development component demands inclusion in this section.

A 1995 process evaluation (Urban Institute 1995) considered only economic outcomes. Most of the economic development grant money was spent on loans and grants to private businesses. The recipient businesses were generally small, and 37 percent of these businesses were minority owned. These loans seemed to perform better than the nongeographically targeted Small Business Administration loans. According to the U.S. Department of Housing and Urban Development (HUD) report, these loans were more important to the business activities of the recipients than the enterprise zone tax incentives,[8] but neighborhood residents held a comparable number of the newly created jobs under both programs (approximately 30 percent).

An effort was made to provide a before-and-after study of 250 census tracts in the CDBG program, using a survey on all CDBG funding and census data from 1980 and 1990. This study found a clear relationship between the level of funding and tract income: tracts that saw an increase in income received $1,247 per capita, tracts that were stable between the two time periods received $844 per capita, and tracts that declined received $737 per capita. Improvement in low-income tracts usually only occurred through gentrification or emigration of low-income people, but in several instances the arrival of major industrial facilities resulted in an increase in income for the tract residents.[9]

In more general terms, the researchers concluded that the existence of an income mix among neighborhood residents and a healthy commercial district appeared to help development. Within the context of this review, these factors could signal the existence of a certain level of social control that would allow community programs to be effective. Neighborhoods without income diversity and a strong commercial center may not have enough social capital to take advantage of any community-based program.

WEED AND SEED

Perhaps the middle class moves out and commercial districts become dilapidated because of the decline in well-paid employment. People have moved; school quality has declined; other related businesses have closed; and crime, particularly drug dealing, may well have replaced manufacturing as a major source of income for young men. In fact several authors have attempted to link the rise of crack in inner city neighborhoods in the mid-1980s to the loss of manufacturing jobs (Currie 1993; Hagedorn 1988). Even if there is no relationship between the two, it is a case of very bad timing, since the development of crack cocaine markets in many of these urban areas exacerbated many of the problems first caused by the loss of jobs. Furthermore, the increase in incarceration due to the "war on drugs" contributes to the social problems by disrupting families and reducing the number of productive males in an area. In these communities, as many as one-fourth of the men are under active supervision of the criminal justice system (Freeman 1999).

The net effect of many years of decline is that these neighborhoods are not attractive places to locate businesses. Evidence from Bostic (1996) shows that places with high crime rates have the hardest time attracting employers. Perhaps as suggested by Stewart (1986) in his classic, *The Urban Strangler,* the problem of crime has to be addressed before businesses will invest in an area. This line of reasoning represents the basic premise of Operation Weed and Seed.

Operation Weed and Seed represents an ambitious federal, state, and local effort to improve the quality of life in targeted high crime zones in urban areas. Launched in 1991 by the Department of Justice, Weed and Seed programs can be found in over 200 sites nationwide, with an average funding level of about $225,000 per site. Key components of this strategy include (1) enhanced coordination among local actors to solve local problems, (2) "weeding" out criminals from target areas through concentrated efforts of local law enforcement, (3) proactive community policing intended to maintain a stable low crime equilibrium, and (4) "seeding" efforts consisting of human services provisions and a neighborhood revitalization effort to prevent and deter further crime.

A major national evaluation of Weed and Seed was released in 1999. This evaluation has a weak design, consisting of a before-and-after study of only eight Weed and Seed sites.[10] Weeding activity usually accounted for most of the funds, with increased special operations for targeted law enforcement. In general, local prosecutors' offices were not brought into the program, resulting in many arrests that were dismissed by the prosecutor or court. The Boston Gun Project has clearly demonstrated the value of including the prosecutor's office in any local law enforcement crackdown (Kennedy, Piehl, and Braga 1996). A wide array of youth programs, including job training, usually dominated the seeding activity, followed by neighborhood beautification programs. Adult employment and economic advancement programs only played a minor role in most sites. Seeding activity tended to be less well implemented relative to weeding and usually followed the weeding program sequentially, instead of occurring simultaneously. Weeding activities without seeding tended to alienate community residents. In terms of the desired outcomes, five of the eight sites had decreases in Index 1[11] offenses reported to the police four years after the implementation of Weed and Seed. These decreases exceeded the rates of decline in the cities as a whole. This comparison is not wholly satisfying, as the authors recognized, because of the differences between a small inner city neighborhood (the target area) and a large metropolitan area. It is noteworthy that the pattern of crime in the Weed and Seed site was consistently in the same direction as the observed pattern for the city as a whole, making it possible that the observed pattern is simply the result of citywide changes in crime rates.

Results of a neighborhood survey conducted at two-year intervals showed that in four sites many fewer residents perceived the neighborhood to be in decline, but only one site showed a decline in the victimization experiences of the respondents. In general, although there were no negative findings, the survey results showed little impact.[12]

A fair review of Weed and Seed based on this evaluation must conclude that there has been little sustained impact. This could be the result of many factors, including the relative paucity of the funding initiative, the lack of coordination of the Weed and Seed components, and the relative failure of the seeding initiatives. An amount of $225,000 per area may simply not be enough money to make a difference in such a large and structurally complex problem.

MOBILITY AND DISPERSION PROGRAMS

Perhaps government programs, at least politically feasible ones (that is, relatively inexpensive), cannot directly change the labor market in inner cities. An alternative approach is to transport the workers who live in these areas to jobs in a different physical location. This is the idea behind housing dispersal and mobility programs.

Policy makers have recently begun to develop ways to change the supply of labor by bringing inner city residents who want to work to suburban jobs, instead of bringing jobs to inner city residents. One way to do this is to physically relocate inner city residents to the suburbs (housing dispersal programs).

The first published outcome evaluation of the housing dispersal concept is based on what is known as the Gautreaux housing mobility program in Chicago. Starting in 1979, the Gautreaux program has given 6,000 inner city families (primarily single mothers) vouchers that allow them to relocate to low poverty neighborhoods throughout a six-county area in and around Chicago. The program, started as the result of a federal court ruling in a housing discrimination case, also allowed families to move within the city of Chicago. Families were assigned to the suburbs or the city based on the location of apartment openings when they became eligible for the program. Because the waiting list was long, and because families were placed at the back of the list if they rejected an opening, Rosenbaum (1992) claims that very few families rejected an apartment when it was offered, regardless of the location.

This created a type of natural experiment whereby the movers were roughly comparable with the nonmovers. Rosenbaum (1992) took advantage of this natural experiment to compare the employment and educational outcomes of the city movers with the suburban movers. It is not clear that a truly random sample of movers was located in each case, given that Rosenbaum was trying to locate movers several years after they had been given vouchers. Given that caveat, the women he located who moved to the suburbs were 28 percent more likely to be employed than the women he located who moved inside the city 5.5 years after moving, on average. This was true even though the wage gains attributed to the move were the same for all women who worked, regardless of their location. In addition, he found that nine years (on average) after the move, the children of the suburban movers were doing significantly better than the children of the city movers.[13] Although criminal activity was not measured, the children of the suburban movers dropped out of high school only 25 percent as often as the city movers, were in college track courses 1.6 times as often as the city movers, were 2.5 times as likely to attend college, were more than 4 times as likely to earn $6.50 an hour if working, and only 38 percent as likely to be unemployed. These results suggest that for children in these environments, relocation can be an effective tool to change their focus toward positive outcomes, such as meaningful employment.

These large positive results have encouraged policy makers to fund programs relocating poor families to nonpoverty areas. Several programs modeled on the Gautreaux program were spawned and now operate in Cincinnati, Memphis, Dallas, Milwaukee, and Hartford. In 1992, HUD provided $168 million to fund Moving to Opportunity (MTO) as a demonstration program for the housing mobility concept. MTO has sites in five large cities—Baltimore, Boston, Chicago, New York, and Los Angeles—and is funded for at least ten years. The project has been set up with a rigorous evaluation component. Households are randomly assigned to one of three groups—the treatment group, who are given a housing voucher which is only valid in places with less than 10 percent poverty along with extensive relocation counseling and assistance; a comparison group, who are given a voucher that is valid any place the tenant can find a suitable apartment; and a control group, who are allowed to remain in public housing in the central city.

Several evaluations of these programs are listed in Table 8.1. Perhaps not surprisingly, in each case, households assigned to the experimental treatment were less likely to move than the households assigned to the comparison group, suggesting that moving to low poverty neighborhoods is a nontrivial exercise for impoverished single-parent households. The Katz, Kling, and Liebman (1999) study of the Boston experiment found that the families who were assigned to move to low poverty neighborhoods had better life outcomes than the control groups and the unrestricted movers, despite the fact that less than half of the assigned households actually moved. In general, the mothers had significant improvements in their mental health, feelings of safety, and victimization relative to the control group. The boys in the sample had a 10–15 percent reduction in their problem behavior relative to the boys in the control group.

Ludwig et al. (1999, 2000) evaluate the MTO experiment in Baltimore. Once again, only half of the experimental households actually take advantage of the vouchers to move. They find that, three years after moving, the mothers in the experimental settings were 9.2 percent less likely to be on welfare than the control groups. Children in the treatment and comparison groups were both less likely to be arrested for violent

Table 8.1
Moving to Opportunity

STUDIES	DESCRIPTION OF INTERVENTION AND FINDINGS
Ludwig, Duncan, and Pinkston 2000, MTO – Baltimore	Eligible families with children who resided in public housing were randomly assigned to a control group or one of two treatment groups: The experimental group received housing subsidies valid only in low poverty areas; the comparison group received unrestricted housing subsidies. Experimental treatment relative to controls had a 6.7% decrease in welfare receipt the first year post program (9.2% decrease three years post program) and a 5.6% increase in welfare-to-work exits. A smaller decrease was found for comparisons relative to controls.
Katz, Kling, and Liebman 1999, MTO – Boston	Experimental treatment relative to controls had a 10.6–15.0% reduction in problem behavior in boys; a 6.5% reduction in criminal victimization; and similar improvements in feelings of safety, child's physical health, and adult's mental health. Smaller changes were found for comparisons.
Ludwig, Duncan, and Hirschfield 1999, MTO – Baltimore	Treatment families that relocated had children at higher risk for criminal involvement. Experimental treatment relative to controls had a 7% decrease in violent crime arrests (a 10% decrease for comparisons relative to controls) in first year post program, but property crime arrests increased 8% for experimental youths. No change was found among comparisons.

NOTE: MTO = Moving to Opportunity.
SOURCE: Authors.

crimes than the children in the control groups. Contrary to predictions, members of the treatment group had higher arrest rates than the comparison group. In addition, children in both groups had more arrests for property offenses than the control group, perhaps because of the increased opportunity.

The authors warn against making too much of these early results, but it would appear safe to conclude that moving to lower poverty areas does have the potential to at least marginally help poor urban women and their children isolated in inner city public housing communities. It is also important to note that housing dispersal programs have met significant opposition from suburban residents afraid of the impact of poor minority families on their communities. For example, the expansion of MTO to include more than 1,300 families was defeated after it became a political issue in the 1994 election. The Mount Laurel decision in New Jersey, a two-decade-old, court-enforced dispersal strategy, is now being undermined by legislators. In addition, minorities sometimes voice a concern that the dispersal of minorities to the suburbs will weaken minority political power (Hughes 1993). According to Kale Williams, former director of the Gautreaux program in Chicago, part of the success of Gautreaux was because "it hasn't been large enough to threaten anyone and hasn't been concentrated enough to arouse apprehension." Given these problems, it seems politically unlikely that housing mobility programs will ever include a large fraction of the residents of poor, inner city neighborhoods.[14]

This reality, however frustrating, suggests that perhaps a strategy aimed at integrating workplaces instead of neighborhoods might be easier to implement. Using this logic, a useful approach to the problem of inner city poverty is mobility programs that provide transportation for inner city residents to the suburbs (Hughes 1993). Such a program recognizes and takes advantage of the power of the suburban labor markets to increase residents' incomes while avoiding the political problems associated with housing dispersal. This idea is relatively new and, as a result, only a small number of programs are in operation in the United States.[15]

HUD funded a $70 million dollar demonstration program in five sites that started providing housing in 1994, and stopped providing new housing assistance in 1999. By 1999, 3,170 families had been offered Section 8 housing certificates under the program, and a total of 1,650 families had obtained new housing under the program. The strategy has three main components: a metropolitan-wide job placement service to connect inner city residents with suburban jobs, a targeted commute mechanism to provide transportation to the jobs, and a support services mechanism to try to ameliorate some of the problems that may result from a long-distance commute into a primarily white suburban location. Rigorous evaluation with random assignment is currently being undertaken by Public/Private Ventures. Midstream process evaluations (all that are available now) suggest that implementation and operation of this type of program is difficult, particularly in tight labor markets. Tight labor markets mean that motivated workers can find decent jobs close to where they live on their own. The remaining workers often need serious training and skill development. As a result, these reverse commuting programs are spending time and resources on both worker training and job development. In other words, these programs are reaching the conclusion that the problem is not one of demand for labor, but rather the supply of labor. In the next section, we will begin a discussion of the relationship between labor supply and crime.

In summary, no program aimed at boosting the demand for labor in high crime communities—whether focused on increasing investment in those areas or on giving opportunities for residents of those communities to find jobs elsewhere—has a record of strong positive findings. Thus they are unlikely to reduce crime in these areas. To be fair, these programs are difficult to evaluate because of their community focus and the multitude of interventions typically implemented simultaneously. In addition, the United States has not yet tried the truly massive infusion of funds suggested by Wilson (1996).[16] The only programs with a positive record of success are housing dispersal programs—which do nothing positive for the environment (as opposed to the people) that is the focus of this chapter. This approach is not likely to be politically feasible on a large scale. We will provide our interpretation of this finding at the end of the chapter.

SUPPLY-SIDE PROGRAMS

Fairly strong evidence indicates that an individual's criminal behavior is responsive to changes in his or her employment status, independent of what is occurring with the demand for labor at a macro level. Sampson and Laub (1993) used data from the Gluecks' 1939 Boston cohort to show that job instability from age seventeen to age twenty-five was correlated with higher arrest rates from age twenty-five to age thirty-two, even after controls for stable individual differences were included in the model. Thornberry and Christenson (1984) found unemployment positively correlated with more arrests, especially for minority youths in Wolfgang's 1945 Philadelphia cohort. Farrington et al. (1986) used data from the Cambridge Study of Delinquent Development to show that the probability of conviction for property crime increased when an individual was unemployed, provided that the individual was predisposed to criminal behavior. Needels (1996) used data from a ten-year follow-up of ex-offenders in Georgia to show that crime and wages were negatively related. Finally, Uggen and Thompson (1999) showed that legal earnings have a negative effect on illegal earnings using data from a contemporary sample of Minnesota youth.

These results suggest that individuals participate in crime at least partially as a response to their labor market experiences. The flip side is therefore also possible—individuals' legal labor market participation is influenced by their criminal activities.[17] Many neighborhoods in the inner city have significant drug activity; and although self-reports on illegal income are hard to verify, there is some evidence to suggest that these illegitimate opportunities can be a significant source of income. For example, Viscusi (1986) found that average annual crime income for inner city black youth was $1,607 in 1980, roughly 25 percent of what they made on average from legal jobs.

Reuter, MacCoun, and Murphy (1990) interviewed convicted drug dealers in Washington, D.C., during the mid-1980s and found that the hourly rate for drug dealing was $30. Although drug dealers deal relatively few hours, this compared with the $7 per hour median legal earnings in the same sample. The median annual earnings from dealing was approximately $10,000. This was substantially more than what someone could earn working forty hours a week for a year at a minimum wage job ($6,968 before taxes). In a review of these studies, Freeman (1999) concludes that, with one exception (Wilson and Abrahamse 1992), all studies over the previous twenty years concluded that crime (especially drug dealing) pays more on an hourly basis than legal work. This conclusion is certainly consistent with the high numbers of young men who have been arrested for drug dealing in some communities. For example, Reuter, MacCoun, and Murphy (1990) estimate that an astonishing 33 percent of black males born in 1967 in Washington, D.C., had been arrested for drug selling between the ages of eighteen and twenty-one.

Reuter, MacCoun, and Murphy (1990) also report that a substantial proportion of the youth arrested for drug selling have legal jobs as well. This runs counter to the conventional wisdom that an individual supplies labor either to the legal labor market or the illegal labor market. Clearly, many persons supply labor to both. However, involvement in crime may affect performance in legitimate jobs. Even if there were no other deleterious effects from crime, involvement in the criminal justice system (court dates and such) interferes with working in the legal labor market.

In addition, labeling theory (Lemert 1951; Sampson and Laub 1993) predicts that employers are less likely to hire ex-offenders because of their ex-offender status, which could lead to increased crime as individuals— shut out from legitimate activity—form a criminal identity. Substantial empirical evidence now demonstrates that there is in fact a stigma attached to a criminal history record in the legal labor market. Bushway (1996) showed that arrests for minor offenses could lead to instability for the offender in the job market. Fagan and Freeman (1999) showed that men who have been incarcerated have a lower rate of employment than they did before they were incarcerated. Kling (2000) used official record information on federal prisoners in California to show that there are only minor effects on employment, but substantial impact on earnings (about 30 percent lower) among a seriously disadvantaged sample. Grogger (1995) estimated that one-third of the racial difference in employment can be attributed to the effect of arrest and incarceration on subsequent employment. Holzer (1996) showed that those firms willing to hire ex-offenders tend to offer lower wages and fewer benefits.

Even if employers did not tend to shy away from ex-offenders, long-term involvement in criminal activity, especially if started at an early age, may mean that an individual becomes "embedded" in criminality (Hagan 1993). Thornberry (1987) describes the process as follows:

> [A] behavioral trajectory is established that predicts increasing involvement in delinquency and crime. The initially weak bonds lead to high delinquency involvement, the high delinquency involvement further weakens the conventional bonds (represented, during adolescence, by attachment to parents, commitment to school, and belief in conventional values), and in combination both of these effects make it extremely difficult to reestablish bonds to conventional society at later ages. (p. 883)

Legal employment and marriage are the two most prominent ties to conventional society for adults. We know that most incarcerated individuals have extremely low levels of educational achievement and very limited job skills. According to the U.S. Bureau of Justice Statistics, only 59 percent of state prison inmates had a high school diploma or its equivalent (compared to 85 percent for the adult population as a whole), and only two-thirds of inmates were employed during the month before they were arrested for their current offense. This process of criminal embeddedness could be heightened and accelerated for people in some communities as the result of the permanent loss of jobs discussed in the previous labor demand section.

The observation that many at-risk individuals lack basic job skills prompted interest in the early 1960s in assessing whether recidivism might be reduced by providing at-risk individuals with additional educational and job skills. Numerous programs have been developed to provide basic education, vocational training, and work experience for youths in high crime and high unemployment communities. The Training and Employment Services division of the Employment and Training Administration of the Department of Labor spends large sums ($5.5 billion in FY 2000[18]) on skills-developing programs aimed at increasing the employment prospects of individuals who are at high risk of being persistently unemployed. Most of these interventions target youths, particularly adolescents, on the reasonable (but not unassailable) assumption that early interventions have higher payoff if successful. Another large set of interventions, funded separately by the various components of the criminal justice system, targets those already involved with the criminal justice system.

Job Training and Education Programs for At-Risk Youth

Programs aimed at youths mostly fall into one of three categories, arrayed below in order of increasing expense and program intensity.

1. The provision of summer work or other forms of subsidized employment in either public or private sector organizations.[19] These programs typically cost about $1,000 (in terms of 1995 dollars) per participant and last about three months for the individual. The Summer Youth Employment and Training Program (SYETP) is the Department of Labor's current summer jobs program, providing minimum wage summer jobs and some education to hundreds of thousands of disadvantaged youths, aged fourteen to twenty-one. Less typical is the more intense Supported Work program from the late 1970s, which provided about one year of full-time public sector employment to minority high school dropouts aged seventeen to twenty with job search assistance at the end of the work period.

2. Short-term training with job placement for out-of-school youth. These programs typically last about six months and cost $2,500 to $5,000 per participant. For example, the federal government's principal program for disadvantaged youth, the Job Training Partnership Act (JTPA) program, enrolled 125,000 out-of-school youth aged sixteen to twenty-one for five months, during which they received on-the-job training, classroom training, and job search assistance. JOBSTART was a large-scale demonstration program, designed as a more intensive version of JTPA, lasting seven months and including more classroom training at a cost of $5,000 per participant.

3. Long-term, intensive residential programs providing vocational and life skills training, general education, and job placement after graduation. The most prominent of these programs is Job Corps, a residential program aimed at extremely disadvantaged populations. In 1999, Job Corps received $1.3 billion and enrolled 60,000 new youth in tailored, one-year programs that included classroom training in basic education and vocational skills, and a wide range of supportive services (including health care), at a cost of roughly $15,000 per student.

Table 8.2 provides a summary of these results. Very few evaluations of these programs measure change in criminal behavior, simply because crime prevention is not generally a primary explicit objective and its measurement requires substantial and complex additional data collection.[20] Crime control is a secondary effect which may result from increased employment, the primary objective.

Subsidized work programs are the cheapest and least intensive of any of the training programs targeted to at-risk youth. Although all subsidized work programs show a marked increase in employment for the targeted population over the time period of the subsidy, no evaluation has shown any long-term effect on employment (for example, Piliavin and Masters 1981). The evaluators point to the failure of most participants to complete the program as one of the sources of error in the study. Overall, the conclusions from this literature seem robust—subsidized work does not increase productivity in any appreciable way and these types of jobs do not appear to be supportive of noncriminal behavior.[21]

The picture is only slightly less gloomy for short-term skills training programs. None of the rigorous evaluations in this category have shown any lasting impact on employment outcomes, although some of the programs show a short-term gain in earnings. It is again not surprising then that the one evaluation that looked at crime shows no lasting impact (JOBSTART). These programs are generally unable to increase productivity in any meaningful way within the constraints of a short-term nonintensive program.

Table 8.2
Noncriminal Justice System: At-Risk Youth

AUTHOR AND PROGRAM	DESCRIPTION OF INTERVENTION AND FINDINGS
Ahlstrom & Havighurst 1982, Kansas City Work / Study	Combines work experience program with a modified academic program. There appeared to be a negative effect on arrest, as the experimental group was more likely to be arrested by the age of 16 than was the comparison group (51% versus 36%).
Cave & Quint 1990, Career Beginnings	Services of Career Beginnings include summer jobs, workshops and classes, counseling, and the use of mentors lasting from the junior year of high school through graduation. Experimentals were 9.7% more likely to attend college than controls (statistically significant); they therefore worked less and earned less.
Farkas et al. 1982, YIEPP	The program guaranteed full-time summer jobs and part-time school year jobs to disadvantaged youth who stayed in school. School year employment doubled from 20% to 40%, while summer employment increased from about 35% to 45%; however, YIEPP was unable to attain its goals of increased school enrollment and success despite the school enrollment requirement.
Grossman & Sipe 1992, STEP	The program, lasting 15 months, involves remediation, life skills, summer jobs over two years, and school year support. STEP had little or no impact on youth's educational experience and had not altered employment patterns for either in-school or out-of-school youth.
Maynard 1980, Supported Work	Structured transitional employment program which offers limited term employment at relatively low wage rates for up to 12 or 18 months, combined with peer group support and close supervision. Up to 18 months post program, there was a significantly larger percentage of treatment group youth employed; there was no significant impact on arrest rate of youths.
Summer Youth Employment and Training Program (SYETP)	This program provides summer jobs for youth. It appears to greatly increase summer employment rates among disadvantaged youth in sites where jobs are provided. No investigation has been done to see whether or not SYETP creates positive long-term impacts on employment after participants leave their summer jobs.

Table 8.2
Noncriminal Justice System: At-Risk Youth (Cont.)

Short-term	Description of intervention and findings
Kemple and Snipes 2000, Career Academy (CA)	Academic and career-related high school (HS) courses provided students with work-based learning experiences. CAs produced little change in outcomes for students at low or medium risk of HS dropout. For students at high risk of HS dropout, CA was associated with a 33.9% lower rate of school dropout, a 36.6% lower rate of arrest, and higher rates of school performance and attendance.
Fogg and Sum 1999, Youth Opportunity Areas (YOAs)	YOAs targeted out-of-school youths in high poverty neighborhoods for education, employment, and training programs. Pre / post comparison found a 6.3% increase in labor force participation, a 6.9% decrease in unemployment, and similar increases in weekly hours of employment and wages. There was also a 9.2–21.0% decrease in high school dropout, a 7.0–63.1% increase in high school graduation, and a similar increase in postsecondary education. No significance testing was reported.
Needels, Dynarski, and Corson 1998, Youth Fair Chance (YFC)	YFC provided one-stop employment and education services to persons living in high poverty areas. Youths in YFC areas relative to youths in non-YFC areas had an increase in employment (12.5% vs. –1.8%) but a decrease in school enrollment. No differences for rates of public assistance, substance abuse, criminal or gang involvement, or single parenthood were found.
Bloom et al. 1994, JTPA	JTPA is the federal government's major training program for disadvantaged youth, which provides an average of 5 months of services including on-the-job training, classroom training, and job search assistance (an average of 420 hrs. of service). After 30 months no increase in earnings was found, and there was no decrease in crime rates.
Hahn, Leavitt, and Aaron 1994, Quantum Opportunities Program (QOP)	QOP offered disadvantaged high school students mentoring combined with financial incentives. QOP youths, relative to control youths, were 53.8% less likely to be in trouble with police, less likely to need help with a substance abuse problem, and 54% less likely to be HS dropouts. QOP youths were also more highly involved in school and volunteer activities, and were more optimistic about the future.

Table 8.2
Noncriminal Justice System: At-Risk Youth (Cont.)

SHORT-TERM (CONT.)	DESCRIPTION OF INTERVENTION AND FINDINGS
Cave et al. 1993, JOBSTART	JOBSTART provides instruction in basic academic skills, occupational skills training, training-related support services, and job placement assistance. JOBSTART led to a significant increase in the rate of GED attainment, or completion of high school. In the final two years of the follow-up, experimentals' earnings appeared to overtake those of controls, but the magnitude of this impact was not significant.
Wolf et al. 1982, 70001 Ltd.	This program provides job search assistance, educational services, and job preparation classes to high school dropouts (an average of 80–90 hrs. of services are given). On long-term follow-up (24–40 months.), there were no significant earnings impacts reported; however, there was significant positive impact on GED attainment.
INTENSIVE	
Mallar et al. 1982, Job Corps	This residential program provides intensive skills training, basic education, support services, and job placement for one year. The average over the first five years after program exit was a 15% earnings increase and a 15% reduction in serious (felony) crime. Also, a large and significant increase in GED attainment and college enrollment was found.
Schochet, Burghardt, and Glazerman 2000, Job Corps (JC)	Experimental evaluation was done on average 22 months after enrollment. JC youths, relative to non-JC youths, had a 16% lower rate of arrest or being charged with a criminal complaint and a 21% lower rate of conviction. JC youths were more likely to receive a GED or high school diploma and to be employed at 30 months post-assignment, but were no more likely to attend college. There was an 8% increase in earnings by the end of the follow-up period.
Wolf, Leiderman, and Voith 1987, California Conservation Corps (CCC)	CCC combines work sponsored by various public resource agencies with youth development activities for up to one year. CCC is not an effective way of raising the earnings of all participants when they first enter the labor market; however, it did improve earnings of disadvantaged residential corps members and significantly increased their hours worked, post program.

NOTES: JTPA = Job Training Partnership Act; STEP = Specialized Training and Employment Project; YIEPP = Youth Incentive Entitlement Pilot Project.
SOURCE: Authors.

The most rigorously evaluated program, and one of the longest lasting, is Job Corps, a long-term, primarily residential training program with emphasis on academic and vocational credentials. The residential component is seen as a key component of the program because it provides people who are drawn from very disordered environments with the experience of living in a structured community committed to learning. The idea is that this environment is what makes the vocational and educational components actually work. The nonresidential programs are seen as a way to reach individuals—primarily women with children—who would otherwise not be able to take advantage of Job Corps. Job Corps is by far the most intensive and expensive nonmilitary training sponsored by the federal government. The high cost is a consequence of the residential element of the program and its severely disadvantaged population (over 80 percent are high school dropouts).

Two major evaluations of Job Corps have been done, one in 1982 (Mallar et al. 1982) and one in 2000 (Schochet, Burghardt, and Glazerman 2000). The earlier, nonexperimental evaluation found that four years after graduating from Job Corps enrollees earned on average $1,300 more per year than the control group, a difference of 15 percent. These achievements corresponded with real increases in educational achievement. Enrollees were five times as likely to get a GED or finish high school, and twice as likely to go to college. Also, arrests for serious crimes, especially theft, declined significantly. However, there was also an unexplained increase in minor arrests, especially traffic incidents.

The 2000 evaluation (Schochet, Burghardt, and Glazerman 2000) was a large experiment involving random assignment based on all 80,883 applicants who applied to Job Corps between November 1994 and February 1996.[22] As in many of the more structured programs, many people did not complete the program—over 50 percent of the study group either did not start the program or lasted less than three months. The average participant enrolled for eight months and received roughly one additional school year of education, including vocational training. The participants were 70 percent more likely to receive a GED or high school degree, and more than twice as likely to have vocational certification than nonparticipants. In contrast to the earlier evaluation, Job Corps participants were found to be no more likely to attend college.

Employment is more difficult to evaluate, since participants were less likely than nonparticipants to work during their participation in Job Corps. As a result, it takes the Job Corps workers some time to "catch up" to peers who could have been working the entire time period. It appears that this finally occurred in the last four months of the study. Job Corps participants were only 3 percent more likely to be working than nonparticipants, but the weekly wages of Job Corps participants were 8 percent higher than the control group. This is comparable to the academic estimates of a 5–8 percent increase in wages for every additional year of schooling. It remains to be seen if these gains are stable over a longer period of time.

In the thirty-month follow-up period, 23.3 percent of the treatment group were arrested compared to 27.7 percent of the control group, a difference of 15.9 percent. The treatment group was also 17 percent less likely to be convicted. As in the 1982 study, the biggest difference occurs during the first-year follow-up, when the treatment group is enrolled in Job Corps. Because Job Corps is a highly structured program that is usually residential, this finding is not surprising. It is tempting to dismiss this finding as the result of "incapacitation" rather than real behavioral change.[23] However, if, as suggested above, involvement in the criminal justice system leads to future problems through labeling, this small difference could be meaningful for later outcomes. Furthermore, unlike in the 1982 study, it is also true that there is a 17 percent difference in arrests during the last six months of the thirty-month follow-up, when virtually all applicants have graduated from Job Corps. This result is at least suggestive of a true impact of this program on criminality. The 2000 study also replicates the finding from the 1982 study that Job Corps participants who do commit crimes tend to be involved in less serious events than the nonparticipants who commit crimes.

The link between employment gains and crime reductions is an encouraging sign that real progress is being measured. However, there was little meaningful difference between participants and nonparticipants in lifestyle issues like drug use, family formation, and place of residence. This finding raises some doubt about the lasting impact of this program since lower drug use, movement out of disadvantaged neighborhoods, and better family relationships are thought to be highly correlated with long-term declines in criminality. We will return to some of the potential lessons from Job Corps in the conclusion.

Mentoring is another way of increasing both youth skills and workforce attachment. The strongest positive evaluation for a mentoring program is for the Quantum Opportunities Program (QOP), a demonstration program offering extensive academic assistance, adult mentoring, career and college guidance, a small stipend, and money set aside for a college fund. The rigorous evaluation of 100 students in four sites found that

42 percent of the QOP students were in post-secondary education versus only 16 percent of the controls; a total of 63 percent of the QOP students graduated from high school, versus only 42 percent of the control group (U.S. Department of Labor 1995). Unfortunately, there was no evaluation of criminal activity. Adult mentors were assessed to be the most important element. Apparently, the mentors provide the necessary focus and motivation for students to change their behavior and perform better in school.

JOB TRAINING PROGRAMS CONNECTED TO THE CRIMINAL JUSTICE SYSTEM

Targeting human capital development programs at offenders while in, or just leaving, the criminal justice system has the merit of focusing resources on the highest risk group. It is a human services equivalent of Willie Sutton's famous line about the banks; in this case, we are going where the crime is. Like Sutton's strategy, it also has an obvious weakness; just as banks are well guarded, so offenders in the criminal justice system have already developed behavior patterns that are difficult to reverse with educational programs.

Secondary reviews from the early 1970s, after these programs had been around for roughly ten years, were uniformly negative. The Department of Labor's Manpower Administration sponsored research on these vocational programs in prisons, and provided a comprehensive review of the research in 1973 (Rovner-Pieczenik 1973). Despite strong commitment and great enthusiasm by program operators, the study reluctantly reported that very few programs led to a substantial decline in recidivism. By way of explanation, the report highlighted problems in persuading correctional institutions to focus on education and post-release objectives. The report also highlighted the great educational deficits of the offenders, generally high school dropouts reading several years below grade level with no discernible job skills. The author concluded, "[W]e entertain no fantasies about the degree of change which manpower projects for the offender can help to bring about. Some offenders will remain unemployed and unemployable no matter what programs are available" (Rovner-Pieczenik 1973, 77).

These disappointing conclusions were communicated to a much broader audience with Martinson's (1974) widely read review of 231 rehabilitative (including employment-based) programs. Martinson concluded that "with few and isolated exceptions the rehabilitative efforts that have been reported so far have had no appreciable effect on recidivism" (p. 25). This report has often been held responsible for the decline of the rehabilitative model in corrections and has limited the research done on these programs.

The sheer numbers of offenders, however, have led correctional officials to continue their efforts to curtail recidivism by attempting to reintegrate ex-offenders into the workforce. Evaluators have also continued their efforts to identify the causal impact of these programs on recidivism. In this section, we rely on a recent comprehensive review / meta-analysis of fifty-three experimental or quasi-experimental treatment-control comparisons based on thirty-three evaluations of prison education, vocation, and work programs by Wilson, Gallagher, and MacKenzie (In press). This list includes nineteen studies conducted during the 1990s.

Wilson and colleagues (In press) report that most of the evaluations find that participants in the treatment programs are less likely to recidivate than those who do not participate in a treatment program. The average effect is substantial. If we assume that the nonparticipants have a recidivism rate of 50 percent, the program participants have a recidivism rate of 39 percent, a reduction of more than 20 percent. Moreover, the studies that include a measure of employment find that program participants are substantially more likely to be employed than nonparticipants. Finally, the programs with the largest employment effect tend to also have the largest reduction in recidivism, validating in some sense the mechanism by which these types of programs are thought to reduce recidivism.

Wilson and colleagues (In press), however, include a strong caveat to these findings that is consistent with our earlier report (Bushway and Reuter 1997). These results are based on studies that are methodologically extremely weak. What this means in practice is that there are very poor controls for preexisting differences between program participants and nonparticipants. Unobserved differences in motivation (or other factors) could account for much of the resulting change in behavior attributed to the training programs. Only three studies used an experimental design and only one of the nonexperimental studies (Saylor and Gaes 1996) used what Wilson et al. considered to be strong statistical controls for selection bias between the participants and nonparticipants. Clearly, even the best of these evaluations has limited scope and serious methodological limitations. As noted by Wilson et al., it would be foolhardy to conclude on this type of limited evidence that vocational programs for incarcerated offenders work. The only reasonable conclusion is a two-fold statement that (1) it is possible that vocational programs aimed at inmates can reduce recidivism, and (2) rigorous evaluations of existing programs need to be implemented to verify that these programs increase employment and reduce recidivism.

The evaluations of these programs also show serious implementation and participation problems that are even larger, not surprisingly, than for programs outside of the criminal justice system. Attrition among staff and prisoners alike is a significant impediment both to program implementation and to adequate evaluation.

Given that the prison environment is at least part of the problem, it seems reasonable to provide work-based assistance to ex-offenders upon their exit from prison, when the need to transition to a life of noncrime becomes a reality. A large number of transitional assistance programs are, in fact, available in almost every state for ex-offenders after they leave prison. These programs tend to give some combination of the following services: (1) job search assistance, (2) remedial education, (3) occupational skills, (4) work experience, (5) on-the-job training, or (6) customized training for a particular employer. The National Institute of Justice website lists at least three different recent publications profiling programs at the state level that attempt to reintegrate offenders back into society through some type of work program. However, as in the case of in-prison training, there has been very little rigorous evaluation. Descriptions of what happens within these programs are provided, but it is impossible to assess what would have happened if the program had not been available.

One exception is an evaluation of ex-offender participation in the federal Job Training Partnership Act (JTPA) program by Finn and Willoughby (1996). They looked at all 521 ex-prisoners who enrolled in JTPA training programs in the state of Georgia for one year starting in July 1989. These enrollees were compared to 734 nonoffender JTPA participants. The researchers found no sign of any difference in employment outcomes for the two groups, either at program termination or fourteen weeks after termination. This result is hard to interpret. Other studies have shown a consistent difference between ex-offenders and other workers. Perhaps the finding of no difference indicates that JTPA programs have helped eliminate some of the stigma of offending. However, since JTPA programs are generally regarded as only minimally effective at improving employment outcomes, that conclusion is hypothetical at best. No existing evidence uniformly supports work-based transitional programs, but rigorous evaluations of any of the current breed of programs might provide support for this approach.

One exception to this blanket conclusion is the finding that transitional programs apparently have an impact for older ex-offenders. A recent review of the Supported Work experiments from the 1970s (Uggen 2000) built upon the initial report (Piliavan and Masters 1981) to show that the programs had significant and substantial work and crime effects for male ex-offenders over the age of twenty-six. Older subjects in the Baltimore Life experiment also recidivated less often relative to their controls than did younger subjects. The authors of the Supported Work program review conclude, "[T]he evidence in this experiment and elsewhere suggests older disadvantaged workers, including those who are known offenders, may be much more responsive (than younger workers) to the opportunity to participate in employment programs" (Piliavan and Masters 1981, p. 45).

This result makes sense to us in terms of the motivation of the offenders. The growing literature on desistance from crime emphasizes that the first step in the process involves some type of personal change in motivation away from crime and toward more prosocial goals (Fagan 1989; Maruna 2001; Shover 1996). After this change has occurred, outside forces such as relationships or work can help the individual maintain this change in orientation.

Mother Nature has her own way of changing motivation: aging. It is possible that the same individuals who are not reachable as at-risk youth may be reachable by similar programs when they have reached adulthood. These older adults may have a reduced propensity to commit crime due to maturation. As a result, the number of crimes prevented by such a program might be less than for younger participants, but at the same time these individuals may be finally ready to take advantage of training programs that are offered. In reviewing the extensive literature on job training for the general population, Heckman (1994, p. 112) concludes the following:

> Employment and training programs increase the earnings of female AFDC recipients. Earnings gains are (a) modest, (b) persistent over several years, (c) arise from several different treatments, (d) are sometimes quite cost-effective. . . . For adult males the evidence is consistent with that for adult women.

We conclude, based on this evidence, that modest but meaningful gains can be had for motivated individuals, including motivated ex-offenders.

It is hard to over-emphasize the importance that evaluators place on the individual motivation when they discuss the success and failure of work-related programs. It is also hard to overstate how difficult it is to deal with the motivation of these individuals in these programs. The high dropout rates for these programs can be tied directly to the lack of a work orientation on the part of the clients. Youths are likely to be less work oriented than the average adult. As a result, in the same review, Heckman

(1994) concludes that no program has been shown to be effective at increasing the earnings of youth. Job Corps, which according to the recent evaluation may be an exception to this conclusion, might succeed because its focus is not just on job skills but on changing the personal orientation of the participants. This is a much more difficult task than simply increasing someone's human capital. We will discuss this problem further in the conclusion.

CONCLUSION

Our review of the labor demand problem began with the observation that cyclical changes in unemployment cannot explain the concentration of crime found in depressed urban areas. Yet permanent job loss, especially of well-paid, low-skill jobs, may in fact be responsible for a great deal of the social problems and the high crime rates in these communities. It is possible, therefore, that job creation programs such as enterprise zones, or economic development programs such as Community Development Block Grants, may be able to change the levels of crime found in these communities. Yet our review shows that none of the current set of evaluations has shown a sustained impact. While leaving hope that more expensive and extensive programs such as the Federal Empowerment Zone programs will have an impact, the current conclusion must be that economic development in these high poverty areas is a very difficult proposition.

Although there is little argument that the lack of labor market demand has worsened many of the problems in these communities, a cycle of decline has been set in motion by job loss that has led to a situation that jobs by themselves will not solve. The problems are no longer just economic, but social, and therefore require solutions that deal with social problems such as alcoholism, lack of family cohesion, welfare dependency, lack of community leadership, and other elements of what is sometimes referred to as social capital. While a healthy business area would help generate some of this social capital, employers are unwilling, and perhaps even unable, to locate in places with the levels of social disorganization found in the high crime, impoverished neighborhoods that are the focus of this chapter. Job creation appears to work best in communities that have some structure and leadership that can encourage and then capitalize on the economic engine represented by jobs. Moreover, a study of reverse commuting programs designed to bring people to jobs has found that at least in the boom of the late 1990s the problem is not lack of jobs but rather the lack of prepared individuals.

Our review of programs aimed at increasing the skills of the labor supply follow the same pattern as our review of labor demand. Ample empirical evidence suggests a link between individual employment and crime. As a result, there is reason to believe that job-training programs should help increase employment of individuals at risk of becoming or remaining involved in crime. Yet, the overwhelming evidence from thirty years and billions of dollars of government spending is that it is very difficult to change an individual's employment status and earnings level (and therefore their crime participation), especially for those individuals most embedded in criminal activity. We believe the primary reason is that they themselves need to be motivated to work before things like job skills can make a difference; although unemployment may have contributed to their criminal activity, a job opportunity (and job skill training) by itself does not solve the problem. Instead, the policy focus must be on shifting the orientation of the individual away from crime and back toward legitimate employment. This may be especially difficult if the individual has developed alcohol and drug dependencies while involved with crime, or if illegitimate activities such as drug dealing remain lucrative. The only completely convincing mechanism that has been identified to change motivation is age (Uggen 2000).

Very intense, expensive residential programs such as Job Corps may also be effective. Mentoring programs also focus directly on giving youth in particular alternative, positive role models on which to shape their lives. As in Job Corps, mentoring programs provide routine contact with adults who project a positive attitude about legitimate activities. It is impossible within the context of the current literature to determine if mentoring is better able to change the motivation of the at-risk youth than a program that involves some type of work training. However, it is clear that creating a focus on obtaining meaningful and productive employment as an important goal is necessary before youth will / can take advantage of job training or schooling.

We believe that the problem of individual detachment is inextricably linked to the problem of poor social structure identified in the labor supply section. In one particularly insightful process evaluation, counselors in a four-month-long job-training program for offenders concluded that they could not change the attitude of offenders toward work in four months, *especially since participants typically lived in criminogenic environments removed from the world of work* (Hillsman 1982). In other words, an individual's lack of work orientation can be directly tied to the social problems of their neighborhoods. The net result is that job programs, whether they are focused on supply or demand, may not be the cure-all that policy makers hope them to be. This is unfortunate, since increased employment as a policy goal creates little opposition. Everyone can agree that employment is good. Other policy "levers" based on criminological evidence are not as value free or easy to implement.[24]

But, based on our review of the literature, we feel safe concluding that the problems of individuals and communities are not solely economic. As a result, programs, even programs with an economic intent such as employment training, need to address social and psychological issues confronting the communities and individuals they are intended to help.

Yet any program is working against a powerful force, the pull of peer pressure and community norms. Criminological research has identified no more powerful element correlated contemporaneously with crime than the actions of one's peers (for example, Warr 1993). Although the causal meaning of that correlation is unclear, it is undeniable that the actions of people in these neighborhoods constrain and influence the actions of other individuals. As a result, detaching one individual from that community and attaching them to the legal world of work means that the policy maker must work against powerful social and psychological forces.

Of course, it might be possible to reorient these forces by focusing not on reattaching one individual to the world of legitimate work, but on reattaching an entire community. But implementation of programs at the community level is difficult by definition. The program that best reflects this goal of reattaching a community, Weed and Seed, has had difficulty implementing the seed (which includes job training) part of the program systematically. Detaching a community from crime without providing alternatives is unlikely to be effective, and will probably antagonize local residents.

One reason that implementing programs at the community level is more difficult than implementing programs for individuals is simply scale. It is usually easier to effect change with one person rather than with 1,000 people. But we do not believe that the problem is just one of scale. It is also possible that, at the community level, the process is not linear. In other words, one cannot expect to reconnect people to legal work one at a time until the majority of people in the community are focused on work rather than on crime or other enterprise. Perhaps, instead, it is necessary to create a large-scale change before any people are willing to tackle the types of changes these types of programs will inevitably inspire. This problem is a natural result of the type of neighborhood effects discussed earlier. Since what your neighbors do matters, policy makers might need to get substantial numbers of people moving together, in order to allow them to support one another. This conclusion is the basis for the U.S. Department of Labor (1995, 63) recommendation that poor neighborhoods should be saturated with a range of interventions intended to alleviate poverty so that "the employment outcomes of some person within a community can lead to 'spillover effects' as other people in the neighborhood are influenced by the positive actions of their peers."

Youth Opportunity Act is the Department of Labor's response to that charge. The goal is to saturate low-income, high crime communities with educational, employment, and training programs aimed at sixteen- to twenty-four-year-old out-of-school youth. The level of funding is impressive ($250 million a year targeted at forty-two sites). For the first time ever, community-level outcomes will be studied along with individual-level outcomes, formally recognizing the link between individual-level and community-level outcomes. Results from a three-site pilot study started in 1996 are cautiously optimistic. An audit of the process at the three pilot sites, however, showed once again that implementing intensive programs in highly disadvantaged areas can be a very difficult process, a lesson learned earlier in the Community Development Block Grant Program and Weed and Seed (Office of Inspector General 2000).

It may not be strictly necessary to create programs specifically focused on these communities to have an impact. Perhaps no policy innovation in recent times has attracted such intense analytic interest as the effort to fundamentally alter the longstanding basic federal welfare program, Aid to Families with Dependent Children (AFDC), now converted to Temporary Assistance for Needy Families (TANF), and made principally a state responsibility. The centerpiece of welfare reform is an effort to move women at risk of becoming long-term welfare recipients into employment. This has potentially enormous consequences for them and their children. If it is successful, a large number of young males will grow up in households that have regular contact with the workplace rather than with welfare checks. On the other hand, if welfare reform fails and large numbers of single mothers become even poorer and more reliant on illegal earnings, this may well have criminogenic effects on their children.

The fact that welfare participation has declined by 50 percent in six years must be seen as evidence that a major social change could be occurring, one with the potential to affect behavior, including the full range of delinquent behavior. To our knowledge, little attention is being given to the crime-prevention consequences of this change. We think this unfortunate, and would encourage researchers and policy makers to at least consider the possibility that this national policy change might in fact have a communitywide impact on norms and attitudes which could be utilized with other comprehensive programs designed to aid people in their transition to work.

Within this same domain, it is possible that a large-scale economic boom that leads to substantial and *permanent* increases in employment and wages for workers in depressed urban areas, especially for African-American youth, could lead to substantial decreases in crime. Freeman and Rodgers (1999) claim that the boom of the late 1990s did in fact lead to a substantial change in the workforce participation of young people in these target areas, which has led to a decline in crime. Several other recent papers (Gould, Weinberg, and Mustard 1998; Raphael and Winter-Ebmer 1998) make a similar point using data that specifically focus on young African-American men in depressed urban areas during the 1990s. These results have substantially larger effects than previously estimated. We find these results interesting, but not completely convincing.[25] If these results can be replicated, we believe they provide an important opportunity to understand what is different about the boom of the 1990s that might have led to changes not observed during previous economic upturns. It is possible that there has been an increased demand for low-skill labor that has resulted in increased wages, which, when combined with decreased drug prices and high levels of incarceration, has led to a widespread change in motivation from crime to more legitimate pursuits. At this point, we believe such an argument, currently given by several scholars as an explanation for the decline in crime during the late 1990s (for example, Bernstein and Houston 2000), has not been proven, and we invite researchers to examine this claim more carefully. In particular, we hope that researchers pay special attention to the noneconomic changes in these neighborhoods that might explain wholesale changes in behavior.

For policy makers, the message of this chapter is clear but complicated. Labor markets matter, and finding ways of raising employment and wages in high crime communities is potentially an important means of reducing crime. But, it is far from clear what policies are likely to be effective in improving job market outcomes in those communities. It may well be that "only everything works," that is, that labor market interventions must be part of broader policies in these communities. Understanding how these policies interact and how to best implement these policies together is an important task for the next generation of policy makers.

9

THE COMMUNITY

Robert J. Sampson

Public discourse on crime policy has traditionally been dominated by calls for the ever-greater penetration of official control—especially more police, more prisons, and longer mandatory sentences. Public-health approaches have begun to challenge this emphasis on reactive strategies by the criminal justice system, advocating instead crime prevention (Reiss and Roth 1993; Earls and Carlson 1996). In thinking about the prevention of crime, policymakers have turned to programs that attempt to change individuals (e.g., Head Start; job training) or families (e.g., child-rearing skills; conflict resolution).

Although individual- and family-level prevention are welcome partners in crime control, there is another target of intervention that until recently has been widely neglected in public policy circles—the community. This level of social inquiry asks how community structures and cultures produce differential rates of crime. For example, what characteristics of communities are associated with high rates of violence? Are communities safe or unsafe because of the persons who reside in them or because of community properties themselves? Perhaps most important, by changing communities can we bring about changes in crime rates?

As implied by these questions, the goal of community-level research is not to explain individual differences in criminal behavior, but to identify characteristics of neighborhoods, cities, or even regions that lead to high rates of criminality. A community-level perspective also points out how federal, state, and local governmental policies not directly concerned with crime policy may nonetheless bear on crime rates. In particular, not enough attention has been paid to "noncrime" policies—especially on housing, families, and child development—and how they influence the link between crime and the community.

In an attempt to address this imbalance, I describe in this chapter a sociological perspective on crime and the social organization of urban communities. My first goal is to review the major findings produced by research on the characteristics of communities that foster high (or low) rates of crime. I thus begin by highlighting the broad continuities that run throughout community-level research.[1] I also consider the reciprocal effect of crime on the social organization of communities. I then turn to the implications of such an approach for urban crime policy.

THE SOCIAL ECOLOGICAL MODEL OF CRIME

Research conducted in Chicago earlier this century provided the impetus for modern American studies of the social ecology of crime. In their classic work—*Juvenile Delinquency and Urban Areas*—Shaw and McKay (1942) argued that low economic status, ethnic heterogeneity, and residential instability led to the disruption of local community social organization, which in turn accounted for variations in crime and delinquency. Shaw and McKay (1969) also demonstrated that high rates of delinquency in Chicago persisted in certain areas over many years, regardless of population turnover. More than any other, this finding led them to question individualistic explanations of delinquency and focus on the processes by which criminal patterns of behavior, especially group-related, were transmitted across generations in areas of poverty, instability, and weak social controls (see also Bursik 1988).

After a hiatus in ecological research during the mid part of this century, the past two decades have witnessed a sharp increase in research focused on community-level variations in urban crime rates.[2] Although many factors have been studied, the following stand out.

Poverty and Inequality

Not surprisingly, a large number of recent neighborhood-based studies of crime have emphasized poverty or economic inequality. Unlike Shaw and McKay, however, the majority of these have attempted to estimate the explanatory role of economic structure independent of other factors such as population composition. Overall, the results have been mixed—some studies show a direct relationship between poverty and violence (e.g., Block 1979; Curry and Spergel 1988) whereas others show a weak or insignificant independent relationship (Messner and Tardiff 1986; Sampson 1985, 1986).[3]

Interestingly, some evidence suggests that the effect of poverty is conditional on neighborhood contexts of mobility. For example, in an evaluation of Shaw and McKay's (1969) theory, Smith and Jarjoura (1988) discovered a significant interaction between mobility and low income in explaining violence across 57 neighborhoods in three cities. Mobility was positively associated with violent crime rates in poorer neighborhoods but not in more affluent areas. The main effects of mobility and income were not significant when this interaction term was included. Smith and Jarjoura (1988) concluded that communities characterized by rapid population turnover and high poverty have significantly higher violent crime rates than mobile areas that are more affluent, or poor areas that are stable.

Mobility and Community Change

Consistent with this finding, one of the fundamental claims made by Shaw and McKay (1969) was that population turnover had negative consequences for the social control of delinquency. A high rate of mobility, especially in areas of decreasing population, was inferred to increase institutional disruption and weaken community controls. The research on mobility is not as extensive as that on economic status, but it has been revealing. For example, Block's (1979, p. 50) study of Chicago revealed large negative correlations between residential stability and the violent crimes of homicide, robbery, and aggravated assault. Victimization data from the National Crime Survey also show that residential mobility has significant positive effects on rates of violent crime (Sampson 1985). Even after adjusting for other neighborhood-level factors, rates of violent victimization for residents of high-mobility neighborhoods are at least double those of residents in low-mobility areas (Sampson 1985, p. 30; 1986, p. 44). And as noted above, Smith and Jarjoura (1988) found a positive effect of residential mobility on robbery and assault victimization in low-income neighborhoods.

Taylor and Covington's (1988) study of poverty, instability, and violent crime (murder and aggravated assault) paints a similar picture. They examined ecological changes in economic status and family status for 277 Baltimore city neighborhoods in the period 1970–1980. Taylor and Covington (1988, p. 561) hypothesized that neighborhoods experiencing declines in relative economic status and stability should also experience increases in violence. In support of this notion, they found that the increasing entrenchment of urban poverty among disadvantaged minority areas was linked to increases in violence. Especially in neighborhood contexts of poverty, then, residential instability appears to have important consequences for violence.

Heterogeneity and Racial Composition

Although ethnic heterogeneity was accorded a central role in early ecological research, in their writings, Shaw and McKay (1969: 153) referred mostly to population composition. This is not surprising, because their data showed that delinquency rates were higher in predominantly black and foreign-born areas than in areas of maximum heterogeneity. For example, in Shaw and McKay's (1969, p. 155) data the delinquency rate in areas with over 70 percent black/foreign-born was more than double the rate in areas of maximum heterogeneity (e.g., 50–59 percent black/foreign-born).

Later research on violence has focused mainly on racial composition. A consistent finding has been that the percentage of blacks in a neighborhood is positively and strongly related to rates of violence. Block (1979) showed that rates of violence had significant and large correlations with percent black, as did Messner and Tardiff (1986), Sampson (1985), Roncek (1981), and Smith and Jarjoura (1988). The dispute arises over the independent effect of racial composition on rates of violence. Specifically, several studies report a sharply attenuated effect of neighborhood racial composition on rates of violence once family structure and socioeconomic factors are accounted for (e.g., Block 1979; Messner and Tardiff 1986; Sampson 1985). While percent black is a significant correlate of violent crime, it is thus questionable whether neighborhood racial composition has unique explanatory power.

Housing and Population Density

Though infrequently studied, research has highlighted the potential role that the physical structure and density of housing may play in understanding patterns of violent crime. Roncek (1981) found that the percentage of units in multiunit housing structures was a consistent and strong predictor of block-level variations in violent crime in Cleveland and San Diego. Land area in acres, population size, and the percent of primary individual households also had significant effects on violence despite age and race composition. As Roncek (1981, p. 88) summarizes, "the most dangerous city blocks are relatively large in population and area with high concentrations of primary individuals and apartment housing." In a similar vein, Schuerman and Kobrin (1986, p. 97) found that increases in multiplex dwellings and renter-occupied housing predicted increases in crime rates in Los Angeles neighborhoods.

Roncek (1981, p. 88) argues that such findings are consistent with the idea of anonymity because primary-individual households and high proportions of multi-unit structures increase the number of residents who do not know one another. For example, as the number of households sharing common living space increases, residents are less able to recognize their neighbors, to be concerned for them, or engage in guardianship behaviors (Roncek 1981, p. 88). These arguments were supported in studies of violent victimization using neighborhood characteristics data and the National Crime Survey (Sampson 1985). Several studies also report a significant and large association between density and violent crime despite controlling for a host of social and economic variables (see Sampson and Lauritsen 1994). Housing and population density are thus linked to violent crime regardless of compositional factors.

Family Structure

Largely ignored in early ecological research, several modern studies have examined the community-level consequences of family "disruption" (e.g., divorce rates, female-headed families with children). Family disruption has been posited to facilitate crime by decreasing networks of informal social control, such as observing or questioning strangers, watching over each others' property, and assuming responsibility for supervision of general youth activities (see e.g., Sampson and Groves 1989; Taylor et al. 1984). This conceptualization focuses on the community-wide effects of family structure and does not require that it is the children of divorced or separated parents that are engaging in crime. For instance, youth in stable family areas, regardless of their own family situation, have more controls placed on their leisure-time activities, particularly with peer groups (Sullivan 1989, p. 178). Neighborhood family structure may thus influence whether neighborhood youth are provided the opportunity to form a peer-control system free of supervision by adults.

Felson and Cohen (1980) also note the potential influence of family structure not just on the control of offenders, but also on the control of criminal targets and opportunities. They argue that traditional theories of crime emphasize the criminal motivation of offenders without considering adequately the circumstances in which criminal acts occur. Predatory crime requires the convergence in time and space of offenders, suitable targets, and the absence of effective guardianship. The spatial and temporal structure of family activity patterns plays an important role in determining the rate at which motivated offenders encounter criminal opportunities. For example, singles and those who live alone are more likely to be out alone (going to work, restaurants, clubs, etc.) than married persons and are thus more vulnerable to personal crimes of violence, such as rape and robbery.

The salience of family structure has been supported by studies reporting a large and positive relationship between measures of family disruption (usually percent female-headed families or divorce rate) and rates of violence. For example, Sampson (1985, 1986) found that rates of victimization were two to three times higher among residents of neighborhoods with high levels of family disruption compared to low levels, regardless of alternative predictors of violent victimization, such as percent black and poverty. In fact, the percentage of female-headed families helped to explain in large part the relationship between percent black and violence. Namely, percent black and percent female-headed families were positively and significantly related, but when percent female-headed families was controlled, percent black was not significantly related to violent victimization.

Similarly, Messner and Tardiff (1986) found that when percent divorced and percent poverty were controlled, the relationship between percent black and homicide rates was insignificant. Smith and Jarjoura (1988) also report that family structure, especially percent single-parent families, helps account for the association between race and violent crime: racial composition was not significantly related to rates of violent crime when percent single-parent families was controlled.

COMMUNITY SOCIAL DISORGANIZATION

Although the empirical evidence reviewed above clearly points to a number of neighborhood-level correlates of crime rates, it does not answer what is potentially the most important question. Why does community structure matter? Put differently, what are the mechanisms and social processes that help explain why factors such as family disruption, residential mobility, and poverty lead to increases in crime and violence? It is to these questions that criminologists have increasingly turned their attention, especially those working in the Chicago-school tradition of social disorganization theory.

In general, social disorganization has been defined as the inability of a community structure to realize the common values of its residents and maintain effective social controls (Sampson and Groves 1989). The social disorganization approach views local communities and neighborhoods as a complex system of friendship, kinship, and acquaintanceship networks, and formal and informal associational ties rooted in family life and ongoing socialization processes (for further elaboration, see Bursik 1988). From this view, both social organization and social *dis*organization are inextricably tied to systemic networks that facilitate or inhibit social control.[4] When formulated in this way, social disorganization is analytically separable not only from the processes that may lead to it (e.g., poverty, residential mobility), but from the degree of criminal behavior that may be a result. This conceptualization also goes beyond the traditional account of community as a strictly geographical phenomenon by focusing on the social networks and voluntary associations of residents.

A major dimension of social disorganization is the ability of a community to supervise and control peer-groups—especially adolescent gangs. It is well-documented that delinquency is primarily a group phenomenon (Thrasher 1963; Shaw and McKay 1969; Reiss 1986), and hence, the capacity of the community to control group-level dynamics is a key theoretical mechanism linking community characteristics with crime. Moreover, the majority of gangs develops from unsupervised, spontaneous play groups (Thrasher 1963, p. 25). Shaw and McKay (1969) thus argued that residents of cohesive communities were better able to control the teenage behaviors that set the context for gang violence. Examples of such controls include the supervision of leisure-time youth activities, intervention in street-corner congregation (Thrasher 1963, p. 339; Shaw and McKay 1969, p. 176–185), and challenging youth "who seem to be up to no good" (Skogan 1986, p. 217; Taylor et al. 1984, p. 326). Socially disorganized communities with extensive street-corner peer groups are also expected to have higher rates of adult violence, especially among younger adults who still have ties to youth gangs (Thrasher 1963).

Another dimension of community social organization is the density and "connectivity" of local friendship and acquaintanceship networks. Systemic theory holds that locality-based social networks constitute the core social fabric of human ecological communities (Bursik 1988). When residents form local social ties, their capacity for community social control is increased because they are better able to recognize strangers, and are more apt to engage in guardianship behavior against victimization (Taylor et al. 1984, p. 307; Skogan 1986, p. 216). The greater the density and overlapping nature of interpersonal networks in a community, the greater the constraint on deviant behavior within the network.

The social networks among adults and children in a community are particularly important in fostering the capacity for collective socialization and supervision. One of the most important factors according to Coleman (1990,

p. 318–320) is the closure (i.e., connectedness) of social networks among families and children. In a system involving parents and children, communities characterized by an extensive set of obligations, expectations, and social networks connecting the adults are better able to facilitate the control and supervision of children. The notion of closure helps us to understand parent-child relations that extend beyond the household. For example, when closure is present through the relationship of a child to two adults whose relationship transcends the household (e.g., friendship, work-related acquaintanceship), the adults have the potential to "observe the child's actions in different circumstances, talk to each other about the child, compare notes, and establish norms" (1990, p. 593). This form of relation can also provide reinforcement for disciplining the child, as found when parents in communities with dense social networks and high stability assume responsibility for the supervision of youth that are not their own (Coleman 1990, p. 320; Sampson and Groves 1989). The closure of local networks can therefore provide the child with norms and sanctions that could not be brought about by a single adult alone, or even married-couple families in isolation.

Collective Efficacy

Social networks and closure are not sufficient to understand local communities, however. Networks are differentially invoked, and dense, tight-knit networks may even impede social organization if they are isolated or weakly linked to collective expectations for action. At the neighborhood level, the willingness of local residents to intervene on behalf of public safety depends, in large part, on conditions of mutual trust and shared expectations among residents. In particular, one is unlikely to intervene in a neighborhood context where the rules are unclear and people mistrust or fear one another. It is the linkage of mutual trust and the shared willingness to intervene for the common good that defines the neighborhood context of what Sampson et al. (1997) term *collective efficacy*. Just as individuals vary in their capacity for efficacious action, so too do neighborhoods vary in their capacity to achieve common goals. Moreover, just as self-efficacy is situated rather than global (one has self-efficacy relative to a particular task or type of task), neighborhood efficacy exists relative to collective tasks such as maintaining public order. Collective efficacy is thus a task-specific construct that refers to shared expectations and mutual engagement by residents in local social control (Sampson et al. 1999).

Moving from a focus on private ties to social efficacy signifies an emphasis on shared beliefs in neighbors' conjoint capability for action to achieve an intended effect, and hence an active sense of engagement on the part of residents. As Bandura (1997) argues, the meaning of efficacy is captured in expectations about the exercise of control, elevating the "agentic" aspect of social life over a perspective centered on the accumulation of "stocks" of social resources. Distinguishing between the resource potential represented by personal ties, and the shared expectations among neighbors for engagement in social control represented by collective efficacy, may help clarify the systemic model. In particular, social networks foster the conditions under which collective efficacy may flourish, but they are not sufficient for the exercise of control. In this way collective efficacy may be seen as a logical extension of systemically based social disorganization theory. The difference is mainly one of emphasis: systemic friend and kinship networks may enhance neighborhood social organization, but the collective capacity for social action, even if rooted in weak, personal ties, constitutes the more proximate social mechanism for understanding between-neighborhood variation in crime rates.

A systemic-based model of social organization and collective efficacy need not ignore institutions, or the wider political environment in which local communities are embedded. Many a community exhibits intense private ties (e.g., among friends, kin) and yet still lacks the institutional capacity to achieve social control (Hunter 1985). The institutional component of social control is the resource stock of neighborhood organizations and their linkages with other organizations, both within *and* outside the community. Kornhauser (1978, p. 79) argues that when the horizontal links among institutions within a community are weak, the capacity to defend local interests is weakened. Vertical integration is potentially more important. For example, Bursik and Grasmick (1993) highlight the capacity of local community organizations to obtain extra-local resources (e.g., police, fire services, block grants) that help sustain neighborhood social stability and local controls.

Empirical Evidence

Although it is difficult to study the intervening social mechanisms and collective processes, a new generation of research has emerged in the last decade that attempts to measure directly the theory's structural dimensions. For example, Taylor et al. (1984) examined variations in violent crime (e.g., mugging, assault, murder, rape) across 63 street blocks in Baltimore. Based on interviews with 687 household respondents, Taylor et al. (1984, p. 316) constructed block-level measures of the proportion of respondents who belonged to an organization to which co-residents also belonged, and the proportion of respondents who felt responsible for what happened in the area surrounding their home. Both dimensions of informal social control were significantly and negatively related to rates of violence, exclusive of other ecological factors (1984, p. 320). These results support the hypothesis that organizational participation and informal social control of public space depress criminal violence.

Simcha-Fagan and Schwartz (1986) collected rich survey-based information on 553 residents of 12 different neighborhoods in New York City. Although the number of neighborhoods was small, they found a significant negative relationship between the rate of self-reported delinquency and rates of organizational participation by local residents. A limited multivariate analysis provided further support for this pattern—"level of organizational participation and residential stability have unique effects in predicting survey-reported delinquency" (1986, p. 683).

In a study conducted in Great Britain in 1982 and 1984, Sampson and Groves' (1989) showed that the prevalence of unsupervised teenage peer-groups in a community had the largest effect on rates of robbery and violence by strangers. The density of local friendship networks also had a significant negative effect on robbery rates, while the level of organizational participation by residents had significant inverse effects on both robbery and stranger violence (1989, p. 789). Central to present concerns, variations in these structural dimensions of community social (dis)organization transmitted in large part the effects of community socioeconomic status, residential mobility, ethnic heterogeneity, and family disruption in a theoretically consistent manner. In particular, socioeconomic status was significantly related to increased levels of organizational participation.

In a more recent study from the United States, Elliott et al. (1996) examined survey data from neighborhoods in Chicago and Denver. A multilevel analysis revealed that a measure of "informal control" was significantly and negatively related to adolescent problem behavior in both sites. Like the British results, informal control mediated the prior effects of neighborhood structural disadvantage—declining poor neighborhoods displayed less ability to maintain social control, and they in turn suffered higher delinquency rates. A number of studies have also used survey data from over 5,000 Seattle residents nested within 100 census tracts to investigate the connection between social processes and crime. Warner and Rountree (1997) found a significant negative association between assault rates and the proportion of respondents in white neighborhoods who engaged in neighboring activities with one another—including borrowing tools or food, having lunch or dinner, or helping each other with problems. In a subsequent study, Rountree and Warner (1999) examined the gendered nature of neighboring and found that the proportion of females engaging in neighboring activities was behind the association with lower rates of violent crime. Bellair (2000) approached the same data with a somewhat different perspective on social processes. He assumed that neighboring activities affect crime rates only indirectly, by increasing the likelihood that neighbors will engage in informal surveillance of one another's property. These causal paths were consistent with the empirical results he obtained.

A large-scale research program in Chicago ("Project on Human Development in Chicago Neighborhoods") has as its primary objective the study of criminal behavior in community context. A major component of this study entailed a community survey of 8,782 residents of 343 Chicago neighborhoods in 1995. Sampson et al. (1997) developed a two-part scale from this survey to examine rates of violence. One component was shared expectations about "informal social control," represented by a five-item Likert-type scale. Residents were asked about the likelihood ("Would you say it is very likely, likely, neither likely nor unlikely, unlikely, or very unlikely?") that their neighbors could be counted on to take action if: (i) children were skipping school and hanging out on a street corner, (ii) children were spray-painting graffiti on a local building, (iii) children were showing disrespect to an adult, (iv) a fight broke out in front of their house, and (v) the fire station closest to home was threatened with budget cuts. The second component was "social cohesion," measured by asking respondents how strongly they agreed (on a five-point scale) that "People around here are willing to help their neighbors"; "This is a close-knit neighborhood"; "People in this neighborhood can be trusted"; and (reverse coded): "People in this neighborhood generally don't get along with each other"; "People in this neighborhood do not share the same values." Social cohesion and informal social control were closely associated across neighborhoods, suggesting that the two measures were tapping aspects of the same latent construct. Sampson et al. (1997) combined the two scales into a summary measure of "collective efficacy."

Using this measure, Sampson et al. (1997) found that collective efficacy had a strong negative relationship with the rate of violence in the neighborhood, controlling for concentrated disadvantage, residential stability, immigrant concentration, and a set of individual-level characteristics (e.g., age, sex, SES, race/ethnicity, home ownership). The results showed that, whether measured by official homicide events or violent victimization as reported by residents, neighborhoods high in collective efficacy had significantly lower rates of violence. This finding held up even when controlling for prior levels of neighborhood violence, which may have depressed later collective efficacy (e.g., because of fear). In this model, a two standard-deviation elevation in collective efficacy was associated with a 26 percent reduction in the expected homicide rate (Sampson et al. 1997, p. 922). Concentrated disadvantage and residential stability were also strongly related to collective efficacy in theoretically expected directions, and the association of disadvantage and stability with rates of violence was significantly reduced when collective efficacy was controlled. The cross-sectional nature of the study and the possibility of reciprocality (e.g., crime may reduce collective efficacy) means that causal effects could not be determined. Nonetheless, the patterns are consistent with the inference that neighborhood structural characteristics influence violence in part through the social mechanism of collective efficacy.

Although there are serious methodological limitations to neighborhood-level studies (see Sampson and Lauritsen 1994, pp. 75–85), their cumulative results support the notion that neighborhoods characterized by (a) mistrust and perceived lack of shared expectations, (b) sparse acquaintanceship and exchange networks among residents, (c) attenuated social control of public spaces, (d) a weak organizational and institutional base, and (e) low participation in local voluntary associations, are associated with an increased risk of interpersonal crime and public disorder within their borders. Moreover, the data are consistent in suggesting that these dimensions of community social organization and collective action are systematically structured (although not determined) by neighborhood structural differentiation. In particular, collective efficacy appears to be undermined by concentrated disadvantage, racial segregation, family disruption, residential instability, and dense population concentration.

THE ECOLOGICAL CONCENTRATION OF RACE AND POVERTY

A community-level perspective also reveals the extent to which race, urban poverty, and social disadvantage are intertwined. Although approximately 70 percent of all poor non-Hispanic whites lived in non-poverty areas in the ten largest U.S. central cities in 1980, only 16 percent of poor blacks did. Moreover, whereas less than 7 percent of poor whites lived in extreme poverty or ghetto areas, 38 percent of poor blacks lived in such areas (Wilson 1987). This trend of ecological inequality by race has continued into the 1990s and beyond. At the national level in 1990, 25 percent of poor blacks lived in concentrated poverty neighborhoods, compared to only 3 percent of poor whites (see Jargowsky 1997, p. 41). These differential ecological distributions mean that relationships between race and individual outcomes are systematically confounded with racial differences in community contexts.

The combination of urban poverty and family disruption concentrated by race is particularly severe. Sampson and Wilson (1995) searched for cities where the proportion of blacks living in poverty was equal to or less than whites, and where the proportion of black families with children headed by a single parent was equal to or less than white families. Although it is known that the average national rate of family disruption and poverty among blacks is higher than whites, in not one city over 100,000 in the United States do blacks live in ecological equality to whites when it comes to these basic features of economic and family organization. Accordingly, racial differences in poverty and family disruption are so strong that the "worst" urban contexts in which whites reside are considerably better off than the average context of black communities (Sampson and Wilson 1995).

In short, differential ecological distributions by race lead to the systematic confounding of correlations between community contexts and crime with correlations between race and crime. Analogous to research on urban poverty, comparisons between poor whites and poor blacks are confounded with the fact that poor whites reside in areas that are ecologically and economically very different from those of poor blacks. This means that observed relationships involving race are likely to reflect unmeasured advantages in the ecological niches that poor whites occupy (see Wilson 1987, pp. 58–60). For example, regardless of whether or not a black juvenile is raised in an intact or single parent family, or rich or poor home, he or she is not likely to grow up in a community context similar to whites with regard to family structure and the concentration of poverty. Hence the returns on a black family's educational and economic resources in terms of neighborhood environment are usually much less than a white family with similar resources.

EFFECTS OF CRIME ON SOCIAL AND ECONOMIC ORGANIZATION

It is important to recognize as well that crime and its consequences (e.g., fear) may themselves have important reciprocal effects on community structure. Skogan (1991) has provided an insightful overview of some of the "feedback" processes that may further increase levels of crime. These include

- physical and psychological withdrawal from community life
- weakening of the informal social control processes that inhibit crime
- decline in the organizational life and mobilization capacity of the neighborhood
- deteriorating business conditions
- importation and domestic production of delinquency and deviance
- further dramatic changes in the composition of the population

For example, if people shun their neighbors and local facilities out of fear of crime, fewer opportunities exist for local networks and organizations to take hold. Relatedly, street crime may be accompanied by residential out-migration and business relocation from inner city areas. As a result, crime itself can lead to simultaneous demographic "collapse" and a weakening of the informal control structures and mobilization capacity of communities, which in turn fuels further crime.

Although the number of empirical studies is relatively small, the evidence is rather consistent that crime does in fact undermine the social and economic fabric of urban areas. One of the most important findings is that crime generates fear of strangers and a general alienation from participation in community life (Skogan 1986, 1991; Rosenbaum, D. 1991; Sampson and Raudenbush 1999). Besides weakening neighborhood social organization, high crime rates and concerns about safety may trigger population out-migration. For example, Bursik (1986) found that delinquency rates are not only one of the outcomes of urban change, they are an important part of the process of urban change. Studying Chicago neighborhoods, Bursik (1986, p. 73) observes that "although changes in racial composition cause increases in the delinquency rate, this effect is not nearly as great as the effect that increases in the delinquency rate have in minority groups being stranded in the community." In a study of 40 neighborhoods in eight cities, Skogan (1991) also found that high rates of crime and disorder were associated with higher rates of fear, neighborhood dissatisfaction, and intentions to move out. And in a study of Dallas neighborhoods, Katzman (1980, p. 278) found that high rates of property crime lead to out-migration from crime-ridden areas. Sampson and Raudenbush (1999) found a reciprocal negative relationship between collective efficacy and rates of violence across neighborhoods in Chicago.

These general trends are observed at the city level as well. In a study of the nation's 55 largest cities, Sampson and Wooldredge (1986) report that crime rates were negatively related to population change from 1970 to 1980, especially nonwhite population change. Crime rates had significant lagged effects on net migration patterns as well. That is, net of fertility and mortality differences, serious crime led to decreases in central city populations and thereby migration to suburbs (see also Frey 1979). Sampson and Wooldredge's (1986) findings persisted despite controls for the effects of other important factors in population migration such as region, per capita tax rate, employment, racial composition, manufacturing base, population density, and poverty.

Evidence on relocation decisions by businesses as a function of crime rates is extremely scarce. However, one study of 62 manufacturing firms that moved from New York City to New Jersey does shed light on the matter. When asked for reasons why they moved, many of the surveyed manufacturing firms cited perceived safety concerns. For example, 9 percent claimed crime was the single most important reason for moving, while 21 percent cited crime as one among several other reasons. Less than 5 percent said that a lower crime rate was the most important reason for moving to New Jersey rather than the outer boroughs of New York City, but 19 percent did say that less crime was one of the factors increasing the desirability of New Jersey relative to alternatives in New York. The report concluded "Security, taxes, 'quality of life' issues, and image problems all contribute to a marketability gap which places many outer borough locations at a competitive disadvantage when compared to New Jersey" (INTERFACE 1985, p. iv). Hence, while business decisions appear to be less sensitive to crime rates than residential ones, they are not immune from the social disorganization, fear, and social incivilities associated with street violence.

Although the empirical base is limited, the overall picture painted by prior research on the effects of crime is one of population abandonment of urban neighborhoods, business relocation to the suburbs, loss of economic revenue, a decrease in economic status and property values, and escalating levels of fear in central cities. Moreover, many cities—especially in the North and Midwest—have not only lost population but also have become increasingly poorer and racially isolated (Wilson 1987). An important part of this racially selective decline in population and economic status apparently stems from violent crime. As Skogan (1991) has emphasized, crime is a salient event that has important symbolic consequences for perceptions of the inhabitability and civility of city life. By undermining social and economic organization, crime generates a reciprocal, feedback effect that may further increase crime. Breaking the cycle of violence in communities is thus crucial to a general strategy for urban policy.

LIMITATIONS OF THE COMMUNITY APPROACH

Like any complex phenomenon, numerous problems plague research on communities and crime. Among other limitations, the use of varying and sometimes highly aggregated units of analysis, potentially biased sources of information on violence (e.g., official data), feedback or reciprocal effects from crime itself, widely varying analytical techniques, and high correlations among social variables all hinder the attempt to draw inferences about the unique explanatory power of community characteristics.

Furthermore, prior research has mostly inferred the existence of intervening social processes, even though the correlation of crime with community characteristics is consistent with many different theoretical perspectives. As noted, studies typically show that percent black, poverty, and family disruption predict rates of crime. While useful as a preliminary test, this strategy does not go much beyond the steps taken by Shaw and McKay over forty years ago. As Kornhauser (1978, p. 82) argues, most criminological theories take as their point of departure the same independent variables (e.g., socioeconomic status). The variables that intervene between community structure and violence are at issue, and to test adequately competing theories one must establish the relationship to violence of the interpretive variables each theory implies. This objective becomes problematic in the majority of studies relying on census data that rarely provide measures for the social variables hypothesized to mediate the relationship between community structure and violence. Fortunately, as reviewed above, a new generation of studies has emerged to directly assess social processes and collective properties.

Another problem in community research is that an apparent ecological or structural effect may arise from individual-level causal processes. For example, an observed result such as the correlation of median income or percent black with violence rates may simply represent the aggregation of relationships occurring at lower levels of social structure and not a manifestation of processes taking place at the level of the community as a whole. Even though rates of crime may not be used to make inferences about individuals, individuals commit the crimes that constitute the rates. Consider further the basic facts on delinquency. Research has consistently demonstrated the early onset of delinquency and its long-term stability

(Glueck and Glueck 1950; Robins 1966). Differences among individuals that are stable over time have direct implications for an ecological study of crime. Antisocial children tend to fight, steal, become truant, drop out of school, drift in and out of unemployment, live in lower-class areas and go on to commit adult crime. The causal nature of the relationship between achieved adult characteristics (e.g., employment status) and adult crime is thus fraught with methodological difficulties. In fact, in *Deviant Children Grown Up,* Lee Robins (1966) offered the provocative hypothesis that antisocial behavior predicts class status more efficiently than class status predicts antisocial behavior.

If area differences in violence rates result from the characteristics of individuals selectively located in those communities (Kornhauser 1978), the findings derived from community-level research must be questioned. Is the correlation of concentrated poverty with violence caused by an aggregation of individual-level effects of class, a genuine community-level effect, or is it simply a differential selection of individuals into communities based on prior (e.g., antisocial) behavior? Or is it that common third factors cause individuals to both commit violence and perform poorly in the occupational sphere? And if violent and antisocial tendencies are formed at early (preteen) ages, what plausible roles can community labor markets and economic stratification play in understanding violence? Simply put, community-level research is not immune to questions concerning the level at which causal relations operate. The level at which a causal relation occurs is a complex issue that is not solved simply by the nature of how variables are measured or the unit for which they are measured. To make matters more complicated, the concrete actions of individuals also feed back to shape the collective environment (Tienda 1991). Thus the unit of analysis does not define the level of causal explanation, and social processes do not necessarily generate the information contained in aggregate data.

Perhaps most disturbing, there seems to be a consensus in evaluation research that community crime prevention programs have achieved only limited success (Bursik and Grasmick 1993, pp. 148–75; Rosenbaum 1991; Hope 1995). The most common crime-prevention approach has been the so-called "neighborhood watch," where attempts are made to increase residents' participation in local efforts at social control (e.g., community meetings, neighborhood patrols). More ambitious interventions have tried to increase social interaction among neighbors and instill concern for the public welfare of local residents (see Greenberg et al. 1985). There have also been even more general efforts to change neighborhood opportunity structures such as the classic Chicago Area Project patterned after Shaw and

McKay's (1942) theory. Yet evaluations of these programs are for the most part pessimistic about concrete reductions in crime (Rosenbaum, D. 1991; Bursik and Grasmick 1993; Greenberg et al. 1985).

Although disappointing results from evaluation research could mean that neighborhood-level theories are wrong, another possibility is that programs were not implemented correctly. We know, for example, that community crime prevention is especially hard to implement in the areas that need them the most—poor, unstable neighborhoods with high crime rates. Participation levels also tend to fall off quickly once interventions are removed. On the other hand, efforts to reduce crime are more likely to succeed if they are embedded in more comprehensive programs for neighborhood stabilization that local residents support. That is, "one shot" interventions that are externally "imposed" and simply try to reduce crime in the short run without confronting other key aspects of the neighborhood are, not surprisingly, highly susceptible to failure (Hope 1995). Whether the poor track record of community interventions (similar, I should note, to the poor track record of individual interventions) is due to a failure of theory or a programmatic failure of implementation is thus unknown. It is also possible that neighborhood-level interventions have attempted to pull the wrong levers of change.

A confluence of factors—selective decisions to live in different communities, misspecification due to population composition effects, overlap among ecological variables, a static conceptualization of community structure, the early onset of many forms of violence, indirect measurement of community characteristics, and weak intervention results—clearly suggest caution in the interpretation of community-level research. Nevertheless, I believe that a community-level perspective not only improves our understanding of the etiology of crime and violence, but that it expands our conceptual apparatus to think about fresh policies for the public agenda on crime.[5] Indeed, what seem most promising are policies that embed a concern for crime reduction in larger, more systemic efforts to improve the social organizational capacities of the neighborhood. The following section builds on this idea.

PUBLIC POLICY IMPLICATIONS: CHANGING PLACES, NOT PEOPLE

Having outlined both the strengths and weaknesses of a community-level perspective on crime and social organization, I now examine some policy-related implications that attempt to move beyond past efforts. I focus primarily on community-level correlates of crime reviewed above that are related, both directly and indirectly, to the policy decisions of public officials. For the most part, these are policy domains that focus on crime prevention and the enhancement of community social organization from other than criminal justice agencies. Initiatives that rely on the police, prisons, and other agencies of social control have been reviewed at length many times, and hence I do not cover them here except as they interface with community-level efforts. For example, I do not cover the traditional literature on neighborhood watch and community crime prevention (see Rosenbaum, D. 1991; Bursik and Grasmick 1993; Hope 1995). Rather, my strategy is to begin discussion with alternative neighborhood-level policies most directly related to crime, and then build toward more comprehensive strategies that attack "root causes" of crime but that are still amenable to public policy.

1. Identify Neighborhood "Hot Spots" for Crime

One area of promise is simple yet powerful. Research has long demonstrated that crimes are not randomly distributed in space. Rather, they are disproportionately concentrated in certain neighborhoods and "places" (e.g., taverns, parking lots). Ecologically oriented criminologists have dubbed these areas "hot spots" of crime (Sherman et al. 1989; Sherman 1995). Drawing on community theory and advances in computer mapping technology, the argument is that policing strategies can be more effective if they are implemented using information on ecological hot spots (see also Reiss and Roth 1993, p. 17). In Chicago, for example, Block (1991) has pioneered the use of what is termed an "early warning system" for gang homicides. By plotting each homicide incident and using sophisticated mapping and statistical clustering procedures, the early warning system allows police to identify potential neighborhood crisis areas at high risk for suffering a "spurt" of gang violence (Block 1991). With rapid dissemination of information, police can intervene in hot spots to quell emerging trouble. Places may also be modified or watched so as to reduce the opportunities for crime to occur. Sherman and colleagues (Sherman 1995; Sherman et al. 1989, p. 48) have considered "place" interventions based on hot spot data such as differential patrol allocations by place, selective revocation of bar licenses, and removal of vacant "crack" houses.

The idea of hot spots suggests a neighborhood-level response that in the end may be much more effective than policies that simply target individuals or even families. By proactively responding to neighborhoods and places that disproportionately generate crimes, policing strategies can more efficiently stave off epidemics of crime and their spatial diffusions.

2. Reduce Social Disorder Physical "Incivilities"

Both the logic of social disorganization theory and the extant evidence suggest that "incivilities" such as broken windows, trash, public drinking, and prostitution increase fear of crime (Skogan 1986, 1991). Incivilities and signs of disorder may increase not just fear but crime itself. One possibility is that potential offenders recognize such deterioration and assume that residents are so indifferent to what goes on in their neighborhood that they will not be motivated to confront strangers, intervene in a crime, or call the police (Wilson and Kelling 1982). Another possibility is that physical and social elements of disorder comprise highly visible cues to which all neighborhood observers respond, potentially influencing migration patterns, investment by businesses, and overall neighborhood viability. Thus if disorder operates in a cascading fashion by encouraging people to move (increasing residential instability) or discouraging efforts at building collective responses, it would indirectly have an effect on crime (Sampson and Raudenbush 1999). To foster a climate of "safety," public order, and hopefully social organization, policy should consider collective strategies in the community that might:

- clean up graffiti, trash, needles, vials, and the like
- stagger bar closing times; enact strict zoning/licensing
- "picket" public drinking, drug use, prostitution, and other disorder crimes
- organize walking groups for adults in public areas

There is limited evidence on these strategies, although various neighborhood-based cleanup interventions have been found to increase perceptions of safety (Rosenbaum, D., 1991). The Police Foundation also conducted an interesting study where a specially trained group of officers performed a variety of disorder-reduction tasks within a Newark experimental area (Skogan 1991). The results were mixed, but they did indicate that crime was lower under conditions of aggressive field interrogations. The implications for general citizen involvement are broader—the community must take partial responsibility for stemming the spiral of decay. Indeed the optimal strategies are those that involve both police *and* the community in the planning and execution of crime control measures (e.g., community policing that focuses on reduction of incivilities and the local production of collective efficacy).

3. Build Informal Social Control and Collective Efficacy

As described earlier, a major dimension of social organization is the ability of a community to supervise and control teenage peer-groups. Communities characterized by an extensive set of obligations, expectations, and social networks connecting the adults are better able to facilitate this task. For example, when the parents' friends or acquaintances are the parents of their children's friends, the adults have the potential to observe the child's actions in different circumstances, talk to each other about the child, compare notes, and establish norms (see Coleman 1990). This form of relation can provide reinforcement for inculcating positive youth outcomes, as found when parents in communities with dense social networks and high stability assume responsibility for the supervision of youth that are not their own. Closure of local networks provides the child with social resource of a collective nature—a social good that is created when relations among persons facilitate action. One can extend this model to closure among networks involving parents and teachers, religious and recreational leaders, businesses that serve youth, and even agents of criminal justice (Sampson 1992).

Programs that might foster informal social controls and collective efficacy include:

- organized supervision of leisure-time youth activities
- observation/reduction of street-corner congregation
- staggered school closing times to reduce peer-control system
- parent surveillance/involvement in after-school and night-time youth programs
- adult-youth mentoring systems; adult acquaintanceship

The key here is to increase positive connections among youth and adults in the community. Stricter sanctions such as curfews for adolescents in public areas may also be necessary, but the focus is on informal social controls that arise from ongoing social interactions and community support. For example, Meares and Kahan (1998) describe the emergence of a "working trust" between the police and residents of Chicago's poverty-stricken west side in the creation of zones of safety. Policies including juvenile curfews and policing of minor disorders were supported by residents largely because of the leadership role of the local police commander, who was a longtime resident. In fact, the police commander led a prayer vigil to protest the occurrence of drug dealing and crime in the community. Over 1,000 residents participated, and in groups of ten they marched and reclaimed street corners where drug dealers had previously dominated. Following the prayer vigil, over 7,000 residents retired to a local park for a celebration. Such a coalition is surely controversial, but from the perspective of collective efficacy theory coupled with the undisputed strength of the black church as a site for collective-action strategies (Pattillo 1998), the Chicago alliance is a fascinating development that bears watching. Indeed, it appears that participation by residents in a newly constituted and legitimized community policing effort was in itself an action that increased community solidarity and collective efficacy.

4. Promote Housing-Based Neighborhood Stabilization

A more general option for enhancing social organization is to focus on joint public/private intervention programs to help stabilize and revitalize rapidly deteriorating inner city neighborhoods. My focus is primarily on investment in the physical structure of declining but still-reachable communities. As noted above, a long history of community-based research shows that population instability and housing decay are linked to crime and social problems among youth (see also Sampson and Lauritsen 1994). The implication is that community-based policy interventions may help to reverse the tide of social disintegration in concentrated poverty areas. Among others, these policies might include:

- resident management of public housing
- tenant buy-outs
- rehabilitation of existing low-income housing
- strict code enforcement
- low-income housing tax credits

For example, inner city neighborhoods have suffered disproportionately from severe population and housing loss of the sort that is disruptive of the social and institutional order. Bursik (1989) has shown that the planned construction of new public housing projects in Chicago's poor communities in the 1970s was associated with increased rates of population turnover, which in turn were related to increases in crime independent of racial composition. More generally, Skogan (1986, p. 206) has noted how urban renewal and forced migration contributed to the wholesale uprooting of many urban black communities, especially the extent to which freeway networks driven through the hearts of many cities in the 1950s destroyed viable, low-income communities. In Atlanta one in six residents were dislocated through urban renewal, the great majority of who were poor blacks (Logan and Molotch 1987, p. 114). Nationwide, fully 20 percent of all central city housing units occupied by blacks were lost in the period 1960–1970 alone. Recognizing these patterns, housing policies should focus more on stabilization of existing areas—especially those dominated by single-family homes.

Municipal code enforcement and local governmental policies toward neighborhood deterioration are also relevant. In *Making the Second Ghetto: Race and Housing in Chicago, 1940–1960,* Hirsch (1983) documents how lax enforcement of city housing codes played a major role in accelerating the deterioration of inner city Chicago neighborhoods. Daley and Meislen (1988) argued that inadequate city policies on code enforcement and repair of city properties contributed to the systematic decline of New York City's housing stock, and in some cases, entire neighborhoods. When considered with the practices of redlining and disinvestments by banks and "block-busting" by real estate agents (Skogan 1986), local policies toward code enforcement—which on the surface are far removed from crime— have nonetheless contributed to crime through neighborhood deterioration, forced migration, and instability.

In short, by acting to reduce population flight, residential anonymity, and housing deterioration, the hope is that neighborhood stabilization and ultimately a more cohesive environment for youth socialization will emerge. This general strategy is quite compatible with that of Community Development Corporations (CDCs). Although CDCs focus on more comprehensive economic development, there are recent examples that such efforts are revitalizing previously declining areas and building social stability and hopefully safer neighborhoods in the process (Briggs et al. 1996).

5. Deconcentrate Poverty; Scattered-Site New Housing

This strategy is linked to that above, but it is more focused on promoting certain forms of class and race integration. As Wilson (1987) shows, the social transformation of the inner city has resulted in a disproportionate concentration and segregation of the most disadvantaged segments of the urban black population—especially poor, female-headed families with children. The social transformation of the inner city in recent decades has no doubt been fueled by macrostructural economic changes related to the de-industrialization of central cities where disadvantaged minorities are concentrated (e.g., shift from goods-producing to service-producing industries; increasing polarization of the labor market into low-wage and high-wage sectors). But perhaps more important, the steady out-migration of middle and upper-income black families from core inner city areas may have removed a former source of institutional supports. Consistent with a social organizational approach, Wilson (1987, p. 56; 1996) argues that the basic institutions of a neighborhood (e.g., churches, schools, stores, recreational facilities) are more likely to remain viable if the core of their support comes from more economically stable families.

An understanding of concentration effects must also recognize not just voluntary migration decisions but the negative consequences of policy decisions to concentrate minorities and the poor in public housing. Opposition from organized community groups to the building of public housing in "their" neighborhoods, de facto federal policy to tolerate segregation against blacks in urban housing markets, and decisions by local governments to neglect the rehabilitation of existing residential units, have led to massive, segregated housing projects which have become ghettos for the minorities and disadvantaged (Massey and Denton 1993). Although a community-level intervention cannot change the macrostructural economy or declining industrial base, the ecological concentration of poverty and racial segregation can be addressed by housing policies. Building on strategy Number 4, two approaches are:

• dispersing of concentrated public housing
• scattered-site, new, low-income housing

The evidence that dispersion policies and scattered-site housing can work is small but still encouraging (Massey and Denton 1993). For example, the Chicago Housing Authority is embarking on an ambitious plan to "scatter" (on a voluntary basis) more than 1,000 units of high-rise public housing in the city's ghetto as a means to break down the severe segregation that presently exists. There is also quasi- and experimental evidence that offering inner city mothers on welfare the opportunity to relocate to more thriving neighborhoods improves the social outcomes of both the mothers and their children (Rosenbaum and Popkin 1991; Ludwig et al. 2001). These results suggest the positive outcomes of housing policies that encourage (but do not require) increased integration among classes and races.

6. Maintain and Build Municipal Service Base

The provision of city municipal services for public health and fire safety—decisions presumably made with little if any thought to crime and violence—appear to have been salient in the social disintegration of poor communities. As Wallace and Wallace (1990) argue based on an analysis of the "planned shrinkage" of New York City fire and health services in recent decades: "The consequences of withdrawing municipal services from poor neighborhoods, the resulting outbreaks of contagious urban decay and forced migration which shred essential social networks and cause social disintegration, have become a highly significant contributor to decline in public health among the poor" (1990, p. 427). The loss of social integration and networks from planned shrinkage of services may increase behavioral patterns of violence, which cause further social disintegration (1990, p. 427). This pattern of destabilizing feedback (see Skogan 1986) appears central to an understanding of the role of governmental policies in fostering the downward spiral of low-income, high-crime areas. Housing and community-based policies should thus be coordinated with local policies regarding fire, sanitation, and other municipal services.

7. Integrate Community and Child Development/Health Policy

Although often neglected in policy discussions, research has demonstrated a substantial connection between structural disadvantage and childhood development. One link comes in the form of physical abuse and maltreatment. In a study of 20 subareas and 93 census tracts within a city, Garbarino and Crouter (1978) found that poverty, residential mobility, and single-parent households accounted for over 50 percent of the variation in rates of child abuse. Coulton et al.'s (1995) analysis of Cleveland showed that children who live in neighborhoods characterized by poverty, population turnover, and the concentration of female-headed families are at highest risk of abuse. The influence of concentrated poverty extended to adolescent risk factors as well, including the teen birth rate, delinquency, and high-school dropout rate. Similar to Shaw and McKay (1942), they suggest that child maltreatment is a manifestation of community social disorganization and that its occurrence is related to the same underlying social conditions that foster other urban problems.

Additional evidence consistent with social disorganization theory is found in a series of studies by Wallace and colleagues of community-level variations in low-birth-weight babies and infant mortality (Wallace and Wallace 1990). These authors document the strong upsurge in infant mortality and low birth-weight in the late 1970s in New York City, especially in devastated areas of the Bronx. In particular, they found that poverty, overcrowded housing, and rapid population change were the main predictors of increased rates of low birth-weight starting in 1974. Community instability coupled with concentrated poverty predicted increased infant mortality beyond what was expected based on migration.

There is thus evidence that concentrated urban poverty and social disorganization combine to increase child abuse/neglect, low birth-weight, cognitive impairment, and other adjustment problems, which in turn constitute risk factors for later crime and violence. In particular, recent data suggest that child neglect and physical abuse are prime risk factors for long-term patterns of violence among adults (Widom 1989). For these reasons, community-based interventions are needed to foster prenatal health care, infant/child health, and support programs for prosocial family management (e.g., child-rearing skills; conflict resolution). Community-level interventions of this sort appear promising, and may prove even more important in the long run than housing-based policies (see Sampson 1992).

8. Increase Community Power/Organizational Base

Stable interlocking organizations form a major linchpin of community solidarity and effective social control. When local organizations are unstable and isolated, and when the vertical links of community institutions to the outside are weak, the capacity of a community to defend its local interests is thus weakened. As Bursik and Grasmick (1993) argue along similar lines, public control refers to the regulatory capacities that develop from the networks among neighborhoods and between neighborhoods and public/private agencies. More specifically, this dimension "refers to the ability to secure public and private goods and services that are allocated by groups and agencies located outside of the neighborhood" (1993, p. 19). It follows that interventions promoting public control might:

- enhance community "empowerment"
- increase local involvement in community organizations
- promote the vertical integration of local institutions with extralocal resources
- promote collective action and awareness of local power

Although it cannot be said that massive changes will result from this type of mobilization, success at the margins produces cumulative changes that may ultimately promote a more stable and long-lasting social organization.

CONCLUSION

What seem to be "noncrime" policies—that is, where or if to build a housing project; enforcement of municipal codes; reduction in essential municipal services; rehabilitation of existing residential units; the dispersement of concentrated poverty building social connections among adults and youth increasing collective efficacy to achieve common goals—may have important effects on crime. As detailed above, residential instability and the concentration of poor, female-headed families with children appear to have been shaped by planned governmental policies at local, state, and federal levels. This conceptualization diverges from the natural market assumptions of the early social ecologists (e.g., Shaw and McKay 1942) by considering the role of political decisions in shaping local community structure.

Crime also generates a reciprocal feedback effect by undermining social and economic organization, which in turn leads to further increases in crime. Even decisions to relocate businesses appear to be shaped in part by the corrosive impact of serious crime on the quality of life for workers and customers alike. Hence policies on urban development can ill afford to ignore the symbolic and economic consequences of crime for the habitability, civility, and economic vitality of city life.

On the positive side, the implication of this paper's community-level perspective is that policy-manipulable options may help reverse the tide of community social disorganization in concentrated poverty areas. Indeed, the unique value of a community-level perspective is that it cautions against a simple "kinds of people" analysis by suggesting a focus on how social characteristics of collectivities are interrelated with crime. Based on the theory and research reviewed above (see also Sampson and Lauritsen 1994), it seems that policymakers should pay special attention to integrating crime-targeted interventions (e.g., early-warning systems, "hot spot" identification; reduction of social disorder) with more general policies that address:

- the interaction of concentrated urban poverty with other structural features of urban areas (e.g., population loss, family disruption)
- mediating processes of social organization (e.g., density of friend/ acquaintanceship; intergenerational ties and age integration; control-of-street-corner peer groups; organizational participation and mobilization; collective efficacy)
- the political economy of place, especially how concentrated poverty is influenced by public policies regarding housing and municipal services
- the effects of concentrated poverty on child, adolescent, and consequently adult developmental outcomes
- the reciprocal relationship between crime and urban socioeconomic development

Only then can we expect a more lasting effect of neighborhood-based interventions on the reduction of crime and disorder.

Overall, the community-level approach proposed in this paper points to simultaneous investment in the physical and social infrastructure of local communities. Given the nature of American society, much of this investment will probably have to come from communities themselves—that is, residents must come together and join forces with the criminal justice system to establish and maintain social order. This strategy relies on a vision of community based on shared values for a safe and healthy environment (see also Sampson et al. 1997; Sampson 1999; Meares and Kahan 1998)—not on divisive policies that separate by race and class.

10

Rehabilitation and Treatment Programs

Francis T. Cullen

"Is rehabilitation dead?" The voicing of this question, which occurred repeatedly in the mid-1970s (see, e.g., Halleck and Witte 1977; Serrill 1975), signaled the collapse of the paradigm of "individualized treatment" that had dominated correctional thinking throughout the twentieth century (Rothman 1980; Rotman 1990). Shortly before this time, it was taken for granted that the chief purpose of state intervention was to treat offenders. We were the nation, after all, that had "invented the penitentiary," built "reformatories," created a juvenile court to "save wayward children," and transformed prisons into "correctional" institutions where "therapeutic communities" could envelop offenders. Writing in 1972, Judge Marvin Frankel (1972, p. 7) captured the hegemony of the treatment paradigm when he observed that it is "fashionable nowadays to say that only rehabilitation can justify confinement." Indeed, criminologists believed that treatment was the logical extension of the scientific study of crime: find the causes of persistent criminality and then develop interventions to cure offenders of their criminogenic influences. As Gibbons (1999, p. 32) suggests, "It seemed to many criminologists that they were about to become 'scholar princes' who would lead a social movement away from punitive responses to criminals and delinquents and toward a society in which treatment, rehabilitation, and reintegration of deviants and lawbreakers would be the dominant cultural motif" (see Toby 1964).

A sea change in thinking, however, ended such delusions of grandeur. Scarcely at the end of the 1970s, Gottfredson (1979, p. 39) would observe that "the conventional wisdom in criminology is that rehabilitation has been found to be ineffective." In fact, criminologists' antipathy toward rehabilitation had become so intense that Gottfredson was able to document the "treatment destruction techniques"—the biased methodological critiques, the ex post facto arguments—that scholars would unfairly invoke to scuttle evaluation studies showing program effectiveness.

Criminologists, it seems, were politicized by the events of that day— by a Civil Rights movement that did not achieve all its goals and left racial inequality intact, by the waging of the Vietnam War, by the shootings at Kent State and Attica, by the Watergate scandal, and so on. Confidence in government plummeted generally in society during this time (Lipset and Schneider 1983), but mistrust in academia was so feverish that many scholars became "enemies of the state." Because the rehabilitation justified giving "the state"—judges and correctional officials—near unfettered discretion to individualize interventions, criminologists took special aim at rehabilitation. Their intellectual project thus turned from the science of rehabilitation to the deconstruction of rehabilitation. Where once rehabilitation was seen as reflecting "good intentions," now the appearance of "benevolence was really a mask for coercion" and the pursuit of class interests; correctional counselors, probation officers, and parole boards became "state agents of control"; extending services to troubled youths was portrayed as "net widening"; the ideal of "individualized treatment" was transformed into "state-enforced therapy"; and prison programs became an insidious attempt to "discipline the minds" of inmates (Binder and Geis 1984; Cullen and Gendreau 1989, 2001).

Outside criminology, elected officials and policymakers hardly embraced the view that rehabilitation was an instrument of state repression; if they had, they might have been more supportive of it. Instead, "treatment" was seen as yet another social welfare program that undermined individual responsibility and that separated bad behavioral choices (in this case, criminal acts) from unpleasant consequences (in this case, punishment). Rehabilitation "coddled offenders" by making life inside prison comfortable; it also allowed inmates to escape the full sting of a stiff prison sentence by conning a parole board that they were "cured" and deserving of an early release. Criminals, they argued, needed to be disciplined and punished (Cullen and Gilbert 1982; see, more generally, Garland 1990).

Much to the chagrin of offenders, criminologists did not become "scholar princes," and they wielded less power than elected officials. As result, the well-being of offenders receded in importance as one "get tough" law after another was passed to inflict more discomfort on "career criminals" and "super-predators." After a while, criminologists came to blame this "penal harm movement" (Clear 1994)—especially the sixfold increase in the prison population—on elected officials and not on rehabilitation. Still, their affection for treating offenders had passed, and they remained convinced that nothing they could ever do would make rehabilitation "work."

Given these developments, one might have expected that rehabilitation would, in fact, have "died." A quarter-century later, however, it is now clear the requiem planned for rehabilitation proved premature. To be sure, the legitimacy once enjoyed by the treatment paradigm is shaky and must be constantly reinforced. Virtually every state has changed its sentencing system to be more punitive and mindful of public safety; many probation departments place a priority on the surveillance of offenders, what one officer called the "pee 'em and see 'em" approach to supervision (drug testing and monitoring); and many jurisdictions have cut back on treatment services. Even so, virtually every prison continues to have an array of rehabilitation programs—perhaps to keep inmates busy, perhaps because it would have been too much effort to get rid of them; probation officers continue to deliver or broker services when they can; and public support for treatment, especially for juveniles, remains high (Applegate, Cullen, and Fisher 1997; Cullen, Fisher, and Applegate 2000; Cullen and Moon forthcoming; Moon et al. 1999).

The key issue, however, is what the future will hold for the rehabilitative ideal and for treatment programs. Although the handiwork of a limited number of criminologists, one exciting development is the emergence of a much clearer idea, based on empirical evidence, of "what works" to inhibit offender recidivism. These insights on effective correctional intervention were largely produced by a new statistical technique called *meta-analysis,* and by a bunch of Canadian psychologists who liked their government and never became "enemies of the state." This story of how rehabilitation was "saved," so to speak, will be told below. An effort will also be made, however, to detail the special challenge facing corrections: how to use this emergent knowledge and implement effective treatment programs. This essay concludes with some thoughts about the broader issue of whether we *should* retain rehabilitation as an integral part of our correctional system.

Before proceeding, it is necessary to convey how the concept of "rehabilitation" or "treatment" will be defined in this essay: *a planned correctional intervention that targets for change internal and/or social criminogenic factors with the goal of reducing recidivism and, where possible, of improving other aspects of an offender's life.* Rehabilitation may be conducted in conjunction with different types of criminal sanctions (e.g., imprisonment versus probation) and in different correctional settings (e.g., in an institution versus in the community). The type of sanction or setting, however, does not define whether treatment is being delivered. Instead, the key ingredient to rehabilitation is that a conscious effort is made to design an intervention whose expressed purpose is to provide some service to offenders that will change them in such a way as to make recidivism less likely. Typically, then, we speak of placing offenders in "programs." But it also is possible that treatment may be a "component" of a correctional program, such as a "boot camp" or "intensive supervision," whose goals include but are not limited to rehabilitation (i.e., they may include "control" or "deterrence") (Taxman 1999). Finally, unlike the punishment-oriented goals of retribution, deterrence, and incapacitation, which seek to inflict pain on or cage law-breakers, rehabilitation attempts to cure, fix, or otherwise improve offenders. Palmer (1992, pp. 22–23) has captured the essential features of rehabilitation in the following way:

> [Treatment] usually tries to reach its socially centered and offender-centered goals by focusing on such factors and conditions as the offender's *adjustment techniques, interests, skills, personal limitations, and/or life circumstances.* It does so in order to affect his or her future behavior and adjustment. That is, treatment efforts focus on any of several factors or conditions and are directed at particular future events. These efforts may be called treatment *programs* or *approaches* insofar as they involve specific components and inputs (e.g., counseling or skill development) that are organized, interrelated, and otherwise planned so as to generate changes in the above factors and conditions—changes which, in turn, may help generate the desired future events (e.g., reduced illegal behavior). [Emphasis in original.]

BEYOND MARTINSON

"With few and isolated exceptions," wrote Robert Martinson (1974a, p. 25), "the rehabilitation efforts that have been reported so far have had no appreciable effect on recidivism." This technical-sounding conclusion would soon come to be known as the "nothing works" doctrine in corrections—that is, that "nothing works" in treatment to change the law-breaking into law-abiding. It would also have enormous ramifications. Two years following Martinson's declaration, Adams (1976, p. 76) captured its impact when he observed that the "Nothing Works doctrine . . .

has shaken the community of criminal justice to its root . . . widely assorted members of the criminal justice field are briskly urging that punishment and incapacitation should be given much higher priority among criminal justice goals" (see, also, Blumstein 1997). Even today, Martinson's study is viewed as prompting a dramatic shift in correctional policy away from rehabilitation (Cose 2000). Others continue to offer Martinson's findings as solid evidence that treatment programs are ineffective—that their "record for repairing and reconstructing souls has been abysmal" (Reynolds 1996, p. 7). As Glaser (1995, p. 123) notes, "conservatives still cite [the study] as grounds for imposing punishments determined only by 'just deserts.'"

Martinson (1974a) presented his assessment of rehabilitation programs in his classic essay, published in *The Public Interest*, entitled "What Works? Questions and Answers About Prison Reform." This work was a provocative precursor to a more judicious 736-page coauthored book published the next year, *The Effectiveness of Correctional Treatment* (Lipton, Martinson, and Wilks 1975). This project involved an analysis of 231 studies, conducted between 1945 and 1967, which evaluated the effectiveness of rehabilitation programs. Although almost half the studies surveyed showed reductions in recidivism (Palmer 1975), Martinson suggested that no *category* or modality of treatment—such as counseling, skill development, or psychotherapy—reliably "worked" to cut criminal involvement. In practical terms, corrections was unlike medical treatment where, for example, diseases were combated with proven cures. Instead, the extant research could give no advice to correctional officials on specific treatment programs that could, with any certainty, diminish recidivism.

Martinson recognized that the pessimistic results from his analysis might be due to poorly conducted research studies or to treatment programs that were sound in principle but inadequately implemented. But he was moved to ask, "whether all these studies lead irrevocably to the conclusion that *nothing works,* that we haven't the faintest clue about how to rehabilitate offenders and reduce recidivism" (p. 48; emphasis added). He then suggested that the treatment enterprise might be inherently futile. "It may be," he warned, "that there is a radical flaw in our present strategies—that education at its best, or that psychotherapy at its best, cannot overcome, or even appreciably reduce, the powerful tendency for offenders to continue in criminal behavior." Martinson stopped short in the essay of explicitly saying that "nothing works," but this was the message being conveyed. Indeed, Martinson (1974b, p. 4) soon clarified that he believed that "rehabilitation was a myth. That is a conclusion I have come to . . . based on the evidence made available by this volume."

For its time, the Martinson study was credible and not inconsistent with contemporary reviews of the treatment-evaluation literature (see, e.g., Bailey 1966; Greenberg 1977; Logan 1972; Robison and Smith 1971). Most noteworthy, a panel of scholars commissioned by the National Academy of Sciences examined research on rehabilitation generally and, in particular, conducted a detailed analysis of a 10 percent random sample of the studies assessed by Martinson. The panel concluded that Martinson and his colleagues Lipton and Wilks were "reasonably accurate and fair in the appraisal of the rehabilitation literature" (Sechrest, White, and Brown 1979, p. 31). Based on the existing body of studies, they shared his view that it was not possible to make "recommendations about ways of rehabil-itating offenders . . . with any warranted confidence" (p. 102). However, given the methodological problems of many evaluation studies and the failure of agencies to implement programs as designed, the panel also cau-tioned that "neither could one say with justified confidence that rehabilitation cannot be achieved, and, therefore, no drastic cutbacks in rehabilitative effort should be based on that proposition" (pp. 102–03). This judicious assessment—that is, the panel's call for more rigorous research before prematurely jumping to conclusions and scuttling treat-ment programs—would not be heeded by the many criminologists who came to embrace the "nothing works" doctrine.

In any case, Martinson's study was formidable in its scope, and it would be unfair to characterize his account of the status of treatment pro-grams as based on a gross misreading of the extant evaluation studies. Even so, as is the case with social science research on virtually any topic, Martinson's conclusions were hardly definitive or the "last word" on treat-ment effectiveness. First, as noted, many of the studies he reviewed reduced recidivism (Palmer 1975), a finding that is inconsistent with a "nothing works" conclusion. This was true as well of the other reviews at this time that, on grounds similar to Martinson, also questioned the value of treatment programs (Andrews and Bonta 1998; Gottfredson 1979). Second, Martinson's research is commonly believed to have assessed 231 studies. What is less known, however, is that the analysis covered only 138 measures of recidivism, of which fewer than 80 measures were linked to interventions that could legitimately be categorized as a "treatment program" as opposed to a "sanction" such as imprisonment or probation (Cullen and Gendreau 2000; Gottfredson 1979). Accordingly, only a lim-ited number of studies fell into any of the treatment categories created by Martinson, and often they were a mixed bag of interventions that had little in common with one another (Klockars 1975). Third, his study did not contain a category for behavioral or cognitive-behavioral interventions. This omission is especially telling because research now shows that this treatment modality is associated with meaningful reductions in recidivism (Andrews and Bonta 1998; Gendreau 1996; MacKenzie 2000; MacKenzie and Hickman 1998; McLaren 1992; Pearson et al. 2000; see also Gaes et al. 1999).

Now more than a quarter of a century after Martinson's essay, we should recognize his study for what it was: an important and sobering reminder that correctional treatment is a difficult enterprise fraught with many failures. It was not, however, a project that was flawless or capable of fully settling the issue of treatment effectiveness. We might have expected, in fact, that scholars would have greeted the publication of his essay with "organized skepticism," a core norm of science that prescribes that provocative findings be subjected to careful scrutiny by the discipline's community of scholars (Merton 1973). Instead, with the exception of a few lonely voices (e.g., Cullen and Gilbert 1982; Gendreau and Ross, 1979; Palmer 1975), Martinson's study was readily accepted by criminologists as incontrovertible proof that "nothing works" in correctional treatment (see also Martinson 1979). This doctrine thus became a "conventional wisdom," and contrary views either were dismissed out of hand or, when addressed at all, were rejected as "obviously" based on methodologically flawed evidence (Gottfredson 1979). In short, it became standard operating procedure in the discipline to discredit correctional treatment, not to conduct a value-free assessment of its effectiveness (however, see Sechrest, White, and Brown, 1979).

The willingness to accept the "nothing works" view and the withering scrutiny given to positive research findings on treatment were not based on fair-minded scientific criteria but were ideologically inspired (Cullen and Gendreau, 2001). By the time Martinson's essay appeared, many criminologists already had rejected or, at the least, had serious doubts about correctional programs. As noted previously, their suspicions were rooted in the fact that the "state" was administering these interventions. In the rehabilitative ideal, which emerged in the early 1900s in the Progressive Era (Rothman 1980), government officials were accorded the discretion to "individualize treatment," much as a physician does with medical interventions. Judges were given wide latitude in whether to sentence offenders to prison and, if so, for how long; for offenders in the community, probation and parole officers were to help those amenable to rehabilitation but also were expected to pick out which "bad apples" should be "revoked" and sent to prison; once in prison, release was to depend on being cured, and a parole board would determine who would, or would not, be granted their freedom.

But what if this "ideal" was nothing but a "noble lie" (Morris 1974)— a benevolent set of good intentions that masked the disquieting practices that really went on in the justice system? Or, still worse, what if rehabilitation was, underneath its cloak of benevolence, an insidious system of power used by the state to discipline deviants and the disadvantaged (Foucault 1977)? And this is precisely what many scholars were prepared to believe at this historical juncture. A series of cataclysmic sociopolitical events and the continuing turbulence in the 1960s and early 1970s had coalesced to diminish Americans' confidence in their government (Lipset and Schneider 1983). Affected by this social context, many criminologists lost their trust in the state and feared the power it exercised over offenders. They were prepared to believe that judges were using their discretion not to individualize treatments but to discriminate against poor and minority defendants; that parole was a lottery—run by a board of political appointees with no criminological expertise—in which release from prison was unrelated to the risk of recidivating; and that treatment programs were used not to cure inmates but to coerce them to behavior while incarcerated, lest they "rot" in prison until they buckled under to institutional rules. They mistrusted the motives of judges and correctional officials, now seeing them as "state agents of social control" who used their discretionary power to reinforce an unequal and unjust social order that benefited the rich, not the poor (Binder and Geis 1984). They embraced policy positions that minimized control over offenders, mindlessly favoring, for example, community sanctions over imprisonment and "radical nonintervention" over any type of state penalty (Schur 1973). Not surprisingly, Martinson's findings of "no appreciable" treatment effects were hardly an occasion for dispute but rather were easily interpreted as showing what they already knew: that "nothing works" in state enforced therapy (Cullen and Gendreau 1989; Cullen and Gilbert 1982).

Criminologists had good reasons to be concerned about the reality of correctional rehabilitation programs. State officials often had virtually unfettered discretion over offenders' lives, often had little or no expertise in rehabilitation, and often made decisions based on ignorance, hunch, or bias (Kittrie 1971; Rothman 1980). Still, the collateral argument that "nothing works" in rehabilitation did not follow from these legitimate concerns about how rehabilitation was being implemented. Most unfortunate, criminologists closed their minds to the possibility that treatment programs—or other interventions carried out by the criminal justice system—could reduce crime. As a discipline, criminologists were more committed to showing that nothing that the state did could diminish crime rates than to building knowledge on what could work to limit offenders' criminality (Cullen and Gendreau, 2001; more generally, see Maruna 2001).

In any case, it is time for criminologists—and others concerned about corrections—to move beyond Martinson's view of rehabilitation. His study's exalted status was never deserved and has served to stifle debate and scientific progress in the study of treatment effectiveness. If we have learned anything over the past quarter-century, it is that rehabilitating offenders, while a daunting challenge, is feasible. Revisionist scholars engaged in the study of correctional rehabilitation have rejected the "nothing works" doctrine and are hard at work in discerning "what works" to change offenders. It is to this exciting development that we now turn.

BIBLIOTHERAPY FOR CYNICS: LESSONS FROM META-ANALYSIS

In 1979, Gendreau and Ross furnished a systematic review of effective treatment programs (see, also, Gendreau and Ross 1987). They hoped, in their words, that this review would provide "bibliotherapy for cynics" who endorsed the "nothing works" doctrine. Although some scholars took notice, most criminologists resisted the "bibliotherapy." In part, their resistance stemmed from their ideology—from their mistrust of the state and its supposed attempt to "coerce" offenders into treatment. But the failure to take seriously Gendreau and Ross's assessment also was made easier by the type of review they conducted: a "narrative review" or a qualitative summary and discussion of what the "research shows."

Until recently, scholars reviewed research in an area in one of two ways. First, in the narrative review, the scholar compiled studies, analyzed them, and then—like Gendreau and Ross—drew conclusions. Second, in the "ballot box" or "vote counting" review, the scholar would find all relevant studies and then would count, one by one, whether a study showed that a treatment program worked or did not work to reduce recidivism. At least with regard to rehabilitation, the difficulty with these approaches was that they often provided mixed results. The question of whether the glass was half empty or half full inevitably emerged. Whereas Gendreau and Ross could identify a host of programs that reduced recidivism, critics could point to a host of programs that were ineffective. The imprecision of the review technique thus encouraged competing interpretations that would be difficult to falsify. In short, the notion that "treatment works" could be dismissed as Gendreau and Ross's "opinion" about what the studies meant.

Research on the accuracy and consistency of narrative or qualitative reviews of scholarly studies reveals that such assessments can draw erroneous conclusions of the extant empirical evidence. In such reviews, authors analyzing the same set of studies are prone to classify these studies differently and to reach contrasting conclusions (Glass, McGraw, and Smith 1981). In such a situation, "conclusions are influenced by prejudice and stereotyping to a degree that would be unforgivable in primary research itself" (p. 18). It might be argued that this interpretive divergence is simply a by-product of the nature of social science research—that is, that methodological imprecision and the inability to replicate findings makes the accumulation of research knowledge difficult and the interpretation of studies more art than science. In an illuminating analysis of research findings in physics and psychology, however, Hedges (1987, p. 443) contends that "the results of physical experiments may not be strikingly more consistent than those of social and behavioral experiments." Even with the inherent limitations of social science methodology taken into account, the problem in understanding what a cumulative body of research shows may lie not in the sample of studies conducted but in the method used to organize and analyze them (Gendreau, Goggin, and Smith 2000, Forthcoming; Glass, McGraw, and Smith 1981; Hedges 1987).

In this regard, over the last decade or so, a new way of "making sense" of a body of research has emerged: the *meta-analysis* or a *quantitative* synthesis of studies. In this approach, each study is coded to determine the statistical relationship—the *effect size*—between the treatment intervention and recidivism. The researcher then computes what is analogous to a batting average across all studies, or what is known as an *average effect size*. This is a precise point estimate of the impact of treatment on recidivism. Usually, the effect size statistic is reported as a Pearson's r and its confidence interval. The r value can most often be interpreted on its face value. An effect size of .20 would mean that there was a 20 percentage point difference in recidivism between the treatment and control groups (Gendreau, Goggin, and Paparozzi 1996). Or, if one were to assume a base recidivism rate of 50 percent, the recidivism rate for the treatment group would be 40 percent and for the control group it would be 60 percent (Andrews and Bonta 1998). Finally, in a meta-analysis, it is possible to introduce *moderators,* or factors that might be seen as influencing the effect size. For example, one might see if the effect size varies by the quality of a study's methodology or by the quality of the treatment delivered.

Meta-analysis is not without its own limitations, the largest one being the "garbage in, garbage out" problem: that is, that the quality of the review will be shaped by the quality of the studies that are quantitatively synthesized. Even the most sophisticated meta-analysis cannot derive sound conclusions from a set of methodologically unsound studies. There is also the possibility of selection bias to the extent that the studies reviewed are not representative of all existing programs or of all evaluations that have been conducted (e.g., evaluations tend to be performed on innovative programs, or published studies tend to report statistically significant findings). Nonetheless, meta-analysis largely eliminates the bias that often emerges when two scholars differentially interpret what a study "really found." Further, because coding criteria and decisions are made public, any given meta-analysis is open to replication.

Overall Treatment Effects

Importantly for the debate over the effectiveness of rehabilitation, meta-analysis has provided a way out of the "half-empty or half-full" assessment of the extant literature. Again, as a quantitative approach, it can provide an "effect size" estimate of the relationship between rehabilitation—or different types of treatment interventions—and recidivism. It is noteworthy that although not beyond dispute, these favorable results have been far more influential than previous narrative and vote counting reviews in persuading criminologists that "rehabilitation works."

On a broad level, it is perhaps useful to begin by asking whether planned interventions are able to improve a range of behaviors, including mental health problems, educational performance, and developmental difficulties. If not, then one might conclude that human conduct, once deeply ingrained, cannot be changed. But if interventions can be beneficial, then one would have to wonder why criminal behavior, among all human problems, would be unique in its resistance to reformation. In a review of 302 meta-analyses, Lipsey and Wilson (1993, p. 1,181) discovered that across a variety of psychological, educational, and behavioral outcomes, the interventions had "a strong, dramatic pattern of overall effects." The average difference in success rates between the treatment and control groups was 24 percentage points. It seems that human conduct, including that deemed as an unfortunate affliction or as a wayward choice, is amenable to alteration. "The number and scope of effective treatments covered by this conclusion are impressive," concluded Lipsey and Wilson, "and the magnitude of the effects for a substantial portion of those treatments is in a range of practical significance by almost any reasonable criteria" (p. 1,199).

We should note that in this review, Lipsey and Wilson included 10 meta-analyses that were conducted on offenders. They did find that the effect sizes for meta-analyses on treatment programs for criminal conduct were lower than for other problem behaviors. Still, consistent with their more general findings, there was no evidence that offenders cannot be rehabilitated.

In this regard, in a review of 13 meta-analyses of offender rehabilitation programs published between 1985 and 1995, Losel (1995) reported that the mean effect size varied from a low of .05 to a high of .18 (see also Redondo, Sanchez-Meca, and Garrido 1999; McLaren 1992). He estimated that the "mean effect size of all assessed studies probably has a size of about .10" (1995, p. 89; see, also, Losel, Forthcoming). In practical terms, this would mean that the recidivism rate for the treatment group would be 45 percent compared to 55 percent for the control group.

It is possible, moreover, that these figures may underestimate the true influence of treatment programs, for two reasons. First, treatment groups are not always compared to control groups who receive "no intervention." Because some criminal justice sanctions might include a rehabilitation component, members of the control group might experience an unmeasured treatment effect (Losel 1995). Second, most studies rely on official and dichotomous measures of recidivism (e.g., either were or were not arrested). According to Lipsey (1992, p. 98), this measurement strategy may attenuate the effect size of treatment because "it is largely a matter of chance whether a particular delinquent act eventuates in an official recorded contact with an agent of law enforcement or the juvenile justice system." He estimates that when this fact is taken into account, the true effect size for treatment interventions may double. We should note that some commentators suggest that other methodological considerations may diminish the treatment effects reported thus far (Gaes et al. 1999; Losel, Forthcoming). Nonetheless, even when a range of methodological factors are taken into account, it appears that the positive effects of treatment found in the extant meta-analyses are sustained (Lipsey 1992, 1999a, 1999b; Lipsey and Wilson 1998).

Heterogeneity of Treatment Effects

Thus far we have been reviewing the impact of rehabilitation on recidivism across a panoply of programs. If we might use a medical analogy, this would be akin to testing whether it was possible to cure strep throat by giving ill patients such diverse interventions as penicillin, aspirin, mouthwash, and bloodletting. Across all of these "treatments," one might find a small positive treatment effect when compared with doing nothing with the patients. Clearly, though, calculating the overall treatment effect would mask the potent impact of some interventions (e.g., penicillin and its derivatives) and the impotence of other interventions (e.g., aspirin, mouthwash, bloodletting). In other words, the treatment effects would, in this case, be *heterogeneous*—some would be strong, others weak. Further, it would seem that searching for "strong effects" would be necessary if one wished to avoid medical quackery, in which useless interventions were dispensed regardless of their failure to cure patients.

It is inadvisable to assume that correctional treatment will ever be as precise as medical treatments of this sort, unless, of course, some crime-curing pills are suddenly invented! If we were to draw a more appropriate medical analogy, it would be to the search for treatments for cancer and AIDS. This search has made important advances, but it is still plagued by substantial failure rates and by the need for ongoing research to do better in saving patients' lives. In a similar manner, correctional interventions will invariably be beset by higher than desired recidivism rates and by the need for continuing experimentation in what really works to divert offenders from criminal conduct. However, in both cases—the treatment of cancer/AIDS and of criminality—the standard of success is not high cure rates but rather doing better than alternative interventions that are available.

In any event, meta-analyses of treatment programs have moved into a "second generation." Beyond computing an effect size across all interventions, scholars are now documenting heterogeneity in effect sizes—that is, they are seeking to differentiate treatment programs that work from those that do not. This enterprise seems commonsensical, but systematic research in this direction remains in the beginning stages (Losel, Forthcoming). Making strides is hindered by three considerations.

First, many evaluations do not describe or measure the intervention with enough specificity to know what exactly was done. In particular, unless process evaluations are conducted, "what went on" in the course of the treatment delivery is difficult to assess with any certainty. Second, the categories used to create homogenous treatment types or modalities are often not theoretically derived (see Andrews et al. 1990). Instead, treatment types are grouped by labels that have long existed, such as "individual counseling" or "life skills." Although not without some value, the weakness of this approach is that a modality such as "individual counseling" may have as much within-group or within-category variation as between-group variation. For example, individual counseling that is behaviorally oriented may have more in common with a token economy than with other types of psychological counseling (e.g., psychoanalytic or client-centered therapy). Third, although hundreds of evaluation studies are now available for meta-analysis, when divided up into specific categories, the number of studies in any one category can become limited. Drawing firm conclusions on the effects of a few evaluations—especially when they are of varying methodological quality—can be risky.

With these caveats in mind, the meta-analysis evidence is reasonably clear about what treatment programs are most successful in reducing recidivism: interventions that are based on social learning or behavioral principles, are structured rather than nondirective, seek to build human capital in offenders, and use more than one treatment modality to address the multiple problems that offenders may be experiencing. In contrast, interventions that are loosely structured, are based on psychoanalytic or client-centered therapy, and/or that target for change factors unrelated or weakly related to recidivism (e.g., self-concept) do not have meaningful effects on recidivism. Thus, as Losel (1995, p. 91) notes, based on his review of existing meta-analyses, "it is mostly cognitive-behavioural, skill-oriented and multi-modal programmes that yield the best effects." Echoing these views, MacKenzie (2000, p. 464) concludes that meta-analyses "have supported the finding that effective programs are structured and focused, use multiple treatment components, focus on developing skills, and use behavioral (including cognitive-behavioral) methods (with reinforcements for clearly identified, overt behaviors as opposed to nondirective counseling focusing on insight, self-esteem, or disclosure)." She also observes that "effective programs . . . must be designed to address the characteristics of offenders that are associated with criminal activities and can be changed." Based on these results and on a priori theoretical views, some criminologists have derived "principles of effective intervention"—an issue we return to below (Andrews 1995; Gendreau 1996).

It might also be useful to pause for a moment to define "cognitive-behavior" programs—another topic we will revisit in this essay (see Spiegler and Guevremont 1998). These programs are based on the view that cognitions—what and how we think—are learned and affect behavioral choices, including the choice to break the law. As Lester and Van Voorhis (1997) point out, cognitive-behavioral programs fall into two categories, although interventions may include both types of approaches (see also Andrews and Bonta 1998). "Cognitive restructuring" programs attempt to change the content of what offenders believe, such as their procriminal attitudes and rationalizations for why law violations are acceptable (e.g., externalizing blame). "Cognitive skills" programs attempt to change the structure or way offenders reason, such as how to cope with and control anger or impulsive urges. Cognitive-behavioral treatments often involve the reinforcement of prosocial attitudes and behavior and efforts to show prosocial coping strategies through modeling, role-playing, and structured group learning (e.g., anger management classes).

Equally salient from a policy standpoint, meta-analysis research also reveals that deterrence-oriented and "character building" interventions—such as "scared straight" programs, shock incarceration ("boot camps"), and "wilderness" programs—do not blunt criminality and might, in fact, be associated with slight increases in recidivism (Andrews et al. 1990; Gendreau et al. 2000; MacKenzie 2000; Lipsey 1992; Lipsey and Wilson 1998; see, also, Finckenauer and Gavin 1999). Similar results have been found for "intermediate sanctions"—punishments that lie "between prison and probation" (Morris and Tonry 1990). In the 1980s, an array of community-based programs were introduced to exert control over and presumably deter offenders free in society—programs such as intensive supervision, drug testing, and electronic monitoring/home incarceration. A meta-analysis of these programs by Gendreau et al. (2000) reported an effect size of zero. This result confirms the conclusions based on the best experimental studies (see, e.g., Petersilia and Turner 1993) and on narrative reviews of the literature (Cullen, Wright, and Applegate 1996; Fulton et al. 1997; Gendreau, Cullen, and Bonta 1994; MacKenzie 1997, 2000; Petersilia 1998). Finally, it is noteworthy that, although suggestive, the evidence also indicates that control-oriented programs only reduce recidivism when they include a treatment component (Bonta, Wallace-Capretta, and Rooney 2000; Cullen, Wright, and Applegate 1996; Petersilia and Turner 1993).

ASSESSING COMMONLY USED TREATMENT PROGRAMS

The section after this one will present an attempt by Canadian criminologists to develop a research-based theory of effective correctional intervention. The value of their theoretical enterprise is that it endeavors to move beyond empirical descriptions of treatment effectiveness to provide both a rationale for why certain interventions reduce recidivism and a blueprint for future program development. An exclusive focus on this undertaking, however, would be misleading, in that it would ignore the wealth of interventions that occur every day within the correctional system. Some of these programs manifest principles of effective treatment; some do not. In any event, they are the kinds of treatment that offenders most often receive, and thus it seems incumbent to consider their effectiveness. In this section, we consider three types of treatment programs that are found in virtually every state correctional system: 1) education and work programs, 2) drug programs, and 3) sex-offender programs.

Education and Work Programs

"Education and work programs," observe Gaes et al. (1999, p. 398), "are the cornerstones of correctional intervention" (see also Lin 2000; Silverman and Vega 1996). Each year, prisons in the United States spend an estimated $412 million on educational programs (*Corrections Compendium* 1997). A survey conducted in 1995 revealed that nearly one-fourth of state and federal prison inmates were enrolled in some type of educational program (Stephan 1997). About four-fifths of U.S. prisons offer the General Equivalency Development (GED) program; in 1996, more than 37,000 inmates earned their GEDs. Three-fourths of the nation's prisons provide adult basic education, which involves learning in such core areas as mathematics, literacy, language arts, and social studies. More than 50,000 inmates are enrolled in such basic education (*Corrections Compendium* 1997). Due to 1994 federal legislation that excluded inmates from securing Pell Grants to fund more advanced study, participation in college degree programs is declining (Tewksbury, Erickson, and Taylor 2000). Still, college education courses may be available in as many as one-third of correctional institutions. In 1996, over 14,500 inmates received a two-year associate's degree, and 232 received a bachelor's degree (*Corrections Compendium* 1997).

Vocational education programs are also found in about half of all correctional institutions. In 1994, a survey of 43 correctional systems reported that more than 65,000 inmates were enrolled in training programs aimed at equipping them with the vocational skills that would enhance post-release job prospects (Lillis 1994). It also is estimated that nearly two-thirds of all inmates are given a work assignment (Stephan 1997). A 1999 survey indicated that in adult correctional facilities, 55 percent of inmates were assigned to the category of "other work," which would mainly involve institutional maintenance (e.g., cleaning, sweeping floors, food service). Another 5.1 percent were assigned to prison farms. Only 6.1

percent of offenders had jobs in prison industries, although this figure jumped to 18.4 percent in the Federal Bureau of Prisons (Camp and Camp 1999; see, also, Flanagan 1989; Wees 1997b). In raw figures, over 70,000 inmates were assigned to prison industry programs. (Camp and Camp 1999). In 1994, the average prison industry budget across states was almost $26 million, whereas for the nation this budget exceeded $1 billion (Wunder 1994).

Inmates work an average of seven hours daily, with wages ranging from $2.17 to $8.94 a day; in programs administered by private companies, the wages range from $26.35 to $35.62 a day. The most common categories of prison industry products and services include agriculture and food (e.g., bakery goods, beef, milk), garments and textiles (e.g., flags, mattresses, clothing), vehicular (e.g., ambulances, auto repair, tires), furniture and other wood products (e.g., picnic tables, reupholstering), paper products and printing (e.g., binding books, signs), metal products (e.g., license plates, traffic signs), janitorial supplies (e.g., mops, paint), electronic products (e.g., CD-ROMs, computers), and the provision of services (e.g., data entry, landscaping, laundry, telemarketing) (Camp and Camp 1999, pp. 110–12).

Most institutions have a unique combination of education and work programs. A sample of program offerings at three correctional facilities in the state of Ohio illustrates this point. At the state's main maximum-security institution, the 1,438-inmate Southern Ohio Correctional Facility at Lucasville, program options are comparatively restricted. Prison industries are limited to the print and shoe shops, while the lone vocational training available is in masonry. Academic alternatives include only adult basic education, the GED, and a building maintenance apprentice program (see http://www.drc.ohio.gov/web/socf.htm). In contrast, at the 2,559-inmate Chillicothe Correctional Institution, industrial programs include the chair and mattress factories, vehicle modification, recycling, packaging tourism information for the state, and remanufacturing laser printing cartridges. Vocational programs include carpentry, building maintenance, welding, upholstery, and heating/ventilation/air conditioning. The academic options encompass not only basic education and the GED—as at the Lucasville prison—but also literacy education and classes from a technical college (see http://www.drc.ohio.gov/web/cci.htm). Finally, the 2,099-offender Ohio Reformatory for Women in Orient has industrial programs in computer-aided drafting, the print shop, and the garment shop. There is vocational training in business office communications, building maintenance, plumbing, graphic arts, and electronics. Academically, the offerings range from literacy and basic education to the GED and then to technical college courses in culinary arts, automotive parts, and landscaping and tree care (http://www.drc.ohio.gove/web/orw.htm).

Beyond programs within adult institutions, there are community-based work and education interventions. For example, two surveys conducted in the 1990s revealed that an estimated 20,000 inmates left the institution each day to participate in work-release programs (Davis 1993; Wees 1997a; see, also, Turner and Petersilia 1996). For offenders on probation, there are also programs aimed at providing career counseling, job placement, and general "job development" (Bushway and Reuter 1997; Camp and Camp 1999). Academic programs and vocational education are commonplace as well in juvenile facilities (Lillis 1993). In the community, there also have been programs aimed at diverting at-risk youths from crime by improving their labor-market prospects (Bushway and Reuter 1997).

Why, however, should education, improving vocational skills, and/or actual work experiences reduce criminal involvement? In part, Americans have long believed that the discipline inherent in diligent study and in particular hard work builds sound character and instills appropriate social habits (Phillips and Sandstrom 1990). For example, when correctional leaders met in Cincinnati for the now-famous 1870 National Congress on Penitentiary and Reformatory Discipline, one of the core "principles" they formally adopted was that "education is a vital force in the reformation of fallen men" (Wines 1871, p. 542). Likewise, they encouraged "industrial training" because "work is no less an auxiliary to virtue, than it is a means of support. Steady, active, honorable labor is the basis of all reformatory discipline" (p. 543). In more contemporary times, the idea of character formation has been complemented with the sense that in modern society, a conventional life is not possible without adequate education and a good job. Virtually every criminological theory has an explanation for why this is so (Cullen et al., Forthcoming; Piehl 1998; Uggen 1999). Education and work are seen to prevent crime because they provide legitimate opportunities (strain theory), foster commitment and informal social control (social bond theory), are conduits for prosocial learning (differential association theory), blunt stigma and enhance reintegration (labeling/shaming theory), make the choice of "going straight" more beneficial (rational choice theory), and so on. Added to these ruminations is the stubborn reality that offenders earn fewer years of education and have poorer work histories than members of the general public (Silverman and Vega 1996; Wilson, Gallagher, and MacKenzie 2000).

In this context, it seems only a matter of "common sense" that access to education and work would diminish criminal participation.

Complexity, however, is often the victim of common sense, and how crime is shaped by schooling and jobs is, if anything, complex. Indeed, numerous considerations caution against the facile assumption that equipping offenders with human capital and occupational opportunities will invariably diminish their criminal involvement: the roots (or "early predictors") of serious criminality emerge before or coterminous with entry into school and surely before the age of adult employment; associations between education/job problems and crime may, due to preexisting individual differences, be partially, or wholly, spurious; educational attainment and employment, though not unimportant, are generally not the strongest predictors of recidivism; many offenders are employed at the time of their crimes; and jobs can furnish opportunities to commit crimes and to develop antisocial friendships that amplify offending outside the workplace (Andrews and Bonta 1998; Wright and Cullen 2000; Fagan and Freeman 1999; Gendreau, Little, and Goggin 1996; Hirschi and Gottfredson 1995; Lipsey and Derzon 1998; Piehl 1998; Uggen 1999).

Despite the long-standing prevalence of work and education programs, the research evidence on whether this treatment modality reduces recidivism is limited and of low quality. A number of useful reviews are now available, but they generally conclude by cautioning against drawing definitive conclusions and by calling for more well-designed studies (Bouffard, MacKenzie, and Hickman 2000; Bushway and Reuter 1997; Flanagan 1994; Gaes et al. 1999; Gerber and Fritsch 1995; MacKenzie and Hickman 1998; Pearson and Lipton 1999a; Wilson, Gallagher, and MacKenzie 2000; Wilson et al. 1999). The main difficulty is that the research designs used typically cannot rule out "selection bias"—that is, that positive treatment results may be due not to the impact of the intervention but to preexisting differences that make members of the treatment less likely to recidivate than those in the control group (e.g., more motivated to change, unmeasured, prosocial, psychological traits). Still, the effects of education and work programs do seem to be "encouraging" (Gaes et al. 1999, p. 398).

Four main conclusions are suggested by the existing evaluation literature. First, there is evidence that participation in education and work education programs may decrease inmates' disciplinary problems while incarcerated. By contributing to social order, programs thus may also serve as a management resource (Lin 2000). Second, although less clear, involvement in these prison programs may increase prosocial activities in the community such as employment and increased schooling (Gaes et al. 1999). Third and most salient, it appears that across existing studies, education and work programs reduce recidivism. Again, this finding is qualified by the dearth of experimental randomized studies that would rule out selection bias. Raising this methodological concern, however, does not obviate the fact that more evidence exists that these programs "work" than exists that they are inconsequential.

Wilson, Gallagher, and MacKenzie's (2000) meta-analysis of 33 educational, vocational, and work programs is most instructive (see also Wilson et al. 1999). They calculated that "assuming a 50 percent recidivism rate for nonparticipants, [program] participants recidivate, on average, at a rate of 39 percent" (p. 361). They also concluded that education programs appeared to achieve a larger reduction in recidivism than work programs. Insights can also be drawn from a systematic review of this literature by Bouffard, MacKenzie, and Hickman (2000). Although cautious about the methodological limitations of the extant research, they suggest that three interventions likely reduce recidivism: 1) vocational education, 2) "multi-component" correctional industry programs that combine employment with other "components" such as vocational education and job search assistance, and 3) community employment programs such as work-release or job search assistance outside the prison.

Finally, the research suggests a fourth conclusion: treatment effects may be modified by offender and program characteristics. Thus, in a study of more than 14,000 Texas inmates released from prison in 1991 and 1992, Adams et al. (1994) found that prison education programs tended to be most effective in reducing recidivism for inmates who initially had low levels of educational achievement. They also uncovered a treatment "dose" effect: education only began to diminish reoffending once inmates had spent a minimum of 200 hours in the program. On a broader level, it also seems likely that programs aimed at creating human capital will be more effective if they are able to link offenders not merely with employment but also with *quality* jobs. There is at least some evidence that while merely having a job does not foster desistance, quality employment is related—net of individual differences—with lower recidivism (Uggen 1999; see also Currie 1985; Sampson and Laub 1993).

Drug Treatment Programs

Drug use and crime are behaviors that often co-occur in the same individuals. The precise causal relationship of involvement in drugs and other illegal conduct is debated, but it appears that drug use amplifies criminality (Lurigio 2000). There also is evidence that offenders are more likely to ingest drugs, especially heroin and cocaine, than the general population (Bureau of Justice Statistics 1992; Lurigio 2000). As might be anticipated, a high proportion of the offenders under correctional supervision have a history of drug use and/or related criminal activity (Maruna 2001). Thus, about one in five state prison inmates and three in five federal inmates are incarcerated for drug-related offenses (Gilliard and Beck 1998). Equally illuminating, psychological evaluations of a nonrepresentative sample of offenders admitted to federal prisons during a one-week period in 1988 found that about four in ten offenders had a "moderate to severe" drug problem (Bureau of Justice Statistics 1992, p. 196).

Self-report surveys of offenders in prison, in jail, and on probation conducted in the 1990s also show the prevalence of drug use among correctional populations (Mumola 1998; Mumola and Bonczar 1998; Wilson 2000). For example, in a survey of inmates in state prisons, approximately seven in ten reported using drugs "regularly" at some point in their lives. More instructive, 57 percent used drugs in the month before being arrested for their current offense, while 33 percent were using drugs at the time of the offense. Similar figures were found for convicted jail inmates. For offenders in federal prisons, the percentages were lower but still substantial: 33 percent used drugs the month before being arrested, 22 percent at the time of arrest. One-third of probationers also reported drug use in the weeks leading up to their current offense; 14 percent said they were on drugs when taken into custody. These figures, moreover, do not include offenders' involvement with *alcohol*. Thus, to take but one statistic, over one-half of state prison inmates were using drugs or alcohol when they were arrested (see Mumola 1998; Mumola and Bonczar 1998; Wilson 2000).

In response, jurisdictions have increasingly subjected convicted offenders, including those incarcerated, to drug tests. In a 1995 survey, about half of all offenders on probation reported being tested for drugs during their current period of supervision (Mumola and Bonczar 1998). In 1998, prison inmates were subjected to more than 1.3 million drug tests, with 4.6 percent testing positive (Camp and Camp 1999). Analyses of existing studies reveal that drug testing, even in conjunction with threats of punishment (e.g., revocation), generally fail to decrease offenders' risk of recidivating (see, e.g., Cullen, Wright, and Applegate 1996; Gendreau et al. 2000; MacKenzie and Hickman 1998). As Prendergast, Anglin, and Wellisch (1995, p. 72) note, "supervision is not enough. For offenders with serious drug problems, it is treatment, not merely supervision, however intensive, that is needed."

Reflecting this reality, drug treatment programs are found throughout the correctional system. Among probationers, for example, 17.4 percent report participating in a drug treatment or drug abuse program during their current sentence. This figure, however, rises to 42.2 percent for offenders who reported using drugs in the month prior to being arrested (Mumola and Bonczar 1998). Similarly, among state prisoners, almost a quarter of inmates stated that they had been involved in a drug-related program since being admitted; this figure climbed to one-third for those who used drugs in the month prior to committing their current offense (Mumola 1998). A survey to which 41 state correctional agencies applied found that 172,747 inmates were in drug treatment programs (Camp and Camp 1999). Still, the need for drug treatment seems to outstrip the supply (Lurigio 2000). Of offenders in prison, seven in ten who reported using drugs "regularly" before institutionalization were receiving no drug-related programming (Mumola 1998).

Within corrections, common forms of treatment include self-help/peer counseling (e.g., Narcotics/Cocaine Anonymous), drug-abuse education classes, counseling by a professional, and a residential facility or unit (Mumola 1998; Mumola and Bonczar 1998; Wilson 2000). A residential unit devoted solely to the treatment of drug and substance abuse is commonly called a "therapeutic community" or "TC" (Wexler, Falkin, and Lipton 1990). The state of Ohio, which has several of these units in its prisons, describes therapeutic communities in this way:

> . . . long-term (6-12 months) residential Alcohol and Other Drug (AOD) treatment programs. The TC approach views AOD abuse as a reflection of chronic deficits in social, vocational, familial, economic, and personality development. The aim of the Therapeutic Community is to promote prosocial behavior, attitudes, and values as a method to attain abstinence from alcohol and other drugs and eliminate antisocial behaviors. (See http://www.drc. ohio.gov/web/pci.htm)

Again, the critical issue is whether drug treatment programs in the correctional system are effective in reducing drug/criminal recidivism. The results seem, in the least, to be promising (Gaes et al. 1999; Lurigio 2000; Prendergast, Anglin, and Wellisch 1995; Taxman 1999). There is a growing consensus that intervention is likely to be successful when it adheres to certain "principles": the program is intensive, long-term, structured, backed up by penalties for nonparticipation (including criminal sanctions); multimodal, so as to deal with other problems that offenders have; and followed by aftercare services (Lurigio 2000; Prendergast, Anglin, and Wellisch 1995; Taxman 1999).

These principles are met most fully in prison-based "therapeutic communities." A meta-analysis by Pearson and Lipton (1999b) found that across seven "TC" studies, the treatment effect size was .133, which can be interpreted in practical terms as a success rate for the experimental versus the control group of 56.7 percent versus 43.4 percent (see also Gaes et al. 1999). Although based on a limited number of studies, they also suggested that treatment options deserving of further study include methadone maintenance for offenders addicted to heroin, cognitive behavioral therapy, and 12-step programs (similar to Alcoholics Anonymous programs). In contrast, Pearson and Lipton's meta-analysis revealed no support for the effectiveness of boot camps for drug offenders and for group counseling. Finally, MacKenzie and Hickman (1998, p. 58) conclude that currently there is "little evidence" that "community-based outpatient programs" reduce recidivism among drug offenders.

Sex-Offender Programs

It is estimated that approximately a quarter of a million sex offenders are under the supervision of the correctional system (Gallagher, Wilson, and MacKenzie 2000). Of these, more than 100,000 are incarcerated (Wees 1996). Within prisons, the most common types of treatment programs are group counseling, individual counseling, and inmate support groups. Less prevalent are medical interventions and programs that seek victim-offender reconciliation. A 1996 survey of 45 state correctional agencies found that over half had special facilities for sex offenders (e.g., therapeutic communities, diagnostic centers) (Wees 1996). One residential sex-offender program in Ohio is described in this way:

> The residential Sex Offender Program is for those inmates that have committed sex offenses in the past or the present, and for those who are not in denial and want to work towards maintaining stability. The program consists of three phases, which last from a minimum of two years to three years. These phases are the Sex Education and Addiction, the Relapse Prevention Plan, and the After Care. Before an inmate can move on to the After Care phase, several modules in social skills and victim empathy must be completed. Once these are completed the inmates then participate in

the After Care phase, which lasts about six months. After the six months of mandatory attendance has been completed, the inmate elects to attend fewer sessions a month. (See http://www.drc.ohio. gov/web/seci.htm)

Reviews of research are now showing that modest, but meaningful, reductions in recidivism can be achieved by sex-offender programs. According to MacKenzie (2000, p. 465), for example, there is evidence that treatment "provided outside of prison in a hospital or other residential setting using cognitive-behavioral methods" reduces sex-offender recidivism. A meta-analysis by Gallagher, Wilson, and MacKenzie (2000) also is revealing (see, also, Gallagher et al. 1999). Across 26 studies, sexual reoffending was, on average, 12 percent for the treatment group and 22 percent for the control group. They offered two additional conclusions. First, it appears that hormonal injections in conjunction with psychotherapy—an intervention that is typically used outside justice agencies—have reduced recidivism among samples of exhibitionists and noninstitutionalized pedophiles. Second, cognitive-behavioral programs that include relapse prevention—an intervention common in the correctional system—have reduced recidivism among samples of rapists and institutionalized pedophiles.

The most comprehensive evaluation of the effectiveness of psychological treatment for sex offenders—mostly cognitive behavioral programs—has recently been completed by Hanson et al. (2000). Their meta-analysis assessed 42 studies, including 15 that they judged to have "credible research designs." Based on this latter subset of studies, they concluded that the psychological treatments were effective. Compared to control groups, offenders receiving treatment had only about half the recidivism rate for sex offenses (9.9 percent versus 17.3 percent) and a lower overall recidivism rate for any offense (32.3 percent versus 51.3 percent). Treatments delivered in the community and prison had similar effects for sex reoffending, but there was a tendency for community-based programs to achieve greater reductions in recidivism for crime in general.

BUILDING A THEORY OF EFFECTIVE REHABILITATION

Although criminology is rich in contemporary theories of crime (Cullen and Agnew 1999; Paternoster and Bachman 2001), true theories of correctional intervention are in short supply. One can find descriptions of successful programs and attempts to show how various counseling approaches apply to offenders (Cullen and Applegate 1997; Van Voorhis, Braswell, and Lester 1997). Even so, one searches in vain in mainstream criminology journals and textbooks for new *systematic* theories of intervention and for empirical tests of these perspectives. Why is this so?

Discussions of how criminologists think about rehabilitation cannot yet escape Martinson's "nothing works" legacy. Martinson framed the debate over offender treatment as an *empirical* issue: does rehabilitation work or not? Developing theories of effective intervention seemed ill-advised if there was, in essence, no "treatment effect" to be explained. Believing that rehabilitation was a euphemism for punishment and a hoax to boot, criminologists had no compelling reason to embark on theoretical inquiry.

Beyond Martinson, however, the politicization of criminology resulted in theories of crime that were not conducive to uncovering the proximate causes of crime—the kinds of factors that treatment programs might change. Again, for criminologists in the Martinson era, the state was transformed from an instrument of good into an instrument of oppression. Theories that blamed the state for "criminalizing" the wayward and "creating criminals"—labeling and conflict theories, for example—suddenly flourished. Explanations of crime not based in the unanticipated consequences of state control focused on the "evils" of American society, especially such structures as capitalism, patriarchy, and inequality. Theories of individual differences were dismissed as "blaming the victim" and as "pathologizing" people whose only crime was being born into an unjust society. Campaigning for social justice, not theorizing and designing effective treatment programs, was seen as the solution for the crime problem.

It is perhaps not surprising, then, that the most prominent effort to build a theory of effective correctional intervention came from a group of scholars—most notably Don Andrews, James Bonta, Paul Gendreau, and Robert Ross—who are not American criminologists. Instead, they are Canadians; at some point in their career, they either worked for or consulted with the government; and they are psychologists by training who saw the contention that behavior—including criminal behavior—could not be changed as inconsistent with a wealth of scientific evidence to the contrary. For them, rehabilitation was still a means to humanize corrections, improve offenders, and protect public safety. American criminologists' views on treatment struck them as ideological, as unscientific, and as bad social policy. Instead, free from the constraints imposed by the professional ideology of U.S. criminology (Cullen and Gendreau 2001), they sought to develop a coherent theory of rehabilitation that they typically have labeled the "principles of effective correctional treatment" (Andrews 1995; Andrews and Bonta 1998; Andrews et al. 1990; Cullen and Gendreau 1989; Gendreau 1996; Ross, Antonowicz, and Dhaliwal 1995; Ross and Fabiano 1985).

The Canadians' Theory of Rehabilitation

This perspective starts with the assumption that a theory of rehabilitation should be based on the social psychology of offending (Andrews 1995; Andrews and Bonta 1998). In this approach, individual and social/situational factors intersect to create in offenders values, cognitions, and personality orientations that foster crime. To a large extent, these ways of thinking and responding are learned and reinforced, and thus become, in effect, individual differences in criminal propensity. This social-psychological approach rejects psychodynamic and psychoanalytical theories of behavior as being too asocial and inconsistent with the empirical literature on crime (a point we will revisit shortly). It also rejects structural theories that link crime to "root causes" whose origins lie in the organization of society; after all, root causes are not amenable to change by correctional programming (see, also, Wilson 1975). Indeed, from the Canadians' standpoint, structural factors can only have effects to the extent that they produce, within individuals, the antisocial values, cognitions, and orientations that are the proximate causes of criminal conduct. Accordingly, while broader reforms may alleviate the distal structural sources of crime, treatment interventions must target those criminogenic factors that are within, or close to, offenders and thus within the reach of the kinds of programs the correctional system can undertake.

The Canadians also readily embraced positivist criminology, arguing that correctional interventions must be rooted in empirical knowledge about the sources of criminal conduct. It has long been asserted that, similar to medicine, rehabilitation programs should seek to change what causes crime (Cullen and Gendreau, 2001). Taking this commonsensical insight seriously, these scholars used reviews of the evidence, including meta-analyses, to document the major *known predictors of recidivism* (Andrews 1995; Andrews and Bonta 1998; Gendreau, Little, and Goggin 1996). This research revealed that the major predictors include 1) "antisocial/procriminal attitudes, values, beliefs and cognitive-emotional states (that is, personal cognitive supports for crime)"; 2) "procriminal associates and isolation from anticriminal others (that is, interpersonal supports for crime)"; and 3) antisocial personality orientations such as low self-control, impulsiveness, risk-taking, and egocentrism (Andrews 1995, p. 37). Recidivism also is predicted by a history of antisocial conduct extending to childhood, by families that lack proper parenting (e.g., inadequate support and supervision of children), and by "low levels of personal educational, vocational or financial achievement," including an "unstable employment record" (Andrews 1995, p. 37).

Importantly, the Canadians noted that some predictors of crime are "static" and cannot be changed, such as a past history of misconduct. However, other predictors, such as antisocial values, are "dynamic" and thus are theoretically amenable to change. If most predictors were static, then there would be nothing to change and rehabilitation would be impossible. As it turns out, the most important predictors of recidivism are dynamic and thus might conceivably be treated or "cured." The Canadians called these dynamic risk factors "criminogenic needs." They also argued that instruments used to classify the "risk level" of offenders should measure not only static risk factors but also these criminogenic needs (Bonta 1996). If so, these classification instruments could be employed in treatment programs to assess whether interventions had altered criminogenic needs. In short, these instruments could serve both a public safety function (estimating risk) and a treatment function (helping to diagnose offender needs and change).

These considerations lead to the question: what, precisely, should treatment programs target for change? This issue is critical because the Canadians' theory of rehabilitation argues that offender behavior will not change if factors weakly related or unrelated to recidivism are the main focus of an intervention (e.g., self-esteem). In fact, a major reason that treatment programs fail is because they either target the wrong factors for intervention or are unspecific as to what is to be altered (i.e., they have no underlying theory of crime guiding the program). In contrast, interventions should focus on the known predictors of recidivism (listed above). If they did, then "promising targets" for change would include "changing antisocial attitudes; changing antisocial feelings; reducing antisocial peer associations; promoting familial affection/communication; promoting familial monitoring and supervision; promoting identification/association with anticriminal role models; increasing self-control, self-management and problem solving skills . . ." (Andrews 1995, p. 55).

The next step is to determine what type or modality of treatment would be most effective in changing the factors that a program targets for rehabilitation. In the Canadians' scheme, "general responsivity" is the use of a treatment modality that is "responsive to" or capable of changing the major known predictors of recidivism. Given their social psychological theory of crime, which emphasizes social learning and antisocial values/cognitions, they hypothesized that the "best modes of service are *behavioural*" (Andrews 1995, p. 56; emphasis in original). These programs thus should "employ the cognitive-behavioral and social learning techniques of modeling, graduated practice, role playing, reinforcement, extinction, resource provision, concrete verbal suggestions (symbolic modeling, giving reasons, prompting) and cognitive restructuring" (Andrews 1995, p. 56; see, also, Ross, Antonowicz, and Dhaliwal 1995; Van Voorhis, Braswell, and Lester 1997; more generally, see Spiegler and Guevremont 1998). In these programs, it is also advised that positive reinforcements outweigh negative reinforcements by a four-to-one ratio (Gendreau 1996).

This theory of rehabilitation has the advantage of predicting not only what does work but also what does not work to reform offenders. According to Andrews (1995, p. 56), these include "programs designed according to the . . . principles of deterrence and labeling, innovative alternative intermediate punishments, non-directive, client-centered counseling, and unstructured psychodynamic therapy." Again, these interventions would be ineffective either because they do not target the appropriate factors for change and/or they are unresponsive to—incapable of altering—the major criminogenic needs.

Beyond general responsivity, the Canadians' model proposes that treatment will be more effective if it pays attention to "specific responsivity." Depending on their characteristics (e.g., intelligence, levels of anxiety), offenders may have different learning styles and thus respond more readily to some techniques than others (e.g., more or less structure in a program, the method through which program information is relayed) (Andrews 1995; Andrews and Bonta 1998; Gendreau 1996). For example, offenders with lower IQs might be more amenable to treatment if a program was less verbal, relied on tangible reinforcers, and conveyed content in a repeated, gradual way. Notably, specific responsivity does not mean—as some commentators are prone to say—that "some forms of treatment work for some types offenders some of the time." Rather, it only means that the degree to which interventions based on the principle of general responsivity will be effective can be further increased if specific responsivity considerations are be taken into account. This situation is analogous to one in which a certain drug is effective in combating an infection, but its impact will be stronger if the physician considers the specific characteristics of the patient in prescribing the frequency and dose with which the medicine is given. In any event, specific responsivity is a way of fine-tuning treatment delivery. It is not meant to make the matching of treatments to offenders so individualized as to render the delivery of effective intervention unfeasible within the context of the resources available to correctional agencies.

The Canadian scholars have argued as well that interventions will be more effective if they are directed to offenders that a risk-needs classification instrument categorizes as "high risk" (Andrews and Bonta 1998). This principle both violates and is explained by "common sense," showing that common sense can account for both sides of most empirical relationships! Thus, common sense would suggest that low-risk offenders are more amenable to treatment because they are less "hardened" in their criminality. But common sense would also suggest that high-risk offenders are more amenable to treatment because they are in a sense "sicker" and thus have more about them that potentially can be changed. The Canadians contend that the latter version is accurate and thus recommend devoting most resources to the treatment of high-risk offenders. Low-risk offenders, they argue, may be made more criminogenic by intrusive interventions.

Finally, the Canadian model makes a number of other recommendations for increasing treatment effectiveness (see Andrews 1995; Andrews and Bonta 1998; Gendreau 1996). These include staff delivering treatment in an authoritative way (warm but restrictive, firm but fair); structured aftercare to give offenders a treatment "booster shot"; program "therapeutic integrity" that involves the use of detailed training manuals, the training and supervision of staff, adherence to the prescribed treatment modality, and a treatment dosage of sufficient duration and intensity to affect the criminogenic needs targeted for change; and a host agency that is supportive of the program's implementation and operation.

In brief, the Canadians' theory of rehabilitation involves the following principles: 1) use a social psychological perspective to focus on the proximate causes of crime; 2) based on empirical data, target for change known predictors of recidivism that are dynamic, not static—that is, focus on "criminogenic needs"; 3) use cognitive-behavioral treatment programs, because these are "generally responsive" to changing the major criminogenic needs; 4) where possible, develop programs that can be "specifically responsive" to the learning styles and characteristics of offenders; 5) focus interventions on high-risk offenders, with risk level determined by classification instruments that measure static risk and dynamic risk factors; and 6) ensure that intervention programs have therapeutic integrity.

Testing the Canadians' Theory of Rehabilitation

The Canadian scholars have not simply constructed a theory of rehabilitation but also have dared to test it through meta-analyses of the existing program evaluation literature. In an initial effort, Andrews et al. (1990) categorized 80 studies in terms of whether the intervention conformed to the principles of effective treatment. If the treatment intervention adhered to these principles, it was defined as providing "appropriate service" (see Andrews et al. 1990, p. 379).

Across all studies in the sample, they found that the effect size was .10, a result consistent with other meta-analyses (Losel 1995, Forthcoming). When they examined "appropriate" treatments, however, the effect size rose to .30 or the equivalent of a 30 percentage-point difference in the recidivism rate between the treatment and control groups. This assessment was later extended to include 230 studies, with similar results. Programs conforming to the principles of the theory of effective intervention had an effect size of .26 (Andrews and Bonta 1998; Andrews, Dowden, and Gendreau 1999: see, also, Antonowicz and Ross 1994). Although based on a smaller number of studies, these results also are found for programs involving female offenders (Dowden and Andrews 1999).

The Canadians' theory is important because it organizes much knowledge about treatment effectiveness. In particular, it tells us not only what works and why but also what doesn't work and why. Most salient, it makes strong predictions about the *ineffectiveness* of control-oriented interventions that seek to specifically deter offenders through surveillance and threats of punishment. Because these control-oriented programs do not target for change the known predictors of recidivism and do not conform to the principle of general responsivity (i.e., do not use cognitive-behavioral treatments), they will not reduce recidivism. As noted previously, the existing literature shows that control-oriented programs are ineffective (see, e.g., Cullen and Gendreau 2000; MacKenzie 2000).

The Canadians' theory of rehabilitation would gain added credence if it were systematically tested by other scholars (Gaes et al. 1999). Further, some contrary results have emerged. For example, studies do not uniformly show that treatment interventions are more effective with high-risk offenders (Gaes et al. 1999; Ross, Antonowicz, and Dhaliwal 1995). Still, the evidence from existing meta-analyses largely support the principles of effective treatment outlined by the Canadians. "It is interesting," observes Lipsey (1992, p. 123), "that the treatment types that show this larger order of effects are, with few exceptions, those defined as most 'clinically relevant' in the Andrews et al. review" (see also Lipsey 1995, pp. 77–78). Similarly, in a replication of the Andrews et al. study, Pearson, Lipton, and Cleland's (1996) meta-analysis found that programs that delivered "appropriate correctional services" were more effective in reducing recidivism than "unspecified" and "inappropriate" programs. The effect size for appropriate programs was not as high as that reported by Andrews et al. (1990), but the results were in the same direction. Further, consistent with the theory of rehabilitation, there is growing evidence that cognitive-behavioral treatment is efficacious in lowering reoffending (see Losel 1995; MacKenzie 2000; Pearson et al. 2000).

In closing, Andrews, Bonta, Gendreau, Ross, and their fellow Canadian coauthors have made an impressive contribution to the study of offender treatment. They have constructed a model of rehabilitation that is rooted in theoretical and empirical criminology, that organizes much of what is known about effective interventions, and that is largely supported by existing meta-analyses of the treatment literature. As with any social science paradigm, this theory warrants our organized skepticism and rigorous empirical scrutiny (see Gaes et al. 1999; Duguid 2000; Whitehead and Lab 1989). Even so, few criminological perspectives have been developed with such clarity as to their core assumptions and with such respect for the extant data. Until rival perspectives meet these standards, it seems likely that the Canadians' theory of rehabilitation will serve as a Kuhnian (1962) paradigm that shapes how treatment research and, potentially, practice are undertaken.

THE CHALLENGE OF TECHNOLOGY TRANSFER

Technology transfer refers to the transmission of scientific knowledge from the producers to the potential consumers of this information. In the social sciences, technology transfer typically involves the dissemination of research findings to practitioners and policymakers so as to improve the effectiveness of service delivery and the soundness of policy initiatives (Backer, David, and Soucy 1995). In some fields, such as medicine, technology transfer is institutionalized through professional training, continuing education, and expectations that scientific journals will be consulted (Blumstein and Petersilia 1995, p. 470). In fact, the failure to receive current scientific knowledge and to incorporate it into medical decision making can expose physicians to legal liability and professional sanctions for malpractice.

In human service fields, however, scientific "technology" is often not transmitted. Take, for example, the treatment of alcohol problems. A review of existing research led Hester and Miller (1995, p. xi) to conclude that "a number of treatment methods were consistently supported by controlled scientific research." However, they were "dismayed to realize that virtually none of these treatment methods was in common use within alcohol treatment programs in the United States."

This situation is commonplace in the delivery of correctional rehabilitation. Criminologists share much of the blame, because they have been substantially in the grips of a "nothing works" ideology for 25 years and thus lax in developing treatment-program technology that could be transferred (Cullen and Gendreau, 2001). Indeed, if not for the research of scholars—mostly psychologists—outside traditional criminology, it is not clear that we would have any meaningful body of scientific knowledge on rehabilitation to share (see, e.g., Andrews and Bonta 1998; Henggeler et al. 1998; Loeber and Farrington 1998; Palmer 1992; see, also, Cullen and Applegate 1997). Still, much of the blame for the lack of technology transfer must be shouldered by policymakers and practitioners. They have often been skeptical of research findings and prepared to privilege "personal experience" over scientific knowledge in deciding which programs to implement (Blumstein and Petersilia 1995). The result has been a form of correctional malpractice or quackery in which ineffective, if not harmful, interventions have been embraced (Cullen and Gendreau 2000). Meanwhile, calls for "evidence-based corrections" have fallen on deaf ears (Cullen and Gendreau 2000; MacKenzie 2000).

The saga of "boot camps" is a recent case in point (for another example, see Latessa and Moon 1992, on the use of acupuncture with drug offenders). An invention of the 1980s, boot camps proposed to expose offenders to a military-style boot camp in hopes of "breaking them down and building them back up." This intervention built on the long-standing narrative in American culture, often represented in films such as *An Officer and a Gentleman*, in which rag-tag, irresponsible young men are inculcated with backbone and maturity under the watchful tough love of a gruff drill sergeant. These programs appealed in particular to elected officials who had, in their minds, been transformed by the discipline of boot camps and believed that their personal experience of being whipped into shape would generalize to offenders (Cullen, Wright, and Applegate 1996; Selcraig 2000).

Amazingly, millions of dollars were spent to implement boot camps without any thought given to the existing criminological technology on program effectiveness. No one involved in the boot camp movement seemed to question the amorphous, if not ridiculous, notion that offender change involved "breaking people down" and then "building them back up"—whatever that means. No one asked what known predictors of recidivism the program was targeting. No one wondered whether such a program, which involved threatening confrontations and punishment in the name of discipline, was a "responsive" treatment for the population to which it was directed—low-risk offenders. No one paused to consult the literature showing that military service has, at best, a modest and complex impact on criminal propensities, with no evidence that boot camps per se have any ameliorative effects (Cullen, Wright, and Applegate 1996). And no one raised the opportunity costs of building boot camps instead of using resources to initiate rehabilitation programs rooted in the principles of effective intervention. In fact, there is no evidence that anyone did any library research on "what works" with offenders or picked up the phone and called Canada to see if they had any scholars that knew anything about changing law-breakers for the better!

Fortunately, there are signs that the field of corrections is becoming more open to technology transfer. To be sure, boot camps persist, with a majority of states still operating one or more facility (Camp and Camp 1999). But their advocates—now faced with near incontrovertible evidence of their failure (MacKenzie 1997)—are on the defensive (Selcraig 2000). More generally, major professional organizations in corrections have embraced the value of technology transfer. The International Community Corrections Association, for example, now regularly sponsors "what works" conferences and related publications (see, e.g., Harland 1996). Similarly, the American Correctional Association has published a compilation of programs that are the "best bets" for effective intervention (Rhine 1998). Still, much work remains to be done.

To assess the quality of programming delivered by agencies, the Canadian scholars designed the Correctional Program Assessment Inventory or CPAI (Gendreau and Goggin 1997; Gendreau, Goggin, and Smith, Forthcoming). Developed on the basis of their theory of rehabilitation, the CPAI is a 75-item instrument that can be used to assess six features of an agency delivering a treatment program: 1) program implementation and leadership, 2) offender assessment and classification, 3) characteristics of the program, 4) characteristics and practices of the staff, 5) evaluation and quality control, and 6) "other" items (e.g., confidentiality of records) (see, also, Latessa and Holsinger 1998). The CPAI can be employed to judge whether agencies are marked by major programming deficits or by the effective delivery of services.

Three studies using the CPAI have assessed, in combination, more than 280 programs in Canada and the United States. The results have not been encouraging. According to Gendreau, Goggin, and Smith (Forthcoming), "the blunt truth is that 70 percent of all programs . . . 'failed' according to the CPAI" (see also Lipsey 1999a). Latessa and Holsinger (1998, p. 26) summarize common problems found by the CPAI in the area of "characteristics of the program":

> Since programs are rarely designed around a theoretical model, it was not surprising to find a lack of a consistently applied treatment model in place. In general, the major shortcomings . . . include lack of programmatic structure; incomplete or nonexistent treatment manuals; few rewards to encourage program participation and compliance; the ineffective use of punishment; staff being allowed to design their own interventions regardless of the treatment literature base; and a host of very obvious and definable, yet ineffective, treatment models. . . . Finally, many programs failed to provide aftercare services or booster sessions.

The CPAI findings are troubling because they show how much correctional practice is doomed to failure because it is based on incorrect "technology." But these results also offer some basis for optimism. It is clear that a number of programs in the "real world" are being conducted largely in accordance with the principles of effective treatment. Lipsey (1999a) reports similar findings in an analysis of "practical" juvenile interventions—programs conducted in agency settings that were not designed and/or operated by researchers. Although still in the minority, these programs supply important evidence that well-designed and effective programs can be administered in correctional agencies.

Lipsey (1999a, p. 641) reminds us, however, that "such beneficial effects do not come automatically—a concerted effort must be made to configure the programs in the most favorable manner and to provide the types of services that have been shown to be effective, and avoid those shown to be ineffective" (see, also, Lin 2000). Again, motivating correctional agencies to make such an effort will require, at least in part, persuading staff that doing so makes good sense. In this context, technology transfer is important in showing clearly why certain correctional practices are almost certain to fail and in pointing out how other intervention strategies can achieve meaningful reductions in recidivism. As Van Voorhis (1987) points out, there is a "high cost to ignoring success" in offender treatment—an observation that gives technology transfer an inherent rationality.

In this exchange, the challenge for criminologists will be to construct a knowledge base—likely built off the Canadians' theory of rehabilitation—that provides clearer guidance both on "what works" and on strategies to implement such principles in the real world. The challenge for policymakers and practitioners will be to become more willing partners with criminologists in the development of effective programs, both receiving and helping to create new offender-treatment "technology."

CONCLUSION: REAFFIRMING REHABILITATION

This essay has been informed by the assumption that treatment programs and the goal of rehabilitation are integral to the correctional enterprise. In the face of various attacks on offender treatment—especially the "nothing works" doctrine—it has been argued, in essence, that rehabilitation should not be abandoned but rather "reaffirmed" (Cullen and Gilbert 1982; Cullen and Moon, Forthcoming). This view rests on three contentions, which will be shared—albeit briefly—as a way of concluding our discussion on offender treatment.

First, rehabilitation programs reduce recidivism overall and, when implemented according to the principles of effective treatment, potentially reduce reoffending substantially. In short, "rehabilitation works." This is not to say that correctional treatment is a panacea or easily accomplished. We need to be far more judicious than the early advocates of the rehabilitative ideal who often were naïve about the difficulty of changing wayward behavior (Rothman 1980). Effective intervention must be based on more than good intentions; it must reflect good science, good policy, and good practice. Still, the empirical evidence is fairly convincing—and growing stronger as time passes—that treatment interventions are capable of decreasing recidivism. The influence of these programs is also likely to be "general." That is, with some variation in effects, they work with serious offenders, drug-offenders, and sex-offenders; with juveniles and with adults; with males and with females; in the community and in prison. In contrast, correctional programs based on the principles of specific deterrence are notoriously ineffective. In the end, the utility of rehabilitation argues for its retention as a core goal of corrections.

Second, the public supports rehabilitating offenders and expanding treatment programs. There is little doubt that there is an ample reservoir of punitive sentiments among the American public to prompt citizens' support for a range of "get tough" policies. Public opinion polls, for example, regularly show that upwards of three-fourths of Americans believe that the courts in their area do not "deal harshly enough with criminals" (Cullen, Fisher, and Applegate 2000). Even so, there is another side of public opinion about corrections. Study after study shows that Americans support rehabilitation as a central goal of imprisonment. In forced-choice questions, a substantial minority selects treating offenders as their preferred goal. When asked to rate the role of treatment in prisons, four in five see rehabilitation as "important" or "very important." A high percentage of citizens also endorses expanding treatment services. Support for rehabilitation is especially pronounced for juvenile offenders. Early intervention programs are strongly advocated, with citizens preferring to spend tax funds on these programs as opposed to building more prisons (Applegate, Cullen, and Fisher 1997; Cullen, Fisher, and Applegate 2000; Cullen and Moon, Forthcoming; Cullen et al. 1998; Moon et al. 1999). In short, the "public will" is not only to punish offenders but also to rehabilitate them.

Third, attempting to rehabilitate offenders is the right thing to do.
Admittedly, sustaining this argument is more difficult because ultimately it reflects the choice of a particular moral compass and is based less on data and more on speculation. A different view is defensible. Thus, those rejecting rehabilitation are often troubled by its paternalism and by its implicit message—broadcast to the larger community—that the harmful behavior of offenders is to be understood, if not excused. In contrast, punishment unadulterated by utilitarian goals is held to clearly demarcate right from wrong, thus setting firm moral boundaries. Punishment also affirms the dignity of offenders, because it treats them "as responsible human beings who must accept the consequences of their actions" (Logan and Gaes 1993, p. 258).

My difficulty with this line of reasoning is twofold (Cullen and Applegate 1997). First, the "messages" offender rehabilitation broadcasts are, at the least, in the eye of the beholder. Where other commentators see paternalism and the excuse of wrongdoing, others might well see rehabilitation as reflecting not the attenuation of moral values but a shared social purpose—"a society in which the dominant groups possess high confidence in their definitions of character and their standards of good behavior" (Allen 1981, p. 11). Or perhaps they might see the call for treatment as showing a legitimate concern for social justice—as evidence that the poor and minority offenders concentrated in the nation's prisons are not to be treated as human refuse but as people with dignity who deserve the opportunity for self-improvement.

Second and more important, I am troubled by what transpires when the correctional system starts to forfeit the rehabilitative ideal and embrace starkly punitive principles—much as has occurred in various jurisdictions in the United States over the past quarter century. I find it difficult to sustain the view that the absence of a firm commitment to offender treatment fosters more justice and dignity for offenders. Indeed, if anything, the contemporary historical record is disquieting in showing that in recent decades, elected officials gave short shrift to the ideals of justice and instead competed to see who could make sentences longer and prison life harsher (Clear 1994). In contrast, by showing concern for the welfare of offenders—with the exchange being that investing in the wayward advances public safety by reducing their risk of recidivating—rehabilitation provides one of the few rationales for not imposing unnecessary pains on those under correctional supervision. In the current context, I suggest that whatever humanity the practice of rehabilitation brings to the correctional enterprise is much needed. And if reaffirming rehabilitation makes corrections a bit more paternalistic and kindhearted, I am all for it.

11

Gun Control

PHILIP J. COOK, MARK H. MOORE,
AND ANTHONY A. BRAGA

In the search for public safety, establishing more stringent controls on gun commerce and use has the broad support of the American public. Thousands are killed by gunfire each year (including almost 12,000 homicides in 1998) and hundreds of thousands more are threatened or injured in robberies and assaults. Developing and implementing government programs to make guns less readily available, especially to those inclined toward violence, deserve a high priority in the quest to save lives and reduce the burden of crime on our society.

But not everyone accepts this perspective on guns. Some argue that guns are the mere instruments of criminal intent, with no more importance than the brand of shoes the criminal wears. If the weapon type does not matter, then policy interventions focused on guns are futile. Another path leading to the same conclusion of futility posits that in a society already saturated with guns, it is simply not feasible to prevent determined criminals from obtaining a gun if they want one. Furthermore, if guns provide law-abiding citizens with an important means of self-defense against crime, then government attempts to restrict gun availability may be perverse rather than merely futile. Of course each of these assertions about the actual or potential consequences of gun control has been extensively debated.

But the debate over gun control is not only concerned with factual issues. If this were true, empirical research might, in principle at least, resolve the matter, and the proper choice of gun-control measures would become clear. In reality, however, there are important value conflicts as well, conflicts concerning the proper relationship between the individual, the community, and the state. Even a definitive empirical demonstration that a gun-control measure would save lives will not persuade someone who believes in an absolute individual right to keep and bear arms.

The purpose of this essay is to provide a foundation for understanding the "Great American Gun War," and to consider the next steps that could be taken in the search for an effective gun-control policy. We begin with a review of the more-or-less uncontroversial facts about trends in gun ownership and use, and the reasons why Americans are inclined to arm themselves. A discussion follows of the more contentious issues, whether and how guns influence levels or seriousness of crime. We then identify the important values at stake in adopting any gun-control policy, and go on to describe the existing policies and the mechanisms by which they and other such measures have their effect. Finally, we make recommendations about promising next steps.

GUN OWNERSHIP, USE, AND MISUSE

Guns are versatile tools, useful in providing meat for the table, eliminating varmints and pests, providing entertainment for those who have learned to enjoy the sporting uses, and protecting life and property against criminal predators. They are an especially common feature of rural life, where wild animals provide both a threat and an opportunity for sport. As America has become more urban and more violent, however, the demand for guns has become increasingly motivated by the need for protection against other people.

Patterns of Gun Ownership

The annual General Social Survey, conducted by the National Opinion Research Center, has long included questions on gun ownership. In 1999 just 36 percent of American households owned at least one firearm, down from nearly 50 percent in 1980 (Smith 2000, p. 55). Surprisingly, there is no such trend in the prevalence of individual ownership among adults, which has remained near 30 percent since 1980. The drop in household ownership reflects the trend in household composition during this period; households are less likely to include a gun because they have become smaller and, in particular, less likely to include a man.

The *number* of guns in private hands has been increasing rapidly. Since 1970, total sales of new guns have accounted for over half of all the guns sold during the twentieth century, and the total now in circulation is on the order of 200 million (Cook and Ludwig 1996). The influx of new guns has been more than needed to equip the expanding population. The "extra" guns have gone to increase the number of guns in the average owner's arsenal (Wright 1981). The most detailed national survey on the subject (the National Survey of the Private Ownership of Firearms, or NSPOF) found that gun-owning households average of 4.4 guns in 1994, up substantially from the 1970s (Cook and Ludwig 1996).[1]

One addition for many gun-owning households has been a handgun. The significance of this trend toward increased handgun ownership lies in the fact that while rifles and shotguns are acquired primarily for sporting purposes, handguns are primarily intended for use against people, either in crime or self-defense. The increase in handgun prevalence corresponds to a large increase in the relative importance of handguns in retail sales: The Bureau of Alcohol, Tobacco, and Firearms (ATF) estimated that half of the new guns sold in the United States in the early 1990s were handguns, up from one-third in the early 1970s. In the late 1990s, however, the handgun share of all new gun sales fell back to about 40 percent (ATF 2000a).

Some of the increased handgun sales have been to urban residents who have no experience with guns but are convinced they need one for self-protection, as suggested by the surges in handgun sales after the Los Angeles riots and other such events (Kellermann and Cook 1999). But while the prevalence of handgun ownership has increased substantially over the past three decades, it remains true now as earlier that most who possess a handgun also own one or more rifles and shotguns. The 1994 NSPOF found that just 20 percent of gun-owning individuals have only handguns, while 36 percent have only long guns and 44 percent have both.

These statistics suggest that people who have acquired guns for self-protection are for the most part also hunters and target shooters. Indeed, only 46 percent of gun owners say that they own a gun *primarily* for self-protection against crime and only 26 percent keep a gun loaded. Most (80 percent) grew up in a household with a gun.

The demographic patterns of gun ownership are no surprise: most owners are men, and the men who are most likely to own a gun reside in rural areas or small towns and were reared in such places (Kleck 1991). Blacks are less likely to own guns than whites, in part because the black population is more urban.[2] The likelihood of gun ownership increases with income and peaks in middle age.

The fact that guns fit much more comfortably into rural life than urban life raises a question. In 1940, 49 percent of teenagers were living in rural areas; by 1960 that percentage had dropped to 34 and by 1990, to 27. What will happen to gun ownership patterns as new generations with less connection to rural life come along? Hunting is already on the decline: the absolute number of hunting licenses issued in 1990 was about the same as in 1970 despite the growth in population, indicating a decline in the percentage of people who hunt (U.S. Department of the Interior 1991). Confirming evidence comes from the National Survey of Wildlife-Associated Recreation, which found that 7 percent of adults age sixteen and over were hunters in 1997, compared with 9 percent in 1970.[3] This trend may eventually erode the importance of the rural sporting culture that has dominated the gun "scene." In its place is greater focus on the criminal and self-defense uses of guns.

Uses of Guns Against People

A great many Americans die by gunfire. The gun-death counts from suicide, homicide, and accident have totaled over 30,000 for every year from 1972 to 1998. In 1998 there were approximately 30,700 firearms deaths, a rate of 11.4 per 100,000 U.S. residents. All but 1,500 were either suicides or homicides. While homicides make the headlines, there were actually 5,600 more gun suicides than homicides. The remainder was classified as accidents, legal interventions, or unknown (www.cdc.gov). Various points of reference help calibrate these numbers. In terms of Americans killed, a year of gun killing in the United States is the equivalent of the Korean War. Another familiar reference is the highway fatality rate, which is about 25 percent higher nationwide.

It is criminal homicide and other criminal uses of guns that cause the greatest public concern. Gun accident rates are an order-of-magnitude lower,[4] and suicide seems more a private concern than a public risk. Fortunately the homicide rate (both gun and nongun) has been dropping rapidly in recent years, but from twentieth century highs in 1980 and 1991 of over 10 per 100,000. The rate was just 6.6 in 1998. Between 60 and 70 percent of homicides are committed with guns, mostly (80 percent) handguns.

Homicide is not a democratic crime. Both victims and perpetrators are vastly disproportionately male, black, and quite young. With respect to the victims, homicide is the leading cause of death for black male youths. The gun homicide rate in 1997 for Hispanic men ages 18 to 29 was seven times the rate for non-Hispanic white men of the same age; the gun homicide rate for black men 18 to 29 was 133 per 100,000, around 25 times the rate for white males in that age group (Cook and Ludwig 2000). (Most male victims in the high-risk category are killed by people of the same race, sex, and age group.) About 75 percent of the homicide victims in this group were killed with firearms. The disparity between the demography of gun sports and of gun crime is telling: sportsmen are disproportionately older white males from small towns and rural areas, while the criminal misuse of guns is concentrated among young urban males, especially minorities.[5]

Of course, most gun crimes are not fatal. For every gun homicide victim there are roughly six gun-crime victims who receive a less-than-mortal wound (Cook 1985) and many more who are not wounded at all. Indeed, the most common criminal use of guns is to threaten, with the objective of robbing, raping, or otherwise gaining the victim's compliance; relatively few of these victims are physically injured, but the threat of lethal violence and the potential for escalation necessarily make these crimes serious. According to the 1998 National Crime Victimization Survey (NCVS), there were 150,000 gun robberies, 394,000 aggravated assaults (of which 52,000 caused injury) and 13,000 rapes in that year, for a total estimated volume of gun crimes of about 557,000. And these gun crimes are only a fraction of all robberies, aggravated assaults, and rapes, as shown in Figure 1. When a gun is used, it is most likely (85 percent) a handgun.

While guns do enormous damage in crime they also provide some crime victims with the means of escaping serious injury or property loss. The National Crime Victimization Survey is generally considered the most reliable source of information on predatory crime, since it has been in the field since 1973 and incorporates the best thinking of survey methodologists. From this source it would appear that use of guns in self-defense against criminal predation occurs approximately 100,000 times per year (Cook, Ludwig, and Hemenway 1997).[6] Of particular interest is the likelihood that a gun will be used in self-defense against an intruder. Cook (1991), using the NCVS data for the mid 1980s, found that only 3 percent of victims were able to deploy a gun against someone who broke in (or attempted to do so) while they were at home. Since about 45 percent of all households possessed a gun during that period, we conclude that it is relatively unusual for victims to be able to deploy a gun against intruders even when they have one nearby.

Gary Kleck and Marc Gertz (1995) have reported far higher estimates of 2.5 million self-defense uses each year, based on their own nationwide telephone survey. Indeed, on the basis of comparing this estimate of self-defense uses with the gun-crime victimization rate from the NCVS, they conclude that guns are used more commonly in self-defense than in crime. But other authors have noted that when the comparison is made using NCVS data alone for both victimization and self-defense, the criminal uses predominate. The same is true in other surveys that have asked about both victimization and self-defense (Hemenway, In press).

Kleck and Gertz's high estimate may result from a relatively high false-positive rate (Hemenway 1997). Of course, even if we had reliable estimates on the volume of such events, we would want to know more before reaching any conclusion. It is quite possible that most "self-defense" uses occur in circumstances that are normatively ambiguous: chronic violence within a marriage, gang fights, robberies of drug dealers, encounters with groups of young men who simply *appear* threatening. Indeed, drug dealers and predatory criminals do face extraordinarily high risks of being assaulted (Levitt and Venkatesh 2000; Cook and Ludwig 2000). In one survey of convicted felons in prison, the most common reason offered for carrying a gun was self-defense (Wright and Rossi 1994); a similar finding emerged from a study of juveniles incarcerated for serious criminal offenses (Smith 1996). Self-defense conjures up an image of the innocent victim using a gun to fend off an unprovoked criminal assault, but in fact many "self-defense" cases are not so commendable.

INSTRUMENTALITY AND AVAILABILITY

Do "guns kill people" or do "people kill people"? In murder trials the killer's motivation and state of mind are explored thoroughly, while the type of weapon—usually some type of gun—is often treated as an incidental detail. Yet there is compelling evidence that the type of weapon matters a lot in determining whether the victim lives or dies. If true, then depriving potentially violent people of guns would save lives, an essential tenet of the argument for restricting gun availability. But then a second question arises. How can we use the law to deprive violent people of guns if such people are not inclined to be law abiding? The saying "If guns are outlawed, only outlaws will have guns" may ring true.[7] There is also some evidence on this matter, suggesting that some "outlaws'" decision of what weapon to use is indeed influenced by the difficulty and legal risks of obtaining and using a gun (Wright and Rossi 1994).

In this section we develop the evidence on these two issues, designated "instrumentality" and "availability." The same two issues should also be raised in an assessment of the self-defense uses of guns, and we do so in the third part of this section.

Instrumentality

In some circumstances the claim that the type of weapon matters seems indisputable. There are very few drive-by knifings, or people killed accidentally by stray fists. When well-protected people are murdered it is almost always with a gun; over 90 percent of lethal attacks on law enforcement officers are with firearms, and all our murdered presidents have been shot. When lone assailants set out to kill as many people as they can in a commuter train or schoolyard, the only readily available weapon that will do the job is a gun. But what about the more mundane attacks that make up the vast bulk of violent cases?

The first piece of evidence is that robberies and assaults committed with guns are more likely to result in the victim's death than are similar violent crimes committed with other weapons. In the public health jargon, the "case-fatality rates" differ by weapon type. Take the case of robbery, a crime that includes holdups, muggings, and other violent confrontations motivated by theft. The case-fatality rate for gun robbery is three times as high as for robberies with knives, and ten times as high as for robberies with other weapons (Cook 1987). For aggravated (serious) assault it is more difficult to come up with meaningful case-fatality estimate, since the crime itself is in part *defined* by the type of weapon used. (A threat delivered at gunpoint is likely to be classified as an aggravated assault, while the same threat delivered while shaking a fist would be classified as a simple assault.) We do know that for assaults where the victim sustains an injury, the case-fatality rate is closely linked to the type of weapon (Zimring 1968, 1972; Kleck and McElrath 1991), as is also the case for family and intimate assaults known to the police (Saltzman et al. 1992).

Case-fatality rates do not by themselves prove that the type of weapon has an independent causal effect on the probability of death. It is possible that the type of weapon is simply an indicator of the assailant's intent and that it is the intent, rather than the weapon, that determines whether the victim lives or dies. In this view—which has been offered as a reasonable possibility by Wolfgang (1958); Wright, Rossi, and Daly (1983); and others—the gun makes the killing easier and is hence the obvious choice if the assailant's intent is indeed to kill. But if no gun were available, then most would-be killers would still find a way. Fatal and nonfatal attacks form two distinct sets of events with little overlap, at least in regards to the assailant's state of mind.

Perhaps the most telling response to this argument is due to Franklin Zimring (1968, 1972), who concluded that there is actually a good deal of overlap between fatal and nonfatal attacks: Even in the case of earnest and potentially deadly attacks, assailants commonly lack a clear or sustained intent to kill. Whether the victim lives or dies then depends importantly on the lethality of the weapon with which the assailant strikes the first blow or two. For evidence on this perspective, Zimring notes that in a high percentage of cases the assailant is drunk or enraged, unlikely to be acting in a calculating fashion. Zimring's studies of wounds inflicted in gun and knife assaults demonstrate that the difference between life and death is evidently just a matter of chance, determined by whether the bullet or blade found a vital organ. It is relatively rare for assailants to administer the *coup de grace* that would ensure their victim's demise. For every homicide inflicted with a single bullet wound to the chest, there are two survivors of a bullet wound to the chest, and similarly for knife attacks.

Zimring's argument in a nutshell is that robbery murder is closely related to robbery, and assaultive homicide is closely related to aggravated assault; death is in effect a probabilistic byproduct of violent crime. While the law determines the seriousness of the crime by whether the victim lives or dies, the outcome is not a reliable guide to the assailant's intent or state of mind. One logical implication of this perspective is that there should be a close link between the overall volume of violent crimes and the number of murders. Confirmatory evidence is provided by a study that demonstrated by use of data on changes in crime rates in forty-four cities that an increase of 1,000 gun robberies is associated with three times as many additional murders as an increase of 1,000 nongun robberies (Cook 1987). "Instrumentality" provides a natural explanation for this pattern.

Zimring's reasoning can be extended to a comparison of different types of guns. In the gun-control debate the prime target has been the handgun, since handguns are used in most gun crimes. But rifles and shotguns tend to be more lethal than handguns: A rifle is easier to aim and the bullet travels with higher velocity than for a short-barreled weapon, while a shotgun blast spreads and may cause a number of wounds when it strikes. To the extent that assailants substitute rifles and shotguns for handguns in response to handgun-control measures, the result may be to increase the death rate (Kleck 1984).[8] Unfortunately, there is little systematic evidence on the question of whether effective handgun-control would lead robbers and other violent people to substitute long guns (more lethal) or knives (less).[9] "Instrumentality effects" are not limited to differences in case-fatality rates. The type of weapon also appears to matter in other ways. For example, gun robbers are far less likely to attack and injure their victims than robbers using other weapons, and are less likely to incur resistance (Conklin 1972; Cook 1976, 1980; Skogan 1978). (In cases where the victim is attacked and injured, the likelihood of death in gun robberies is far higher than with knives or blunt objects, which accounts for the relatively high case-fatality rate in gun robbery.) We also have evidence that aggravated assaults follow similar weapon-specific patterns (Kleck and McElrath 1991). The most plausible explanation for this pattern of outcomes is simply that a gun gives the assailant the power to intimidate and gain his victim's compliance without use of force, whereas with less lethal weapons the assailant is more likely to find it necessary to back up the threat with a physical attack.

The intimidating power of a gun may also help explain the effectiveness of using one in self-defense. According to one study of NCVS data, in burglaries of occupied dwellings only 5 percent of victims who used guns in self-defense were injured, compared with 25 percent of those who resisted with other weapons.[10] Other studies have confirmed that victims of predatory crime who are able to resist with a gun are generally successful in thwarting the crime and avoiding injury (Kleck 1988; McDowall, Loftin, and Wiersema 1992a). But the interpretation of this result is open to some question. Self-defense with a gun is a relatively unusual event in crimes like burglary and robbery, and the cases where the victim does use a gun differ from others in ways that help account for the differential success of gun defense. In particular, other means of defense usually are attempted after the assailant threatens or attacks the victim, whereas those who use guns in self-defense are relatively likely to be the first to threaten or use force (McDowall, Loftin, and Wiersema 1992b). Given this difference in the sequence of events, and the implied difference in the competence or intentions of the perpetrator, the proper interpretation of the statistical evidence concerning weapon-specific success rates in self-defense is unclear (Cook 1986, 1991).

In sum, we postulate that the type of weapon deployed in violent confrontations appears to matter in several ways. Because guns provide the power to kill quickly, at a distance, and without much skill or strength, they also provide the power to intimidate other people and gain control of a violent situation without an actual attack. When there is a physical attack, then the type of weapon is an important determinant of whether the victim survives, with guns far more lethal than other commonly used weapons.

Availability

If the type of weapon transforms violent encounters in important ways, as suggested in the preceding discussion, then the extent to which guns are available to violence-prone people is a matter of public concern. "Availability" can be thought of in terms of time, expense, and other costs.

Violent confrontations often occur unexpectedly, and in such cases the weapons that will be used are among those that are close at hand; the relevant question is whether a gun is *immediately* available. But in other cases, robberies and assaults are planned, or at least expected, and the relevant time frame for obtaining a gun is hours or days.

Arthur L. Kellermann and his associates (1992, 1993) provide evidence on the importance of "availability" in the first scenario, where the question is whether a gun is close at hand. In case-control studies of violent events occurring in the home, they found that the likelihood of both suicide and homicide are greatly elevated by the presence of a gun in the home. The authors selected each "control" from the same neighborhood as that in which the killing occurred and through their matching criteria and use of multivariate statistical techniques attempted to control for other differences between the cases and controls. There is no guarantee that this effort to control for other factors that might be confounded with gun possession was successful, so the proper interpretation of these findings remains controversial.[11] If we accept the authors' interpretation, then two propositions follow:

1. If a member of the household owns a gun, then at-home suicide attempts and armed assaults are more likely to involve a gun than otherwise.
2. A gun is more deadly than other weapons would have been in these circumstances (an instrumentality effect).

From the more-aggregate perspective, we can ask whether the extent to which guns are readily available in the community influences the mix of weapons used in violent crime. A cross-national comparison for eleven countries found a strong positive correlation (.72) between the household prevalence of gun ownership and the fraction of homicides committed with a gun (Killias 1993), perhaps because the overall scarcity of guns in a country influences weapon choice in violent events. Some skeptics have questioned whether guns are in any sense scarce in the United States, suggesting that anyone (most especially youths and violent criminals) would find it little more difficult to obtain a gun than, say, a kitchen knife. But regional comparisons indicate otherwise.

The prevalence of gun ownership differs rather widely across urban areas, from around 10 percent in the cities of the Northeast to upwards of 50 percent in the Mountain states. (One explanation for these large differences has to do with the differing importance of rural traditions in these cities.)[12] The overall prevalence of gun ownership is highly correlated with the percentage of homicides, suicides, and robberies that involve guns in these cities (Cook 1979, 1985). Thus, where gun ownership is prevalent in the general population, guns are also prevalent in violence. A natural explanation for this pattern is in terms of inter-city differences in scarcity. Predatory criminals obtain most of their guns from acquaintances, family members, drug dealers, thefts from homes and vehicles, and other street sources, rather than from licensed dealers (Decker, Pennell, and Caldwell 1997; Sheley and Wright 1995; Smith 1996). The ease of making such a "connection" will be greater in a city where guns are prevalent.

Duggan (In press) reports the most extensive analysis to date of how the prevalence of gun ownership influences homicide rates. Using annual data on states from 1980 to 1997, he relates the change in the prevalence of gun ownership (proxied by the subscription rate to *Guns & Ammo* magazine) to the change in the homicide rate. He finds strong evidence that an increase in gun ownership is followed by an increase in homicide. The reverse is also true, although the effect of homicide on gun ownership is much smaller proportionately.

It helps in thinking about the availability of guns to realize how frequently they change hands. For youthful criminals, acquiring a gun is typically not a one-time decision. One interesting statistic from a survey of inner-city male high-school students helps make the point: 22 percent said they currently owned a gun, while an additional 8 percent indicated that they had owned one or more guns in the past, but did not at the time of the interview. Further, the number who said they carried a gun on occasion exceeded the number who owned one, suggesting loans and other temporary arrangements are important features of this scene (Wright, Sheley, and Smith 1992). In this environment, a realistic objective for policy may be to reduce the percentage of a delinquent career in which the typical youth is in possession of a gun, rather than to strive to deprive delinquent youth of guns entirely. Where guns are relatively scarce and expensive, a youthful criminal may be slower to acquire a gun and quicker to sell it when he does, simply because keeping the gun will have higher opportunity cost.

Of course, for a gun to be available for use during a violent encounter, it is not enough for the assailant to have a gun—he must also be carrying it at the time. Since most violent crime occurs away from home, one important aspect of gun availability is the propensity to go armed. The majority of states allows carrying concealed (if the carrier has obtained a permit) but do not treat violations as serious offenses. A notable exception is the Bartley-Fox Amendment in Massachusetts, which in 1975 imposed a mandatory one-year prison sentence for anyone convicted of carrying a gun without a license. This mandatory-sentence provision was widely publicized at the time it was implemented. The immediate impact was clear: thousands of gun owners applied for licenses required to carry a handgun legally. Several studies analyzed subsequent trends in violent crime. Pierce and Bowers (1981) concluded that the short-term impact was to reduce the fractions of assaults and robberies involving guns and, presumably as a consequence, to reduce the criminal homicide rate (see also Deutsch [1979]). Apparently some streetwise people were deterred from carrying, and as a result were more likely to commit their robberies and assaults, when the occasion arose, with weapons other than guns. The result was to reduce the death rate in these attacks (the instrumentality effect). More recently, the Kansas City Gun Experiment was designed to reduce gun availability on the streets through aggressive patrolling against illegal carrying. These patrols were instituted in one high-crime area of the city but not in another area that had a similar number of drive-by shootings at baseline. The "treatment" area experienced a 49 percent reduction in gun crimes during the study period, while gun crimes increased by 4 percent in the comparison area (Sherman, Shaw, and Rogan 1995). These results are suggestive but not definitive, given that the crime trends in the "control" area were somewhat different than in the "experimental" area even before the intervention.

In sum, while guns are certainly a prevalent feature of the mean streets of American cities, they are not yet at the point of saturation or beyond control. It is a remarkable fact that less than one-fifth of noncommercial robberies are committed with a gun, despite the relative profitability of gun robbery (Cook 1976; Bureau of Justice Statistics 2000, Table 66); the legal and other costs of obtaining, possessing, and carrying a gun are sufficient to discourage some violent people from doing so, at least some of the time.

One important question remains. While the general availability of guns appears to influence the choice of weapons in violent crime, and the likelihood that a violent crime will result in the victim's death, does gun availability influence the overall *volume* of violent crime? The available evidence provides little reason to believe that robbery and assault rates are much affected by the prevalence of gun ownership (Cook 1979; Kleck and Patterson 1993). The fact that the United States is such a violent country[13] does not have much to do with guns; the fact that our violent crimes are so deadly has much to do with guns (Zimring and Hawkins 1997).

Self Defense

It is not just street criminals who carry guns, of course—sometimes their potential victims do as well. The practice of going armed in public has been facilitated in recent years by changes in the concealed-carry laws of a number of states; by the mid-1990s over 30 states had liberal provisions that enable most adults to obtain a license to carry. The laws are often called "shall issue," since they require the local authorities to issue a concealed-carry license to anyone who meets certain minimum conditions. A study by two economists (Lott and Mustard 1997) found evidence that states that liberalized their concealed-carry regulations in this fashion enjoyed reductions in violent-crime rates as a result, presumably because would-be assailants were deterred by the increased likelihood that their victims would be armed. This study, expanded into a best-selling book (Lott 2000), has been extraordinarily influential with the public and with state legislators. It is now routine for the potential "antideterrent" effect of any proposed gun-control measure to be a prominent consideration in the public debate.

In his first study, Lott (working with David Mustard) utilized a multivariate estimation procedure[14] applied to annual panel data on counties for the period 1977 to 1992, generating estimates of the effects of a state's adopting a shall-issue concealed-carry law. Their dependent variables were the Part I crimes of the FBI's Uniform Crime Reports. The independent variables in their specification included a dummy variable indicating whether a shall-issue law was in effect in that state and year, a dummy variable for each of the 3000-plus counties, the arrest rate for the crime in question, and several demographic covariates. In addition to the results based on the county data, they also reported estimates based on state-level panel data. Since the publication of this article, Lott (2000) has re-estimated the original equations with two additional years of data (1993 and 1994). He then extended the data set through 1996 and generated estimates using a different approach, where dependent variables are entered in change form (percent increase relative to the previous year) rather than in "level" form. The two approaches reflect two quite different conceptions of how the "shall issue" laws would likely affect crime rates: In the "levels" analysis, the presumption is that the "shall issue" law would cause a permanent once-and-for-all shift in the level of the crime rate, while in the "change" analysis, the presumption is that the shall-issue law would change the trend in crime rates with no effect on the level of crime at the time of passage.

The original results (Lott and Mustard 1997) suggested that the implementation of shall-issue laws had the effect of reducing violent crime rates (homicide, aggravated assault, rape, and robbery) while generally increasing property crime rates (especially larceny and auto theft). But these results proved somewhat sensitive to the time period, the specification, and whether the variables measure levels or percentage changes from the previous year.

Of particular interest are Lott's results for the crime of homicide, because of its importance, and for robbery, since the "deterrence" argument seems more plausible for that crime than others. It seems reasonable to suppose that "shall issue" laws would be most effective in increasing the deterrent threat to criminals in public spaces (where robberies usually occur), since access to guns for self-protection in private homes and commercial establishments is relatively unaffected by these laws. Thus, if the results computed by Lott were in fact due to the causal deterrent effects of "shall issue" laws, among the different violent crimes that he studies, we would expect to observe the strongest effect for robbery. But as shown in Table 1, his results for robbery are inconsistent, differing depending on the details of the estimation procedure. In the first four sets of results, the estimated effects are either negative and marginally significant (by the usual standards), or actually positive. These results appear to be a weak basis for conclusions about whether shall-issue laws deter robbery. On the other hand, his reported results for homicide are consistently negative and usually significant.

Given the prominence and political influence of Lott's research on gun control, it is not surprising that it has been widely attacked by gun-control advocates. He recounts these attacks, some of which have been completely off base, and his responses in Lott (2000). His work has also engendered a more measured response from scholars. Scholarly criticism has been primarily methodological, concerned with the accuracy of his data and with the properties of his statistical methods. For example, Black and Nagin (1998) present a series of results indicating Lott and Mustard's (1997) findings are sensitive to minor changes in the specification and data. Further, they conduct a specification test that suggests that the states that adopted shall-issue laws would have experienced reductions in violent crime (relative to other states) even *without* that legislation. In effect, then, it appears that adoption of these laws has not been exogenous to the process which generates crime; if so, then Lott and Mustard's (1997) findings are biased.[15] Ludwig (1998) utilizes a different estimation strategy that relies on youths as the "control group" in assessing the effects of the shall-issue laws, arguing that minors get

Table 11.1

Summary of Estimated Effects on Robbery and Homicide of Adopting "Shall Issue" Law (County-level panel data)

DEPENDENT VARIABLE TIME PERIOD COVARIATES SOURCE: LOTT (2000)	SIGN OF COEFFICIENT ON SHALL-ISSUE VARIABLE	STATISTICALLY SIGNIFICANTLY DIFFERENT FROM ZERO IN TWO-TAILED TEST?
Log of crime rate 1977–1992 Covariates Table 4.1 in Lott (2000)	R: Negative H: Negative	R: Yes, 10% level H: Yes, 1% level
Log of crime rate 1977–1992 Standard covariates plus burglary rate Table 4.5 in Lott (2000)	R: Positive H: Negative	R: No H: Yes, 1% level
Annual change in log of crime rate 1977–1992 Standard covariates Table 4.6 in Lott (2000)	R: Negative H: Negative	R: Yes, 11% level H: No
Log of crime rate 1977–1994 Standard covariates Table 4.13 in Lott (2000)	R: Positive H: Negative	R: No H: Yes, 1% level
Annual percent change in crime rate 1997–1996 Standard covariates Table 9.1 in Lott (2000)	R: Negative H: Negative	R: Yes, 1% level H: Yes, 1% level

NOTE: The "standard" list of covariates includes demographic variables and the arrest rate, as well as dummy variables for county and year.

little protection from these laws because concealed-carry permits are only issued to adults. Ludwig finds that the shall-issue laws have a negligible effect on homicide. These and other studies are summarized in the comprehensive review by Ludwig (2000). More recently, Duggan (In press) observes that Lott and Mustard (1997) are inconsistent in what date they assign to the adoption of a shall-issue law; when that problem is corrected, the effect of adoption on homicide is no longer statistically significant.

Many analysts are skeptical of Lott's findings because they find them implausible:

1. Lott and Mustard's original findings suggested that shall-issue laws deter violent crime but stimulate property crime, particularly auto theft and larceny. Their account of this odd result was that criminals who were deterred from committing robbery (the one violent crime that is motivated by financial gain) then switched to other kinds of theft that did not require face-to-face confrontation with a potentially armed victim. However, as shown in Table 11.1, Lott's results for robbery are not strong or even (necessarily) of the "right" sign—it is the other types of violent crime that consistently appear with significant negative effects. It seems quite implausible that auto theft is a substitute for rape or assault. In any event, Lott's recent reversal, where he now (based on a longer time series and different statistical approach) reports negative effects on property crime rates, has disarmed this challenge, while raising a new question.

2. The effect of the new laws on the prevalence of carrying by likely victims may be too small to plausibly account for the very large effects on homicide and rape that Lott has estimated. Most states with shall-issue laws had permitted less than 2 percent of the adult residents during the period of Lott's data, and few of the people who are seeking and obtaining permits are in demographic groups that mark them as at high risk for violent victimization. Further, many people were carrying guns, including concealed guns, without benefit of a permit before adoption of shall-issue laws, as is clear from arrest statistics and survey data. So Lott is in effect claiming that a rather small change in the risks facing would-be violent criminals has had remarkably large effects on their behavior. While that is not logically impossible, it does create a reasonable basis for skepticism and a demand for strong evidence (Robuck-Mangum 1997; Hood and Neeley 2000; Ludwig 2000).

Given the available evidence, we conclude that the "shall issue" laws have had little effect on violent crime or property crime.

THE VALUES AT STAKE

Used in the manner of our rural sporting tradition, a gun provides recreation, food, and, arguably, a way of learning a sense of responsibility. When kept behind the counter of a small grocery in a high-crime neighborhood, a gun may help stiffen the owner's resolve to stay in business while serving as part of the informal social-control system for local youth. When used as an instrument of gang warfare, a gun becomes part of the nation's nightmare of crime that terrorizes urban residents and cuts short far too many lives.

These different uses of guns all have value to those who use them in these ways. Society as a whole, however, values some uses less highly than do the individual owners. The "Great American Gun War" is an ongoing debate and political struggle to determine which uses will be protected, and which sacrificed to achieve some greater social good. There is widespread consensus that disarming the gangs would be a step in the right direction (a conclusion that the gang members themselves may or may not agree with), but the social value of preserving current opportunities for self-defense and sporting use is far more controversial.

The debate over gun-control policy makes broad use of both consequentialist and deontological arguments. A consequentialist framework is concerned with ascertaining and valuing the consequences of proposed reform, while the deontological framework is concerned with how a proposed reform measures up in terms of its assignment of civic rights and responsibilities. Advocates on both sides tend to make use of both consequentialist and deontological claims. Control advocates typically argue their case both by pointing to the reductions in fatalities engendered by the proposed reform and by insisting that gun owners, as a matter of principle, should be willing to relinquish some of their rights to own guns in the interests of achieving these benefits. The anti-control advocates argue that gun ownership serves to reduce crime rather than increase it, and that in any event they have a constitutional right to own guns.

Much of the rhetoric in the debate stems from three broad perspectives. Two of these, the public-health and welfare-economics perspectives, are predominantly consequentialist, while the third is primarily deontological.

The Public Health Perspective

Public health advocates are primarily concerned with the loss of life and limb caused by the use of guns against people. They are not much concerned with whether any particular shooting is criminal or not; all loss of life is equally serious. Lives lost to gun accident, suicide, and criminal homicide are of equal public concern (Moore et al. 1994).

Assigning suicide the same importance as homicide is profoundly important in evaluating the gun "problem." There are more gun deaths from suicide than homicide, and the demographic incidence of suicide is quite different than homicide.[16] Looking at homicide statistics we conclude that guns are a far greater problem in cities than elsewhere, especially in minority communities, and we are led to focus gun-control efforts there. But including suicide as an equally important prevention target suggests that guns are a major problem in suburban and rural areas as well, and pose a considerable threat to older whites as well as to black and Hispanic youths (Cook and Ludwig 2000).

In any event, the bottom line in the public-health framework is whether a proposed control measure would reduce the incidence of injury and death. There is little concern with the value of sporting uses of guns. From this perspective, the modest pleasures associated with recreational shooting and the dubious benefits from self-defense should yield to society's overwhelming interest in reducing gun deaths. Preserving life is the paramount value in this scheme.[17]

The Welfare Economics Framework

Like the public-health framework, the welfare-economics framework is predominantly consequentialist, but with a wider array of consequences and greater attention to individual preferences. It leads us to view the gun "problem" in terms of the harm inflicted on others, with much less attention to suicides and self-inflicted accidents. The socially costly uses are virtually coterminous with those that are prohibited by law. But there is no presumption that punishing criminal uses is an adequate response, and there remains the possibility that the benefits of preemptive controls on guns, such as a ban on carrying concealed, would outweigh the costs (Cook and Leitzel 1996). The costs of such controls include the public costs of enforcement and the private costs of compliance (or evasion) of these regulations.

In principle we could determine whether a particular gun-oriented measure is worthwhile by comparing the cost with the benefits stemming from whatever reductions in gun crime are accomplished. A direct comparison requires that benefits be expressed in monetary terms, and since much of the value of living in a safer community is subjective, this translation requires an assessment of preferences. In that spirit, Cook and Ludwig (2000) asked respondents from a national sample how much they would be willing to pay for a reduction in their community's gun-violence rate of 30 percent. Based on their responses, the authors estimated that such a reduction would be worth about $24 billion nationwide.

In this calculus of cost and benefit, where does self-defense fit in? For most gun owners, the possibility that the gun will prove useful in fending off a robber or burglar is one source of its value.[18] Indeed, if guns had no value in self-protection, a ban on possession of guns in the home would quite likely be worthwhile, since other, sporting uses of guns could be preserved by allowing people to store firearms in shooting clubs and use them under regulated conditions. This arrangement would be akin to the military policy for controlling the use of rifles and ammunition by servicemen on military bases, and is somewhat more liberal than the current policy governing fireworks in most states (and far looser than policies regulating the distribution of high explosives). So we believe that the self-defense uses of guns are more important than sporting uses in assessing the costs of restrictions on home possession and carrying in urban areas.

Some have even argued that the private valuation of guns in this respect understates their public value, because the widespread possession of guns has a general deterrent effect on crime (Snyder 1993; Kleck 1991; Lott 2000). Indeed, one survey of imprisoned felons found that a paramount concern in doing their crimes was the prospect of meeting up with an armed victim (Wright and Rossi 1994). What we do not know is whether the predominant effect on criminals is desistance from predatory crime, or displacement to victims who are less likely to be armed, or adoption of a more aggressive style to preempt effective self-defense. If the latter two predominate, then the externality is negative rather than positive (Clotfelter 1993).

Thomas Jefferson offered another reason why gun ownership and use may be undervalued in private decisions, as explained in this quotation: "A strong body makes the mind strong. As to the species of exercises, I advise the gun. While this gives a moderate exercise to the body, it gives boldness, enterprise and independence to the mind. Games played with the ball and others of that nature, are too violent for the body and stamp no character on the mind."[19]

If gun sports are especially suited to building character, then perhaps these sports should be viewed as "merit" goods on a par with the opera or schooling, and deserving of subsidy by the public. But Jefferson would surely have changed his mind about the relative merits of guns and ball games if he could have foreseen the invention of basketball.

The "Rights and Responsibilities" Perspective

The welfare-economics framework helps organize the arguments pro and con for gun controls, and suggests a procedure for assigning values. But for those who believe in the "right" to bear arms, it is not a completely satisfactory approach. The debate over gun control can and should be conducted, at least in part, in the context of a framework that defines the appropriate relationship between the individual, the community, and the state.

Very much in the foreground of this debate lies the Second Amendment, which states, "A well regulated Militia, being necessary to the security of a free State, the right of the people to keep and bear Arms, shall not be infringed." The proper interpretation of this statement has been contested in recent years. Scholars arguing the constitutionality of gun-control measures focus on the militia clause, and conclude that this is a right given to state governments (Henigan 1991; Wills 1995). Others assert that the right is given to "the people" rather than to the states, just as are the rights conferred in the First Amendment, and that the Founding Fathers were committed to the notion of an armed citizenry as a defense against both tyranny and crime (Kates 1983, 1992; Halbrook 1986; van Alstyne 1994).[20] The Supreme Court ruled only once during the twentieth century on a Second Amendment issue, in which it adopted the "state militia" interpretation (Ehrman and Henigan 1989; Vernick and Teret 1999).[21] In *United States v. Miller*, 307 U.S. 174 (1939), the Court held that the "obvious purpose" of the Amendment was "to assure the continuation and render possible the effectiveness . . . " of the state militias. It further wrote that the Amendment "must be interpreted and applied with that end in view." Indeed, as of this writing, no federal appeals court has overturned a gun-control law on Second Amendment grounds.

Regardless of the concerns that motivated James Madison and his colleagues in crafting the Bill of Rights, the notion that private possession of pistols and rifles is a protection against tyranny may strike the modern reader as anachronistic—or perhaps all too contemporary when one recalls such groups as the Branch Davidians and the Aryan Nation. More compelling for many people is the importance of protecting the capacity for self-defense against apolitical assailants.

Some commentators go so far as to assert that there is a public duty for private individuals to defend against criminal predation, now just as there was in 1789 (when there were no police).[22] The argument is that if all reliable people were to equip themselves with guns both in the home and out, there would be far less predatory crime (Snyder 1993; Polsby 1993). Other commentators, less sanguine about the possibility of creating a more civil society by force of arms, also stress the public duty of gun owners, but with an emphasis on responsible use: storing them safely away from children and burglars, learning how to operate them properly, exercising good judgment in deploying them when feeling threatened, and so forth (Karlson and Hargarten 1997). In any event, even if there is an individual right to bear arms then, like the right of free speech, it is surely not absolute but subject to reasonable restrictions. The appropriate extent of those restrictions, however, remains an unresolved issue.

In conclusion, these three perspectives—public health, welfare economics, and civic rights and responsibilities—each provide arguments about the public interest that seem familiar and important. Each is well represented in the ongoing debate over the appropriate regulation of firearms. In practice, the public health perspective helps focus greater attention on suicide, while the perspective that stresses civic rights strengthens the case for protecting self-defense uses of guns. We are not inclined to argue the relative merits of these differing perspectives in the abstract, but will have more to say about policy evaluation in the next sections.

ALTERNATIVE GUN-CONTROL POLICIES

Commerce in guns and the possession and use of guns are regulated by federal, state, and local governments. To assess the options for reform it is first helpful to understand the current array of controls and why they fail to achieve an acceptably low rate of gun violence.

The Current Array of Policies

The primary objective of federal law in this area is to insulate the states from one another, so that the stringent regulations on firearms commerce adopted in some states are not undercut by the greater availability of guns in other states. The citizens of rural Wyoming understandably favor a more permissive system than those living in Chicago, and both can be accommodated if transfers between them are effectively limited. The Gun Control Act of 1968 established the framework for the current system of controls on gun transfers. All shipments of firearms (including mail-order sales) are limited to federally licensed dealers who are required to obey applicable state and local ordinances, and to observe certain restrictions on sales of guns to out-of-state residents.[23]

Federal law also seeks to establish a minimum set of restrictions on acquisition and possession of guns. The Gun Control Act specifies several categories of people who are denied the right to receive or possess a gun, including illegal aliens, convicted felons and those under indictment, people ever convicted of an act of domestic violence, users of illicit drugs, and those who have at some time been involuntarily committed to a mental institution. Federally licensed dealers may not sell handguns to people younger than twenty-one, or long guns to those younger than eighteen. And dealers are required to ask for identification from all would-be buyers, have them sign a form indicating that they do not have any of the characteristics that would place them in the "proscribed" category, and initiate a criminal-history check. Finally, dealers are required to keep a record of each completed sale and cooperate with authorities who seek to trace the sequence of ownership of guns used in crime.

In addition to these federal requirements, states have adopted significant restrictions on commerce, possession, and use of firearms. A number of states require that handgun buyers obtain a permit or license before taking possession of a handgun, a process that may entail payment of a fee and some waiting period. All but a few state transfer-control systems are "permissive," in the sense that most people are legally entitled to obtain a gun. In a few jurisdictions, however, it is very difficult to obtain a handgun legally. In Chicago and Washington, D.C., only law enforcement officers and security guards are eligible to obtain a handgun. A variety of more modest restrictions on commerce have been enacted as well: for example, several states have limited dealers to selling no more than one handgun a month to any one buyer.

State and local legislation tends to make a sharp distinction between keeping a gun in one's home or business and carrying a gun in public. All but one state (Vermont) either bans carrying a concealed firearm or requires a special license or permit. Local ordinances typically place additional restrictions on carrying and discharging guns inside city limits.

Some types of firearms are regulated more stringently than others in federal and state law. The National Firearms Act of 1934 mandated registration and a $200 tax on all transfers of gangster-style firearms, including sawed-off shotguns and automatic weapons (such as the Tommy gun); more recently Congress has prohibited the manufacture of such weapons. The Gun Control Act of 1968 banned the import of small, cheap handguns,[24] and subsequent legislation has banned the importation and manufacture of certain "assault" weapons (Roth and Koper 1997). States typically regulate handguns more closely than long guns, since the former account for most of the firearms used in crime.

Beyond this array of legislated restrictions on gun commerce and use are a variety of other approaches to reducing gun violence. Some sense of the variety of possibilities here is suggested by this list of recent efforts, proposed or adopted, to extend additional control over firearms commerce and use:

1. Raising the federal excise tax on ammunition or guns
2. Establishing a "best practice" industry code of conduct for manufacturers, distributors, and retailers
3. Limiting handgun sales to no more than one per month per customer
4. Requiring that gun buyers pass a test demonstrating their knowledge of the law and good practice in handling a gun
5. Imposing minimum requirements for safe functioning on guns introduced in commerce
6. Trying local drug dealers in the federal courts if they are in possession of a gun at the time of their arrest
7. Organizing a gun buy-back program, offering cash or other considerations in exchange for guns
8. Establishing minimum mandatory sentences for carrying a gun illegally
9. Developing public education campaigns and the cooperation of the television industry to stigmatize storing unlocked, loaded guns in households
10. Giving the police power to revoke gun licenses and search intensively for guns in residences where court restraining orders have been issued against spouses
11. Using magnetometers to keep guns out of schools and other public buildings
12. Disseminating a "parents compact" to promote parent's efforts to prevent their children from possessing or carrying guns

In the face of the rather daunting array of possibilities, policymakers need guidance on which approaches hold the most promise of reducing firearms violence, and at what cost to legitimate owners. Reliable information is difficult to obtain; even when particular control measures have been evaluated in some fashion (and such evaluations are rare in practice) the results are not going to be definitive. There will always be some degree of uncertainty in estimating the consequences of any one intervention, since there is no such thing as a controlled experiment in this area. Further uncertainty arises when we attempt to predict the consequences of implementing a similar intervention in another time and place. Still, some evidence is available concerning which general approaches show the most promise.

In searching for worthwhile reforms, we find it useful to classify alternative gun-control measures into three generic strategies (cf., Zimring 1991; Wintemute 2000b):

1. Those designed to raise the price of guns and reduce general availability
2. Those designed to influence who has these weapons
3. Those designed to affect how the guns are used and with what effect

We offer a general assessment of each of these strategies below.

Strategy 1: Raising the Price, Reducing Availability

Many gun-control measures have an effect on the overall supply of guns or ammunition. If guns (or ammunition) become less readily available, or more expensive to purchase, then some violence-prone people will arguably decide to rely on other weapons instead, and gun violence will be reduced.

Commentators have suggested that this strategy is doomed by the huge arsenal of guns currently in private hands. How can we discourage dangerous people from obtaining guns when there are already enough in circulation to arm every teenager and adult in the country (Wilson 1994; Polsby 1994; Wright 1995)? In response, we note that the number of guns in circulation is only indirectly relevant to whether supply restrictions can hope to succeed; of direct consequence is the price and difficulty of obtaining a gun.

Basic economic reasoning suggests that if the price of new guns is increased by raising the federal tax or other means, the effects will ripple through all the markets in which guns are transferred, including the black market for stolen guns (Cook and Leitzel 1996). If the average prices of guns go up, some people—including some violence-prone people—will decide that there are better uses for their money. Others will be discouraged if, in addition to raising the money price, the amount of time or risk required to obtain a gun increases. While there are no reliable estimates of the elasticity of demand for guns by violence-prone people, we submit that they are likely to be more responsive to price than to more remote costs (such as the possibility of arrest and punishment). Those who argue that offenders will do whatever is necessary to obtain their guns may have some hard-core group of violent gang members and drug dealers in mind, but surely not the much larger group who get into fights from time to time (Sheley and Wright 1995; Smith 1996).[25]

An indirect approach to raising prices is to impose safety requirements on gun manufacturers (Cook 1981). Proposals in this area include "child-proofing" guns so that they are inoperable by children; requiring that domestically manufactured guns meet the same safety requirements as imports, including protections against accidental discharge; and requiring safety devices such as trigger locks and loaded chamber indicators (Teret and Wintemute 1993). As it is now, firearms manufacturers are remarkably free of safety regulation, in part because the Consumer Product Safety Commission has no authority over personal firearms. While safety regulations may be welcomed by gun buyers worried about gun accidents, they would have little direct effect on suicide and criminal misuse of firearms. To the extent that such regulations made guns more costly, however, there could be some indirect effect comparable to raising the federal tax (Cook and Leitzel 1996).

A more far-reaching proposal is to encourage the manufacture of guns that are "personalized," in the sense that they would be equipped with an electronic sensing device that would "recognize" a ring on the owner's finger, or even the owner's fingerprint. Such devices are currently under development. If they prove reliable, law enforcement agencies may adopt them to protect officers from being assaulted with their own guns. If all new handguns were equipped with such devices, it would gradually reduce the number of gun accidents and reduce the profitability of stealing guns (Robinson et al. 1998).

The argument against requiring that new guns meet minimum design standards follows from the fact that such standards would take the cheapest guns off the market, thus making it more costly for poor households to enjoy whatever protection a gun conveys. Since it is the poorest households that generally face the greatest threat from predatory crime, this argument is not easily dismissed.

Finally, both government and nonprofit groups have shown enthusiasm for reducing availability through gun buy-back programs. Research on these programs, which are typically short-duration offers of cash or goods in exchange for guns, has suggested that these approaches are not effective at reducing gun violence (Kennedy, Piehl, and Braga 1996a; Romero, Wintemute, and Vernick 1998; Rosenfeld 1996). There is even a theoretical possibility that a permanent gun buy-back policy might increase the prevalence of gun ownership because by increasing the resale value of the gun, it would reduce the cost of owning one for a while (Mullin 2001). But a note of caution is in order. The effects of a gun buyback will likely depend on the circumstances. Australia's recent buyback of semi-automatic rifles may constitute a best-case scenario; in that case the buyback was a prelude to a near-comprehensive ban on private ownership of these weapons. Thus owners could not exploit the buyback to exchange their old gun for a new one, nor were the sellers to the buyback limited to those who had no further use for the weapon. But at this point there is no systematic evidence on the effects of the Australian buyback on gun violence.

Strategy 2: Restricting Access

The second broad class of gun control policy instruments are those designed to influence who has access to different kinds of weapons. The intuitive notion here is that if we could find a way to keep guns out of the hands of "bad guys" without denying access to the "good guys," then gun crimes would fall without infringing on the legitimate uses of guns. The challenges for this type of policy are, first, to decide where to draw the line and, second, to develop effective barriers to prevent guns from crossing this line.

Who should be trusted with a gun? Federal law is guided by the premise that owning a gun is a right granted to all adults[26] who are legal residents of the United States, unless they do something to disqualify themselves, such as committing a serious crime. A quite different approach would be to treat gun ownership as a privilege, as is the case, say, with driving a vehicle on public highways.[27] And as in the case of the driving privilege, one eminently sensible requirement for those who seek to acquire a gun is that they demonstrate knowledge of how to use it safely and legally.[28] It is an intriguing possibility that such a requirement would engender considerable growth in the National Rifle Association's safety training programs, since many of those wishing to qualify for a license would need to enroll in such a course (Moore 1983).

Wherever the line is drawn, there is the serious problem of defending it against illegal transfers. That task is currently being done very poorly indeed. The major loopholes stem from scofflaw dealers, the difficulty in screening out ineligible buyers, and, most important, a vigorous and largely unregulated secondary market in which used guns change hands. We discuss each of these three areas in turn.

Scofflaw and Negligent Dealers. The U.S. Bureau of Alcohol, Tobacco, and Firearms (ATF) is the agency charged with the regulation of federally licensed gun dealers. It is a small agency whose jurisdiction includes regulatory inspections of gun dealers and criminal investigations of violations of federal gun laws, as well as both regulatory surveillance and criminal investigation of the explosives, alcohol, and tobacco industries. For many years understaffed and lacking political support for its firearms mission, ATF rubber stamped applications for firearms-dealers licenses, and by 1993 there were over 280,000 people who had obtained one—far more than were genuinely in the business of selling guns to the public (Violence Policy Center 1992). Thus, the federal licensing system, which was intended to act both as the gatekeeper in the federal system for insulating the states from each other and as a system for keeping particular groups of dangerous people from obtaining guns, was not performing as originally intended. But changes in application requirements ordered by the new administration in 1993, combined with the hefty increase in fee mandated by Congress in 1994 (from $30 to $200), have had the effect of reducing the number of federal licensees to one third of the peak level, thereby enhancing ATF's ability to serve its regulatory function (Pierce, Briggs, and Carlson 1998).

What can effective regulation and criminal enforcement accomplish? Licensed dealers' access to large numbers of firearms makes them a particular threat to public safety when they fail to comply with the law (Wachtel 1998; Siegel 1999). A recent review of ATF firearms-trafficking investigations revealed that corrupt licensed dealers were involved in under 10 percent of the trafficking investigations but were responsible for the illegal diversion of nearly half of the total number of firearms trafficked in the ATF investigations (ATF 2000b). The average number of guns trafficked by a corrupt licensed dealer in any one case was over 350. These dealers were engaged in an assortment of violations, including making false entries in their record books, selling firearms "off the books," knowingly transferring firearms to convicted felons, conducting illegal out-of-state sales, and illegally selling National Firearms Act weapons such as machine-guns, grenades, and sawed-off shotguns.

ATF's efforts are now guided in part by the results of systematic data on the origins of guns used in crime. Police departments submit confiscated guns to ATF for tracing. The tracing process is cumbersome since there is no central database on gun sales, and only about half of all trace requests are successful to the point of identifying the dealer who first sold the gun at retail (Cook and Braga 2000). Nonetheless these trace data have proven useful in pinpointing targets for investigation. Analysis of trace data has determined that some dealers are greatly overrepresented as a source of crime guns—in 1998, for example, just 1.2 percent of dealers accounted for 57 percent of all traced firearms. This concentration is explained only in part by differences in sales volume (Wintemute 2000a).

Besides an improved regulatory effort, a recent spate of lawsuits filed by cities and counties directed at manufacturers, distributors, and dealers may ultimately force greater dealer compliance with regulations governing transfers (Siebel 1999; Kairys 2000; Vernick and Teret 1999). The suit brought by Chicago and other jurisdictions assert negligent marketing practices by the firearms industry, which serve to undercut the regulations of tight-control jurisdictions. Chicago in particular has banned the acquisition of handguns by residents since 1982, and yet handguns purchased from suburban dealers flow into the city. It seems feasible for the industry to police itself if it were required to by court order; other industries dealing in hazardous products have been successful in this regard (Siebel 1999, p. 277).

Screening. The Brady Handgun Violence Prevention Act, implemented in 1994, required that anyone seeking to buy a handgun from a dealer is required to submit to a criminal-history background check. (Beginning in 1998 the background-check requirement was expanded to include transfers of rifles and shotguns.) A number of states also impose more stringent requirements for handgun transfers, including a waiting period and a more thorough check of records. If the dealer complies with this requirement, there is some chance that disqualified buyers will be identified and screened out. But the reliability of the screening process in identifying proscribed applicants is limited by the generally poor quality of criminal history records and inaccessibility of mental-health records, and by the fact that in most jurisdictions would-be buyers are identified only through a driver's license or other document that is readily forged.

Nonetheless, studies of California data suggest that the screening process there has been effective in keeping guns out of the hands of some violent criminals (Wright et al. 1999; Wintemute et al. 1999). And our experience with Brady background checks certainly demonstrates that a considerable number of proscribed people do attempt to buy handguns from licensed dealers without concealing their identity: between 1994 and 1998, Brady background checks resulted in about 320,000 requests for purchase being denied, with 220,000 of the rejections due to prior felony convictions or pending indictments (Bureau of Justice Statistics 1999). Other would-be handgun purchasers may have been discouraged from trying, knowing that they would be blocked as a result of the background check.

Realistically, however, there is no guarantee that those who were prevented from purchasing a handgun from a dealer remained unarmed. They could buy one in the secondary market from an acquaintance or unlicensed dealer.[29] Alternatively, they can buy from a licensed dealer by use of a qualified "straw man" purchaser, or perhaps find a licensed dealer who is willing to sell guns off the books.

According to one evaluation, the direct effect of the Brady Act on homicide rates was statistically negligible (Ludwig and Cook 2000). The evaluation took advantage of the "natural experiment" created by the fact that only 32 states were required to change their procedures as a result of the Brady Act: the remaining 18 states already required background screening at the time that the Act went into the effect. This "control" group evidenced the same trend in homicide rates before and after implementation of the Act as the "experimental group" of states that were required to adopt a waiting period and background check for handgun transfers—hence the authors' conclusion that the Act was ineffective at reducing homicide. Closing the secondary-market loophole may be a necessary precondition for effective screening.

Secondary Markets. There is a remarkably active and open market for used guns which is largely unregulated, a market where buyers and sellers find each other through word of mouth, the Internet, classified ads, or gun shows. These transactions, constituting 30 to 40 percent of all firearms transactions (Cook and Ludwig 1996), are often entirely legal—someone who sells a gun or two on occasion is not subject to any federal requirements except that they not knowingly sell to a felon, a minor, or other person prohibited from possessing a gun.

This legal loophole could be closed by a requirement that all transactions be processed through a licensed dealer (or a law-enforcement agency) and include the same record-keeping and background-check requirements as the sale of a gun by a dealer. However, compliance with this requirement would likely be low unless there were some incentive to sellers or buyers. In the case of motor vehicles, the registration requirement coupled with liability serves that purpose (Cook, Molliconi, and Cole 1995), and could conceivably be applied to firearms, although there are a number of practical concerns about this arrangement (Jacobs and Potter 1995, 1998). A requirement that sellers at gun shows conduct background checks of would-be buyers is a modest step in the right direction, recently adopted by several states.

Whether or not the legal loophole is closed, the intentional diversion of guns to proscribed people will remain a problem. In that regard, it is useful to distinguish between transfers that move guns from the licit to the illicit sectors, and transfers within the illicit sector (Koper and Reuter 1996). Licensed dealers figure to a surprising extent in the former category, together with theft and secondary-market sales.

The importance of licensed dealers in supplying crime guns has been established on the basis of analyses of firearms-trace data. The rather surprising finding is that guns recovered by the police are not representative of the stock of guns in private hands; a relatively large percentage are quite new, although rarely in the hands of the person who is recorded as the original buyer (Zimring 1976; Cook and Braga 2000; ATF 1997). That, together with other information, suggests that many of the guns used in crime may have moved rather directly from dealer to criminal user, by way of a straw purchase or trafficker. That evidence suggests that the supply of guns to crime can be curtailed by closer regulation of dealers (as explained above), as well as such measures as requiring that dealers report multiple purchases, and the prohibition adopted by several states on selling more than one handgun to a customer per month. Indeed, "one gun a month" laws in Virginia and Maryland caused the number of guns recovered in Washington, D.C. with Virginia and Maryland origins to drop dramatically, though the number of crime guns recovered from other source states increased (Weil and Knox 1996; Teret et al. 1998).

Reducing theft may be more difficult, yet with over 500,000 guns a year being transferred this way each year (Cook and Ludwig 1996), it is just as important. To shrink this source of crime guns, it may be possible to impose some obligation on gun dealers and gun owners to store their weapons securely (as we now do on pharmacists who sell abusable drugs), or to step up enforcement against "fences" who happen to deal in stolen guns.

There is evidence that some of the thefts supplying criminal use are organized. More than a quarter of ATF gun-trafficking investigations involved the theft of firearms from residences, licensed dealers, and common carriers (such as the United Parcel Service) (ATF 2000b). Organized rings of thieves that specialized in stealing firearms often characterized these cases. To the extent that stolen guns are channeled to the street through theft rings and fences, law enforcement agencies can work to identify these criminal networks (through informants, proffers to criminals caught in the possession of stolen guns, and the like) and disrupt these supply lines.

A technological "fix" for gun theft may be feasible. If guns were designed so that they were "personalized," as discussed above, then their value to thieves would be reduced to an extent that depends on the cost of "re-keying" them. If the personalization device is readily replaced, as is the case, say, for motor vehicles today, then theft would remain an important source of guns to proscribed users. But if the device was costly to re-key, or the re-keying process were only accessible through specially authorized dealers, then theft of new guns would cease to be a problem.

Interdicting transfers *within* the illicit sector has been a low-priority mission for most police departments. Because there has been so little experience with local investigations directed at stopping the redistribution of guns among youths, drug dealers, and others in the illicit sector, it is not clear what can be accomplished in this arena. The analogy to drug enforcement may provide some guidance (Koper and Reuter 1996). But gun markets appear quite different from heroin and cocaine markets for several reasons.

First, the supply of guns to this market is diffuse, involving myriad potential sellers who enter the market when they happen to have an extra gun or two, rather than the more concentrated illicit supply system that characterizes the cocaine and heroin markets. Every burglar who steals a gun then has the opportunity to become a dealer for the purpose of disposing of the gun, selling to other youth they know. Alternatively, they may sell to middlemen, including drug dealers. And police investigations occasionally turn up a licensed dealer who has been active in making illicit sales. But it appears that the bulk of the sales in the black market are by people who have no commitment to this line of business.

Second, because guns are a durable good, and are both purchased and used less frequently than drugs, the total number of transactions in the market is much smaller than in the illicit drug market (Koper and Reuter 1996). There are also fewer repeat buyers. This means that the illicit gun markets are less visible than drug markets in local communities, but relatively easy to penetrate by the police informants and undercover agents.

Third, because in most areas there is a large legal market standing alongside the illicit market, the prices that can be charged in the illicit market are typically lower than in other markets for guns, just as is true for stolen jewelry or televisions. The exception may be in very tight control jurisdictions, such as New York and Boston, where prices are apparently high enough to motivate a good deal of gun-running from jurisdictions with weaker controls. There is some evidence that these gunrunning operations tend to be small (Moore 1981). More than 40 percent of ATF gun-trafficking investigations involved the illegal diversion of ten guns or less (ATF 2000b).

Thus, the illicit gun market appears to be made up for the most part of relatively small and unspecialized enterprises, with easy entry and exit. While shutting down particular trafficking operations may be of little consequence in such a regime, law-enforcement efforts directed at illicit trafficking can be effective to the extent that they discourage entry by creating a general deterrent.

Our bottom line is simply that the potential for attacking the secondary market in guns has scarcely been tested, and until it is tested in systematic fashion, no firm conclusions are warranted.

Strategy 3: Controlling Uses

The third broad class of gun-control-policy instruments is concerned with limiting unsafe and criminal uses of guns. These include both design regulation and law enforcement.

Design regulation has been discussed at several points above; federal law currently limits commerce in sawed-off shotguns, fully automatic guns, and some types of "assault" weapons, and the list could be extended in various ways (Wintemute 1996; Teret et al. 1998). For example, certain small-cheaply-made guns, often called Saturday Night Specials, are banned from importation by the federal Gun Control Act of 1968, but domestic manufacturers have been free to make such guns. Maryland has banned a list of such domestic guns since 1988, apparently with substantial effect (Vernick, Webster, and Hepburn 1999), and other states are now considering legislation of this sort.

A number of commentators have pointed out the logic in treating guns the same as most other consumer products, which are subject to ongoing review and regulation by federal agencies including the Consumer Product Safety Commission and the National Highway Traffic Safety Administration (Bonnie, Fulco, and Liverman 1999). Again by analogy to other products, it seems appropriate that this type of design regulation be supplemented by the threat of civil liability for unsafe design.

The criminal law and enforcement do play prominent roles in deterring the misuse of firearms. Most prominent are sentencing-enhancement provisions for the use of a gun in crime. One clear advantage of this approach as compared with other gun policies is that it does not impinge on legitimate uses of guns. One analysis of crime trends in jurisdictions that adopted such sentencing provisions provides evidence that they can be effective in reducing the homicide rate, although there is no consensus on this matter (McDowall, Loftin, and Wiersema 1992b).[30]

Another and more controversial tactic is to focus local law-enforcement efforts on illegal possession and carrying. The potential effectiveness of this approach is suggested by the success of the Bartley-Fox Amendment in Massachusetts, discussed earlier. This sort of gun enforcement typically requires proactive policing, and police departments differ widely in how much effort they direct to halting illegal possession and gun carrying (Moore 1980). The controversy over enforcement stems in part from the concern that police, if sufficiently motivated, may conduct illegal searches in the effort to get guns off the street. Nonetheless, gun-oriented patrol tactics have the potential to reduce gun violence (Sherman, Shaw, and Rogan 1995; Fagan, Zimring, and Kim 1998; Sherman 2000).

Rather than a general effort to get guns off the streets, a more focused effort can be directed at prohibiting guns in particularly dangerous locations such as homes with histories of domestic violence, or bars with histories of drunken brawls, or parks where gang fights tend to break out, or schools where teachers and students have been assaulted. In seeking to reduce the presence of weapons in these particularly dangerous places, groups other than the police may be mobilized to help make the laws effective. Victimized spouses or their advocates might help enforce rules against guns in violence-prone households, liquor-licensing agencies might be enlisted to help keep guns out of bars, the recreation department might be mobilized to reduce gun carrying in public parks, and so on. The point is that there may be some particular "hot spots" for gun offenses that could be targeted as places to concentrate gun enforcement efforts much as we focus a great deal of attention on keeping guns and bombs out of airplanes.

There have been some promising developments in the use of deterrence-based strategies to reduce illicit gun use, first incorporated in the Boston Gun Project. Beginning in 1995, an interagency working group composed of Harvard University researchers, members of the Boston Police Department, and other criminal justice agencies conducted research and analysis on Boston's youth violence problem, designed a problem-solving intervention to reduce youth violence, and implemented the intervention. The research showed that the problem of youth violence in Boston was concentrated among a small number of serially offending gang-involved youth (Kennedy, Piehl, and Braga 1996b; Kennedy, Braga, and Piehl, 1997). The key problem-solving intervention that arose from the research diagnoses was known as the "pulling levers" focused deterrence strategy. This approach involved deterring violent behavior by chronic gang offenders by reaching out directly to gangs, saying explicitly that violence would no longer be tolerated, and backing that message by "pulling every law enforcement lever" legally available when violence occurred (Kennedy 1997; 1998).

The "pulling levers" approach attempted to prevent gang violence by making gang members believe that gun use by any one member of the gang would result in legal problems for all members. The intent was to create an incentive for gang members to discourage each other from gunplay, thus reversing the usual group norm in support of violence. A key element of the strategy was the delivery of a direct and explicit "retail deterrence" message to a relatively small target audience regarding what kind of behavior would provoke a special response and what that response would be. The deterrence message was delivered by talking to gang members on the street, handing out fliers in the hot spot areas explaining the enforcement actions, and organizing forums between violent gang members and members of the interagency working group (Kennedy 1997, 1998). An evaluation of the Boston strategy to prevent youth violence found it to be associated with significant decreases in youth homicides, shots fired, and gun assaults (Braga et al. 2001). A number of cities have begun to experiment with variations on this approach and have experienced some encouraging preliminary results. These cities include Minneapolis, Baltimore, Indianapolis, Los Angeles, Bronx, Winston-Salem, Memphis, New Haven, and Portland, among others (see Kennedy and Braga 1998; Coleman et al. 2000).

Drawing from the Boston experience, the Project Exile program in Richmond, Virginia, mandated that any felon caught in the possession of a firearm would be prosecuted federally and, if convicted, receive five years in federal prison. This prosecution strategy was accompanied by a vigorous publicity campaign, which warned potential violators of the new risks associated with being a felon in possession of a firearm through television commercials, billboard advertisements on buses and buildings, and business cards. The communications campaign and the aggressive prosecution strategy were designed to deter felons and others from illegally possessing and carrying firearms. No formal evaluation has been undertaken as of this writing.

Finally, several jurisdictions have implemented specialized courts for firearms-related offenses based on the premise that deterrence is enhanced when punishment is administered soon after the offense is committed and with a high degree of certainty.

CONCLUSION: WHAT'S TO BE DONE?

Given the important value conflicts and empirical uncertainties surrounding gun-control policies, some caution in recommending public or governmental action is warranted. But recommending caution is far from recommending inaction. Indeed, we think that it is time to get on with the business of actively exploring alternative gun-control initiatives to develop more effective interventions than those we now rely upon. Exploration and experimentation are urgent for several reasons.

First, the current toll of gun violence demands action. Interventions to restrict the availability of guns are unlikely to have much effect on the overall rate of violence, but they do have the potential to reduce the number of fatalities. A substantial portion of the thousands of gun homicides each year can surely be prevented without infringing too heavily on the public fisc or individual rights. A "war on gun violence" seems a far more promising avenue to saving lives than the costly war on drug abuse.

Second, it is only through trying alternative approaches that we can hope to develop confident conclusions about what works. Learning from experience is not automatic, but it can happen if reforms are coupled with systematic evaluation. With additional evidence may come a shift in the politics of gun control as well. Currently advocates on both sides mix value statements concerning rights or social welfare with factual claims concerning potential efficacy. For example, those who assert an individual right to bear arms usually also claim that widespread private ownership of guns reduces crime, implying that the value at stake here (freedom from government interference) can be preserved without social cost. If the factual claims were sufficiently robust that advocates had to accept the fact that their position entailed real costs, we would begin to learn something about how strongly these values are actually held.

The goal of gun-control policy over the next decade should be to develop and evaluate specific gun-control measures that can reduce gun crimes, suicides, and accidents, while preserving as much legitimate use of guns as possible. There is no reason to believe that there is a single best policy. Rather, we are looking for a portfolio of policies that reflects the full array of gun "problems." To some extent this portfolio should differ according to local circumstances and values, with a greater emphasis on suicide prevention in Iowa and on street violence in Washington, D.C.

Our suggestions are organized according to level of government.

Action at the Federal Level

The Federal Government is best positioned to make guns more valuable and harder to obtain, while insulating the states from one another's supply of guns. Among the next steps that appear most promising are these:

1. Raising the tax on guns and ammunition to make the cost of acquiring and owning particular kinds of guns more accurately reflect the social costs and benefits of having them. Incidentally, we would favor converting the current excise tax, which is proportional to the wholesale price, to a flat tax. Cheap handguns do as much or more damage as expensive ones. On the one hand, we recognize that this tax is repressive, and will be particularly burdensome on poorer people who want a gun. On the other hand, the benefit of such a tax, reductions in gun crimes and accidents, will also accrue disproportionately to the poor, who are vastly overrepresented among the victims of gunshot wounds.

2. Requiring all gun transfers to pass through federally licensed dealers, with the same screening and paperwork provisions as if the gun were being sold by the dealer.

3. Stepping up criminal enforcement efforts against gun-running operations.

4. Providing funding and technical know-how to enhance the quality and completeness of state and federal criminal-history files and facilitating access by law enforcement agencies to these files.

5. Enhancing cooperation with the local law-enforcement efforts in investigating and prosecuting those who deal in stolen guns and those who engage in illegal gun trafficking.

6. Mandating that new guns meet minimum safety requirements to reduce gun accidents, while encouraging research in devices to personalize guns.

The federal government is also in the best position to accumulate the national experience with gun-control policy initiatives. Much as the National Institutes of Health try to accelerate learning about what is effective in dealing with cancer by monitoring treatments and outcomes in nationally established protocols, so the National Institute of Justice should expedite the search for more effective gun-control policies by continuing to support evaluation of the diverse policy interventions that will be launched at different levels of government over the next few years. To facilitate such evaluations, better data are needed. The Fatal Accident

Reporting System is a good model. It has provided the raw material for evaluation research in traffic fatalities. A similar system for intentional violent injuries could be implemented without much difficulty.

Beyond this, the surgeon general and attorney general together should continue using their "bully pulpit" to help create an environment in which local governments, community groups, and private individuals would begin to change their attitudes and behaviors with respect to guns. Such measures have proven effective over the long run in reducing smoking, drunk-driving, and drug use; perhaps they could become effective in changing behavior with respect to guns. Specifically, it is important to remind gun owners of the need to keep their weapons secure from theft, to transfer them only to responsible others, to keep them out of the hands of their children, and so on. The message should be: guns are dangerous, particularly in an urban environment, and it behooves owners to learn how to store them safely and use them responsibly.

Action at the State Level

The agenda for each state will and should depend on its circumstances. In the past the states have been the laboratory for instituting a variety of licensing and regulatory programs, as well as establishing different sentencing schemes for use of guns in crime and for carrying illegally. Technology transfer can take place only if these innovations are subjected to careful evaluation.

A battle has been engaged over the extent of liability for manufacturers, sellers, and owners of guns when a gun is used to injure someone. Lawsuits based on a variety of liability theories are moving through the courts, initiated in many cases by cities. The implicit threat posed by these lawsuits is that if manufacturers and sellers are held responsible for the damage done by handguns, the monetary liability would be prohibitive. This possibility is appealing to those who are impatient with the more moderate results achievable through the political process. In a number of cases, however, state legislatures have intervened to block cities from suing.

The most notable victory for the plaintiffs to date was in the Maryland courts (*Kelly v. R. G. Industries*), where the jury found the manufacturer of a small cheap handgun liable for an injury it caused (Teret 1986). In that case the Maryland legislature enacted a law that exempted the manufacturers against such claims but at the same time established a process for banning commerce in certain types of small, cheap handguns. Thus the plaintiff's lawyers were successful in improving the terms of political trade by changing the status quo, and the result, while still quite moderate, went farther to control guns than otherwise would have been possible.

Action at Metropolitan or Municipal Level

Perhaps the greatest opportunities to work on reducing gun violence in the immediate future lie in the cities where the toll of gun violence—especially criminal violence, and particularly youth violence—is so high. It is there that the scales balancing the competing values of rights to gun ownership on one hand, and the social interest in reducing gun violence on the other tilts most significantly toward reducing gun violence. It is there that one might expect gun owners to willingly surrender some of their privileges, or to accept a greater public responsibility in the ways that they acquire, possess, use, and transfer their weapons.

What works against this outcome, of course, is fear of crime and the fervent belief by some that a gun will provide protection. Thus, one important goal of gun-control policy at the local level should be not simply to reduce the availability of guns but to find other, less socially costly means that people can use to produce security and reduce fear. In many cities, this is one of the important goals of shifting to a strategy of community policing. Community policing is designed to help mobilize citizens into effective self-defense groups that can work in partnership with the police forces. If such groups became common, the need for individual gun ownership might abate. Another goal of community policing is to work directly on the fear of crime as well as on actual criminal victimization. To the extent that these efforts help to dissipate some ill-founded fears, these measures, too, might reduce the felt need for individual gun ownership, and with that, increase the range of feasible and desirable gun-control policies.

The particular targets of city efforts against gun violence that seem important to us are three:

1. Reducing gun carrying by offenders on city streets
2. Reducing youth access to and use of all kinds of weapons
3. Keeping guns out of places that have records of violent conflicts such as rowdy bars, homes where domestic violence often occurs, or other community "hot spots"

Exactly how to accomplish these particular objectives remains unclear, but it is not hard to list particular actions one could imagine police departments undertaking. Indeed, bringing gun crime down would be a good exercise in problem-solving to turn over to an innovative police agency. The Boston Gun Project, which established a cooperative arrangement between local, state, and federal agencies, is an important model.

Action at the Community and Household Level

Our emphasis on government action in no way denies the potential importance of activists, private professionals, and volunteer groups in changing the culture and norms of acceptable behavior around guns. The problem of gun violence, and the role of guns in contributing to that violence, may be eased as individuals become more responsible and more attentive to their own and their neighbors' interests in deciding whether to own a gun, how to store and use it, and to whom to transfer it. If we get together to deal with the threat of violence, the fear that leads many to keep a loaded firearm handy may abate, thus sparing their households from this particular hazard. And in particularly risky circumstances, where there is ongoing domestic violence or a member of the household is suicidal, neighbors, counselors, and social workers must be prepared to insist that any guns be removed from the premises.

The challenge of finding the best portfolio of gun-control measures is daunting in the face of our considerable uncertainty about what works and the profound disagreements about which values should be paramount. But with continuing attention to the evidence generated by the state and local innovations, and a vigorous public dialogue on the importance of both rights and responsibilities in this arena, there is every hope of doing better.

12

Substance Abuse Policy from a Crime-Control Perspective

DAVID A. BOYUM AND MARK A. R. KLEIMAN

Discussions about crime control, whether at cocktail parties, in classrooms, or on Capitol Hill, inevitably turn to the subject of drugs. No one doubts that drugs and policies to control them are linked to nondrug crime: all the varieties of theft, assault, and offenses against public order. But the precise nature of those links remains obscure, and what to do about them remains controversial.

One of the few universally accepted propositions about crime in the United States is that active criminals are disproportionately substance abusers. In Manhattan, urine tests indicate that over three-quarters of those arrested have recently taken one or more illicit drugs; in few major cities is the proportion less than half (National Institute of Justice 2000). A majority of state and federal prisoners report that they were under the influence of alcohol or other drugs (or both) at the time of their current offense (U.S. Department of Justice 1999).

Statistics about crime related to drug dealing are harder to come by, but scholarly studies echo newspaper headlines about "drive-by shootings" in attributing changes in homicide rates to the rise and fall of open markets for illicit drugs and the patterns of weapons acquisition, carrying, and use associated with them (Cork 1999).

The dominant view among citizens and elected officials sees these facts as proof of the need for vigorous enforcement of the drug laws. If drug trafficking is inherently violent, and if illicit drug use catalyzes criminal and other delinquent behavior (immediately, as intoxication reduces inhibition and stimulates aggression, and in the longer term, through the impacts of long-term substance abuse on character, life-style, and non-criminal opportunities), then it seems to follow that enforcement efforts to suppress drug-selling and drug-taking will tend to reduce crime (Office of National Drug Control Policy 1994).

But a strongly held dissenting view sees drug policy, and not drug abuse, as principally responsible for the observed drugs-crime connection (Nadelman 1988). Drug laws and their enforcement make illicit drugs more expensive. Since many heavy users of those drugs commit crimes to finance their habits, those higher prices increase, rather than decreasing, nondrug crime. As to violent crime among dealers, that is even more obviously attributable to prohibition; when alcohol was an illicit drug, alcohol dealers settled their differences with firearms, just as cocaine dealers do today. But two contemporary liquor store owners are no more likely to shoot one another than are two taxi drivers.

Exponents of this dissenting view argue that the drug laws, being criminogenic, should be repealed, or less drastically, that drug law enforcement should be radically cut back and the problems of drug abuse addressed in ways designed to minimize individual and social harm rather than the rate of drug consumption.

But "drug warriors" and "legalizers" alike (to use the terms the two sides apply to one another) ground their policy recommendations on partial and one-sided analyses of the relationship between drugs and crime. By creating black markets, prohibition can cause crime. But so too can intoxication and addiction, even when the underlying drug is legal. Thus, the answer to the question "Do drugs, or drug laws, cause crime?" is "Yes."

The right question, from a crime-control perspective, is "What set of drug laws, enforcement practices, and other policies would cause the least crime?" Of course, the crime-minimizing set of drug policies might not be the best set of policies, all things considered; other components of the public health and welfare are also involved, along with questions about morality and civil liberty. Those broader questions are outside the scope of this chapter.

Even the narrower problem of designing drug policies to minimize nondrug crime is complicated enough, with causal chains that look like loops, evidence that remains stubbornly ambiguous, and policies whose effects, even as to their direction, may depend on difficult-to-predict details of implementation. It might turn out, for a given drug, that an intelligently implemented prohibition would outperform any practicable system of legal availability, but that the imperfect legalization that would actually emerge if the current laws were repealed would outperform the imperfect prohibition system we actually have (or vice versa). More obviously, the crime-control costs and benefits of various drug policies are likely to vary sharply from drug to drug, even among those currently illicit, in somewhat complicated ways.

Nevertheless, this chapter attempts a systematic exploration of the myriad ways in which drugs and drug policy might, as a conceptual matter, cause or prevent predatory criminal behavior, and reviews what evidence there is about the existence and effect sizes of the logically possible effects. From there, it will turn to a review of drug abuse control policies, asking how the legal status assigned to various drugs, the enforcement of drug laws, policies to deal with intoxicated behavior, prevention efforts, treatment programs, and policies aimed at drug-involved offenders, as applied to a variety of drugs, are likely to influence the levels of predatory crime. Last comes the question of what all this suggests for the design of crime-minimizing drug policies.

THE DRUGS-CRIME CONNECTIONS

There seem to be three links between drugs and crime. First and most obvious are the crime-facilitating effects of drug use itself: the intoxication and addiction that, in certain circumstances, appear to encourage reckless and combative behavior. The second and third drugs-crime connections stem from policies of drug prohibition and enforcement: the crimes that attend the workings of the black market—violence among dealers, crime incident to the disorderly conditions that surround open illicit markets, the corruption of law enforcement—and the crimes committed by users to obtain money with which to buy drugs.

Abuse-Related Crime

More crimes—and in particular, more violent crimes—are committed under the influence of alcohol than under the influence of all illegal drugs combined (U.S. Department of Justice 1999). That alcohol, a legal and inexpensive drug, is implicated in so much crime suggests that substance abuse itself, and not just economic motivation or the perverse effects of illicit markets, can play a significant role in crime. This hardly comes as a surprise. Anything that weakens self-control and reduces foresight is likely to increase lawbreaking (and other risky activities that promise immediate benefits and only the possibility of future costs) (Wilson and Herrnstein 1985). Most of us know individuals who, when drunk or high, become reckless and aggressive. Moreover, although aggressiveness is often an unwanted or at least unintended side effect of intoxication, those who intend to act aggressively sometimes become intoxicated to unleash their rage or to steel themselves for a violent encounter.

Yet the claim that drugs cause aggressive behavior is hard to prove. Of all psychoactive substances, alcohol is the only one that has been shown in behavioral experiments to commonly (though not invariably) increase aggression (Roth 1994; Reiss and Roth 1993). Heroin and marijuana, for example, seem to generate pacific rather than aggressive pharmacological effects, although short tempers are common during withdrawal from opiate addiction (Martin 1983; Dewey 1986). Sweeping assertions about intoxication and aggression rarely withstand close scrutiny; the relationship only holds for people with certain types of personalities, using certain substances, in certain settings (Fagan 1990).

But the immediate effects of intoxication are not the only, or necessarily the most significant, effects of drug-taking on offending. Both the pharmacology of various drugs and the sociology of their acquisition and use may alter the behavior of heavy users in ways that increase their propensities toward offending, even when not under the influence. Chronic intoxication impairs school and job performance, makes its victims more present-oriented and less prone to delay gratification, and damages relationships with friends and family. All of this, one would assume, makes violent and other criminal behavior more likely by decreasing its actual and perceived disadvantages.

At least where cocaine is concerned, there is a chemical aspect to the matter as well. Stereotypes are rarely devoid of truth, and it is hard to dismiss the widespread belief among inner-city residents and drug treatment personnel that chronic cocaine and crack abuse produce paranoid, irascible behavior (Weiss and Mirin 1987; Post 1975). From a pharmacological perspective, cocaine and amphetamines are quite similar, and amphetamine abuse is clearly related to aggressive behavior (Bejerot 1970; Grinspoon and Bakalar 1985). Indeed, the difference in the levels of violence between the active street heroin markets of the 1970s and the active street cocaine markets of the late 1980s and early 1990s seems to reflect in part the irritability that tends to characterize chronic heavy cocaine users. That in laboratory experiments cocaine has failed to consistently stimulate violent behavior is not conclusive here; if the connection between cocaine and violence is conditionally causal—meaning that cocaine use encourages violence, but only in particular contexts, and perhaps only after long-term abuse—then experiments will necessarily have a hard time identifying a cocaine-violence link. Moreover, in real life, though not in experiments, cocaine use is often accompanied by alcohol use, and the combination may be more-than-additively potent in unleashing aggression.

Crime Attributable to Drug Markets

Some transactions involving illicit drug markets have high propensities for violence. Because selling drugs is illegal, business arrangements among dealers cannot be enforced by law. Thus territorial disputes among dealers, employee discipline (punishment for stealing, informing, or not paying debts), and disagreements over the price, quantity, and quality of drugs are all subject to settlement by force. Since dealers have an incentive to be at least as well-armed as their competitors, violent encounters among dealers, or between a dealer and a customer, often prove deadly. Moreover, perpetrators of inter-dealer or dealer-customer violence are unlikely to be apprehended: enforcement drives transactions into locations that are hidden from the police, and victims—themselves involved in illegal behavior—are unlikely to complain to the authorities.

We should expect drug dealers to be more commonly and more heavily armed than entrepreneurs and employees in other lines of work, because dealing provides both the motivation and the wherewithal for weapons acquisition. In homicides in New York City in 1984 that the police called drug related, 80% of the victims were killed with a handgun, compared with only 47% in homicides not considered drug related (Goldstein and Brownstein 1987). While guns can be a deterrent, perhaps reducing the number of violent encounters, their presence tends to raise the lethality of incidents that do take place. The net effect is probably a decrease in black eyes, an increase in fatalities (see Chapter 11 in this volume). In addition, the fear generated by gun violence among drug dealers may encourage gun acquisition among other residents of drug-involved neighborhoods; survey reports that a significant proportion of inner-city high school students carry guns for self-protection may represent evidence of such an effect (Sheley and Wright 1993; Kennedy 1994).

It is not clear how much of the violence among drug dealers is attributable to the drug trade itself, as opposed to the personal propensities of the individuals employed in it, or to the economic, political, social, or cultural conditions of drug-impacted communities. Violent drug dealers tend to live and work in poor, inner-city neighborhoods, where violence is common, independent of the drug business. On an individual level, a willingness to engage in violence is part of the implicit job description of a drug dealer in many markets. And the logic of natural selection suggests that active dealers (as opposed to those who are dead, incarcerated, or scared out of the business) are those who were best able to use violence, intimidation, and corruption to protect their position.

Even the degree to which the drug trade provides the immediate pretext for violence among drug dealers is hard to pin down. Many violent incidents that are commonly assumed to be drug-related in this narrow sense—because they occur between dealers, between members of drug-dealing gangs, or at a known dealing location (Goldstein et al. 1990)—are in interpersonal rather than commercial in motive, involving an insult, a woman, a sideways look, or seemingly nothing at all. Or it may involve gang territory; in studying street gang crime in Chicago from 1987 to 1990, Carolyn and Richard Block (1993) concluded that gang-motivated homicides were most often turf-related (gang turf, not drug turf), while only 8 of 288 homicides were related to drugs. Observers note that the combatants are easily provoked—"live wires" is a common description—especially when they are themselves chronic crack smokers. (Spending one's working life in a violent business, or living in a violent community, also contributes to having a short fuse.)

Other researchers stress the role of an inner-city culture in which respect is earned through violence, and where the cost of backing down from a confrontation is not only loss of face but an increase in future vulnerability (Ferguson 1993). "In fact, among the hard-core street-oriented," writes sociologist Elijah Anderson (1994, p. 92), "the clear risk of death may be preferable to being 'dissed' by another." Still others note that those involved in violent incidents typically have a history of delinquency (including violence) dating back to early childhood (Wasserman 1993). While data on these kinds of factors are difficult to assemble, Jeffrey Fagan came up with some revealing evidence in a survey of over 500 active drug dealers in the Central Harlem and Washington Heights neighborhoods of New York City. Fagan reports, among these dealers, an association between violent activity within the drug trade and violence and criminal activity outside of the drug business. "It appears," he concludes, "that processes of self- and social-selection result in the participation of generally violent and criminally active people in drug-selling" (Fagan 1992, p. 117).

The drug trade also contributes to crime by diverting inner-city youths away from legitimate pursuits of school and employment (Inciardi and Pottieger 1991). Not only does the drug business introduce them to criminal enterprise, it also increases their risk of substance abuse and weakens their prospects for legitimate work (prison time makes for a bad résumé entry), all of which make it more likely that they will engage in criminal activity even outside the drug business.

In addition to diverting individuals away from the above-ground economy, the drug trade also drains the resources of the criminal justice system.

This too may encourage crime. There are approximately 1.5 million drug arrests a year in the United States; without question, this imposes a tremendous burden on police, courts, and prisons. More than 60% of the residents of federal prisons are committed for drug offenses; in state prisons, the figure is roughly 20% (U.S. Department of Justice 2000). In a world of finite criminal justice resources, drug law enforcement reduces the risks of committing nondrug crimes—and thus the legal deterrent to doing so—and the number of persons imprisoned for nondrug offenses (Blumstein 1993).

It would seem, then, that increasing the resources devoted to drug law enforcement would inevitably exact a price in terms of increased non-drug crime. That is surely true with respect to deterrence. The picture with respect to incapacitation is somewhat less clear, because most of those incarcerated for drugdefined crimes (possession or sale) also have very high rates of nondrug offending. Indeed, there is some evidence that, on average, those incarcerated for drug offenses and those incarcerated for other crimes have committed nondrug offenses with the same frequency (Cohen and Nagin 1993). So using a prison cell to house an arrested drug offender may buy, in incapacitation, as much reduction in non-drug crimes as would using that prison cell to house someone caught for a nondrug offense. If making drug arrests involves less police work than making nondrug arrests, arresting and prosecuting individuals for drug offenses might turn out to be an efficient approach to reducing nondrug crime. The same might be true if suppressing some forms of retail drug-dealing contributed to crime control through the reduction of disorder.

However, the sheer use of resources is not the only way in which drug law enforcement could compete with enforcement against predatory crimes.[1] One of the terrors imprisonment holds for offenders is the social stigma attached to being, or having been, incarcerated. That stigma is likely to decrease in intensity as the rate of imprisonment rises, simply because prisoners and ex-prisoners become less uncommon. Thus imprisoning more drug dealers will tend to reduce the deterrent effect of any given level of nondrug imprisonment.

Moreover, from a crime-control perspective, the costs of arresting, prosecuting, and imprisoning the significant minority of drug offenders with little or no other criminal activity (couriers, many low-level marijuana and hallucinogen dealers), are deadweight losses. In any case, very long sentences as provided by federal drug laws and many state drug laws for a wide range of offenses are likely to be crime-increasing for two independent reasons. First, the deterrent value of any given amount of punishment can be increased by spreading it more evenly across the class of those eligible to be punished, increasing certainty at the expense of severity (Cook 1981). Long sentences do the opposite. Second, the incapacitating effect of isolation depends on the "personal crime rates" of those incarcerated, and offending tends to diminish with age. The longer the sentence, the older the offender during its later years, and the fewer the offenses that are prevented by his (rarely her) incarceration. ("Three strikes and you're out" laws, which provide for life imprisonment without parole for repeat serious offenders, are especially subject to this objection.)

Economically Motivated Crimes by Users

The proposition that drug-abusers commit crimes to get money to buy drugs is straightforward enough. The desire for drugs among habitual users can be an extraordinarily powerful one, and for many heavy users of expensive drugs, crime is the only feasible source of sufficient funds. Once again, there is plenty of circumstantial evidence. Fred Goldman (1976, 1977, 1981) found that among heroin addicts, 90 cents of each criminally earned dollar was spent on heroin. In studying New York City heroin addicts, Bruce Johnson and his colleagues found a close match between criminal income and drug expenditures (Johnson et al. 1985; Johnson, Anderson, and Wish 1988). Similar correlations have been found for criminally active cocaine users (Collins, Hubbard, and Rachal 1985).

Yet, like many conjectures about the drugs-crime connections, the idea that users commit crime for drug money is hard to prove. What we know is that there is a clear association between heavy use of expensive drugs and income-generating crime, and that this relationship holds for individual users, who commit more crime during periods of heavy use and less crime during periods of lower use or abstinence (Chaiken and Chaiken 1990).

But there are other possible explanations for the observed relationship between drug use and crime. Drug use itself may induce antisocial behavior (including crime), and there may be other factors, such as indifference to risk and willingness to deviate from established norms, that cause both drug abuse and crime. Lastly, there could be the "paycheck effect": just as some heavy drinkers splurge at the local bar on payday, drug-involved offenders may buy drugs because crime gives them the money to do so. Thus income-generating crime may cause drug use, as well as the other way around.

Despite this methodological difficulty, there is no reason to doubt that a nontrivial amount of crime among addicts is economically motivated.

And many drug-involved offenders acknowledge this: according to a 1989 survey of convicted jail inmates, 39% of cocaine and crack users claimed to have committed their current offense to get money to buy drugs (U. S. Department of Justice 1992).

What can also be said, with more certainty, is that economic motivation is an incomplete theory of crime among heavy drug abusers. First, the survey of jail inmates just cited also implies that 61% of cocaine and crack users committed their current offense for reasons *other* than drug money. Second, there is a substantial body of research indicating that, while drug use does appear to intensify and perpetuate criminal behavior, it usually does not initiate it (Ball, et al. 1981; Weisman, Marr, and Katsampes 1976). Most street drug users appear to have been involved in crime before drug use. So while the need for drug money may be a motivating factor for some crime among criminally active users, it did not, in most cases, cause them to become criminals. Third, most crime, even among drug addicts, appears to be opportunistic rather than planned, a complicating fact for a theory that assumes some level of economic rationality (Cook 1986). Fourth, as noted earlier, more crimes are committed under the influence of (inexpensive) alcohol than under the influence of all illegal drugs combined (U.S. Department of Justice 1999).

Making Sense of the Drugs-Crime Connections

All drug-related crime can be categorized according to a highly influential typology of drug-related violence developed by P. J. Goldstein (1985). In this schema, a crime is categorized as *psychopharmacologic* if caused by the short- or long-term effects of drug use (as distinct from expense or illegality), as *economic-compulsive* if driven by the need for money to acquire drugs, and as *systemic* if caused by conditions of illicit trade.

This framework is a good starting point for thinking about the drugs-crime connection, but it can obscure phenomena as well as clarifying them. To whatever extent there is a genuine drug-crime connection—that is, insofar as the observed patterns of association are causal rather than spurious—one or more of the named effect types must account for it.

However, what seem to be mutually exclusive logical categories are less neat and clean when one attempts to identify them with empirical observations. The killing of one crack dealer by another in a business dispute appears "systemic," but it may in fact stem from the effects on both of them of their chronic cocaine abuse and their consequent irritability. In contrast, a killing with no obvious nexus to the illicit business—over an insult or a pair of sneakers—may employ the weapons and reflect the personal operating styles acquired in the drug trade. Moreover, there are apt to be important contributory non-drug causes that are not captured at all by Goldstein's framework. Perhaps the key factor is an inner-city culture that does not allow either party to a dispute to walk away peacefully without a loss of self-esteem that may be devastating and a loss of reputation that may be life-threatening (Anderson 1994, 1999).

Another danger posed by such a framework is the tendency to overgeneralize. Some scholars, for example, have pointed out the great variability in drug trade violence, noting that it is difficult to generalize across time and drugs and emphasizing the role of context-specific factors (Watters, Reinarman, and Fagan 1985). Ansley Hamid, for one, has argued that "the rate, type and volume of violence attaching to the use or distribution of any particular drug result from its unique impacts upon particular neighborhoods" (Hamid 1990, p. 32). Hamid stresses that much violence in inner-city neighborhoods was peculiar to the particular circumstances surrounding the growth of crack markets. In addition to the economic and social deterioration of inner-city communities, he points to aspects of the crack trade that are not typical for other illegal drug businesses—very young dealers, centralized retail distribution operations, curbside sales. Indeed, the shift from cocaine to cannabis as the most popular drug among young men in some inner-city neighborhoods seems to have broadly coincided with the decline in violence in those neighborhoods.

A final danger of any such framework is that it can highlight differences that may not matter from a policy perspective. Consider the evidence that drug users commit more crime during periods of heavy addiction and less during periods of abstinence or reduced use. Is this because heavy drug use increases the economic motivation to commit crimes, or is the heightened criminal activity the product of the intoxicating and demoralizing effects of some patterns of drug use? For certain policy decisions, the answer may be irrelevant. Either explanation implicitly endorses policies that reduce drug use, for a reduction in drug use will, other things being equal, reduce crime. In driving a car, it is enough to know that depressing the brake pedal, and not the accelerator, causes it to slow down; the physics involved is interesting, but not directly relevant.

DIFFERENCES AMONG DRUGS

Many nonspecialists talk about illicit drugs as if they were a single substance. While this is convenient, it often obscures important differences.

Illicit drugs vary in pharmacological effects, patterns of use, price, and availability.

Surely, the nature of the connection between drugs and crime must vary across drugs. Of the three major illicit drugs of abuse (marijuana, cocaine, and heroin), one would expect marijuana to be the least implicated in crime. Marijuana habits are cheap compared to cocaine and heroin habits, and so there is probably much less economically motivated crime committed by its users. Marijuana dealing is comparatively discreet and therefore relatively peaceful, in part because marijuana users make fewer purchases than do heroin or cocaine users. (Because they do not typically engage in the sort of binge use that stops only when their drug supply is exhausted, marijuana smokers are able to buy in bulk and hold an inventory.) Finally, marijuana does not appear to generate much abuse-related crime. Those high on marijuana are not typically violent, and marijuana is less likely to bring its users into a criminal subculture. Accordingly, the ratios of measured drug use among arrestees to self-reported drug use in the population as a whole suggest that a cocaine or heroin user has a much higher annual chance of being arrested for a predatory crime than does a marijuana user, although the rate of positive tests for marijuana among arrestees has been rising as the fashion in high-crime neighborhoods shifts from cocaine to marijuana. (Golub and Johnson [1997] report very sharp reductions in cocaine initiation starting, in some cities, as early as 1986.)

The differences between cocaine and heroin are less clear. Although there are some indications that heroin use is on the rise (primarily in population subgroups with relatively low arrest rates), active criminals are still much more likely to use cocaine in some form. Violence is still more common in the cocaine business. Pharmacologically, cocaine addicts are more prone to aggression, and thus, presumably to violent crime. Criminally active heavy cocaine and heroin users probably commit income-generating crime at roughly similar rates; in dollar terms, their drug habits appear comparable. However, chronic heroin users appear to be more persistent in their habits than chronic cocaine users (though estimates of the average span of active cocaine use are rising); if this translates into longer criminal careers, lifetime offending rates could be higher among heroin abusers.

DRUG ABUSE CONTROL POLICIES

In what follows, we survey a variety of drug abuse control policies, discussing their likely impacts on both drug abuse and crime. For purposes of taxonomy, policies are grouped into three categories: legal status, law enforcement, and prevention and treatment. While these classifications parallel the custom of distinguishing drug policy strategies as either supply reduction or demand reduction, that distinction is less straightforward than it seems.

Surely, drug consumption is a function of demand and supply: of individuals' desire to use drugs and of the expense, difficulty, and risk of obtaining them. But the line between demand reduction and supply reduction policies is harder to draw. Typically, drug enforcement is considered supply reduction, while prevention (i.e., persuasion) and treatment are placed on the demand side. But suppose high drug prices, stemming from drug enforcement, convince an addict he can no longer support his habit, prompting him to enter a treatment program that reduces his appetite for drugs. And what if, relieved of the financial pressures of his addiction, the addict gives up dealing as well, thereby reducing the supply of drugs? Has enforcement become a demand-side policy and treatment a supply-side one?

Legal Status

The sale and possession of heroin and cocaine (with the exception of the tiny market in pharmaceutical cocaine) is a criminal offense everywhere in the United States. Other substances—such as alcohol, tobacco, and opiate pain relievers—are not completely prohibited, but their purchase and sale is more or less regulated. Drugs also vary by the extent of enforcement directed at their users and sellers, with marijuana well below cocaine and heroin. There is no sharp line distinguishing prohibition from decriminalization or regulation; all limit the legal access to drugs. Morphine, PCP, codeine, and cocaine are all listed under Schedule II of the Controlled Substances Act, yet we generally think of cocaine and PCP as prohibited and codeine and morphine as regulated. Prohibition is nothing more than extremely tight regulation, and regulation is simply targeted prohibition.

Drug policy can use regulation to control a variety of behaviors connected to drug sales and use. Laws can regulate intoxicated behavior, such as driving while intoxicated (DWI) or public drunkenness. Laws can regulate commerce, placing restrictions on potency and form and on commercial behavior, limiting the times and places of sale. Beer and whiskey are allowed to have only a certain alcohol content; cigarettes cannot be advertised on television. There can be limits on the purpose of use, as we now have for prescription drugs. There can be restrictions on who uses, such as the prohibition for minors, although enforcing those restrictions is harder than announcing them.

Prohibition is less discriminating in its approach. It threatens all sellers, buyers, and users, rather than some, with criminal penalties. It also expresses a collective sentiment that drug use is dangerous, if not wrong in itself (Moore 1991). Decriminalization tries to find a middle ground between regulation and prohibition. It threatens sellers as in a prohibitory regime, but by and large lets users alone. (This was the regime called Prohibition when applied to alcohol.)

In comparison to a legal, unregulated regime, the prohibition, decriminalization, or regulation of drugs will reduce consumption, and thereby the crime that is attributable to the pharmacology of drug consumption. Legal status may also have an impact on user crime, apart from the effect on consumption. For instance, the fact that decriminalization does not brand apprehended users criminals may make them less prone to break other laws.

Regulation will usually result in a smaller black market than prohibition or decriminalization, although a well-enforced prohibition could easily have a smaller illicit market than poorly enforced regulation. (This is in part a matter of how one defines "illicit market"; more adolescents obtain alcohol than buy any illicit drug, but the alcohol supply system for juveniles does not involve professional illicit dealers.) Other things being equal, decriminalization will tend to result in the largest black market; there is no legal market, and buyers are not as strongly deterred as they would be by a prohibitory regime. Size matters: other things being equal, a large black market for a given drug will tend to entail more black market-related crime than a tiny market for the same drug. But the marijuana market, with more customers than the heroin market (and comparable total expenditures), is much less violent.

Despite the vast territory of potential policy that lies between complete prohibition and virtually free legal commerce, drug policy is commonly framed as a matter of prohibition versus legalization (Kleiman 1992b). This has a censoring effect on drug policy discourse; discussants are labeled and divided into warring camps, and middle-ground policies that do not jibe with either the extreme (prohibition or legalization) go unnoticed for that reason or are summarily dismissed by each side as being steps on the slippery slope to the other's position. Nonetheless, the legalization question is too prominent for us to ignore, and so we will comply with convention before turning to what seem to us more immediately pressing questions. To explore the crime-control issues at stake and the range of possible effects, we consider in turn the legalization of three currently illicit drugs: marijuana, PCP, and cocaine.

Changing Legal Status (I): Legalizing Marijuana

Making marijuana legally available to adults on more or less the same terms as alcohol would tend to reduce crime: certainly by greatly shrinking the illicit market and possibly by reducing alcohol consumption via substitution (if smoking marijuana acts, on balance, as a substitute for drinking alcohol, [as found in DiNardo 1991; Model 1991, 1994] rather than a complement to it [Pacula, Forthcoming]); since drinking seems to have a greater tendency to unleash aggression than does cannabis use, substituting cannabis for alcohol would tend to decrease violence. Insofar as some marijuana users are now committing income-producing crimes to pay for their habits, the price reduction that would follow legalization would also tend to decrease crime if, as seems likely given the low cost of an hour "stoned," cannabis demand is relatively inelastic to price. In addition, if marijuana is a "gateway" to other illicit drugs primarily because it is illicit (Clayton and Voss 1981), the legalization of marijuana, by breaking the link between marijuana users and illicit drug dealers, would be expected to somewhat reduce the number of cocaine and heroin users. The conditional probability of cocaine use given cannabis use—that is, the probability that someone who smokes marijuana will go on to use cocaine—is substantially, though not spectacularly, lower in the Netherlands, where buying and selling small amounts of cannabis are effectively legal, than in the United States (MacCoun and Reuter 2001). Substitution effects might work in the same direction. It is rather difficult to see any effects of marijuana legalization that would be crime-increasing, unless legalization for adults increased use by teenagers in ways that decreased either their prudence or their legitimate opportunities.

This does not, by itself, imply that marijuana legalization on the alcohol model would be, on balance, desirable. The almost inevitable increase in overall intoxication, and in the number of persons who become heavy, chronic marijuana users, would create offsetting non-crime costs. Either the current prohibition, or some legalization under much stricter controls on quantity and on intoxicated behavior than now apply to alcohol (Kleiman 1992b), or a ban on commercialization alone, permitting possession and production for personal use, might be the better course. But if crime control were the only social objective, marijuana prohibition, at least as currently implemented, could not stand.

Changing Legal Status (II): Legalizing PCP

By contrast, the legalization of phencyclidine (PCP) would almost certainly increase crime. The illicit markets in PCP remain small, both in the number of users and in the revenues involved. (Revenues are small in part because PCP, which is easily synthesized, remains cheap even as a forbidden commodity.) Thus legalizing PCP would not eliminate much illicit-market crime, avoid much economic crime by users, or free much in the way of law enforcement resources. Even a small increase in crime related to intoxication and addiction would make PCP legalization a net crime-increaser.

It is quite possible that PCP does not fully deserve its evil reputation as the generator of bizarrely aggressive behavior; some of that effect surely relates to the demography of its users rather than the pharmacology of the drug. Evidence for this is that ketamine, a pharmacologically quite similar drug used by a much more sophisticated and less impoverished group of users, has no such reputation. It is also possible that other chemicals produced in the course of careless illicit synthesis and mixed with what is sold on the street as PCP are responsible for a considerable share of PCP-related crime. Still, given that PCP today represents a tiny contributor to crime, legalizing it as a measure of crime control would be a far-fetched notion. Thus, marijuana and PCP form the two ends of the spectrum of drugs in terms of the effects of legalization on crime rates.

Changing Legal Status (III): Legalizing Cocaine

But, of course, the main event on the legalization fight-card is not marijuana or PCP, but cocaine. It is cocaine whose trafficking and consumption in the face of prohibition causes enormous amounts of crime and a massive hemorrhage of enforcement resources. Would legalizing cocaine reduce crime?

No one knows. Even were the details of the "legalization" better specified than they usually are by proponents or opponents (Who could buy? At what price? With what, if any, limits on quantity?), the effects of cocaine legalization would be so numerous, so profound, and so unpredictable that any strongly expressed opinion on the subject must reflect some mix of insufficient intellectual humility and simple bluff. No one knows, and there is no plausible way of finding out, short of actually legalizing cocaine over a wide region for a long time. (Even then one couldn't be sure, as other factors would be changing.) A survey of the likely effects of cocaine legalization will provide a basis for this sweeping negative claim.

If cocaine were sufficiently legal that heavy users, who account for the vast bulk of illicit purchases, could obtain legal supplies—which would mean, in effect, selling unlimited quantities, as is now the case with alcohol—illicit cocaine dealers would be put out of business. In the short run, this might increase predatory crime, as some turned to theft as the next-best alternative to honest work in the absence of an illicit cocaine market and others tried to muscle in to the remaining illicit drug markets (if any). Also in the short run, the supply of guns purchased for use in the cocaine trade, or with the proceeds from it, would remain in the hands of young men with short fuses.

In the long run, however, smaller illicit-market revenues would translate into less illicit-market crime, and the shrinking of the illicit business with the greatest attractiveness to young men with few marketable skills would tend to increase their job-market participation and decrease the proportion of them with prison records and expensive weapons. At the same time, about 20% of the nation's law enforcement, prosecution, and corrections resources would be freed up to deter and punish predatory crime instead of cocaine dealing. (As already noted, the resulting reduction in the incarceration rate would tend to increase the stigma on incarceration and thus its deterrent value.) The legalization of cocaine would have two large crime-decreasing effects, one via the crime associated with illicit markets and the other through relieving the strain on criminal justice institutions.

Whether cocaine legalization had a similar effect on the income-producing crime of cocaine users would depend on its details, and especially on the price set by taxation. Legalization near current black-market prices (about $100 per gram) would presumably increase user crime, since there would be more users due to reduced stigma and enforcement risk and increased availability but no less need of money among those who did become heavy users. Moreover, some of the income needs of heavy users now satisfied by dealing would have to be satisfied by theft instead.

At prices closer to the free-market price ($5 per gram, or about 25 cents per rock of crack), income-motivated crime by users would probably decrease; since habits would be much cheaper to finance, a smaller proportion of chronic users would resort to crime as a source of income, and it is doubtful that total spending on cocaine would go up (which would require a greater than twenty-fold increase in cocaine use). But how about intoxicated crime, and the crime resulting from the long-term effects of addiction? On this score, legalization at a high price is almost certainly worse than prohibition, and legalization at a low price substantially worse than that. Since cocaine (as opposed to coca leaf) has never been legal anywhere since the invention of cocaine-smoking, there is no compelling way to estimate the number of people who would try it if it were legal and cheap, or the proportion of them who would go on to establish, and persist in, habits of very heavy use. Nor is it possible to predict the proportion of heavy users who would become aggressive either under the immediate influence of the drug, by combining it with alcohol and other drugs, or due to its chronic effects. While this would probably be a smaller proportion than now do so—given the reduction of economic pressures, the elimination of the need to deal with black-market criminals, and the dilution of the cocaine addict pool by persons with less initial commitment to criminal lifestyles—how much smaller is anyone's guess.

Anyone who doubts that the horrible cocaine/crime situation of today (or even of a decade ago) could get worse might contemplate the alcohol/crime problem, and then recall that alcohol plus cocaine is a frequent drug combination. Even without the nightmare fantasy of developing as many cocaine addicts as there now are alcoholics, cocaine legalization could greatly increase the level of cocaine abuse and the level of alcohol abuse, thus creating a double pharmacological source of crime increase to set off against the likely decreases in economic and systemic crime.

On the pharmacological level alone, putting aside the legal risks and expense, chronic heavy cocaine use can be an intense misery for the user and his or her intimates and neighbors. It is extremely likely that any thoroughgoing legalization would increase substantially the number of persons going through that experience. Though legality would somewhat decrease the misery of cocaine addiction and the collateral damage it inflicts, those addicted under the new regime who would have escaped addiction under the old regime would represent a very substantial toll in suffering, a toll it would require a noticeable crime decrease to offset.

Agnosticism in terms of crime-control effects thus suggests opposition to cocaine legalization as an overall proposition. However, against this one must offset the sheer volume of imprisonment resulting from current cocaine enforcement; imprisonment, like addiction, is a source of suffering for those immediately subject to it and those who care about them or depend on them. Moreover, since the burdens of prohibition fall largely inside poor inner-city neighborhoods, while the burdens of legalization would fall largely outside, (Boyum 1998; Brownsberger 2000), distributional considerations, and the race-relations and civil-liberties costs of drug law enforcement, would weight the argument in the other direction.

For what our opinion is worth, we regard cocaine legalization as, on balance, a thoroughly bad idea, but that view is based in part on our belief that better-focused policies could maintain most of the advantages of prohibition without constantly keeping 300,000 people behind bars on cocaine charges.

Changing Legal Status (IV): Getting Serious About Alcohol Supply

An observer from Mars would find the treatment of alcohol in the American drug-policy debate hard to understand. Drug policy reformers routinely cite the example of alcohol as an argument for changing the legal statuses of some or all of the currently prohibited substances, pointing out how much more damage alcohol does than any of them, or for that matter all of them combined. Drug warriors tend to respond with some variation on "Don't change the subject," though some of them have the wit to respond that, if the one legal addictive intoxicant does more damage than all the illegal addictive intoxicants combined, there would seem to be reason to doubt that legalization tends to minimize aggregate harm. The two sides tend to tacitly agree that no change should be made in current policies toward alcohol. But again, since those policies seem to be producing quite miserable results—there are seven or eight persons meeting clinical criteria for alcohol abuse or dependency for every one person meeting those criteria for any other drug—this agreement seems, on reflection, very strange.

According to surveys of jail and state prison inmates, more crimes, and especially violent crimes, are committed under the influence of alcohol than under the influence of all illicit drugs combined (U.S. Department of Justice 1999). Arguably, alcohol-related crime represents the single largest external cost of substance abuse. As discussed below, raising the prices of the currently illicit drugs is both difficult to accomplish and of questionable benefit in terms of crime control. But there is one drug for which higher prices would clearly be crime-decreasing, and for which a price increase requires no more effort than changing a few figures in the tax code: alcohol.

Alcohol consumption, and especially consumption by heavy drinkers, who spend a large proportion of their personal budgets on drink, is responsive to price (Cook and Tauchen 1982). At present, the federal and state tax burden on the average drink is only about 10 cents, roughly one-tenth of its total price. Both economic efficiency and fairness dictate that alcohol taxes should be high enough to cover the costs that drinkers impose on others. They are not even close; even studies that exclude the costs of alcohol-related crime suggest that drinkers pay for only a third of their external costs (Manning et al. 1989). A good case can thus be made for alcohol taxes at the level of a dollar per drink (Kleiman 1992a). The effect on alcohol-related crime (including domestic violence and child abuse) would likely be substantial.

Of course, such a tax would have disadvantages. Trafficking and consumption of "moonshine" and other illegal alcohol products would increase, bringing with it damage from black market crime and adulterated drinks. But evidence from those foreign countries where alcohol is taxed more highly than in the United States—and from the early 1950s, when U.S. alcohol taxes were, in purchasing-power terms, several times higher than they are now—suggests that these effects would present only minor problems. It appears that the safety and convenience of legal alcohol, and loyalty to legal brands, are sufficient to overwhelm the cost advantage of untaxed products.

A more radical step would be to reduce the availability of alcohol. This runs into the fact that most adults (including most voters) are alcohol consumers, and that the vast majority of them are not problem users. That raises the question of whether availability could be limited selectively. Current laws attempt such a selective limitation by age, though with very partial success. There is at least as strong a justification for limiting access according to prior conduct. It seems curious that someone who drinks and drives should be deprived of his or her driving license, while the "license" to drink is treated as irrevocable.

Like the current age limit, a ban on drinking by those previously convicted of alcohol-related offenses—in effect, a selective, rather than a blanket, prohibition—would have to be enforced primarily on sellers, rather than on buyers (Kleiman 1992b). Naturally, compliance would be well short of perfect, though both sellers of alcohol and law enforcement personnel might be willing to treat violations of such a ban somewhat more seriously than they do the widespread adolescent practice of buying alcohol with false identification documents. A certain amount of inconvenience would be imposed on all drinkers by the need to show a driver's license before buying (where those who had lost their drinking privileges as a result of a conviction would carry driver's licenses with different markings). Such a program, even with its imperfections, would almost certainly be crime-reducing, perhaps substantially so; in addition, it might free police resources by reducing the population of chronic inebriates repeatedly arrested for minor public order offenses.

That such a relatively modest step remains well outside the bounds of political discussion, let alone political feasibility, is a commentary on the relative roles of practical concerns—including substance abuse as well as crime control—as against symbolic politics—in framing policy towards alcohol and other drugs.

Law Enforcement

Drug-dealing is a transactional crime, in which buyers and sellers seek one another out, in contrast to predatory crimes, whose victims seek to avoid their victimizers. This distinction is not identical to that between crimes with and without victims, or that between an act wrongful in itself (what the old jurisprudence called *malum in se*) and one wrongful only because forbidden (*malum prohibitum*), nor yet again to the distinction between what is forbidden at all times and everywhere and what is forbidden only by local custom (MacIntyre 1981). (For example, dumping toxic waste into a river from which drinking water is taken is, we would assert, both an act with victims and an act wrongful in itself; yet the legal ban on it is recent, and the provision of "midnight dumping" services is, in its operation, a purely transactional crime.) So the fact that drug dealing is transactional does not, in itself, imply anything about the moral culpability of the participants or the extent to which, as a matter of moral philosophy, punishing them ought to be considered a worthwhile action, aside from its practical consequences.

But the predatory/transactional distinction is of the highest importance in understanding what those practical consequences are likely to be. When the perpetrator of a transactional crime is imprisoned, both deterrence and incapacitation effects lead us to believe that the result will be a lower incidence of that crime, if we hold constant the precautions taken by potential victims (Cook 1986). Crucially, there is nothing about deterring or incapacitating one predatory victimizer that encourages another such to take his place, unless the supply of victims is for some reason so limited that predators must compete with one another in seeking them.

But when law enforcement puts a purveyor of a forbidden commodity out of business, either directly by imprisoning him or indirectly through the threat of punishment, the result is to create a market niche for a new supplier or for the expansion of effort (e.g., hours of work) by an existing supplier (Kleiman 1997a; see Reuter, MacCoun, and Murphy 1990 on the prevalence of part-time dealing).

The same thing applies when it is drugs, rather than their dealers, that are seized. As long as there are retail dealers ready to sell them and customers ready to buy them, the drugs themselves can be replaced, at a price. Thus while imprisoning a burglar directly prevents burglary, taking drugs and drug dealers off the streets does not directly prevent drug selling in anything like the same fashion. "The best estimate of the incapacitation effect (number of drug sales prevented by incarcerating a drug dealer) is zero" (Piehl and DiIulio 1995).

Insofar as drug law enforcement reduces drug-dealing, drug-taking, and the associated non-drug crimes, it does so by changing conditions in the illicit markets. It influences the prices at which drugs are sold by imposing costs on dealers at all levels (Reuter and Kleiman 1986); it influences the social and spatial distribution of retail dealers by imposing different risks on different times, places, and styles of dealing; it influences the conduct of the industry, including such factors as the use of violence, by the policies and legal rules according to which enforcement risks and penalties are determined.

By doing so, drug enforcement influences both the money prices of drugs and the nonmonetary costs and risks of drug acquisition: how much time, effort, and know-how it takes to find a seller and how risky it is to purchase, including the risks of robbery, the risk of being sold poor-quality goods, and the legal and social risks to buyers from the threat of arrest for possession and the threat of drug testing and sanctions imposed by employers, schools, and probation and parole authorities. These nonmonetary costs help make up what is often referred to as "availability" as opposed to "price" (Moore 1973; Rocheleau and Kleiman 1993). The result of all this on crime is conceptually complex and empirically obscure, with the consensus of experts having shifted dramatically over the past two decades.

Enforcement Aimed at Availability

Increases in the nonmonetary costs of buying and using drugs will tend to reduce not only the volume consumed but the dollars spent by drug users. Insofar as crimes are committed for money to buy drugs, then reduced availability unambiguously tends to reduce non-drug crimes by users. On that point there is little dispute, and there has been no change of views among researchers. There remain differences of opinion about the extent to which enforcement can have lasting effects on availability, with the standard skeptical view that retail enforcement can move markets around but not shrink them being challenged by scattered success stories (e.g., Kleiman et al. 1988; Kennedy 1993) and by dramatic differences in user-reported difficulty in purchasing drugs in New York after its well-publicized crackdown on retail drug-dealing by comparison with other cities (Riley 1997). Academic proponents of retail-oriented enforcement strategies emphasize the importance of disrupting the markets, rather than merely making many arrests, and argue in consequence for concentration, rather than dispersion, of retail enforcement activity. In yet-unpublished work, David Kennedy has begun to explore arrest-minimizing techniques for disrupting markets, in recognition of the fact that the cost (in police and court resources) of drug crackdowns represent one of the most important barriers to their widespread use, and costs are roughly proportional to the number of arrests made.

If, as seems natural, the level of violence is roughly proportional to some combination of the volume of transactions and the revenues of the industry, increasing search time would tend to decrease violence. On the other hand, a shrinking market might lead to increased levels of violent disputes among market participants, especially if dealers from a market forced out of existence by a crackdown attempt to poach on others' established sales territories.

Since availability is directly determined by the numbers, social and spatial distribution, and behavior of retail sellers, rather than that of large-scale distributors, this would seem to put a premium on retail-level drug law enforcement as a means of controlling nondrug crime. However, in the absence of a well-worked-out and empirically tested theory of how the various levels of the different drug traffics relate to each other, one cannot rule out the possibility, fervently believed in by some enforcement officials, that enforcement directed at high-level dealers could, under some circumstances, decisively influence availability, and do so far more cost-effectively than retail-level strategies.

Enforcement Aimed at Raising Money Prices

While decreases in illicit drug availability appear unambiguously crime-reducing, increases in money costs have more ambiguous effects. The following line of reasoning, once held by most researchers, remains a commonplace in popular discussions.

Drugs are addictive. (Or, to put the matter somewhat more subtly and accurately, a very large proportion of the volume of drugs consumed and money spent involves those whose drug use is frequent and heavy, meeting clinical criteria for drug abuse or drug-dependency disorders, for whom drug-taking is not under perfect volitional control.) Addiction, on this account, means that the volume of drugs used is determined by a user's habit size, independent of price; that is, drugs for addicts act economically like necessities, whose consumption is hard to reduce and for which demand is therefore largely insensitive to price. Since the quantity is more or less fixed, any increase in price will lead to an increase in expenditure, and thus in the revenues of dealers. If the money for drugs comes largely from crime by users, and the money spent on drugs leads to crime among dealers, higher prices will necessarily lead to higher crime rates. Thus, insofar as drug enforcement increases prices—which would seem to be the primary impact of enforcement directed far up the supply chain—it may help public health by preventing addiction, but at least in the short run it must increase predatory crime. The less sensitive drug consumption is to price, the greater the short-run crime-control damage done by rising drug prices.

The key to the connection between drug prices and crime is thus the strength of the relationship between drug prices and consumption: what economists call the price-elasticity of demand. If the percentage change in consumption is smaller than the percentage change in price (i.e., less than unit elasticity), total expenditures go up along with prices, and we would expect to see users committing more crimes for drug money. Higher prices and greater revenues would also be expected to increase drug-related violence. Even in this case, it is in principle possible that the fall in abuse-related crime would be greater than the combined increases in crime committed by dealers seeking competitive advantage and crime perpetrated by users looking for drug money, but the arithmetic of relatively inelastic demand is discouraging.

If, on the other hand, the demand for drugs is more than unit elastic, effective drug enforcement will have more positive consequences. Higher prices will cause a more-than-proportional drop in consumption, lowering total expenditures on drugs. This should cause a decline in crime connected to abuse and in crime motivated by economic need, and leave dealers with fewer illicit dollars to fight over (and potential dealers with fewer illicit opportunities to divert them from licit employment).

The price-elasticity of demand for a given drug is not an unchanging constant, like its molecular weight. It varies from user to user, and thus may rise and fall as the mix of users changes. It also varies with the price itself; other things being equal, one would expect the price-elasticity of demand to rise with price, since the impact of, say, a 10% price increase on a user's budget will tend to be greater if the drug is already expensive. It varies as well with the availability and price of substitutes (in the economic sense of that term): other drugs, other recreations, and help in shedding unwanted drug habits.

Moreover, the short-run price elasticity—the effect of today's price change on today's consumption—is different from the long-run elasticity, which takes into account the effect of price change on consumers' habits and personal routines. In the case of gasoline during the two oil shocks of the 1970s, for example, the stock of automobiles and the distribution of commuting distances were both fixed in the short run. Over time, though, higher fuel prices led people to buy more efficient cars and to move closer to work (or find work closer to home). The long-run elasticity was near unity, though the short-run elasticity was only about 0.1 (Pindyck 1979).

So even if the short-run elasticity of demand were small, leading to an upsurge in user and dealer crime as a result of a price increase, the long-term effect of higher drug prices on nondrug crime might be good rather than bad, through its influence on initiation, intensification, quitting, and relapse, the four processes that influence the size of the addict population over time. By reducing drug purchases by new, nonaddicted users or former addicts in remission, and by increasing the rate of treatment entry or "spontaneous" desistance from heavy drug-taking, higher prices might reduce the number of addicts in the future (Moore 1990; however, Trebach, in Trebach and Inciardi 1993, denies any importance to these long-term effects).

As logically compelling as the argument for inelastic drug demand may be at first blush, its premises are shaky both theoretically and empirically. Poor addicts of expensive drugs spend virtually all their disposable income on the drugs, notoriously scanting what others treat as necessities: food, clothing, shelter, health care. Thus, they can't maintain their drug habits by cutting back on other expenditures, and their ability to maintain their habits in the face of rising prices depends on their having substantial, previously untapped earnings potential.

(Note that the discussion of this issue in terms of the price-elasticity of drug demand is somewhat inaccurate terminologically, since the standard microeconomic definition of "elasticity" holds incomes fixed.)

Given the notoriously insatiable character of heavy drug-taking, it seems implausible that many addicts would be able to maintain their drug consumption in the face of increased prices by increasing their work effort, licit or illicit.

Empirically, two studies from the 1970s seemed to support the thesis that higher prices for a drug (in this case, heroin in Detroit and New York) lead to increased predatory crime (Brown and Silverman 1974; Silverman and Spruill 1977). But a contemporary study in Washington, D.C., found that sharp increases in heroin prices brought about similarly sharp decreases in heroin-related overdoses (DuPont and Greene 1973; Boyum 1992), which seems to contradict the idea of inelastic demand. Part of the explanation may have been the availability of treatment in Washington; a price increase that would increase crime in the absence of treatment might reduce it if treatment were widely available. In economic terms, treatment is a substitute for drugs, and the availability of a substitute will tend to increase the price-elasticity of demand for the good for which it substitutes.

More recently, results from examining the effects of various temporary price "spikes" in the cocaine market, such as the one occasioned by the demise of the Medellin "cartel" in 1989, found higher cocaine prices correlated with lower crime rates (Hyatt and Rhodes 1992), suggesting greater than unit elasticity.

While a decade ago it was universally believed that the short-term price-elasticities of demand for cocaine and heroin were below unity, meaning that a 1% increase in price would lead to less than a 1% decrease in volume, pushing total revenues up, more recent studies tend to find values at or above unity, meaning that a 1% increase in price would lead to more than a 1% decrease in volume, thus decreasing total expenditures and revenues (Caulkins 1996; Pacula and Chaloupka, Forthcoming).

The more elastic drug demand is to price, the greater the benefit of price-increasing enforcement efforts. Thus, the old critique of high-level drug law enforcement as counterproductive in terms of predatory crime seems to have been mistaken. If we remained confident that more, or better, drug law enforcement could substantially raise prices, boosting such enforcement in the cocaine and heroin markets would now appear to be an effective, and perhaps a cost-effective, crime control measure.

However, confidence in the ability of enforcement to raise prices has been slipping, even as appreciation of the value of such price increases has been growing. That more drug enforcement meant higher drug prices once seemed too obvious to be worth arguing. Empirically, illicit drug prices are obviously many times free-market prices. (Pharmaceutical-grade cocaine, prepared and packaged according to demanding FDA manufacturing standards, sells for about $5 per gram; black-market cocaine, a much shoddier product, trades at retail for about $100 per gram, whether as powder or as crack.) Theoretically, the law of zero long-run, pure profit in a competitive industry required that, in the long run, the total revenues of the industry should equal its total costs, including the value traffickers assign to the enforcement risks they face (Reuter and Kleiman 1986). The only questions seemed to be how much prices would increase for a given amount of enforcement effort and how that amount might vary for different kinds of enforcement activity.

In effect, the period from the early 1980s through the present represents an empirical test of that theory. The level of enforcement activity rose sharply, not only in absolute terms but also compared to the volume of the traffic, probably the more relevant measure. As the volume of cocaine sold in the United States rose approximately tenfold, from 1980 to its peak a few years ago, the number of cocaine dealers in prison rose about thirty-fold, for what should have been roughly a trebling of enforcement pressure per gram. And yet the price fell steadily as volume expanded through the 1980s, then more or less leveled off (if anything, continuing to drift downward) as cocaine volume stabilized or began to fall slightly. Today's price, adjusted for inflation, is somewhere between one-fifth and one-eighth of its 1980 levels, or something like a twentieth of the level that would have been predicted if one assumed that prices would rise proportionately to enforcement activity. The figures for heroin are roughly comparable. Only in the case of cannabis did the enforcement push of the 1980s lead to a substantial and sustained increase in price, a fact that may be accounted for by the bulkiness of cannabis shipments and the consequent capacity of border interdiction efforts to force the relocation of the growing trade from overseas to the United States, where costs are higher and enforcement tougher. (Enforcement seems to have been comparably effective with respect to the East Coast heroin market in the late 1960s and early 1970s and, more transiently, the West Coast heroin market a decade later. In each case a single foreign source country dominated the traffic, which is no longer the case for either cocaine or heroin.)

While it remains likely that the price decrease would have been even more dramatic in the absence of the run-up in enforcement pressure, the hope that enforcement effort can substantially and lastingly raise the price of a drug with an established mass market has been greatly dimmed by the evidence of the past 20 years. This pessimism is not restricted to scholarly observers; enforcement agencies, notably the federal Drug Enforcement Administration, have tacitly conceded that increasing prices is not their mission. Where DEA used to call its time-series on the purity-adjusted price of heroin the Performance Measurement System, interpreting high heroin prices as reflecting its own success, both that label and the claim it represents have been abandoned, and any attempt to use drug prices as performance measures for enforcement activity is now strongly resisted. (In

1982, then-Associate Attorney General Rudolph Giuliani told a group of reporters present for the announcement of the Organized Crime/Drug Enforcement Task Force [OCDETF] program that the program ought to be considered a success if the price of cocaine rose. By the end of that decade, when the Office of National Drug Control Policy issued the set of measurable goals demanded by Congress, drug prices were nowhere to be found, and in fact are not measured in any official governmental report.)

We have gone from thinking of drug price increases as achievable but perhaps undesirable on crime-control grounds to thinking of them as clearly desirable, but perhaps not achievable by enforcement.

Enforcement Aimed at Changing Market Conduct

Price and availability are aspects of what the economists who study industrial organization call the "performance" of an industry: roughly speaking, what it provides to consumers. But enforcement can also influence illicit-industry "conduct"—how business is carried on—in ways that change the impact of the illicit drug trade on nondrug crime. It can do so by selectively winnowing out those dealers whose conduct, beyond delivering illicit drugs, creates the most noxious social side-effects and by influencing the incentives facing the remaining market participants, in particular the risks they face from enforcement itself: arrest, conviction, prison time, and asset seizure. Since these risks are the most important costs of selling illicit drugs, there is every reason to hope that making them vary systematically with the behavior of dealers and dealing organizations could significantly change that behavior.

Drug dealers and drug-dealing organizations vary in their capacity and willingness to employ violence, though there is little systematic knowledge about the patterns or extent of that variation. The probability that a given dealing organization will be the subject of enforcement action depends in part on its vulnerability—how hard it would be for an enforcement agency to make a case—and in part on its perceived importance. If the importance of a drug case is defined largely by the drug involved and its quantity, as it is, for example, in the federal sentencing guidelines, then an organization of a given size trafficking in a given drug has little capacity to move itself up or down the enforcement-priority list. In that context, if the use of violence makes an organization somewhat less vulnerable (perhaps by reducing the willingness of employees and outsiders to become police informants), the organization has every incentive to acquire and use guns.

If, by contrast, enforcement were focused, and known to be focused, on the most violent organizations, a dealer would have to weigh the benefits of violence in reducing enforcement vulnerability to the risk that violence will move him or his group up the enforcement target list. Moreover, those organizations and individuals most prone to violence would be taken out of the trade by enforcement action at a higher rate than their less violent rivals. Insofar as the acquisition and use of capacities for violence by rival organizations have some of the characteristics of an arms race, there might also be indirect benefits, as the reduction in the average level of violence through selective deterrence and incapacitation led to a reduction in the optimal level of violence for any given organization.

Dealing organizations, and the markets they create and inhabit, also vary in flagrancy. At one extreme is highly discreet hand-to-hand selling to a limited customer base in a private, multiuse setting (such as a dealer's apartment) or, in a more recent style, door-to-door delivery, pizza-style, based on pager messaging. At the other is dealing in the open, or in dedicated drug locations such as crack houses. Flagrancy is of concern not only because it increases the availability of drugs to those not (yet) deeply knowledgeable about how to acquire them or strongly committed to their acquisition, but also because flagrant dealing is linked in two ways to non-drug crime. First, flagrant dealers face greater risk of robbery than discreet dealers, and thus have stronger incentives to become armed. Second, flagrant dealing creates the disorderly conditions which not only directly diminish neighborhood quality of life but can also attract serious criminal behavior to the area by creating the (partially self-fulfilling) impression that the risks of arrest and punishment for offenses committed there are low (Wilson and Kelling 1982).

To some extent, flagrancy is its own punishment, because it increases vulnerability to enforcement. (This is less true when open markets become so crowded with buyers and sellers that they inadvertently protect one another by competing for enforcement attention) (Kleiman 1993). But there remains considerable scope for enforcement agencies to increase the costs of flagrancy to dealers by deliberately focusing their attention on those forms of flagrant dealing that create the most criminogenic disorder. Police should also think hard about how tough they want to be on the more discreet dealing styles facilitated by new communications technology.

Some organizations, more than others, employ juveniles as dealers or helpers of various kinds. In part, this is a perverse effect of the policy of protecting juveniles from the full rigors of the criminal justice system. That protection makes them more attractive dealing accomplices, because they are less likely to face sufficient pressure from threatened prison time to become informants.

The employment of juveniles in drug dealing is arguably more criminogenic than the employment of adults (Kleiman 1997b). The ill effects of dealing (and punishment for dealing) on future licit opportunities may be stronger at younger ages; dealing competes with schooling at a highly vulnerable life-moment. Moreover, if juvenile dealers turn over faster than adults, and if the damage done to licit opportunity by a spell of dealing grows less than proportionately to the length of the spell, engaging juveniles will increase the total number of participants in dealing, and thus the number of people for whom continued crime, including nondrug crime, seems the most attractive option. For all these reasons, discouraging the use of juveniles in dealing should be crime-reducing.

Perhaps for this reason, but more likely because the thought of using children to help commit crimes is so intuitively disgusting, federal sentencing guidelines provide enhanced penalties for the use of a juvenile in a drug conspiracy. In principle, this should discourage the activity in two ways, both by raising the potential penalty if caught and by increasing the risk of being caught by increasing the enforcement priority accorded to the conduct in question. (Agents and prosecutors are known to use sentence length as a rough measure of case significance.)

However, the primary factors in federal drug sentencing remain drug and quantity, and the sentences imposed for the basic offense are so severe that prosecutors usually omit charges under the special provisions about employing juveniles, thus sparing themselves the problems of proof at trial. This prosecutorial behavior is then reflected in enforcement agency choices; they see little point in investing investigative effort in a charge unlikely to be charged. As a result, the disincentive for employing juveniles remains small, and it would require affirmative decisions by enforcement agencies, backed by prosecutors, to change that situation.

Sentencing Policy

The problem of sentencing cuts across all the various reasons for and techniques of drug law enforcement. Sentencing influences which drug dealers are out of prison at any one time, and the threat of sentencing influences the behavior of the rest. Sentencing also influences the behavior of agents and prosecutors. (One reason gun trafficking is grossly underinvestigated and underprosecuted compared to drug trafficking is the relatively mild sentences involved, which make gun cases seem not worth the effort to those who would have to work to make them and take them to trial.) Finally, sentencing determines the cost, in money and suffering, created by imprisonment.

Not all drug offenders inflict the same level of damage on society. A small number of them are among the very most active and vicious criminals; among them, they account for the lion's share of the violent and property crime perpetrated by drug offenders. These individuals ought to be a particular focus of criminal justice efforts.

Given limited prison capacity, it makes sense to give priority to housing the most active and violent offenders. Current federal policy is perhaps the most prominent example of the wrong approach. Under the law, relatively minor participants in drug-trafficking, some with no prior arrests, frequently face long mandatory prison terms. According to a Department of Justice analysis in the early 1990s (when drug offenders accounted for a smaller share of the federal prison population than today), 21% of all federal prisoners were "low-level drug law violators" with no record of violence or prior incarceration. Of these, 42% were drug couriers (or "mules"), rather than dealers or principals in trafficking organizations (Heymann 1994). Since those cells could instead be holding more dangerous offenders, the result of long mandatory sentences for minor drug offenders is to increase crime. Even if long sentences were given to offenders worth locking up, deterrence theory suggests that they would not be the best way to employ limited cell capacity to deter drug dealing: certainty (maximized by handing out many shorter sentences) is more important than severity (Cook 1981).

Varying Enforcement over the Epidemic Cycle

While drugs such as alcohol, nicotine, and (a borderline case) cannabis are consumed in patterns that tend to persist over time, and with increases and decreases following no particular pattern, the consumption of drugs with smaller user bases tends to rise and fall much more sharply, and in a pattern similar to that of an epidemic disease:

- A period of quiescence at a low level.
- An accelerating rise in initiation rates as satisfied new users help recruit additional new users, fueling an even more dramatic change in the total user base.
- Progression among some users from recent or casual use to chronic,

heavy use and the development of increasing levels of problems, leading to a worsening reputation for the drug.

- A fairly sudden reversal of initiation rates leading to a very rapid
plunge. This results from the combination of the exhaustion of the
"susceptible" population and the change in reputation. Since it is
recent initiates who are most likely to proselytize, the decline in initiation rates feeds on itself, just as the rise did.

- A long period where the number of users falls, though far less rapidly
than initiation rates, while the number of problem users, total quantity consumed, and related problems continue to rise.

- An even longer period of declining problems.

Since both total volume consumed (and thus illicit revenues) and crime by
users are more closely related to the number of problem users than to the
total number of users, the period of high initiation rates tends to be over
by the time the crime problem connected with a drug becomes significant.
(Methamphetamine, with its very rapid progression to problem use, is a
partial exception here.)

The effectiveness of a given level of enforcement pressure on a market
is inversely proportional to the size of that market (Kleiman 1993), so
there is a great potential advantage to deploying enforcement resources
against a drug as early as possible in its rise. This observation is reinforced
by the relative ease of preventing initiation (by limiting availability) compared to the difficulty of reducing consumption among those with
established use patterns (and established "connections"), and by the fact
that the rise of the user base coincides with the proliferation of retail distribution channels, which at should be more vulnerable to enforcement
before they are well established.

However, in the absence of well-functioning "early warning" systems
tracking the rise of new, or newly popular, substances, exploiting this
potential advantage is difficult operationally, and made more so politically
by the fact that it is drugs in the latter phases of their epidemic cycles that
are generating violence among dealers and income crimes by users.
Moreover, mature markets yield more and better cases per unit of enforcement effort than emerging markets, creating strong disincentives for
individual agents and agencies to shift attention early. Thus the temptation
to "fight the last war" tends to be overwhelming. This was the pattern as
cocaine use exploded during the late 1970s and very early 1980s; heroin
was still thought to be the more important target. Nowadays it is cocaine
that gets most of the attention, even as there is evidence that heroin is

making a comeback (though not, or not yet, in the poor minority urban neighborhoods where it used to be most common).

Logically, enforcement (and prevention efforts) ought to be allocated to lead the epidemic cycle, while treatment should be allocated to lag it (Tragler, Caulkins, Feichtinger 2001; Behrens et al. 2000). More realistically, it would make sense to move enforcement into a new drug quickly once its rise is evident, and more importantly to relax enforcement once an epidemic is on its way down. Whatever the value of enforcement directed at cocaine trafficking in 1985, that value would have been much higher five years earlier and is very much lower today.

Controlling Intoxicated Behavior

Much of the social damage caused by drug users occurs while they are intoxicated. As noted earlier, a majority of jail and state prison inmates report that they were intoxicated when they committed their current offense. Even allowing for the possibility that intoxication contributes to the likelihood of arrest, it seems that something like half of all crimes are committed under the influence of alcohol or other drugs.

While some of the crimes committed under the influence would surely have been committed even if the offender had remained sober, some of them would not. Being drunk or high clouds judgment and diminishes self-control. For some individuals, in certain circumstances, the ambient level of punishment threat is a sufficient deterrent to crime when they are sober but inadequate when they are intoxicated.

The taxation and regulation of alcohol, and the prohibition of other drugs with the attendant enforcement effort, all aim at reducing the frequency of intoxication. So do the "demand-side" prevention, treatment, and control efforts discussed below. But intoxication and intoxicated behavior can also be targeted directly.

One approach to combating intoxication-generated crime is to discourage intoxication in the first place, or at least intoxication in settings where damaging behavior is especially likely. Such a policy can take one of three forms: the law can proscribe intoxication per se (which often in law, and almost always as a practical matter, means intoxication in public) or it can cast its net less widely, either with respect to persons (forbidding intoxication only to those who have committed crimes under the influence) or conduct (forbidding only dangerous or harmful intoxicated behavior). In practice, the last approach could involve two steps: first, punishing intoxicated individuals who are engaged in activities (such as driving) where their intoxication significantly increases risks to others; second, treating intoxication as an aggravating, rather than a mitigating, factor in punishing crimes (either in sentencing or crime definition). However, such policies raise difficult moral questions.

It is not difficult to justify laws against intoxication, at least intoxication in public. Becoming drunk or otherwise high is (for most people) voluntary behavior, and insofar as the risks it imposes on others are substantial, it amounts to reckless endangerment. But in only a small percentage of cases does intoxication lead to criminal or other antisocial acts, and it is hard to justify severe punishments for intoxication by itself. It might seem at first blush as if punishment for intoxication would be pointless as crime control unless the punishment for being intoxicated were at least comparable to the punishment for the crime to be prevented, but this need not be so; the decision to become intoxicated (or to begin the drug use session that might lead to intoxication) is taken sober, a state in which the person in question is presumably more deterrable than is the case once he or she becomes intoxicated.

Making intoxication an aggravating circumstance in crime commission is more problematic. Deterrence theory supports the idea: if intoxication weakens self-command, then logically it requires the threat of a greater punishment to deter someone who is drunk or high than to deter someone who is sober. However, is it really more blameworthy to commit a crime in a semiconscious, drunken stupor than when stone-cold sober? If anything, notions of culpability are more consistent with intoxication being a mitigation, rather than an aggravation of responsibility; the criminal law recognizes diminished capacity, and intoxication can contribute to behavior we would consider unrepresentative of a person's character.

There are probably variations on these policies that would be more palatable to our sense of justice. For instance, the law could proscribe, and punish with some severity, reckless intoxication, rather than intoxication per se. Implicit in such an approach is the notion that intoxication increases the likelihood of socially irresponsible or criminal behavior, and so those who get intoxicated have a duty to do so in a setting that minimizes these risks. Being armed while intoxicated, for example, could reasonably be forbidden.

Another avenue is to target only those previously convicted of offenses committed while intoxicated. In this way, the law would acknowledge both that not all individuals are crime-prone while intoxicated and that intoxication or intoxicated behavior is not always characteristic of an individual. With multiple offenses, the "I wasn't myself" defense is no longer convincing. John Stuart Mill, while opposing drug controls generally, advocated such a specific prohibition:

> Drunkenness, for example, in ordinary cases, is not a fit subject for legislative interference; but I should deem it perfectly legitimate that a person, who had once been convicted of any act of violence to others under the influence of drink, should be placed under a special legal restriction, personal to himself; that if he were afterwards found drunk, he should be liable to a penalty, and that if when in that state he committed another offense, the punishment to which he would be liable for that other offense should be increased in severity (Mill [1859] 1989, p. 98).

However, while Mill's proposal to forbid intoxication to those convicted of intoxicated offenses is unexceptionable, the suggestion for enhanced penalties seems dubious on retributive grounds. Given that intoxication weakens judgment and self-control, it is hard to argue that committing a crime when drunk is worse than committing the same crime when sober, even when the perpetrator has a checkered past. Ultimately, any policy that treats intoxication as an aggravation has to be justified on the grounds that its deterrent value outweighs the violation of retributive principles. Given that a majority of violent crimes, including perhaps two-thirds of homicides, are committed under the influence of drugs and alcohol, such a claim deserves consideration.

There is also a practical problem with Mill's proposal. In effect, it tells problem drinkers that they can drink, but not get drunk, a bad strategy according to most substance-abuse counselors. Perhaps it is better to require those with a history of drinking problems (such as committing a crime while drunk) to follow a course of abstinence, which gets us back to the idea of a seller-enforced, individual-specific prohibition.

The "Demand Side": General Considerations

The demand for drugs can be reduced in two ways: by altering the subjective states of users and potential users (attitudes, opinions, and preferences), or by changing the objective conditions of drug use to make it less pleasant or more hazardous. Even if attitudes were systematically harder to influence than objective conditions, there are at least two reasons that attitudes might nonetheless be the object of policy intervention, either among those not, or not yet, drug abusers (generically, "prevention") or among those with established patterns of problem use (usually thought of in terms of "treatment," though this term is probably too narrow to cover the full range of possibly useful policies).

First, given the constraints of the justice system, supply-reduction strategies have only limited capacity to raise the prices or reduce the availability of mass-market drugs. Second, in a liberal society, it is generally preferable that citizens behave responsibly and obey the laws for reasons of internal, rather than external, motivation. It is better, for instance, if our fellow citizens refrain from mugging us because they believe mugging is wrong, and not because they are afraid of getting caught. (It does, of course, matter how attitudes or values are internalized. Big Brother-like tactics might be useful in preventing drug abuse, but at substantial cost to civic and republican values. In the view of many, even some of the current anti-drug messages tread rather close to the line, both as to their freedom with the facts and their employment of prejudice and fear [Gersh 1988; Trebach in Trebach and Inciardi 1993]).

Changes in attitudes can influence drug abuse and its consequences in several ways. First, attitudes can reduce initiation, either because potential users believe drug use to be wrong or dangerous or because drug use is stigmatized. However, a worry here is that the same attitudinal changes that reduce initiation may increase the rates of progression to heavy use, and of misbehavior, among those who do initiate. If the existence of patterns of (more) moderate and responsible drug use is acknowledged, prevention effectiveness may be compromised. If it is denied, those who use drugs despite the warnings may be at greater risk of behaving unwisely both in their drug use patterns and in their intoxicated behavior.

Second, attitudes can affect the progression to habitual use, or influence the time, place, and character of intoxicated behavior. An obvious helpful example is the practice of choosing a "designated driver," or norms against drinking alone or before lunch. A less obvious illustration is the Japanese perspective that intoxication is something to be flaunted rather than concealed, as is typical in Western societies; this makes it easier for those who are intoxicated to acknowledge their incapacities and for those who are sober to identify them.

Third, attitudes can influence the frequency and duration of cessation. Attitudes about addiction, attitudes toward ex-addicts, and beliefs about the probability and difficulty of successful cessation all matter.

Last, attitudes can influence involvement in drug dealing, which in turn affects drug use and its consequences. When potential dealers enter the drug trade, they increase the availability and lower the price of drugs.

They also tend to increase their own risks of involvement in illicit drug use and nondrug crime.

PREVENTION

Prevention programs are an effort to change knowledge and attitudes about drug use in ways that reduce its prevalence (primary prevention), the rate of progression to problem use or to more dangerous drugs (secondary prevention), or the health and behavioral damage that accompanies problem use (tertiary prevention).

By contrast with supply-reduction programs, which can have crime-increasing as well as crime-decreasing effects, even modestly successful prevention programs are unambiguously beneficial in reducing crime. They offer the benefit of reduced drug use and reduced drug-dealing without any of the unwanted side effects of enforcement.

That's the good news about prevention. The bad news is that few prevention programs have demonstrated that they can consistently reduce the number of their subjects who use drugs. In addition, the positive results that have accompanied some pilot programs have often proven difficult to replicate in other settings (Haaga and Reuter 1995, Caulkins et al. 1998).

Large-scale, long-term evaluations, which would be required to measure the effects of prevention programs on progression to heavy or chronic drug use of expensive addictive drugs are methodologically difficult and costly, simply because such progression is a relatively rare event and tends to occur years after initiation. As a result, the most common measure of prevention effectiveness is a program's effect on early initiation to tobacco, alcohol, and cannabis use. The strong correlation between early initiation and subsequent problems argues that retarding initiation is a useful measure of program effectiveness, but no one knows the extent to which that correlation is causal and therefore exploitable for policy purposes. It might be the case that early initiation is a sign, rather than a cause, of personal and environmental characteristics that predict later getting into trouble.

By this measure, results from the top tier of programs are significant, though not spectacular: reductions of about 25% in rates of early initiation. Since even the best programs cost relatively little, these modest gains, if they were to carry over into reductions in heavy, chronic use of heroin and cocaine, or even into reductions in alcoholism, would make prevention highly cost effective as a means of reducing substance abuse and, presumably, crime as well. But no existing prevention program has been shown to achieve dramatic changes; the programs are cost effective not because they are effective but because they do not cost much. (Caulkins et al. 1998).

Added to this concern about efficacy are concerns about some of the methods employed; many prevention instructors and some antidrug advertising disseminate or broadcast demonstrably false information about the physical and psychological effects of drug use (Horgan 1990). The programs would have to be marvelously effective to justify this kind of misinformation.

The best known and most widely employed drug abuse prevention program is also the one that directly engages the police: Drug Abuse Resistance Education (DARE). The basic DARE program consists of 13 hour-long classroom sessions delivered once per week in the fifth grade; additional programming has been developed for older students. DARE instructors are specially trained police officers, and in most jurisdictions their time is contributed by their departments without any financial recompense from the schools. This, along with federal subsidies for the materials, has made DARE especially attractive to financially-pressed school departments. DARE is also highly popular among the officers involved, among students and alumni, and among their parents, and has been singled out by Congress for federal subsidy.

Unfortunately, none of the published evaluations has shown DARE to be effective in reducing substance abuse initiation among students who go through it, when compared to matched controls (Dukes, Ullman, and Stein 1996; Brown and Kreft 1998). (A new DARE curriculum introduced in 2001 awaits evaluation.)

Insofar as DARE competes with other drug prevention programs with higher demonstrated efficacy, its continued high prevalence represents a problem. Formal evaluations agree with anecdotal reports in finding that DARE tends to greatly improve student attitudes toward police—and police attitudes toward children—especially in low-income and minority neighborhoods, and this may be more than ample justification for its continued deployment. But that effect is not the same as substance-abuse prevention, nor a close substitute for it.

It is possible that continued research, development, and evaluation will eventually come up with substantially more effective substance abuse prevention programs, but there seems no strong basis for optimism on that score. Perhaps—this is speculation, not based on any convincing evidence—a narrow focus on substance abuse works less well than would a broader focus on self-management, health maintenance, and the avoidance of risky behaviors.

It is also possible that the virtually complete focus on primary prevention—the prevention of initiation—is suboptimal by comparison with a policy that allocated some resources to secondary and tertiary prevention programs, which aim to prevent intensification to problem use among those who have already initiated and reduce health and other consequences among those engaging in problem use who do not wish to quit. Secondary and tertiary programs are more directly and immediately relevant to crime control than is the primary prevention effort. However, secondary and tertiary prevention efforts, especially aimed at schoolchildren, are too politically and ideologically problematic to have much chance of becoming widespread, because they tacitly or explicitly presume that their audiences engage in, or will engage in, the use of drugs. Current federal policy, for example, denies federal funds to any alcohol-prevention program that so much as mentions responsible drinking.

Another potential target for prevention efforts would be the prevention of drug-dealing (Kleiman 1997b). Again, the crime-control benefits of such prevention efforts, were they successful, could be immediate and substantial. The risks of dealing are much greater than the risks of initiating drug use, and may be underestimated by potential dealers, who may also grossly overestimate its rewards.

DRUG ABUSE TREATMENT

From a crime-control perspective, successful treatment of drug-involved offenders is, like prevention, an unequivocal winner. The criminal activity of addict-offenders seems to rise and fall in step with their drug consumption, and importantly, the relationship holds whether reductions in drug use are unassisted or are the product of formalized treatment and whether participation in treatment is voluntary or coerced (Anglin and Speckart 1986; Nurco et al. 1988; Anglin and Hser 1990). Moreover, a treatment-induced reduction in demand does not bring with it the side effects of an enforcement-induced reduction (higher drug prices, depletion of criminal justice resources). Lastly, many drug-involved offenders sell drugs in addition to using them, and some may exit the drug trade if they gain control over their own habits. Thus treatment has supply-reduction as well as demand-reduction benefits.

While most popular and much scholarly discussion of treatment focuses on the rates of "success"—conventionally defined as complete abstinence at one-year follow-up—treatment can have powerful crime-control effects without having any lasting effect on drug use. Findings from the Treatment Outcome Prospective Study (TOPS)—to date the most comprehensive evaluation study of treatment effectiveness—indicate that the largest reductions in criminal activity, by a wide margin, occur *during* treatment. Among TOPS subjects treated three months or longer, about 60% of residential clients and about one-third of outpatient methadone and outpatient drug-free clients reported criminal activity in the year prior to entering treatment. Yet fewer than 10% of the outpatient clients and only 3.1% of the residential clients reported committing predatory crimes during treatment. In fact, this reduction in criminal activity is so large that on cost-benefit grounds it would probably justify the treatment costs even if treatment had no effect on post-treatment behavior (Hubbard et al. 1989).

In light of all this, the inadequate availability and poor quality of substance abuse treatment—created in part by the reluctance of public and private health insurance to finance treatment for substance abuse and dependency on the same terms as treatment for other disorders—constitutes a major missed opportunity for crime control. Advocates of drug treatment, including the providers themselves, are understandably frustrated and outraged that, in a political atmosphere where the punitive side of the crime-control effort, including drug law enforcement, enjoys widespread support and growing funding—where money is recklessly spent, liberty recklessly compromised, and suffering recklessly imposed in the name of providing public safety and protecting potential victims—drug treatment, which demonstrably reduces crime, remains neglected and underfunded.

A special source of outrage is the underprovision and overregulation of opiate maintenance therapy. In terms of crime-control efficacy and other measurable improvements in the behavior and well-being of its clients, methadone treatment is by far the most dramatically successful kind of drug treatment. Unlike most treatment modalities, it has little trouble attracting and retaining clients. Yet only about one-eighth of U.S. heroin addicts are currently enrolled in methadone programs.

Because it does not promise or even attempt to "cure" addiction, methadone, along with other maintenance therapies, remains bitterly controversial. The controversy stems in part, but only in part, from the way methadone was oversold—by its political advocates rather than by its practitioners—as a way to "wean" heroin addicts away from opiate use, rather than as a frank substitution of a less dangerous addictive drug under less dangerous conditions for the purchase and use of illicit heroin on the street, and from the reluctance of some methadone providers to insist that their clients desist from either selling their doses on the street or continuing to buy and use illicit heroin and cocaine. Much of it derives from the sense that it is simply wrong to help opiate addicts remain opiate addicts.

The manifestations of the controversy are ubiquitous. New York Mayor Rudolph Giuliani tried to shut down the methadone clinics in that city; Senator John McCain, as a presidential candidate, proposed a lifetime limit of six months' methadone treatment; many drug courts, while mandating their clients into such unproven drug therapies as acupuncture, refuse to allow them to remain in methadone programs. All this is in the face of research showing that methadone clients forced out of treatment face substantial risks of relapse to active heroin addiction, a condition with annual mortality rate of about 2%.

The Narcotic Addict Treatment Act and the regulations implementing it have limited methadone treatment to specialized clinics, unavailable in most nonurban areas and difficult to site, due to understandable not-in-my-back-yard sentiments, even in big cities. (By contrast, methadone can be prescribed for pain control, as opposed to maintenance, by any physician.) Enforcement and regulatory agencies, led by the federal Drug Enforcement Administration have been concerned—perhaps excessively so, given the apparent rarity of primary methadone addiction, suggesting that almost all diverted methadone goes to individuals with established opiate habits, rather than to new users—about the admittedly widespread phenomenon of methadone clients selling doses illicitly. The result has been pressure on the clinics to limit methadone dosages to levels below those shown by research to be clinically optimal, increasing the risk that methadone patients will continue to purchase heroin as well.

Several developments over the past few years have brightened the picture somewhat. One of the problems with methadone maintenance is the need for daily dosing. This means either forcing clients to come in every day, at considerable inconvenience to them and expense to the clinic and effectively preventing clients from traveling out of town, or allowing take-home doses, thus risking diversion. Consequently, the National Institute on Drug Abuse invested considerable money and time in the development of a longer acting analog: l-alpha-acetyl-methadol (LAAM). Since LAAM remains active for 72 hours rather than 24, it promised a considerable relaxation of these problems. Unfortunately, it ran into the conservatism of regulators, providers, and patients alike. Even after the Food and Drug Administration approved LAAM, the drug then had to pass muster with state regulators, a process that has consumed years. Despite the lack of evidence that LAAM would be in demand as an illicit drug, concerns about diversion have limited the extent to which it can be provided on a take-home basis, thus in some cases reversing what should have been one of its great advantages. Consequently, its market share remains tiny. Still, over time, resistance to LAAM is being worn away. A parallel battle is being fought over the use of buprenorphine, which seems to be a more appropriate drug for those with shorter histories of heroin use and less profound addictions than is typical of methadone clients. After great bureaucratic pulling and hauling, new regulations under the Narcotic Addict Treatment Act were at last promulgated in 2000, under which a wider range of qualified practitioners and institutions would be allowed to compete with specialized methadone clinics in prescribing and dispensing methadone and other maintenance therapies. These largely unpublicized changes have far more promise for preventing crime (and, let us not forget, saving lives) than much better known initiatives such as drug courts.

Parity for substance abuse in health insurance and managed care plans, better funding for drug treatment for those without health insurance, improvement in medical education regarding substance abuse, and relaxation of the regulations that limit opiate maintenance would all reduce nondrug crime. The extent of the potential gains, however, is not as clear as some treatment advocates would claim.

The drug-treatment literature is as methodologically problematic as the drug-prevention literature, though for different reasons. In the absence of double-blind experimental studies—difficult to carry out for both ethical and operational reasons—it is hard to tell how much of the well-documented correlation between entering and staying in treatment on the one hand and reducing drug use on the other ought to be regarded as an effect of the treatment itself, as opposed to the motivation that leads someone to seek treatment and continue in it. (This methodological problem might be overcome by systematically varying *access* to treatment, but those studies have not been done.) Moreover, treatment programs vary widely in terms of approach, cost, and quality for any given drug. The most clearly and consistently successful treatment approach—methadone or other opioid maintenance for heroin addiction—has no parallel for any other drug. No one doubts that interaction effects between program type and client characteristics must matter in determining outcomes, but attempts to systematize that intuition and demonstrate it empirically have been disappointing.

Moreover, the current treatment literature tells us only about the effects of treatment provided at close to the current scale. While the findings are uniformly favorable (Anglin and Hser 1990; Gerstein and Harwood 1990; Gerstein et al. 1994), the effects of doubling or more than doubling the size of the effort—which is what would be required to bring availability in line with estimated "need for treatment" as determined by the clinical criteria for substance abuse or dependency—cannot easily be known without actually trying it. If those most amenable to treatment are also the most diligent in seeking it out, the benefits of providing twice as much treatment might be substantially less than the benefits of providing the current level. That casts doubt on strong claims about the cost-effectiveness of treatment compared to enforcement (for example, in Rydell and Everingham 1994).

Any such claim must also deal with the possible contributions of enforcement to the treatment process. The criminal justice system is among the most powerful mechanisms for getting drug-involved offenders into treatment; high effective prices can convince users that maintaining their habits is too costly, and courts can offer or compel treatment as a condition of parole or probation. Many drug-involved offenders will only enter treatment if coerced; simple availability is often not a sufficient enticement.

While shortages of treatment capacity—especially for such difficult-to-treat clients as women with young children and persons suffering from serious mental illness as well as substance abuse disorders—remain significant, as reflected in long waiting lists for some treatment programs, adding more resources by itself would not make treatment a panacea. Not all substance abusers want to stop their drug-taking, though many would prefer to have better control over their use patterns. Even in those who do want to stop, that desire may be transient or may not survive confrontation with the difficulty of achieving and sustaining recovery. Almost all treatment programs—methadone and other maintenance programs for heroin addicts are the major exception—have dropout rates near or above the 50% level. Attempts to develop a comparable therapy for those dependent on cocaine and methamphetamine have so far come up dry, perhaps for fundamental reasons related to the differences between opiates and stimulants. (If the taste for opiates is satiating, so that each dose during a use session reduces the desire for the next, while the taste for stimulants is kindling, then the search for stimulant maintenance therapy is doomed to futility: as one researcher remarked, "You can't maintain a disturbance.")

For maximum crime control, treatment resources should be aimed at drug-involved offenders. Arguing against this approach is the fact that criminally active drug users are often poor candidates for treatment, at least as evaluated by treatment providers who face evaluation based on their success in achieving long-term abstinence. There is also something perverse about giving offenders preference in the allocation of a scarce good.

Treatment in Prison

For those offenders in prison, however, the case appears quite different, at least at first blush. The problem of attracting users to treatment, and keeping them in treatment, would seem to be much less when they are literally a captive audience. The incremental costs of providing treatment, once the subject is already confined, are likely to be smaller than providing treatment on the outside, especially compared to residential programs. Programs on the therapeutic community (TC) model, for example, tend to have high success rates (among the minority of entrants who complete them), but since they provide room and board their costs are several times those of even intensive outpatient treatment: about $20,000 per participant per year. By contrast, the incremental cost of providing TC treatment in prison is only a few thousand dollars per year, and the completion rate might be expected to be higher when dropping out means returning to a cellblock rather than to the street.

Moreover, the recidivism rate among prisoners is so high (typically 40% to 60%, and higher among heroin and cocaine abusers) and the cost of imprisonment itself so great, that even rather expensive treatment would have its full costs recouped by even rather modest reductions in recidivism, which would likely follow from even modestly successful treatment programs.

On the other hand, prison-based treatment programs do not have the benefit of reducing the criminal activity of participants during treatment; in order to prevent crime, they must have lasting behavioral effects. Discouragingly, most prison-based drug treatment programs have not been shown to reduce recidivism rates (Gerstein and Harwood 1990). This may be due to the poor quality of the programs themselves. But probably it also reflects a deeper problem. The prison environment is so different from the outside world that behavior patterns learned in prison are likely to carry over very imperfectly once prisoners have left. If the goal is for an offender to learn how not to use drugs in the community, much of that learning probably has to take place in the community.

Accordingly, the small number of demonstrably successful in-prison treatment programs, mostly on the TC model, all have strong links to follow-up treatment in the community after the subject leaves prison (Lipton 1994). The gains from such programs easily cover their costs, even if we consider only reductions in future imprisonment; the gains to the offender, his or her family, and potential future victims come for free.

ENFORCEMENT VERSUS TREATMENT?

The notion that the drug control budget is out of balance and that funds should be moved from enforcement to treatment enjoys widespread support. It might be said to represent the minimally "dovish" position on drug-control policy. But it is not obviously sound, either conceptually or empirically.

As argued above, the claim that treatment is generically more cost-effective than enforcement cannot be taken at face value; at minimum, it depends on details about what kind of enforcement is to be cut back and what kind of treatment (in terms of quality, program type, and client base) is to be provided in its place. Probably some enforcement activities are far more cost-effective as crime control than the average treatment activity, while others are far less effective or even counterproductive. A complete cost-effectiveness analysis would also require facts not in evidence about the likely benefits of the marginal, as opposed to the average, treatment episode and the quantitative relationship between enforcement pressure and treatment entry.

Still, it seems reasonable to think that the crime-minimizing allocation of drug control resources, if constrained to the current total budget, would provide somewhat more treatment and somewhat less enforcement than now occurs; drug treatment is unambiguously crime-reducing, while the effects of drug-law enforcement on nondrug crime are far less clear. Moreover, given the current budget situation, a small decrement (about 10%) in enforcement would fund a doubling of publicly paid drug treatment. However, all of this implicitly assumes that there is a budget for drug abuse control that some decision-maker then allocates among its component parts. While, as a matter of calculation, such a budget can be assembled (though with considerable uncertainty as to the actual numbers), it is rather remote from political and managerial reality. In practice, at the federal, state, and local levels, budgets are made for law enforcement agencies, health care agencies, and social service agencies, then allocated to various purposes within those agencies. Moving money from drug enforcement to drug treatment is not within the power of any one decision maker. If enforcement budgets were cut, there is no assurance that drug enforcement would bear the brunt of those cuts. Similarly, if money were moved into health care and social services, drug treatment might not be the primary beneficiary.

The disproportion between drug enforcement spending and drug treatment spending does not come about because, as a society, we spend more on law enforcement activities than on health care activities; the reverse is true, by about 5: 1 if we look at public resources only, and by

10:1 if we count private efforts as well. Drug law enforcement outspends drug treatment because enforcement agencies devote a much larger fraction of their (much smaller) total budgets to drug control efforts than does the health care system (Kleiman and Satel 1997). It might make more sense to ask whether the attention of law enforcement agencies might usefully be reallocated from drug law violations to other crimes, and whether health care resources ought to be reallocated from the treatment of other diseases toward substance abuse and dependency. But those changes cannot be made by waving a budgetary wand; detailed work and political and managerial effort would be required to change the factors that have led to the existing allocations, such as the low professional status of drug abuse treatment within the world of medicine and medical education.

TREATMENT IN LIEU OF PRISON: DIVERSION PROGRAMS AND THE DRUG COURT

While many drug-involved offenders will not seek out treatment voluntarily, perhaps they could be induced to enter and remain in treatment if the alternative were prison. As a means of incapacitation, drug treatment is far more cost-effective than incarceration, reducing the rate of criminal activity among participants during the treatment period by much more than half at perhaps a seventh of the cost of a prison cell. Some deterrence is sacrificed in the trade, but on the other hand there is some hope that treatment will have long-run rehabilitative effects, which no one much expects of prison anymore.

Such is the thinking behind two sets of programs: the long-established "diversion" programs and the more recent drug treatment courts. Both rely on the threat of prison as a lever to secure treatment entry, retention, and compliance. Some such programs are limited to those charged with drug offenses, but others—sensibly, from a crime-control perspective—engage drug-involved offenders arrested for other offenses as well. The notion that drug addicts need treatment rather than prison is highly popular, as illustrated by the passage of Proposition 200 in Arizona in 1996 and Proposition 36 in California in 2000, both of which mandate treatment rather than incarceration for minor drug offenders.

While there is great variety among diversion programs, most take place under the administrative authority of probation departments. Offenders who fail to live up to their side of the bargain risk being found in violation of the terms of probation and incarcerated. Many probation departments contract with nonprofit organizations (frequently under the rubric TASC,

Treatment Alternatives to Street Crime) to provide placement and monitoring services for diversion clients.

Since probation is the neglected stepchild of the criminal justice system, with most probation agencies underfunded, understaffed, short on technology, and demoralized (Reinventing Probation Council 1999), the reliance of diversion on the probation system constitutes a major problem. Not only are probation departments overwhelmed, with caseloads often in the hundreds, but they lack the capacity to impose sanctions without going to court, at significant cost in work effort, delay, and uncertainty about outcomes. This discourages aggressive supervision. The scarcity of treatment slots is both a genuine problem for diversion clients truly seeking treatment and a handy excuse for diversion clients who prefer to go back to drug use. Moreover, many treatment providers, though willing to accept diversion referrals, do not fancy themselves in the law enforcement business, and consequently are reluctant to report even egregious noncompliance by their clients to criminal-justice agencies. Even when noncompliance comes formally to the attention of probation departments, sanctions are rare; often, the reaction is merely to record the failure, which will count against the offender if he or she is arrested again for a fresh crime. Consequently, the "mandate" to treatment under many diversion programs remains merely nominal, with half or more of diversion clients never even entering treatment, let alone remaining in it or complying with the advice of the treatment providers (Prendergast, Anglin, and Wellisch 1995; Anglin, Longshore, and Turner 1999).

Even so, diversion may often represent the best of a poor set of alternatives. For offenders whose current offense and criminal history do not warrant incarceration, probation with a mandate to seek treatment is probably better than probation alone; after all, some offenders comply. Some of those who would have been sent to prison had diversion not been an option are low-rate, minor offenders who didn't belong there in any case; if the existence of a nominal treatment mandate allows the judge and the prosecutor to save face without wasting cells, that too is a benefit (just as "alternative" health care practices whose actual efficacy is tiny, or even nonexistent, may contribute to health problems if their existence keeps patients with minor, imaginary, or untreatable conditions from demanding surgery or antibiotics).

Still, it's hard not to regret that diversion—conceptually such a good option from the viewpoint of the offender, the overcrowded prison system, the public budget, and potential future victims—cannot be made to work because it leans on such a weak administrative reed.

Treatment drug courts reflect this frustration. They draw on the power of the judge—over both offenders and other agencies inside and outside the criminal justice system—to make diversion to treatment real. Drug-court participants, (who, like diversion-program participants are volunteers in the sense that they could, as some do, choose to accept standard processing instead), have their behavior periodically reviewed by the judge, with the prospect of condign praise or rebuke in open court and, to an extent varying considerably from court to court, sanctions for departure from the judge's rules. Moreover, drug-court participants face a day of reckoning; after some period, the judge decides whether to release the offender from supervision (and, in some states, expunge the record of the case) or instead to sentence the offender on the original charge. As a result, the treatment mandate issued by a drug court is more than nominal. While outcome evaluations have been distinctly mixed, there seems little doubt that some drug courts are performing quite well, at modest cost, and that the judges involved tend to be passionate advocates of their program (Office of Justice Programs 1998).

Still, the significance of the drug-court movement, like that of the therapeutic communities, is nowhere near as large as the attendant publicity would suggest. The brute fact of scale tells most of the story: the total number of drug-court participants at any time is in the low tens of thousands, while the number of seriously drug-involved offenders is about a hundred times as large. This is not a problem that could be resolved simply by adding more drug courts. Advocates and observers agree that a key to successful drug-court implementation is the skill and dedication of the judge; the number of skilled and dedicated judges may not be easily expansible. Moreover, the drug-court's capacity to commandeer resources from elsewhere, in particular probation officers and drug treatment slots, would run into capacity constraints were the number of such courts to grow substantially.

Moreover, most drug courts limit their client base to those without any history of violence. This no doubt improves their chances of success (and reduces the risk of a "Willy Horton" incident), but at the same time it limits the potential contribution of the drug court to reducing the most serious crime problems.

Diversion, then, is often better than the alternatives, and the treatment drug court is usually better than diversion. But, at least in the current institutional environment, neither of them seems capable of making a major dent in the problem of drug-involved offenders.

DRUG TESTING-AND-SANCTIONS PROGRAMS

Several factors limit the capacity of drug treatment, whether voluntary or coerced, to reduce crime: the limited availability of treatment; deficiencies in technique and quality; the reluctance to undergo treatment (or at least ambivalence about it) of many drug-involved offenders; and the administrative and procedural difficulties involved in coercing treatment entry, retention, and compliance. If it were the case that all users of expensive illicit drugs were sufferers from clinically diagnosable substance abuse or dependency disorder, and that sufferers from such disorders have no volitional control over their drug-taking, and that such disorders are invariably chronic and go into remission only with professional intervention, the limits on treatment would also be the limits on the capacity of the criminal justice system to influence the drug-taking of those under its jurisdiction.

Happily, however, not one of those propositions is true. Many users, even frequent users, of cocaine, heroin, and methamphetamine do not meet clinical criteria for substance abuse or dependency. ("Substance abuse" as a legal matter merely means using a prohibited drug, or using a prescription drug for nonmedical reasons or without a valid prescription; "substance abuse" as a medical matter is defined by criteria such as escalation of dosage and frequency, narrowing of the behavioral repertoire, loss of control over use, and continued use despite adverse consequences.) Even for those who do meet clinical criteria, actual consumption depends in part on availability and on the consequences, especially the more-or-less immediate consequences, associated with use—it is not a constant. Incentives influence drug use, even within the treatment context; monitoring drug use by urine-testing enhances outcomes (Hser, Longshore, and Anglin 1994), as does the provision of even very small rewards for compliance (Higgins et al. 1994; Higgins 1997). Moreover, while the minority of substance-abusing or substance-dependent individuals suffering from chronic forms of those disorders makes up a large proportion of the population in treatment, the most common pattern of substance abuse is a single period of active disease followed by "spontaneous" (i.e., not treatment-mediated) remission (Heyman 2001).

That being the case, persuading or forcing drug-using offenders into treatment is not the only way to reduce their drug consumption. An alternative to mandating treatment is to mandate instead desistance from the use of expensive illicit drugs for persons on probation or parole. This mandate can be enforced by frequent drug tests, with predictable and nearly immediate sanctions for each missed test or incident of detected drug use.

While in the long term, drug-involved offenders who remain drug-involved are highly likely to be re-arrested and eventually incarcerated, those long-term and probabilistic threats, even if the penalties involved are severe, may be less effective than short-term and virtually certain threats of much less drastic sanctions.

For those offenders whose drug use is subject to their volitional control, testing-and-sanctions programs can reduce the frequency of that use. Those unable to control themselves, even under threat, will be quickly identified, and in a way that is likely to break through the denial that often characterizes substance abuse disorders. That will both direct treatment resources to those most in need of them and help create a "therapeutic alliance" between providers and clients (by giving clients strong incentives to succeed, as opposed to merely wanting the therapists off their backs).

Since probationers and parolees account for substantially more than half of all the cocaine and heroin sold in the United States, and therefore for most of the revenues of the illicit markets, an effective testing-and-sanctions program would have a larger impact on the volume of the illicit trade—and presumably on the side-effects it generates, including the need for drug law enforcement and related imprisonment—than any other initiative that could be undertaken: by one estimate, a national program of this type could reasonably be expected to shrink total hard-drug volumes by 40% (Kleiman 1997c).

To succeed, such a program would need money and facilities for drug testing, small enough probation caseloads to monitor compliance and impose sanctions, either judges willing to sanction predictably or authority for probation departments to impose administrative sanctions, police officers (or probation officers with arrest authority) to seek out absconders, capacity for carrying out sanctions (such as supervisors for "community service" labor and confinement capacity appropriate for one- and two-day stays), and treatment capacity for those who proved unable to quit without professional help. If it were possible to provide rewards for compliance (if only the remission of previously imposed fines), as well as punishments for noncompliance, that should improve success rates and reduce overall costs. The key to success is the immediacy and certainty of the sanctions (and rewards). This in turn depends on keeping the population assigned to the program small compared to the resources available, until the program has had a chance to establish the credibility of its threats. That credibility will minimize violation rates and thus the need for the actual imposition of sanctions. (Maryland's well-publicized venture in this direction, under the rubric "Breaking the Cycle," seems to have suffered from a lack of sanctions credibility, caused by a combination of lack of administrative follow-through and judicial reluctance to punish detected drug use.)

It has been estimated that all of this can be provided for about $3,200 per offender per year, suggesting that a national program of this type might be implemented for between $6 billion and $8 billion per year, a sum that would be more than saved by the consequent reductions in imprisonment for both the drug-involved offenders and the drug dealers who would have to leave the business as their best customers were denied them.

Testing-and-sanctions is not a new idea. (DuPont and Wish 1992; Kaplan 1971). It has had at least one very noisy academic advocate for more than a decade (Kleiman 1997c, 2001). Even those who think that advocates of testing-and-sanctions have been over-promising (Brownsberger 2001) do not deny that it has substantial potential. Where it has been tried, even imperfectly, it has substantially reduced drug use without the heavy use of sanctions (Harrell, Cavanagh, and Roman 1999; Gallegher 1996, 1997). It was adopted as policy by the Clinton administration, and a provision designed to encourage its use by the states was enacted into law in 1996. The editorial page of the *Wall Street Journal* went so far as to praise Al Gore for endorsing the idea during the 2000 presidential campaign.

Yet to date only Maryland has tried to move testing-and-sanctions beyond the pilot-program phase. The need for cooperation among multiple agencies—some state, some county, some municipal, some judicial, some administrative, some nongovernmental—greatly increases the difficulty of a successful implementation. Formulaic sanctioning requires either limiting judicial discretion, getting the judges out of the process entirely, or persuading judges to put their actions on autopilot; the first two are unpopular with judges, who remain quite influential in making policy, and the third is extremely problematic (Harrell, Hirst, and Mitchell 2000): as one researcher remarked after evaluating such a program, changing addict behavior is easy, but changing judge behavior is hard. Ideologically, testing-and-sanctions tends to be too tough-sounding and insufficiently therapeutic to appeal to treatment advocates—who are morally outraged at the notion that someone with a disease could be punished for manifesting one of its symptoms—and yet not draconian enough to excite the drug warriors, who would prefer to use drug-testing results as the basis for revoking probation or parole status and incarcerating or reincarcerating the offender for periods of months rather than hours, an approach operationally inconsistent with either certainty or swiftness in sanctioning. Some promoters of drug-courts see testing-and-sanctions programs as a competitor for resources.

Whether the idea's operational potential is great enough to overcome these barriers remains to be seen. In advance of a full-scale test, the actual results of a national implementation remain debatable. What is not debatable is that testing-and-sanctions offers a plausible prospect for greatly reducing the extent of drug abuse, drug-related crime, and imprisonment, and that no other operationally feasible idea yet put forward can make the same claim.

SUMMARY OF POLICY IMPLICATIONS

Because so much crime appears to be connected to the sale and chronic use of drugs, and because crime is widely thought the most serious of the harms associated with drug abuse, many Americans consider drug policy to be a massive crime prevention program. This view, which does not see any trade-offs between reducing drug abuse and reducing crime, is analytically unsound. Any drug policy that includes efforts to limit or hinder access to drugs will generate, along with its benefits, unwanted side effects. Specifically, such policy will decrease some types of crime while increasing other sorts; in principle, the net effect can go either way.

Moreover, there is no reason to assume a consistent relationship between particular drug policy strategies and crime. More likely, policy effects are highly sensitive to the specific circumstances of implementation and vary across drugs, cities, and time periods. To take one example: enforcement that results in increased heroin prices might lead to lower crime in cities where methadone maintenance is readily available and higher crime where methadone programs are scarce.

Given such uncertainties, we are agnostic on some of the most hotly debated issues of drug policy, such as whether legalizing cocaine in some form would reduce crime. At the end of the day, what can be said with any colorable show of confidence can be briefly said:

Reducing the incidence of drunkenness will reduce crime, unless the control measures create a substantial illicit market. Increased taxation (up to some multiple of current rates) and a campaign of persuasion to make drunkenness less fashionable both seem like good candidates. Forbidding alcohol to those who have committed crimes under the influence would be harder to implement, but the potential rewards would be large.

Reducing the volume of cocaine, heroin, and methamphetamine consumed without raising their prices will also reduce crime. Making treatment more available to offenders is one way to do so.

Opiate maintenance therapy (methadone, LAAM, and buprenorphine) is a proven crime-control strategy. It needs more money and fewer regulations.

Long sentences for minor, nonviolent drug offenders increase predatory crime by wasting prison cells without much influencing the price or availability of drugs.

Reducing marijuana consumption is less likely to reduce crime than reducing consumption of alcohol, cocaine, methamphetamine, or heroin.

Police tactics to disrupt certain kinds of flagrant drug-dealing can reduce crime even if they do little to reduce drug consumption.

Other things equal, drugs in the rising phase of their epidemic cycle (currently methamphetamine and heroin) are better targets for enforcement efforts than drugs in the declining phase (currently cocaine).

Using the probation and parole systems to coerce abstinence among persons under their supervision could greatly reduce crime committed to buy drugs, and the violence and disorder co-incident to drug-dealing.

While this list of relatively firm conclusions is short, each item on it is of potentially great significance. If drug abuse control policy were made primarily for practical reasons and primarily with an eye to the control of predatory crime, the result would probably be a substantial reduction in crime.

However, those who rely for their careers on the support of the public have found that, like Calvin Coolidge's preacher in his attitude toward sin,[2] they can get along on drugs and crime by being "against it." Only a change in public attitudes is likely to remedy that situation, and such changes are not, alas, brought about by essays on policy analysis.

13

Fair and Effective Policing

LAWRENCE W. SHERMAN

Social science research has given police agencies substantial guidance on how to accomplish their goals. Research has also gotten police into a lot of trouble. Both consequences of research flow from police applying the statistical concept of *risk*. By guiding police to concentrate more efforts on people, places, times, and situations with high risks of crime, social science has arguably made policing more effective. Yet from London to Los Angeles, those same risk-focused policing practices are under increasing attack for being unfair. No one will be surprised that a social scientist's solution to this problem is more research, not less. For as some police agencies have already discovered, the same kind of risk analysis they use to reduce crime can be employed to reduce perceptions—and realities—of unfairness.

Research alone is never likely to resolve the underlying social conflicts about the "necessary evil" (Wills 1999) of government intrusion into public and private life. These conflicts fed a long debate (from roughly 1750 to 1850) about whether to even establish police forces in England and the United States. The debate was settled by a wave of moralistic political reform that gave birth to the modern police, as well as to public schools, abolition of slavery, and the end of capital punishment for most felonies (Miller 1977, p. 6). Social conflicts over police powers continue to wax and wane along with other factors driving such historical periods of great moral "awakenings." Whether or not the late twentieth century was such a period (Fogel 2000), it was an era of increasing sensitivity to matters of police fairness and effectiveness, especially for racial minorities.

Research shows that Americans, like Australians, the English, and others, think more highly of their police than they do of many other institutions (Sherman 2001). The fact that public trust in government has declined in so many democracies (Ingelhart 1997) obscures the fact that substantial majorities prefer their police to courts and lawyers. Americans even think that police are more effective at solving social problems than churches, let alone other branches of government (Morin 2001). But these majorities are not found among African Americans, especially younger males. Because the highest risk crime areas in the United States are often the most segregated minority communities, the concept of risk-focused policing takes on a twin meaning: high risk for both crime and allegations of police unfairness. In these areas as well as in the wider society, police are faced with the dilemma of criticism for doing too much to fight crime, as well as doing too little.

This chapter examines the basic issues in police using risk factors to reduce crime in a multiracial society. It identifies some of the key questions about the consequences of police actions, and summarizes some of the answers provided by social science research to date. It concludes with an agenda for research, development, and management that can move policing closer to meeting the challenge of exercising authority in egalitarian democracies.

This chapter considers the following key questions. The answers are summarized here and given in detail in the sections below.

1. *How many police should each community have?* Communities vary widely in the number of police they employ, but the number of police may not matter as much as what the police do.

2. *What can police do to prevent crime?* In general, policing is most effective when focused on the places, times, situations, and people with the highest risk of crime.

3. *How can police identify crime risks most fairly?* A new management process called "COMPSTAT" provides a means for objective, citywide analysis of crime risks, focusing police resources with crime mapping, crime-by-time analysis, and *offense* rather than *offender* profiling.

4. *Does crime risk analysis cause racial profiling?* Not if it is done correctly. Policing for crime risks may create an appearance of racial profiling— a tactic that relies solely on race as the reason to stop and investigate people—but race is only a correlate, not the cause, of policing based on objective methods of offense analysis.

5. *What is the evidence for racial discrimination in policing?* Race is associated with decisions to stop, search, arrest, and shoot people, but in complex ways.

6. *What makes police appear discriminatory when they are not?* The gruff, bossy manners many police use in talking to citizens are out of date in an egalitarian, consumerist culture, where minorities in particular define such manners as unfair.

7. *How can police build trust and respect?* Listening more to victims, offenders, and other citizens, especially in the context of specific criminal incidents, is a proven strategy for increasing respect for police.

8. *How can police leaders foster fairer policing?* Extending the COMP-STAT strategy to the risk analysis of police unfairness could reduce crime and complaints at the same time.

9. *How can elected officials foster fairer and more effective policing?* Reinventing the police institution in big cities, with better-paid, better-educated police, could replace industrial-age bureaucracy with information-age performance accountability.

1. HOW MANY POLICE SHOULD EACH COMMUNITY HAVE?

The number of police in each community is shaped by many historical and cultural factors, as well as by the risk of crime. In Europe, for example, cities near the Mediterranean have historically had far more police than cities in northern Europe (Fosdick [1915] 1969, pp. 401–02). Stockholm had 2.4 police per 1,000 residents in 1914, when Rome had twice as many (4.8). These differences are still found across the world today: Paris has 15 police officers per 1,000 residents, while New York City has only 5 and Japan has only 2 (Rybczynski 1995, p. 18; Miyazawa 1992, p.13).

Whether these differences in the number of police have an effect on the number of crimes is hard to say. Although some statisticians claim that adding more police reduces crime (Marvell and Moody 1996), it is very difficult to control for other causes of the numbers of crimes. The weight of the research shows that the effect of police on crime depends heavily on what police actually *do*, rather than how many are on the payroll. In some police departments officers spend most of their time on the streets looking for opportunities to prevent crimes or enforce the law; in others police spend a lot of time in station houses or other locations where their presence can have little effect. Even the assignment of police varies widely, with the percent of officers assigned to uniformed patrol ranging from more than half to less than a quarter of all sworn police.

The number of police each community needs also depends on the community's *risk factors* for crime, such as alcohol use, poverty, and racial conflict. The number of major crimes per police officer, for example, is over twice as high in Japan as in the United States, but social factors in Japan keep crime rates much lower there than in the U.S. Communities may need to hire more police when risk factors for crime increase, as New York did in the early 1990s, when its homicide rates were rising rapidly during the crack-cocaine epidemic. By 1998, the total number of police employees had risen by about 20%, and the homicide rate had dropped by two-thirds (from 29 to 9 per 100,000 per year). Yet risk factors can change just as quickly in the opposite direction. Over the same time period in San Diego, the numbers of police remained about the same, while the San Diego homicide rate dropped by three-quarters—even further than it dropped in New York (FBI 1992—1999). Thus, it is difficult to distinguish changes in crime risk factors from changes in numbers of police.

Many serious scholars were once convinced that police visibility was irrelevant to the crime rate. That conclusion was based on a highly influential experiment conducted by the Kansas City, Missouri, police in the early 1970s. That experiment systematically compared crime rates in three groups of patrol beats. One group was given two to three times as much patrol coverage as usual. Another group had patrol entirely withdrawn, except to answer calls for service. A third group was left unchanged, at normal patrol coverage. The results showed no difference in crime across the three groups (Kelling et al. 1974). Despite methodological criticisms of the experiment (Larson 1975), many mayors and police chiefs concluded from this evidence that increasing police patrols would not be cost effective.

Since that experiment was done, a new generation of police research has led to the opposite conclusion: that adding police to perform certain kinds of police work can indeed prevent crime.

2. WHAT CAN POLICE DO TO PREVENT CRIME?

In general, this research shows that the more precision police use in focusing on the risks of crime, the more crime they can prevent with the same numbers of police. This increased precision has been made possible by far greater use of computerized analysis of crime patterns. These analyses suggest how to increase police activity where risk is high by reducing it where risk is low. Research on each of the units of risk analysis has discovered a wide range of police activities that can prevent crime, from simple patrol presence to field interrogations and undercover arrests.

High-Risk Places and Times: The "Hot Spots of Crime"

One prime example was learned by analyzing crimes more precisely than by comparing large neighborhoods to each other. Once computers made it possible to compare crime rates from one street address to the next, a very different picture of crime risks emerged.

Over half of all crime comes from less than 3% of the addresses in a city, and crime at those "hot spot" addresses is bunched by "hot" days of the week and times of day. Thus, most addresses, and even most blocks, in any city go for years without any crime—even in high-crime neighborhoods (Sherman et al. 1989). Spreading patrol visibility or even undercover police evenly across space and time means applying police officers *un*evenly to crime. While all citizens get their "fair share" of policing equally, this strategy may be as useful as giving everyone their fair share of penicillin—regardless of whether they are sick. And by reducing the "penicillin dosage" received by those who are "sick," its net effect may be to raise crime for everyone. The Kansas City patrol experiment tested that (old-fashioned) strategy, spreading police out fairly evenly across the hot and cool spots of spatial and temporal risks of crime. Like standard American policing, the experiment invested most police time on the low-crime cool spots and offered little extra presence on the high-crime hot spots. Regardless of the scientific issues with the Kansas City experiment, it is this illogical (but politically attractive) "fair share" strategy that may be at fault.

A more sensible question, then, is whether police activity can make a difference if concentrated at high-crime places and times. So far, at least, the answer is yes. When police have taken that approach, evaluation findings have generally shown police can reduce, or at least displace, the targeted crime problems (Sherman 1997). Police visibility may matter immensely, but not with the "fair share" approach that many civic groups want. Concentrating police visibility where the crime is may protect those civic group members much better than the "spread-out" strategy they demand, for all citizens are more likely to be attacked by stranger-crime in public hot spots than in their own homes. One hundred percent of the robberies in one year in Minneapolis, for example, occur at just 2% of that city's addresses (Sherman et al. 1989).

The need for "hot spot" police visibility has increased as the population has become less dense over the past half century. Many crimes can only occur at the small number of locations where people or property is highly concentrated, like commercial centers. Modern zoning has segregated high-density commercial activity from low-density residential land use far more markedly than ever before, giving police two choices. One choice is to dilute police presence to virtual invisibility by patrolling low-crime residential areas. The other is to make police omnipresent in crime hot spots. Two kinds of evidence suggest that this strategy might work: evaluations of police "crackdowns" and a controlled experiment in hot spot patrol.

Crackdowns and Displacement

Police crackdowns are defined as sudden, massive increases in police presence or enforcement activity. They have produced substantial short-term reductions in crimes as diverse as drunk driving, robbery, drug-dealing, prostitution, and youthful disorder, usually in small geographical areas. Whether these crimes have all been pushed to other locations is impossible to say for sure, but the evidence is against it. A review of 18 police crackdowns around the United States and in five other countries shows that 15 were successful, with little clear evidence of displacement (Sherman 1990). A London prostitution crackdown, for example, found no indication that the prostitutes pushed from one area had opened up business in any other area of central London.

Further evidence against displacement comes from two sources. One is the observation in many evaluations of just the opposite effect. Rather than displacing crime to surrounding areas, crime prevention measures reduce crime in areas where they have not been implemented and at hot spots after police patrols are gone (Koper 1995). The "phantom" or carryover effect may reflect the second source of evidence against displacement: the concentration of crime in hot spots. That is, if criminal opportunities are limited to hot spots, the prevention of crime in one hot spot seems unlikely to displace crime outside of a hot spot. If any displacement occurs, it should be to another hot spot providing a similar opportunity structure. But if police visibility is high in all hot spots in a community, the potential for displacement is theoretically much lower.

The key to making crackdowns work is to keep them short and unpredictable. Long-term police crackdowns all show a "decay" in their deterrent effects over time. Short-term crackdowns, in contrast, show a free bonus of "residual deterrence" after the crackdown stops, while potential offenders slowly figure out that the cops have left. Random rotation of high police visibility across different short-term targets can accumulate free crime-prevention bonuses and get the most value out of police visibility. Even if displacement to other hot spots occurs, the unpredictable increases in police presence at any hot spot may create generally higher deterrent effects from the same number of police officers.

The Hot Spots Patrol Experiment

The theory of increased but unpredictable police presence was put to the test in the Minneapolis Hot Spots Patrol experiment in 1988–1989 (Sherman and Weisburd 1995). Three hours a day of intermittent, unpredictable police presence was applied to a randomly selected 55 out of the worst 110 hot spot intersections in the city. The other 55 received normal patrol coverage, primarily in response to citizen calls for service. The net difference was about 250% more police presence, confirmed by more than 6,000 hours of observations by an independent research team. The effect on all reported crime was modest but statistically significant at 13%, and even greater for some serious crimes such as robbery (more than 20%). The level of disorder, including fights and disturbances, noted by independent observers was 50% lower at the hot spots with higher police visibility than at the control group. Similar findings were reported from a randomized controlled experiment in policing drug markets in Jersey City (Weisburd and Green 1995).

Further analysis of the Minneapolis experiment (Koper 1995) showed the value of frequent rotation of police across different hot spots, rather than long spells of patrol at any one hot spot. The independent observations made it possible to measure how long it took from the time a police car left the hot spot until the first act of crime or disorder was observed there. The analysis showed that the longer the police stayed, the longer the hot spot was crime-free after the police departed—but only up to a point: five minutes was more effective than one minute, and ten minutes better than five. But much more than ten minutes produced diminishing returns. Merely driving through the hot spot had almost no measurable benefit. Thus, the optimal way to use police visibility may be to have police travel from hot spot to hot spot, staying about ten minutes at each one.

High-Risk Persons

Computerized analysis of crime risks has also shown that police prevent crime by focusing on "repeat offenders" or "career criminals." Well known to police for decades, research showed just how large a portion of crime a small percentage of all offenders commits (Wolfgang et al. 1972). The concentration of offending among repeaters was so great that the research prompted widespread review of police policies toward such criminals. Computers enabled police to make fine distinctions among different kinds of repeat offenders, with different levels of seriousness and frequency of prior offending. Computers also allowed police to keep closer track of who was being released from prison. By the time this idea had led to other analyses of repeat offenders and "career criminals" (Blumstein et al. 1986), police had already developed and tested the idea of focusing a special unit on persons believed to be committing crime at very high rates of frequency. A controlled experiment in Washington, D.C., found that such units could substantially increase the odds of active offenders being returned to prison (Martin and Sherman 1986), and a similar experiment in Phoenix found similar results (Abrahamse et al. 1991).

Despite these early successes, the idea of repeat offender units failed to catch on. Few if any police agencies currently operate surveillance or decoy units aimed at specific individuals based on high rates of prior offending. This is not due to public criticism of the units: few if any fairness complaints arose from policing people based on their known prior crimes. It is more likely that the idea died because of the rising influence of political lobbying on police to address highly visible situational crime patterns rather than the less visible individuals committing crimes.

High-Risk Situations

In the 1970s, the English government developed a comprehensive new approach to risk factors called "situational crime prevention" (Clarke 1997). While this approach has been more successful in dealing with some crime risks than others (Buerger 1993), it provides a clear framework for public demands to "do something" about specific crime patterns, especially making more arrests. The organization Mothers Against Drunk Driving, for example, lobbied police to increase their arrests of drunken drivers. Domestic violence advocates lobbied police to arrest more spouse abusers. Business leaders lobbied police to arrest more panhandlers and graffiti artists. Community groups in high crime neighborhoods lobbied police to raid more drug houses and seize more guns off the streets.

These demands are made in a general context of police using their arrest powers far less often than they could. Legally trained observers consistently find that police make arrests in less than half of all cases where they have adequate legal cause and in only slightly more than half of all felony cases (Reiss 1971; Black 1980; Smith and Visher 1981). When police do make arrests, the reasons may vary from the seriousness of the offense to the rudeness of the offender. When they do not make arrests, it is often because they can find other "solutions" to the situation, such as restitution or separation. For example, police could persuade a suspect to return the property or leave the scene for the night. Police scholars call this "peacekeeping," in contrast to "law enforcement."

Research has shown that the effect of increasing arrests in these situations varies widely, depending on both the kind of situation and the kinds of people involved. But where the arrests can be focused precisely on the situations where they will be effective, the evidence suggests they can prevent crime.

Domestic Violence

In 1984, a controlled experiment found that misdemeanor domestic violence was reduced in Minneapolis when police made arrests rather than using alternative "peacekeeping" strategies (Sherman and Berk 1984). This result received widespread publicity, and helped prompt a nationwide effort to increase the arrest rate for misdemeanor domestic assault (Sherman and Cohn 1989). Fortunately, the National Institute of Justice decided not to stop at one experiment but to further test the hypothesis in other cities. The results of the replications were even more important, although far less publicized and influential than the original Minneapolis experiment. Taken together with the Minneapolis results, three experiments now show evidence of a deterrent effect of arrest, while three others show evidence of a criminogenic effect (Sherman 1992).

Further analyses shed some light on the different results. While there were no consistent differences between the two groups of experiments, there were consistent differences within at least four of them. In Milwaukee, Omaha, Dade County (Florida), and Colorado Springs, arrest consistently deterred *employed* batterers but increased repeat violence among *unemployed* men (Pate and Hamilton 1992; Berk et al. 1992; Sherman and Smith 1992). A further re-analysis of the Milwaukee experiment suggests that this pattern may have more to do with the neighborhoods where arrests are made than with individual employment status. That is, even employed people in neighborhoods where the unemployment rate is high become more violent when arrested than when warned, and even unemployed people in neighborhoods with low unemployment tend to be deterred by arrest (Marciniak 1994). Whatever the reasons for these results, they show that more arrests are no simple guarantee of less crime. In order to be effective, arrests must be used in situations where they will reduce crime, while alternatives to arrest must be sought in situations where arrests would backfire.

Carrying Concealed Weapons

The leading situational risk factor for serious injury and death in the United States is handguns. A great deal of evidence shows a strong connection between the gun density of a community and its rates of gun injury (Reiss and Roth 1993). More important may be the rate at which people carry guns illegally on the streets—especially people likely to use them. The rise and fall of homicide in recent years seems to track available measures of gun carrying. Yet it also tracks police efforts against guns, with homicides dropping when police nationally increased arrests for weapons-carrying offenses (Sherman 2000). Carrying a gun, even for "self-defense," makes that gun more likely to be used. When guns are available, disputes otherwise settled by fists may be settled by bullets. For that reason, some police scholars have long theorized that increased enforcement of laws against carrying concealed weapons would reduce gun crime (Moore 1980; Wilson 1980, 1994).

Two tests of that hypothesis have found that traffic enforcement in gun-crime hot spots increases gun seizures and reduces gun crime. The first was in a high-homicide patrol beat in Kansas City, Missouri. When police added 2,200 officer-hours of patrol—(slightly more than one officer-year) in gun-crime hot spots in one target neighborhood for three months, the number of guns seized rose to 11 per 1,000 residents, compared to only 4 per 1,000 residents in a high-homicide rate control group area in another precinct. Gun-related crimes in the target area dropped by 58% from the prior year, compared to only a 29% drop in the control group area. Shots fired in the target area dropped by 81%, compared to only a 32% drop in the control group area. By both measures, doubling the gun recovery rate in the Kansas City gun experiment was associated with more than doubling the reduction in gun violence (Sherman and Rogan 1995a). A similar result was found in a replication of the Kansas City gun experiment by the Indianapolis Police Department (McGarrell *et al.* 2000).

It is also interesting to note what did *not* work in Kansas City. A more traditional "community involvement" strategy of door-to-door visits seeking anonymous gun tips was implemented very thoroughly by officers in the target beat—an area with one drive-by shooting every two weeks and a homicide rate 20 times the national average. Making contact in 80% of the 1,000 dwellings through more than 1,400 visits in 35 days of regular patrol time, the officers handed out flyers with the telephone number of a gun-tips hotline. The middle-aged, predominantly African American homeowners told the officers (all of whom were white), and an independent evaluator, that they were delighted with the program (Shaw 1995). But the program failed to produce gun tips and had no effect on crime. The more direct methods of field interrogations and traffic stops were required in both Kansas City and Indianapolis to increase guns seized and perhaps reduce gun carrying as the crucial risk factor for gun crime.

Raiding Drug Houses

One high-risk situation in which police efforts have failed to prevent crime effectively is the residential premises used for street-level (retail) drug dealing. In another experiment in Kansas City (Sherman and Rogan 1995b), some 200 drug houses were identified through undercover purchases of narcotics. Sufficient evidence was obtained to justify search warrants for all locations. But only half of them were subjected to a "raid" to conduct an authorized search; the other half were selected at random from the list to be left alone for at least 30 days after a warrant could have been issued. A comparison of the two groups showed that crime on the block dropped sharply in the days right after a raid, compared to crime on the blocks where raids were postponed. But the drop in crime on the "raided" blocks lasted for only twelve days, after which it came right back up to the levels of crime on the unraided blocks. The amount of police effort expended was substantial, but the measurable effect on crime was only transient.

Drug raids may have had other effects on crime, both positive and negative. The raids may have saved lives by reducing the availability of high-powered weapons; many drug raids resulted in the seizure of small arsenals. The raids may have also increased resentment against police, however, given the large numbers of children and other innocent parties who were caught up in the raids. In this respect, the drug raid strategy shares a dilemma with a larger class of arrest strategies: whether maximum enforcement of laws against minor offenses reduces crime by maintaining order or increases crime by undermining the perceived fairness of the police.

"Broken Windows" and Zero Tolerance

Since the early 1980s, police practices have been influenced by the "broken windows" theory (Wilson and Kelling 1982), which states that police failure to enforce laws against minor public order offenses is a risk factor for serious crime. This theory was derived in part from the findings of a foot-patrol experiment done by social scientists and police administrators in Newark, New Jersey (Police Foundation 1981). Its name came from an earlier experiment in which an abandoned car was left untouched in a high-crime area as long as its windows were intact, but was quickly demolished after just one window was broken (Zimbardo 1969, as cited in Wilson 1982). The foot-patrol experiment found that there was less crime in the areas where foot-patrol officers actively prevented minor public disorder, although they rarely used arrests to do so.

The "broken windows" theory of public order as the *goal* spawned a corollary theory of arrests as the *means*. Police called this theory "Zero Tolerance": full enforcement of all laws, no matter how minor, would reduce serious crimes as well. This was a far cry from what the broken windows theory had said. Nor did the Zero Tolerance theory retain Wilson and Kelling's tight focus on disorder in high-risk places and times for crime. From Australia to Arizona, the Zero Tolerance theory was interpreted as a high-arrest strategy for all times and places. Stated this way, Zero Tolerance was just the opposite of risk-factor policing. It discarded the core idea of efficient allocation (and conservation) of resources for the high-crime times and places where they could have the greatest return on investment. The absence of a risk focus also reduced the apparent legitimacy of police intrusions necessary to intercept criminals for violating "risk laws," such as those against carrying guns or driving while intoxicated.

As yet, there is no rigorous evaluation of either the "broken windows" theory or the alternative Zero Tolerance theory. The most relevant research addresses the question of field interrogations and arrests for traffic offenses. A San Diego police experiment in the early 1970s found that cutbacks in field interrogations were followed by increases in street crime, which was reduced to pre-cutback levels when the interrogations were resumed (Boydstun 1975). These field stops, however, did not necessarily mean increases in arrests. In a less powerful correlational study, Sampson and Cohen (1988) found that cities with higher arrest rates for traffic offenses and disorderly conduct had lower rates of robbery. Whether these arrest rates have any effect on long-term willingness to comply with law is a question that no research has directly answered. But the legitimacy of arrests for minor offenses, like arrests for domestic violence, may depend on who is being arrested and whether they think the procedure for arresting them is fair and impartial.

3. HOW CAN POLICE IDENTIFY CRIME RISKS MOST FAIRLY?

A century of race discrimination in American policing left a legacy of distrust in the fairness of police discretion. In some cities, police once refused to provide even minimal services in black areas. In others, blacks were subjected to high levels of arrest and brutality in certain times and places, including police-sanctioned lynching. Counteracting this legacy may require more public accountability for the processes by which police select crime-prevention strategies and risk factor targets.

One rapidly growing mechanism for accountability is the police management system called COMPSTAT. This system combines computerized crime mapping with regular discussions of crime trends and patterns. The mapping software became widely available for personal computers in the early 1990s, bringing back a police practice found at least as early as 1850 in Philadelphia (Johnson 1979). The speed with which computers could generate new maps finally made crime statistics useful for rapid deployment of police. New York, Indianapolis, and other cities sped up the reporting of crime statistics from a nine-month lag to a one-week lag, in order to map recent crime trends to guide police operations. These maps then empowered top police managers to hold mid-managers accountable for what they were doing about crime.

For the first time, crime maps were accompanied by bar graphs, pie charts, and trend lines, showing the days of the week and the times of day in which crimes were concentrated. The data were broken down by specific types of crimes and even further—by specific kinds of victims and situations. Domestic violence, robbery/purse snatch from pedestrians, shootings in drug-dealing areas, home invasion robberies of Puerto Rican grocery store (bodega) owners who kept their cash under the mattress: these and other crime patterns were plotted, by time of day, against patterns of police activities such as arrests made or patrols on duty. When the times for police activity did not match the times for criminal activity, the graphs dramatically implied how police operations should be rescheduled.

The most dramatic change occurred in New York, where COMPSTAT was invented in the Transit Police and later established in the City Police (Bratton 1998) before spreading to Philadelphia, Baltimore, New Orleans, Washington, D.C., Los Angeles, Indianapolis, several counties in Maryland, and elsewhere. Here is how some observers described the initiation of the practice in New York in 1994–1995:

Commanders would be questioned on the crime conditions in their particular areas of jurisdiction. In the room, long tables lit by green lamps, were set up in a horseshoe, facing a lectern. . . . A high-tech console flashed maps and graphs on . . . video screens. Commanders were called to the rostrum to make their presentation, then grilled with reference to the map. Crime by crime, sector by sector, a precinct would be scoured by laser pointer.

> It was a new experience for the bosses, and many fumbled and stumbled. Some were obviously unacquainted with the most basic facts about crime in their areas. A precinct commander might be asked, for example, why his burglary rate was up. If he said he didn't know, he was in trouble. Who was committing the burglaries? Had the captain perhaps noticed a concentration of daytime burglaries around a large public high school? To emphasize the point, the laser beam would sweep over the locations under discussion, like an accusing finger (Lardner and Reppetto 2000, p. 324).

This relentless focus on the places and times of crime often led to assignments of additional officers, just as the controlled experiments had shown would be effective. Some commanders used them effectively, focusing them on highly specific assignments in relation to precise locations. Other commanders merely sent the extra officers out to patrol at their own discretion, with little clear evidence of effectiveness. In New York, COMPSTAT was followed by a near-doubling in the number of arrests, with a somewhat slower rise in complaints against police. Meanwhile, crime dropped dramatically, but without a clear explanation for the decline.

As a management system, COMPSTAT puts all the incentives into preventing criminal events. Unlike previous police management practices that focused on arrests, the COMPSTAT focus is on the ultimate issue of public safety. Arrest activity is no excuse for increased crime. Thus there seems little incentive for discrimination in arrest activity, or singling out socially powerless groups for "easy" arrests to meet a quota. (This is not, of course, the case in the state police highway patrols, where many allegations of racial profiling have been directed.) Where policing practices are driven solely by concerns for public safety, using uniform criteria for risk analysis throughout the city, risk factors can be selected in a demonstrably fair manner. This is even more likely to occur in cities like Philadelphia, where the COMPSTAT sessions are open to the public and the news media.

Offense versus Offender Profiling

COMPSTAT is one category of the general strategy of statistical offense profiling. This strategy for identifying risk factors stands in sharp contrast to television shows and movies about offender profiling. In practice, *offender* profiling is a rarely used method to solve crimes that have already occurred, may occur, or are occurring. Using subjective methods, offender profiling is wide open to prejudice and bias. *Offense* profiling is the more widely used objective method to predict where, when, and by what kinds of people offenses are likely to be committed. It is offender, not offense, profiling that has been widely associated with racial discrimination.

In the early 1980s, FBI agents developed an investigative technique they called "offender profiling" (Hazelwood and Burgess 1987; Ressler et al. 1988). This method was designed to infer the likely characteristics of the person who has committed a particular crime or series of crimes. The logic of narrowing the pool of suspects made a great deal of sense, and the idea caught on rapidly all over the world. Unfortunately, it had no basis in research evidence or empirical data. Sometimes called a "ouija board" approach by its critics, the *clinical* approach to offender profiling was based on logic and experience rather than systematic analysis. Famously, it predicted that the Unabomber would be found to have a blue-collar background and minimal education. The person ultimately convicted of the Unabomber's crimes, however, Ted Kaczynski, was a Harvard graduate and former professor of mathematics at U.C. Berkeley.

Despite substantial publicity, offender profiling is used quite rarely. While exact estimates are unavailable in the United States, one English study found that it was used in only 75 cases in 1994 (Copson 1995). The same study found that clinical profiling had helped to solve the crime in only 14% of the cases and to identify the offender in just 3% of cases. Given the subjective character of the clinical profiling method, these low rates of success are not surprising.

Much higher success rates have been found with an alternative approach to clinical profiling called *statistical* profiling. Cambridge University criminologist David Farrington and his colleague Sandra Lambert (2000) have developed a method of identifying specific individuals as likely suspects of specific crimes based upon repeated patterns (or "modus operandi") of the crimes for which they were previously arrested. Coding such fine details as which door or window a criminal uses to break into a house, what kind of tools they use, what time of day or type of premises the individual is arrested on, Farrington and Lambert have shown how police data can be analyzed to identify people who have high probabilities (risk) of being the criminal sought in specific, unsolved crimes. They demonstrate how the use of this method could have been far more successful than standard investigative procedures in solving such rare crimes as the "Yorkshire Ripper" murders, as well as more common crimes of burglary and violence. The success of this method, however, has not made it anymore widely used than clinical profiling.

Neither statistical nor clinical profiling of individual suspects in past crimes constitutes "profiling" in the sense it has been used in lawsuits, presidential debates, and police operations. When Wilson (1994) recommended enforcing laws against carrying guns in places and times where gun crimes repeatedly occur, he was proposing a strategy of offense profiling. The critique of police implementation of this strategy is that it ultimately became offender profiling, in which suspects were chosen solely because of their race. But the evidence suggests that apparent racial bias is often likely to be a coincidental by-product rather than a guiding force in police decisions to stop and investigate people.

4. DOES CRIME RISK ANALYSIS CAUSE RACIAL PROFILING?

Public concern over racial profiling is a result of badly drawn *offender* profiles, which have been used to challenge more precisely drawn *offense* profiles. The claim that American police single out racial minorities for harassment and arrest has a long history, but it rose to epidemic proportions in the 1990s. A "tipping point" (Gladwell 2000) of public concern about racial profiling was reached in New Jersey and soon grew into a national issue that led state legislatures to pass new laws regulating police conduct. These laws require that police keep records of the race of people they stop for investigative purposes, as well as of the people they arrest or ticket. The wave of public concern also prompted a series of federal lawsuits brought by the Civil Rights Division of the U.S. Department of Justice against police agencies in Los Angeles; Columbus, Ohio; Pittsburgh; and other places in addition to the New Jersey State Police.

Ironically, the federal lawsuits challenged practices that had been adopted at the suggestion of the U.S. Justice Department itself. In some 91,000 pages of documents the New Jersey State Police (NJSP) turned over to the Justice Department, the conflicting direction from Washington during different administrations and from different branches of the agency was evident (Kocieniewski and Hanley 2000). In 1987 to 1989, the federal Drug Enforcement Administration had given seminars to NJSP troopers encouraging them to stop drivers who fit a drug courier *offender* profile. This profile was apparently clinical rather than statistical in nature, emphasizing certain late model cars, rental car license plates (which can be identified before police decide to stop a car), and the ethnicity of major drug gangs, including Jamaicans. Enforcement practices concentrated heavily in two NJSP stations resulted in rates of searches and arrests of blacks far in excess of their percentages among speeding drivers (based on social science observation research samples). Despite internal legal opinions that offender profiling was an unconstitutional basis for stopping cars, the agency allowed the practices to continue for some years. The governor eventually fired the state police superintendent, and the State admitted that it had engaged in racial profiling: stopping people solely because of their race (*Philadelphia Inquirer* 2000).

A high rate of stopping blacks in an integrated environment like a major highway is indicative of racial profiling. A high rate of stopping minority groups in segregated minority environments, however, indicates something very different, especially in places where offenses are shown to be highly concentrated. In such areas, some evidence suggests that racial profiling works to reverse discrimination: while most blacks are not stopped, police do stop most whites found in the area (Shaw 1995). Thus, a fair treatment of racial profiling requires an examination of how race relates to place.

PROFILES IN RACE AND PLACE

Crime risks based on place are often correlated with race, but the correlation is a coincidence rather than a cause. A clear example of this point is found in Australian airports, where (according to the November 22, 2000, broadcast of National Public Radio's *Morning Edition*) officials subject 7,000 Korean couples to intensive policing and luggage searches each year. These searches are not based on the race of the suspects, but on the place from which they have just come: Korea. Koreans coming from Paris or the United States are not subjected to these searches unless they appear to be newlyweds, an additional risk factor in the statistical offender profile.

These place-based searches are designed to detect not guns or drugs but chestnuts, which virtually all newlyweds in Korea are given to take on their honeymoons. Newlywed Koreans in Australia pose a very high risk of infecting Australian vegetation with chestnut blight, a disease that could destroy many kinds of trees in Australia and reduce its rainfall, threatening human habitation on the continent. In order to protect Australian forests from this threat, customs authorities require young Korean couples to submit all their baggage to be x-rayed, a method that readily identifies the chestnuts. The law enforcement officers then seize and destroy the chestnuts, releasing the couples with a warning. The more equitable alternative of scanning every suitcase entering Australia—a practice that Korea itself uses for all travelers—would delay all other travelers and be far more costly than the selective targeting of persons identified as high-risk based on their age, marital status, and ethnicity. Neither Koreans nor Australians apparently object to this spatial profiling with a racial correlation, given the high risk of danger of those being searched and the seriousness of the danger itself.

The most important difference between "honeymooning while Korean" in Australia and "driving while black" in the United States, of course, is the history of slavery and Jim Crow laws in the U.S. The Korean newlyweds have no history of subjugation or oppression by Australians, while American minority groups—especially blacks—have experienced more than a century of brutality, prejudice, and unequal treatment by police.

Airports are also a highly secured environment, in which intrusion of all sorts is routine, and even expected, given the threat of terrorist bombings. In most American environments, however, being stopped by police is a far more volatile event than an Australian baggage search. It is also a very rare event in most areas, at most times. Now more than ever, municipal police concentrate their resources for stopping pedestrians and motorists at the places and times where crime is most likely to occur. These concentrations produce a striking disparity between the proportions of racial minorities stopped by police and the proportion in the residential population. That disparity is often taken as prima facie evidence of discrimination. The reality, as research reveals, is more complex.

The Denominator Debates

The central issue in the racial fairness of police stopping decisions is the selection of an appropriate "denominator." The racial denominator for prison sentences, for example, is the racial composition of persons convicted of crimes. If blacks are more likely than whites to be imprisoned for the same offenses, other things being equal, we would conclude that the sentencing was racially unfair. The denominator for conviction might be prosecution, for prosecution it might be arrest, and for arrest it might be persons observed to be or accused of breaking laws.

The appropriate denominator for stopping people is far less clear, but it can be made clearer through research. Research showed that the proportion of speeding drivers in New Jersey who were black was far lower than the proportion of drivers stopped and asked to consent to a search, which suggests that discrimination is present. Research might also show, however, that discrimination is absent. If the racial proportions of persons present in high-crime "hot spots" at high-crime times closely matches the racial proportions of persons stopped or arrested, then there is no disparity between numerator and denominator. The use of a "persons present" denominator, whatever it shows, is arguably more appropriate than the use of a residential population denominator.

As Philadelphia Police Commissioner John Timoney argued after a report accused his officers of discrimination in stopping minorities in 1999, the residential population includes people of all ages in all neighborhoods, high-crime and low-crime. Older people tend to stay home at night, and different races have different age structures. If minorities have somewhat higher concentrations of young people who spend time in high-crime public places at night, he suggested, then the proportion of 60% of persons stopped who were black would not necessarily show discrimination against the 44% of residents who were black. In the absence of a systematic observation study of the user population in the same locations where COMPSTAT directs police to for reasons of crime risk, however, it is impossible to know exactly what a more appropriate denominator would show.

A lawsuit against the Albuquerque, New Mexico, Police Department provides one example of such a study. The suit claimed that police were discriminating against Hispanics because some 70% of the juveniles ejected from a shopping mall for trespassing without being arrested were Hispanic. This compared to only 35% of the residential population that was Hispanic, and 58% of all persons arrested in the city who were Hispanic. Yet a systematic observation study of more than 4,000 juveniles actually present on mall premises found that 68% of the males appeared Hispanic to a Hispanic researcher (Gonzalez 2001). Thus, the percentage of the population of users closely matched the population of those evicted, reducing the appearance of discrimination. A similar (but unpublished) observation study has been conducted at hot spot street corners for an English police agency, with similar results.

In this matter, as in others, the research that leads police to concentrate resources increases risks for police themselves. The solution appears to be yet more research. Unless more research is done to measure the racial breakdowns of *user populations,* the police risk losing their legitimacy in the eyes of the public. If that research shows that disparity in the numerator of persons stopped and frisked (e.g., Spitzer 1999) is not matched by a disparity in race, sex, and age of those persons present in hot spots at hot times, the fairness of police would be even more suspect. Research showing a close match between the race of users and persons stopped could demonstrate a fair basis for police practices. Yet, for research to have that effect, it may need to be done frequently and independently.

The risk of appearing unfair when concentrating resources is all the greater if every other stage of the criminal justice process, including arrest itself, is biased by race. Only by addressing that concern can police show that policing for offense risks does not lead to discrimination based on racial profiling of offenders.

5. WHAT IS THE EVIDENCE FOR RACIAL DISCRIMINATION IN POLICING?

Considerable evidence suggests that there is indeed racial discrimination or disparity in arrest decisions by police, even when appropriate denominators are employed. This evidence comes from three main sources. One source is systematic observation of arrest decisions in field settings by legally trained observers. A second source is the comparison of self-reported offending to officially detected offending rates. The third source is comparisons of victim accounts of offender race compared to police arrest data. All three sources are now rather dated, but no new research has yet challenged the conclusions these sources of evidence suggest.

Systematic Observations of Police Arrest Decisions

Two major systematic observation studies, conducted in 1966 and 1977, found that police are more likely to arrest blacks than whites, even when other factors are taken into account. This can occur even when police making arrest decisions are themselves black (Friederich 1977), because police normally exercise substantial discretion in their decisions to arrest. Even when the evidentiary basis sufficient to justify arrest was present, police chose not to arrest in about half the cases. Whether these patterns from twenty-four years ago have continued will be clearer when results of similar studies conducted in 1995–1996 are reported.

In the 1966 sample, there were 143 cases in which the police had sufficient basis for arrest. Observers found that police decided not to make an arrest based on citizen testimony in 44% of felony accusations and 69% of misdemeanor accusations (Black 1980, p. 91). The police choice of who got arrested and who did not in that analysis was clearly influenced by race. In felony cases blacks were arrested at the rate of 60% of those legally eligible, compared to 45% for whites. In misdemeanors the arrest rates were 47% for blacks and 38% for whites (p. 95). That study was conducted in Boston, Washington, and Chicago in the summer of 1966 (Reiss 1971), and was replicated in 1977 in the suburban and center city police agencies in three other metropolitan areas: Rochester, New York; St. Louis, Missouri; and Tampa-St. Petersburg, Florida. The replication also found that, even when holding other factors constant, suspects who were black stood a significantly higher chance of being arrested (Smith and Visher 1981, p. 167).

Self-Reported Crime Versus Official Arrests and Convictions

There is a substantial discrepancy between the black-white differences in rates of criminal activity found in official records and anonymous social science surveys of self-reported offending. The differences between blacks and whites are much smaller in the self-report surveys than they are in the official statistics, although the comparison is complicated by the documented failures of many respondents to self-report crimes for which they were officially arrested or convicted (Blumstein et al. 1986, pp. 40–41).

Victim-Reported Crime Versus Official Arrests and Convictions

A study that compares the race of the assailant in personal crimes as measured in surveys of victims also shows substantially smaller black-white differences in rates of criminal offending than are reported by FBI data on official arrests (Hindelang 1978, p. 93). While this study still shows higher rates of offending in robbery and assault among black males than among white males, the difference is not nearly enough to account for the much higher rates at which blacks are arrested for those offenses than whites. That difference may be due, however, to race-neutral, crime-risk policies that place more police in high-crime areas, in which black offenders are more spatially concentrated than white offenders. Discrimination and spatial inequality in housing may be more important in accounting for this difference than police decisions, given the concentration of black poverty relative to the dispersion of white poverty (Sampson 1987).

6. WHAT MAKES POLICE APPEAR DISCRIMINATORY EVEN WHEN THEY ARE NOT?

The evidence of discriminatory arrest practices reveals the importance of respect in police-citizen encounters. Some analysts conclude that police make arrest decisions based not on race but on the suspect's manifest disrespect of the police. Other analysts conclude that the disrespect follows rather than precedes police decisions to arrest. What seems clear to observers of police culture is that arresting the disrespectful is a race-blind practice, when it is practiced at all. One recent indication of this is an officer who was disciplined for marking traffic tickets with smiling or frowning faces to record the attitude the suspect manifested to the officer.

Even when police are not disposed to let race influence their discretion in any way, their perception of a hierarchy between police and citizen can create an appearance of discrimination. White people stopped by police often comment on the gruff, didactic manner of police officers, both black and white. While white citizens may call this rudeness, minority citizens may call it racism. Minorities often assume that police do not treat white people so rudely. Police, for their part, do not define such conduct as rude but as rudimentary—a means of establishing authority in a potentially volatile situation. In an increasingly egalitarian age, the acceptability of direct orders by parents, teachers, doctors, and employers has been greatly undermined. The police may be the last authority figures who still give orders and act "bossy." While police may think that is their right, the practice may threaten police ability to command public trust in their fairness.

This claim may be challenged by reference to the high levels of public support for police by the population in general (Sherman 2001). Yet the population surveyed rarely has any contact with police. Among the small fraction of people who have had recent contact with police, the opinion of police fairness is much lower. A decade of research by psychologist Tom Tyler (1990, 1998) shows that there is a close connection between police bossiness and perceived unfairness, especially among minority group members. Tyler's surveys show that when police treat citizens with apparent courtesy, taking time to explain their decisions and listen to the citizen's views on the matter, they gain high citizen ratings on fairness—even if they arrest or ticket the citizen. But when police do not appear to show respect or listen to citizens, they get low ratings for fairness, even if the police decide not to arrest or ticket them. Tyler finds a clear distinction between police manners, which he calls "procedural justice," and police decisions, which he calls "distributive" or "outcome justice."

The importance of procedural justice may be so great that it directly affects the rate of crime. One study, for example, found that when police arrested domestic violence offenders more politely, it reduced their subsequent domestic violence (Paternoster et al. 1997). Defendants interviewed in jail within an hour of being arrested for misdemeanor violence were asked how they were treated by police during the arrest process. Police, in turn, were asked how the defendants behaved during the arrest. Offenders who said police treated them well by listening to their side of the story were 40% less likely to reoffend in six months than those who said police had refused to listen to them. This analysis controlled for the offenders' prior records and indicators of their attitudes.

Similarly, when New Jersey State Police, in 1999, first installed cameras on patrol cars and wore microphones to speak to drivers they stopped on the New Jersey Turnpike, the first 40 complaints of racist police language were disproved. Yet it is possible that the complaints were inflated by drivers who reacted not to racist language, but to a mere attitude of hierarchy which police take to be appropriate to the circumstances. While that attitude breaks no law or regulation, it may be that the more egalitarian and explanatory style many officers use is less likely to fuel anger and allegations of police unfairness.

This research suggests a major hypothesis about the movement against racial profiling. The hypothesis is that criticism of the police is caused more by the manners police use than by the decisions they make. In a context of much lower trust in police among African Americans than among whites (Sherman 2001), the bossy manners some police use on everyone are taken as evidence that police are picking on minorities. This climate then obscures the facts in an important public discussion about how police resources should be allocated.

7. HOW CAN POLICE BUILD TRUST AND RESPECT?

One proven means of increasing respect for police among victims and offenders is listening more to people. The famous gruff instruction to "tell it to the judge" is a statement that police do not want to listen to accused offenders trying to explain their conduct. Crime victims and witnesses often get similar instructions, especially in the context of an arrest situation. Yet under the widespread practice of plea-bargaining, there is rarely an opportunity for anyone but the lawyers to say anything to a judge. As the procedural justice research suggests, giving citizens the chance to be heard by police in the immediate aftermath of a crime can make a great deal of difference in how much respect citizens will have for police. That respect, in turn, can increase citizen compliance with the law.

Other evidence that listening to citizens builds public respect comes from four Australian experiments in police-led community justice conferences. These conferences, developed by Australian police in the early 1990s, follow the principles of "restorative justice" that have recently become part of a worldwide social reform movement. To the extent that conferences foster restorative policing encounters with victims and offenders, they create situations in which police are given time and training to listen.

Restorative justice is legitimated by a convergence of many religious traditions, which should reinforce the morality and perceived fairness of police adopting the practice. Closely aligned with the liberal peace churches such as Mennonites and Quakers (Sherman 2001), restorative justice principles have also been endorsed by the more militant denominations that gave rise to the police institution in the "Great Awakening" of the mid-nineteenth century. Restorative justice has also been endorsed by the Roman Catholic Church (National Conference of Catholic Bishops 2000) in a more general attack on retributive punishment. As the American Baptist Convention (2000) puts it, restorative justice focuses on the harm done by crime, what needs to be done to repair the harm, and who is responsible for repairing the harm. Retributive justice, in contrast, focuses on what law has been broken, who is responsible for breaking the law, and what punishment is appropriate. The rising global protest at retributive justice seems to unite right and left in its concern for helping crime victims, a task retributive justice quite openly rejects. The spread of restorative justice in the late 1990s was so rapid that by mid-2000 the United Nations had drafted its own "Basic Principles on the Use of Restorative Justice Programmes in Criminal Matters" (www.restorativejustice.org/conference/UN/RJ_UN.htm).

The Australian Police have tested the effects of restorative justice in four randomized controlled experiments (Sherman et al. 2000). One experiment tested the practice used with offenders under age 30 charged with violent crimes. A second tested the effects on juvenile offenders charged with property crimes involving personal (rather than institutional) victims. A third experiment focused on juvenile shoplifting suspects. The fourth sample was drawn from adult offenders charged with drinking and driving. In each experiment, offenders who conceded their guilt were randomly assigned to either criminal prosecution in court or diversion from criminal prosecution to a police-led conference. If the conference reached an agreement for the offender to repair the harm, and if police confirmed that the offender fulfilled the agreement, the police were able to drop the charges. Interviews conducted with offenders and victims shortly after both conference and court treatments measured their attitudes toward police and the legal system, as well as other issues. Observations of most offenders in both court and conference measured what happened in the two settings.

The most important fact about these experiments is that the *severity* of punishment in both restorative and conventional justice was generally comparable. Prison sentences were almost never imposed in either group. While the crimes ranged from shoplifting to armed robbery and life-threatening assaults, the sentences were typically fines, community service, or probationary supervision of some sort. Thus what was tested in the experiments was not the *substance* of justice but the *procedures* used to determine that substance. The fact that most offenders did not go to prison is also consistent with American practices for those offenses, including the violent offenses, most of which were misdemeanor or minor felony assaults that rarely receive prison terms upon conviction in U.S. courts.

The most striking difference between court and police-led conferences was the time each procedure took. Court lasted about ten minutes, adding up all the time offenders spent before a judge over the course of repeated appearances. Conferences lasted more than an hour in all four experiments. The difference in time meant that offenders in conferences, compared to those in court, spent much more of their official contact actually talking and being listened to. Victims had an even greater difference in participation, since they were almost never invited to the court appearances but were given ample opportunity to speak in conferences. The conference procedure allowed everyone present to offer opinions of the crime and what should be done to repair the harm. Conducted in an egalitarian circle, the conferences were a sharp contrast to the hierarchy of a courtroom with a judge up on a high bench.

The interviews of both offenders and victims showed a strong preference for restorative justice conferences over court. Those attending conferences, in comparison to those in cases going to court, showed increased respect for police and the legal system. Victims also felt safer and had less fear or anxiety after restorative justice conferences than after court dispositions (Strang 2000). While the conferences only reduced repeat offending in one experiment, that one dealt with the most serious crimes. Violent offenders going to conferences had 38% fewer repeat offenses in the year after the conference than the violent offenders sent to court (Sherman et al. 2001). None of the experiments showed increases in repeat offending in the restorative justice group.

An Indianapolis test of a similar procedure also found repeat offending reductions compared to juvenile court prosecution of a group of very young property offenders (McGarrell 2000). These findings are not necessarily unique to Australia. Further research is under way in England and other American cities.

What remains to be seen is whether widespread use of this practice by American police could increase public trust and respect for the fairness of police practices. The research so far suggests that it might, especially if a large proportion of the population participates in the conferences as friends, family, or colleagues of the charged offenders. Spotlighting the police as calm discussion leaders may be just the right way to demonstrate a less "bossy" manner and to develop among police the kind of interpersonal style that Americans expect from government in the twenty-first century.

8. HOW CAN POLICE LEADERS BUILD FAIRER POLICING?

While restorative justice may help build trust in police, it cannot overcome the effects of police conduct in the core business of police agencies: field encounters under stress, with victims, suspects, and witnesses. The stress on citizens in these encounters creates frequent challenges to police authority, which in turn may provoke stern police responses that escalate citizen stress. The cycle of shame and rage that police and citizens may feel in these situations is not easy to deal with. But it is predictable. It is also something that some officers deal with far better than others.

Like doctors, lawyers, and other professionals, police are often reluctant to acknowledge criticisms of their colleagues, even when they know that the colleagues are at fault. To the extent that problems from citizen-police encounters are heavily concentrated in a small proportion of each police department, a decision to take action against those problems may not cause great disruption in the social cohesion of the agency. The 1990s saw many police executives taking that view. Moreover, they took action by using computerized risk analysis of police-citizen conflicts to identify officers with disproportionately high rates of conflicts.

One example of risk analysis of police began as something quite different. In the early 1990s, an analysis of repeat victims revealed that 12 of the most frequent 50 victims were police officers. These officers had named themselves as victims injured by offenders they arrested, usually in conjunction with an injury to the arrestee. The police chief's reaction to the list was to call in each of the 12 officers and threaten them with dismissal if they did not reduce the frequency with which the suspects they arrested were injured. He then used the same database to establish an award-winning "early warning system" for police officers who were showing high risk of unwarranted violence against citizens. Over the ensuing decade, many other police departments established such officer-based warning systems, using complaints against police and other indicators to broaden their detection tools.

By 1997, the New York City Police Department had broadened the monitoring of citizen complaints from the individual officer to entire precincts. At COMPSTAT sessions, precinct commanders could be asked about trends in citizen complaints against precinct officers just as easily as they could be asked about armed robbery. The emphasis on reducing complaints was focused on high-risk precincts, and commanders who reduced complaints were given high praise. While the NYPD in that era took much criticism over tragic encounters with young black men, long-term indicators such as the number of people killed suggest success in reducing police use of force. Whether these systems changed the manner of police conversations with citizens was harder to measure. Some agencies call back samples of citizens who called the police to take a "customer satisfaction" survey. New York commissioned a regular public opinion poll, much like presidential approval ratings. This poll found that in the first year of a new police commissioner, for example, the public approval rating rose from 43% to 50% overall. While approval by blacks and Hispanics was much lower than that of whites, black citizen approval of the police almost doubled that year, from 17% to 31%, and black disapproval dropped from 75% to 59% (Flynn 2001).

The Newark, New Jersey, police had pushed the measurement of police fairness issues even further by late 2000. Separate COMPSTAT meetings were established on a regular basis just to review data on police use of force and citizen complaints against police (Shalev 2001). Analyses of police conduct data by day of week, time of day, police beat, and district, as well as by supervisor and officer, all revealed the high-risk profiles for citizen distrust of police. Risk factors other than police conduct, of course, shape these complaints, just as they shape crime itself. Whether police can develop explicit statistical models that factor out the other causes of complaints against police remains to be seen (Sherman 1998). But American police are clearly moving in the direction of precise risk analyses of the problems of fair policing, just as they have in finding more effective responses to crime.

9. HOW CAN ELECTED OFFICIALS BUILD FAIRER AND MORE EFFECTIVE POLICING?

No matter how much police leaders try to shape the conduct of their officers, they face many barriers to reaching their goals. These barriers are inherent in the legal and governmental framework for the police, including residency requirements, civil service law, and police unions. These barriers prevent police chiefs from hiring the kind of people they want, promoting the kind of people they want to manage the agency, and disciplining or firing police when they think it necessary.

The American police institution now stands in between its industrial-age past and its information-age future. Crime, justice, and even democracy may depend on police departments shaking off the factory model that prevents them from adopting an entrepreneurial model that will move them forward. Despite the major efforts to graft information-driven management onto assembly-line practices, police organizational structures no longer "fit" well with the egalitarian culture they serve. While public support for police in democracies remains high, both police officers and the public seem to want an institution that gives them more respect.

The question of what police can do about crime in an egalitarian world depends heavily on the organizational design of the police. If the police organization is forced by union contract to have virtually equal numbers of officers working each day of the week, despite heavy concentration of serious crime on weekends, that fact severely limits what police can do about crime. If the police organization is forced by civil service law to retain top managers in positions of power despite poor results in crime reduction, that fact limits the extent to which better information will guide police operations. If the police organization is unable to reward work groups with salary bonuses for better or more equitable service to the public, that fact limits officers' incentives to work for those results.

These barriers help explain why police earned little praise for the drop in American crime rates in the late 1990s. Rather than applauding the growth of information-age practices to reduce crime, news coverage was dominated by allegations of industrial-age partisanship: abuse of blacks and immigrants, callous treatment of women, and even police harassment of voters at the polls. Against a backdrop of objective measures showing police to be more nonpartisan and restrained than ever before, these attacks may seem misguided. But they are a predictable part of the rising public expectations for perfectionism in all services, including business, medicine, and government. Only an organizational design that can cope with these demands seems likely to maintain the legitimacy police need to elicit voluntary compliance with the law. Creating an information-driven police institution, operating internally and externally on egalitarian principles, may require nothing less than reinventing the police.

Most proposals to transform police departments make the fatal assumption that this must be done in the current organizational framework. What may be far more effective is creating an entirely new agency on completely different principles. This agency could be developed at the same time that the traditional police department winds down, reducing its cost to the city through attrition and retirement. Meanwhile, a new "public safety department" could assume more and more of the old "police department" tasks. This could start with such specialized tasks as crime analysis and move on to complete transfer of authority for one police district at a time. Spread out over a period of 10 to 20 years, this gradual evolution would avoid putting the public at risk. Over the long run, it could protect the public far better than the current organizational design.

A new public safety department could implement many of the blue-ribbon recommendations that could never be implemented by industrial-age policing:

- All police should hold bachelor's or master's degrees
- Police should be appointed on three-year renewable contracts, not be tenured
- Each officer should be paid twice the salary that current officers are paid
- Officer schedules should concentrate patrols at high-crime times and days
- Far fewer officers would be able to produce the same results for the same total budget
- Each officer and work group should share in rewards for creating more public safety in their assigned areas than risk factors would predict is possible
- Work groups should be given broad flexibility to design lawful strategies

- Officers should be recruited nationwide, with race and gender diversity key goals

The prospect of closing down civil service police agencies in favor of results-driven public safety departments exemplifies the choices facing America's cities, especially those losing large portions of their population. These cities can continue to levy high taxes and suffer high crime rates while jobs and residential population both decline. Or they can redesign their governments around the tools and human capital of the information age, reducing taxes and increasing the quality of life. Substantial increases in police fairness and effectiveness may be unlikely unless the elected leadership of those cities make it possible.

14

Physical Environment, Crime, Fear, and Resident-Based Control

Ralph B. Taylor

A syllogism adopted for the last three decades by some researchers and policymakers alike goes as follows: There is more crime in some places than in others. The physical environment (PE) is different from place to place, therefore the PE is somewhat responsible for these place-to-place differences. Therefore, by implication, if we change the PE in high crime places, crime there will decline.

Is this syllogism correct? Can we achieve crime prevention through land use or environmental design changes? If the syllogism is not correct, where does it break down? Could it be correct but incomplete, and if so, in what ways? Does it depend on the scale of the location in question?

This chapter explores the above questions, by implication touching on a broader split in criminology and criminal justice generally.[1] For about a decade now, some leading researchers have argued that we know more about the places of crime than the people who commit crimes; therefore we should move toward a place-centered rather than person-centered focus for research, policy, and practice (Weisburd 1997; Sherman 1995, pp. 36–37). Will a place-focused policy framework help us more effectively promote public safety than a person-focused perspective? And if so, for what crimes? Or to put the point less dramatically, in what ways should a place-focused framework complement person-centered concerns?

We should rely on the opening syllogism only if each of several challenges can be addressed successfully. Can we go from observing location-to-location differences in crime to isolating the key physical differences between high- and low-crime locations to changing those physical features to realizing crime prevention benefits? And if these changes can have prevention impacts but those impacts are partially or completely contingent on other setting conditions, can we isolate and then assess those contingencies so that we target interventions at locales where positive benefits are expected?

The concern here on the outcome side includes not just crime but also related ecological processes such as social and physical problems thought to be crime related (also called *social and physical incivilities*), related psychological dynamics like fear of crime and residents' concerns about neighborhood viability, and related social dynamics such as residents' willingness versus unwillingness to intervene (Maccoby, Johnson, and Church 1958), either by acting directly to maintain order on the street, or by calling the police.

The material reviewed in this chapter will suggest two points. First, the above syllogism is correct but incomplete. Extensive empirical work shows PE does link to crime or related outcomes. A much slimmer volume of empirical work suggests changes in PE link to changes in crime or related outcomes. But the work also suggests that for both cross-sectional and longitudinal work, these connections often surface only under specific setting conditions. In other words, a broader contextual dynamic usually shapes the relevant processes (Sampson 1993). What happens on the block or in the neighborhood depends on the surroundings.[2]

Such a contingent, contextual dynamic appears to refute architectural determinism—the belief of many planners or architects that PE features will determine or at least substantially shape the behaviors of those using that space (Broady 1972). Such a view is implicit in the opening syllogism and is generally not applicable to a wide range of everyday settings.[3] Once we recognize that this view is misleading, the important practice issues then expand beyond just identifying the relevant physical features. We must also ask: are social and/or cultural setting conditions present that would enable crime prevention changes or fear changes or resident behavioral changes to emerge from shifts in the physical setting? If the enabling conditions are not present, could they be developed with a cost-effective amount of outside assistance or guidance? Can we outline the micropolitical, community-input processes, and interagency arrangements needed to appropriately involve key stakeholders in the planning for and implementation of physical design changes?

Suggesting that PE-crime connections are sometimes contingent may prove troubling for decision makers. Policy planners far prefer the "one size fits all" approach when it comes to crime prevention (Rosenbaum 1987, 1988). But these contingencies are unlikely to be random. We can understand the patterns in these contingencies if we draw on a broader theoretical perspective supplied by theories of ecological psychology (Taylor 1997c), or environmental psychology (Gifford 1997), including territorial functioning

(Taylor 1988). Stated differently, to build a more comprehensive policy framework it is vital to complement the theoretical perspectives applied to crime-environment links that are site-level or microlevel with theoretical perspectives considering settings more broadly and considering processes over time. By thoughtfully melding these micro and macro perspectives we can better understand the contingencies the research has shown and better target proposed interventions. That broader integration has not yet taken place.

The second major point suggested by the review is that we know much more about cross-sectional relationships than we do about longitudinal ones. This is also generally true in the broader disciplines within which these questions are nested: environmental criminology, environmental psychology, ecological psychology, and urban studies generally. Theories are often developed and may even include a longitudinal flavor, based on cross-sectional findings. But it is not unusual to find that those same findings do not resurface in identical form when recast within a longitudinal framework (e.g., Miethe and Meier 1994, p. 138). Generally, it is much more demanding and time consuming to conduct longitudinal studies requiring primary data collection, and current external funding practices and academic production norms sometimes create additional barriers. Further, this is especially difficult when examining PE changes for two reasons. It means tracking a number of settings, not just individuals, over time. Also, these changes are taking place in real environments, and complicated planning and negotiating processes depending on numerous parties planning and executing the changes (Donnelly and Majka 1998).

Nonetheless, because a cross-sectional finding has not yet been evaluated in a longitudinal context, or because a static finding may have failed to replicate in longitudinal studies in a single location or a small number of locations, does not necessarily mean that the longitudinal relationship does not hold. It could be that the longitudinal relationship appears but is weak, and thus will not show consistently; or that it depends on setting conditions that have not yet been fully specified; or that we do not yet fully understand the time frame within which these longitudinal processes operate, and thus are not sure how long it takes for the positive effects of PE changes to appear. Stated differently, a theoretical perspective developed in a cross-sectional relationship cannot be readily installed in a longitudinal framework. Rather, the installation itself raises a number of additional questions that need to be addressed. The work on PE change and crime change has generally not addressed these issues.

This chapter considers the relationships between physical environment and crime primarily at the streetblock and neighborhood levels.[4] These relationships, once we move beyond connections based on target hardening and situational crime prevention (Clarke 1992), are likely to be carried or mediated by offender-based dynamics or user- or resident-based dynamics. Offender-based dynamics span issues such as perceptions linked to costs and benefits associated with the target, victim, or surroundings and behaviors shaping the relationship between offender locations and target or victim locations. The resident- or user-based dynamics encompass social, face-to-face, and organizational group dynamics, as well as a number of person-place bonds. Understanding the PE-crime connections is not just a matter of identifying "what works," or as suggested by the discussion of context effects immediately above, clarifying "what works where." Rather, it is a question of gauging both what works where *and* specifying in what time frame *and* identifying the responsible processual dynamics—and their contextual dependence—leading to the outcome. Policy planners increase the likelihood of framing a successful implementation and intervention if they give thought to the "in between" steps leading to the desired ultimate outcomes and the issue of timing. The issues are: what works where, because of what micro-macro connections, because of what underlying processes, over what time period?

The chapter begins by briefly reviewing four meta-orientations to PE-crime links. Two perspectives concentrate mostly on resident-user-based or setting-user-based dynamics: territorial functioning and the incivilities thesis. Another perspective, behavioral geography, concentrates mostly on offender-based dynamics. The final one (discussed first here), routine activities theory and the "life-style" variant, consider both offenders and victims or targets. These perspectives provide different outlooks on what specific dynamics may lead to which specific outcomes. Certain PE changes may lead to beneficial outcomes because the intervention is likely to tap into *several* of the dynamics postulated as relevant by the different orientations. If several different frameworks each suggest that a certain specific PE feature is likely to activate a certain process, it seems more likely that that feature will have crime-prevention benefits than if the feature is targeted by only one of the frameworks.

THE META-ORIENTATIONS ON PHYSICAL ENVIRONMENT AND CRIME

Rational Offender Perspective

Offenders often seem to operate in a rational fashion (Clarke 1983), preferring to commit crimes that require the least effort, provide the highest benefits, and pose the lowest risks. Risks are lower if entrance time to the crime site is shorter, exit time is shorter, chances of coming under surveillance are lower, and the offender can more easily, completely, or quickly "read" events taking place at and around the site. Physical features play important roles in shaping those risks. Researchers have applied this rational offender perspective to a range of crimes (Clarke 1983; Clarke and Cornish 1985; Cornish 1994). Included within the rational offender perspective are both the life-style theory (Hindelang, Gottfredson, and Garofalo 1978, 1979; Titus 1995), concentrating largely on the victim's behavior, and routine activities theory, attending to both offender and target characteristics. In its earlier versions, routine activities theory proposed that crimes occur when three things come together in space and time: a motivated offender, a suitable target, and the *absence* of a capable guardian (Felson 1994). [5] A house is likely to be burglarized if more motivated burglars live closer, it is clear the house contains expensive goods, and the owners are away.

More recently, theorists have added three more pieces to the model (Felson 1995). First, motivated offenders have "handlers": relatives, friends, or acquaintances who can discourage the motivated offender from committing the crime without resorting to force for their persuasion. In addition to guardians who are focused on protecting a particular target, settings often have "place managers": people who discourage crime and disorderly behaviors by controlling places. This modification merges routine activities theory with ecological psychology and human territorial functioning (Taylor 1997a, 1997c, 1988: chapter 8), described below. With the introduction of the place manager, routine activities theory develops into a perspective clearly focused on small-scale locations. It tells us about differences across sites, not across communities, over time (Eck 1995). "[S]pecific places should be a focus of research . . . for small time increments" (pp. 795–96).

Miethe and colleagues in a third elaboration of the theory clarify and integrate the structural-versus-choice elements of the theory into a "structural choice" model (Miethe and Meier 1990, 1994, p. 40). The structural elements, determined by potential victim settlement and routine activity patterns, and offender settlement and routine activity patterns, determine the exposure of potential victims or targets to potential offenders and the proximity of the motivated offenders. Choice, in accord with a rational perspective on offender decisionmaking (Clarke and Cornish 1985; Cornish and Clarke 1986), enters as potential offenders choose targets, deciding that the utility of one is greater than another and that the effectiveness of one guardian is greater than another. In short, macroscale features shape the overall opportunity structure; how potential offenders evaluate the opportunity structure is subjective, based on rational or at least satisfactory decision-making processes (Simon 1996). The structural choice model could be elaborated to include handlers and place managers as well.

Recent reviews of routine activities have pointed out the *contingent* nature of the theory; it specifies that if there is an attractive target *and* a motivated offender *and* if capable guardians are lacking, then crime is most likely (Bursik and Grasmick 1993; Eck 1995, p. 72).[6] This represents an important conceptual distinction between routine activities and systemic control models (Bursik and Grasmick 1993, p. 72). Not all theorists, however, portray routine activities as a theory solely of moderated or contingent impacts (e.g., Hough 1987).

Another important suggested difference in interpretation is in scale. Some have argued that routine activities perspective describes situations at an exceedingly small scale, where the time perspective is in minutes and the spatial perspective is in feet (Eck 1995). Elaborations that add in handlers and place managers seem congruent with this contention.

The practical issues raised by this question of scale are significant. If the appropriate scale is at the more micro level, then prevention programs are to be planned, implemented, and evaluated at the streetblock or building level rather than the community level.

Behavioral Geography/Crime Pattern Theory

This approach keys on the daily activities of potential offenders and how these activities structure offenders' behavior space (the total set of locations they frequent) and their awareness space (the total set of locations about which they are knowledgeable) and how these two spaces shape offenders' search space (the locations they will explore, consider, and evaluate as potential offending locations, when they have a particular crime in mind) (Brantingham and Brantingham 1981). Offenders go to jobs, visit friends, come home, shop at the store, and carry out other daily activities just like the rest of us. Within this activity space motivated offenders search for likely targets for the type of crime they hope to commit. For example, suburban burglars may look for worthwhile houses to break into that are not too far off their route between home and work (Rengert and Wasilchick 1985). Urban, drug-using burglars may choose sites near drug markets (Rengert 1996). Crime pattern theory integrates ideas about offenders' movement through space with a consideration of target distributions through space (Eck and Weisburd 1995). It links places with desirable targets and the context in which they are found by offenders.

Whereas the routine activities perspective concentrates on evaluations of potential victims, guardians, and place managers at an offense site, the behavioral geographic view focuses on the chances that the potential offender will even be likely to consider the site in the first place. Therefore, PE proves most relevant as it influences both physical distance and functional distance. Physical distance between an offender and an offense site could be measured by looking at straight line or city block distance; functional distance could be measured by looking at the shortest route traveled, on foot, by car, or by public transport, between offender worksite—or home or shopping location—and an offense site.

The behavioral geography perspective seems more or less applicable depending on the crime in question and depending on the locale in question. More specifically, applicability seems strongest when considering property crimes such as burglary, motor vehicle theft, and (although perhaps to a lesser extent) larceny. These are crimes where offenders often have particular types of targets or particular goals in mind, although they are certainly capable of changing their noncriminal plans when opportunity arises (Rengert and Wasilchick 1985). In addition, applicability seems strongest in communities where offenders and targets are not equally mixed. More specifically, the crime patterns in locations that are home to few offenders but are popular locations for committing offenses may be more easily understood using this view than would be the crime patterns in locations with large numbers of both targets and offenders.

Human Territorial Functioning

Serious misconceptions abound about human territorial functioning (Taylor 1988: chapter 4). These serious misconceptions and concomitant misapplications make it difficult to clearly appreciate the roles that territorial functioning plays in everyday settings. Human territorial functioning refers to an interlocked system of sentiments, cognitions, and behaviors that are highly place specific, socially and culturally determined and maintaining, and that represent a class of person-place transactions concerned with issues of setting management, maintenance, legibility, and expressiveness (Taylor 1988, p. 6).

Extensive empirical work has established that territorial functioning is limited to small, face-to-face social groupings (Taylor 1988, p. 84). Although the term has been misapplied (e.g., Sack 1986) to phenomena of widely varying scales, ranging up to nation states, the empirical work and the relevant evolutionary underpinnings only support its application to small, face-to-face groups (Taylor 1988 pp. 315–16). Cultural, physical, individual, intra-, and intergroup factors shape how users view a particular place (p. 92). Part of those views are territorial cognitions: a subset of place-specific attitudes and sentiments addressing responsibility for and control over the locale, including matters of upkeep, regulating the behavior of users, and controlling entry and exit. These cognitions include, "How responsible I feel for what happens there; how concerned I am about its appearance and upkeep; how much privacy I expect to have there; what kinds of persons I expect to encounter and how I may respond to them" (p. 94). Relevant territorial behaviors include, most prototypically, "those intentional behaviors aimed towards notifying others of occupancy, excluding others, asserting control, or asking others to conform to setting standards. Such behaviors aim to directly influence the behavior of others in the setting" (p. 94). Also relevant are nonverbal behaviors, setting-changing or -maintaining behaviors that influence the behaviors of users (Taylor 1987). There are short-term benefits that result from this person-place behavior system, including allowing individuals to freely carry out the activities associated with the site and making social interaction "more organized and predictable" (Taylor 1988, p. 95). Longer-term consequences are social (maintaining group functioning and viability and reducing intergroup conflict) as well as ecological (allowing settings to "run" more smoothly) and psychological (reducing intrapersonal stress) (Taylor 1988, pp. 95–96, 117–31).

Researchers in environmental psychology (Proshansky, Ittelson, and Rivlin 1970) and ecological psychology (Barker 1968) have described the strong supporting roles that place managers can play in maintaining a setting; their contributions affect setting stability, including the likelihood of offending or victimization, because they contribute significantly to the territorial functioning in the site. The place managers described in the latest version of routine activity theory are involved in just such territorial functioning, even though the researchers fail to refer to the extensive work there. Territorial functioning has played a key role in defensible space theory (Newman 1972; Taylor, Gottfredson, and Brower 1980; Newman and Franck 1980, 1982) with earlier misconceptions being replaced by more appropriate views about residents.

The territorial perspective provides guidance on design and management issues surrounding a current pressing policy issue—vacant housing. In large older cities, among the most crucial policy choices confronting urban leaders are those relevant to the demolition or renovation of vacant housing. Vacant housing problems are particularly intense at this time, following three if not four or five decades of declining population in larger, older cities, and decades of scarce city funding for housing. Especially in lower income, inner-city locations, the pattern that cities choose when razing structures dynamically affects territorial functioning on the streetblock in question and on adjoining streetblocks. Because it directly addresses resident-based informal control, the territorial perspective provides the clearest directive on how to respond. Wholesale demolition of one side of a streetblock is undesirable because the created nonresidential space is too large for residents to manage informally, unless the space is deeded to the residents, funds are provided for effectively closing and securing the space at certain times, and residents are given assistance on planning and managing uses in that space—whether for small playgrounds or urban gardens.

We know a lot about what can go wrong with such spaces (Brower 1988, pp. 97–139) and the design guidelines needed to make these spaces work (pp. 161–172). Sawtooth demolition—taking down vacant houses and leaving standing alternate, occupied dwellings—may be preferable under certain conditions. With this demolition pattern, public officials need to 1) allow and fund the bounding (fencing) of such open spaces; 2) ensure the unquestioned structural integrity of the remaining buildings; and 3) figure out, perhaps through tax incentives, how to link management of the spaces to the occupants remaining in the occupied dwellings.

With declining city populations in many large cities, vacant housing policies afford opportunities to transform residential streetblocks into settings that support a more diverse array of activities while also supporting residents' control over these locations and discouraging detrimental uses and users. In these settings the dialectic between residents and regular users and legitimate activities versus marginal users, unacceptable behaviors, or criminal behaviors is endemic and will never disappear (Taylor 1987). Real opportunities exist in big cities with problems like this to act in ways that create more manageable and safer streetblocks.

The Incivilities Thesis

In the last few years, one group of researchers and policy scholars have modified a model of human ecology to address resident fear, neighborhood crime changes, and neighborhood decline (Taylor 1999).[7] The sociological version of human ecology theory focuses on population, social, policy, and physical factors at the community level that contribute to social disorganization—the inability of the residents of a community, or of the groups representing those residents, to solve their common problems and work toward shared solutions (Bursik and Grasmick 1993; Taylor, Forthcoming). The scholars developing the incivilities thesis have put the human ecology model through the following changes: they have "psychologized" the basic social disorganization model, added a physical component, and then "re-ecologized" it while adding additional outcomes linked to neighborhood change (Skogan 1990). Within this family of models are several different variations, generally referred to as "broken windows," "crime and grime," "decline and disorder," or the "incivilities thesis" (Taylor 1997b, 2001).

The kernel of the original idea as developed by James Q. Wilson, and Garofalo and Laub, was that some residents are more surrounded by, and more bothered by, disorderly social and physical conditions (Garofalo and Laub 1978; Wilson 1975). These disorderly conditions inspired fear among residents who had not been criminally victimized. According to this idea, as disorderly conditions increased, so too would residents' fear. This idea surfaced as analyses of some of the first nationwide crime, victim surveys of the mid-1970s started showing far more residents fearful about crime than were victimized (e.g., Cook and Skogan 1984). The social conditions include unruly teens, "hey honey" hassles, public drug sales or drug usage, public drinking or drunkenness, and so on. Linked physical conditions include more extensive litter, graffiti, abandoned houses, abandoned cars, weedy vacant lots, and houses in disrepair.

The first theorists paying attention to these conditions suggested that those viewing such would feel vulnerable and at risk of being victimized (Garofalo and Laub 1978). Others suggested it was the lack of repair to deteriorated physical conditions that sparked residents' concerns—the broken window that wasn't fixed (Perkins, Meeks, and Taylor 1992; Wilson and Kelling 1982). The theory further evolved to encompass how these dynamics would unfold over time (Taylor 1999). The window isn't fixed or the graffiti isn't erased, and residents become more fearful and withdraw from efforts to control events on the streetblock, local rowdies act bolder and vandalize further, and the process spirals onward.

Further, as noted above, the model was "reecologized." Researchers began suggesting that the outcomes applied to neighborhoods, not just individuals. So outcomes such as neighborhood fear, neighborhood economic decline, increasing neighborhood instability, and neighborhood out-migration became of interest. Some suggested that disorderly social and physical conditions could independently cause neighborhoods to go down the tubes (Skogan 1990).

Relevance of Physical Environment Features May or May Not Be Differential across Theories

The different theoretical perspectives provide markedly different perspectives on how PE proves relevant to crime and related outcomes (see Table 14.1). They differ in their spatial focus, their temporal focus, and whom they define as the most relevant actors. The perspectives also differ in the range of physical features they define as relevant to crime and related outcomes and as to how those physical features might prove relevant. But there are also points of overlap, physical features that *several* theoretical perspectives suggest should prove relevant to crime. Most commonly pointed to by the different theoretical orientations are two sets of design features: circulation restrictions, including both boundaries and decreased ease of internal circulation; and segregation of nonresidential from residential land uses.

EMPIRICAL WORK: HOUSING DESIGN FEATURES AND BLOCK LAYOUT

Can housing design and block layout make residents less vulnerable and feel safer? The originally formulated Jane Jacobs/defensible space idea is that physical features that offer better surveillance, delineation between public and private space, segmentation of outdoor space into locations controlled by smaller groups, and proximity to well-used locations enable stronger resident-based informal control of outdoor, near-home spaces. Such control should lead to less delinquency, less fear, and less victimization (Jacobs 1961; Newman 1972, 1976; Newman and Franck 1982; Poyner 1983).

Studies of varying quality began testing these ideas in the early 1970s and continued at a rapid pace for the next dozen years. In 1980, with further theoretical elaboration of the theory, distinctions were drawn between "first generation" and "second generation" defensible space (Taylor, Gottfredson, and Brower 1980). The latter work confirmed that in public housing communities (Murray 1982) and on residential streetblocks (Taylor, Gottfredson, and Brower 1984), defensible space features contributed to lower levels of violence and lower fear. For example, in lower rise public housing buildings, with fewer households per entryway, residents socialized more in outdoor locations, knew one another better, and reported lower fear.

Proving harder to demonstrate have been the impacts of changes in housing design and layout on crime changes or fear changes (Murray

Table 14.1

Differences Between Various Meta-Orientations to Physical Environment-Crime Links

Theoretical Perspective Issue	Routine Activities	Behavioral Geography	Territorial Functioning	Incivilities Thesis
Spatial Focus	Feet (Eck 1995) or community level to site level (Miethe and Meier 1990)	Community level to site level	Site level to streetblock level	Streetblock level to neighborhood level
Temporal Focus for Changes	Seconds (Eck 1995) to years (Miethe and Meier 1990)	Period in which potential offenders acquire aware-ness space; period in which background distribution of targets and victims changes	Days to years	Not specified (weeks or months to years?)
Most Relevant Actors	Potential offend-ers and their handlers, resi-dents or users, place managers and guardians	Potential offend-ers	Regular residents or users of settings	Regular residents or users of settings vs. delinquents and potential offenders
Most Relevant Physical Features	Those affecting distribution of targets, availability and effectiveness of place managers and guardians	Those affecting spatial behavior of potential offenders and the background distribution of potential targets	Those facilitat-ing density of "caring eyes" on the street; making for gradual transitions in resident- or user-based con-trol; expressing group identity, care, watchful-ness, or solidarity	Those indicating deterioration, lack of upkeep

1995). Many of the studies completed were demonstration projects, rather than quasi-experimental research projects, and failed to take into account sufficiently important features of the local social and cultural context (Taylor, Gottfredson, and Brower 1980).

Practical Implications

This work led to implementation of specific design elements in numerous locations. These ideas have proved broadly influential in housing policy, leading the U.S. Department of Housing and Urban Development (HUD) in the 1990s to fund millions of dollars to demolish high rises and replace them with low-rise housing more in accord with the design guidelines described here (Popkin et al. 2000). Of course, design changes in public housing communities cannot be considered by themselves; their contribution deserves attention in the context of numerous policy and managerial issues. Design of other types of structures has been affected as well; for example, parking garage stairwells with outer walls of glass (Crowe 1991).

Limitations

One of the major limitations to expanding the number of defensible space designs has been the lack of research about how potential offenders view or use the physical features in question. Researchers have recently recast the discussion of defensible space features into a threefold grouping of physical features: prospect, refuge, and escape (e.g., Fisher and Nasar 1992):

- Settings with high refuge offer concealment for the potential offender.
- Settings with high prospect allow the legitimate user to survey a wide area.
- Settings with high escape potential offer easy escape for the legitimate user.

This view of defensible space focuses explicitly on potential victim–potential offender dynamics in specific locations. Research confirms that fear is higher in locations that offer good refuge for the potential offender and low prospect and escape for the user.

An additional limitation is that the effectiveness of defensible space features depends in part upon the immediate social and cultural context. In some contexts, defensible space can be left "undefended" (Merry 1981).

Extreme cultural or subcultural heterogeneity may be one setting condition that makes it harder to defend defensible spaces. More knowledge is needed about the characteristics of context that allow defensible space features to more effectively support resident-based control. In all fairness, however, this limitation applies to all perspectives that link PE features with crime and related outcomes, and it is not unique to this theoretical perspective. This is not a problem per se, but just a limitation encountered when we move away from unrealistic assumptions of architectural determinism.

Land Use and Circulation Patterns

All four perspectives reviewed above suggest that the internal layouts, boundary characteristics, and traffic patterns of neighborhoods may encourage or discourage different types of crime. By implication, changes in land uses, boundaries, and traffic patterns may result in higher or lower crime rates because they affect both potential offenders and users (Rengert and Wasilchick 1985).

NEIGHBORHOOD LEVEL

Cross-sectional and longitudinal works both suggest strong connections between these physical features and crime levels. Cross-sectional studies in Atlanta (Greenberg and Rohe 1986; Greenberg, Williams, and Rohe 1982), Minneapolis (Bevis and Nutter 1977), and Richmond, Virginia (White 1990), found that the internal layouts of low-crime neighborhoods were less permeable—more one-way, narrow, and low-volume streets—than those found in higher crime neighborhoods.

Because public housing communities are often denser settlements than the surrounding neighborhoods, there will be more circulation in and around such communities. Studies using different methodologies reveal inconsistent patterns of effects. The siting of public housing may result in later destabilization of a community and higher delinquency (Bursik 1989). A study with detailed geo-coded crime data suggests a complex relationship. In the Bronx it appears that public housing communities stimulate higher crime rates in immediately adjoining areas while, at the same time, crime in those adjoining areas makes crime rates in the public housing communities higher (Fagan and Davies 1997). The pattern is particularly hard to pin down because areas surrounding public housing communities not only have high through-traffic levels, they also are likely to host numerous service establishments.

Longitudinal research in Hartford (Fowler and Mangione 1986; Fowler, McCalla, and Mangione 1979), Akron (Donnelly and Majka 1998), Dayton (Donnelly and T. Majka 1996), and unpublished and published evaluations in Miami (Atlas and LeBlanc 1994; Ycaza 1992), suggest that physical changes to internal circulation patterns and boundaries were followed by lower crime rates.

In the studies involving redesign, however, local social or organizational dynamics have often accompanied planned changes (Donnelly and T. Majka 1996). Although it seems likely that design changes themselves have at least been partially responsible for the impact observed (Donnelly and Majka 1998), researchers have not yet precisely estimated their independent contribution to lowering crime, fear, or perceived risk. How much of the benefit has been due to the redesign, and how much has been due to the social and organizational changes surrounding the planned change?

Practical Implications

There are several practical implications of this research at the neighborhood level. (1) Social and organizational conditions are important when changes in layout, traffic, or land use are being considered (Donnelly and Majka 1998). Community involvement of residents, neighborhood organizations, and local businesspeople is essential for developing a plan free of adverse effects on major interest groups. (2) Local involvement may be an important precondition not only for rational, maximally beneficial change but also for achieving a redesign that will actually reduce crime. One study suggests that changes in layout, under conditions of community mobilization, appear to have been partially responsible for decreases in some crimes (Fowler and Mangione 1986). But the crime-preventive benefits of changes in layout appear to weaken as community mobilization wanes. (3) An early step in planning redesign to prevent crime is understanding offender location. For some offenses, such as auto theft, offenders may come from other neighborhoods. For other offenses, such as drug-dealing, offenders may live in the area. If they come primarily from outside the neighborhood, can residents readily distinguish between these potential predators and individuals who are in the neighborhood for legitimate purposes? If they can make the distinction, physical impediments to entry and circulation may result in fewer crimes being committed by certain types of offenders. Under some conditions, restricting neighborhood entrances and making internal circulation patterns more difficult for outsiders should result in safer neighborhoods.

There are three important further caveats to such a circulation reduction approach. The limits cannot impair the ability of local public agencies to deliver services such as fire suppression, trash collection, and policing. In addition, the distinctions drawn between insiders and potential offenders from outside must have some empirical foundation and not be driven solely by residents' class- or ethnic-based fears and concerns. Finally, these changes, even if they have an empirical foundation, can exacerbate between-neighborhood conflicts (Taylor 2001: chapter 8).

Of course, such an implication needs to be tempered by the recognition that crime prevention is just one objective of land-use planning. Other agendas, such as economic development or equal housing opportunities, may conflict at times with crime-prevention or fear-reduction goals.[8]

STREETBLOCK LEVEL

Streetblocks—the two sides of the street bounded by cross streets—are behavior settings (Barker 1968) with established norms and temporal rhythms (Taylor 1997c). They are units over which informal social groups of residents, as well as formal organizations such as block clubs, exert control (Prestby and Wandersman 1985). As such, they represent important arenas not only in residents' lives but for potential policy interventions. Since at this level there are many units with no crime whatsoever from year to year, police calls for service are often used as the crime proxy variable.

At the streetblock level, two related but distinct features of the PE may interfere with residents' ability to manage activities on the block and to recognize people who belong to the neighborhood: nonresidential land uses and high traffic volume. Residents living on higher vehicle traffic streets use their front yards less and withdraw from neighbors (Appleyard 1981). High vehicle volume makes it harder to get to know the people across the street and makes sitting out front less pleasant. As a result, residents' ability to distinguish who does and who does not "belong" on the block, and perhaps their willingness to intervene, seems likely to be lower. Studies directly connecting police calls for service and street traffic volume have not been conducted, but we do know that social integration is weaker on these streets and residents' fear is higher (Hunter and Baumer 1982).

The policy implications for vehicle traffic, however, are not straightforward. As Appleyard's work in San Francisco in the 1970s showed, if you reduce traffic somewhere, it has to go somewhere else, and those residents somewhere else might not like it (Appleyard 1981).

Higher levels of foot traffic, often associated with nearby commercial or institutional land use, also can cause the same social cocooning (Baum, Davis, and Aiello 1978). The question of which nonresidential land uses are troublesome in a predominantly residential setting is an open one. Certainly, there are some nonresidential land uses, such as bars and schools, where crime will be higher (Roncek 1981; Roncek and Bell 1981; Roncek and Faggiani 1985; Roncek and Maier 1991; Roncek and Pravatiner 1989). Sites like these are likely to be both crime generators and crime attractors. A crime generator generates lots of opportunities for crime as a by-product of large volumes of pedestrian traffic—the potential victim flow is enhanced (Gardiner 1976, p. 10). A crime attractor draws in lots of potential offenders because of the reputation of the site. But once we move beyond clearly troublesome land uses like bars, opinions differ about whether they are good in a predominantly residential context.

Territorial Signage and Physical Features Promoting Territorial Functioning

As described above, nonresidential land use can be problematic on street-blocks because it can weaken territorial functioning. Streetblock analyses in two cities—Baltimore and Philadelphia—confirm strong connections between the relative dominance of nonresidential land use and assessed, on-site physical deterioration (Taylor et al. 1995). Blocks with more stores or small businesses or institutional uses, in a predominantly residential context, are more run down. It is not clear if this is a result of the higher foot traffic levels, lower levels of resident-based maintenance efforts as they withdraw, or both. In the second study, conducted solely in an inner city Philadelphia neighborhood, results showed that nonresidential land use and not physical deterioration weakened residents' informal control and their willingness to call the police for assistance (Kurtz, Koons, and Taylor 1998).

Thinking about psychological and social/psychological outcomes, residents living on blocks with higher levels of nonresidential land use are more concerned for their personal safety and less likely to intervene if they see something suspicious; they experience higher victimization rates and call the police more often. These links have been supported by evidence from numerous studies conducted in different cities around the country (Kurtz, Koons and Taylor 1998; McPherson, Silloway and Frey 1983; Perkins et al. 1990; Roncek 1981; Roncek and Bell 1981; Roncek and Faggiani 1985; Roncek and Lobosco 1983; Roncek and Maier 1991; Roncek and Pravatiner 1989; Taylor et al. 1995).

This does not mean that stores and small businesses should be removed from residential settings. Residents may depend on these services. Further, in settings where proprietors have long tenancy or are culturally similar to residents, they may make important contributions to the safety and orderliness of street life (Jablonsky 1993, p. 80). Nevertheless, in locations where sizable "gaps" exist between residents and entrepreneurs, steps may be needed to draw the personnel staffing nonresidential land uses into contributing to overall street order.

Understanding the effects of nonresidential land use on informal control on the streetblock is limited by a lack of recent work examining relationships between entrepreneurs and residents in inner-city neighborhoods. There are several excellent recent ethnographies of inner-city life by, among others, Elijah Anderson, Elliot Liebow, Terry Williams, and Phillipe Bourgois. Some provide some insight into relations between storeowners and residents. Bourgois (1996) describes how storeowners are recruited by dealers so that drugs can be stashed at the bodega. Simon and Burns (1997) describe extremely fractious relationships between Asian store personnel and African American residents in a Baltimore neighborhood (Simon and Burns 1997). But a lot more attention is needed to these topics before we can understand the contingencies affecting the relationship between nonresidential land use and crime and related outcomes.

Evidence supporting the territorial perspective on safe streetblock functioning comes from several cross-sectional studies linking territorial markers, territorial cognitions, local social involvement, and control over nearby public spaces (Brower 1988; Greenbaum and Greenbaum 1981; Taylor 1997c). Residents perceive that stronger markers indicate a safer environment: the more threatening the environment, the more markers required to make residents feel safe (Brower, Dockett, and Taylor 1983). On blocks where territorial cognitions are stronger, residents feel safer (Taylor 1997c).

Practical Implications

In keeping with territorial ideas, planners and designers want to create delimited, semipublic spaces that can easily be overseen by residents and are likely to be used by residents. The popularity of gardening on vacant lots in inner-city neighborhoods testifies to what people can do with a space they are allowed to manage. The garden gives them a reason to keep an eye out on the street and involves them more in the neighborhood.

Even if residents can't garden, a series of studies done in a public housing community in Chicago suggests that the presence of outdoor trees and grass results in less fear and stronger local ties (Kuo et al. 1998) because residents use the outside spaces more (Coley, Kuo, and Sullivan 1997); trees and grass may also link to less deterioration (Brunson, Kuo, and Sullivan 2000) and less reported crime (Kuo and Sullivan, 2000). In short, greener outdoor spaces are more heavily used by residents, leading to more effective territorial functioning because residents know one another better and feel safer and potential offenders avoid the locale.

In addition, officials may want to publicly support local initiatives that encourage resident-based territorial strategies. Many local community groups already promote extensive efforts to encourage residents to get involved with cleanup and beautification (e.g., Taylor 1988, p. 193). Local officials do not want to "take over" these activities. Nevertheless, community groups and residents may be appreciative if officials recognize and support the contributions they are making to create safer blocks and overall neighborhood viability.

The Question of Physical Incivilities

Space constraints preclude a detailed review of the empirical work linking physical incivilities with crime and crime-related outcomes such as attenuated neighborhood commitment or fear of crime. More detailed treatment can be found elsewhere (Taylor 2001). This section summarizes what seems to be the current direction given the most recent work.

Numerous studies connect residents' perceptions of local incivilities with higher fear of crime, weaker attachment to place, and weaker residential satisfaction. But this is a connection that operates primarily at the individual level, not the ecological level—primarily between neighbors and not between neighborhoods. Residents who see more problems than the average neighbor on their block or in their neighborhood are also more afraid than that average neighbor. Further, it is not known if the connection is partially spurious, driven by another psychological variable, such as personal pessimism or anxiety, for example.

Cross-sectional, bivariate links appear quite strong at the neighborhood level. For example, one study of more than 40 neighborhoods in several different cities linked perceived incivilities with outcomes like robbery victimization and fear of crime (Skogan 1990). But the independent contribution of incivilities to these outcomes, net of basic neighborhood fabric, was not established (Harcourt 1998). Another study of more than 100 neighborhoods in five different cities found strong links between perceived incivilities and outcomes like fear and neighborhood satisfaction, but the connection was cut in half after controlling for neighborhood status, race, and stability (Taylor 1999). At the streetblock level, assessed incivilities influence outcomes such as perceived crime problems (Perkins, Meeks, and Taylor 1992), and this contribution persists after controlling for block layout, stability, and racial composition. In short, at both the neighborhood and streetblock level there are cross-sectional connections between incivilities and crime-related outcomes, although questions persist about just how strong these are after we remove the influence of status, stability, and race.

Turning to the longitudinal question, a quasi-experiment in Oakland, California looking at streetblocks, found that a program involving police and other city agency personnel to encourage physical cleanup and evictions of troublesome renters resulted in enhanced safety. The study design did not permit isolating the effect of the physical changes themselves, however.

A longitudinal but nonexperimental study looking at data from 30 Baltimore neighborhoods spanning two decades suggested that assessed or perceived incivilities contribute moderately to later changes in some aspects of fundamental neighborhood fabric, moderately but inconsistently to later changes in crime, and minimally to later changes in residents' reactions to crime such as fear and avoidance, after controlling for other features of neighborhood (Taylor 2001). The patterns of impacts observed depend in part on the specific outcome in question and the specific indicator used for incivilities. So grime does contribute to later decline, as the longitudinal incivilities thesis hypothesizes, but the contributions are weaker than anticipated and do not surface regardless of how we measure incivilities. Results also showed that incivilities were far less important than neighborhood fundamentals, especially neighborhood status and racial composition. Further, over time, crime seemed to more strongly influence grime than the reverse.

Presuming the above-described results hold up following replication attempts, policy implications would seem to be as follows. Physical incivilities deserve attention in efforts to stabilize neighborhoods and prevent decline, but such attention ought not to crowd out attention to programs promoting neighborhood stability and quality more generally. Reducing incivilities, as we have seen repeatedly when looking at other features of the PE, will not "do it all" when it comes to reducing crime, stabilizing the neighborhood, and making residents feel safer.

Community policing initiatives include a wide array of different types of programs. It appears from the attention lavished on the incivilities argument the past few years that policymakers have widely presumed that incivility-reduction initiatives will prove more potent than other types of community-policing efforts. The most recent work implies this may not be the case. Therefore policy planners and police decision makers ought not to crowd out other traditional or community-policing initiatives on the perhaps faulty assumption that initiatives geared to physical incivility reduction would have more long-term impact than other initiatives. Such pressure surfaced in Baltimore in the mid-to-late 1990s as city council leaders tried to force (then) Commissioner Frazier to give incivility reduction some of the highest priorities.

CONCLUSIONS

We know that the numerous site-level features of PE, including those investigated as part of situational crime prevention (Clarke 1995; Jankowski 1992) are linked to crime and crime changes. We also know that at a higher level of aggregation—the streetblock or the neighborhood—a broader array of PE features, including land use mix, circulation patterns, features representing physical neglect, and features representing resident investment and caring, link to crime, crime-related outcomes, and reactions to crime. But the streetblock or neighborhood connections may not surface in all settings, or may not surface equally strongly, but rather may be contingent on a range of social, cultural, and surrounding contextual features. Further, the extent to which the linkage observed stands alone, as opposed to reflecting broader local dynamics, may vary across settings. In short, sometimes there may be questions about PE impacts being moderated by other features, about the spuriousness of the PE-outcome connections, or both. But it is clear that at some times and in some locations PE features contribute independently to crime or related outcomes.

The physical features that would appear most relevant—land use mix and circulation patterns—are those features that connect to processes specified by *several* theoretical perspectives, rather than just one. There are numerous reasons to expect the features would "work." In a residential context, the most relevant features for prevention at the neighborhood and streetblock levels appear to be restricting access, reinforcing neighborhood boundaries, making circulation patterns less permeable, and reducing the mixing of many residential and nonresidential land uses. Putting such suggestions in a broader historical context, these suggestions sound like scaling down defensive structures usually associated with cities (Weber 1950), and incorporating them at the community level. Decreasing neighborhood permeability, however, may negatively affect intercommunity relations. Presumed crime-prevention benefits to be gained by such physical shifts need to be weighed against adverse social impacts at a higher level.

One reason it is necessary to be so cautious in our conclusions derives simply from the independent variables in question. It is exceedingly difficult, using an experimental or rigorous quasi-experimental design to simultaneously change a large number of PE features on a block or in a neighborhood. Case studies (Dayton, Miami Shores) and two quasi-experiments (Hartford, Oakland) showed that PE changes resulted in improved safety. One longitudinal study suggested physical features contribute independently to crime changes over time. Given the scale of many of the features at issue here, research is unlikely to learn precisely about causal connections as features change. Once neighborhood layout is established, or a suburban development built, it cannot be changed wholesale.

But there is also the suggestion in some of these works that improvements may be contingent on local social and political processes. We can better understand these contingencies by more closely integrating work on PE and crime with the broader theoretical perspectives that have been described above.

15

Deterrence

STEVEN D. LEVITT

O pportunities to commit crime are everywhere: Each house is a potential burglary target; every store is a place to shoplift; and each person passed on the street offers the prospect of a robbery. In practice, however, crime is extremely rare. Crime is infrequent for many reasons, but one of the most important factors is likely to be fear of punishment (especially in a country like the United States, where over 2 million people are incarcerated at any given time). Deterrence, which is the subject of this chapter, is the formal term for the idea that criminal behavior can be affected by the threat of punishment.

Deterrence can operate in many ways. For instance, increases in the number of police on the streets may raise the likelihood that a crime will lead to an arrest. Stiffer prison sentences also will increase the costs of crime. But deterrence need not operate only through the criminal justice system. If a criminal knows that a potential robbery victim is armed with a gun, the criminal may be afraid to attempt the robbery. Neighborhood watch groups that actively report crimes to the police will increase the chances that a criminal is caught, reducing the attractiveness of the illegal act.

The chapter is structured as follows. First, I examine the theoretical underpinnings of deterrence. Although the theory of deterrence is straightforward, misconceptions nonetheless persist. For instance, many criminologists mistakenly believe that criminals must be "rational" for deterrence to exist.

I then discuss the reasons why testing for deterrence in the data is not nearly as straightforward as it might initially appear. There are three main reasons. First, the deterrence model is a description of individual behavior, but most tests of the model rely on aggregate data due to data limitations. Second, it is often difficult to separate correlation and causality. To the extent that public policy on crime is itself affected by the level of crime (for example, more police are hired in response to a crime wave), standard statistical approaches like ordinary least squares regression do not reliably test the effectiveness of deterrence. Third, it is often extremely difficult to differentiate between deterrence and other competing hypotheses. In particular, incapacitation—a reduction in crime due to the fact that prisoners are quarantined from society at large and thus cannot commit crimes while incarcerated—is in most cases indistinguishable from deterrence. Thus, most purported tests of deterrence are in reality joint tests of deterrence and incapacitation.

The bulk of the chapter is devoted to assessing the existing empirical evidence on deterrence. In particular, I focus on four different settings where deterrence might be expected to arise: increases in the size of the police force, the scale of imprisonment, the death penalty, and victim precaution. Although there is an enormous empirical literature on the subject, many of these studies shed little light on deterrence as a consequence of failure to deal adequately with one or more of the pitfalls described above. As a result, the emphasis in this chapter is on a highly selective set of papers which I believe are most successful in overcoming these inherent empirical difficulties. More exhaustive surveys of the empirical research on issues related to deterrence can be found in Cameron (1988) and Nagin (1998). The best available evidence suggests that deterrence plays a nontrivial role in explaining differences in crime rates across time and space, but by itself deterrence falls far short of providing a complete explanation for the observed patterns of crime.

THE THEORY OF DETERRENCE

The idea underlying deterrence—that criminals respond to the costs and benefits of crime—featured prominently in the thinking of classical writers such as Bentham and Beccaria. In the modern era, however, deterrence received little attention from those studying crime until the seminal contribution of Becker (1968), which provided the first formal mathematical model of deterrence. Since that time, deterrence has been the focus of a great deal of research, both theoretical and empirical, especially among economists (for example, Stigler 1970, Ehrlich 1973, Posner 1977, Polinsky and Shavell 1984, Kaplow and Shavell 1999). Because the Becker model has so greatly influenced the way economists think about crime, it is sometimes simply referred to as the "economic model of crime."

Becker's model is one in which potential criminals are rational utility maximizers (in the sense that they use all information available in optimally choosing actions). Furthermore, there is complete information, that is, potential criminals know precisely the likelihood with which they will be caught if they commit a crime, as well as the punishment. The decision to commit crime is weighed against the best legitimate job opportunity. If the payoff to crime exceeds that of the best legitimate opportunity, then the crime is committed.

The Becker model is not intended to be an accurate, literal reflection of the world. In real life, people are not perfectly rational in their actions (especially when under the influence of drugs and alcohol as are many criminals at the time of their crimes). Individuals have less than perfect information about the probability they will be caught and the punishment they will receive if convicted.

Indeed, many of the specific predictions of the Becker model do not match real-world experiences well. For example, the model predicts that fines will be used as punishment rather than imprisonment and that all crimes will be punished with the maximum penalty, but with varying probabilities of apprehension. The primary contribution of the Becker model was not its predictions, but rather that it provided researchers with a simple framework for thinking about how the costs and benefits of crime influence criminal behavior. As a consequence, extensions of the Becker model do succeed in generating predictions that are consistent with various stylized facts in criminal justice: stiffer penalties for more severe offenses (Stigler 1970), harsher penalties for repeat offenders (Polinsky and Rubinfeld 1991), less than maximal penalties (Andreoni 1991), the use of prisons rather than fines (Levitt 1997b). Clotfelter (1978) and Shavell (1991) further extend the economic model of crime to incorporate a role for victim precaution (for example, installing car alarms or carrying concealed weapons).

In the simplest versions of deterrence, the key determinant influencing crime is the "expected punishment," which is simply the amount of prison time an offender will serve on average for committing a particular crime. The expected punishment, expressed mathematically, is the probability that a criminal is caught multiplied by the punishment if caught. Certainty and severity of punishment play equal roles in deterring crime in such models. Although not discussed as frequently, the swiftness of punishment is also likely to influence crime. The benefits of crime accrue immediately, but punishment is delivered with a delay. Because individuals tend to discount the importance of future events relative to the present, the faster punishment can be administered, the greater the predicted reduction in crime.

Because formal models of deterrence generally assume both that criminals are rational and that they have detailed knowledge of the certainty and severity of punishment, a misconception has arisen that deterrence cannot work in the absence of these restrictive assumptions. This claim, however, is patently false. The only requirement for deterrence to be present empirically is that criminals *on average* must respond to changes in the costs and benefits of crime. Some potential criminals may greatly understate the true likelihood of punishment and therefore go undeterred; other criminals may have exaggeratedly high estimates of the probability of detection and thus be "excessively" deterred. It is not rationality that is required for deterrence, but rather that people—including criminals—are capable of responding to incentives. This would seem to be a minimal hurdle to clear as incentives are a ubiquitous element of everyday life: People study to get good grades, work hard to get promoted, consume more of a good when the product's price falls, and so on. Even pigeons and rats show the ability to respond to incentives in laboratory experiments.

DIFFICULTIES IN TESTING
THE DETERRENCE HYPOTHESIS

Despite the simplicity of the logic underlying deterrence, it has proven surprisingly difficult to estimate the magnitude of deterrence empirically. As noted briefly at the beginning of this chapter, there are three primary obstacles that need to be overcome. First, deterrence is a model of individual-level behavior, but almost all relevant crime data are at the aggregate level such as those for cities, counties, states, or nations. When individual-level data on criminal activity are available, for example in the longitudinal data sets analyzed by Wolfgang et al. (1972) and Sampson and Laub (1993), all of the subjects are drawn from localized geographic areas. For example, in the classic Glueck and Glueck (1950) data set reanalyzed by Sampson and Laub, all of the subjects are from the Boston metropolitan area. Consequently, all individuals in the sample presumably face similar punishment regimes, making it difficult to test for deterrence. Tauchen et al. (1994) attempted to overcome this problem in data on a cohort of Philadelphia youths collected by Wolfgang et al. (1972) by using a particular individual's own arrest history as a proxy for expected punishment. This approach, however, is subject to criticism because past punishment history is likely to be correlated with unobserved factors that also influence an individual's criminal propensity. A similar criticism can be leveled at Witte (1980). The overwhelming majority of studies, however, have used aggregate data. While there is nothing inherently flawed in such an approach, aggregate data necessarily provide only an indirect test of individual-level behavior, leading to possible misinterpretation. This is especially true given that the available aggregate data based on reported crime statistics suffer from important weaknesses: For example, many crimes are never reported to the police and thus are not included in official records (O'Brien 1985).

The second difficulty in testing deterrence is differentiating between correlation and causality. If two variables are correlated, it simply means that they tend to move together. It does not necessarily demonstrate the presence of a causal relationship, or identify the direction of causality. Both for the purposes of testing a hypothesis and developing good public policy, only causal relationships are relevant. Standard empirical approaches typically used in studies of deterrence (for example, simple correlations or ordinary least squares regression analysis), however, identify correlations between variables, not causal relationships. The issue of correlation versus causality proves to be especially important in measuring deterrence because crime policy emerges from a political process. When crime is high, more money tends to be spent on the criminal justice system. As one example, large cities tend to have both many more police officers per capita and higher crime rates than smaller cities. Thus, there is a positive correlation between police and crime in a cross-section of cities, but it cannot plausibly be argued that the greater numbers of police *cause* the high crime. Rather, the reverse is true. If one wishes to determine the impact of police on crime, an alternative approach must be identified.

A third factor making it hard to test adequately the deterrence hypothesis is that empirically deterrence and incapacitation are very difficult to distinguish. Unlike deterrence, incapacitation is not a behavioral theory of crime, that is, incapacitation can exist even if no individual alters his or her behavior in response to incentives. Incapacitation simply asserts that repeat offenders will be unable to commit further crimes when imprisoned because they are isolated from society at large. The number of crimes prevented through incapacitation will be closely related to the expected punishment for crime, just like deterrence. As a consequence, most studies of the impact of criminal justice resources (which are hypothesized to impact crime through increases in expected punishment) are not tests of deterrence, but rather are joint tests of the combined crime-reducing impact of deterrence *and* incapacitation. Given that there is overwhelming evidence that many prisoners are frequent offenders when not incarcerated (Chaiken and Chaiken 1982, DiIulio and Piehl 1991), studies that attribute all of the crime reduction associated with increased punishment to deterrence are likely to overstate the true magnitude of the deterrent effect.

THE IMPACT OF POLICE ON CRIME

A logical place to begin a discussion of the impact of the criminal justice system on crime is with police, who represent the first line of defense against crime. An enormous literature on this topic emerged in the 1970s. Some of the earliest evidence comes from a quasi-randomized experiment conducted in Kansas City (Kelling et al. 1974). Five "proactive" beats were assigned two to three patrol cars per beat; five "reactive" beats were given no routine preventative patrols, although police of course responded to calls for service; and five beats maintained the standard level of patrol: one car per beat. The experiment ran for one year. A number of outcome variables were analyzed including reported crime rates, victim-derived crime rates, and citizen perceptions. Few statistical differences were found across the beats. The experiment, however, has been criticized on numerous grounds by Larson (1976). Perhaps most troubling is the fact that police response times were unaffected by the experiment. Thus, the practical differences in police services provided to the treatment and control beats, at least along one of the most important dimensions, was negligible. As a consequence, most researchers view this experiment as inconclusive.

A great number of studies were published that compared the relationship between crime rates and the number of police across cities or states at a given point in time (known as cross-sectional studies). Of the twenty-two studies of this type that Cameron (1988) surveys, eighteen find either no relationship or a *positive* relationship between the number of police and the crime rate. A positive relationship between police and crime means that places with more police also tend to have more crime. This result is contrary to the prediction of deterrence. The clear weakness of these studies is the failure to distinguish correlation from causality, a point made quite definitively by Fisher and Nagin (1978). Places with more severe crime problems respond by hiring more police. This induces a positive correlation between police and crime, but says little about the causal impact of hiring more police. The research conducted by Fisher and Nagin (1978) was part of an extremely influential National Academy of Sciences panel on deterrence that called into question the validity of all of the empirical work on the subject up to that time. Following the release of the scathing report of this panel, research on the impact of the number of police on crime virtually disappeared for almost two decades. Sherman (1992), in surveying the literature on police and crime, relegates discussion of this entire question to a footnote, devoting his attention instead to studies of policing strategy—that is, how to most effectively use a fixed number of officers.[1]

It was not until the 1990s that researchers returned to the task of estimating the impact of police on crime with a range of solutions to the difficulties raised by Fisher and Nagin (1978). Levitt (1997a) attempts to solve the question of reverse causality using an "instrumental variables" approach. The goal in such research is to identify a "natural experiment" which systematically affects the size of the police force, but is otherwise unrelated to crime. Levitt (1997a) uses mayoral and gubernatorial elections as such a source of variation in police forces. Empirically, it is shown that increases in the size of big-city police forces are disproportionately concentrated in election years, presumably engineered by politicians seeking the maximum electoral benefit. Having controlled for other government spending, demographic factors, and the state of the local economy, it seems plausible to argue that the impact of elections on crime through channels not taken into account in the analysis will be negligible, as is necessary for the instrumental variables strategy to yield interpretable results. Although imprecisely estimated, Levitt (1997a) finds additional police to be extremely effective in reducing crime: A 10 percent increase in the size of the police force is associated with a decrease in crime of 3–10 percent.

Marvell and Moody (1996) attack the same problem in a very different manner, but uncover similar results. Marvell and Moody (1996) employ a Granger-causality approach. One variable is said to "Granger-cause" another if changes in the first variable are associated with future changes in a second variable. Thus, Granger causality does not reflect causality in the typical sense of the word, but rather a temporal relationship between changes in two variables.[2] Using panel data for both U.S. states and large cities, Marvell and Moody (1996) find strong evidence that increases in police lower crime with a lag.[3] The magnitude of the effects are comparable to Levitt (1997a). While not direct causal evidence, the analysis of Marvell and Moody is nonetheless quite compelling.

A recent study, Corman and Mocan (2000), adopts yet another approach to answering this question. Corman and Mocan (2000) note that the problem of distinguishing correlation and causality in studies of police and crime arises partly as an artifact of using annual data. Police hiring occurs only with a lag after a rise in crime (empirically, they find the lag to be approximately six months). Using annual data, however, a rise in crime in the beginning of the year can trigger an increase in police later in the year, leading to spurious results. On the other hand, if one uses monthly data, a rise in crime will not trigger an increase in police immediately, allowing one to identify a short-run causal impact of police on crime. Corman and Mocan (2000) use monthly data for New York City covering the period 1970 through the 1990s. Their results suggest that a 10 percent increase in the size of the police force reduces crime by roughly 10 percent—the same magnitude as found in Levitt (1997a) and Marvell and Moody (1996).

Although each of the studies described above has limitations, it is remarkable that three papers employing such different approaches and data sets yield such consistent results. Together, these studies provide convincing evidence that increases in the number of police reduce crime.

Is the Decline in Crime Associated with More Police due to Deterrence?

The extent to which the decline in crime from more police is attributable to deterrence (as opposed to incapacitation, for instance) is an issue that has not been the subject of much research. If more police lead to more arrests and higher rates of imprisonment, then the impact of police need not be due to deterrence. Note, however, that the deterrence model has an ambiguous prediction, which may surprise the uninitiated, as to whether more police will lead to an increase or decrease in *arrests*. If criminals know that the probability of arrest for any particular offense has risen because of more police, fewer crimes should be committed. Thus, depending on the relative magnitude of those two effects (more arrests per crime, fewer crimes committed), the absolute number of arrests made may either rise or fall as the number of police rises.

The most compelling (albeit indirect) evidence to date on this issue comes from a clever study by McCormick and Tollison (1984), which uses a change in the number of referees in college basketball as a natural experiment for analyzing the response of behavior to increases in the probability of punishment. In this context, more referees correspond to more police, and the number of fouls called parallels the number of arrests made. McCormick and Tollison (1984) demonstrate that the switch from two to three referees per game is associated with a reduction in fouls called of over 30 percent. This result strongly suggests a deterrent effect in basketball, although it is unclear whether this result can be generalized to police.

Another study that attempts to disentangle the deterrence and incapacitation effects of arrests is Levitt (1998a). In general, it is difficult to do so because an increase in the expected punishment for a given crime, say robbery, is associated with a reduction in that crime through both channels, making it difficult to distinguish the two effects. Levitt (1998a), however, points out that when the expected punishment for robbery rises, deterrence predicts an *increase* in crimes that are substitutes for robbery (like burglary), but incapacitation predicts burglary should *fall*, as long as criminals are generalists.[4] Thus, by looking at how changes in punishment for one crime affect other crimes, deterrence and incapacitation can be isolated. Levitt (1998a) finds that deterrence is more important than incapacitation in explaining the link between arrest rates and crime, particularly for less serious offenses.

EXPECTED PUNISHMENT AND CRIME RATES

It is critical to the deterrence hypothesis that longer prison sentences be associated with reductions in crime. Because of both conceptual and data issues regarding the measurement of expected sentences, much of the research to date, however, has relied on other, less explicit tests of the link between expected punishment and crime. In particular, the focus of research has been on the relationship between the overall size of the prison population and crime rates.

The early literature on the subject, which focused exclusively on time-series patterns in the data, emphasized the fact that in spite of enormous increases in the U.S. prison population in the United States since the 1970s, crime rates did not begin to systematically fall until the 1990s (for example, Zimring and Hawkins 1991). Based on this evidence, these authors argue that both deterrence and incapacitation effects must be inconsequential and call for a dramatic reduction in the prison population. These analyses, however, fail to distinguish correlation from causality.[5] Assuming that the expected punishment per crime remains constant, any increase in the crime rate (for example, due to changing demographics [Wilson and Herrnstein 1985], economic fluctuations [Freeman 1995], or a decline in stable families and communities [Wilson 1987]) will translate one-for-one into an increase in the prison population. There is an essentially mechanical relationship binding the crime rate to the prison population. Thus, it is not at all surprising that aggregate crime and imprisonment rates might be positively correlated in some time periods.

More recent research has been far more careful in analyzing this issue. Marvell and Moody (1994), utilizing a panel-data set of U.S. states, demonstrate that the positive relationship between imprisonment rates and crime disappears when looked at within a state over time, as opposed to using cross-sectional data. Marvell and Moody (1994) estimate that a 10 percent increase in the size of the prison population reduces crime by about 1.5 percent.

While the research methodology employed in the preceding paragraph is superior to that of earlier studies, it goes only part of the way in isolating a causal link between prisons and crime. To more convincingly identify causality, a natural experiment approach has been utilized. Levitt (1996) uses prison-overcrowding litigation filed by the American Civil Liberties Union (ACLU) as an "exogenous" shock to the state prison population. In response to widespread prison overcrowding, the ACLU filed lawsuits against state prison systems on the basis of cruel and unusual punishment inflicted by the poor prison conditions. Years later, when these lawsuits had finally wound their way through the legal process, courts ordered these states to ameliorate prison overcrowding. This was often accomplished by releasing prisoners who otherwise would have been held. As Levitt (1996) demonstrates, crime rates jump sharply coincident with the release of prisoners in states affected by the lawsuits. The magnitude of the estimated relationship between the number of prisoners and crime is two to three times greater than that obtained by Marvell and Moody (1994).

The results above, while consistent with a deterrent effect of imprisonment, are extremely weak tests of deterrence because of the potential incapacitation effects of prisons (Chaiken and Chaiken 1982, DiIulio and Piehl 1991, Spelman 1994). The distinction between deterrence and incapacitation is of paramount importance in this context because of the differing implications that these two channels have for the effectiveness of policies such as "three strikes and you're out." Under such policies, repeat offenders are sentenced to extremely long prison terms designed to keep them off the streets permanently. If incapacitation is the operative factor, "three strikes" is not an efficient use of prison space. Eventually, prisons will be overflowing with aging inmates, most of whom no longer pose a threat to society as a result of the natural declining age crime profile (Blumstein et al. 1986). Greenwood et al. (1994), for instance, projected that annual prison expenditures in California would almost triple if "three strikes" were fully implemented. Such doomsday scenarios, however, completely ignore the role of deterrence. If deterrence works, then "three strikes" is an extremely attractive policy because the threat of punishment deters the potential criminal from committing the crimes in the first place. Since fewer crimes are committed, the prison population may actually decline when "three strikes" is implemented. The experience of California since the adoption of "three strikes" certainly appears to be more consistent with the predictions of deterrence than with the projections of Greenwood et al. (1994). Between 1994 and 1998, California's prison population grew at a rate only slightly above the national average (29 percent vs. 23 percent) and California's violent crime rate per capita fell 30 percent, compared to 20 percent for the rest of the nation.

Two further studies provide evidence for a deterrent effect of increases in expected punishment. Kessler and Levitt (1999) evaluate the impact of Proposition 8 in California, which instituted sentence enhancements for particular crimes, for example, crimes committed with a gun. Because those convicted of such crimes virtually always received prison sentences even without the sentence enhancements, Proposition 8 had no immediate effect on incapacitation. Only after the conventional prison term expires and the longer sentence due to the enhancement takes effect will the incapacitation effect begin to operate. Thus, any immediate decline in crime associated with passage of Proposition 8 must be due to deterrence, not incapacitation. Consistent with a deterrent effect, Kessler and Levitt (1999) find that crimes covered by Proposition 8 appear to fall immediately by about 4 percent relative to other states, whereas crimes not covered by Proposition 8 are unaffected. Crimes covered by the law continue to fall over time, suggesting that incapacitation is reducing crime once the sentence enhancements take hold.

A second study suggesting deterrence from increased punishment is Levitt (1998b), which looks at changing crime involvement with the transition from the juvenile to the adult criminal justice system. In those states in which the adult system is substantially more punitive than the juvenile system, criminal activity falls sharply when the age of majority is reached, whereas this is not the case in states where the juvenile and adult systems are similar in severity. The immediacy of the drop in crime when juveniles become subject to more severe adult sentences strongly suggests deterrence is at work, especially since juvenile records are sealed in most states so that criminals making the transition to the adult system start with clean records.

The studies discussed above attempt to infer the presence of deterrence based on observed criminal behavior. An alternative research strategy is to ask potential criminals about how the threat of punishment affects their behavior. This survey approach has the attractive feature of being quite direct. Survey responses, however, may not adequately reflect true behavior if criminals provide intentionally misleading answers, or if they are simply unaware of the reasons why they do or do not engage in certain patterns of behavior. By and large, survey responses are consistent with a deterrent effect of punishment, although the relationship is sometimes weak and deterrence is typically not the most powerful explanatory variable (see, for example, Saltzman et al. 1982). As an example of how deterrence appears in these surveys, two-thirds of prisoners interviewed by Van Voorhis et al. (1997) say that they agree or strongly agree with the statement that being sent to prison has "taught them a lesson" and that they "have given up criminal activity forever." A slightly different approach is adopted by Glassner et al. (1983), which reports the findings of a series of interviews with adolescents in New York who self-report a dramatic reduction in criminal involvement at the age of majority, that is, the age at which they become subject to the punishments of the adult court. As one youth who recently turned sixteen (the age of majority in New York) says, "When you are a boy, you can be put into a detention home. But you can go to jail now. Jail ain't no place to go." Another adolescent, interviewed in a juvenile detention facility, saw his one-to-four year sentence as "easy. I'll just do my year and get out; it ain't nothing." But he advised his friend who continued his criminal activity to stop "because he's 16 now; he'll go to jail."

CAPITAL PUNISHMENT

The deterrent effect of capital punishment has been the subject of extensive, spirited academic debate for more than two decades.[6] On the surface, capital punishment would appear to be an ideal means of testing deterrence. Because the alternative to execution is likely to be life in prison without parole, incapacitation is not an issue. Whether the prisoner is executed or not, he is unlikely ever to be released from prison.

On further reflection, however, it is clear that the rarity with which executions occur and the long lag between the crime and the eventual execution suggest that a rational criminal's decision-making is unlikely to be greatly affected by the presence of the death penalty. In 1997, seventy-four prisoners were executed in the United States—the highest total in thirty years. At the end of 1997, there were 3,335 inmates under a sentence of death, meaning that only about 2 percent of those on death row were executed. The execution rate on death row is only slightly greater than the rate of accidental and violent death for black males between the ages of 15 and 34. Among the subsample of individuals engaged in illegal activities, the death rates outside of prison are likely to be at least as high. Levitt and Venkatesh (2000) report a death rate of 7 percent annually for street-level drug sellers in the gang they analyze. Kennedy, Piehl, and Braga (1996) estimate violent death rates to be 1–2 percent annually among all gang members in Boston. Based on these figures, it is hard to believe that in modern America the fear of execution would be a driving force in a rational criminal's calculus. Furthermore, given the high discount rates of many criminals (Wilson and Herrnstein 1985) and the fact that many homicides are committed by individuals under the influence of alcohol or drugs that further foreshorten time horizons, it is hard to believe that punishment with such a long delay would be effective.

Given the infrequency of executions, it is not surprising that empirical estimates of any deterrent effect are extremely sensitive to modeling assumptions. Much of the evidence arguing in favor of a deterrent effect of capital punishment is based on the work of Ehrlich (for example, Ehrlich 1975, Ehrlich 1977, Ehrlich and Liu 1999). Ehrlich (1975), using national time-series data for the period 1932–1970, estimates that between one and eight lives are saved per execution. These results, however, depend critically on the years of data included in the analysis. If the sample ends in the mid-1960s, or is extended to include later years, the results often disappear (Passell and Taylor 1977, Forst et al. 1978, Leamer 1983). The importance of the late 1960s to the results is particularly worrisome because that was a time of sharp increases in all types of crime. Presumably, the death penalty only has a deterrent effect on crimes that are punished by death, so it is not plausible that the rise in property crime, robbery, and aggravated assault can be attributed to declining use of the death penalty in the late 1960s.

Ehrlich (1977) uses cross-sectional state-level data for the year 1940 and for the year 1950 to obtain estimates of the deterrent effect of capital punishment that are similar to his time-series estimates. As was noted in the earlier discussion of police, heterogeneity across states is an important concern, particularly since the use of the death penalty is heavily concentrated in a small number of Southern states. Cameron (1994) summarizes a number of articles that question the findings of Ehrlich (1977). Perhaps the most interesting of these studies is Bailey (1982), which finds no impact of the death penalty on police killings. One might expect police killings to be the type of homicide that is most sensitive to capital punishment since the death penalty is much more likely to be invoked against cop killers than murderers more generally.

Panel-data estimates of the impact of executions also yield mixed results. Lott and Landes (1999), using data from the 1970s to the 1990s, report finding that a one percentage point increase in the probability of execution for those committing murder is associated with a 7 percent reduction in the homicide rate. Katz et al. (2000), however, find that panel data estimates of the impact of the death penalty are very sensitive to the time period examined and the way in which one controls for unobserved differences across states and time periods.

Thus, it appears that the death penalty, at least as exercised in the United States, offers little concrete evidence either for or against deterrence.[7] Even if a substantial deterrent effect does exist, the amount of variation in crime rates induced by executions may simply be too small to be detected. Assuming a reduction of seven homicides per execution (a number consistent with Ehrlich 1975), observed levels of capital punishment would have a trivial impact on overall homicide rates. Even in Texas, the state that has executed far and away the most prisoners in recent years (a total of 144 executions between 1976 and 1997), executions would be predicted to have reduced the annual number of homicides in Texas by about fifty, or 2 percent of the overall rate. Given that the standard deviation in the annual number of homicides in Texas over this same time period is over 200, it is clearly a difficult challenge to extract the execution-related signal from the noise in homicide rates.

VICTIM PRECAUTION

Although the usual focus of deterrence is government expenditures on criminal justice, any action that raises the potential costs of committing crime would be predicted to have a deterrent effect. In the case of victim precautions, a critical distinction is required between actions that are or are not observable to the criminal prior to committing the criminal act (Clotfelter 1978, Shavell 1991). In the case of observable precautions, such as enclosing one's house with a fence, putting "The Club" on a steering wheel, or posting a "beware of dog" sign, criminals are likely to substitute other victims, for example, the house next door, for the protected targets. Such precautions may have "specific" deterrence (that is, protect the person who erects the fence), but may have little or no impact on aggregate crime because of substitution by criminals to other available victims. In stark contrast, unobservable victim precaution (for example, silent alarms or carrying concealed weapons) may have "general" deterrence since the criminal will not know in advance whether a particular victim is protected or not.

The possible deterrent effect of laws allowing citizens to carry concealed weapons has been the focus of heated debate in recent years. Lott and Mustard (1997) and Lott (1998) present panel-data evidence which argues for extremely large crime reductions associated with the passage of such laws. For instance, Lott (1998) estimates that states that allow citizens to carry concealed weapons experience a 7.7 percent decline in homicide and a 5.3 percent decline in rape (although only a 2.2 percent decline in robbery—the crime one might expect to fall the most).

The results in Lott and Mustard (1997) and Lott (1998) have been strongly challenged by a series of critics. Ludwig (1998) notes that juveniles are never allowed to carry concealed weapons. Thus, in states that pass laws allowing adults to carrying concealed weapons, criminals should substitute away from adult victims toward juvenile victims. In fact, however, Ludwig demonstrates that juvenile victimizations actually fall more with the passage of such laws than does adult victimization. Black and Nagin (1998) and Duggan (2000) both find that the evidence in favor of concealed weapons is sensitive to the construction of the sample, the precise econometric approach used, and the way the law is coded in the analysis. Duggan (2000), for instance, demonstrates that the statistical significance of the Lott and Mustard (1996) estimates disappears when one takes into account that data from counties within a state are not independent of one another as Lott and Mustard (1997) and Lott (1998) implicitly assume in their analysis. Ayres and Donohue (1999) find that extending the original sample, which ended in 1992, to include more recent data reverses the results: The passage of laws allowing for the carrying of concealed weapons appears to be associated with increasing rather than declining crime.

Unfortunately, outside of concealed weapons, there has been little empirical research on the issue of victim precaution. One exception is Ayres and Levitt (1998), which analyzes a different form of unobservable victim precaution: an anti-theft radio transmitter known as "Lojack." This device, hidden inside a vehicle, allows specially equipped police vehicles to remotely track a vehicle that has been stolen. There is no indication anywhere on the vehicle that Lojack has been installed, making it a prototypical example of unobservable victim precaution. Ayres and Levitt (1998) find that auto theft falls sharply when Lojack is introduced into a city, consistent with deterrence. The key to Lojack's effectiveness is attributable to the fact that Lojack leads police directly to "chop shops," where large numbers of stolen vehicles are stripped for parts. Without Lojack, finding such chop shops is extremely difficult for police. Other crimes do not appear to be strongly affected by Lojack, suggesting that auto thieves are not substituting into other crimes in large numbers. Nor is there evidence that the auto theft is being displaced geographically. If the estimates in the paper are correct, the number of cars equipped with Lojack is far below the social optimum—little of the benefit of deterrence accrues to the owner of the actual vehicle that has Lojack installed (the car may still be stolen because Lojack is unobservable). Instead the benefits are dispersed across all car owners.

CONCLUSION

Empirical evidence from a wide range of settings is consistent with the presence of a substantial deterrent effect. There is evidence that increases in police, the number of prisoners, sentence lengths, and victim precaution are all associated with reductions in crime through a deterrence channel. Deterrence alone, however, cannot adequately explain the differences across place and time in crime rates. Given the most reliable estimates of the impact of the criminal justice system on crime rates and the fraction of that impact that is attributable to deterrence, it seems unlikely that any more than 25 percent of the observed fluctuations in crime rates either across geographic areas or over time is due to deterrence. Thus, while deterrence is an important consideration in the development of public policy, it appears that other factors—family, community, demographics, and so on—are at least as influential. Nonetheless, to the extent that deterrence is a factor that can be readily influenced by public policy through changes in the criminal justice system, it may represent the quickest and most efficient way for government to influence criminal activity in the short run.

16

Prisons: A Policy Challenge

Alfred Blumstein

ESCALATING PRISON POPULATIONS

In a precursor to this volume, I began my essay[1] on prisons with the observation that "the most critical administrative problem facing the United States criminal justice system through the 1980s will be that of crowded prisons. Pressure will continue to mount for more and harsher prison sentences, seriously straining the already limited capacity of penal institutions."

That essay from which I quoted was written in 1981, and the period of the 1980s—and continuing into the 1990s—certainly bore out that forecast. That impact is displayed most vividly in Figure 16.1, which depicts the United States' incarceration rate (prisoners per capita) from 1924 to 1999. The fifty-year period from the early 1920s to the early 1970s was characterized by an impressively stable incarceration rate averaging 110 per 100,000 of general population (or 0.11 percent of the population) in prison at any time, with a coefficient of variation (the standard deviation of the series of annual observations divided by the mean of the series) of only 8 percent.

Indeed, that stability through a period that included such disruptive events as the Great Depression (when incarceration rates increased somewhat) as well as World War II (when the nation had greater needs for men of imprisonment age, and perhaps even better means for controlling them) was so striking (and was consistent with similar stability in a number of other countries) that it suggested a homeostatic process leading to this stability.[2]

Especially in light of what has happened more recently, the homeostatic process proposed seems to have been a reasonable characterization of that period, when incarceration policy was largely within the control of functionaries within the criminal justice system: When prisons got too

451

crowded (presumably because crime rates were climbing), then those functionaries could simply raise the threshold of the kind of offending behavior that warranted imprisonment, or lower the threshold of the assurance of "rehabilitation" before a prisoner was released on parole. Similarly, when more slack capacity became available (perhaps because crime rates were declining), then those shifts in threshold could be reversed.

However valid that explanation might have been for those first fifty years, it certainly did not explain the past twenty. Clearly, some fundamental societal and political changes gave rise to the steady climb seen in the right-hand portion of Figure 16.1. The 1999 incarceration rate of 476 per 100,000 (involving 1,366,721 prisoners in state and federal institutions)[3] was over 4.3 times the rate that had prevailed for the earlier fifty years. The nation had entered a new regime in which prison populations kept climbing, a clear replacement for the previously stable punishment policy.

In this chapter, we would like to identify some of the factors contributing to this changed environment, to explore some of the costs and benefits of this growth, and then to consider whether some policy changes might be appropriate. Some of the factors that are natural candidates for having contributed to that growth include crime rate changes (all else

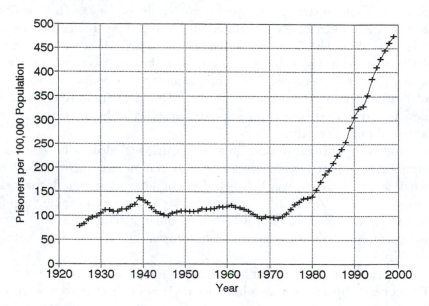

Figure 16.1
U. S. Incarceration Rate by Year, 1924–1999

equal, more crime should lead to more prisoners), demographic changes (more people in the crime-prone demographic groups, even with no change in demographic-specific criminal tendencies, should lead to more prisoners), and performance or policy changes within the criminal justice system (greater police effectiveness in arresting offenders or more punitive sanction policies should lead to more prisoners). A central policy shift that we have to consider is the "war on drugs" that became particularly intense in the late 1980s. That was a major new policy initiative, stimulated, of course, by the growth of the crack cocaine usage that began in the mid-1980s.

Once we identify the factors contributing to the growth of incarceration, we will examine some approaches that are being used or that might be considered to try to address the seemingly uncontrolled growth.

Growth of Incarceration by Crime Type

The growth in the incarceration rate has been far from uniform across all crime types. Figure 16.2 presents data on the growth in the adult[4] incarceration rate from 1980 to 1996 for six different types of crime, with particular emphasis on the six crime types that account for three-quarters of state prison populations: murder, robbery, aggravated assault, burglary, drugs, and sexual assaults.[5] In terms of the number of prisoners, there were 234,000 prisoners for the six offenses in 1980. By 1996, this total had grown to 860,000, a 268 percent increase.

The most striking observation from Figure 16.2 is the growth in the incarceration of drug offenders. In the 17 years from 1980 to 1996, drugs climbed from the single offense with almost the fewest prisoners to the one with by far the largest number. There were an estimated 23,900 state and federal prisoners for drug offenses in 1980, which represented an incarceration rate of less than 15 per 100,000 adults. By 1996, that incarceration rate had grown to 148 per 100,000, more than a ninefold increase. The drug incarceration rate in 1996 was about equal to the rate that had prevailed for fifty years for the entire U.S. prison system.

Two other offense types that have grown appreciably are aggravated assault (from 14 inmates per 100,000 adults in 1980 to 50 per 100,000 in 1996) and sexual assault (from 13 per 100,000 to 52 per 100,000 in 1996), about a quadrupling for each. The rate for murder grew from 22 per 100,000 adults to a rate of 57, a growth rate of 164 percent. The other offense types (robbery and burglary) grew over that period, but by less than 100 percent: 54 percent for robbery and 81 percent for burglary.

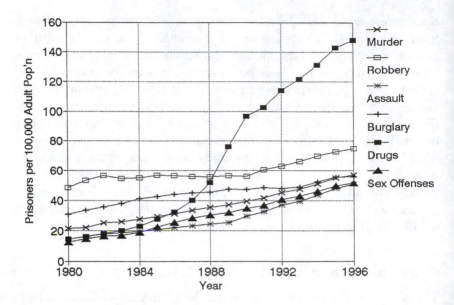

Figure 16.2
Incarceration Rate for Six Types of Crime, 1980–1996

It is clear that a major component of the overall growth is attributable to the increase in the drug offending. About 45 percent of the growth in the total incarceration rate for these six offenses from 1980 to 1996 is attributable to an increase in the number of drug offenders. If one includes all other crime types, such as other violent offenses (e.g., negligent manslaughter, reckless endangerment, kidnapping), other property offenses (e.g., motor-vehicle theft, fraud, arson, and larceny) and public-order offenses (e.g., drunk driving, weapons offenses, and the various non-drug vice crimes), then this reduces the contribution of the growth in drug incarceration to 33 percent of the total growth in incarceration.

Trends in Crime Rates

In order to examine the first of these alternative explanations—the growth in crime rates—we can examine the Uniform Crime Reports (UCR) crime rates. These rates are tabulated by the FBI each year based on reports submitted by police departments, which in turn receive reports of crimes, usually from individual victims.[6] The two crime types for which the reports are probably most reliable and well-defined are those for murder and robbery; these are also the two most prevalent violent crimes in prison, accounting respectively for 11.8 and 14.0 percent of prison inmates in 1999.[7]

Figure 16.3 presents a graph of the annual reported rates of robbery and of murder (whose rate is scaled up by a factor of 25 to bring it into the same numeric range as robbery for ease of comparison). As is evident from the figure, the reported crime rates for these two crimes over this period of dramatic growth in prison population have fluctuated somewhat, but have generally remained within a fairly confined range of 200 to 250 per 100,000 population for robbery and 8 to 10 per 100,000 for murder. Both the murder and the robbery rates peaked in about 1980, declined through the early 1980s, and then climbed again during the late 1980s with the spawning of the crack epidemic and the "war on drugs." Both rates peaked in 1991, and have since declined quite steadily, although murder had a slight blip in 1993. By 1999, both had reached levels that were the lowest seen in over 30 years, and well below the window of oscillation that prevailed from 1972 through1995. The prison population continued to grow despite—or some would argue because of—these strong downward trends in the crimes. Indeed, sorting out the causal direction involved here is a major challenge.

Figure 16.4 compares the time series of the reported crime rate for the six offenses considered in Figure 16.2. Since imprisonment involves adults almost exclusively, in examining trends in offending we are interested primarily in the *adult* offending rate. This is obtained by partitioning the UCR reported crime rate in proportion to the fraction of arrestees for that crime type who are adults. That adult fraction varies across the crime types, lowest for burglary (63 percent) and robbery (73 percent) and highest for murder (89 percent) and drug offenses (88 percent).

With this focus on adults, we can examine the trend in the offense rate (per 100,000 adults) for each crime type based on UCR reports. Since there is no comparable independent information on trends in the rate of drug *offending* other than through arrest, we display for the drug "offense" rate the adult *arrest* rate.

The first observation from Figure 16.4 is that only two offense types— drugs and assault—show a clear upward trend over this period. The drug arrest rate has the sharpest growth overall; the rate rose rapidly during the 1980s, peaked in 1989 at almost 2.5 times the 1980 rate, hit a trough in 1991 to 1993, and began to rise again, almost reaching the 1989 peak again in 1996. Because "drug offending" is measured through arrest rather than through reported crimes as with the other crime types, and because

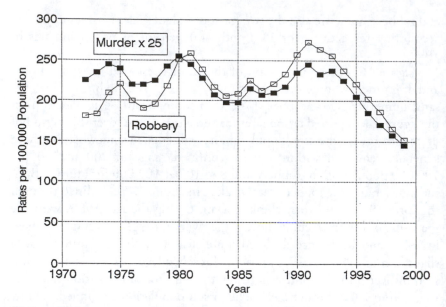

Figure 16.3
UCR Murder and Robbery Rates, 1970–1999

drug arrest policies can be highly discretionary, it is difficult to distinguish how much of the trend is attributable to an increase in drug offending and how much is due to changes in drug enforcement and arrest policies.[8]

The growth in aggravated assault is probably associated, at least in part, with an upward trend in the official recording of domestic assaults, especially beginning in the mid-1980s.[9] It is also possible that the inevitably subjective threshold between "aggravated" and "simple" assault in police reports to the UCR has been shifting downward. In a comparison of assaults reported to the police in the UCR and as reported by victims in the National Crime Victimization Survey (NCVS),[10] the trends for the other crimes are much closer to each other and are much flatter. Murder and robbery, the two most serious violent crimes being considered here, are seen to track each other fairly closely (as they did in Figure 16.3), and to be relatively flat following the declines in the early 1980s. Sexual assault, here measured by reports of forcible rape, also follows a somewhat similar pattern.

Burglary is the only crime type with a clear downward trend, first in the early 1980s and subsequently in the 1990s. Baumer et al. (1998) attribute this to a preference for robbery over burglary by crack users: they were in a

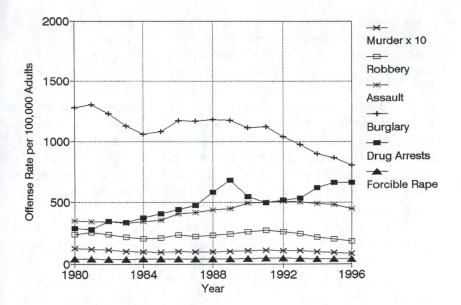

Figure 16.4
Offense Rate for Six Crime Types, 1980–1996

hurry to get the money to buy their drugs, and robbery offers a much shorter time interval than burglary from offense to ready cash. Also, because there were significant increases in sanctions for burglary from 1980 to 1996 that were unmatched by changes in robbery sanctions, the relative unattractiveness of robbery from the perspective of deterrence was diminished. All of these considerations could contribute to the substitution of robbery for burglary, especially for drug users anxious to get buy money.

Aside from drug offenses, murder, robbery, and burglary are the three most prevalent offenses represented in prison, together accounting for over half of the prisoners. It is clear that the rates of these three crimes have not increased dramatically over the past twenty years, thereby making it very unlikely that the growth in prison population was a consequence of growing crime rates.

As a further, related observation, until the late 1990s, crime rates have also not *decreased* dramatically either, perhaps suggesting that the considerable growth in prison population (more than quadrupling over the past twenty-five years) has not succeeded in significantly *reducing* the crime rate. But finding the reasons for that limited response to the increase in sanctions is complex. Much of the increase in prison population is attributable to the dramatic increase in incarceration for drug offenses. Inmates sentenced for a drug offense accounted for 29 percent of the increase in the prison population from 1980 to 1996 (Blumstein and Beck, 1999, Table 3), more than twice the contribution of any other crime type. While that incarceration is unlikely to have had much impact on the rate of drug offending (largely because drug offending is predominantly demand driven, and so the market readily recruited replacements—primarily inner-city juveniles—for incarcerated or deterred drug sellers by new recruits), it should have had an effect of incapacitating the other offenses that at least some of the incarcerated drug offenders may have committed if they were free.

The crime trends of the late 1990s, with steady declines from 1994 through 1999 (see Figure 16.3 for the declines in murder and robbery) have prompted some observers to point to the negative association between that crime decline and the growth in incarceration during the same period (the most recent portion of Figure 16.1) and claim that incarceration explains the crime decline. It should be evident that that so simplistic an analysis cannot provide the basis for generating an estimate of its impact. After all, in the late 1980s, during the period of the sharpest growth in imprisonment, violence was also increasing rather sharply. A much more subtle analysis examining the crime reduction from what it might otherwise have been, during periods of crime increase as well as decline, is heeded.

Two different approaches to such analyses are undertaken in Blumstein and Wallman (2000) by Spelman (2000) and Rosenfeld (2000). Spelman pursues a "top-down" approach using estimates from the literature of the "elasticity" of crime with respect to incarceration rates (i.e., the percent crime reduction associated with a 1-percent increase in incarceration rate). Spelman uses an elasticity measure of 0.35 to estimate a reduction from what the crime rate would have been if the incarceration rate had not increased. Thus, he can attribute an incarceration effect on crime rates even during the periods when crime rates were increasing. One result of his calculation is an estimate that about one-quarter of the crime drop of the 1990s can be attributed to the growth in incarceration during that period, the other three-quarters attributable to the other factors emphasized in Blumstein and Wallman (2000)—primarily the mutually supporting combination of control of guns in young people's hands, the decline in new users in crack and the consequent reduction in the recruitment of young people as sellers, and the robust economy which provided legitimate employment and the associated incentive for conformity to the young people who might otherwise have been recruited into drug markets.

A different "bottoms-up" approach was taken by Rosenfeld to estimate the contribution of the incapacitative effect of incarceration on the crime drop. He estimated that the rate at which people in prison would commit homicide if they were on the outside would be comparable to the homicide rate in the most disadvantaged neighborhoods of an urban area, and he estimated that rate to be 150 per 100,000 or about 25 times the rate for the nation as a whole. With that estimate, he also attributes about 25 percent of the crime drop in the 1990s to this incapacitative effect, an estimate similar to Spelman's. But he also notes that the cost of that effect is considerable—about $13.3 million dollars to incarcerate 100,000 offenders at a cost of $20,000 per year to avert 150 homicides (or to incarcerate 667 offenders to avert one homicide).

These issues highlight the contradiction to the simplistic arguments that incarceration accounts for all or none of crime changes. It certainly should account for some reduction of what the crime rate would have been in the absence of the prison growth. but still leaves us with the difficult question of isolating the other exogenous factors contributing to crime changes. These could include economic conditions, especially in the poorest neighborhoods where street crime is most prevalent; policing efforts to control crime, especially to keep guns away from the most irresponsible hands like those of juveniles and felons; activities of drug markets and the crime associated with them, both by drug users to get money to buy the drugs and by drug sellers who resort to violence for dispute resolution because they are precluded from participating in normal civil forums to resolve their disputes.

It is also possible that the effects of incarceration are muted by the criminalization effects of imprisonment. Golub (1992), for example, suggests that the incapacitative effect is counteracted by a delay in the termination of criminal careers of those incarcerated. Then, when they leave prison, they resume their criminal career at the point they left them when they went in to prison, with no evidence of termination in prison. More generally, it is possible that the criminalization experience of prison (resulting from interacting intensely with a criminal subculture and developing associated skills and network connections) contributed to an increase in criminal propensity to the large numbers of people being released from prison. This effect would have been amplified by their difficulty in finding legitimate employments because of their prison record. This would be expected especially to be the case with the sizable fraction of drug prisoners who were not involved in other forms of criminality.

Shifts in Policies

It is clear, however, that there has been a real increase in sanctions imposed per crime committed. This is reflected in an increase in the probability of incarceration following a crime as well as an increase in time served.[11] The increase in incarceration probability has been documented by Langan (1991), and the increase in both probability of incarceration and time served by crime type by Cohen and Canela-Cacho (1994). These shifts should have had some deterrent effect on crime rates, and almost certainly had an incapacitation effect on these crimes.

Blumstein and Beck (1999) examined the factors contributing to the growth in prison population from 1980 to 1996 at four possible stages: 1) increase in crime, 2) increase in arrests per crime (a measure of police effectiveness), 3) increase in prison commitments per arrest (a measure of prosecutorial effectiveness and judicial punitiveness), and 4) increase in time served (a measure of judicial punitiveness—sometimes required by legislative mandates—and parole restrictiveness in delaying a release or forcing a recommitment, especially for technical violations). They analyzed the growth at each of these stages for each of six crime types (murder, robbery, assault, burglary, drug arrests, and sexual assault) that account for over 75 percent of state prison populations.

The previous section notes that virtually none of the increase was attributable to an increase in crime with the exception of the "drug arrests," which certainly did increase. They found no significant trend for any of the five crime types (other than drugs) in arrests per crime, a measure of police effectiveness; this was somewhat surprising in light of the important changes in police management and in police technology that have occurred over that period.

The dominant changes have been in the later two stages of the system, commitments per arrest and time served.[12] For the five crime types other than drugs, commitments accounted for 42 percent of the growth and time served accounted for 58 percent (Blumstein and Beck, p. 43). When one includes drugs, the relative contributions are reversed, since the commitments per arrest for drugs grew more rapidly than time served. Time served was a particularly important contributor to prison population growth in the 1990s, as is evident from Figure 16.5. Important contributors to the growth in time served were longer sentences, often mandated

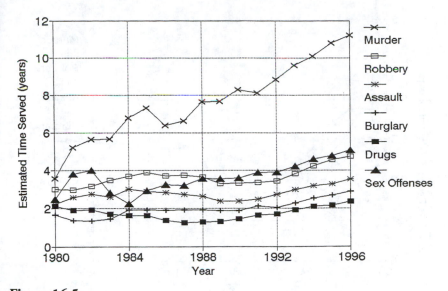

Figure 16.5
Estimated Time Served in Prison for Six Crime Types, 1990–1996
Note: This includes time served for parole violations; time served is estimated for
each year as the ratio of current prisoners to new commitments in that year.

by mandatory-minimum sentencing laws and by federal incentives offered
through the Truth in Sentencing Act, which awarded funds to states that
kept their offenders—particularly those serving time for violent offenses—
in prison for at least 85 percent of their sentences.

Perhaps an even more important contributor has been the growing
toughness on the part of the parole system. This has resulted in longer
delays before individuals are let out on parole; perhaps more important,
there has been a greater readiness to recommit a parolee to prison for technical violations. One of the important technical requirements of parole is
abstention from drugs, an entirely reasonable requirement since an estimated 80 percent of prisoners face a drug problem. Since drug testing has
become such a widespread aspect of parole, recommitment for dirty urine
has become a major contributor to the prison growth. This growth in
parole's contribution to admissions is evident in Figure 16.6, which displays the ratio of parole violators to the total prison admissions for each
crime type. Murder is the crime type with the lowest percent of parole
violators; murderers rarely receive parole, and they are rarely released until
the parole authorities are quite confident of their low risk. Sex offenders
have the highest ratio of parole violators; as shown in Figure 16.6, over 50

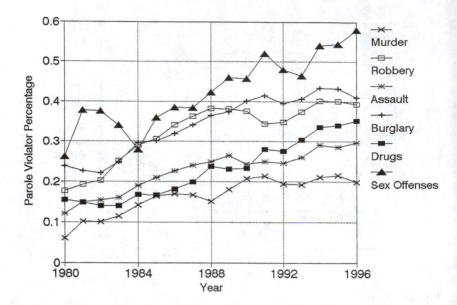

Figure 16.6

Parole Violators Admitted to Prisons for Six Crime Types, 1990–1996

Note: This includes parole violators plus new court commitments in that year.

percent of the sex offenders admitted to prison come in as parole violators. It is not clear how much this is attributable to their high rates of recidivism in sex crimes or to the special surveillance of sex offenders by parole authorities due to the public's sensitivity to those offenses.

Since the growth is so sensitive to policy shifts, it is important to explore the factors that have contributed to those shifts. The period of the 1980s and beyond saw a major shift in the political environment, and hence the policies related to imprisonment. For most of the first two-thirds of the twentieth century, the dominant perspective on imprisonment viewed it as a vehicle for "correction" or "rehabilitation." The notion was that upon release, a prisoner should be less likely to commit crimes. Prison professionals would recommend an offender's release when he was judged to be "rehabilitated."

But the faith in rehabilitation was severely challenged in the early and mid-1970s by a succession of experimental studies that evaluated a variety of alternative rehabilitative strategies. The dominant finding of these studies of adults was a "null effect," that is, that no particular approach consistently works any better than any other in changing post-release criminal behavior.[13] The implication was that individual traits of offenders and of the environment to which they are returned after release may have far more influence on subsequent recidivism than exposure to any particular rehabilitative program.

Controversy remains between those who contend that prison makes criminals better and those who believe it makes them worse. The former group argues that prison improves some criminals by virtue of its "specific deterrent" effect (i.e., its unpleasantness discourages future criminality by the individual who is imprisoned) or its rehabilitative effects (i.e., the prisoner is taught skills that enable him to function more effectively in the community). The rehabilitative argument has largely diminished since rehabilitative programs in prisons are far less prevalent than they once were, perhaps because of a loss of faith in their effectiveness or because of tightness of resources as prison populations have grown to consume all available space in the institution.

Others argue to the contrary that prison is harmful because it socializes prisoners, especially younger ones, into a hardened criminal culture. The frequent null-effect finding does not necessarily invalidate either of these positions, but it does suggest that there is probably merit on both sides, and that the opposing effects roughly balance each other in the aggregate. Some individuals emerge from prison with sufficient distaste for the experience—and sufficient control over their own subsequent behavior—to avoid the risk of subsequent imprisonment by desisting from crime. Others are socialized into a criminal culture—or at least are frustrated by the limitations they find in the legitimate labor market—and may then commit more and more serious crimes than they might otherwise have committed.

If one had a sure means of distinguishing those who would benefit from prison from those who would be harmed by it, and if judges were willing to employ such means (recognizing that inequitable treatment would result), then there might be a more significant rehabilitative effect from imprisonment. So far, however, criminal justice authorities have been saved from having to face the legal and ethical dilemmas involved in making such decisions by the inability of anyone to offer a valid method of identifying the appropriate candidates for rehabilitation through imprisonment.

The loss of confidence in rehabilitation has contributed significantly to the growth in prison populations. It is ironic that the initial assault on the rehabilitation approach came from a de-incarceration perspective which argued that because there was so little the criminal justice system could do to change behavior, there should be less intervention with offenders. They also claimed that those exercising the release authority—parole boards and their associated professionals—were engaged in an arbitrary exercise of power over individuals' liberty, and so declaimed the disparity of treatment that resulted.

To some degree, these arguments about disparity were accepted, and there were a variety of attempts to limit discretion over the time served by prisoners. Some of these emerged from the parole boards themselves, and included structured parole guidelines, with formulations on the additional time to be served based on attributes of the offender as well as on the court's sentence. Legislatures passed determinate-sentencing laws, initially intended to prescribe by statute the time to be served for each offense category, with "enhancements" for certain aggravating factors like gun use or inflicting serious bodily injury.

Rather than diminish or even limit the use of imprisonment, as the initial advocates wished, this political shift transferred the emphasis away from rehabilitation to the more explicitly punitive deterrent and incapacitative effects of prison as the only means left to the criminal justice system to address the objective of reducing crime. This reflected a pressure for greater retribution and an intensified desire by the public for crime control. Judges have also felt the influence of the growing public hostility toward criminals and of increasing demands for severe punishment, and have undoubtedly responded to those pressures.

The standards for what level of punishment constitutes "just deserts" have thus been increasing. Parole boards especially, which were subject to criticism in the 1980s for releasing prisoners before they served their "full sentences," responded to the political environment and became more cautious about who they released and when they did so. They also became more aggressive about returning parole violators to prison. All these changes brought control over sanction policy out of the criminal justice system and into the open political arena. It opened the door for changes in legislation and in practice that have contributed to the uncontrolled growth of prison populations that characterized the late 1970s through the 1990s.

Once the policy moved into the political arena, little could be done to recapture concern for limiting prison populations. The public, concerned as it always is about crime, has little sympathy for the offenders, and responded with enthusiasm to political calls for increasing sentence severity. Wherever judges are elected, the campaign commercial involving a prison cell door being slammed shut has become a widespread cliché. In a modern age of rapid media response, many political figures find it attractive to follow the report of any heinous crime with a call for increasing the sentence for that kind of crime. If some judge was found to have sentenced an offender to probation, then that was taken as evidence of the irresponsible leniency of the entire judiciary, and so a bill calling for mandatory minimum sentences would be introduced. In an evolving political environment where every campaign manager is looking for ways to label an opponent as "soft on crime," once such bills got to the floor of a legislature, they would be passed with overwhelming majorities. It was left largely to the legislative skill and political courage of the chairs of the judiciary committees to bottle up bills that were irresponsible.

The result of this process has been a major transfer of discretion within the criminal justice system to the prosecutor, mostly from the judge. It is the prosecutor who decides what charges to file in a particular case, what charge revisions to accept in exchange for a guilty plea, and how the charge relates to various laws limiting sentencing discretion in particular cases. Since prosecutors tend to deal with each case as a discrete entity, it is difficult to get them to pay particular attention to aggregate effects like impacts on prison populations. Also, since prosecutors are almost always elected to office, and usually have ambitions for higher office, it is consistent with their professional responsibilities as well as their political ambition to be seen demanding higher sanctions. Even if they agree that such sanctions may not apply in a particular case, it strengthens their negotiating position in a plea bargain to be able to threaten a charge that would result in a severe sanction if the defendant does not accept the plea bargain.

There have been some attempts to restrain this process. The most notable is the creation of sentencing commissions, either by action of the judiciary or by statute. The first sentencing commission was established in 1978, and commissions now exist in 19 states, the District of Columbia, and the federal government. Such commissions are given the assignment of creating a coherent schedule of sentences that reflect both the gravity of the offense committed and the prior record of the convicted offender. In some cases, the commissions are expected to assure that their sentencing schedule is compatible with the available capacity of the state prison system. Most, whether required to do so or not, take some account of the impact of their sentencing schedules on prison populations, and can recommend additional construction to the legislature if that is needed.

One of the intentions in creating sentencing commissions has been to take the establishment of sentencing out of the hands of the legislative process and its political pressures. That has not prevented legislatures, including the Congress, even after creating a sentencing commission, from enacting mandatory-minimum sentences, even when that would distort the coherence of the established sentencing schedule. Such legislation inevitably takes precedence over the rules of a sentencing commission.

The structural arrangements for decision-making in legislatures or within the criminal justice system regarding sentencing policy are such that the costs associated with increased punitiveness (i.e., prison crowding, larger corrections budgets) are almost never faced directly by those who act punitively (e.g., legislators, prosecutors, judges). Thus, it is easy for these decision-makers to respond to the public's demands for harsher measures. In the legislative process, when new sentencing legislation is proposed, it is almost always addressed by a judiciary committee, and, in most cases, never has to face an impact estimate on either prison population or budget expenditure, thereby insulating the judiciary committee members from any direct concern for such impacts. That makes it easier for the legislation to pass, and the appropriations committee simply has to provide the funding for its impact, usually several years later. In most states, this has contributed to the steady increase in the severity of sentences and the growth in prison populations.

The Crack Cocaine Epidemic and the Drug War

The other major element that has driven the issue of prison populations is the emergence of the crack-cocaine epidemic that began in the early 1980s and led to a massive criminal-justice response to that problem.

The drug problem is clearly an issue of serious concern to the American public. Many people are debilitated by taking drugs, and there is particular concern by parents that their children, whom they see as particularly vulnerable, will become captured by drugs. Further, there is a profound nexus between drugs and crime more generally. In 1997, 49 percent of state prisoners reported that they had ever used cocaine or crack, the single most popular drug other than marijuana, 34 percent reported that they had used cocaine or crack regularly, and 15 percent reported that they were using cocaine or crack at the time they committed the crime that led to their current imprisonment.[14]

Given the seriousness of the problem, the American public in the mid-1980s vigorously demanded that something be done about the drug problem. Democratic political systems require a strong response to such vigorously articulated demand—even when there is no clear means of effective response. Unfortunately, our political system has learned an overly simplistic trick: it responds to such pressures by sternly demanding increased

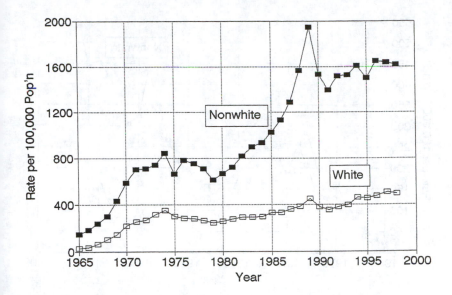

Figure 16.7a
Drug Arrest Rate, Adult

punishment. This approach has been found to be strikingly effective—not in solving the problem, but in alleviating the political pressure to "do something." The public generally seems to accept this approach to almost any behavior it finds objectionable, and without much questioning as to whether it will be effective in the particular context of concern.

As a result, there has been a succession of punitive efforts to attack the drug trade. Many states have adopted mandatory-minimum sentences for drug dealing that are comparable to the sentences for homicide. The consequence of these efforts has been a dramatic growth in the number of arrests for drug offenses and the filling of prisons with drug offenders.

Figures 16.7a and 16.7b show the growth from 1965 to 1992 in arrest rates for adults and juveniles for drug offenses, by race.[15] Since the early 1970s, the rate for white adults has been fairly steady, rising slowly to about 500 per 100,000. On the other hand, the rate for nonwhites (primarily African-Americans) rose rapidly between 1980 to 1985, and then accelerated exponentially at an annual rate of about 15 to 20 percent per year until it reached a peak in 1989, and then continued at a high rate.

The growth in drug arrests for juveniles, depicted in Figure 16.7b, is rather different from that for adults. From 1965 until about 1980, arrest rates for white and nonwhite juveniles were very similar; indeed, from

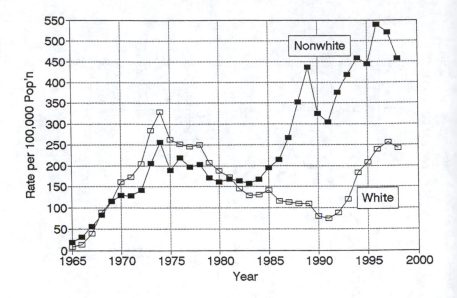

Figure 16.7b
Drug Arrest Rate, Juveniles

1970 until 1980, the arrest rate for whites was higher than for nonwhites, quite an unusual occurrence in arrest statistics. But arrest rates for both groups were growing from a rate of about 10 per 100,000 juveniles in 1965 to a peak about 30 times higher in 1974 (329 for whites and 257 for nonwhites).

Most of the arrests of juveniles during that period were for marijuana offenses. Following the 1974 peak there was a degree of decriminalization of marijuana that gave rise to a steady decline in the arrest rate for whites until it began to climb again in 1992. The rate for non-white juveniles also declined, but it began a sharp rise in 1985, more than doubling by the 1989 peak. Comparing 16.7b with Figure 16.2 suggests that the response by the drug markets to the major growth in incarceration of drug offenders was the recruitment of non-white juveniles from inner-city neighborhoods as replacements for the incarcerated older sellers in order to meet the growing demand for crack that characterized the mid-1980s.

The intensity of the crackdown on drug offenders shows itself in prison populations. In 1998, 58 percent of the prisoners in federal prisons and 21 percent of those in state prisons were there on a drug charge.[16] This contrasts sharply with the rates in 1986, twelve years earlier, when drug offenders accounted for only 8.6 percent of state prisoners.[17] As shown in

Figure 16.2, the growth since 1980 has been very dramatic, and represents a considerable cost to the criminal justice system. The 300,000 prisoners in federal and state prisons on drug charges represent an annual operating cost of about $6 billion.

Despite the enormous magnitude of the efforts and the impacts on the criminal justice system, accepting those costs would not necessarily be unreasonable if the approach was truly effective in reducing drug abuse. There is, however, no indication that the efforts have been at all successful. Of course, that result is not at all surprising. Anyone who is removed from the street is likely to be replaced by drawing from the queue of replacement dealers ready to join the industry. It may take some time for recruitment and training, but experience shows that replacement is easy and rapid.

A similar situation applies to general deterrence. One of the rationales most frequently cited for increasing the level of drug sanctions is that sellers will be deterred from engaging in drug transactions. There is little question that some actual or potential sellers, learning of the severe sanctions, are indeed deterred. But as long as there remain willing replacements, that deterrent effect is of little import. As long as the market demand persists and there is a continued supply of sellers, there should be little effect on drug transactions. Reports from the streets in the 1990s (e.g., Johnson et al. 2000) indicate the importance of group norms in having the most powerful effect on drug demand: as word spread of the negative effect of crack on parents and older siblings, crack use became very unfashionable and demand by new users dropped markedly.

It is difficult to discern whether the continued escalation of sanctions has been carried out in ignorance of these basic insights, or whether the policies have been adopted more cynically. It is not unreasonable to believe that the people who establish the high-sanction policies fully understand the limitations of the policies but need some means to respond to the public pressure to "do something." Lacking any better alternative to propose, they merely increase the sanctions, not so much because they think it will work, but because they have come to realize that it is an effective way to relieve the political pressure.

The basic observation about drug markets is that they are inherently demand driven. As long as the demand is there, a supply network will emerge to satisfy that demand. While efforts to assault the supply side may have some disruptive effects in the short term, the ultimate need is to reduce the demand in order to have an effect on drug abuse in the society. This require efforts in treatment of current users and prevention of potential users.

Demographic Effects on Prison Populations

Oddly, the growth of the prison population through the 1980s came at a time when the prospects appeared reasonably bright with respect to crime, at least initially. Crime rates, which are extremely age-sensitive, were expected to decline during the 1980s as the large birth cohorts of the post-war baby boom (those cohorts born in the period 1947 to 1962) passed out of their late teens (the years of most active criminal activity) into their early twenties and beyond.

The age-sensitivity of criminal activity is illustrated by the age-crime curves (age-specific arrest rates), which peak in the 16–18 age range, and then drop quickly, falling to about half the peak rate in the early 20s for the property crimes and for robbery (which is certainly a property crime from the viewpoint of the offender, even though its violent nature has it classed as a "violent crime" in UCR tabulations), and in the mid-30s for the personal assault crimes.

Since age is so salient a factor in crime commission, we also need information on the changing age composition of the American population.[18] This is reflected in Figure 16.8, which depicts the number of people at each age in the U.S. population in 2000.[19] If we think of 18 as being a peak crime age, then the people who were 18 in 1980 are 38 in 2000. From Figure 16.8, it is apparent that those people (and those slightly older) were among the largest cohorts in U.S. demographic history. Thus, if the age-specific rates were unaffected by cohort size, then larger cohorts should give rise to a larger number of crimes. In fact, there is some evidence[20] that larger cohort sizes lead to an increase in the age-specific crime rates for those cohorts, amplifying the composition effect of the larger cohort size alone. Easterlin (1980) argues that if there are more people in the high-crime ages, they reinforce each other in their crime-committing propensity, and also tend to overwhelm the formal and informal forces of control.

These demographic effects on crime and on prison populations were examined in a study that used data reflecting demographic changes and policy choices of the 1970s.[21] Data from Pennsylvania were used to make projections about crime and prison populations based on trends displayed during the 1970s. During that time, policy was fairly stationary, so that the results were driven strongly by demographic shifts,[22] which were changing rather rapidly as the baby boom generation passed through their teens and twenties. The study estimated that crime rates would reach a peak in 1980 and then decline subsequently. The predicted peak actually occurred in Pennsylvania and in the United States generally, as shown in Figure 16.3.

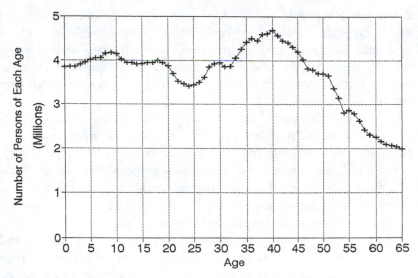

Figure 16.8
Age of U.S. Population in 2000

Based on those demographic considerations, the downturn of the early 1980s was expected to continue until the early 1990s, when the "echo boomers"—the children of the "baby boomers"—were expected to enter the peak crime age. As can be seen from Figure 16.8, the smallest age cohort relevant to the crime problem in the United States is the cohort born in 1976; this group was about 24 in 2000, and so its criminal activity should diminish subsequently. But subsequent cohorts will be larger, and so demographic factors should re-emerge as contributing to crime growth in the first decade of the twenty-first century.

Of course, demographic shifts are only one of the many factors influencing crime rates. Even though crime rates in the early 1980s followed demographic influences, other factors assumed much greater importance in the late 1980s, particularly the crack-cocaine epidemic—and all its consequences—that began in the mid-1980s, reached a peak in the early 1990s, and declined subsequently.

The age shift that contributed to an easing of crime rates in the early 1980s also contributed to *growth* in the prison populations. This seeming paradox results from the difference between the peak crime ages and the peak imprisonment ages. Arrest rates peak between the ages of 16 and 18, but, in contrast, the peak imprisonment ages are the late-20s, with a median age of prisoners in the early 30s. The difference results mainly from the fact that very few people under 18 are sent to prison, which is intended primarily for adults.[23] Also, those in the adult age ranges who are convicted of crimes are generally put on probation for their first—or first few—convictions for all but the most serious crimes. By the time they have accumulated a sufficient number of convictions to become serious candidates for prison, they are well into their 20s.

As a result, even though crimes were expected to decline, prison populations were expected to increase over the 1980s as the bulge of the baby boom (with a peak at about the 1960 cohort) continued to flow through the high-imprisonment ages. But it was also expected that, by the early 1990s, those cohorts would also be past the peak imprisonment ages, and so prison populations were expected to begin to decline—at least based on these considerations of the age composition of the population.

Of course, all projections are based on a number of assumptions, and do not countenance new developments that cannot be foreseen at the time the projections are made. The emergence of the crack epidemic of the late 1980s was an important factor in the reversal of the anticipated decline in crime rates. Also, the changing policy environment surrounding crime and punishment during the 1980s and 1990s could override any influence of demographics alone.

RESPONSES TO THE PRISON-POPULATION GROWTH

The major growth in prison populations since the mid-1970s can be attributed predominantly to the growth in punitiveness, most visibly in the execution of the drug war, but to punitiveness generally for all crime types. This growth came at a time when many state budgets were under severe fiscal stress: taxpayer revolts have been manifested in various tax-limitation referenda and voters' rejection of initiatives to increase prison capacity, whether through bond issues or through tax increases. Corrections budgets to accommodate the prison-population growth were often the single fastest growing item in state budgets, and their growth was most often accompanied by reductions in state expenditures on higher education. For example, governmental expenditures (in 1992 dollars) on corrections grew from $14 billion in 1982 to $31 billion in 1992, an increase of 320 percent; over that same period, state expenditures on higher education grew from $38 billion in 1982 to $45 billion in 1992, an increase of only 18 percent.[24] In the face of these severe pressures, governments would very much like to find ways to respond to the growth in prison population.

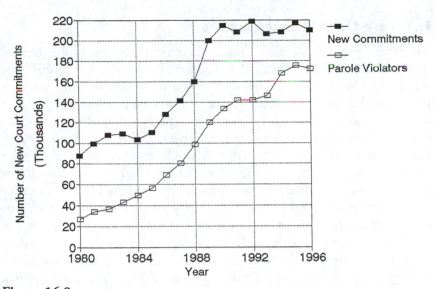

Figure 16.9

Total Prison Admissions for Six Crime Types, 1980–1996
Note: This includes parole violators and new court commitments.

There are some indications that the growth period that has lasted over 25 years may be slowing. Figure 16.9 indicates the composition of prison admissions for the six crime types of murder, robbery, assault, burglary, drugs, and sex offenses. It is evident from Figure 16.9 that the flow of new commitments from courts has been strikingly stable since about 1990, that only parole violators have been increasing over that time, and even that flow may be reducing. These indications of slowing in admissions do not represent a reduction in punitiveness, but rather a reflection of the reduction in crime rates since 1993 and the waning of the crack epidemic. It is clear, however, that the growing tendency to recommit parole violators is continuing to keep prison populations over capacity.

It is also possible that the political power of the punitiveness response, while still strong, may be beginning to mellow somewhat. This may be reflected, for example, in the strong majority votes for referenda supporting medical uses of marijuana in at least eight states.[25] This seems to be a statement by the public that the zero tolerance positions are excessively rigid. If that is any indicator of softening yet to come, then there will be a search for approaches that might serve to reduce prison population and provide resources for other governmental purposes—including crime prevention—without endangering public safety.

Intermediate Punishments

There are important reasons—principally those of cost and of the time lag from a decision to build until the additional capacity is operational—for states to be hesitant to address their crime problems primarily through increasing their prison capacity. Yet the continuing growth of incarceration suggests a need for using the available capacity more effectively. This requires a view of prison capacity as a scarce resource, and allocating that resource more effectively and efficiently. There seems to be a growing consensus that the focus of the incarceration should be on the violent offender—the individual who is not likely to be deterred by any threat of a criminal sanction, and who, at least during his period of violent activity, can be removed as a threat to the community only through incarceration.

Intermediate punishment (IP) provides one opportunity for dealing with the non-violent offender. IP involves a variety of approaches for controlling those who represent a relatively smaller threat in the community, but who require some kind of punishment involving restraint, partly for retributive reasons, and partly to make it clear to them that they cannot continue their criminal activity with impunity.

The approaches involve some combination of finding who is most appropriate for the IP, and then selecting from an array of IP alternatives to assign an appropriate IP to that individual. The array of alternatives has been enumerated by Morris and Tonry,[26] and are discussed more extensively elsewhere in this volume. They include community-service requirements; intensive probation supervision with much closer surveillance than is possible under normal probation supervision with its excessive numbers of cases; work release; house arrest enforced through electronic monitoring with a bracelet placed on the offender that links him electronically to his telephone in order to monitor whether he is at home; or "boot camps," which invoke the rigorous discipline of Marine recruit training, but for a much shorter time than would normally be served in prison.

Unfortunately, there has been little careful evaluation of these approaches. One striking exception has been the randomized field experiments conducted by Petersilia and Turner[27] in 16 jurisdictions to evaluate intensive supervision programs (ISP). As with so many other experimental evaluations, they find no major impact on the recidivism of the persons placed in ISP. They do find a greater risk of technical violation as a result of the more intensive surveillance of the individuals in the programs. They also find that, even though the programs might have been introduced with the intention of diverting prisoners to a lesser level of control, the people assigned tend to be offenders who would otherwise have been more likely to be assigned to probation. As a result, even the anticipated cost saving is frustrated because the ISP results in an escalation of an average routine-supervision cost of $4,700 to an ISP cost of $7,200, rather than the anticipated savings from a typical $20,000 prison cost. They do find, however, that ISP is attractive for drug offenders at an early stage of their criminal careers.

Thus, for first-time offenders, and especially for drug offenders, or for others who represent no direct threat of danger to the community, such approaches seem to offer important possibilities. They would be consistent with a general strategy of continual monitoring of individuals under the control of the criminal justice system. As they conform, they would be put under conditions of looser control; as they are found to be failing, either through reports of criminal activity, or even with urinalysis when drug abuse is an important part of their behavioral problem, they can then be moved to a tighter form of control. Ultimately, of course, prison will be necessary for many of these.

Increasingly, we can expect the introduction of more sophisticated tracking capability than what is available through the house arrest link through the home telephone. The telephone's tracking role is lost when the individual leaves home, even if he is permitted to do so for work or school. Installing a GPS (Geographic Positioning System, which measures location to less than 20 feet based on triangulation on satellite signals) can provide continuous tracking. The lightweight GPS system can maintain the record of its position or it can be linked with an automated cell-phone ankle bracelet to report position to a central computer at regular short intervals. If the system approaches within some specified distance of a prohibited location (e.g., a former victim's home or a prohibited bar), an alarm signal can be sent to the central computer, and from there to the police or to an appropriate parole or probation officer. If the person being controlled is found to have been in the contemporaneous vicinity of a crime that matched his offending history, he could be called on to explain that coincidence. Such a system is undergoing test and development in the Colorado parole system.[28]

Increasingly, these intermediate punishments are being incorporated into sentencing guidelines. The problem in implementing them, however, is that an infrastructure of capability to manage the intermediate punishment programs is needed, and most jurisdictions do not have that capability. States seem ready to spend whatever it takes (an average of $20,000 per prisoner-year) to maintain an offender in prison, but are much more reluctant to make the much smaller investments in community-based programs. Thus it is likely that judges will continue to be confronted with a choice between meaningless probation and excessive control in prison for many convicted people.

Sunsetting Mandatory-Minimum Sentences

As the economy sours and state budgets become more strained, many states will feel the power of the opportunity costs associated with large prison populations and will seek more rational means of allocating their prison cells. They will presumably want to make that allocation to maximize the protection of public safety, by keeping in prison those who represent the greatest current threat to public safety, and releasing those for whom the risk is least. Indeed, to some degree, that was presumably the approach taken by the parole boards in the period before the politicization of crime policy.

While the corrections agencies that operate prisons and make release decisions have considerable discretion on which prisoners they release, statutes usually prohibit them from releasing prisoners under mandatory-minimum sentences. The growing prevalence of such laws—usually enacted to serve a political rather than crime-control need—severely limits the ability of the releasing authorities from addressing matters of public safety.

One form of mandatory-minimum law is the "three-strikes" laws enacted by half the states and the federal government, all passed since Washington set the trend in 1993. These generally impose severe sentences—usually life—after the third (sometimes second) conviction of a limited set of most serious crimes. In most of the states, only a handful of persons were convicted under these laws—an indication of their political rather than crime-control orientation, or perhaps of the recognition by prosecutors of the general inappropriateness of their draconian nature and an indication of a reluctance to invoke them. In California, however, 40,511 persons were convicted under the multi-strike law in the four years subsequent to enactment, mostly for a second "strike," but including 4,468 under a life sentence for a third strike.[29]

Research on deterrence has consistently supported the position that sentence "severity" (i.e., the time served) has less of a deterrent effect than sentence "certainty" (the probability of going to prison).[30] Thus, from the deterrence consideration, there is a clear preference for increasing certainty, even if it becomes necessary to do so at the expense of severity. This suggests a preference for shortening sentences (that diminish severity) in order to strengthen certainty when capacity constraints force a choice.

This perspective is also supported from the standpoint of incapacitation. The longer the time served, the more likely it is that the individual would have terminated his criminal activity. In this sense, additional prison time is "wasted" after his career is terminated. Studies of the duration of criminal careers suggest that property offenders "retire" from crime at a rate of 10 to 20 percent per year (with a criminal career in the range of five to ten years), and at a lower rate for violent offenders,[31] and that this termination rate increases appreciably after they pass their early forties. In any given year, then, one might expect about 10 percent of the individuals in prison to have terminated their criminal activity if they were on the outside. It is, however, difficult to identify just which of those prisoners have terminated at any time. Because of this process of termination of criminal careers, incapacitation is best accomplished by incarcerating individuals during the period when they are most likely to be criminally active, which is the period closest to the time of conviction. From the perspective of incapacitation as well as that of deterrence, prison capacity should be allocated to more, shorter sentences, which will be more effective at crime control than allocating to fewer, longer ones. These considerations do not preclude the value of long sentences for retributive reasons, but it should be recognized that use of long sentences for punishment may well result in diminished efficiency in the use of limited prison resources for crime reduction.

Aside from their inefficiency in terms of crime control, the long mandatory-minimum sentences deprive the judge of the discretion to treat distinctive cases differently. Some felonies will be less serious than others. The California three-strike law was invoked for a theft of a pizza. There may be mitigating factors in an individual's background in the victim provocation in a situation. All of these are denied when the offender is convicted of the mandatory-minimum charge. There is widespread agreement, especially among the judiciary, that the mandatory-minimum laws distort efforts to deliver just sentences, and the entire process would be much better without them. But it would be extremely difficult to get any legislature to repeal them because of the widespread political fear of being labeled "soft on crime."

One approach that would partially mitigate these problems is to address the mandatory-minimum laws through a generic "sunset" law that put all the mandatory-minimum laws under a specified lifetime (say, three years), after which they would expire if not re-enacted. This would recognize that they were enacted to address a particular crime problem at a particular time, and that they could then safely fade away. Most sunset laws involve an analysis of the effectiveness of the law as it is about to retire, and provides an opportunity for the law to be retained or modified rather than merely expire. This would be seen as an act of good government rather than softness on crime, and should stand a much better chance of getting through a legislative process than simple repeal.

Capacity-Sensitive Policies

One approach to controlling prison-population growth is through sentencing policies—statutes or guidelines—that require sentencing policies to be consistent with available prison capacity. This requires consideration of the construction and operating cost of developing policies that cannot be accommodated with existing facilities.

One good example of a planned policy sensitive to prison capacity is the original set of sentencing guidelines developed by the Minnesota Sentencing Guidelines Commission. The commission's work followed from an explicit legislative mandate to "take account of prison capacity" in developing its sentencing guidelines, and used prison capacity as a specific constraint on the sentencing schedule that emerged. If commission member wanted to increase the prescribed sentence for robbery, he had to identify the offenses for which he would like to reduce the sentences in exchange. Such a procedure requires a technology (such as some kind of simulation or impact-estimation model) that enables the policy group to calculate the prison capacity each possible sentencing schedule would consume. This in turn requires information on the expected number of convicted offenders in each category within the sentencing schedule (typically based on an offense gravity score and on the seriousness of the offender's prior conviction record) in order to estimate the prison capacity that the schedule would consume.

The existence of this prison-capacity constraint imposes a rare discipline on the policy debate. In most settings where sanction policies are debated, advocates of tougher sentences gain political benefits without having to consider the costs of their actions. But the availability of this discipline has undoubtedly contributed to making Minnesota the state with the second lowest incarceration rate in the nation in 1991—78 prisoners per 100,000 population in 1991, when the national rate was 310 per 100,000 population, and 125—the lowest in the nation—in 1999 when the national rate was 476.[32]

It is also possible to introduce a policy that employs a population-responsive "safety valve" that releases prisoners when overcrowding becomes excessive. Under that approach, a corrections commission is charged with monitoring the population of the state's prisons in relation to their capacity, and with reporting to the governor when the population of the prisons exceed their capacity for longer than thirty days. Upon receipt of such a report, the governor is then mandated to reduce the minimum sentences of every prisoner by up to ninety days, thereby increasing the population eligible for parole. This does not represent an automatic release of all these prisoners because they still have to appear before the parole board, which can still retain the dangerous convicts until their maximum sentences expire. This strategy was explicitly designed to diffuse the political cost of accommodating prison population to capacity. The legislature enacts the law; the independent corrections commission declares the condition of overcrowding; the governor orders the reduction of minimum sentences; and the parole board orders the actual release. This approach was intended to provide all participants with a politically palatable means of acting responsibly to avoid the consequences of prison overcrowding. Nevertheless, even this carefully designed scheme failed to survive the Michigan political environment when the governor refused to exercise his mandated obligation to reduce the minimum sentences.

There might be more radical approaches to rationing the limited number of prison spaces. One is suggested by a former corrections commissioner in Connecticut, John Manson. A "ration" of prison cells is allocated to each court and its judges or prosecutors, who must then take their limited allocation into account in making their own sentencing decisions or recommendations.[33] When a court has used up its allocation and wants to send an additional convicted offender to prison, the court is required to identify which cell from among its allocation should be vacated. The judge must then release a current occupant in order to obtain the needed space for the new one. This approach forces the judge (or the prosecutor before him) to assume concern for the political costs of facing up to the problem of prison crowding, and to take those costs into account in making sentencing decisions. So far, no jurisdictions have adopted this approach, for reasons that are fully understandable. But it does force a focus on the allocation issues of concern, and directs attention to the other, more conventional approaches.

All of these approaches to controlling the prison population require an explicit formulation of the excessively flexible concept of "prison capacity." As long as double- or triple-celling is a possibility, capacity remains a very poorly defined notion, and represents no constraint whatsoever on any of the policy- or decision-makers within the criminal justice system. When considerations such as reasonable limits on prisoner capacity become more explicit and are taken into account, then capacity does become a more meaningful limit, and explicit policy statements can be formulated to define it. This can be done by a commission, including representatives of the legislature, the judiciary, the correctional administration, and prosecutors.

DEVELOPING A RATIONAL STRATEGY FOR THE USE OF PRISONS

Any development of a rational strategy regarding prisons must recognize several key facts:

- There has been a massive growth in prison populations since the early 1970s, with no comparable effect on crime rates.
- There has been a major growth in the use of imprisonment for drug offenders, and prison has not at all demonstrated its effectiveness for diminishing drug selling or drug abuse.
- Prisons are expensive, costing about $20,000 per year, per prisoner to operate, and these funds are diverted from other needs (such as education or economic development, or even in juvenile institutions where rehabilitation is most likely, with the right programs and resources applied), which might have some possibility of diminishing the future calls for prison.
- Prisons are generally ineffective for rehabilitation of adults and may have serious criminalizing effects on those who come out.
- While the threat of a lengthy prison sentence is undoubtedly very effective at deterring white-collar crimes that tend to be committed by middle class individuals, they are probably far less effective in deterring the crimes committed by under-class individuals, who are the primary occupants of prisons, and for whom the increment of pain associated with prison time may be far less severe than it would be for those ensconced in a comfortable job.
- Incapacitation through imprisonment is probably the only effective means of restraining the violent crimes that are committed by some individuals otherwise out of social control, and so incarceration of these people should be a high priority for the use of limited prison capacity.
- It is important to find ways to remove prison policy from a primarily political agenda that reacts to the crime of the moment, and to develop a coherent schedule and process of imposing punishment and controlling offenders.

With these basic observations, and in recognition of the public concern over violence, particularly by young people, we can begin to develop a mixture of short- and long-term strategies for dealing with the prison problem.

For the short-term, there is little we can do but respond to violence with arrest, conviction, and incarceration, at least for the period when the individual can be expected to continue to act violently. In order to do this, we must make room in our prisons for those who are likely to engage in violence on the outside, for whom prison is most appropriate for reasons of incapacitation. A variety of risk-prediction scales have been developed over the years, and they can provide useful guidance on the risk of individual offender's recidivism, which must be weighed along with the seriousness of the kinds of offenses in which they are likely to recidivate.

In order to provide that capacity, we should seek to make much greater use of intermediate punishments for those accused of nonviolent offenses, and especially of drug dealing. Doing this requires that communities receive the resources and expertise to enable them to carry out their responsibilities in these intermediate punishments. In particular, there could be much better use of police and their presence, along with greater access to modern information systems, and individual tracking systems and telecommunications for control of people on intermediate punishment (including those on probation and parole release) within the community.

We should find the means to do away with mandatory-minimum sentencing laws, which were passed in the passion of some issue at one point in time, and may no longer be appropriate. In general, one finds those sentenced under mandatory-minimum sentencing laws to have appreciably less serious prior records than those sentenced otherwise, and so, at the margin, prison might be better used for offenders that are more like the latter group. If politics preclude outright repeal, then we should pass a generic "sunset" law causing all mandatory-minimum laws to expire automatically three years after enactment unless explicitly re-enacted. This is especially necessary for the mandatory-minimum laws that apply to drug offenses, which are of doubtful effectiveness and account for the majority of prisoners serving time on mandatory sentences.

More generally, we have to reconsider the inappropriate use of prison for the problem of drug abuse. Certainly, drug abuse is a serious problem to be addressed, but there is no indication that the attacks by the criminal justice system on the supply side of the market have been successful in dealing with it. Indeed, it could well be that the crime and violence problems created by the replacements brought into the drug markets are more severe than those created by the imprisoned sellers or perhaps even the abusive drugs they sell. There should be a gradual transformation of those efforts to a public-health model with prevention and treatment focused on the demand side, and tight regulation of the supply side. This is not a problem that will be solved in the short term, but the long-term strategies must be addressed in the short term.

For the intermediate term, it would be most desirable to find ways to take the issue of punishment policy out of the rabid political arena, where the conditions under which the debate occurs can lead to the enactment of irresponsible policy. One means for achieving that is through the creation of sentencing commissions, even though they are also affected by political pressures. But, since they are explicitly charged with the development of a coherent sentencing structure, they are more likely to maintain a reasonable degree of coherence in the sentences they develop. The major distortion to most sentencing commissions' schedules have been associated with the mandatory-minimum laws passed by legislatures, often even after establishing the sentencing commission.

For the longer term, it seems essential that we focus on some of the major factors that contribute to important and large segments of our nation's population having no stake in legitimate conformity. These people reinforce each other in greatly diminished sensitivity to the sanctions available to the criminal justice system. When large segments of a group in the society find themselves convicted—or even given the penultimate sanction of incarceration—then the stigma effect of the sanctions is largely diminished, and may even be replaced by a view that the sanction is merely another rite of passage. It would not be surprising if that effect were taking place among young black males in their late twenties, more than 8 percent of whom are in a state or federal prison on any given day. If that is the case, the effects of the high level of sanction could well be counter-productive.

Society will have to consider how that has come about—how it may derive from inadequate socialization and how society can remedy those problems—by enhancing parental skills or by taking over some aspects of the socialization functions. Any such efforts, of course, are likely to be expensive, perhaps enormously so, and the benefits are still very uncertain. But even if successful, they are not likely to be realized for at least ten years, when another political administration is in office.

In light of the short political planning horizons and the very limited availability of funds for such efforts, we are not likely to see significant progress of this sort pursued in the near future. In that event, it is likely that we will continue to need appreciably more prison capacity in the decades to come.

17

Community Corrections

JOAN PETERSILIA

A fundamental fact about punishment in the United States is that the vast majority of those under correctional supervision are *not* behind bars, but living in the community. At year-end 1999, 6.4 million adults were under some form of correctional supervision—incarcerated in jails and prisons, or supervised on probation or parole. Just 1.9 million of them were physically in custody. The remaining 4.5 million persons (*or 70 percent of all adult criminals under sentence*) are on probation or parole (Beck 2000a). In addition, nearly 600,000 juveniles were placed on probation in 1996—56 percent of all cases that received a juvenile court sanction (Snyder and Sickmund 1999). These nonprison programs are known as community corrections, because they permit an offender to reside in the community while serving a criminal sentence. Today, the U.S. criminal justice system is primarily a system of community-based sanctioning.[1]

Probation and parole are the core of the community corrections system. While the terms are often used interchangeably, probation is a dispositional *alternative* to prison, whereas parole implies that the offender has already served a portion of his sentence incarcerated. There are two other important differences:

- Probation is a sentencing option available to local judges, who determine the form probation will take. Parole results from an administrative decision made by a legally designated paroling authority. Under parole, the power to determine when an offender may be released, and to fix supervision conditions, passes from the hands of the court to an agency within the executive branch of the state.
- Probation can be a state or local activity, administered by one of more than 2,000 separate agencies in the United States. Parole is always a state function and administered by a single agency.

Table 17.1
Adults under Correctional Supervision, 1990–1999

Year	Total estimated correctional population	Community supervision		Incarceration	
		Probation	Parole	Jail	Prison
1990	4,348,000	2,670,234	531,407	403,019	743,382
1995	5,335,100	3,077,861	679,421	499,300	1,078,542
1996	5,482,700	3,164,996	679,733	510,400	1,217,528
1997	5,725,800	3,296,513	694,787	557,974	1,176,564
1998	6,126,300	3,670,591	696,385	584,372	1,224,469
1999	6,367,700	3,773,624	712,713	596,435	1,284,894
Percent change 1990–1999	46.5%	41.3%	34.1%	48.0%	72.8%
Average annual percent change 1990–1999	5.2%	3.9%	3.3%	4.5%	6.3%

SOURCE: *Bureau of Justice Statistics 2000: At A Glance,* (Washington, D.C.: Bureau of Justice Statistics, August 2000), p. 19.

In other major respects, probation and parole are similar. In both, information about an offender is gathered and presented to a decision-making authority, and that authority has the power to release the offender under specific conditions; and a new crime or technical violation of these conditions may lead to enhanced restrictions or incarceration. The goals of probation and parole supervision are also identical: to protect the community and help rehabilitate offenders. These dual functions are referred to as the "law enforcement" function, which emphasizes surveillance of the offender and close control of behavior, and the "social work" function, which attempts to provide supportive services to meet offenders' needs. Both have always been part of community corrections, and debating which should be of higher priority has always caused strain. Currently, the social work function has given way to the law enforcement function, and probation and parole officers are less interested today in treating clients than in controlling their behavior (Petersilia 1999).

The fact that most active offenders are not incarcerated, but instead on probation or parole, means that these community corrections agencies are potentially central in any serious crime-control strategy. As (former) U.S. Assistant Attorney General Laurie Robinson observed:

> How can we have a conversation about public safety in this country and not talk about the . . . 3.9 million people on probation and parole. That's about three times the number of people behind bars. (Dickey and Smith 1998, p. 1)

Truth is, community corrections should be generating a great deal of debate and analysis. But it is not. We spend inordinate amounts of time debating prison policy—who should go, for how long, under what conditions—and are relatively unconcerned and vastly uninformed about community corrections, which in the long run may have more to do with crime. Community corrections research (particularly on parole) is weak; and we know relatively little about the risks posed by such offenders, or how they are supervised or assisted while under supervision. Moreover, while most agree that the nation's community corrections system is woefully inadequate, until recently there has been little discussion about how to make it better.

This chapter is designed to provide an overview of current parole and probation practice. It presents data on the growth of probation and parole populations, and what is known about offenders' crimes, personal backgrounds, and court-ordered conditions. Data is presented on the average size of probation/parole caseloads, offender contact requirements, and the annual costs of supervision. This chapter also describes the collateral consequences of parole, recidivism outcomes, and the results of a decade of experimenting with intermediate or "middle-range" punishments. Finally, it identifies some current thinking on how to "reinvent" probation and parole, and identifies some of the more promising community corrections strategies.

OFFENDER CHARACTERISTICS, CASELOADS, AND COMMUNITY CORRECTIONS FUNDING

The disproportionate number of criminals serving sentences in the community is not new. There have always been more people convicted of crimes in the U.S. than there are prison cells to hold them (Clear and Dammer 2000). In fact, despite mandatory minimum sentences, "three strikes and you're out" legislation, and other tough-on-crime policies of the past decade, the absolute numbers of offenders serving sentences in the community is larger than ever before in our history (probation up 41 percent since 1990), and the percentage of the total correctional population under community supervision (vs. incarceration) has declined only slightly in that period—from 74 percent to 71 percent (Bonczar and Glaze 1999).

The truth is that, as the U.S. population has grown, more citizens are being arrested and convicted, and *all* corrections populations (for example, prisons, jails, probation, and parole) have grown simultaneously (see Figure 17.1). The number of offenders on probation and parole is now so large that the U.S. Department of Justice estimates that 2.2 percent of *all* adult residents in the United States are serving criminal sentences in the community—about 1 in 27 men, 1 in 160 women.

Fifty-one percent of the probationers were convicted of felonies (as opposed to misdemeanors), as were 100 percent of the parolees. The personal characteristics of offenders under community supervision mirror

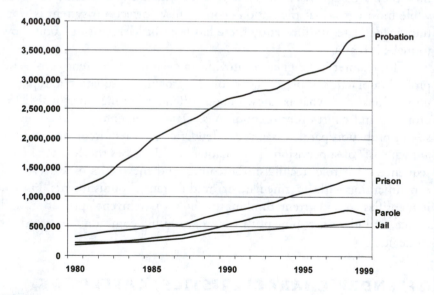

Figure 17.1
Adult Correctional Populations, 1980–1999
SOURCE: *Bureau of Justice Statistics 2000: At A Glance,* (Washington, D.C.: Bureau of Justice Statistics, August 2000), 20.

those of the larger body of offenders: 37 percent are African American and 62 percent are white. Eighteen percent are of Hispanic origin. Women make up 21 percent of the nation's adult probationers and 12 percent of parolees (Bonczar and Glaze 1999).

Probation and parole populations have not only grown in numbers, but the characteristics of persons under supervision have become more serious. Surveys of probation and parole officials consistently show that they believe their current caseloads (the number of offenders an officer is responsible for supervising) are becoming more difficult to manage because more of their populations are drug users or sexual offenders, are mentally ill, have gang affiliations, and have few marketable skills (Petersilia 1998). Beck (2000b) recently reported that 74 percent of prisoners reentering the community within the next twelve months are drug or alcohol involved, 15 percent are mentally ill, and 11 percent have co-occurring disorders (substance abuse and mental illness). Beck also reports that just 22 percent of the alcohol or drug abusers will have participated in treatment while in prison, while 60 percent of those having a mental illness will have received treatment.

Despite wide usage and its essential role in supervising serious offenders, community corrections enjoys little public support and is often the subject of intense criticism. It suffers from a "soft on crime" image and is often depicted as permissive, uncaring about crime victims, and committed to a rehabilitative ideal that ignores the reality of violent, predatory criminals. Public opinion surveys show that Americans have very low confidence in and little knowledge of probation and parole. A national survey conducted by Longmire and Sims (1995) found that roughly 60 percent of those surveyed reacted favorably to the performance of the police while only 25 percent expressed confidence in probation. In a 1996 national poll, 53 percent of the sample "agreed" that "community corrections programs are evidence of leniency in the criminal justice system" (Cullen, Fisher, and Applegate 2000). Citizen surveys repeatedly show that the public thinks that prisons and jails make people worse, but it does *not* believe that probation and parole make them better, hold offenders accountable, or protect the public (Reinventing Probation Council 2000).

Their poor public image leaves probation and parole agencies woefully underfunded, and unable to compete effectively for scarce public funds. Nationally, probation and parole receive about 15 percent of state and local government expenditures for corrections, even though they supervise 70 percent of correctional clients (Bureau of Justice Statistics 1993). And, despite the fact that community corrections populations have grown at a rate similar to that of prisons and jails, funding for prisons and jails has increased significantly while spending for probation and parole remains unchanged from what it was in 1977 (Langan 1994). Annual expenditures per prisoner in the United States are $20,261, compared to $1,890 per parolee and $1,497 per probationer (Camp and Camp 1999).

The increase in populations, coupled with stagnant or decreasing funding, means that caseloads keep increasing, and probation and parole officers are unable to monitor compliance with court-ordered conditions (for example, no drug use, maintain employment, perform community service, pay victim restitution). In such situations, probation and parole may actually mean freedom from supervision. While the 1967 President's Crime Commission recommended that ideal caseloads should be about 35:1, national averages for probation are now 175:1, and for parole, 70:1 (Camp and Camp 1999).

In large urban counties, the situation is particularly acute and the average caseload size noted above does not convey the seriousness of the situation. Consider, for example, the Los Angeles County Probation Department, the largest probation department in the world. In 2000, its 900 line officers were responsible for supervising 90,000 adult and juvenile offenders. Since the mid-1970s, county officials have repeatedly cut the agency's budget, while the number of persons granted probation has grown. As a result, 70 percent of all probationers in Los Angeles are now supervised on "automated" or banked caseloads—no supervision, services, or personal contacts are provided.[2]

A more detailed analysis found that nearly 10,000 violent offenders (convicted of murder, rape, assault, kidnap, and robbery) are supervised on any given day by probation officers in Los Angeles, and half are on "automated minimum" caseloads with no reporting requirements (Los Angeles County Planning Committee 1996). As Clear and Braga (1995, 423) wrote: "Apparently, community supervision has been seen as a kind of elastic resource that could handle whatever numbers of offenders the system required it to."

Of course, there is wide variation among jurisdictions regarding the extent and quality of services provided probationers and parolees. Some smaller jurisdictions have more resources and a historical commitment to providing rehabilitation and/or surveillance. Some of them operate solid community corrections programs, and a description of some promising (but seldom evaluated) programs can be found in Wilkinson (2000). In most large jurisdictions, however, it is safe to say that the overall services and monitoring are woefully inadequate to meet the needs of today's community corrections clients.

Ironically, while caseloads have grown and funding has declined, the proportion of offenders subject to special conditions has increased. The public's more punitive mood, combined with the availability of inexpensive drug testing and a higher number of offenders having substance abuse problems, contributes to the increased number of conditions imposed. The Bureau of Justice Statistics (BJS) reports that nearly half of all probationers had five or more conditions to their sentence required by the court or probation agency. A monetary requirement was the most common condition (84 percent), and more than 2 of every 5 probationers were required to enroll in some form of substance abuse treatment. Nearly a third of all probationers were subject to mandatory drug testing—43 percent of felons and 17 percent of misdemeanants (Bonczar 1997). Parole requirements are more stringent. Rhine et al. (1991) found that 80 percent of parolees were required to have "gainful employment," 61 percent "no association with persons of criminal records," 53 percent "pay all fines and restitution," and 47 percent "support family and all dependents." It is estimated that more than a third of *all* U.S. probationers and parolees have court-ordered drug testing conditions (Camp and Camp 1999).

Although research shows that reducing caseloads does not necessarily reduce recidivism, it is also evident that such large caseloads make it difficult to provide services or maintain anything but superficial and infrequent contacts with offenders (Petersilia and Turner 1993). Annually, probation and parole officers have an average of twenty face-to-face contacts with probationers and parolees—*or about one every 2 weeks*.[3] As Kleiman notes, even if officers were able to deliver two face-to-face contacts per week to each offender, each lasting thirty minutes, offenders would *still* have close to 125 hours per week of (awake) unsupervised activity. This simple arithmetic—which would require a quadrupling of current U.S. probation/parole contact levels and associated staff—shows how difficult it is for probation and parole officers to exert much control on unwilling offenders using face-to-face contacts alone (Kleiman 1999). As one Washington, D.C., police officer succinctly put it: "I've never run into a criminal who was very afraid of probation."

Such "supervision" not only makes a mockery of the justice system, but leaves many serious offenders unsupervised and undoubtedly contributes to high recidivism rates. Langan found that nearly half of all probationers do not comply with the terms of their sentence, and only a fifth of those who violate their sentences ever go to jail for their noncompliance. It is also true that thousands of probationers and parolees abscond (that is, whereabouts unknown) from supervision. The BJS estimates that in 1990 just 1 percent of all adult probationers and parolees had absconded from supervision, but by 1998 fully 10 percent of them had (Bonczar and Glaze 1999). In California the figure is even higher: On any given day in 1999, 20 percent of all parolees had absconded supervision (Petersilia 2000). While a majority of jurisdictions issue warrants for such violators, funding shortages mean that little is done systematically to locate absconders.

It is also worth noting that probation and parole officers play a vital role to crime victims, providing them information about the offender's whereabouts, conditions of supervision, and other issues affecting victim safety. When offenders abscond, the victim's peace of mind and safety are compromised.

PUBLIC SAFETY AND RECIDIVISM

With few services and little surveillance, most probationers and parolees do not succeed. For the probation population as a whole, we do not know the percentage who are re-arrested while on probation because 48 percent of all adult probationers have been convicted of misdemeanors and have not been the subject of recidivism research. For *felony* probationers, the best recidivism data come from the BJS study by Langan and Cunniff. They found that within three years of sentencing, while still on probation, 43 percent of felons were re-arrested for a crime within the state. Half of the arrests were for a violent crime or a drug offense (Langan and Cunniff 1992).

Parolees fare no better. The BJS tracked a national sample of parolees released from prison in 1983 (Beck and Shipley 1989). They found that within three years, 62 percent of them had been re-arrested for a felony or serious misdemeanor (23 percent for a violent crime), and 47 percent were returned to prison or jail. More recent BJS analyses showed similarly disappointing results: 42 percent of parolees in 1999 were returned to incarceration during their parole period (Bureau of Justice Statistics 2000b). For both probationers and parolees, the risk of recidivism is highest in the first year after sentencing or release on parole (Langan and Cunniff 1992; Beck and Shipley 1989).

Recidivism rates, like other aspects of community corrections, vary greatly among states. Texas recently reported that its three-year reincarcerate rate has dropped from a high of nearly 50 percent for 1992 releases to a low of 31 percent for 1997 releasees. Similarly, Pennsylvania has reported its three-year reincarcerate rate has also declined from 50 percent for 1994 releases to 39 percent for 1996 releases. Why failure rates are declining in certain states is subject to several possible explanations. Some believe it is attributable to longer lengths of stay and the associated aging of the prisoner release cohorts. It could also be due to widely divergent approaches to measuring recidivism, better employment conditions for parolees, or mere changes in revocation practices as prison systems become crowded (Austin 2000).

Research has also consistently shown that a number of factors are associated with recidivism. The best predictors of probation recidivism were recently summarized by Morgan (1993): conviction crime (property offenders have higher rates), prior criminal record (the more convictions, the higher the recidivism), employment (unemployment is associated with higher recidivism), age (younger offenders have higher rates), family composition (persons living with spouse or children have lower rates), and drug use (heroin addicts have highest recidivism rates). Similar factors have been found to predict parole outcomes (Petersilia et al. 1986).

Petersilia and Turner found that although these factors were shown to be *correlated* with probation/parole recidivism, the ability to *predict* recidivism was limited (Petersilia et al. 1986). Knowing the above information and using it to predict who would recidivate and who would not resulted in accurate predictions only about 70 percent of the time. The programs the offender participated in, along with factors in the environment in which he was supervised (for example, family support, employment), predicted recidivism as much or more than the factors present at sentencing and often used in recidivism prediction models.

Another way to examine the risks posed by current probation and parole populations is to look at their contribution to the overall crime problem. The best measure of this comes from various data sources compiled by the BJS, which are summarized in Figure 17.2. Importantly, it shows that, of all persons arrested for felony crimes in 1990, 17 percent were on probation and 8 percent were on parole at the time of their current arrest. When viewed this way, *a quarter of all serious crime arrests made in the United States were attributable to persons who were on probation or parole at the time of the offense.* Moreover, BJS data reveal that 44 percent of persons in prison report being on probation or parole at the time of the crime that landed them in prison (up from 34 percent in the 1979 survey). Leaving probationers and parolees "unattended" is not only bad policy, it leaves many victims in its wake.

Such high recidivism rates have led to the common perception that "nothing works." Of course, it is important to remember that the availability of treatment, both in and out of custody, lags behind the demand

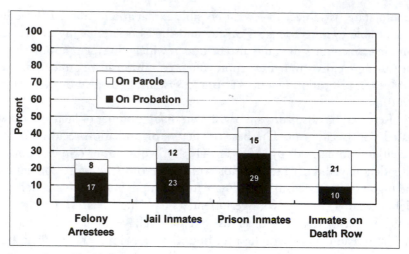

Source: Petersilia 1999

Figure 17.2
Percent of Offenders on Probation or Parole at Time of Offense
SOURCE: Petersilia 1999

for services. Of the inmates that report mental illness, only 17 percent of state prisoners, 11 percent of jail inmates, and 12 percent of probationers receive treatment for mental illness. Of the estimated 70 to 85 percent of state inmates who need substance abuse treatment, only 12 percent were treated in 1997 (Hurwitz 2000). These numbers represent the known population of offenders with mental illness and substance abuse, and may actually underestimate the need for treatment.

When offenders are released to probation and parole, it is unlikely that their participation in treatment will increase. Offenders will be met with long waiting lists, financial constraints, and inadequate community-based programs. Ninety percent of probationers and parolees will be placed on "regular" caseloads where they are seen less than twice per month by their probation/parole officer. The dollars available to support their supervision and services are generally less than $2,000 per offender—when effective treatment programs are estimated to cost $12,000 to $15,000 per year, per client (Institute of Medicine 1990). It is no wonder that recidivism rates are so high—in a sense, we get what we pay for, and as yet, we have never chosen to invest sufficiently in community-based programs. As Kleiman recently concluded:

> Under current conditions, probation and parole are probably best thought of as legal statuses allowing swifter incarceration or reincarceration when fresh offenses are detected rather than as programs with independent incapacitative or rehabilitative effects. (Kleiman 1999, 1917)

Even though many court-ordered conditions are not actively enforced, the probation/parole population is so large that even revoking a few percent of them or revoking all those who are re-arrested can have a dramatic impact on prison admissions. In fact, offenders who fail under community supervision are the fastest growing component of the prison population. In 1980, parole violators constituted 18 percent of all admissions; but by 1998, nearly 40 percent of all persons admitted to state prisons were parole violators—60 percent of them having been arrested for or convicted of a new offense. Overall, the increase in the number of probation and parole violators accounted for 42 percent of the growth in total admissions to state prisons between 1980 and 1994 (Blumstein and Beck 1999).

Probation and parole, systems developed in the United States more by accident than by design, now threaten to become the tail that wagged the corrections' dog. Corrections populations continue to rise; more offenders are required to be on parole or parole supervision, where fewer services and work programs exist due to scarcity of resources (often diverted from community corrections to fund prison expansion). A greater number of probation/parole violations (particularly drug use) are detected through monitoring and drug testing, and community corrections officers have increasingly less tolerance for failure. Revocation to prison is becoming a predictable (and increasingly short) transition in the criminal justice revolving-door cycle.

THE COLLATERAL CONSEQUENCES OF PAROLE FAILURES

Inadequate community supervision not only threatens public safety and impacts corrections costs, but also contributes to a number of adverse social consequences. Criminologists have begun to write about some of these consequences, but the literature is still fragmentary. Tonry and Petersilia (1999) and Petersilia (2000) have identified at least five kinds of collateral consequences that accompany parole release.

First, there are the effects of imprisonment on prisoners' later employment prospects. Sizable economic and smaller ethnographic literatures (see Reuter, this volume) convincingly show that parole reduces ex-offenders' subsequent incomes and employment. A policy literature shows that various state and federal laws deny parolees the right to vote or hold office in some places, the opportunity to engage in certain occupations in some places, and the right to receive various public benefits and services in some places (Fellner and Mauer 1998).

Second, various literatures show that imprisonment and parole affects family stability and childhood development. Imprisonment often leads to the breakup of families and social relationships and to lessening of parents' involvement with their children (Hagan and Dinovitzer 1999). Since 1991 the number of minor children with a parent in state or federal prison rose by over 500,000—from 936,500 to 1,498,800 in 1999 (Bureau of Justice Statistics 2000a).

We know little about the effects of a parent's incarceration and release on childhood development, but it is likely to be significant. Mothers released from prison have difficulty finding services such as housing, employment, and childcare; and this causes stress for them and their children. Children of incarcerated and released parents often suffer confusion, sadness, and social stigma; and these feelings often result in school-related difficulties, low self-esteem, aggressive behavior, and general emotional dysfunction (Hagan and Dinovitzer 1999). Children of incarcerated parents are five times more likely to serve time in prison than are children whose parents are not incarcerated (Beck, Gilliard, and Greenfeld 1993).

Third, while we have no data on involvement of parolees' in family violence, it may be significant. Risk factors for domestic violence and child abuse and neglect include poverty, unemployment, alcohol/drug abuse, low self-esteem, and poor health of parents—common attributes of parolees.

Fourth, parole certainly impacts the larger community. As a greater number of parolees recycle in and out of inner-city neighborhoods, the social characteristics of those neighborhoods—and their ability to exert informal social controls to reduce crime—diminish. Sociologist Elijah Anderson explains the breakdown of social cohesion in socially disorganized communities and how returning prisoners play a role in that process and are affected by it. Moral authority increasingly is vested in "street smart" young men for whom drugs and crime are a way of life. Attitudes, behaviors, and lessons learned in prison are transmitted to the free society. He concludes that as "family caretakers and role models disappear or decline in influence, and as unemployment and poverty become more persistent, the community, particularly its children, becomes vulnerable to a variety of social ills, including crime, drugs, family disorganization, generalized demoralization and unemployment" (Anderson 1990, p. 4).

Prison gangs also appear to have growing influence in inner-city communities. Sociologist Joan Moore notes that because prisons are violent and dangerous places, new inmates seek protection and connections. Many find both in gangs. Inevitably, gang loyalties are exported to the neighborhoods when inmates are released. The revolving prison door strengthens street gang ties. She warns that as more young people are incarcerated earlier in their criminal career, more of them will come out of prison with hostile attitudes and will exert strong negative influences on the neighborhoods to which they return.

Researchers explored similar effects by looking at crime rates in Tallahassee, Florida, one year after offenders who had been sent to prison from there had returned to that community. Rather than reducing crime (through the deterrent or rehabilitative effects of prison), releasing offenders into the community in 1996 led to an increase in crime the following year, even after other factors were taken into account (Rose, Clear, and Scully 1999). One explanation focuses on individuals, contending that offenders "make up for lost time" by resuming their criminal careers with renewed energy. But the researchers who studied Tallahassee offer another explanation, one focusing on the destabilizing effect of releasing a large number of parolees on the community's ability to influence its members. They argue that "coerced mobility," like voluntary mobility, is a type of "people-churning" that inhibits integration and promotes isolation and anonymity—factors associated with increased crime.

Fifth, the poor health of parolees, combined with escalating community health care costs, has public health experts worried about the spread of infectious diseases (especially such conditions as tuberculosis, hepatitis, and HIV) (McDonald 1999). Prisoners and parolees have significantly more medical and mental health problems than the general population because they often live as transients in crowded conditions, tend to be economically disadvantaged, and have high rates of substance abuse, including intravenous drug use. While in prison, inmates have access to state-provided health care, but upon release most cannot easily obtain health care.

At year end 1997, 2.1 percent of all state and federal prison inmates were known to be infected with HIV, a rate five times higher than in the general population (Hammett, Harmon, and Maruschak 1999). Public health experts predict the rate will continue to climb; and eventually HIV will manifest itself on the street, particularly as more drug offenders—many of whom use drugs intravenously and share needles, or trade sex for drugs—are released on parole.

THE EMERGENCE OF INTERMEDIATE SANCTIONS

To address the direct and collateral consequences of a weak community corrections system, most jurisdictions have implemented a variety of "intermediate" sanction programs—mid-range punishments that lie somewhere between routine probation/parole supervision and incarceration with respect to their restrictions and costs. Various intermediate sanction programs (often referred to as "ISPs") have been developed in recent years, including intensive probation or parole, house arrest, electronic monitoring, boot camps, drug courts, day reporting centers, community service, and specialized (mostly drug-related or sex offender) probation and parole caseloads. In and of themselves, ISPs do not imply any particular type of program. Rather, "ISP" is a generic term that simply means "more than" what offenders in that location would have received in the absence of the ISP.

Between the years 1985 and 1995, hundreds of intermediate sanction programs were started, often with a great deal of ceremony. But Petersilia (1999) estimated that despite all of the programs implemented only about 10 percent of all adult probationers and parolees participated in intermediate sanction programs.

Still many intermediate sanction programs were implemented, and several good evaluations were conducted. The results have been summarized in Tonry and Lynch (1996), Petersilia (1999), and Clear and Braga (1995). Despite differences in the programs, the agencies that implemented them, and the characteristics of offenders who participated, the research findings are incredibly consistent. The four major findings are as follows:

1. Most ISPs have been probation-*enhancement* programs rather than prison or jail *diversion* programs. They seek a "tougher" probation/parole to replace traditional methods, and they target the "toughest" probation/parole cases. The stringent conditions and strict enforcement associated with most ISP programs mean they produce a *higher* failure rate of technical violations. As a result, most ISPs implemented to date have not saved money—since the intermediate sanction is usually more expensive than the routine probation/parole programs they supplant.

2. Well-implemented ISPs *do* restore credibility to the justice system, and provide a much-needed spectrum of punishments to match the spectrum of risk posed by criminals. Policymakers, judges, corrections

practitioners, and the public strongly support intermediate sanctions for nonviolent offenders. Offenders judge certain ISP programs as more punitive than short incarceration terms. This is particularly true in ISPs which include mandatory work and drug-testing requirements.

3. Intermediate sanctions may offer promise as a way to get and keep offenders in drug and other treatment programs. With drug treatment programs at least, there is evidence that coerced treatment programs can reduce both later drug use and later crimes, and there is evidence in the ISP and boot camp literatures that these programs can increase treatment participation.

4. The most important finding from the intermediate sanctions literature is that programs must deliver high "doses" of *both* treatment and surveillance to assure public safety and reduce recidivism. "Treatment" alone is not enough, nor is "surveillance" by itself adequate. Programs that can increase offender-to-officer contacts *and* provide treatment have reduced recidivism. Petersilia and Turner (1993) found that offenders who received drug counseling, held jobs, paid restitution, and did community service were arrested at rates 10 to 20 percent lower than others.

These research findings are being used to redesign many of the more promising community corrections programs, which are discussed in the next section.

WHAT NEEDS TO BE DONE? REINVENTING PROBATION AND PAROLE

Everyone agrees that the current system of community corrections is failing to protect the public or rehabilitate offenders. Adequate resources and staffing are certainly critical for doing an effective job, but increasing resources alone will not solve the problem. Correctional leaders, policy analysts, and scholars are all now calling for "reforming," "reinventing," and "restructuring" community corrections. But exactly *how* would one go about reforming probation and parole?

Three separate study groups, each composed of leading academics and corrections practitioners, convened between 1998–2000 for purposes of facilitating strategic discussions on the future of probation and parole. All three groups have issued reports, and there is a great deal of overlap in their recommendations (Dickey and Smith 1998; Reinventing Probation Council 2000; Tonry 1999). In addition, the American Correctional Association (Rhine 1998) and the Association of State Correctional

Administrators (Rhine 1998; Wilkinson 2000) have each conducted surveys to identify promising programs in community supervision. A reading of these reports, as well as the authors' own thinking, suggests an emerging consensus about what needs to be done. It involves at least five steps:

1. Identify the most dangerous and violent offenders, for whom surveillance through human and technological means is a top priority.
2. Deliver quality treatment (particularly for substance abuse) and job training programs to the subgroup of offenders for whom research shows it could be most beneficial.
3. Create the ability to identify and respond quickly to probation and parole violations, particularly those involving drug use.
4. Establish an array of credible intermediate sanction programs to divert true technical violators away from expensive prison cells.
5. Commit to a community-centered approach to offender supervision and management, which means getting officers out of their offices and having them work interactively with victims, law enforcement, offenders, and families.

Greater Monitoring of High-Risk Violent Probationers and Parolees

There can be no doubt that the public, aided by private industry, will continue to demand and receive an increased level of control over certain violent, predatory offenders living in the community. The most visible sign of this is the expanded registration of parolees, originally begun for sex offenses, but now expanding in terms of types of crimes and how accessible the information is to the public. Connecticut recently expanded its parolee registration to include kidnapping for sexual purposes, public indecency, and fourth-degree sexual assault. Its entire list is now posted on the Internet. Florida and New Jersey also allow citizens to have complete access to inmate release information through an Internet site maintained by each state's Department of Corrections.

A New York City-based crime victim's advocacy group, using information from the State Department of Correctional Services, now places on the Internet the names of inmates soon to be *eligible* for parole from New York State prisons. In addition to including inmates' names, criminal background, and parole eligibility dates, the Internet site includes press clippings of the crime if they are available. The site encourages citizens to contact the New York State Division of Parole with comments.

In California, the State Department of Justice developed a CD-ROM database with the pictures, names, and whereabouts of the state's more than 50,000 registered sex offenders. Visitors to any local police station in the state are able to type in their ZIP codes and find out if a sex offender lives nearby. When the data was first released, many local newspapers published the pictures and addresses of local sex offenders. Los Angeles County announced that since few residents are using the CD-ROMs, they would begin mass mailings to residents informing them of the location and names of sex offenders living in their neighborhoods. As of January 1, 1999, California school districts also have direct access to the CD-ROM and permission to distribute the information directly to the public. New York and California both also now have 900-number hotlines set up to allow residents to check if someone is a registered sex offender. Before that, it was illegal for a law enforcement officer to notify citizens about a sex offender living in the neighborhood.

Sophisticated electronic tracking and location systems are also assisting police and corrections officers in keeping better track of offenders in the community. As the Cold War wound down, the defense industry, along with the developing computer and electronic industries, saw community corrections as a natural place to put its energies—a growing market. Today, electronic monitoring—either the old-fashioned bracelets that communicate through a device connected to telephone lines or more modern versions based on cellular or satellite tracking—is in use in most states (Fabelo 2000).

Florida, New Jersey, and Michigan are now using Global Positioning Satellite (GPS) to track offenders on community supervision. Their GPS systems are connected to satellites owned by the U.S. government. These satellites orbit above the earth constantly transmitting the precise time and their position in space. GPS receivers can determine when an offender is in the community 24 hours a day, as well as the direction and speed the offender is moving. One of the most important benefits of satellite tracking is the increased protection it offers crime victims. For instance, when the court orders a sex offender to have no contact with the victim, exclusionary boundaries can be set at an appropriate distance around the victim's residence and place of employment. If the perimeters are broken, an early warning can be sent to the victim. GPS can send an alarm if the offender is in an area where he or she is not allowed (exclusion zone), or if the offender leaves an area in which he or she must stay (inclusion zone). With GPS, everything is archived, so if it is necessary to know an offenders' whereabouts in the past that information is available. The Florida chief judge who is using the system indicated that it appears to be the "ultimate means of protecting the community" (Wilkinson 2000, p. 235). The cost per day to place an offender on Florida's GPS system is $9.26, compared to $3.00 per day for regular electronic monitoring.

A recent survey of correctional officers in Florida showed that they are very supportive of the GPS system and believe it is ideal for violent (particularly domestic violence offenders) and sex offenders, but may be a waste of money for drug offenders (because the offender could be using narcotics in his or her own home and GPS would have no way of indicating that a violation had occurred). Fabelo (2000) worries that such devices will expand the net of state control and reduce the rehabilitation efforts of probation and parole, but there is no doubt that corrections technology will accelerate in the coming years and allow community corrections the option of becoming more surveillance oriented.

Delivering Effective Treatment and Work Programs to Offenders

Treatment Programs. The public seems to have isolated its fear and punitiveness to violent and sexual offenders, and seems more willing to tolerate treatment programs for nonviolent offenders, particularly substance abusers (Cullen, Fisher, and Applegate 2000). This softening of public attitudes seems to have resulted from knowledge about the high costs of prisons, combined with emerging evidence that some treatment programs are effective for some offenders under certain empirically established conditions (for a complete review, see Cullen in this volume). Gendreau and Andrews (1990) found that effective programs, for both juveniles and adults, had the following features:

- They were intensive and behavioral. Intensity was measured by both the absorption of the offenders' daily schedule and the duration of the program over time. Appropriate services in this respect will occupy 40–70 percent of the offender's time and last an average of six months. Behavioral programs will establish a regimen of positive reinforcement for prosocial behavior and will incorporate a modeling approach including demonstrations of positive behavior that offenders are then encouraged to imitate.
- They targeted high-risk offenders and criminogenic needs. Somewhat surprisingly, effective programs worked best with offenders classified as high risk. This effect is strengthened if the program first identifies the

presence of individual needs known to be predictive of recidivism. Targeting needs not proven to be related to criminal behavior (for example, self esteem) will not produce favorable results.

- Treatment modalities and counselor must be matched with individual offender types, for example, matching the learning style and personality of the offender. Matching the style of any therapist/counselor with the personality of the offender (for example, anxious offenders should be matched with especially sensitive counselors) also is critical.

- They provide prosocial contexts and activities and emphasize advocacy and brokerage. Effective programs will replace the normal offender networks with new circles of peers and contacts who are involved in law-abiding.

These principles are influencing prison and parole release programs in a number of states. Perhaps most dramatically, Washington passed the Offender Accountability Act in 1999 and incorporated its principles into all aspects of its Department of Corrections' operations. As of January 2000, each inmate was subject to a risk assessment, which gives higher weights to dynamic (rather than static) risk factors. Priority for treatment programs is given to high-risk inmates. Programs are designed around the cognitive restructuring and intensity of treatment principles outlined above (Lehman 2000b). An evaluation of the program is planned.

A California program is also incorporating the "principles of effective treatment" for a select group of drug offenders on parole. A recent summary of drug treatment effectiveness reported that "a growing body of research" shows that voluntary or mandatory drug treatment can reduce recidivism, especially when treatment is matched to offender needs (Prendergast, Anglin, and Wellisch 1995). A program that attempts to do this, with noted success, is San Diego's Parolee Partnership Program (PPP), which is part of California's statewide Preventing Paroling Failure Program. The San Diego program, begun in 1992, provides substance abuse treatment for parolees in San Diego County. A private vendor operates the program, using principles of client selection, managed care, case management, and case followup. The vendor subcontracts to provide outpatient, residential, and detoxification treatment services and facilities. Support services (for example, education, vocation training, and transportation) are provided directly by the vendor or through referral to other community resource agencies. Typically, the time limit is 180 days of treatment. The participant is then assigned a "recovery advocate," who motivates the offender to continue in treatment for as long as necessary and keeps the parole agent aware of the parolee's progress. The program served about 700 offenders in FY 1995–96 at a total cost of about $1.5 million (about $2,100 per parolee).

An evaluation of the program shows that the PPP was successful with its target group (which was characterized as a hard-to-treat group, who on average had used drugs for about eleven years). The percentage of parolees placed in the PPP who were returned to prison was nearly eight percentage points lower than the return rate for the statistically matched comparison group, and this difference was statistically significant (California Department of Corrections 1997). Los Angeles County operates a similarly successful program. The success of these programs motivated the California state legislature to increase funding for parole substance abuse programs in 1999–2001.

Work Programs. Research has consistently shown that if parolees can find decent jobs as soon as possible after release, they are less likely to return to crime and to prison. Several parole programs have been successful at securing employment for parolees.

The Texas RIO (Re-Integration of Offenders) project, begun as a two-city pilot program in 1985, has become one of the nation's most ambitious government programs devoted to placing parolees in jobs (Finn 1998c). RIO has more than 62 offices with 100 staff members who provide job placement services to nearly 16,000 parolees each year throughout every county in Texas (or nearly half of all parolees released from Texas prisons each year). RIO claims to have placed 69 percent of more than 100,000 ex-offenders since 1985. RIO represents a collaboration of two state agencies, the Texas Workforce Commission, where the program is housed, and the Texas Department of Criminal Justice, whose RIO-funded assessment specialists help inmates prepare for employment and whose parole officers refer released inmates to the program. As the reputation of the program has spread, the Texas Workforce Commission has developed a pool of more than 12,000 employers who have hired parolees referred by the RIO program.

A 1992 independent evaluation documented that 60 percent of the RIO participants found employment, compared with 36 percent of a matched group of non-RIO parolees. In addition, one year after release, RIO participants had worked at some time during more three-month intervals than comparison group members had. During the year after release, when most recidivism occurs, 48 percent of the RIO high-risk clients were re-arrested compared with 57 percent of the nonRIO high-risk parolees; only 23 percent of high-risk RIO participants returned to prison compared with 38 percent of a comparable group of nonRIO parolees. The evaluation also concluded that the program continually saved the state money—more than $15 million in 1990 alone–by helping to reduce the number of parolees who would otherwise have been re-arrested and sent back to prison (Finn 1998c). These positive findings encouraged the Texas legislature to increase RIO's annual budget to nearly $8 million, and other states (for example, Georgia) to implement aspects of the RIO model.

New York City's Center for Employment Opportunities (CEO) project is a transitional service for parolees, consisting of day labor work crews. Assignment to a work crew begins immediately after release from prison, and while it is designed to prepare inmates for placement in a permanent job, it also helps to provide structure, instill work habits, and earn early daily income (Finn 1998b). Most participants are young offenders, released from prison boot camp programs, who are required to enroll as a condition of parole. The descriptive evaluation of this program shows that young parolees associated with the program are more likely to be employed, refrain from substance use, and participate in community service and education while in the CEO program.

The Safer Foundation, headquartered in Chicago, is now the largest community-based provider of employment services for ex-offenders in the United States, with a professional staff of nearly 200 in six locations in two states. The foundation offers a wide range of services for parolees, including employment, education, and housing. A recent evaluation shows that Safer has helped more than 40,000 participants find jobs since 1972, and nearly two-thirds of those placed kept their jobs for thirty days or more of continuous employment (Finn 1998a).

Another highly successful program for released prisoners is operated by Pioneer Human Services, a private, nonprofit organization in Seattle, Washington. Pioneer Services provides housing, jobs, and social support for released offenders, but it also operates sheltered workshops for the hard-to-place offenders. It is different from other social service agencies in that its program is funded almost entirely by the profits from the various businesses it operates, and not through grants. The program places a priority on practical living skills and job training. Most of their clients are able to maintain employment either in the free market or for Pioneer

Services, and the recidivism rates are less than 5 percent for its work-release participants (Turner and Petersilia 1996).

Monitoring and Punishing Probation and Parole Violations

One of the difficulties in monitoring probationers and parolees is that while the court may impose a variety of conditions, correctional officers have few resources to assure that the conditions are being met or, if violations are detected, to punish the behavior. The inability to monitor and punish violations is particularly troublesome when it comes to drug offenders. Mark Kleiman says that controlling probationers' and parolees' drug use is key to the nation's ability to reduce overall demand for illicit drugs. He writes that:

> By one estimate, about three-quarters of all frequent, high-dose users of cocaine and heroin are arrested in the course of a given year, suggesting that some 60 percent of the total volume in those markets is purchased by those who are under the nominal supervision of the community corrections system.
>
> The implication is clear: our chances of shrinking the hard-drug markets, with all that would mean in terms of violence reduction, neighborhood protection, and reduced need for incarceration, depend largely on managing the behavior of those frequent hard-drug users who are also clients of the community corrections system (Kleiman 1999).

Dr. Kleiman suggests a program of "coerced abstinence," where probationers and parolees would be required to take frequent drug tests—say, twice weekly—as a condition of remaining on the street. These tests are inexpensive—urine tests covering up to five drugs at a time can be administered for a total cost of less than $5 per test—and show immediate results. If an offender fails the test, he or she would be placed in jail, initially for a short period (possibly a weekend) and then for longer periods if the initial failure were repeated. Treatment programs at little or no cost to the user would have to be available not only in every prison, but for every drug-dependent probationer and parolee. Efforts to test Dr. Kleiman's proposals are under way in Connecticut and Maryland. At last report, Maryland had more than 16,000 probationers under the program and was claiming good results. A formal evaluation is being conducted.

Intermediate Sanctions for Parole and Probation Violators

States continue to struggle with how they might respond to violations of probation and parole—particularly technical violations that do not involve, of themselves, new criminal behavior. Many believe that for probation and parole to work, sanctions must be in place for violations. Even the smallest violations must be met with a meaningful response from probation/parole officers. But responding with a prison cell may be both unnecessary and expensive. Several states are now restructuring the court's responses to technical violations. In 1988 Missouri opened up the Kansas City Recycling Center, a 41-bed facility operated by a private contractor to deal exclusively with technical violators who have been recommended for revocation. The pilot program proved so successful that the state took over operation and set aside a complete correctional facility of 250 beds for the program. Mississippi and Georgia use ninety-day boot camp programs, housed in separate wings of the state prisons, for probation violators (for other program descriptions, see Parent et al. 1994).

The Delaware Department of Correction noted that 60 percent of its violations from probation and parole were for technical violations, putting significant strain on the state's jail and prison operation. Their solution was to build into the system an intermediate step between probation and incarceration by building Violation of Probation (VOP) centers. Today, they have two such centers in operation, with a third in the planning stages. An offender usually ends up in the VOP center after being arrested by probation officers using an administrative warrant for technical violations of the conditions of supervision. Usually within one working day, the offender is placed on a special VOP court calendar reserved for the program. The intent is to transfer the offender as quickly as possible to the VOP center. First-time offenders serve up to seven days; second-time offenders up to fourteen days; and repeat offenders can serve up to thirty days. There is no limit to the number of times an offender can be sent to the VOP center. The VOP philosophy is similar to that of boot camps. The days are highly regimented, the rules are strict, and the discipline is enforced without exception. The Delaware Commissioner of Corrections wrote: "The goal of the VOP center is to fulfill the need for an immediate, harsh sanction for probation violators" (Taylor 2000, 185).

While empirical evidence as to the effects of these programs is scant, system officials believe that the programs serve to increase the certainty of punishment, while reserving scarce prison space for the truly violent.

Importantly, experts believe that states with "intermediate" (nonprison) options for responding to less serious probation/parole violations are able to reduce new commitments to prison.

Neighborhood-Based Parole and Probation Supervision

Crime and criminality are complex, multifaceted problems; and real long-term solutions must come *from* the community, and be actively participated in *by* the community and those that surround the offender. This model of community engagement is the foundation of community policing, and its tenets are now spreading to community corrections.

At the philosophy's core is the notion that for probation and parole supervision to be effective, they must take place where offenders live and recreate. Proponents of this model argue that community corrections has suffered from "fortress" or "bunker" mentality, where supervision takes place in offices far removed from neighborhoods and the factors that contribute to crime and disorder. As Corbett et al. write:

> The office is rightfully the base of supervision; the neighborhood should be the place of supervision. Firsthand knowledge of where the offender lives, his family, and his immediate and extended environment are critical elements of meaningful supervision. Meaningful supervision also means that it is conducted at times not confined to the traditional 8:00 a.m. to 5:00 p.m., Monday through Friday. To be effective, it must be delivered at nights, on weekends, and on holidays (Clear and Corbett 1999).

This new parole model is being referred to as "neighborhood parole" (Smith and Dickey 1998), "corrections of place" (Clear and Corbett 1999), or "broken windows" probation (Reinventing Probation Council 2000). Regardless of the name, the key components are the same. They involve strengthening community corrections linkages with law enforcement and the community; brokering treatment and work resources; and attempting to change the offenders' lives through personal, family, and neighborhood interventions. At the core, these models move away from managing offenders on conventional caseloads and toward a more "activist supervision," where agents are responsible for close supervision as well as procuring jobs, social support, and needed treatment. Effective supervision then is attentive to the social ecology of community life (Rhine 1998; Clear and Corbett 1999).

The "broken windows" model of community supervision is attracting a lot of attention from professionals in the field.[4] It is being discussed at professional meetings; publications are being produced; and a group of leaders from probation and parole agencies have volunteered their services to provide technical assistance to communities wishing to adopt the model. Boston, Phoenix, and numerous districts throughout Iowa, Maryland, and elsewhere have adopted many of the elements (Reinventing Probation Council 2000).

The "neighborhood parole" model has been most well thought out in Wisconsin, where the Governor's Task Force on Sentencing and Corrections recommended the program. Program proponents realize neighborhood-based parole will be more costly than traditional parole supervision, but are hopeful that reduced recidivism and revocations to prison will offset program costs. In 1998 the Wisconsin legislature allocated $8 million to fund and evaluate two countywide pilot projects (Smith and Dickey 1998).

The Washington State Department of Corrections in Spokane has also developed a program called Neighborhood Based Supervision (NBS). NBS corrections officers share office space with local police officers and other shareholders, along with neighborhood volunteers housed at Community Oriented Policing Substations (COPS). Being located in the neighborhoods' COPS shop enabled the community corrections officers (CCOs) to work cooperatively with police officers and community members while supervising offenders on their caseloads who live in their neighborhoods. The program reports a 35 percent reduction in burglaries since the beginning of the program in 1993. The Washington program is now expanding into other communities (Lehman 2000a).

CONCLUDING REMARKS

While no one can predict the future, it is likely to be characterized by a greater number of probationers and parolees who have increasingly serious social and personal problems. Taxes are unlikely to increase, resulting in fewer social services available to community corrections clients. All of this means that offenders will receive fewer services to help them deal with their underlying problems, assuring that recidivism rates will remain high, and public support for community corrections will remain low.

At the same time, however, there are some real glimmers of hope emerging. However, it is again the practical, rather than the humanistic or reintegrative, appeal of community corrections that is likely to be important. Today, less than half of felony convictions result in a prison term, and the average prison term served is about two years. Yet states are struggling financially to keep up with the demands of imposing that level of imprisonment, and are being forced to make some hard choices regarding spending priorities. Many states must either continue to make cuts in vital social programs to pay for expanded prisons, or take a hard look at who is currently in prison and decide whether some could be punished in tough, but less expensive community-based programs.

So, probation and parole agencies find themselves in a unique position: They are being blamed for the revolving-door justice problem and high levels of crime, and yet they are being asked to solve the problem they are seen as causing. But, for the first time in this author's experience, probation and parole leaders are accepting the challenge. They have become less defensive and are now reexamining the way they do business. They are developing new programs that are research based and are building in measurement systems to track results. Perhaps most importantly, they are reaching out to the rest of the justice system for collaborative partnerships.

One of the critical lessons learned during the past decade has been that no one program—surveillance or rehabilitation alone—or any one agency—police without community corrections, community corrections without mental health, or *any* of these agencies without the community—can reduce crime, or fear of crime, on its own. Community corrections—with its responsibility for supervising three-fourths of all criminal offenders—is critical to any long-term strategy to control crime. But community corrections has been functioning as an entity unto itself. The partnerships and initiatives emerging across the nation promote the idea of interagency collaboration and communication, resulting in enhanced monitoring and improved delivery of services. If evaluations show the programs work, we might finally deliver community corrections programs that live up to their early promises—protecting citizens while fostering offender rehabilitation.

18

Prosecution

BRIAN FORST

INTRODUCTION

Some of the most fundamental and vexing of all public policy questions revolve around what prosecutors should do with people arrested for violating the law. Despite years of increases in prison populations, many still believe that our crime problem is largely the product of a system that is too soft on criminals. How tough are prosecutors really? Do they achieve a proper balance between the rights of the accused and the rights of victims? Is the main problem that offenders too often slip through the system on legal technicalities? Or is it that prosecutors have discretion that is unchecked and exercised arbitrarily, often against the poor and minorities? Should prosecutors be responsible for preventing crimes? How? What are the core problems of prosecution? What can be done about them?

These questions can be addressed by starting with basics. Most agree that case processing should be just, effective, and speedy, but authorities disagree broadly and often bitterly over the specifics. For prosecutors, central questions involve how to allocate scarce resources and how best to proceed for each of a wide variety of cases involving street crime, domestic violence, drug violations, child abuse, white-collar offenses, and repeat offenders in violation of court orders and warrants. The decision about whether and how to charge each arrested person must take into account the often conflicting goals of crime prevention, fairness, reform of the offender and reintegration into the community, and resource conservation.

TYPICAL CASE DISPOSITIONS

Given these various goals, what happens to the approximately three million arrests made each year in the United States for index crimes (homicide, forcible rape, robbery, burglary, aggravated assault, larceny, and

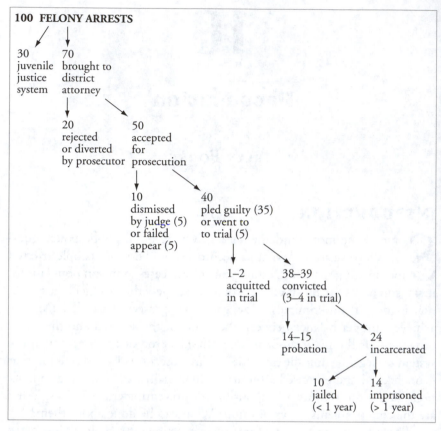

Figure 18.1
Typical Dispositions of 100 Felony Arrests in the United States, 1996

arson)? Just as most offenses do not end in arrest, available data suggest that most arrests do not end in conviction (Brown, Langan, and Levin 1999). Those who are convicted are considerably more likely to be incarcerated, and for longer periods than a few decades ago, due to greater public concern about crime. In 1970, imprisonments amounted to fewer than 1 percent of all reported index crimes. By 1996 the rate had nearly tripled, rising to 2.6 percent.[1]

Figure 18.1 depicts the outcomes of 100 typical arrests for felony offenses in a cross section of jurisdictions throughout the United States.[2]

To begin with, about 30 percent of all felony arrests involve juvenile offenders. Statistics about the outcomes of those cases are not readily available, largely because of a widespread reluctance to maintain juvenile records. To the extent that we do know about the dispositions of the million-plus felony cases involving juveniles annually, we can say that they tend to involve more variation in handling than adult felony cases from jurisdiction to jurisdiction and, generally, fewer long-term commitments.[3]

We know a bit more about what happens to adults arrested for felony crimes. About 30 percent of these cases are either rejected outright at the initial screening stage or dropped by the prosecutor soon afterward; some 70 percent are accepted for prosecution (about 50 of the original 100 felony arrests displayed in Figure 18.1). In about 10 of those 50, the judge dismisses the case due to evidence insufficiency, procedural difficulty (e.g., the prosecutor is not prepared), or the triviality of the offense; five more are eventually dropped because the defendant fails to appear in court after having been released on money bond, personal recognizance, or third-party custody. (About 35 of the 50 defendants whose cases are accepted for prosecution are released prior to trial, and about 5 of those are re-arrested before the case is resolved. [Toborg 1982; Rhodes 1985; Bureau of Justice Statistics 1991]). Some 35 (about 85–90 percent) of the 40 remaining defendants plead guilty, often to obtain a lighter sentence than if found guilty in trial; the other 5 go to trial and are most often found guilty.[4] Most of the 38 or 39 thus convicted are incarcerated, the more serious receiving prison and the others jail terms of less than a year.

One measure of the importance of the prosecutor is revealed in Figure 18.1: for every felony case that a judge presides over in trial, the prosecutor decides the fate of 14 adult felony cases brought by the police.

WHAT FACTORS PREDICT CONVICTION AND INCARCERATION?

The numbers presented above tell us little about the factors that determine *which* cases are selected for prosecution and harsher sanctions in any jurisdiction. We can begin to learn about the factors that influence felony case dispositions by focusing on the cases dropped and the reasons given by prosecutors for rejecting them.

It turns out that the vast majority of all felony cases dropped by the prosecutor are rejected due to insufficiency of evidence—the police fail to produce adequate physical evidence (e.g., stolen property, implements of the crime) or testimonial evidence from victims or eye witnesses (Boland, Mahanna, and Sones 1992). The next major reason given by prosecutors, although far less common than evidentiary insufficiency, is triviality of the offense (often reported as declined "in the interest of justice"). The defendants in these cases are generally not viewed as serious threats to the community. Most are dropped outright, while others are "diverted," often with the stipulation that the defendant must complete a program of counseling or instruction aimed at rehabilitation (Adams and Cutshall 1987).

Many of the cases dropped or diverted are not trivial. Cases of assault and rape, in particular—often cases involving serious injury—are frequently dropped by prosecutors because they arise between people who knew each other prior to the offense, typically in domestic settings. Studies of felony arrest processing in several jurisdictions have shown that in the majority of violent offense cases, the assailant is known to the victim, many involving members of the same family.[5] Prosecutors have traditionally regarded such cases as unattractive; the victims, after having called the police to arrest the offender, are frequently uncooperative.[6] Because of uncooperative witnesses, prosecutors reject arrests for crimes of assault within families at a rate of over 40 percent—nearly three times the rate for assault cases involving strangers.[7] Males with a habit of assaulting their female partners may commit serious crimes in the home as frequently as other offenders with more serious criminal records do on the street.[8] Although considerable progress appears to have been made on this front since 1980, prosecutors still are often reluctant to give the attention to such cases that may be warranted by conventional standards of justice.

Largely because of the importance of the relationship between offender and victim, conviction rates vary substantially from one index crime to another. Recall from Figure 18.1 that some 38 or 39 of a typical cross-section of 100 felony arrestees are convicted. For murder, the number is much higher: 60 out of a typical 100 persons arrested are convicted. About half of all persons arrested for larceny are convicted. For robbery, a crime committed frequently in retaliation by persons known to the victim, about 30 of a typical 100 arrestees are convicted. For aggravated assault, just 13 are convicted (Brown, Langan, and Levin 1999).

It is widely believed that many, if not most, felony cases presented to prosecutors are dropped for another reason—legal "technicalities" related to Fourth Amendment exclusionary rule violations. In fact, fewer than one percent of all felony arrests are dropped on such grounds; most of those are drug cases involving questionable procedures for searching for drugs (Forst, Lucianovic, and Cox, 1977; Brosi 1979; Boland, Mahanna, and Sones 1992). While the exclusionary rule may retard the ability of the police to arrest offenders and bring apprehended offenders to the prosecutor, it does not appear to play a major role in the prosecutor's decision to reject or dismiss cases.[9]

Of course, the reasons for case rejections officially recorded by public agents are not necessarily to be believed. On this question, however, independent empirical evidence exists to validate the official reasons. Convictions are systematically more likely to follow arrest when police produce and document physical evidence in the case than when such evidence is not produced. Likewise, when police produce information about two or more witnesses (including victims), convictions are more likely to follow. And when police make the arrest soon after an offense occurs, physical evidence is more likely to be found and a conviction is more likely to follow than when more time elapses between the offense and the arrest (Forst, Lucianovic, and Cox 1977; Forst, et al. 1981).

It should not be surprising that arrests with the strongest tangible and testimonial evidence are most likely to produce convictions. Old and young audiences alike have seen enough courtroom drama on television and in movies to know that the evidence needed to convict in court must be sufficient to prove guilt beyond a reasonable doubt. More instrumental is the fact that the *police* are responsible for obtaining physical evidence and information about witnesses, as well as for providing information to witnesses that induces them to support the prosecutor in convicting offenders. While the police have little control over the amount and quality of evidence available for processing, it turns out that some police officers consistently produce arrests that end in convictions at a rate substantially surpassing random chance.[10] Interviews have revealed that those officers tend to be more persistent about finding witnesses and more conscientious about follow-up investigation than officers with low rates of conviction (Forst, et al. 1981).

In short, whether an arrest ends in conviction depends in the first place on factors over which the prosecutor has no direct control: the strength of the evidence as presented to the police officer, the effectiveness of the officer in bringing the best available evidence (both tangible and testimonial) to the prosecutor, and the seriousness of the offense. Nonetheless, prosecution resources and practices—and the exercise of discretion—do play a central role in determining whether arrests lead to conviction.

THE PROSECUTOR'S IMPACT ON SENTENCING AND SANCTIONS

Until the 1980s, sentencing decisions were not substantially more predictable than prosecution decisions. The seriousness of the offense, an important factor in prosecution, was found also to be critical in sentencing, as was the offender's prior record, and whether the defendant pled guilty (those who did tended to receive lighter sentences than those similarly charged who took their chances and were found guilty in trial) (Blumstein et al. 1983, pp. 11–12, 18). The sentencing decision was found to have been shaped most decisively, however, by the sentencing judge, more so than all other factors combined. This finding was confirmed both in studies in which identical cases were shown to several judges for an opinion about the appropriate sentence and in studies of sentences given in real cases, using detailed case descriptions from presentence investigation reports to control statistically for other factors influencing sentence severity (Hogarth 1971; Diamond and Zeisel 1975; Forst and Wellford 1981).[11] Judges exercised discretion in determining not only who would be incarcerated and who would be given terms of probation, but also the minimum term before eligibility for parole for persons selected for prison, as well as the extraordinary option of selecting concurrent or consecutive terms of imprisonment for separate conviction charges in individual cases.

The tide shifted in the 1980s, largely because legislators assumed a much larger role in the toughening of sanctions than during any earlier period, as noted in the accompanying chapter by Michael Tonry. It was the product also of research findings—first on the ineffectiveness of rehabilitation programs (Martinson1974),[12] second on disparity in judicial sentencing practices.[13] Support for flexible ("indeterminate") sanctions began to erode when reformers and public entertainments (the movie *A Clockwork Orange* is a classic example) raised questions about the ethics of the rehabilitation model. Even members of the judiciary stepped forward to register complaint about indeterminate sentencing (Frankel 1973).

The replacement of indeterminate sentencing with more structured approaches removed discretion from judges and parole officials, but not from prosecutors. Does this mean a shift in sentencing discretion from judges to prosecutors? Not necessarily. What some see as a shift in discretionary authority from judge to prosecutor, others may see as a net reduction in unwarranted disparity under sentencing guidelines with no absolute increase in prosecutorial discretion. Judges surely have less discretionary authority under the guidelines, but it is not evident that prosecutors have more, either in filing charges or reducing them, than they did before guidelines. One might reasonably expect disparity in the exercise of prosecutorial discretion to be relatively structured at least insofar as assistant district attorneys work for the D.A. Prior to laws that made sentencing practices more uniform, individual judges reported to no one in shaping sentences. If an imbalance of power between judge and prosecutor is regarded as the primary problem of structured sentencing policy, it becomes tempting to find solutions that result in more judicial discretion and a return to disparate sentencing, with no less prosecutorial discretion—a cure that could be far worse than the disease.

One caution is in order to prosecutors interested in the sentencing implications of their charging and case-processing decisions: Severe sentences for offenders with long records, often the product of mandatory minimum and "three-strikes" statutes, can be especially counterproductive. They often work at cross-purposes with the goal of "selective incapacitation"—reserving prison space for the most dangerous and criminally active offenders. The three-strikes statutes may have offsetting deterrent effects,[14] but to the extent that offenders tend to accumulate longer records as they grow older, tough mandatory minimums for persons with long records without regard to age can have the effect of reserving prison space primarily for offenders nearing the ends of their criminal careers. Further losses of incapacitation benefits result when parole boards accelerate the release of dangerous offenders to accommodate the incarceration of less dangerous drug offenders sentenced under mandatory minimum statutes.[1] Prosecutors should be wary of charging and case-processing decisions that produce long sentences for offenders nearing "retirement" from their criminal careers and that hasten the release of more dangerous offenders from prison.

As the prosecutor becomes increasingly influential in determining the sanction imposed on the offender in most jurisdictions, it becomes especially important that prosecution policy be mindful of issues that go beyond the immediate impact of case-processing decisions on the court outcome. Prosecutors should consider also whether the sanction that will follow a conviction is the most effective alternative for the offender and the community. Incarceration may be the most appropriate sanction for some offenders, but other sanctions may be more productive in reducing crime and may do so at a considerable saving to the public. An affluent nation with a high crime rate may be both able and willing to put a larger proportion of its population behind bars than any other in the world—more than 1 percent of the U.S. adult male population, about two million in all (Bureau of Justice Statistics 2000)—but we will do well to consider alternatives to prison and jail for offenders who can be safely and effectively punished in other ways: fines, restitution, forfeiture, and community-based sanctions that encourage community reintegration without substantial risks. These sanctions are less inexpensive to administer, and they tend to produce less stigma than prison, enhancing the offender's prospects for community reintegration. Moreover, some alternatives to incarceration can provide compensation to the victim and, especially in the case of crimes without identifiable victims, to society.

What are these options? The most widely used alternatives to conventional incarceration include *community service, shock probation* (resentencing the prisoner to probation after a short prison term), *intensive probation supervision* (often involving *house arrest* and *electronic monitoring*), and *community-based corrections*. These alternatives, considered more fully in Joan Petersilia's chapter in this volume, have become increasingly important as our prison populations have continued to soar during the 1980s, 1990s and beyond. A serious risk associated with the harsher of these alternatives is that they may not be used as alternatives to incarceration at all that they may be imposed instead on offenders who would ordinarily have received lesser sanctions (a phenomenon commonly referred to as "net widening"), making it more difficult for community reintegration—or that they may be inappropriately used in *addition* to incarceration.

The tough questions for prosecutors in making case-processing decisions that influence the sanction are these:

1. Will the action and resulting sanction best serve the collective interests of the community, taking into account the likely future behavior of the offender and victim(s) in the current case, and that of other prospective offenders and victims?
2. Will it be administered effectively and fairly, so as to make it transparent that the sanction is not out of line with that received by similarly situated offenders and in similarly serious cases?
3. What voice should the victim and offender have in these matters?

Different jurisdictions will inevitably arrive at different answers to these questions. Regardless of those answers, basic notions of justice warrant that they be uniformly applied to offenders within the jurisdiction.

VARIATION IN SCREENING AND PLEA BARGAINING PRACTICES

The practices and outcomes that follow arrest are not uniform across the approximately 2,500 prosecution offices in the United States[16]—prosecutors are free to go about their business in quite different ways from one jurisdiction to another, and even among offices within the same jurisdiction. The Constitution says nothing explicit about prosecutorial rules and standards.[17] As a result, prosecutors in some offices are much more inclined to obtain convictions by plea rather than take cases to trial. Conventional wisdom holds that these differences are due to variations in the workloads per prosecutor from office to office, but that is by no means the whole story. Jurisdictions with huge caseloads often have low ratios of pleas to trials, while those with much smaller caseloads often have high ratios.[18]

Prosecution *policy*—whether to aim for *quality* convictions by being more selective at the screening stage and then putting more effort into bringing cases to trial, or to aim for *more* convictions by accepting more marginal cases and putting greater effort into negotiating guilty pleas in return for charge reductions—appears to be no less important a determinant of the ratio of pleas-to-trials than the press of large caseloads. In screening arrests for prosecution, offices that aim for more convictions are more inclined to apply the arrest standard of "probable cause," while those that aim for quality convictions tend to use a higher standard of "trial-worthiness." Offices with less selective screening policies have been found to have higher plea-to-trial ratios and higher conviction rates, but lower rates of imprisonment, than those that are more selective.[19] Less selective screening practices appear also to reduce the total number of justice errors, although the evidence on judicial errors has been more anecdotal and indirect than systematic.[20] In jurisdictions where the police tend to bring weaker cases, a more selective screening policy appears to be more clearly justifiable (Forst 2001).

Many have argued that plea-bargaining is simply wrong and should be abolished—it deprives defendants of their day in court and deprives victims of the security of long terms of incarceration for offenders (see Jost 1999). But the abolition of or constraints on plea-bargaining practices by legislation or voter referendum has proven to be at best ineffective and often counterproductive.[21] It is clear that little good would be accomplished by attempting to force all cases through the trial process, since many—perhaps most—pleas involve cases in which an offender has no defense and simply wishes to expedite the process, often in exchange for minor concessions by the prosecutor.

Other pleas involve leniency in exchange for information from the defendant against other suspects. Such pleas can be indispensable for bringing offenders to justice, but they can also risk miscarriages of justice, especially when the person offering the information is a greater menace to the community than the person about whom the information is given. Street offenders have been found, in any case, to be less inclined to assist prosecutors by providing such information than other offenders; many have been known to impose sanctions against collaborators who breach a bond of trust that are considerably harsher than those imposed by the criminal justice system (Forst and Lucianovic 1977).

UNBRIDLED PROSECUTORIAL DISCRETION?

The typical urban prosecutor's office, presented with approximately 100 felony cases per attorney each year, obviously cannot give celebrity-status attention to every case. In rationing their time, the attorneys in the office normally exercise considerable latitude in choosing which felony arrests to prosecute, what charges to file, how aggressively to prosecute each case, and what to negotiate with the defense attorney. According to criminologist Albert Reiss (1974), prosecutors exercise "the greatest discretion in the formally organized criminal justice network."

For many if not most cases, the decision whether to prosecute is virtually automatic—cases in which the evidence is either extremely strong or weak and cases involving either very serious or trivial offenses. Numerous studies agree that prosecutors' case-screening and handling decisions have been influenced primarily by the strength of the evidence and the seriousness of the offense (Forst and Brosi, 1977; U.S. Department of Justice 1977; Jacoby 1981; Feeney, Dill, and Weir 1983). In the late 1970s and early 1980s many prosecutors, stimulated largely by federal support, instituted programs to target resources as well on cases involving repeat offenders (Chelimsky and Dahmann 1981). Prosecutors' decisions have been neither random nor incomprehensible.

Within those boundaries, however, there is substantial discretion. In deciding how to allocate their time to various cases, how to proceed in each, and in recommending sentences to judges, prosecutors have considerable room to maneuver. Written policies used in even the most rule-conscious offices do not provide unambiguous instructions about how to handle each and every type of case. Because of this discretion, statistical models of prosecutors' decision-making are incapable of accurately predicting screening, charging, or plea-bargaining decisions in particular cases.

When asked to explain the rationale behind their decisions, prosecutors are often inclined to say that case-handling decisions, like medical decisions, involve both science and craft, and that experienced prosecutors know how to blend the technical requirements of the law with the good judgment that comes from years of practice. Unfortunately, this tells us nothing about the underlying goals that influence their actions. Nor do we know whether prosecutors consciously make case selection and handling decisions with such goals in mind. Most prosecutors argue that while justice, crime control, and speedy case-processing are all worthy goals, each case is unique. Whether to accept a case, what charges to file, how much time to spend preparing it for a court proceeding, what charge or charges to allow the defendant to plead to in return for dropping other charges (or what sentence to recommend to the judge if the defendant pleads guilty to a particular charge) in any given case cannot be determined by pondering over abstract goals or resorting to a formula derived from such goals. Until a strong argument can be made for instituting a more explicit set of rules or guidelines for making case-processing decisions based on well-established factual links between the rules and such tangible goals as crime control and reduced case-processing time, decisions about individual cases are likely to continue to be made in a subjective and largely unpredictable manner.

At some point, however, prosecutors risk pushing the political, if not the ethical[22] and Constitutional limits of their discretion. Authorities from both ends of the political spectrum have long voiced strong objection to the politicization of prosecution policies and practices. The 1990s saw accusations of abusive prosecution made against the independent prosecutor in his pursuit of Bill Clinton (Adams 2000; Will 1994), against Joseph DiGenova in his pursuit of the former Washington, D.C., Mayor Marion Barry following a sensational cocaine bust, and against U.S. attorneys in going after arbitrarily selected Wall Street traders under the amorphous Racketeer Influenced and Corrupt Organization (RICO) statute (Forst 1995, pp. 372, 587 [Note 9]).[23] Much less has been written about cases involving low-level street offenders, but the lack of any recent systematic review of prosecutors' decisions about which cases are filed in court and how much attention is given to each should lead one to wonder about even-handedness in those cases as well.

Prosecutors may in fact be less than clear about the proper goals of prosecution, or about the best way to achieve any particular goal. They are likely to find, however, that the development of guidelines for screening and case-processing decisions can at least produce greater consistency and coherence, if not critical and constructive thinking about the role of the prosecutor in society.

INCENTIVES OF PROSECUTORS

Given the substantial obstacles confronting prosecutors—large case loads, limited resources, and broadly conflicting views about what the system ought to be accomplishing—it seems in order to ask what motivates them. District attorneys are typically publicly elected officials, so they are inclined to conduct themselves in a way that appeals to the general public.[24] But can we be sure that public appeal has much to do with the attainment of justice? Suppose a district attorney is especially conscientious about taking on cases involving highly active offenders, even when those cases require the commitment of additional resources (e.g., giving extra attention to the needs of reluctant witnesses). If as a result the crime rate were reduced by 10 percent, our inability to prove cause and effect would prevent even the district attorney from knowing for certain whether his or her conscientiousness paid off. Another district attorney may routinely drop cases involving repeat offenders unless they happen to be easy cases, taking on only those that do not require much attention; he may then boast of winning a few high profile cases, or perhaps of a conviction rate over 90 percent for the narrow subset of cases that either go to trial or result in guilty pleas. Since information about cases dropped by the prosecutor is not generally made available to the public, a prosecutor's legitimate crime control efforts, or lack thereof, will go unnoticed.

The prosecutor is insulated by the virtual absence of a system of measured public accountability in most states. The success of prosecutors is assessed principally in terms of the public's perception of the prosecutor's ability to convict offenders. These perceptions are shaped primarily by a few prominent cases in the news and by occasional public pronouncements by a district attorney or attorney general asserting toughness against any and all who would dare to violate the law. Unlike other elected officials, whose voting records are readily accessible for public viewing, the prosecutor's case-processing decisions are typically hidden from public view. And unlike police chiefs, who are appointed by and accountable to mayors, prosecutors generally do not report to a higher political authority in a position to call for a more comprehensive system of accountability. The voters do not spontaneously organize to ask for such systems, and political opponents have not been able to distract the general public from its preoccupation with celebrity cases and an obliviousness to the importance of systematic measures of performance. The media, capable of enlightening the public on the folly of weak accountability for the vast majority of felony cases, have not helped either. Rather, they have revealed a strong preference for feeding the public's appetite for information about exceptional cases.

Prosecutors in most jurisdictions do not report information about the numbers and types of arrests received from the police and the dispositions of each type. To put this problem in perspective, imagine a police chief deciding not to provide comprehensive information about reported offenses, arrests, and clearances to anyone outside the office. Imagine him or her justifying such a decision on grounds that such information is too easily misinterpreted to be useful. Asked how, then, the public should hold the chief and the department accountable, suppose the chief responded that his frequent contacts with the public and attention from the local media make him more than sufficiently accountable. Such a stance would be regarded as arrogant and irresponsible. Yet this is essentially the position of most prosecutors in the United States with regard to information about the number and type of arrests brought by the police, the number of those cases accepted for prosecution and filed in the court, and the outcomes of those cases in court.

Most chief prosecutors, while directly accountable to the voters, have it in their narrow interest not to subject themselves to systems of accountability that opponents could use against them. The police chief may benefit from falling crime rates but must also suffer the inevitable upward swings in crime; the prosecutor is rarely called to task by the local press for a drop in the conviction rate. Conviction rates are not routinely reported to a national agency in the same way that crimes reported to the police and arrests made by the police are documented annually by the FBI. The National Judicial Reporting Program (NJRP) reports felony convictions and arrests for about 300 of the nation's 3,195 counties, but the data are aggregates rather than based on individually tracked felony cases (Brown, Langan, and Levin 1999, p. 5). Many of the convictions reported for any given year relate to arrests made in earlier years, which creates distortions especially when the aggregates change from one year to the next. Moreover, the NJRP gives no information about cases rejected or dropped by prosecutors. More than a few people might like to know *why* over 80 percent of all arrests for motor vehicle theft fail to end in conviction, and why about 60 percent of all arrests for robbery and burglary fail as well.

Nor are the prosecutors in most jurisdictions required to provide systematic information about case outcomes to other criminal justice agencies that deal with and rely on the prosecutor, most notably the police and victim-witness organizations. Some prosecutors do provide feedback, but it is usually voluntary and episodic.

Prosecutors occasionally select cases and handle them in a way that gives some political visibility, but this too tends to be opportunistic rather than systematic. Prosecutors in New York have established a tradition of pursuing high-profile cases aggressively, accepting pleas well beyond national norms in other cases, and eventually running for higher public office.[25] A prosecutor's career path can be driven, for better or worse, by the outcome of a single case that attains local or national prominence.

What then does give public visibility to the district attorney? Most conspicuous is the handful of exceptional cases that appear in the daily papers and on news broadcasts. Also important is the image that the D.A. projects in press conferences and public appearances on a variety of crime issues. Many a prosecutor has gained visibility by announcing crackdowns on organized crime or drug dealing. Former U.S. Attorney Rudolph Giuliani adopted such an approach in his high profile targeting of white-collar offenders in the Southern District of New York in the late 1980s. If a prosecutor says he is tough on criminals and appears to put up a good fight in the exceptional cases that make the news, any failures in managing his office efficiently or in dealing effectively with the larger pool of cases involving predictably dangerous offenders—cases that rarely make the news—will not jeopardize his prospects for reelection or advancement to higher political office.

"Career criminal" prosecution programs, created in 1975, illustrate the tension that can arise between the somewhat abstract goals of justice and crime prevention, on the one hand, and the more immediate incentives facing prosecutors on the other. The career criminal programs were initiated by the Justice Department to deal with the problem posed by a relatively few offenders who, as researchers found repeatedly, account for a disproportionate share of cases involving serious crimes.[26] It had been perceived generally that prosecutors did not give special attention to cases involving those more criminally active offenders—cases that were often otherwise unattractive. This perception was later validated empirically (Forst and Brosi 1977). To provide an incentive for prosecutors to target more attorney time on such cases, the Justice Department offered additional resources to local prosecutors for the creation of career criminal programs. Many prosecutors, interested in the additional resources, applied for and obtained them, creating sections of the office in which attorneys worked on fewer cases and processed them through all the stages of prosecution ("vertically") rather than in the production-line process ("horizontally") that characterizes municipal prosecution.

Subsequent evaluations of those programs, however, produced mixed results. On the one hand, career criminal units were found to allocate a much greater concentration of resources to cases involving potential career criminals, by some estimates four or five times more than would have been conventionally applied (Chelimsky and Dahmann 1981; Rhodes 1985). On the other hand, the criteria used by the prosecutors to identify career offenders were often less than optimal. Rather than pinpointing the most criminally active suspects, most jurisdictions developed criteria designed to be easily administered and to produce interesting cases. Career criminal units typically targeted offenders with at least one prior felony conviction and current charges involving a serious crime—often homicide, rape, or assault. Such criteria are better than none, but prosecutors can do even better by basing case selection on criteria that correspond more closely to the actual characteristics of dangerous, high-crime-rate offenders: prior arrests for serious crimes, a juvenile record, youthfulness, drug use, and known involvement in robbery or burglary. Those characteristics had been shown to be the strongest predictors of predatory crime in research at the University of Pennsylvania, the Rand Corporation, and elsewhere (Wolfgang, Figlio, and Sellin 1972, p. 88; Williams 1979; Forst, Rhodes et al. 1982; Greenwood 1982; Chaiken and Chaiken 1982), yet they rarely turned up as career criminal targeting criteria.[27] The public has been deeply concerned about crime and generally supportive of career criminal programs, but in practice career criminal units have tended to employ criteria that focused largely on criminals in the twilight of their careers, bypassing the offenders likely to inflict the most harm on society.

The programs appear, nonetheless, to have improved prosecution, on balance. Career criminal prosecution units atrophied when federal funding disappeared, but an awareness of the need to consider not only the strength of the evidence and the seriousness of the offense but also the dangerousness of the offender has been a legacy of the units that appears to live on in most conventional prosecution systems.

In spite of these improvements, the incentives of prosecutors and the accountability systems that guide their behavior leave substantial opportunity for disparity and inefficiency in the exercise of discretion. The goals of prosecution have not been made sufficiently clear, and detailed, comprehensive information about the decisions made by prosecutors has not been made sufficiently accessible to allow anyone to know whether prosecutors tend to make decisions about individual cases that correspond closely or consistently to any particular standard of justice or efficiency.

RESISTANCE TO REFORM

Ineffective systems of incentives and accountability have not placed prosecutors at the vanguard of criminal justice reform. The end of the twentieth century finds sea changes in every other sector of the criminal justice system. Policing is going through the community-oriented revolution, as well as a transformation in privatization. As recently as 1965 there were more sworn police officers than private security personnel; 30 years later the number of private security personnel was about triple the number of sworn officers (Forst and Manning 1999, p. 16). We have seen equally remarkable changes in sentencing and corrections: the conversion from extensive judicial discretion in sentencing to mandatory terms and legislatively imposed sentencing guideline systems, large-scale shifts from a black-and-white world of either incarceration or probation to one with a myriad of intermediate sanction options ranging from intensive supervision and electronically monitored home detention to more widespread use of community-based sanctions, and the expansion of private alternatives throughout the corrections sector.

Changes in prosecution have been quite modest by comparison. The typical prosecutor's office has a more modern appearance than it did in the mid-twentieth century, with desktop computers supporting operations, access to vastly greater sources of information, and knowledge of complex forensic technologies such as DNA evidence than ever before. Women and minorities play larger roles as prosecutors than in earlier times, paralleling their gains in virtually every other profession. In the 1990s prosecutors started developing community outreach programs that echoed community policing.

The fundamentals of prosecution, however, remain as they have for decades. The basic nature and goals of prosecution, the role of the citizen as victim or witness in a matter between the state and the defendant, the essential steps in processing cases through the courts, and systems of public accountability all remain essentially as they were in 1970.

A 1998 survey of over 500 scientific evaluations of crime prevention programs, sponsored by the National Institute of Justice and conducted by Lawrence Sherman and his former colleagues at the University of Maryland, found just one evaluation of an innovative prosecution program, an experiment run by David Ford that tested three alternative domestic violence interventions in Indianapolis (Ford and Regoli 1993).[28] Innovation was found mostly in other parts of the justice system—programs initiated by the police, social service agencies, schools, drug treatment specialists, housing and correctional authorities.

Prosecutors are not more inherently resistant to change than others. They tend to be well educated, they must understand fine points of the law, and they must be able to decipher diverse and intricate case details quickly and interpret complex human behaviors accurately. Their work demands intelligence and ingenuity, resourcefulness and hard work. They are sworn to serve the public. And many have experienced that innovations can produce welcome political capital.

Still, as elected officials, district attorneys aim to avoid embarrassment. This is usually accomplished by keeping the bulk of their work below the horizon, staying away from risky ventures and drastic departures from conventional modes of office management and from collaborations with researchers on the assessment of policies, procedures, or performance, assessments that could show up as tomorrow's negative headline.

The prosecutor's insulation derives in part from legal training. Prosecutors are trained in an adversarial system of law, not in principles of service delivery or systems of management. To the extent that they receive any administrative training in law school, it pertains to the management of private law practice rather than the administration of a prosecutor's office.

A first rule of prosecution derives from the legal-adversarial culture: Don't divulge the particulars of your case to anyone who's not in a position to help you win it. Prosecutors become accustomed to keeping their options open by revealing little about their objectives and about the information they have and do not have. They typically see little to gain and much to lose in divulging any information that is not required by law. Internal office policy manuals indicating the prosecutor's guidelines for screening cases and negotiating pleas are typically unavailable to the defense bar and the general public.

On at least one critical dimension—prosecutors' decisions whether to file charges in felony arrests brought by the police—we actually know *less* today than we did in the 1970s and 1980s. Detailed information about the decisions made about whether to accept cases, reasons for rejections, extent of charge reductions, diversions, and related matters—collected through the Prosecutor's Management Information System (PROMIS) from Manhattan, Los Angeles County, Washington, D.C., Wayne County (Detroit), Marion County (Indianapolis), Multnomah County (Portland, Ore.), and a host of other jurisdictions—was, for about 15 years, documented and published by the Bureau of Justice Statistics (BJS). Unfortunately, this series was quietly discontinued in 1992, despite the proliferation of PROMIS-like data systems in district attorneys' offices throughout the United States, as part of a revealed BJS preference for aggregate national estimates over local area data. The routine collection of data from these systems could be extremely useful both as a companion and complement to the Uniform Crime Reports and as a resource for research—for example, to permit an assessment of whether initiatives to protect victims of domestic violence are followed by systematic increases in the rates at which such cases are accepted for prosecution.[29]

While many prosecutors are open and honest about the work of their offices, however, the prosecution culture remains resistant to accountability and fundamental reform. Some offices refuse to record arrest charges, and innovative reform efforts of other criminal justice agents have often been thwarted by prosecutors. Sherman et al. (1998), have documented pretrial diversion programs that "tend to get co-opted by prosecutors for purposes other than the intended purpose of rehabilitating offenders." (p. 14) They note that Sally Hillsman has reported finding prosecutors converting an innovative attempt at rehabilitation in New York into a vehicle for controlling offenders who would otherwise have had their cases dismissed following diversion and the completion of job training. These may be exceptional stories, but without the systematic tracking and reporting of felony arrests through prosecutors' offices, we really have no way of knowing.

DIRECTIONS FOR REFORM: STRUCTURING THE EXERCISE OF PROSECUTORIAL DISCRETION

Aware of room for improvement, a few prosecutors, as well as state and federal legislators and criminal justice system reformers, have set out to introduce procedures designed to produce greater uniformity and efficiency in the decisions and practices that follow arrest. In the 1970s prosecutors began to rely on computers for tracking individual cases and caseloads of individual attorneys, printing subpoenas, producing periodic reports showing various aggregate dimensions of office performance, and providing data so that office policy could be analyzed in depth. Lack of information about prosecutor operations prior to the use of computers limited opportunities to measure the benefits of improved information technology.

The proliferation of management information systems in a setting that traditionally has been ambivalent about such technology, however, suggests that prosecutors gain benefits from these systems that exceed the costs. And despite the limitations of career criminal programs noted earlier, the adoption and retention of basic elements of those programs in most offices after the withdrawal of federal support further attests to a growing sense of prosecutorial awareness of their role in serving aggregate abstractions such as crime prevention. Prosecutors, like many other lawyers, have tended to focus traditionally on individual cases and litigation related to them rather than on jurisdiction-wide, or even office-wide constructs of performance

(Szanton 1972). Thoughtfully crafted guidelines and computerized decision-support systems can and have helped prosecutors to make screening and case-processing decisions more uniform and effective. Computerized information systems developed in the 1970s helped district attorneys to shift their thinking from the single-case litigation perspective instilled by conventional legal training to an orientation that considers the aggregate information in the context of goals of prosecution and sentencing. What is arguably the most fundamental and revolutionary aspect of reform in prosecution has been under way for some time now.

DIRECTIONS FOR FURTHER REFORM: THE EFFECTIVE USE OF INFORMATION

Despite the availability of these systems, most prosecutors continue to operate in outmoded and unhelpful statistical environments, uncharacteristic of other major components of the criminal justice system and inconsistent with contemporary standards of management and public accountability. Critical to the effective use of data used to support criminal justice decisions is that the data be *reliable*. Prosecutors are usually quick to express concern, as they should, about the need for prompt, accurate information about evidence from investigators, forensic laboratories, and lineups. A crime-control-oriented prosecutor should show concern as well about the quality of data indicative of defendant dangerousness, including arrest history ("rap sheet") information, juvenile record, and a urinalysis test result to indicate whether the defendant was on drugs at the time of arrest. Prosecutors have not been conditioned to seek out such information to support prosecution decisions, despite widespread concern about "false positives"—people selected for targeting who in fact would not commit another crime if released. The availability and use of reliable information about prior record and current drug use, when combined with existing information, would provide demonstrably more accurate assessments of defendant dangerousness than current information alone is capable of providing; more accurate assessment means *fewer* false positives and greater opportunity to prevent crime.[30]

Data used by prosecutors and courts, properly processed, can also help improve performance in other areas of the criminal justice system. For example, district attorneys can induce the police to bring better arrests by periodically providing information to police supervisors about the outcomes of the arrests brought to prosecution, itemized by department, precinct, and officer. This information could include data about the frequencies of each major type of outcome (such as those displayed in Figure 18.1) and the reasons for case rejections and dismissals. Information about case outcomes could also be given routinely to the victims and witnesses in those cases. The systematic dissemination of information can also nurture cooperation between prosecutors and police, victims, and witnesses. Public support of the criminal justice system is not enhanced by the routine failure of prosecutors to provide feedback to victims and witnesses. Similarly, police incentives to produce better evidence are weakened when prosecutors routinely fail to provide information about arrest outcomes to police officers and their supervisors.[31]

DIRECTIONS FOR FURTHER REFORM: COMMUNITY PROSECUTION

In the 1990s a few chief prosecutors attempted to improve the operations of their offices and improve their relations with the public in the process by introducing "community-oriented" prosecution programs. Patterned after community policing programs that aim to improve police performance by building bridges to the community, these programs assign individual attorneys to cases involving crimes in specific neighborhoods. The basic idea is that prosecutors can be more effective when they become less insular and get to know the neighborhood and its problems better (Forst 1993; Coles and Kelling 1998, 1999). Additional economies are likely to derive from working with the same few police officers who are responsible for particular neighborhoods. The impact of these programs on crime has not been rigorously assessed at the time of this writing, but the programs pass the test of common sense and reflect the spirit that characterizes success in a service economy—generating value by getting closer to the customer.

District attorneys from Boston and Brooklyn to Kansas City and Portland have launched such programs of community outreach, assigning cases to assistant D.A.s by neighborhood rather than in the order they arrive, and encouraging their assistants to spend more time in the community (Boland 1997, 1998, 1999; Coles and Kelling 1998, 1999). A common theme is to redirect service outside the court, with more sensitivity to the cultures and special needs of those served. Other common characteristics include flexible organizational arrangements and innovative use of the law (Boland 1997).

Prosecutors who have publicly embraced these goals of service and grassroots sensitivity are putting a variety of programs in place to achieve them: working more closely with those who understand the unique characteristics of particular neighborhoods, sometimes assigning assistant district attorneys to work out of police precincts or storefronts, supporting community crime prevention programs, and converting from a production line approach that moves cases along impersonally to a system ("vertical prosecution") that reduces the need for traumatized victims to repeat harrowing experiences to a sequence of strangers. A corollary activity has been to deal with crimes involving offenders who operate across communities by collaborating more closely with prosecutors in other jurisdictions.

A focus group commissioned by the Bureau of Justice Assistance developed this definition of community prosecution: "A long term, proactive strategy involving a partnership among the prosecutor's office, law enforcement, the community and public and private organizations whereby the authority of the prosecutor's office is used to solve problems and improve public safety and the quality of life in an identified community" (Stevens 1994, p. 13).

These ideas mirror ones initiated 10 years earlier in policing. Municipal police departments throughout the country have worked to build bridges to the community and improve public relations by moving officers from squad cars to foot and bicycle patrols, sending officers to schools to speak about drugs, and focusing more on prostitution, vandalism, and other crimes of disorder. Anecdotal evidence in support of these activities is compelling, but whether they really reduce serious crime remains unclear. Wesley Skogan's (1990) exhaustive review of the experimental research in several cities has found these efforts to have done more to reduce fear and increase public satisfaction with police service than to reduce crime rates, at least in the short term.[32]

Community policing and community prosecution are rooted more fundamentally in two larger social movements of the 1980s and 1990s: consumerism and communitarianism. The consumer movement itself has two distinct roots, one emphasizing excellence in service delivery, stimulated by the work of Tom Peters and Bob Waterman (1982), the other emphasizing consumer rights, stimulated by the work of Ralph Nader (1965). The combined effects of these influences on the attitudes, expectations, and behaviors of people acting both as public citizens and private consumers paved the way for criminal justice focus on the quality of service. The communitarian roots, stimulated largely by the work of Amitai Etzioni (1993), emphasize people working together more closely in crime watches, community policing and prosecution programs, sentencing nonviolent offenders to community service, and strengthening informal social control mechanisms (pp. 139–41).

By the late 1990s, federal funding became widely available to district attorneys to sweeten the community prosecution pot. Byrne Grant program funds, administered by the Bureau of Justice Assistance, provide support to prosecutors to establish and participate in community prosecution programs generally and community justice centers and multijurisdictional task forces in particular.

Many prosecutors have responded by climbing aboard the community bandwagon. They have done so in much the same way as did police chiefs: first a few brave souls, then others, when the political benefits become more apparent and federal support available. Columnist Robert Samuelson (2000) has referred to community-oriented justice programs that confer benefits on politicians rather than on more traditional special interest groups as "the new pork barrel . . . propaganda disguised as a government program." Most prosecutors may be adopting these programs with noble intentions. There is, in any case, merit in bringing prosecutors down from the ivory tower, to induce greater sensitivity to the lives of the people whose fates are often at the mercy of the prosecutor's decisions. Still, it may be no coincidence that such programs are unheard of in other countries, where prosecutors are appointed rather than elected. Ten years ago it was common to hear police officers complain about learning of their department's conversion to "community policing" on the evening news. Today, assistant district attorneys are telling similar stories.

These patterns vary considerably from place to place. Montgomery County, Maryland, and Fairfax County, Virginia, are two of the most affluent counties in the country[33] and have similar sociodemographic profiles. Both counties have homicide rates less than 1/20 that of the bordering District of Columbia.[34] Yet the two offer stark, illuminating contrasts in their receptivity to community prosecution programs. Douglas Gansler, State's Attorney for Montgomery County, has committed his office to community prosecution, organizing his office along geographic lines corresponding to the County's five police districts, assigning his officers to work with teachers and administrators in every school in the county, and focusing on a variety of crime prevention strategies. Robert Horan, Commonwealth Attorney for Fairfax County, uses vertical prosecution in homicide cases, but he sees community prosecution largely as a fad. Horan prefers to serve his county in the traditional way, which he says has worked quite well throughout his 34 years of tenure in office.[35] Unfortunately, such variations have not been rigorously assessed to learn their effects on crime rates, conviction rates, or reelection rates. They do, in any case, reveal that prosecutors are not of one mind on the effectiveness of community prosecution.

Despite their appeal, it is really not clear that the prevailing bundle of interventions that have become associated with the community prosecution movement are really the most effective ones for giving prosecutors their needed training on sensitivity toward community residents and problems. Should prosecutors be spending much time lecturing to schoolchildren? Assessments of police doing so under the Drug Abuse Resistance Education (DARE) programs have consistently found that those programs have done nothing to achieve the professed objectives of reduced drug use and delinquency (Sherman et al. 1998).

And precisely *how* should prosecutors be working more closely with police officers? It certainly makes sense for prosecutors to engage in ride-alongs with the police and set up operations in precincts and storefronts, to get to know both the neighborhoods and the police better. Yet there is no guarantee that those experiences will ensure that the prosecutors, thus enlightened, will exercise discretion more wisely from the case screening stage through final adjudication. Nor is it clear that prosecution by geography offers a more direct route to justice and crime prevention than priorities based principally on case seriousness and defendant dangerousness.

A basic premise of these programs also warrants questioning: How much time *should* prosecutors spend supporting community crime prevention programs? Surely crime prevention is a worthy goal, but it is not clear that prosecutors are better situated to engage effectively in those efforts than are the police. Targeting resources in court on cases involving repeat offenders in the primes of their criminal careers may be a more productive crime prevention strategy than redeploying those resources into the community. In any case, we have no clue as to the respective contributions to crime control of any given level of resources allocated to the pursuit of convictions and the same level allocated to the pursuit of any particular crime prevention activity.

The post-arrest options associated with community prosecution are another matter: focusing on dispute resolution, mediation, community service, restitution, and other community-based approaches to resolve minor crimes and problems at early stages before they blossom into serious felonies. These programs fit the prosecution mandate more closely than many other crime-prevention programs. In the meantime, prosecutors who win convictions in the ocean of run-of-the-mill cases that do not make the evening news are likely to produce at least an ounce of crime prevention.

Converting from a production-line approach to vertical prosecution may make sense in rape and homicide cases and cases involving victims who are very young or otherwise especially vulnerable. For a variety of less serious crimes, however, large municipal prosecution offices could be wasting resources and losing cases if they were to rely on systems of prosecution better suited to rural settings.

Multijurisdictional task forces may also be an effective way of sharing information to facilitate the solving of crimes and collecting of evidence needed to secure convictions, but it may be much more effective in some settings and for certain types of cases than others. Task force successes appear to depend largely on the unique chemistries of the individuals involved.

Evidence from Boston in the late 1990s is consistent with the idea that interventions associated with community prosecution may reduce crime, especially cooperation between prosecutors and others in positions to prevent and solve crime. A constellation of projects are credited with reducing gun homicides in that city, especially among juveniles. The number of homicides dropped from about 100 annually in the late 1980s, before the projects were launched, to 35 by 1998 and not a single juvenile homicide in that year. The number of shootings also plummeted. Ralph Martin II, the District Attorney for Suffolk County (comprising Boston and immediately surrounding communities), played a pivotal leadership role in these projects.

A centerpiece of the Boston crime reduction efforts was the Safe Neighborhood Initiatives (SNI), which coordinated law enforcement activities, supported neighborhood revitalization efforts, and complemented conventional response activities with a focus on prevention. SNI prosecutors spoke at all the local schools and attended community organization meetings. (Coles and Kelling, 1998, pp. 77–78) They also participated in the Boston Youth Violence Strike Force, which coordinated Martin's SNI with the Massachusetts Attorney General and local U.S. Attorney, as well as with 45 full-time Boston Police Department officers, 15 officers from nearby police departments, and federal agents, together with probation, parole, and other correctional agents (Department of Justice 1999). A third element of collaboration was the Boston Gun Project, which included the close support of agents from the Bureau of Alcohol, Tobacco and Firearms (Kennedy 1999).

In all three projects, coordination among prosecutors provided an array of creative options in determining which charges to file in which court or courts. Cross-deputization of prosecutors provided opportunities to file cases that fell under multiple jurisdiction authority in Suffolk County juvenile court, adult court, or federal court. Coordination with law enforcement officials appears to have been equally important, to ensure that the elements needed to satisfy various charging requirements were met.

A broader set of prosecution strategies emerged from this coordination than had been traditionally applied. The Suffolk County D.A. aggressively filed charges against crimes of disorder—graffiti, truancy, noise, public drinking, and so on—to improve the quality of life, especially in areas of Boston that had suffered from chronic private abuse and public neglect. Federal, state, and local statutes were creatively applied to remove guns from the streets under laws against gun use, possession, and trafficking. The Massachusetts Commonwealth's criminal and civil forfeiture laws were exploited to take over drug dens and permit their renovation into suitable low-income housing. Civil sanctions were also more aggressively applied to target chronic public blemishes, such as mechanics doing major vehicle repairs on the street and commercial establishments improperly disposing of waste.

A variety of interventions thus appears to have reduced crime in Boston, but this is by no means a clear victory for community prosecution. It may be a victory for aggressive programs to remove guns from juveniles and dangerous juveniles from the streets. It may be a victory for a unique way of targeting drugs, or for the influence of inner-city churches. It may even be a victory for prosecutors who are effective at inducing support from others in positions to control crime. Several interventions were used, some having little to do with community prosecution, and we have no way of knowing which ones were the most effective; one or two may have even been counterproductive.

A key ingredient missing from the Boston experience was that the interventions were not individually tested by experimentation. Prosecutors in Boston and elsewhere are spending scarce resources on a loosely defined set of interventions having to do with "community outreach" and "cooperation" without the benefit of systematic evidence validating that some are really more effective than others, or indeed that *any* of those usually associated with community prosecution are useful for achieving the goals of prosecution. The primary problem with community prosecution programs as currently constituted is that even the best of the programs lack systematic bottom-line public accountability.

The Boston interventions make sense, but time and again criminal justice interventions based on common sense and theory—from random police patrols and rapid police response to boot camps and DARE programs—have been found to be ineffective when subjected to properly designed and executed experimental research. In some cases, such as mandatory arrests of unemployed spouse assaulters and three-strikes-and-you're-out for old offenders, the intervention has been shown to be *worse* than neutral (Sherman et al. 1998). Over the years a few courageous police chiefs—Clarence Kelley, Lee Brown, and Darrel Stephens are three notable examples—have distinguished themselves and advanced their calling by allowing researchers to alter normal operations for the sake of learning from experiments what works, and there is no good reason why this should not happen in prosecution.

As they are currently conceived, community prosecution programs do little either to make prosecutors more systematically accountable to citizens for their workaday, behind-the-scene performance in *all* felony cases or to promote a deep, transformational sense of justice. While these programs may offer immediate political advantages for prosecutors, and may even produce marginal gains in crime abatement, they represent no "paradigm shift." They may, in fact, divert attention from reforms that could really serve members of the community most in need of relief from crime. We might do well to consider, instead of or in addition to community prosecution, a truly radical departure from current arrangements. Not just for political gains, but primarily for the sake of victims, and for the well being of the community.

PROSPECTS FOR FUNDAMENTAL REFORM

Two prosecution events dwarfed all others in the 1990s: the prosecution of the O.J. Simpson case and independent prosecutor Kenneth Starr's impeachment investigation of the President. Neither ennobled the stature of prosecution. The latter was especially significant for its revealing a free-wheeling exercise of discretion in building a case against the President; yet remarkably little media attention was paid to the power of prosecutors generally. The fact that Starr's target was no less than the President of the United States is, of course, what made that investigation so remarkable. Still, one might have expected a greater expression of concern about the broader implications of Starr's methods, that extraordinary means are available to prosecutors to damage personal reputations in the name of other ends.

This concern is not new. In 1940 former U.S. Attorney General and Supreme Court Justice Robert H. Jackson observed, "The prosecutor has more control over life, liberty, and reputation than any other person in America" (Jackson 1940, p. 18). Jackson's remark had more resonance 60 years ago than today; a public that has grown intolerant of crime can be expected to accept extremes in the prosecutor's use of authority. But Starr's interests were not about street crime, and there is ample reason to suspect that for all the lip service paid to crime, most prosecutors appear to have other interests that shape their operations.

While the operations of most other institutions, both public and private, are much more open to scrutiny today than in Justice Jackson's time, systematic accounting of the prosecutor's day-to-day operations remain absent from public view. Much of the work of the prosecutor remains subject to abuses of discretion, despite posturing to the contrary. Contemporary standards of accountability warrant the casting of a brighter light on the work of prosecutors, to move beyond rhetoric and strengthen legitimacy by making their operations more transparent and subject to systematic evaluation.

If prosecutors really wish to serve the community, they will subject their new programs to more rigorous assessment and more systematic reporting. They could make data available to the public on the number of arrests in each neighborhood, by offense category, and the disposition of those arrests at each stage of prosecution from the screening room until the case leaves the court. They could routinely communicate information about the status and outcome of each case to the police, victims, and witnesses. They could work more diligently to nurture, maintain, and monitor the cooperation of witnesses and victims.

The potential for truly fundamental change in prosecution goes beyond even the critical matter of accountability. The prospects for such change do not necessarily lie beyond our grasp. Change that could significantly advance the public's interests in justice and order would require a shift from our current system, which treats the victim primarily as a resource for promoting the interest of the state, to one that recasts justice as a matter of balancing the right of the defendant to a fair and full hearing under the presumption of innocence with the fundamental right of the victim to be restored. Under current arrangements, victims are inadequately compensated for costs imposed by the criminal justice system: lost income, time spent with police and court officials, out-of-pocket costs for transportation, child care, and related costs. Victims are not routinely included in a meaningful way in case-processing decisions following arrest. Most significantly, they are rarely compensated for losses associated with the crime, which often has devastating long-term impact on their health, income and wealth, and psychological well being (Macmillan 2000). Victims commonly end up feeling used, like little more than items of evidence, deprived even of basic rights corresponding to those extended to offenders (Cassell 1996).[36] Even when the offenders are convicted, victims rarely benefit in any tangible way from conventional sentences of incarceration and probation. Nor are intermediate sanctions typically of much help to victims: community service does little for the community and less for the victim; fines are rarely collected, and when they are, the proceeds typically do not go to the victim. In the exceptional case in which the judge orders restitution, the court rarely follows up to ensure that the terms of restitution are fully met. Victims are too often left with little incentive to cooperate in subsequent episodes (Rosen1999).

When victims are asked how they have been treated by various components of the criminal justice system, prosecutors fare less well than police, despite the fact that the chief prosecutor is usually an elected official and the police chief is not.[37] Community prosecution programs aim principally to connect the prosecutor more closely to the community, not primarily to restore the victim. These programs leave intact the principle that the prosecutor represents the state, not the victim, in all criminal matters.

A prospect for a truly revolutionary advance in prosecution would be to challenge that fundamental principle. Bruce Benson and others have suggested that a shift to a process resembling our tort system might effectively work to remedy the serious deficiencies of our existing state-versus-defendant system. Genuine opportunities for victims to be restored could well increase their incentives to report crimes to the police, thus reducing recidivism rates and crime costs, stimulating general deterrent effects, and raising the perception of system legitimacy throughout society (Bazemore 1998; Van Ness and Strong 1997).

Whether or not such basic transformation happens, prosecutors should be induced to take a larger, more systemic view of their operations. The one-case-in-a-vacuum perspective of case screening, plea bargaining, and sentencing—and the disparity that that approach engenders—has contributed to cynicism of the administration of justice and doubt about the objectives of the system.

How we use prosecutors to deal with offenders—and victims—will be assessed inevitably on grounds of justice and efficiency. But assessments of our system of prosecution and adjudication transcend the domains of crime, justice, and efficiency. In the end, how we deal with offenders and victims of crime is a reflection of what kind of people we are.

19

Crime and Public Policy

James Q. Wilson

There are two great questions about crime: why do people differ in the rate at which they commit crimes, and why do crime rates in a society rise and fall? You might suppose that the answer to these two questions would be the same. If we can explain why people differ in their criminality, then all we need to do is add up these individual differences in order to know how much crime there is in their society. But in fact, the answers to these questions are not at all the same. The forces that put people at risk for committing crimes overlap only in part with the factors that influence how much crime a nation will experience. For example, we have come to understand that young men are much more likely to break law than are young women (or older men), but most societies have roughly the same share of young men. Despite that, many nations will differ dramatically in their crime rates.

Over the last 40 years, social scientists have made great gains in explaining why some people are more likely than others to commit crimes but far smaller gains in understanding a nation's crime rate. Many of the essays in this book summarize these remarkable new findings that help us understand individual differences in crime rates. We know, for example, much more than we once did about the influence of biological, familial, and neighborhood factors that put people at risk for—or protect them from—criminality. But though we also know much more than we once did about the effect on crime of criminal sentences and the opportunities for reducing crime rates by prevention and treatment methods, we cannot easily extract from this knowledge a good explanation of why some nations have much higher crime rates than others or useful lessons for driving down the crime rate in our nation.

Consider prisons. We are more confident than we once were that the rate at which offenders are sent to prison, other things being equal, will affect the crime rate: The higher the probability of punishment, the lower the crime rate (see Steven Levitt's chapter, 15). But that knowledge does not make it easy to explain why nations differ in their crime rates, in part because the international data we would need to make such judgments are often lacking and in part because there seem to be so many other factors— youth, culture, opportunities, the availability of guns—that also affect crime rates. No one, so far as I am aware, has ever explained a nation's crime rate by taking systematically into account all of the variables that might affect it. (Unfortunately, this inability has not prevented some scholars from confidently explaining to journalists why the crime rate has gone up or gone down.) Moreover, it is no simple matter to drive down crime rates by relying more on imprisonment. Doing that requires changing the effectiveness of policing, altering the behavior of prosecutors and judges, and coping with the costs, tangible and intangible, of having a large prison population.

The same problems confront efforts to reduce the crime rate by means of prevention, employment, and rehabilitation programs. We are getting better at evaluating such efforts and drawing lessons from them, but we have no idea what would be the cumulative effect of putting in place all of the best programs on a large scale. One reason is that the best ones are often hard to make larger. They begin as small, carefully managed efforts that draw on the talents of highly talented, strongly motivated people. Scaling up such programs requires one to believe that what a few skilled people can do can also be done by a large number of less skilled ones and that managing a big program is no different from managing a small one. For example, putting some at-risk young people into imaginative day-care programs, creating job skills for a roomful of juveniles, and making probation a meaningful experience for a few dozen offenders may well reduce the risk of criminality, but doing the same thing for a million youngsters, a million juveniles, or a million probationers is no easy matter.

Moreover, one of the most frequently suggested remedies for crime— keeping unemployment low—turns out to have only a modest effect on the crime rate. There is evidence that higher unemployment does increase the rate of property crime, but that relationship for the United States is quite modest. As Bushway and Reuter point out in chapter 8, property crime rates fall by about 2 percent for every 1 percent cut in the unemployment rate, but this means that if the unemployment rate is cut dramatically—say, from 8 percent to 4 percent—the rate of property crime will only decrease by 8 percent. Now, if the United States had a serious depression and unemployment soared to very high levels, cutting it down to 4 percent would probably make a big difference in property crime, but that has not happened in this country since the 1930s, and that was a time when we had no reliable crime measures with which to test the effect of reducing unemployment. Moreover, the fact that high unemployment rates are found in certain neighborhoods does not explain why the crime rate in those areas is so high. But another aspect of the labor problem— the existence of many people who neither have nor are looking for a job—may well contribute to high crime rates. Understanding the connection between low labor force participation and high crime is complicated, however, because we are not certain in which direction causality runs (does low labor force participation cause crime, or does a lot of crime make illegal activities more rewarding than work?), and we are not certain what underlying factors (such as weak families, poor schooling, strong gangs, or frequent drug use) may simultaneously cause both low labor force participation and high levels of crime.

And dealing with crime means not only preventing it but judging it. Suppose we were confident that either imprisonment or rehabilitation would reduce the crime rate sharply. We are not free to simply put these ideas in place; the reason is that ordinary citizens view crime in moral as well as practical terms. When a person is convicted of a crime, people expect that he or she will be punished in a way that reflects the gravity of the offense and the prior record of the offender as well as in a way that will reduce the crime rate. Suppose we learned that a $5,000 fine, if routinely imposed, would cut the rate at which women are raped. I doubt that many people would agree that the fine was enough punishment, whatever its effect on the frequency of rapes. To most of us, the crime is sufficiently appalling that we would demand that the offender spend a long time in prison whether or not the length of imprisonment had any effect on the rate at which rapes occur. Or to take a different example, suppose that rapists could be cured of their habit by putting them in a treatment program outside of prison, perhaps one located in a clinic. No matter how successful the treatment, people would expect more severe measures to be employed as a way of making clear how gravely society views the offense.

And the same argument can be made in the opposite direction. If a sentence of five years in prison would reduce the robbery rate and a sentence of ten years would add no further deterrent value, would we be justified in increasing the penalty to ten years just because people detest robbers? Perhaps, but a good argument can be made that by doing this we are not only making no difference in the robbery rate we are also consuming scarce prison space that would be put to better use by confining another robber for five years. Morality and utility sometimes lead to the same result, but just as often they may be in conflict.

When we debate public policy toward crime, we are arguing about issues that necessarily combine moral and utilitarian considerations. Social scientists can help people understand the utility of different strategies, but they are not very good at helping people cope with the morality of these efforts. This is not to say that social scientists should avoid making moral judgments; inevitably they will make them, and that is fine so long as those judgments are made explicitly and not left as the hidden subtext of a purportedly scientific claim.

In the remainder of this chapter, I wish to address three questions that concern many readers: Why does America have so much crime? Why did the crime rate go down in the late 1990s? What, if anything, can be done to keep it down? In discussing these issues, I will draw on many of the essays in this volume, but I will do so on the basis of my own judgment. The authors of these essays may well disagree with the use to which I put some of their findings, and so this chapter is in no sense a summary of this book. If you are a student, do not read this chapter to find a condensed version of this book; read the book.

CRIME IN AMERICA

As James Lynch makes clear in chapter 2, Americans should stop thinking of their country as more crime-ridden than is the case in Europe. In general, America has less property crime and more violent crime than do other industrialized nations. There are two ways of calculating crime rates—police reports and victim reports. In general, the two measures lead to roughly comparable results. Using police data, the burglary rate in Australia, Austria, Canada, England, Germany, and the Netherlands is much higher than it is in the United States; only in France and Sweden is it lower. Using victim reports, the differences in burglary rates look much the same except that Germany now has a lower rate than does America. Motor vehicle theft is probably an even better measure of property crime because automobiles are insured, and thus their loss is more likely to be reported to the police. Your car is more likely to be stolen in Australia, Austria, Canada, England, and Sweden than it is in the United States.

But America indisputably has a higher murder rate than does any other industrialized nation. The American rate is three to five times higher than it is in most of Europe. But for another violent crime, robbery, the differences as reported by victims are not very large. The American rate is about the same as it is in Australia, Canada, England, France, and Italy. Of course, robbery rates are harder to measure accurately than are homicide rates: the latter produce dead bodies, while the former may range from minor lunch-yard thefts to armed attacks on banks, making the victims of these widely various crimes differ in their inclination to call the authorities.

We sometimes suppose that our high murder rate is the result of violent television, dangerous drugs, or the widespread ownership of guns. These factors may have some effect (guns almost surely do), but bear in mind that the homicide rate in New York City has been 10 to 15 times higher than that rate in London for at least 200 years (Monkkonen 2001). We were killing each other at a high rate long before movies, television, heroin, and cocaine were invented. And though the availability of guns probably affects the murder rate, please know that the rate at which Americans kill each other *without* using guns—that is, with clubs, knives, and fists—is three times greater than the nongun homicide rate in England. Robberies in this country are more likely to be fatal than robberies in England, in part because American robbers are more likely to be armed, but the death rate from robberies committed by *unarmed* robbers is also much higher in the United States than in England. (Zimring and Hawkins 1997). Even without a gun in their hands, American robbers are more violent than English ones.

We are a violent nation. Why? If you are asked this question on a final examination, you are in luck, because there is a long list of possible answers and precious little scientific evidence as to which one, or which combination of them, is correct. Write down any of the following: We are more violent because the country was settled by immigrants who created farms and villages before there was any government to protect them, and so they defended themselves against each other and against Native Americans. We are more violent because America has never had a landed aristocracy that tended to monopolize violent power; since wealthy knights could not own all the swords and guns, their ownership was spread among everybody, some of whom liked to settle quarrels with their use. We are more violent because for three centuries many people lived on a frontier where they hunted for food and fought against Native Americans. We are more violent because the country was filled by people from many different nations and ethnic groups who struggled, sometimes violently, to define against one another an appropriate standard of behavior. We are a more violent nation because whites used force to subdue black slaves and then slowly put an end to slavery by a war between the North and the South that killed 140,000 soldiers, injured another quarter million, and left a lot of people armed and angry. We are a more violent nation because a culture of honor emerged in the South that placed a high value on maintaining status by means of duels and killings. We are a more violent nation because the government had, for most of its history, only weak powers over people and for many centuries took little notice of crimes committed by African Americans on other African Americans. We are a more violent nation because Prohibition created large criminal gangs that relied on force to maintain their illegal control of the liquor trade. And so on.

THE RECENT DECLINE IN CRIME

Crime rates rose dramatically from the early 1960s until around 1980, leveled off a bit until the mid-1980s, then increased sharply in the late 1980s, and finally, in the late 1990s, dropped just as sharply. Some of this change was the result of changes in the age distribution of the population: in the 1960s we had a lot of young people, in the 1990s we had relatively fewer. Crime went up when there were more young men around and down when there were not so many. But the age explanation only accounts for a small fraction of either the increase or the decrease in crime; by the 1990s, there may have been proportionately fewer young people, but the ones who existed had, per capita, a higher rate of criminality.

One of the puzzles of crime in the 1980s can be solved, as Alfred Blumstein shows in chapter 16, by disaggregating crime along age lines. Murder and robbery rates hit a high around 1980, then started to decline, and then shot up again in the late 1980s and early 1990s. The reason in part is that in the late 1980s and early 1990s young people became more criminal, probably because many were part of the crack cocaine trade. The crime rate was falling for a variety of reasons—the population was getting older, more offenders were in prison—but when the crack drug trade opened up after 1985, many young men got involved in it, acquired guns to defend their illegal activities against competitors, and increased the rate at which they killed people. By the mid-1990s, however, murder and robbery rates were dropping sharply. One of the reasons may have been a drop in crack dealing, as many would-be users turned against a drug that was sending so many addicts to hospitals, prisons, and morgues.

But the age and drug factors are probably only one part of the story. At least two other things happened, and a third may have. The third factor can be mentioned immediately because we have no facts that bear on the matter. Perhaps the crime rate has dropped because the culture has changed. If the public has become more concerned about crime it may, through families, neighborhoods, and schools, invest more heavily in persuading young people to stay out of trouble and in using shame to penalize those who do get into trouble. A good case can be made that the emancipation of the individual from traditional restraints imposed by families and neighbors contributed to the steep rise in crime that occurred in virtually every industrialized nation between the early 1960s and the 1990s despite high and rising levels of economic achievement (Wilson 1983). It is possible that this emancipation was reduced a bit by the popular aversion to crime and a desire to reimpose some older restrictions. We may have moved from an era that let us "do our own thing" to one that urged us to "do what society expects." But this speculation is merely that; we have no way of evaluating it.

A different explanation has more facts to support it. As Americans worried more and more about crime, they invested more heavily in self-defense. They moved to the suburbs or to gated communities, bought condos in buildings with armed guards, equipped their cars with alarms and special locks, and avoided dangerous neighborhoods. No one knows how much these changes affected crime rates, but they surely had some influence, since crime requires, as Ralph Taylor points out in chapter 14, not only an offender but an opportunity to offend. Most ordinary street crime occurs near where offenders live; if the neighborhood becomes harder to attack, there will be less crime, with rather few would-be offenders moving to easier targets some distance away.

But this investment in self-defense also imposes a cost. As Robert Sampson notes in chapter 9, when the middle class moves out of an urban neighborhood in search of a safer life in the suburbs, it leaves behind poorer people who cannot move, and these may become more vulnerable to crime. Crime is more common in unstable neighborhoods where people move in and out frequently, because it is hard to maintain in these places an adequate sense of mutual trust and a shared willingness to intervene in local affairs in order to reduce crime. What Sampson calls the "collective efficacy" of a neighborhood is reduced when people with a stake in and a talent for sustaining that efficacy move away.

Crime is also reduced when a nation increases its use of prisons. This has been a deeply controversial topic among criminologists, with some praising it as a way of deterring crimes and locking up offenders (see chapter 16 and Wilson 1983) and others denouncing it as an excessive reaction. But one can estimate the extent to which imprisonment makes a difference. William Spelman suggests, on the basis of his calculations, that the increased use of prison can explain about 25 percent of the reduction in crime (Spelman 2000). This estimate, though carefully done, is still only an estimate; the real impact of prison could be much higher or somewhat lower. It cannot be zero, however, because we know from many studies that the median nondrug-dealing offender when free on the street commits about 12 crimes a year (Chaiken and Chaiken 1982; DiIulio and Piehl 1991; Spelman 1994). When 1,000 more offenders are taken off the street, there are potentially 12,000 fewer crimes. The actual decrease, of course, is much harder to calculate, since it depends on how many crimes are committed by newly imprisoned (instead of already imprisoned) offenders. That number will vary greatly by state, depending on how tough each state is about the use of prison. A state such as Texas, which sends a high proportion of its offenders to prison, will gain less from sending a few more to prison (because the additional inmates will have less serious crime rates) than will a state that sends only a small fraction of its convicts to prison.

Moreover, national differences in the willingness to use prison may help us understand why nations differ in their crime rates. Many of the European nations where the rates of burglary and auto theft are higher than they are in the United States display less willingness to use prison. In chapter 2, Lynch shows how difficult it is to compare the use of prison across nations in ways that should lead us to beware of such gross simplifications as that America is "the most punitive nation." Much depends on the kind of crime we analyze and whether we look at the stock of people in prison or the rate (or flow) at which people enter prison, and whether we distinguish between the length of sentence and the probability of getting a sentence.

Allowing for all of this, it becomes clear that the United States and most European nations are equally likely to use prison for serious offenders, such as those who commit homicide and robbery, that America is more likely to send burglars to prison than are these other nations, and that until recently the time spent in prison was about the same for America, Canada, and England. But this last factor—how long each offender spends in prison—has gone up in the United States more than in other nations. For both drug crimes and property crimes such as burglary, America is more punitive.

Some scholars (Farrington and Langan 1992; Farrington and Wikstrom 1993) have suggested that America's greater use of prison for burglary and other property crimes may help explain why there are more such crimes committed in nations that do not rely so heavily on prison. The facts are consistent with this view, though of course it is impossible to know whether they prove it. England, for example, had a lower burglary rate than did the United States during the early 1980s. But by the mid-

1980s England's rate had caught up with that of the U.S., and by the early 1990s the former was much higher than the latter. This change in burglary rates between the two nations coincided with an increase in the probability of going to prison here and a decrease in that probability in England. Whether this coincidence amounts to a cause is, of course, impossible to say with any confidence.

Since no nation wants a high crime rate, one may wonder why some nations are more willing to use prison to reduce that rate than are others. The answer, I think, is politics. In the United States, district attorneys and many judges are elected, and in a lot of states the citizens, by voting on initiative issues, can alter the laws affecting punishment. These facts make American officials highly sensitive to what voters want. In England, by contrast, neither prosecutors nor judges are elected, there is no way for the voters to change sentencing laws by means of an initiative measure, and much of the policy toward offenders is determined by appointed officials in the Home Office, who have little interest in how voters think. As a result, America uses prison more than does England.

Some people think that Americans let politics influence sentencing policies too much. The voters, the argument goes, are unduly influenced by horrific crimes and get carried away with a desire for retribution. No doubt this sometimes happens. Voters can insist on increasing the maximum sentence for, say, burglary without realizing that many burglars will get no prison sentence at all; they will be punished by being placed on probation, and so the longer maximum sentence will affect hardly any offenders. Moreover, a long sentence for burglary may add little to the deterrent effect of prison if (as is often the case) the certainty of punishment is more important than its severity. As a result, we may end up with a few burglars growing old in prison while a lot more enjoy probation.

But just as often the voters may get matters right. They may insist on mandatory minimum sentences that reduce the chances of probation for certain offenders (at the cost, of course, of big bills for prison construction), or they may support a way of increasing the deterrent effect of prison. One controversial example is California's "Three Strikes" law, which requires most offenders who have already been convicted of two crimes to spend at least 25 years in prison when they are convicted of a third. The controversy over this law involves several matters: How serious should the crimes be before they count as a strike? How much discretion should prosecutors and judges have in deciding that a prior conviction is not a strike? Will this law actually affect crime, and if so, will it do it at a cost the state can afford to pay?

The last issue has been hotly debated among scholars. One early study (Greenwood et al. 1994) predicted that the law in California would produce a small reduction in crime at the cost of a very expensive prison-building program. This claim was based on the effect of Three Strikes on incapacitating offenders—that is, on reducing crime simply by keeping criminals off the street for longer periods of time. But the law might also have a deterrent effect: it might discourage offenders who have two strikes from taking the risk of getting a third one. The early study had no way of estimating deterrence because the law had yet to be enforced. But since its enforcement, research has suggested that it does indeed have a deterrent value, such that the crime rate in California fell after the law was implemented by more than would have been predicted in the absence of the law (Chen 1998, 2000).

The value of prison will vary depending on the type of crime being committed. For property crimes such as robbery, burglary, and larceny, a higher probability of prison may reduce the number of such crimes. But for drug offenses, there may be no deterrent effect at all. An incarcerated robber is not immediately replaced on the street by a would-be robber who notices that a vacancy has occurred in the robbing business. But an incarcerated drug dealer may well be replaced on the street by a drug-dealing organization that realizes one of its members is locked up and so recruits a new dealer to replace him. It is also possible, of course, that high penalties for drug dealing will discourage any would-be dealers from volunteering for the job. We do not know which process operates, but we certainly have no reason at present for thinking that imprisoning drug dealers will have the same effect on the narcotics traffic as imprisoning robbers has on the robbery business.

In short, some unknown combination of age, culture, prisons, and urban conditions have shaped the American crime rate in ways that are hard to predict.

CAN MORE BE DONE TO REDUCE CRIME?

There is no silver bullet that will reduce crime, much less eliminate it. Indeed, the "crime rate" itself is a misleading number. What people care about is the risk they face in the neighborhoods where they live, and this risk varies dramatically across the country. The murder rate in South Dakota is only one-twelfth of what it is in Louisiana, and in Louisiana the rate in New Orleans is almost ten times higher than what it is in Lafayette. Someone living in Sioux Falls, South Dakota, is 70 times safer from murder than someone living in New Orleans, and within New Orleans some neighborhoods are much safer than others. In 1996, 81 American cities accounted for half of all the murders in the nation. In that same year, one-third of all the robberies in the country occurred in just two states, California and New York. The risks people confront vary so greatly that any responsible criminal justice policy has to be attuned to the needs of particular places. What works in New York City may not work in a New York City suburb.

We have heard a great deal about the effectiveness of the New York City Police Department in sharply reducing the crime rate in that city during the late 1990s. I am persuaded that new management policies and street strategies at the NYPD did have a lot to do with that reduction, but we must bear in mind that the crime rate has also fallen, though not by nearly as much, in cities where no special police efforts were made.

While no one can satisfactorily explain changes in crime rates, there are at least three things that push that rate up—drugs; guns; and personal, familial, and neighborhood factors. The first two forces are objects of much controversy, with some people saying that we ought to legalize drugs and criminalize guns while others argue that we ought to criminalize drugs and legalize guns. The first group believes that legalizing drugs would reduce thefts motivated by a desire to buy drugs, eliminate the need for violence to protect the drug trade, and get rid of the corruption that accompanies illegal trafficking. Accompanying drug legalization, many supporters believe, there should be a sharp reduction in the public's access to guns, because guns, unlike drugs, are inherently dangerous. Their opponents made exactly the opposite arguments: drugs are too dangerous for free consumption to be allowed, while guns are a valuable form of personal self-protection.

The chapters in this book on guns (chapter 11, by Philip Cook, Mark Moore, and Anthony Braga) and drugs (chapter 12, by David Boyum and Mark Kleiman) should have persuaded you that these conventional arguments are too simple. Guns serve legal as well as illegal purposes, and drugs differ greatly in the effects they have on people. Picking a set of useful policies requires one to make some careful distinctions.

The third factor that affects the crime rate—personal, familial, and neighborhood forces—suffers not so much from controversy as from despair. Hardly anyone doubts that our personality, how we were raised, and where we live affect our risk of becoming an offender, but for most people it is impossible to think of any way to make a significant difference in these risk factors. But if you read carefully the essays on the biological basis of crime (chapter 3, by Adrian Raine), the family (chapter 6, by

David Farrington), the neighborhood (chapter 9, by Robert Sampson), and crime prevention with youth (chapter 5, by Patrick Tolan), you will find ideas about how each of these forces can be modified. Let me offer my own suggestions on these topics.

DRUGS

Illegal drugs contribute to crime by causing some people to steal in order to buy them and other people to use force or bribery to maintain their control over the supply.

There is no chance that heroin, cocaine, PCP, or methamphetamines will be legalized, nor do I think there is any good reason why they should be. Since this change will not happen, I shall spare you my arguments about why it should not happen, and ask you to focus on the real strategic options that the country faces. (Chapter 12 contains an excellent explanation as to why no one should be certain that legalized drugs would produce lower crime rates.) There are essentially two strategic factors: reducing demand and reducing supply. It is fair to say that supply reduction—destroying drug supplies abroad, attacking smugglers who bring drugs into this country, and arresting drug dealers on the street—has been the chief strategy that this country has pursued. No doubt there have been some gains from this effort, but any fair assessment of the drug trade will lead you to understand, I think, that as long as there is a demand for drugs a supply of them will be generated. If opium (with which to make heroin) is no longer supplied by Turkey, it will be supplied by Myanmar or Afghanistan; if coca leaves (with which to make cocaine) are no longer produced in Colombia, they will be produced in Peru; if one drug-dealing cartel is broken up, another will rise to take its place; if trucks can no longer smuggle drugs, airplanes will. It is impossible to think of any product for which there is a strong human demand that will not be made available by somebody, somewhere.

Reducing the demand for drugs is difficult but not impossible, provided we focus our energies on people who use drugs at high rates and are vulnerable to social control. Those who meet these two tests are convicted offenders—those in prison, on parole, and on probation. A majority of them report being involved with drugs at the time of their arrest, and they number in excess of 5 million persons. They fall under the coercive power of the state because as inmates they are bound by prison rules, and as probationers or parolees they live in the community subject to certain state controls that can be exercised without violating constitutional bans on unreasonable search and seizure.

These facts suggest the need to expand prison-based drug treatment programs so they are available to and required of every inmate who had a pre-arrest drug problem. It is expensive but essential to do what we can to reduce the dependence on drugs of people under our control. A second implication, one already embraced by more than 400 American cities, are drug courts. These are staffed by judges dedicated to handling offenders on probation who have a record of drug abuse and who have not committed a serious crime. The judges require that these convicts enter and stay in drug treatment programs as a condition of remaining on the street. We do not yet know the long-term effect of drug courts, but they do seem to provide at least short-term benefits to the offenders subject to them.

However, drug courts reach only a small fraction of drug-abusing offenders, because they serve only those who are on probation for having committed minor (as opposed to major) crimes. But many probationers and most parolees have committed major offenses. Therefore, it is important to direct probation and parole officers to keep these people under close watch. Boyum and Kleiman call for this in chapter 12; the program they suggest is called "coerced abstinence." By this they mean frequent drug tests (perhaps twice a week) of probationers and parolees, with those who fail the tests quickly punished by (initially) a brief return to jail with further violations followed by longer returns. The goal of this coercion is not to punish drug users but to make staying in a community-based drug treatment program more attractive than repeated trips to jail. We know from other studies that drug treatment programs are valuable in more or less direct proportion to how long addicts remain in them, and that coercion as a way of inducing participation does not weaken the program's effects and may, in fact, strengthen them (Satel 1999; Anglin and Hser 1990).

For this program to work, the penalties for failing a street drug test must be swift and certain, though not especially severe. But swiftness and certainty cannot be achieved by referring probationers and parolees back to the criminal courts for a new hearing; that takes much too long and has an uncertain outcome. Rather, the (temporary) revocation of probation or parole must be an administrative matter—revoking probation or parole— done on the spot by probation and parole officers. This can be accomplished by a statute that makes clear that no probationer or parolee can refuse a drug test or can remain on the street if he or she fails one.

To create jail or prison space for those breaking the rules governing probationers and parolees on the street, it will be necessary to release many inmates who are now confined solely because they were guilty of possessing illegal drugs. This is no small number; perhaps one-third of all state prison inmates are there on drug charges, and a significant fraction of these have committed no other offense. Since we have no evidence that imprisoning them reduces the drug trade, they are occupying scarce prison space that ought to be used for offenders who have committed property or violent crimes or who have failed to live by the rules governing street life for probationers and parolees.

More can probably be done to reduce drug demand among employees. We know from experience with the military that drug use was cut sharply by a policy of frequent tests accompanied by zero tolerance for drug use. The prevalence of drug use in the military fell from about 27 percent in 1980 to about 3 percent in 1994 (Mehay and Pacula 2000). It is hard, but not impossible, to extend this policy to private employers.

GUNS

Much the same logic ought to govern our effort to reduce the availability of guns to people who are at risk of using them illegally. The vast majority of all guns are owned by people who never commit a crime and for whom gun ownership represents an opportunity to hunt, to shoot at targets, and to enhance their self-defense. Though controversial, the study by John Lott (2000) suggests that states in which people without a criminal or mental health record are allowed to carry concealed firearms on the street reduces the rate at which street crimes occur. Lott's argument is that a would-be offender must take into account the ability of a would-be victim to resist an attack. The chances of effective resistance go up if some unknown but not trivial percentage of would-be victims is armed. Gun carrying thus deters some crimes without, so far as we can tell from the evidence, increasing the rate at which persons authorized to carry weapons harm other people. Even guns kept at home have some deterrent value as is suggested by the fact that "hot burglaries"—that is, burglaries at a time when the owners are at home—are much less common in the United States, where millions of people have guns at home, than they are in England, where very few people have weapons in their residences. The Lott study has been challenged by other scholars (Duggan 2000; Ayres and Donohue 1999; and chapter 11 in this book), and so the ultimate effect of private gun carrying on crime remains in doubt. But the doubt is important to remember because so many advocates of tougher gun control have no doubts at all.

Many people carry weapons illegally. They may be known criminals, or young men looking to protect themselves in a fight, or gang members protecting their turf or looking for a chance to get even. Guns in the wrong hands create problems, as is evidenced by drive-by shootings in which gang members shoot at rivals and miss, killing instead an innocent child or adult standing nearby. Given this, it would be difficult to say that illegally carried weapons cause no harm.

The task of the police is to get such guns off the streets. Doing so would, in my view, have a greater impact on violent crime than further tightening of the rules governing how guns are sold. The vast majority of gun sales are arranged by law-abiding citizens; making the rules tougher for such sales will chiefly affect law-abiding citizens. A significant fraction of all guns used in crimes are stolen or borrowed (Wright and Rossi 1986). If point-of-sale restrictions become much tougher, an even larger fraction of such guns will be acquired by theft or in the black market.

The law governing police searches of ordinary persons is vague. In general, it suggests that the police need only a reasonable suspicion that the citizen has committed or is about to commit a crime in order for them to have the authority to stop and pat down an individual to see if a gun is in his or her clothing. But the police can readily stop and search parolees and probationers for guns, and should do so at every opportunity. Since most persons released from prison commit new crimes, keeping guns out of their hands reduces the risk that those weapons will be used in those crimes. But stopping probationers and parolees is not enough; they must be penalized if they are illegally carrying a weapon. Unfortunately, some research suggests that a large fraction of people from whom illegally carried weapons have been taken are given no meaningful penalty. For them, carrying a gun has no cost.

One new way of dealing with these people has been pioneered in such cities as Baltimore, Birmingham, and Providence. There gun courts, modeled on drug courts, impose sentences on people caught illegally carrying weapons. Some of these courts deal with all offenders, some only with juveniles; some require their defendants and their families to take special firearms safety courses, others send the defendants to boot camps or impose strict probation rules, and yet others do all of these things. We have as yet little published evidence on their effect, but one study suggests that the recidivism rate of juveniles going through the Birmingham gun court is about half that of young people processed in the ordinary way (Braun 2001).

But for citizens who are neither probationers nor parolees, there is at present no obvious way of both seizing illegal weapons and observing their constitutional right to be free of an improper search. That can change if the government proceeds with its efforts to develop a portable device that will enable the police to identify a gun under the clothing of a person from a distance of 20 or 30 feet. Such devices exist in the prototype stage, but are still too large to be of much practical value. With advanced versions of this technology, it will be possible for the police to see not simply a lump of iron in a person's pocket but the precise outline of the weapon. With that information, the police could then stop and question the person. If he or she has a license, they are free to move on; if not, they can be arrested and the gun seized.

The evidence we have so far is that street gun searches make a difference. Lawrence Sherman, in chapter 13, reports that a project in Kansas City encouraged the police to search for guns when they made traffic stops. In one neighborhood that tried this, the number of guns seized almost tripled. Gun-related crimes in that area dropped by 58 percent, compared with only a 29 percent crime decrease in a control neighborhood. Increasing gun seizures seems to cut gun crimes.

There is, of course, a risk in greater police efforts at preventing crime on the streets. Today that risk is called racial profiling, by which is meant an effort to stop and question people on the basis of their racial or ethnic identity. Suppose we ask the police to patrol intensively criminal "hot spots," to focus on known high-rate offenders who are free on the street, and to stop people who are suspected of carrying weapons. This means that a disproportionate share of such stops will involve African Americans and Hispanics. This is *not* racial profiling if the police have good grounds apart from race for making their interventions. It *would* be racial profiling if automobile drivers were stopped simply because they were black or Hispanic. In between these two extremes are many tough cases. In his chapter, Sherman suggests ways by which the police can think through this problem that will prevent obvious racial profiling and still allow race, under certain circumstances, to be taken into account in identifying suspects.

PREVENTION

Everyone would like to prevent people from committing crimes in the first place, but almost everyone also knows that this is not an easy task. *Almost* everyone, for a few people have devoted themselves to designing and running crime-prevention programs that they are convinced will stop young people from becoming serious offenders. The two central questions that such efforts raise are these: Do these programs really work? If they work, can they be made larger? We have learned a great deal about how to answer the first question but not much about how to answer the second.

There are hundreds, perhaps thousands, of crime-prevention programs under way. Many may work (and, of course, all their leaders think they work). But which actually work can only be determined by a rigorous evaluation. Not many have been evaluated in this way. A rigorous evaluation requires four things to be done: First, people must be assigned randomly to either the prevention program or a control group. Random assignment virtually eliminates the chance that those in the program will differ in some unknown way from those not in it. Random assignment is better than trying to match people in the two because we probably will not know (or even be able to observe) all the ways by which they should be matched. Second, the prevention must actually be applied. Sometimes people are enrolled in a program but do not in fact get the planned treatment. Third, the positive benefit, if any, of the program must last for at least one year after the program ends. It is not hard to change people while they are in a program; what is difficult is to make the change last afterward. Fourth, if the program produces a positive effect (that is, people in it are less likely to commit crimes than similar ones not in it), that program should be evaluated again in a different location. Some programs will work once because they are run by exceptional people or in a community that facilitates its success; the critical test is to see if they will run when tried elsewhere using different people.

The Center for the Study and Prevention of Violence at the University of Colorado has been working for many years to identify programs that meet these four tests. They have (so far) found about a dozen prevention programs that, on the basis of rigorous evaluations, seem to work. In his chapter, 5, Patrick Tolan reviews these findings. Among the successful programs are these: Big Brothers/Big Sisters, a national effort to match adults with young people from single-parent homes so as to give, on a part-time basis, serious adult care to youngsters at risk for delinquency or drug abuse; nurse home visitations, a program in several cities that sends nurses to the homes of poor, often unmarried, pregnant women to advise them on child care and parenting; and various school-based and family-oriented programs that teach anger management, ways of resisting peer pressure, and strategies for improving motivation and the acceptance of personal responsibility (Elliott 1998). The ways that other programs may help at-risk children in school are described by Denise Gottfredson and her colleagues in chapter 7. She believes that good schools can help reduce delinquency, but notes how few good evaluations there are of school-based programs. Those that seem to work contain few great surprises: they are the ones that make the school as a whole an effective, well-managed institution with firm but fair discipline and high expectations about student behavior. Small add-on programs—individual counseling, recreational opportunities, many courses designed to "teach" good behavior—often have little effect.

Throughout all the chapters on crime prevention, juvenile delinquency, criminal rehabilitation, and school-based crime reduction programs, one theme is repeated over and over: Cities and states typically do not invest in what works but only in what is popular. A few crime-prevention and criminal rehabilitation programs have passed rigorous evaluation, but these are not widely copied; instead, other programs that have never been evaluated or have failed an evaluation are funded. In chapter 10, Francis Cullen argues that policymakers and politicians favor personal experience or ardent advocacy over scientific knowledge and tested results. For example, two programs aimed at preventing drug abuse and reducing delinquency, DARE (Drug Abuse Resistance Education) and "boot camps," are immensely popular despite the dearth of credible evidence that they make a lasting difference. To their credit, the leaders of DARE have recently announced that they plan to make important changes in their program.

Imagine what would happen if we sold commercial products the way we prevent crime. For a business firm to operate the way crime-prevention programs function, it would have to market a new product without testing it with a small number of consumers, mount advertising for it without finding out whether the ads reach customers, and spend money on the product without wondering whether it ever returned a profit. If you run a corporation that way, the firm will soon be bankrupt and you will be out of a job.

Indeed, the problem is even more profound when we understand how criminal justice money is spent. The police and the prisons get most of it. Criminologists know full well that I am no opponent of either policing or prisons; I have argued for decades in favor of better police strategies and an expansion of prison use. I still believe that they have made a big difference in the crime reduction that has occurred in this country. But if we are to do more, we have to spend more money and design better strategies for the neglected part of the system—probation and parole officers and crime-prevention programs.

There are about 5 million people today under the control of the criminal justice system, but only one-fifth of them are in prison. The rest are on the streets as probationers and parolees, even though most of these offenders have committed serious crimes—one or more felonies. As Joan Petersilia shows in chapter 17, managing people in the community is even more important than managing them in prisons, because while they are on the streets they can harm all of us. And in time most people on parole will return to prison unless we become more skillful at changing their behavior.

But politically improving community-based corrections cannot be done by asking the public for funds to pay for community-based corrections (that sounds much too flabby) or to hire more probation and parole officers (they sound like people who will be too easy on criminals). There is no way, I think, to improve what we do on the street without making crystal clear what specific goals we hope to achieve. We want to reduce the demand for drugs among criminal offenders and get illegally carried weapons out of the pockets of dangerous people. That should be the message that politicians take to the public. As it turns out, the best way to do these things is to hire more probation and parole officers and give them some tough marching orders.

Much the same message needs to be broadcast with respect to crime prevention and rehabilitation. More people support these efforts than believe in community-based corrections, but the political emphasis must be on achieving here, in this city or county, the same gains that we know were achieved elsewhere by a scientifically validated effort. That is hard to do, not because ordinary voters will fight these efforts, but because the people who run programs that do not work will fight hard to keep their share of public money. The chief problems facing crime-prevention programs are three: We have to worry about making a successful small program into an equally successful large one, we have to convince citizens that there are programs that really work, and we have to win an interest-group war with those who run programs that do not work. None of this is easy.

THINKING ABOUT CRIME

But there is another, more ideological war that also must be fought. People who write about crime often think that their political preferences should dictate their policy recommendations. If you are a liberal, you will tend to blame crime on racism and unemployment and argue in favor of more civil rights and better jobs—whatever the facts may be. If you are a conservative, you will tend to blame crime on personal irresponsibility and argue in favor of capital punishment and longer terms in prison—whatever the facts may be. Picking your way carefully through this ideological morass is difficult, and no one, including the authors of this book, is entirely successful at doing it. But trying to think clearly and factually about crime is a goal all of us ought to share.

That goal ought to lie at the heart of the federal government's efforts to control crime. Obviously, federal authorities have important laws to enforce and are ideally situated to deal with crimes that cross state lines or involve international conspiracies. But ultimately, law enforcement remains a local matter. Police, sheriffs, prosecutors, public defenders, prisons, and treatment and prevention programs are overwhelmingly local responsibilities. Cities and counties investigate the vast majority of crimes, arrest the vast majority of offenders, and try and imprison the great majority of inmates.

But there is one thing that local authorities cannot do very well: find out what works. In part this is because city and state leaders will be criticized if they spend scarce money on "research" when the public wants them to attack crime. And in part it is because even if local leaders had the money and the political opportunity to spend on research, those studies would benefit all cities and states and not just the one that spent the money. Moreover, money used to find out if a popular program really cuts crime may well reveal that it does not, and so the authorities that supported the program will be embarrassed by their effort to evaluate it. For all these reasons, state and local expenditures on evaluating crime control projects are costly, risky, and rare.

Federal authorities do not face quite the same constraints. They do not run most crime-prevention programs; cities, counties, and states do. As a result, Washington can evaluate what other people are doing. And since there is only one national government that collects tax money from everybody, whatever lessons about crime control it learns can be shared with every taxpayer (which is to say, with every city, county, and state).

Over the years, Washington has conducted many evaluations, largely through the National Institute of Justice (a part of the Justice Department) and in part through other research agencies concerned with science and public health. But the money it spends on evaluations is typically but a small fraction of what it spends on aiding cities and states to fight crime. And when Congress, following public opinion, becomes worried about crime, it tends to react by telling the FBI to help investigate what the police and sheriffs are already investigating and by creating new, tougher federal penalties for that offense.

Now there is nothing intrinsically wrong with that reaction, though sometimes one worries that Washington is moving in the direction of nationalizing our law-enforcement system. But there is something wrong with not trying to find out what works. Yet when someone proposes such an attempt, some political leader dismisses the idea as "just another piece of research." (Of course, sometimes they are right; crime control, like every piece of social science, is littered with bad research projects that either tell us nothing or have little effect on how law enforcement operates.) What I mean by "research" is chiefly evaluations of ideas about how to reduce crime. Evaluations, as we have already seen in this and other chapters, are not easily done well, but it is vital that good ones be attempted. The chief federal role in domestic law enforcement should be to encourage and fund such research. No one else will do it.

Notes and References

CHAPTER 2

James Lynch

CRIME IN INTERNATIONAL PERSPECTIVE

Notes

1. See Miller (1977) for a discussion of how urbanization and industrialization in England led to the disruption of traditional institutions, a rise in crime, and the development of the modern police.

2. For illustrations of the case-study methodology see Koppel (1992); Dobash and Dobash (1992); Miller (1977). For an illustration of a case study that uses less qualitative information but takes great care getting the statistics right, see Farrington and Langan (1992).

3. For illustration of studies that test quantitative models see Bennett and Lynch (1990); Stack (1984); Gartner and Parker (1990a, 1990b); Messner (1989).

4. The statistical compendia that provide the data for modeling are improving in quality over time. Most notable here are the data available in the European Sources Book in which authors have taken great pains to deal with issues of comparability.

5. For a good discussion of the different types of distortions that various types of statistical systems can introduce see Biderman (1966) and Biderman and Lynch (1991).

6. With somewhat more effort, annual police statistics from individual nations can be used for comparison purposes. Much more information is available in these reports, but they often require translation and extensive work to ensure comparability of crime classes and procedures.

7. Violent crime includes rape, robbery, and various forms of assault, including attempts.

8. In earlier comparisons (Lynch, 1995) more nations had lower rates of burglary than the United States, but the steady drop in burglary rates since 1980 in the U.S. has changed this picture.

9. The National Crime Victimization Survey (BJS 1992) indicates that only 41.5 percent of simple assaults are reported to the police, 58.4 percent of aggravated assaults, 54.7 percent of purse snatching, 28.1 percent of personal larcenies without contact, and 14.6 percent of larcenies involving household property worth under $50.

10. The differences in the proportion of crimes reported to the police are much reduced when the range of countries is restricted to those most similar to the United States. Canadians report 49.8 percent, Americans 52.3 percent, Australians 46.4 percent, and victims in England and Wales report 58.7 percent. This is probably due to the similarity of the crime mix in these countries, as we will see later in this chapter.

11. Unfortunately police statistics do not always clearly differentiate commercial from noncommercial crime. For a discussion of this in the United States see Biderman and Lynch (1991).

12. Teske and Arnold (1982) have made a detailed comparison of legal codes and crime classification schemes for Germany and the United States.

13. Some police data systems can fall substantially short of total coverage for the nation (Biderman and Lynch 1991). This is in some ways the worst of both worlds, since the result is neither a census nor a systematic sample. Moreover, there is good reason to believe that differences in the coverage of these systems is not constant across nations. Coverage in federated nations may be less adequate than in those more politically or administratively centralized.

14. The data used to compute these rates were taken from FBI (1989, 12) and Home Office (1989, p. 75).

15. This is due primarily to the fact that property crime is much more prevalent than violent crime. One interpretation is that wealthier people simply have more to steal than the less wealthy. There is also some evidence that the victim survey methods may underestimate the victimization experience of the less educated relative to the more educated (Hubble 1990; Lynch 1993b). Since income is highly correlated with education, this type of measurement may affect the observed differences between income groups.

16. These standardizations were done with the public use file from the 1988 ICS.

17. The ICS has much more potential to illuminate differences in cross-national rates of property crime. Much more complex standardization can be done. The data are particularly well-suited for multilevel models wherein nation-level variables can be included with the characteristics of victims to provide a much more complete picture of why nations differ with respect to the level of crime. The small sample sizes in the survey will limit what can be done, but pooling the 1988 and 1992 surveys will help in this regard. There are also some questions about sources of measurement error in the survey that may affect cross-national comparisons (Lynch 1993b). These can and must be dealt with if the ICS is to fulfill its potential.

18. In 1978, for example, I noted that only 9 of the 87 persons convicted of murder in Sweden were imprisoned. I wrote to the director of the agency responsible for Swedish prison statistics questioning the accuracy of the data. He responded that the data were indeed accurate. He noted, however, that in the same year, 67 of the persons convicted of murder were sentenced to secure mental institutions for indefinite periods. The decision to include or exclude mental hospitals in the definition of incarceration is the difference between a conviction-based incarceration rate of 87.4 or 10.3.

19. Although flow designs have a number of advantages over stock designs, some of which were mentioned earlier, they also have a number of potential disadvantages. Rather than confounding length of sentence with the propensity to incarcerate as stock studies do, flow designs can confuse delay in court processing with the incarceration rate. The bias introduced by delay can be ignored if we make one of two assumptions—that the bias is offsetting from year to year, or that delay in processing felony offenses is fairly constant across countries. A second source of possible error in flow designs restricted to a specific type of crime results from changes in charge during court processing. Offenders who are arrested for aggravated assault, but plead guilty to and are sentenced for simple assault, drop out of a flow study that is restricted to aggravated assaults. Since the offender is arrested for aggravated assault, his arrest will be included in the denominator of the incarceration rate. Because he is admitted to prison for simple assault, his admission will be excluded from the numerator, thereby arti-

ficially reducing the incarceration rate. If charge reduction practices are reasonably similar across countries, then they should not affect the accuracy of the comparison.

20. Time served in custody is used rather than imposed sentence because the determinacy of the sentencing process varies across nations. Sentences imposed by the court, for example, can later be modified by correctional administrators via "good time," or by parole boards through decisions to grant early release. It is essential that countries be compared as much as possible on the basis of the final decision made on an offender for a particular crime.

21. As incoming cohorts receive longer sentences, fewer of these inmates will appear immediately in the release cohorts. Hence exiting cohorts have fewer of the more harshly sentenced prisoners in them and more persons with relatively short sentences. Albert Biderman (1995) has pointed out that in the case of rapid and substantial increases in sentence length, the time served based on release cohorts would be shorter when the actual time served is increasing.

22. Using crime specific rates does not remove all of the problems inherent in differences in the nature of crime.

23. One of the major difficulties in obtaining crime-specific incarceration rates is selecting the appropriate method for controlling for the volume of crime.

The number of persons convicted for a specific type of crime would be the most desirable base for an incarceration rate, since it includes only those persons who have been found guilty. This would provide the most interpretable measure of the relative punitiveness of sentencing practices cross-nationally. Defining the particular point at which conviction occurs in each country, however, is not simple due to the differences in the structure of the criminal justice process. In the United States, for example, prosecutors can decide not to proceed with a case for reasons other than evidentiary strength. Indeed, there is strong evidence to suggest that the less serious crimes are less likely to be prosecuted (Jacoby et al. 1982), regardless of the evidentiary strength of the case. By deciding not to proceed, the prosecutor makes the decision not to incarcerate.

In systems like that of Germany where prosecutors do not have the same discretion to decline to prosecute (Langbien 1979), the judge may be confronted with many more less-serious cases in his sentencing decision, and fewer convicted persons will be incarcerated. If the two systems were compared using an incarceration rate based on convicted persons, then Germany would appear less punitive than the United States, when the two systems may be quite similar if some decisions not to prosecute are included as decisions not to incarcerate. Since different actors make the same decisions in different countries, there is no unambiguous choice of decision point for assessing the punitiveness of sentencing practices cross-nationally. Convicted persons may be the most appropriate base for an incarceration rate, but determining when conviction occurs in each system is problematic. Moreover, comprehensive and offense-specific data on sentencing are not widely available.

24. Farrington and Langan (1992, p. 14) note that about one-half of the persons receiving a noncustodial sentence for homicide were sentenced to secure mental hospitals. In the United States the proportion sentenced to mental hospitals for homicide is negligible. Consequently, it may be better to use the figure .93 as the probability of custody given conviction in England and Wales rather than .86.

25. In this calculation, arrest in England and Wales was approximated by adding together all those proceeded against in magistrates court and all of those cautioned by the police for drug offenses. Some may object to the inclusion of cautioning as equivalent to arrest in the United States because it is less severe. If cautions are excluded, the incarceration rate for drug offenses is .092. The truth may lie somewhere in between. Under the first assumption the

probability of incarceration given arrest in the United States is 2.69 times that in England and Wales. Under the second assumption, the probability of incarceration in the United States is 1.6 times that in England and Wales. Either way the difference is considerable.

26. Some may argue with using other nations as a standard for the appropriate level of incarceration. Utilitarian standards (e.g., crime levels or reductions) or "just deserts" standards may be more suitable or rational. There is no contesting, however, the fact that cross-national comparisons are widely used to assess criminal justice policy, and, as a result, they merit attention.

References

Archer, Dane, and Rosemary Gartner. 1984. *Violence and Crime in a Cross-national Perspective*. New Haven: Yale University Press.

Australian Institute of Health and Welfare (AIHW). 1998. *National Drug Strategy Household Survey*. Drug Statistic Series Number 1.

Bennett, Richard, R., and James P. Lynch. 1990. "Does a Difference Make a Difference? Comparing Cross-nation Crime Indicators." *Criminology* 28(1) 153-182.

Biderman, Albert. 1966. "Social Indicators and Goals." In *Social Indicators*, ed. Raymond Bauer. Cambridge, Mass.: MIT Press.

Biderman, Albert, and James P. Lynch. 1991. *Understanding Crime Incidence Statistics. Why the UCR Diverges from the NCS*. New York: Springer Verlag.

———. 1995. "Statistics of Average Time Served in Prison are Fallacious Indicators of Severity of Punishment." Paper presented at the Annual Meetings of the American Statistical Association Meetings, Boston, Mass. November 15-18.

Bittner, Egon. 1967. "The Police on Skid Row: A Study of Peace Keeping." *The American Sociological Review*, 32:699-715.

———. 1973. *The Functions of the Police in Modern Society*. Cambridge, Mass.: Oelgeschlager, Gunn and Hain.

Block, Richard. 1992. "Comparing National Surveys of Victims of Crime." *International Journal of Victimology*, 1-20. Bureau of Justice Statistics (BJS). 1992. *Drugs Crime and the Justice System: A National Report*. Washington, D.C.

———. 1998. *National Corrections Reporting Program, 1990*. Washington, D.C. Canadian Centre on Substance Abuse (CSSA). 2000. *Drug Use in Toronto Report*. Research Group on Drug Use.

Cantor, David, and James P. Lynch. 2000. "Self-report Surveys as Measures of Crime and Criminal Justice." In *Criminal Justice 2000; Measurement and Analysis of Crime and Justice*, vol. 4. Washington, D.C.: U.S. Department of Justice.

Clarke, Ronald, and Derek Cornish. 1986. *The Reasoning Criminal: Rational Choice Perspective on Offending*. New York: Springer Verlag.

Clarke, Ronald, and Pat Mayhew. 1988. "The British Gas Suicide Story and Its Criminological Implications." *Crime and Justice: A Review of Research*, ed. Michael H. Tonry and Norval Morris, 10:107.

Cohen, Lawrence, and Marcus Felson. 1979. "Social Change and Crime Rate Trends: A Routine Activity Approach." *American Sociology Review* 44:588–608.

Corkery, John. M. 2000. *Drug Seizure and Offender Statistics, United Kingdom, 1998*. Home Office: Government Statistical Service.

del Frate, Anna Alvazzi, Ugljesa Zvekic, and Jan J. M. van Dijk. 1993. *Understanding Crime: Experiences of Crime and Crime Control*. Rome: United Nations Inter-regional Crime and Justice Institute (UNICRI).

Ditton, Paula M., and Doris James Wilson. 1999. *Truth in Sentencing in State Prisons.* Washington, D.C.: Bureau of Justice Statistics Special Report.

Dobash, R. Emmerson, and Russell P. Dobash. 1992. *Women, Violence and Social Change.* London: Routledge.

Dodd, Tricia, and Paul Hunter. 1992. *The National Prison Survey: Report to the Home Office of a Study of Prisoners in England and Wales.* London Office of Population Censuses and Surveys, Social Survey Division.

Doleschal, E. 1977. "Rate and Length of Imprisonment: How Does the U. S. Compare with the Netherlands, Sweden, and Denmark?" *Crime and Delinquency* 23:51.

European Committee on Crime Problems, ECCP, 1999. *European Sourcebook of Crime and Criminal Justice Statistics.* Strasbourg: Council of Europe.

European Monitoring Centre for Drugs and Drug Addiction (EMCDDA). 1998. *Annual Report on the State of the Drugs Problem in the European Union.* Luxembourg: Office for Official Publications of the European Communities.

———. 2000. *Annual Report on the State of the Drugs Problem in the European Union.* Luxembourg: Office for Official Publications of the European Communities.

Farrington, David P., and Patrick A. Langan. 1992. "Changes in Crime and Punishment in England and Wales and America in the 1980s." *Justice Quarterly* 9(1): 6–46.

Farrington, David P., Patrick A. Langan, and Per-Olof H. Wikstrom. 1994. "Changes in Crime and Punishment in America, England and Sweden Between, the 1980s and the 1990s." *Studies on Crime and Crime Prevention* 3: 104–30.

Federal Bureau of Investigation (FBI). 1989. *Crime in the United States.* Washington, D.C.: U.S. Department of Justice.

Fingerhut, Lois, and Joel C. Kleinman. 1990. "International and Interstate Comparisons of Homicide among Young Males." *Journal of the American Medical Association* 263, no. 24 (June).

Fisher, Bonnie S. and Francis T. Cullen. 2000. "Measuring the Sexual Victimization of Women: Evolution, Current Controversies and Future Research." In *Criminal Justice 2000; Measurement and Analysis of Crime and Justice,* vol. 4. Washington, D.C.: U.S. Department of Justice.

Gartner, Rosemary, and Robert Nash Parker. 1990a. "Cross-national Evidence on Homicide and the Age Structure of the Population." *Social Forces* 69(2): 351.

———. 1990b. "Victims of Homicide: A Temporal and Cross-national Comparison." *American Sociological Review* 55:92–106.

Gurr, Ted. 1977. "Crime Trends in Modern Democracies Since 1947." *The International Annals of Criminology* 16:41–85.

Home Office. 1989. *Police Statistics: England and Wales 1988.* London: Her Majesty's Stationery Office.

———. 1992. *Police Statistics: England and Wales 1990.* London: Her Majesty's Stationery Office.

Hubble, David. 1990. "National Crime Survey New Questionnaire Phase-in Research: Preliminary Results." Paper presented at the International Conference on Measurement Errors in Surveys, Tucson, Ariz., November 11–14.

Interpol. 1988. *International Crime Statistics.* Paris: Interpol General Secretariat.

———. 1999. *International Crime Statistics.* Paris: Interpol General Secretariat.

Jacoby, Joan, L. Mellon, E. Ratledge, and S. Turner. 1982. *Prosecutorial Decisionmaking: A National Study.* Washington, D.C.: National Institute of Justice.

Kaiser, G., H. Kury, and H. J. Albrecht, with the assistance of H. Arnold. 1991. *Victims and Criminal Justice*. Freiburg: Max Planck Institute.

Kalish, Carol. 1988. *International Crime Rates*. Washington, D.C.: Bureau of Justice Statistics.

Killias, Martin. 1993. "Gun Ownership, Suicide, and Homicide: An International Perspective." In *Understanding Crime: Experiences of Crime and Crime Control*, ed. Anne Alvazzi del Frate, Ugljesa Zvekic, and Jan J. M. van Dijk. Rome: United Nations Inter-regional Crime and Justice Institute.

Koppel, David B. 1992. *The Samurai, the Mountie and the Cowboy: Should America Adopt the Gun Controls of Other Democracies?* Buffalo, N.Y.: Prometheus Books.

Langan, Patrick A., and David P. Farrington. 1998. *Crime and Justice in the United States and in England and Wales, 1981–96*. Washington, D.C.: Bureau of Justice Statistics.

Langbien, J. 1979. "Land Without Plea Bargaining: How the Germans Do It." *Michigan Law Review* 78:204-10.

Lynch, James P. 1988. "A Comparison of Prison Use in England and Wales, Canada, the United States and West Germany: A Limited Test of the Punitiveness Hypothesis." *Journal of Criminal Law and Criminology* 79(1): 180–217.

———. 1993a. "A Cross-national Comparison of the Length of Custodial Sentences for Serious Crimes." *Justice Quarterly* 10(4).

———. 1993b. "The Effects of Survey Design on Reporting in Victim Surveys." In *Fear of Crime and Criminal Victimization*, ed. Wolfgang Bilsky, Christian Pfeiffer, and Peter Wetzels. Stuttgart: Enke Verlag.

———. 1995. "Crime in International Perspective." In *Crime*, ed. James Q. Wilson, and Joan Petersilia. San Francisco, Calif.: Institute for Contemporary Studies.

———. 1996. "Clarifying Divergent Estimates of Rape from Two National Surveys." *Public Opinion Quarterly*, vol. 60, no. 3 (Fall).

Lynch, James P., Steven Smith, Helen Graziadei, and Tanutda Pittayathikhun. 1994. *Profile of Inmates in the U.S. and in England and Wales, 1991*. Washington, D.C.: Bureau of Justice Statistics.

MacCoun, Robert J., Aaron Saiger, James P. Kahan, and Peter Reuter. 1993. "Drug Policies and Problems: The Promises of Pitfalls of Cross-national Comparisons." In *Psychoactive Drugs and Harm Reduction: From Faith to Science*, ed. N. Heather, E. Nadelman, and P. O'Hare. London: Whurr Publications.

Maurer, Michael. 1991. *Americans Behind Bars: A Comparison of International Rates of Incarceration*. Washington, D.C.: The Sentencing Project.

Mayhew, Pat, and Philip White. 1997. *The 1996 International Crime Victimisation Survey: Research Findings, No. 57*. Home Office Research and Statistics Directorate.

Mayhew, Pat, and Jan van Dijk. 1997. Criminal Victimization in Eleven Industrialized Countries: Key Findings from the International Crime Victimization Survey. Wetenschappelijk Onderzoek-en Documentatiecentrum.

Messner, Steven. 1989. "Economic Discrimination and Societal Homicide Rates: Further Evidence on the Cost of Inequality." *American Sociological Review* 54:597–611.

Miller, Wilbur. 1977. *Cops and Bobbies: Police Authority in New York and London*. Chicago: University of Chicago Press.

Nettler, Gwynn. 1978. *Explaining Crime*. New York: McGraw-Hill.

Riedel, Marc. 1990. "Nationwide Homicide Data Sets: An Evaluation of the Uniform Crime Reports and National Center for Health Statistics Data." In *Measuring Crime: Large-scale, Long-range Efforts,* ed. D. L. MacKenzie, P. J. Baunach, and R. R. Roberg. Albany, N.Y.: SUNY Albany Press.

Shryock, J., and L. Siegel. 1973. *Methods of Demography.* Washington, D.C.: U.S. Census Bureau.

Sloan, J. H., A. L. Kellerman, D. I. Reay, J. A. Fenis, T. Koepsell, F. P. Rivara, C. Rice, L. Gary, and J. Logerfo. 1988. "Handgun Regulations, Crime, Assaults And Homicide: A Tale of Two Cities." *New England Journal of Medicine* 319:1256–62.

Sproule, C., and D. J. Kennett. 1989. "The Use of Firearms in Canadian Homicides, 1972–1982." *Canadian Journal of Criminology* 30:31–37.

———. 1990. "Killing with Guns in the USA and Canada 1977–1983: Further Evidence for the Effectiveness of Gun Control." *Canadian Journal of Criminology* 31:245–51.

Stack, Steven. 1984. "Income Inequality and Property Crime." *Criminology* 22:229–57.

Substance Abuse and Mental Health Services Administration. 2000. *National Household Survey on Drug Abuse Full Report, 1999.* Office of Applied Studies (August).

Teske, R., and H. Arnold. 1982. "Comparison of the Criminal Statistics of the United States and Federal Republic of Germany." *Journal of Criminal Justice* 10:359.

Tomasevki, K. 1994. *Foreigners in prison.* Helsinki, Finland: European Institute for Crime Prevention and Control.

Tonry, Michael. 1999a. "Reconsidering Indeterminate and Structured Sentencing." *Sentencing & Corrections, Issues for the 21st Century.* Washington, D.C.: National Institute of Justice.

———. 1999b. "The Fragmentation of Sentencing and Corrections in America." *Sentencing & Corrections, Issues for the 21st Century.* Washington, D.C.: National Institute of Justice.

Trebach, Arnold S., and James A. Inciardi. 1993. *Legalize It? Debating American Drug Policy.* Washington, D.C.: American University Press.

van Dijk, Jan, and P. Mayhew. 1993. "Criminal Victimization in the Industrialized World: Key Findings of the 1989 and 1992 International Crime Surveys." In *Understanding Crime: Experiences of Crime and Crime Control,* ed. Anne Alvazzi del Frate, Ugljesa Zvekic, and Jan J. M. van Dijk. Rome: United Nations Inter-regional Crime and Justice Institute.

van Dijk, Jan, P. Mayhew, and M. Killias. 1990. *Experiences of Crime Across the World.* Boston: Klewer.

Waller, I., and Janet Chan. 1975. "Prison Use: A Canadian and International Comparison." *Criminal Law Quarterly* 3:47.

Walmsley, Roy. 1999. *World Prison Population List: Research Findings No. 88.* London. Home Office Research, Development and Statistics Directorate.

Wikstrom, Per-Olof H., and Lars Dolmen. 2000. "Sweden." Paper Draft for *Cross-national Studies in Crime and Justice,* ed. David P. Farrington, and Michael Tonry. Chicago: University of Chicago Press.

Young, Warren, and Michael Brown. 1993. "Cross-national Comparisons of Imprisonment." In *Crime and Justice: A Review of Research,* ed. Michael H. Tonry and Albert J. Reiss. Chicago: University of Chicago Press.

CHAPTER 3

Adrian Raine

THE BIOLOGICAL BASIS OF CRIME

Acknowledgement: This chapter was written with the support of an Independent Scientist Award (K02 MH01114-01) from the National Institute of Mental Health.

Notes

1. This review restricts itself to biological measures. There are many nonbiological measures that have substantial genetic contributions, such as intelligence and personality and that relate to crime, but are not included here because they are not biological measures (see Herrnstein 1995; Wilson and Herrnstein 1985).

2. The reader is referred to other sources for detailed discussions of startle-blink deficits (Patrick 1994), event-related potential deficits, and autonomic responsivity to both neutral and aversive stimuli (McBurnett and Lahey 1994; Raine 1993; Damasio, Tranel, and Damasio 1990; Fowles 1993).

References

Allen, G. 1976. "Scope and Methodology of Twin Studies." *Acta Geneticae Medicae Gemellologiae* 25:79–85.

Archer, J. 1991. "The Influence of Testosterone on Human Aggression." *British Journal of Psychology* 82:1–28.

Arseneault, L., R. E. Tremblay, J. R. Boulerice, J. R. Seguin, and J. F. Saucier. 2000. "Minor Physical Anomalies and Family Adversity As Risk Factors for Violent Delinquency in Adolescence." *American Journal of Psychiatry* 157:917–23.

Bach-y-Rita, G., J. R. Lion, C. E. Climent, and F. Ervin. 1971. "Episodic Dyscontrol: A Study of 139 Violent Patients." *American Journal of Psychiatry* 127:1473–78.

Bennis-Taleb, N., C. Remacle, J. J. Hoet, and B. Reusens. 1999. "A Low-Protein Isocaloric Diet during Gestation Affects Brain Development and Alters Permanently Cerebral Cortex Blood Vessels in Rat Offspring." *Journal of Nutrition* 129:1613–19.

Bohman, M., R. Cloninger, S. Sigvardsson, and A. L. von Knorring. 1982. "Predisposition to Petty Criminality in Swedish Adoptees: I. Genetic and Environmental Heterogeneity." *Archives of General Psychiatry* 39:1233–41.

Brain, P. 1990. "Hormonal Aspects of Aggression and Violence." Symposium on the Understanding and Control of Violent Behavior. Destin, Fla., April 1–4.

Breakey, J. 1997. "The Role of Diet and Behavior in Childhood." *Journal of Pediatric Child Health* 33:190–94.

Brennan, P. A., E. R. Grekin, and S. A. Mednick. 1999. "Maternal Smoking During Pregnancy and Adult Male Criminal Outcomes." *Archives of General Psychiatry* 56:215–24.

Brennan, P. A., A. Raine, F. Schulsinger, L. Kirkegaard-Sorensen, J. Knop, B. Hutchings, R. Rosenberg, and S. A. Mednick. 1997. "Psychophysiological Protective Factors for Male Subjects at High Risk for Criminal Behavior." *American Journal of Psychiatry* 154:853–55.

Brunner, H. G., M. Nelen, X. O. Breakfield, H. H. Ropers, and B. A. van Oost. 1993. "Abnormal Behavior Associated with a Point Mutation in the Structural Gene for Monoamine Oxidase-A." *Science* 262:578–80.

Cadoret, R. J., T. W. O'Gorman, E. Troughton, and E. Heywood. 1983. "Alcoholism and Antisocial Personality: Interrelationships, Genetic and Environmental Factors." *Archives of General Psychiatry* 42:161–67.

Cadoret, R. J., W. R. Yates, E. Troughton, G. Woodworth, and M. A. Stewart. 1995. "Genetic-Environmental Interaction in the Genesis of Aggressivity and Conduct Disorders." *Archives of General Psychiatry* 52:916–24.

Cases, O., I. Seif, J. Grimsby, P. Gaspar, K. Chen, S. Pournin, U. Muller, M. Aguet, C. Babinet, J. C. Shih, and E. de Maeyer. 1995. "Aggressive Behavior and Altered Amounts of Brain Serotonin and Norepinephrine in Mice Lacking MAOA." *Science* 268:1763–66.

Christensen, M. K., and C. J. Frederickson. 1998. "Zinc-Containing Afferent Projections to the Rat Corticomedial Amygdaloid Complex: A Retrograde Tracing Study." *Journal of Comparative Neurology* 400: 375-90.

Cloninger, C. R., and I. I. Gottesman. 1987. "Genetic and Environmental Factors in Antisocial Behavior Disorders." In *The Causes of Crime: New Biological Approaches,* ed. S. A. Mednick, T. E. Moffitt, and S. Stack, Cambridge: Cambridge University Press.

Cloninger, C. R., S. Sigvardsson, M. Bohman, and A. L. von Knorring. 1982. "Predisposition to Petty Criminality in Swedish Adoptees: II. Cross-Fostering Analysis of Gene-Environmental Interactions." *Archives of General Psychiatry* 39:1242–47.

Convit, A., P. Czobor, and J. Volavka. 1991. "Lateralized Abnormality in the EEG of Persistently Violent Psychiatric Inpatients." *Biological Psychiatry* 30:363–70.

Cox, D., R. Hallam, K. O'Connor, and S. Rachman. 1983. "An Experimental Study of Fearlessness and Courage." *British Journal of Psychology* 74:107–17.

Crowe, R. 1974. "An Adoption Study of Antisocial Personality." *Archives of General Psychiatry* 31:785–91.

Dabbs, J. M., R. B. Ruback, R. L. Frady, C. H. Hopper, and D. S. Sgoutas. 1988. "Saliva Testosterone and Criminal Violence among Women." *Personality and Individual Differences* 9:269–75.

D'Agincourt, L. 1993. "PET Findings Support Insanity Defense Case." *Diagnostic Imaging* 15:45–50.

Damasio, A. R. 1994. *Descartes' Error: Emotion, Reason, and the Human Brain.* New York: Grosset / Putnam.

Damasio, A. R., D. Tranel, and H. Damasio. 1990. "Individuals with Psychopathic Behavior Caused by Frontal Damage Fail to Respond Autonomically to Social Stimuli." *Behavioral and Brain Research* 41:81–94.

Davidson, R. J. 1993. "Parsing Affective Space: Perspectives from Neuropsychology and Psychophysiology." *Neuropsychology* 7:464–75.

Davidson, R. J., and N. A. Fox. 1989. "Frontal Brain Asymmetry Predicts Infants' Response to Maternal Separation." *Journal of Abnormal Psychology* 98:127–31.

Davidson, R. J., K. M. Putnam, and C. L. Larson. 2000. "Dysfunction in the Neural Circuitry of Emotion Regulation: A Possible Prelude to Violence." *Science* 289:575–79.

Dawson, M. E. 1990. "Psychophysiology at the Interface of Clinical Science, Cognitive Science, and Neuroscience: Presidential Address, 1989." *Psychophysiology* 27:243–55.

Delville, Y. 1999. "Exposure to Lead during Development Alters Aggressive Behavior in Golden Hamsters." *Neurotoxicology and Teratology* 21:445–49.

Demas, G. E., M. J. Eliasson, T. M. Dawson, V. L. Dawson, L. J. Kriegsfeld, R. J. Nelson, and S. H. Snyder. 1997. "Inhibition of Neuronal Nitric Oxide Synthase Increases Aggressive Behavior in Mice." *Molecular Medicine* 3:610–16.

Drake, M. E., S. A. Hietter, and A. Pakalnis. 1992. "EEG and Evoked Potentials in Episodic-Dyscontrol Syndrome." *Neuropsychobiology* 26:125–28.

Eley, T. C., P. Lichenstein, and J. Stevenson. 1999. "Sex Differences in the Etiology of Aggressive and Nonaggressive Antisocial Behavior: Results from Two Twin Studies." *Child Development* 70:155–68.

Evans, J. R., and N. S. Park. 1997. "Quantitative EEG Findings among Men Convicted of Murder." *Journal of Neurotherapy* 2:31–39.

Eysenck, H. J. 1964. *Crime and Personality,* 1st ed. London: Methuen.

Falconer, D. S. 1965. "The Inheritance of Liability to Certain Diseases, Estimated from the Incidence among Relatives." *Annals of Human Genetics* 29:51–76.

Farrington, D. P. 1987. "Implications of Biological Findings for Criminological Research." In *The Causes of Crime: New Biological Approaches,* ed. S. A. Mednick, T. E. Moffitt, and S. A. Stack, 42–64. New York: Cambridge University Press.

———. 1997. "The Relationship between Low Resting Heart Rate and Violence." In *Biosocial Bases of Violence,* ed. A. Raine, P. A. Brennan, D. P. Farrington, and S. A. Mednick, 89–106. New York: Plenum.

Fishbein, D. H., R. I. Herning, W. B. Pickworth, and C. A. Haertzen. 1989. "EEG and Brainstem Auditory Evoked Response Potentials in Adult Male Drug Abusers with Self-Reported Histories of Aggressive Behavior." *Biological Psychiatry* 26:595–611.

Fishbein, D., and S. Pease. 1994. "Diet, Nutrition, and Aggression." *Offender Rehabilitation* 21:117–44.

Fowles, D. C. 1993. "Electrodermal Activity and Antisocial Behavior." In *Electrodermal Activity: From Physiology to Psychology,* ed. J. C. Roy, W. Boucsein, Washington, D. C. Fowles, and J. Gruzelier. New York: Plenum.

Gale, A. 1975. "Can EEG Studies Make a Contribution to the Experimental Investigation of Psychopathy?" Paper presented at the NATO Advanced Study Institute on Psychopathic Behavior. Les Arc, Sept. 5–12.

Ge, X., R. J. Cadoret, R. D. Conger, J. M. Neiderhiser, W. Yates, W. E. Troughton, and M. A. Stewart. 1996. "The Developmental Interface between Nature and Nurture: A Mutual Influence Model of Child Antisocial Behavior and Parent Behaviors." *Developmental Psychology* 32:574–89.

Gottschalk, L. A., T. Rebello, M. S. Buchsbaum, and H. G. Tucker. 1991. "Abnormalities in Hair Trace Elements as Indicators of Aberrant Behavior." *Comprehensive Psychiatry* 32:229–37.

Goyer, P. F., P. J. Andreason, W. E. Semple, et al. 1994. "Positron-Emission Tomography and Personality Disorders." *Neuropsychopharmacology* 10:21–28.

Grove, W. M., E. D. Eckert, L. Heston, T. J. Bouchard, N. Segal, and D. T. Lykken. 1990. "Heritability of Substance Abuse and Antisocial Behavior: A Study of Monozygotic Twins Reared Apart." *Biological Psychiatry* 27:1293–304.

Guy, J. D., L. V. Majorski, C. J. Wallace, and M. P. Guy. 1983. "The Incidence of Minor Physical Anomalies in Adult Male Schizophrenics." *Schizophrenia Bulletin* 9:571–82.

Halas, E. S., G. M. Reynolds, and H. H. Sandstead. 1977. "Intra-uterine Nutrition and Its Effects on Aggression." *Physiology and Behavior* 19:653–61.

Halverson, C. F., and J. B. Victor. 1976. "Minor Physical Anomalies and Problem Behavior in Elementary Schoolchildren." *Child Development* 47:281–85.

Harpur, T. J., S. E. Williamson, A. Forth, and R. D. Hare. 1986. "A Quantitative Assessment of Resting EEG in Psychopathic and Non-psychopathic Criminals." *Psychophysiology* 23:439.

Henry, B., and T. E. Moffitt. 1997. "Neuropsychological and Neuroimaging Studies of Juvenile Delinquency and Adult Criminal Behavior." In *Handbook of Antisocial Behavior,* J. Breiling, D. M. Stoff, and J. D. Maser, 280–88. New York: Wiley.

Herrnstein, R. J. 1995. "Criminogenic Traits." In *Crime,* ed. J. Q. Wilson and J. Petersilia, 39–64. San Francisco: ICS Press.

Hill, D., and D. A. Pond. 1952. "Reflections on 100 Capital Cases Submitted for Electroencephalography." *Journal of Mental Science* 98:23–43.

Intrator, J., R. Hare, P. Stritzke, K. Brichtswein, D. Dorfman, T. Harpur, D. Bernstein, L. Handelsman, C. Schaefer, J. Keilp, J. Rosen, and J. Machac. 1997. "A Brain Imaging (Single Photon Emission Computerized Tomography) Study of Semantic and Affective Processing in Psychopaths." *Biological Psychiatry* 42:96–103.

Kagan, J. 1994. *Galen's Prophecy: Temperament in Human Nature.* New York: Basic Books.

Kandel, E., and S. A. Mednick. 1991. "Perinatal Complications Predict Violent Offending." *Criminology* 29:519–29.

Kuruoglu, A. C., Z. Arikan, M. Karatas, M. Arac, and E. Isik. 1996. "Single Photon Emission Computerized Tomography in Chronic Alcoholism: Antisocial Personality Disorder May Be Associated with Decreased Frontal Perfusion." *British Journal of Psychiatry* 169:348–54.

Lally, J. R., P. L. Mangione, and A. S. Honig. 1988. "Long-Range Impact of an Early Intervention with Low Income Children and Their Families." In *Parent Education as Early Childhood Intervention,* ed. D. R. Powell, 79–104. Norwood, N.J.: Ablex.

Lewis, D. O., J. H. Pincus, B. Bard, and E. Richardson. 1988. "Neuropsychiatric, Psychoeducational, and Family Characteristics of 14 Juveniles Condemned to Death in the United States." *American Journal of Psychiatry* 145:584–89.

Liu, J. J. and A. Raine. 1999. "Early Health Prevention of Violence." In *Encyclopedia of Violence in the United States,* ed. R. Gottesman and M. Mazon. New York: Charles Scribner.

Loosen, P. T., S. E. Purdon, and S. N. Pavlou. 1994. "Effects on Behavior of Modulation of Gonadotrophin-Releasing Hormone Antagonists." *American Journal of Psychiatry* 151:271–73.

Lubar, J. O. 1989. "Electroencephalographic Biofeedback of SMR and Beta for Treatment of Attention Deficit Disorder in a Clinical Setting." *Biofeedback and Self-Regulation* 9:1–23.

McBurnett, K., and B. B. Lahey. 1994. "Biological Correlates of Conduct Disorder and Antisocial Behavior in Children and Adolescents." In *Progress in Experimental Personality and Psychopathology Research,* ed. D. C. Fowles. New York: Springer.

McBurnett, K., B. B. Lahey, P. J. Frick, C. Risch, R. Loeber, E. L. Hart, M. A. G. Christ, and K. S. Hanson. 1991. "Anxiety, Inhibition, and Conduct Disorder in Children: II. Relation to Salivary Cortisol." *Journal of the American Academy of Child and Adolescent Psychiatry* 30:192–96.

McBurnett, K., B. B. Lahey, P. J. Rathouz, and R. Loeber. 2000. "Low Salivary Cortisol and Persistent Aggression in Boys Referred for Disruptive Behavior." *Archives of General Psychiatry* 57:38–43.

Maliphant, R., F. Hume, and A. Furnham. 1990. "Autonomic Nervous System (ANS) Activity, Personality Characteristics, and Disruptive Behavior in Girls." *Journal of Child Psychology and Psychiatry* 31:619–28.

Mark, V. H., and F. R. Ervin. 1970. *Violence and the Brain.* New York: Harper Row.

McMillan, T. M., and S. J. Rachman. 1987. "Fearlessness and Courage: A Laboratory Study of Paratrooper Veterans of the Falklands War." *British Journal of Psychology* 78:375–83.

Mednick, S. A., W. H. Gabrielli, and B. Hutchings. 1984. "Genetic Influences in Criminal Convictions: Evidence from an Adoption Cohort." *Science* 224:891–94.

Mednick, S. A. and E. Kandel. 1988. "Genetic and Perinatal Factors in Violence." In *Biological Contributions to Crime Causation,* ed. S. A. Mednick and T. Moffitt, 121–34. Dordrecht, Holland: Martinus Nijhoff.

Mednick, S. A., J. Volavka, W. F. Gabrielli, and T. Itil. 1981. "EEG as a Predictor of Antisocial Behavior." *Criminology* 19:219–31.

Milstein, V. 1988. "EEG Topography in Patients with Aggressive Violent Behavior." In *Biological Contributions to Crime Causation,* ed. T. E. Moffitt and S. A. Mednick. Dordrecht, Netherlands: Kluwer.

Moffitt, T. E. 1993. Life-course-persistent and Adolescent-limited Antisocial Behavior: A Developmental Taxonomy. *Psychological Review 100*: 674-701.

Moffitt, T. E. and Caspir. In press.

Moilanen, I. 1987. "Dominance and Submissiveness between Twins." *Acta Geneticae Medicae et Gemellologiae* 36:249–55.

Needleman, H. L., J. A. Riess, M. J. Tobin, G. E. Biesecker, and J. B. Greenhouse. 1996. "Bone Lead Levels and Delinquent Behavior." *Journal of the American Medical Association* 275:363–69.

Nelson, R. J., G. E. Demas, P. L. Huang, M. C. Fishman, V. L. Dawson, T. M. Dawson, and S. H. Snyder. 1995. "Behavioral Abnormalities in Male Mice Lacking Neuronal Nitric Oxide Synthase." *Nature* 383–86.

Neugebauer, R., H. W. Hoek, and E. Susser. 1999. "Prenatal Exposure to Wartime Famine and Development of Antisocial Personality Disorder in Early Adulthood." *Journal of the American Medical Association* 4:479–81.

O'Connor, K., R. Hallam, and S. Rachman. 1985. "Fearlessness and Courage: A Replication Experiment." *British Journal of Psychology* 76:187–97.

Olds, D., C. R. Henderson, R. Cole, J. Eckenrode, H. Kitzman, D. Luckey, L. Pettitt, K. Sidora, P. Morris, and J. Powers. 1998. "Long-Term Effects of Nurse Home Visitation on Children's Criminal and Antisocial Behavior." *Journal of the American Medical Association* 280:1238–44.

Olweus, D. 1987. "Testosterone and Adrenaline: Aggressive Antisocial Behavior in Normal Adolescent Males." In *The Causes of Crime: New Biological Approaches,* ed. S. A. Mednick, T. E. Moffitt, and S. A. Stack, 263–82. Cambridge: Cambridge University Press.

Olweus, D., A. Mattesson, D. Schalling, and H. Low. 1988. "Circulating Testosterone Levels and Aggression in Adolescent Males: A Causal Analysis." *Psychosomatic Medicine* 50:261–72.

Oteiza, P. I., L. S. Hurley, B. Lonnerdal, and C. L. Keen. 1990. "Effects of Marginal Zinc Deficiency on Microtubule Polymerization in the Developing Rat Brain." *Biological Trace Element Research* 23:13–23.

Patrick, C. J. 1994. "Emotion and Psychopathy: Startling New Insights." *Psychophysiology* 31:319–30.

Paulus, D. L., and C. L. Martin. 1986. "Predicting Adult Temperament from Minor Physical Anomalies." *Journal of Personality and Social Psychology* 50:1235–39.

Petersen, I., M. Matousek, S. A. Mednick, J. Volavka, and V. Pollock. 1982. "EEG Antecedents of Thievery." *Criminology* 19:219–29.

Pfeiffer, C. C., and E. R. Braverman. 1982. "Zinc, the Brain, and Behavior." *Biological Psychiatry* 17:513–32.

Pillmann, F., A. Rohde, S. Ullrich, S. Draba, U. Sannemuller, and A. Marneros. 1999. "Violence, Criminal Behavior, and the EEG: Significance of Left Hemispheric Focal Abnormalities." *Journal of Neuropsychiatry and Clinical Neurosciences* 11:454–57.

Piquero, A., and S. Tibbetts. 1999. "The Impact of Pre/Perinatal Disturbances and Disadvantaged Familial Environment in Predicting Criminal Offending." *Studies on Crime and Crime Prevention* 8:52–70.

Pomeroy, J. C., J. Sprafkin, and K. D. Gadow. 1988. "Minor Physical Anomalies as a Biological Marker for Behavior Disorders." *Journal of the American Academy of Child and Adolescent Psychiatry* 27:466–73.

Quay, H. C. 1965. "Psychopathic Personality as Pathological Stimulation Seeking." *American Journal of Psychiatry* 122:180–83.

Raine, A. 1993. *The Psychopathology of Crime: Criminal Behavior as a Clinical Disorder.* San Diego: Academic Press.

Raine, A. 1996a. *Low Resting Heart Rate as a Predisposition to Childhood Aggression.* Paper presented at the Society for Research in Psychopathology. Atlanta, Sept. 26–29.

Raine, A. 1996b. "Autonomic Nervous System Activity and Violence." In *Neurobiological Approaches to Clinical Aggression Research,* ed. D. M. Stoff and R. B. Cairns, 145–68. Mahwah, N.J.: Lawrence Erlbaum.

Raine, A. 1997. "Psychophysiology and Antisocial Behavior." In *Handbook of Antisocial Behavior,* ed. D. Stoff, J. Breiling, and J. D. Maser, 289–304. New York: Wiley.

Raine, A., P. Brennan, and S. A. Mednick. 1994. "Birth Complications Combined with Early Maternal Rejection at Age 1 Year Predispose to Violent Crime at Age 18 Years." *Archives of General Psychiatry* 51:984–88.

Raine, A., P. A. Brennan, and S. A. Mednick. 1997. "Interaction between Birth Complications and Early Maternal Rejection in Predisposing to Adult Violence: Specificity to Serious, Early Onset Violence." *American Journal of Psychiatry* 154:1265–71.

Raine, A., and M. S. Buchsbaum. 1996. "Violence and Brain Imaging." In *Neurobiological Approaches to Clinical Aggression Research,* ed. D. M. Stoff and R. B. Cairns, 195–218. Mahwah, N.J.: Lawrence Erlbaum.

Raine, A., M. S. Buchsbaum, and L. La Casse. 1997. "Brain Abnormalities in Murderers Indicated by Positron Emission Tomography." *Biological Psychiatry* 42:495–508.

Raine, A., M. S. Buchsbaum, J. Stanley, S. Lottenberg, L. Abel, and J. Stoddard. 1994. "Selective Reductions in Pre-frontal Glucose Metabolism in Murderers." *Biological Psychiatry* 36:365–73.

Raine, A., T. Lencz, S. Bihrle, L. La Casse, and P. Colletti. 2000. "Reduced Prefrontal Gray Matter Volume and Reduced Autonomic Activity in Antisocial Personality Disorder." *Archives of General Psychiatry* 57:119–27.

Raine, A., and J. H. Liu. 1998. "Biological Predispositions to Violence and Their Implications for Biosocial Treatment and Prevention." *Psychology, Crime, and Law* 4:107–25.

Raine, A., J. H. Liu, P. H. Venables, C. Dalais, K. Mellingen, and S. A. Mednick. 1999. "Educational and Nutritional Enrichment at Age 3–5 Years Reduces Conduct Disorder at Age 17 Years: Evidence from the Mauritius Child Health Project." Symposium on Prevention Trials Targeting Conduct Disorder or Depression. Society for Prevention Research, New Orleans, June 24–26.

Raine, A., J. R. Meloy, S. Bihrle, J. Stoddard, L. La Casse, and M. S. Buchsbaum. 1998. "Reduced Prefrontal and Increased Subcortical Brain Functioning Assessed Using Positron Emission Tomography in Predatory and Affective Murderers." *Behavioral Sciences and the Law* 16:319–32.

Raine, A., S. Park, T. Lencz, S. Bihrle, L. La Casse, C. S. Widom, I. Al-Dayeh, and M. Singh. In press. "Reduced Right Hemisphere Activation in Severely Abused Violent Offenders during a Working Memory Task as Indicated by fMRI." *Aggressive Behavior.*

Raine, A., G. Reynolds, and C. Sheard. 1991. "Neuroanatomical Mediators of Electrodermal Activity in Normal Human Subjects: A Magnetic Resonance Imaging Study." *Psychophysiology* 28:548–55.

Raine, A., C. Reynolds, P. H. Venables, and S. A. Mednick, and D. P. Farrington. 1998. Fearlessness, Stimulation Seeking, and Large Body Size at Age 3 Years as Early Predispositions to Childhood Aggression at Age 11 Years." *Archives of General Psychiatry* 55:745–51.

Raine, A., J. Stoddard, S. Bihrle, and M. S. Buchsbaum. 1998. "Prefrontal Glucose Deficits in Murderers Lacking Psychosocial Deprivation." *Neuropsychiatry, Neuropsychology, and Behavioral Neurology* 11:1–7.

Raine, A., and P. H. Venables. 1981. "Classical Conditioning and Socialization—A Biosocial Interaction?" *Personality and Individual Differences* 2:273–83.

Raine, A., P. H. Venables, Cyril Dalais, K. Mellingen, and S. A. Mednick. In press. "Early Educational and Health Enrichment at Age 3–5 Years Is Associated with Increased Autonomic and Central Nervous System Arousal and Orienting at Age 11 Years: Evidence from the Mauritius Child Health Project." *Psychophysiology.*

Raine, A., P. H. Venables, and S. A. Mednick. 1997. "Low Resting Heart Rate at Age 3 Years Predisposes to Aggression at Age 11 Years: Findings from the Mauritius Joint Child Health Project." *Journal of the American Academy of Child and Adolescent Psychiatry* 36:1457–64.

Raine, A., P. H. Venables, and M. Williams. 1990. "Relationships between CNS and ANS Measures of Arousal at Age 15 and Criminality at Age 24." *Archives of General Psychiatry* 47:1003–7.

Raine, A., P. H. Venables, and M. Williams. 1995. "High Autonomic Arousal and Electrodermal Orienting at Age 15 Years as Protective Factors against Criminal Behavior at Age 29 Years." *American Journal of Psychiatry* 152:1595–1600.

Raine, A., P. H. Venables, and M. Williams. 1996. "Better Autonomic Conditioning and Faster Electrodermal Half-Recovery Time at Age 15 Years as Possible Protective Factors against Crime at Age 29 Years." *Developmental Psychology* 32:624–30.

Rosen, G. M. 1996. "Iron Deficiency among Incarcerated Juvenile Delinquents." *Journal of Adolescent Health Care* 6:419–23.

Rubin, R. T. 1987. "The Neuroendocrinology and Neurochemistry of Antisocial Behavior." In *The Causes of Crime: New Biological Approaches,* ed. S. A. Mednick, T. E. Moffitt, and S. A. Stack, 239–62. Cambridge: Cambridge University Press.

Rutter, M., H. Giller, and A. Hagell. 1998. *Antisocial Behavior by Young People.* Cambridge: Cambridge University Press.

Scarpa, A., A. Raine, P. H. Venables, and S. A. Mednick. 1997. "Heart Rate and Skin Conductance in Behaviorally Inhibited Mauritian Children." *Journal of Abnormal Psychology* 106:182–90.

Schacter, F. F. and R. K. Stone. 1985. "Difficult Sibling, Easy Sibling: Temperament and within Family Environment." *Child Development* 54:424–35.

Schauss, A. G. 1981. "Comparative Hair Mineral Analysis Results of 21 Elements in a Random Selected Behaviorally 'Normal' 19–59 Population and Violent Adult Criminal Offenders." *International Journal of Biosocial Research* 1:21–41.

Seidenwurm, D., T. R. Pounds, A. Globus, and P. E. Valk. 1997. "Temporal Lobe Metabolism in Violent Subjects: Correlation of Imaging and Neuropsychiatric Findings." *American Journal of Neuroradiology* 18:625–31.

Sigvardsson, S., R. Cloninger, M. Bohman, and A. L. von Knorring. 1982. "Predisposition to Petty Criminality in Swedish Adoptees: III. Sex Differences and Validation of the Male Typology." *Archives of General Psychiatry* 39:1248–53.

Slutske, W., A. Heath, S. Dinwiddie, P. Madden, K. Bucholz, M. Dunne, D. Statham, and N. Martin. 1997. "Modeling Genetic and Environmental Influences in the Etiology of Conduct Disorder: A Study of 2,682 Adult Twin Pairs." *Journal of Abnormal Psychology* 106:266–279.

Soderstrom, H., M. Tullberg, C. Wikkels, S. Ekholm, and A. Forsman. 2000. "Reduced Regional Cerebral Blood Flow in Non-psychotic Violent Offenders." *Psychiatry Research* 98:29–41.

Stuss, D. T., and D. F. Benson. 1986. *The Frontal Lobes.* New York: Raven Press.

Susman, E. J., L. D. Dorn, and G. P. Chrousos. 1991. "Negative Affect and Hormone Levels in Young Adolescents: Concurrent and Longitudinal Perspectives." *Journal of Youth and Adolescence* 20:167–90.

Susman, E. J., L. D. Dorn, G. Inoff-Germain, E. D. Nottelmann, and G. P. Chrousos. 1997. "Cortisol Reactivity, Distress Behavior, Behavior Problems, and Emotionality in Young Adolescents: A Longitudinal Perspective." *Journal of Research on Adolescence* 7:81–105.

Susman, E. J., D. A. Granger, E. Murowchick, A. Ponirakis, and B. K. Worrall. 1996. "Gonadal and Adrenal Hormones: Developmental Transitions and Aggressive Behavior." *New York Academy of Sciences* 794:16–30.

Susman, E. J., and A. C. Petersen. 1992. "Hormones and Behavior in Adolescence." In *Textbook of Adolescent Medicine,* E. R. McAnarney, R. E. Kreipe, D. P. Orr, and G. D. Comerci, 125–30. New York: W. B. Saunders.

Susman, E. J., and A. Ponirakis. 1997. "Hormones—Context Interactions and Antisocial Behavior in Youth." In *Biosocial Bases of Violence,* ed. A. Raine, P. A. Brennan, David P. Farrington, and A. Mednick, 163–74. New York: Plenum.

Tarter, R. E., A. M. Hegedus, N. E. Winsten, and A. I. Alterman. 1984. "Neuropsychological, Personality, and Familial Characteristics of Physically Abused Delinquents." *Journal of the American Academy of Child Psychiatry* 23:668–74.

Tennes, K., and M. Kreye. 1985. "Childrens' Adrenocortical Response to Classroom Activities in Elementary School." *Psychosomatic Medicine* 47:451–60.

Tikal, K., O. Benesova, and S. Frankova. 1976. "The Effect of Pyrithioxine and Pyridoxine on Individual Behavior, Social Interactions, and Learning in Rats Malnourished in Early Postnatal Life." *Psychopharmacologia* 46:325–32.

Timiras, P. S., D. B. Hudson, and P. E. Segall. 1984. "Lifetime Brain Serotonin: Regional Effects of Age and Precursor Availability." *Neurobiology of Aging* 5:235–42.

Turner, C. W., M. H. Ford, D. W. West, and A. W. Meikle. 1986. "Genetic Influences on Testosterone, Hostility, and Type A Behavior in Adult Male Twins." Paper presented at the meeting of the American Psychological Association. Washington, D.C.

van den Oord, E. J. C. G., D. I. Boomsma, and F. Verhulst. 1994. "A Study of Problem Behaviors in 10- to 15-Year-Old Biologically Related and Unrelated International Adoptees." *Behavior Genetics* 24:193–205.

van Goozen, S. H. M., W. Matthys, P. T. Cohenkettenis, F. Gispendewied, T. L. Wiegant, and H. Vanegeland. 1998. "Salivary Cortisol and Cardiovascular Activity during Stress in Oppositional-Defiant Disorder Boys and Normal Controls." *Biological Psychiatry* 43:531–39.

Venables, P. H. 1987. "Autonomic and Central Nervous System Factors in Criminal Behavior." In *The Causes of Crime: New Biological Approaches,* ed. S. A. Mednick, T. Moffitt, and S. Stack, 110–36. New York: Cambridge University Press.

Virkunnen, M. 1985. "Urinary Free Cortisol Excretion in Habitually Violent Offenders." *Acta Psychiatrica Scandinavica* 72:40–42.

Volavka, J. 1987. "Electroencephalogram among Criminals." In *The Causes of Crime: New Biological Approaches,* ed. S. A. Mednick, T. E. Moffitt, and S. Stack, 137–45. Cambridge: Cambridge University Press.

Volkow, N. D., L. R. Tancredi, C. Grant, H. Gillespie, A. Valentine, N. Mullani, G. J. Wang, and L. Hollister. 1995. "Brain Glucose Metabolism in Violent Psychiatric Patients: A Preliminary Study." *Psychiatry Research—Neuroimaging* 61:243–53.

Wadsworth, M. E. J. 1976. "Delinquency, Pulse Rate, and Early Emotional Deprivation." *British Journal of Criminology* 16:245–56.

Wainwright, P., and R. Stefanescu. 1983. "Prenatal Protein Deprivation Increases Defects of the Corpus Callosum in BALB/c Laboratory Mice." *Experimental Neurology* 81:694–702.

Waldrop, M. F., R. Q. Bell, B. McLaughlin, and C. F. Halverson. 1978. "Newborn Minor Physical Anomalies Predict Short Attention Span, Peer Aggression, and Impulsivity at Age 3." *Science* 199:563–64.

Walsh, W. J., H. R. Isaacson, F. Rehman, and A. Hall. 1997. "Elevated Blood Copper/Zinc Ratios in Assaultive Young Males." *Physiology and Behavior* 62:327–29.

Weisman, R. 1986. "Nutrition and Neurotransmitters: The Research of Richard Wurtman." *Journal of Child and Adolescent Psychotherapy* 3:125–32.

Werbach M. 1995. "Nutritional Influences on Aggressive Behavior." *Journal of Orthomolecular Medicine* 7:45–51.

Widom, C.S. 1997. Child Abuse, Neglect, and Witnessing Violence. In *Handbook of Antisocial Behavior,* ed., D.M. Stoff, J. Breiling, and J.D. Maser. 159-170. New York, Wiley.

Wille, R., and K. M. Beier. 1989. "Castration in Germany." *Annals of Sex Research* 2:103–34.

Williams, D. 1969. "Neural Factors Related to Habitual Aggression: Consideration of Those Differences between Those Habitually Aggressive and Others Who Have Committed Crimes of Violence." *Brain* 92:503–20.

Wilson, J. Q., and R. J. Herrnstein. 1985. *Crime and Human Nature.* New York: Simon and Schuster.

Zahn, T. P. and M. J. Kruesi. 1993. "Autonomic Activity in Boys with Disruptive Behavior Disorders." *Psychophysiology* 30:605–14.

CHAPTER 4
Peter W. Greenwood
JUVENILE CRIME AND JUVENILE JUSTICE

References

Altschuler, David M., and Troy L. Armstrong. 1991. "Intensive Aftercare for the High-Risk Juvenile Parolee: Issues and Approaches in Reintegration and Community Supervision." In *Intensive Interventions with High-Risk Youths: Promising Approaches in Juvenile Probation and Parole,* ed. Troy L. Armstrong. Monsey, NY: Willow Tree Press.

Aos, S., P. Phipps, R. Barmoski, and R. Lieb. 1999. *The Comparative Costs and Benefits of Programs to Reduce Crime.* Olympia: Washington State Institute for Public Policy.

Bartollas, C., S. J. Miller, and S. Dinitz. 1976. *Juvenile Victimization: The Institutional Paradox.* New York: John Wiley and Sons.

Blumstein, A., and R. Rosenfeld. 1998. "Explaining Recent Trends in U.S. Homicide Rates." *Journal of Criminal Law and Criminology* 88, no. 4: 1175–216.

Braithwaite, J. 1998. "Restorative Justice: Assessing an Immodest Theory and a Pessimistic Theory." In *Crime and Justice: A Review of Research*, vol. 23, ed. M. Tonry. Chicago: University of Chicago Press.

Brown, J. M., and P. A. Langan. 1998. *State Court Sentencing of Convicted Felons*. Washington, D.C.: Bureau of Justice Statistics, U.S. Department of Justice.

Coates, R., A. Miller, and L. Ohlin. 1982. *Diversity in a Youth Correctional System*. Cambridge, Mass.: Ballinger.

Cohen, Jacob. 1988. *Statistical Power Analysis for the Behavioral Sciences*, 2d ed. Hillsdale, N.J.: Lawrence Erlbaum Associates.

Cook, Philip J., and John H. Laub. 1998. "The Unprecedented Epidemic in Youth Violence." In *Youth Violence, Crime and Justice*, vol. 24, ed. Michael Tonry and Mark H. Moore, 27–64. Chicago: University of Chicago Press.

Deschenes, Elizabeth P., Peter W. Greenwood, and John Adams. 1993. "An Evaluation of the Nokomis Challenge Program in Michigan." *Journal of Contemporary Criminal Justice* 9, no. 2 (May): 146–67.

Elliot, D. S. 1998. *Blueprints for Violence Prevention*. Boulder: Institute of Behavioral Sciences, University of Colorado at Boulder.

Empey, Lamar T. 1979. *American Delinquency: The Future of Childhood and Juvenile Justice*. Charlottesville: University of Virginia Press.

Empey, Lamar T., and Steven G. Lubeck, 1971. *The Silverlake Experiment: Testing Delinquency Theory and Community Intervention*. Chicago: Aldine.

Fagan, J. 1995. "Separating the Men From the Boys: The Comparative Advantage of Juvenile Versus Criminal Court Sanctions on Recidivism Among Adolescent Felony Offenders." In *A Sourcebook: Serious, Violent and Chronic Juvenile Offenders*, ed. J. C. Howell, B. Krisberg, J. D. Hawkins, and J.J. Wilson, 238–61. Thousand Oaks, Calif.: Sage.

Feld, Barry. 1977. *Neutralizing Inmate Violence: Juvenile Offenders in Institutions*. Cambridge, Mass.: Ballinger.

———. 1984. "Criminalizing Juvenile Justice: Rules of Procedure for Juvenile Court." *Minnesota Law Review* 69:141–276.

———. 1989. "The Right to Counsel in Juvenile Court: An Empirical Study of When Lawyers Appear and the Difference They Make." *Journal of Criminal Law and Criminology* 79:1185–346.

Greenwood, Peter W. 1986. "Differences in Criminal Behavior and Court Response Among Juvenile and Young Adult Defendants." In *Annual Review of Criminal Justice Research*, vol. 7, ed. Michael Tonry and Norval Morris, 151–87. Chicago: University of Chicago Press.

———. 1996. "Responding to Juvenile Crime: Lessons Learned." In *The Future of Children*, Vol. 6, Number 3, Winter 1996. R. E. Behrmann, M.D., The Juvenile Court, Center for the Future of Children, The David and Lucille Packard Foundation.

Greenwood, Peter W., Elizabeth Piper Deschenes, and John Adams. 1993. *Chronic Juvenile Offenders: Final Results from The Skillman Aftercare Experiment*, MR-220-SKF. Santa Monica, Calif.: RAND.

Greenwood, Peter W., Albert Lipson, Allan Abrahamse, Franklin Zimring. 1983. *Youth Crime and Juvenile Justice in California: A Report to the Legislature*, R-3016-CSA. Santa Monica, Calif.: RAND.

Greenwood, P. W., K. E. Model, C. P. Rydell, and J. Chiesa. 1996. *Diverting Children from a Life of Crime: Measuring Costs and Benefits*. Santa Monica, Calif.: RAND.

Greenwood, Peter W., and Susan Turner. 1993. "Evaluation of the Paint Creek Youth Center: A Residential Program for Serious Delinquents," *Criminology* 31, no. 2 (May): 263–79.

Griffin, P., P. Torbet, and L. Szymanski. 1998. *Trying Juveniles in Adult Courts: An Analysis of State Transfer Provisions.* Washington, D.C.: Office of Juvenile Justice and Delinquency Prevention, Office of Justice Programs, U.S. Department of Justice.

Hammond, W. R., and B. R. Yung. 1993. "Evaluation and Activity Report: Positive Adolescent Choices Training." Unpublished grant report. U.S. Maternal and Child Health Department, Washington, D.C.

Hawkins, J. D., R. F. Catalano, R. Kosterman, R. D. Abbott, and K. G. Hill. 1998. "Promoting Academic Success and Preventing Adolescent Health Risk Behaviors: Six-Year Follow-up of the Seattle Social Development Project." Seattle: School of Social Work, University of Washington.

Howell, J. C., and J. D. Hawkins. 1998. "Prevention of Youth Violence." In *Youth Violence, Crime and Justice,* vol. 24, ed. M. Tonry and M. H. Moore. Chicago: University of Chicago Press.

Jones, M. B., and D. R. Offord. 1989. "Reduction of Antisocial Behavior in Poor Children by Non-school Skill-Development." *Journal of Child Psychology* 30, no. 5: 737–50.

Karoly, L. A., P. W. Greenwood, S. S. Everingham, J. Hoube, M. R. Kilburn, C. P. Rydell, M. Sanders, J. Chiesa. 1998. *Investing in Our Children: What We Know and Don't Know About the Costs and Benefits of Early Childhood Interventions.* Santa Monica, CA: RAND.

Kazdin, A. E., T. C. Siegel, and D. Bass. 1992. "Cognitive Problem-Solving Skills Training and Parent Management Training in the Treatment of Anti-Social Behavior in Children." *Journal of Consulting and Clinical Psychology* 60:733–47.

Krisberg, Barry, J. Austin, and P. Steele. 1991. *Unlocking Juvenile Corrections.* San Francisco: National Council on Crime and Delinquency.

Lally, R. J., P. L. Mangione, and A. Honig. 1988. "The Syracuse University Family Development Research Program: Long Range Impact of an Early Intervention With Low-Income Children and Their Families." In *Parent Education as Early Childhood Intervention,* ed. D. R. Powell, 79–104. Norwood, N.J.: Ablex.

Lipsey, Mark W. 1991. "Juvenile Delinquency Treatment: A Meta-Analytic Inquiry into the Variability of Effects." In *Meta-Analysis for Explanation: A Casebook.* New York: Russell Sage Foundation.

Lipsey, M. W., and D. B. Wilson. 1998. "Effective Intervention for Serious Juvenile Offenders." In *Serious & Violent Juvenile Offenders,* ed. R. Loeber and D. Farrington, 313–45. Thousand Oaks, Calif.: Sage.

Lipton, Douglas, R. Martinson, and J. Wilks. 1975. *The Effectiveness of Correctional Treatment: A Survey of Treatment Evaluation Studies.* New York: Praeger.

Lipton, Mark. 1991.

MacKenzie, D. L. 1990. "Boot Camp Prisons: Components, Evaluations, and Empirical Issues." *Federal Probation* 54, no. 3.

Menard, Scott, and D. S. Elliott. 1993. "Data Set Comparability and Short-Term Trends in Crime and Delinquency." *Journal of Criminal Justice* 21:433–45.

Olds, D. L., J. Eckenrode, C. R. Henderson, H. Kizman, J. Powers, R. Cole, K. Sidora, P. Morris, L. M. Pettit, and D. W. Luckey. 1997. "Long-Term Effects of Home Visitation on Maternal Life Course and Child Abuse and Neglect: Fifteen-Year Follow-Up of a Randomized Trial." *Journal of the American Medical Association* 278 (August 27): 637–43.

Reiss, A. J., and J. A. Roth, eds. 1993. *Understanding and Preventing Violence.* Washington, D.C.: National Academy Press.

Schwartz, Ira M., and R. Van Vleet. 1992. "Public Policy and the Incarceration of Juveniles: Directions for the 1990s." In *Juvenile Justice and Public Policy*, ed. Ira M. Schwartz, 151–64. New York: Lexington Books.

Schweinhart, L. J., H. V. Barnes, and D. P. Weikart. 1993. *Significant Benefits.* Ypsilanti, Mich.: High/Scope.

Sechrest, L., S. O. White, and E. D. Brown, eds. 1979. *The Rehabilitation of Criminal Offenders: Problems and Prospects.* Washington, D.C.: National Academy of Sciences.

Sickmund, M., A. L. Stahl, T. A. Finnegan, H. N. Snyder, and J. A. Butts. 1998. *Juvenile Court Statistics 1995.* Washington, D.C.: Office of Juvenile Justice and Delinquency Prevention, Office of Justice Programs, U.S. Department of Justice.

Slavin, R. E., N. A. Madden, L. J. Dolan, B. A. Wasik, S. M. Ross, and L. J. Smith. 1994. "Whenever and Wherever We Choose: The Replication of Success for All." *Phi Delta Kappan* (April): 639–47.

Thornberry, Terence P., S. E. Tolnay, T. J. Flanagan, and P. Glynn. 1989. *Children in Custody, 1987: A Comparison of Public and Private Juvenile Custody Facilities.* New York: University at Albany: March 7.

Torbet, P., and L. Szymanski. 1998. *State Legislative Responses to Violent Juvenile Crime: 1996–97 Update.* Washington, D.C.: Office of Juvenile Justice and Delinquency Prevention, Office of Justice Programs, U.S. Department of Justice.

Tremblay, R. E., F. Vitaro, L. Bertrand, M. Le Blanc, H. Beauchesne, H. Boileau, and L. David. 1992. "Parent Child Training to Prevent Early Onset of Delinquency: The Montreal Longitudinal-Experimental Study." In *Preventing Antisocial Behavior: Interventions from Birth through Adolescence,* eds. J. McCord and R. E. Tremblay. New York: Guilford.

U.S. Department of Health and Human Services. 1990. *Health: United States, 1989.* Hyattsville, Md.: Public Health Service, U.S. Department of Health and Human Services.

U.S. Department of Justice. 1999. *Juvenile Offenders and Victims: 1999 National Report.* Washington, D.C.: Office of Juvenile Justice and Delinquency Prevention, U.S. Department of Justice.

CHAPTER 5
Patrick Tolan
CRIME PREVENTION: FOCUS ON YOUTH

Correspondence should be sent to the author at Institute for Juvenile Research, University of Illinois at Chicago, 840, S. Wood, Chicago, IL 60612.

References

Aber, J. L., S. M. Jones, J. L. Brown, N. Chaudry, and F. Samples. 1998. "Resolving Conflict Creatively: Evaluating the Developmental Effects of a School-Based Violence Prevention Program in Neighborhood and Classroom Context." *Development and Psychopathology* 10:197–213.

Aos, S., P. Phipps, R. Barnoski, and R. Lieb. 1999. *The Comparative Costs and Benefits of Programs to Reduce Crime: A Review of National Research Findings with Implications for Washington State,* Version 3.0 (May). Olympia: Washington State Institute for Public Policy.

Barr, R., and K. Pease. 1990. "Crime Placement, Displacement, and Deflection." In *Crime and Justice: A Review of Research,* ed. M. Tonry and N. Morris, vol. 12. Chicago: University of Chicago Press.

Berleman, W. C., J. R. Seaberg and T. W. Steinburn. 1971. "The execution and evaluation of a delinquency prevention program." *Social Problems,* 95, 413-423, 323–46.

Borduin, C. M., B. J. Mann, L. T. Cone, S. W. Henggeler, B. R. Fucci, D. M. Blaske, and R. A. Williams. 1995. "Multisystemic Treatment of Serious Juvenile Offenders: Long-term Prevention of Criminality and Violence." *Journal of Consulting and Clinical Psychology* 63:569–87.

Brantingham, P. J., and P. L. Brantingham. 1991. *Environmental Criminology,* 2nd ed. Prospect Heights, Ill.: Waverland.

Bry, B. H. 1982. "Reducing the Incidence of Adolescent Problems through Preventive Intervention: One- and Five-Year Follow-Up." *American Journal of Community Psychology* 10 (3): 265–76.

Bursik, R. J., and H. G. Grasmick. 1993. *Neighborhoods and Crime.* New York: Lexington.

Cairns, R. B. 1987. "Predicting Aggression in Girls and Boys." *Social Science* 71:16–21.

Clarke, R. V. 1995. "Situational Crime Prevention." In *Strategic Approaches to Crime Prevention: Building A Safer Society,* ed. M. Tonry and D. P. Farrington, 91–150. Chicago: University of Chicago Press.

Cohen, L. E., and M. Felson. 1979. "Social Change and Crime Rate Trends: A Routine Activity Approach." *American Sociological Review* 44:588–607.

Coie, J. D., and K. A. Dodge. 1998. "Aggression and Antisocial Behavior." In *Handbook of Child Psychology,* vol. 3, *Social, Emotional, and Personality Development,* 5th edition, ed. W. Damon and N. Eisenberg, 779–862. New York: Wiley.

Conduct Problems Prevention Research Group. 1999. "Initial Impact of the Fast Track Prevention Trial for Conduct Problems: I. The High Risk Sample." *Journal of Consulting and Clinical Psychology* 67:631–47.

Dangel, R., J. Deschner, and R. Rapp. 1989. "Anger Control Training for Adolescents in Residential Treatment." *Behavior Modification* 13:447–58.

Deschenes, E. P., S. Turner, P. Greenwood, and J. Chiesa. 1996. *An Experimental Evaluation of Drug Testing and Treatment Interventions for Probationers in Maricopa County, Arizona.* Santa Monica, Calif.: RAND Corporation.

Dishion, T. J., K. M. Spracklen, D. W. Andrews, and G. R. Patterson. 1996. "Deviancy Training in Male Adolescents' Friendships." *Behavior Therapy* 27:373–90.

Downes, D., and P. Rock. 1982. *Understanding Deviance.* Oxford: Clarendon.

Dumas, J. E., E. A. Blechman, and R. J. Prinz. 1992. "Helping Family with Aggressive Children and Adolescent? Change." *Journal of Child Clinical Psychology,* 21, 351-375.

Dyal, W. W. 1995. "Ten Organizational Practices of Public Health: A Historical Perspective." *American Journal of Preventive Medicine* 11:6–8.

Elliott, D. S. 1996. "Delinquency, School Attendance, and Dropout." In *The International Library of Criminology, Criminal Justice, and Penology,* vol. 2, *Criminal Careers,* ed. D. F. Greenberg, 377–84. Aldershot, England: Dartmouth Publishing Company.

Elliott, D. S., and P. H. Tolan. 1998. "Youth Violence, Prevention, Intervention, and Social Policy: An Overview." In *Youth Violence: A Volume in the Psychiatric Clinics of North America,* ed. D. Flannery and R. Hoff. Washington, D.C.: American Psychiatric Association.

Fagan, J. 1995. "Separating the Men from the Boys: The Comparative Advantage of Juvenile versus Criminal Court Sanctions on Recidivism among Adolescent Felony Offenders." In

A Sourcebook of Serious, Violent, and Chronic Juvenile Offenders, ed. J. C. Howell, B. Krisberg, J. D. Hawkins, and J. J. Wilson. Thousand Oaks, Calif.: Sage.

Farrell, A. D., and A. L. Meyer. 1997. "Effectiveness of a School-Based Prevention Program for Reducing Violence among Urban Adolescents: Differential Impact on Girls and Boys." Manuscript under review.

Farrington, D. P. 1998. "Youth Crime and Antisocial Behavior." In *The Social Child,* ed. A. Campbell, S. Muncer, et al., 353–92.

Feldman, R. A., T. E. Caplinger, and J. S. Wodarski. 1983. *The St. Louis Conundrum: The Effective Treatment of Antisocial Youths.* Englewood Cliffs, N.J.: Prentice Hall.

Freedman, M. 1993. *The Kindness of Strangers: Adult Mentors, Urban Youth, and the New Voluntarism.* San Francisco, Calif.: Jossey-Bass Inc.

Garbarino, J. 1996. "Youth in Dangerous Environments: Coping with the Consequences." In *Social Problems and Social Contexts in Adolescence: Perspectives across Boundaries,* ed. K. Hurrelmann and S. F. Hamilton, 269–90. New York: Aldine De Gruyter.

Gorman-Smith, D., P. H. Tolan, and D. Henry. 1999. "The Relation of Community and Family to Risk among Urban Poor Adolescents." In *Where and When: Influence of Historical Time and Place on Aspects of Psychopathology,* ed. P. Cohen, L. Robins, and C. Slomkowski, 349–68. Hillsdale, N.J.: Lawrence Erlbaum Associates.

———. In press. "A Developmental-Ecological Model of the Relation of Family Functioning to Patterns of Delinquency." *Journal of Quantitative Criminology.*

Gottfredson, D. C. 1986. "An Empirical Test of School-Based Environmental and Individual Interventions to Reduce the Risk of Delinquent Behavior." *Criminology* 24 (4): 705–31.

Gottfredson, D. C., G. D. Gottfredson, and S. Skroban. 1996. "A Multimodel School-Based Prevention Demonstration." *Journal of Adolescent Research* 11:97–115.

Greenwood, P. W., K. E. Model, C. P. Rydell, and J. Chiesa. 1996. *Diverting Children from a Life of Crime: Measuring Costs and Benefits.* Santa Monica, Calif.: RAND Corporation.

Grizenko, N., and S. Vida. 1988. "Propranolol Treatment of Episodic Dyscontrol and Aggressive Behavior in Children." *Canadian Journal of Psychiatry* 33:776–78.

Grossman, J. B., and J. P. Tierney. 1998. "Does Mentoring Work? An Impact Study of the Big Brothers Big Sisters Program." *Evaluation Review* 22:403–26.

Guerra, N. G., and R. G. Slaby. 1989. "Evaluative Factors in Social Problem Solving by Aggressive Boys." *Journal of Abnormal Child Psychology* 17: 277–89.

Guerra, N. G., P. H. Tolan, and R. Hammond. 1994. "Prevention and Treatment of Adolescent Violence." In *Reason to Hope: A Psychosocial Perspective on Violence and Youth,* ed. L. D. Eron, J. H. Gentry, and P. Schlagel, 383–404. Washington, D.C.: American Psychological Association.

Hawkins, J. D., D. P. Farrington, and R. F. Catalano. 1999. "Reducing Violence through the Schools." In *Youth Violence: New Perspectives for Schools and Communities,* ed. D. S. Elliott, B. A. Hamburg, and K. R. Williams. Cambridge: Cambridge University Press.

Hawkins, J. D., T. Herrenkohl, D. P. Farrington, D. Brewer, R. F. Catalano, and T. W. Harachi. 1998. "A Review of Predictors of Youth Violence." In *Serious and Violent Juvenile Offenders: Risk Factors and Successful Interventions,* ed. R. Loeber and D. P. Farrington, 106–46. Thousand Oaks, Calif.: Sage.

Henggeler, S. W., B. P. Cunningham, S. G. Pickrel, S. K. Schoenwald, and M. J. Brondino. 1996. "Multisystemic Therapy: An Effective Violence Prevention Approach for Serious Juvenile Offenders." *Journal of Adolescence* 19:47–61.

Henggeler, S. W., G. B. Melton, L. A. Smith, S. L. Foster, J. H. Hanley, and C. M. Hutchinson. 1993. "Assessing Violent Offending in Serious Juvenile Offenders." *Journal of Abnormal Child Psychology* 21 (3):233–43.

Henry, D., N. G. Guerra, R. Huesmann, P. H. Tolan, R. VanAcker, and L. D. Eron. 2000. "Normative Influences on Aggression in Urban Elementary School Classrooms." *American Journal of Community Psychology* 28:59–81.

Henry, D., P. H. Tolan, and D. Gorman-Smith. In press. "Longitudinal Family and Peer Group Effects on Violence and Non-violent Delinquency." *Journal of Clinical Child Psychology.*

Howell, J. C., ed. 1995. *Guide for Implementing the Comprehensive Strategy for Serious, Violent, and Chronic Juvenile Offenders.* Washington D.C.: U.S. Department of Justice, Office of Juvenile Justice and Delinquency Prevention.

Institute of Medicine, Committee on Prevention of Mental Disorders. 1994. *Reducing Risks for Mental Disorders:Frontiers for Preventive Intervention Research*, ed. P. J. Mrazek and R. J. Haggerty. Washington, D.C.: National Academy Press.

Lipsey, M., and J. Derzon. 1998. "Predictors of Violent or Serious Delinquency in Adolescence and Early Adulthood: A Synthesis of Longitudinal Research." In *Serious and Violent Juvenile Offenders: Risk Factors and Successful Interventions*, ed. R. Loeber and D. P. Farrington, 86–105. Thousand Oaks, Calif.: Sage.

Lipsey, M., and D. B. Wilson. 1998. "Effective Intervention for Serious Juvenile Offenders: A Synthesis of Research." In *Serious and Violent Juvenile Offenders: Risk Factors and Successful Interventions*, ed. R. Loeber and D. P. Farrington, 313–45. Thousand Oaks, Calif.: Sage.

Loeber, R., and D. P. Farrington. 1998. *Serious and Violent Juvenile Offenders: Risk Factors and Successful Interventions.* Thousand Oaks, Calif.: Sage.

Mayhew, P., R. V. Clarke, and D. Elliott. 1989. "Motorcycle Theft, Helmet Legislation, and Displacement." *Howard Journal of Criminal Justice* 28:1–8.

Mercy, J. A., and P. W. O'Carroll. 1988. "New Directions in Violence Prediction: The Public Health Arena. Special Issue: The Prediction of Interpersonal Criminal Violence." *Violence and Victims* 3 (4):285–301.

Merry, S. E. 1981. *Urban Danger: Life in a Neighborhood of Strangers.* Philadelphia: Temple University Press.

Metropolitan Area Child Study Research Group. 2000. *A Cognitive-Ecological Approach to Preventing Aggression in Urban and Inner-City Settings: Preliminary Outcomes.* Manuscript submitted for publication.

Moffitt, T. E. 1993. "Adolescence-Limited and Life-Course-Persistent Antisocial Behavior: A Developmental Taxonomy." *Psychological Review* 100:674–701.

Moore, R. H. 1987. "Effectiveness of Citizen Volunteers Functioning as Counselors for High-Risk Young Male Offenders." *Psychological Reports* 61:823–30.

Moore, M. H. 1992. "Problem Solving and Community Policing." In *Modern Policing*, vol. 15, M. Tonry and N. Morris. Chicago: University of Chicago Press.

———. 1995. "Public Health and Criminal Justice Approaches to Prevention." In *Crime and Justice: A Review of Research*, vol. 19, *Building a Safer Society: Strategic Approaches to Crime Prevention*, ed. M. Tonry and D. P. Farrington, 237–62. Chicago: University of Chicago Press.

Mulvey, E. P., M. W. Arthur, and N. D. Repucci. 1993. "The Prevention and Treatment of Juvenile Delinquency: A Review of the Research." *Clinical Psychology Review* 13:133–57.

Nagin, D., and R. E. Tremblay. 1999. "Trajectories of Boys' Physical Aggression, Oppression, and Hyperactivity on the Path to Psychically Violent and Non-violent Juvenile Delinquency." *Child Development* 70:1181–96.

Papke, L. E. 1994. "Tax Policy and Urban Development: Evidence from the Indiana Enterprise Zone Program." *Journal of Public Economics* 54:7–49.

Patterson, G. R., J. B. Reid, and T. J. Dishion. 1991. *Antisocial Boys: A Social Interactional Approach,* vol. 4. Eugene, Ore.: Castalia.

Perry, B. 1997. "Incubated in Terror: Neuro-developmental Factors in the 'Cycle of Violence.'" In *Children in a Violent Society,* ed. J. D. Osofsky, 124–49. New York: Guilford.

Reid, J. B., J. M. Eddy, R. A. Fetrow, and M. Stoolmiller. 1999. "Description and Immediate Impacts of a Preventive Intervention for Conduct Problems." *American Journal of Community Psychology* 27:483–517.

Rosenbaum, J. E. 1992. "Black Pioneers: Do Their Moves to the Suburbs Increase Economic Opportunity for Mothers and Children?" *Housing Policy Debate* 2:1179–213.

Sampson, R. J. 1987. "Urban Black Violence: The Effect of Male Joblessness and Family Disruption." *American Journal of Sociology* 93:348–82.

Sampson, R., S. Raudenbush, and F. Earls. 1997. "Neighborhoods and Violent Crime: A Multilevel Study of Collective Efficacy." *Science* 277:918–24.

Schwitzgebel, R. L., and D. J. Baer. 1967. "Intensive Supervision by Parole Officers as a Factor in Recidivism Reduction of Male Delinquents." *Journal of Psychology* 67:75–82.

Shaw, C. R., and H. D. McKay. 1942. *Juvenile Delinquency and Urban Areas.* Chicago: University of Chicago Press.

Sherman, L. W., P. R. Gartin, and M. E. Buerger. 1989. "Hot Spots of Predatory Crime: Routine Activities and the Criminology of Place." *Criminology* 27:27–56.

Sherman, L. W., D. Gottfredson, D. MacKenzie, J. Eck, P. Reuter, and S. Bushway. 1997. *Preventing Crime: What Works, What Doesn't, What's Promising.* College Park: University of Maryland, Department of Criminology and Criminal Justice.

Skogan, W. 1996. "The Police and Public Opinion in Britain." *American Behavioral Scientist* 39:421–32.

Snyder, H. N. (1998). "Serious, Violent, and Chronic Juvenile Offenders—An Assessment of the Extent of and Trends in Officially Recognized Serious Criminal Behavior in a Delinquent Population. In *Serious and Violent Juvenile Offenders*. R. Loeber and D. Farrington (pp. 428-444). Thousand Oaks, CA: Sage.

Styles, M. B., and K. V. Morrow. 1992. *Understanding How Youth and Elders Form Relationships: A Study of Four Linking Lifetimes Programs.* New York.

Thornberry, T. P., D. Huizinga, and R. Loeber. 1995. "The Prevention of Serious Delinquency and Violence: Implications from the Program of Research on the Causes and Correlates of Delinquency." In *Sourcebook of Serious, Violent, and Chronic Juvenile Offenders,* ed. J. C. Howell, B. Krisberg, J. D. Hawkins, and J. J. Wilson, 213–37. Thousand Oaks, Calif.: Sage.

Tolan, P. H. 1987. "Implications of Age of Onset for Delinquency Risk Identification." *Journal of Abnormal Child Psychology* 15:47–65.

———. 1998. "Community and Prevention Research." In *Handbook of Research Methods in Clinical Psychology,* 2nd edition, ed. P. Kendall, J. Butcher, and G. Holmbeck. New York: Wiley.

———. In press a. "Family-Focused Prevention Research: Tough but Tender with Family Intervention Research." In *Family Psychology Intervention Science,* ed. H. Liddle, J. Bray,

D. Santesban, and R. Levant. Washington, D.C.: American Psychological Association.

———. In press b. "Youth Violence and Its Prevention in the United States: An Overview of Current Knowledge." *Journal of International Violence Prevention.*

Tolan, P. H., and C. H. Brown. 1998. "Methods for Evaluating Intervention and Prevention Efforts." In *Violence against Children in the Family and the Community,* ed. P. K. Trickett and C. Schellenbach, 439–64. Washington, D.C.: American Psychological Association.

Tolan, P. H., and D. Gorman-Smith. 1997. "Treatment of Juvenile Delinquency: Between Therapy and Punishment." In *Handbook of Antisocial Behavior,* ed. D. Stoff, J. Brieling, and J. Maser, 405–15. New York: Wiley.

———. 1998. "Development of Serious, Violent, and Chronic Offenders." In *Never Too Early, Never Too Late: Serious, Violent, and Chronic Juvenile Offenders,* ed. R. Loeber and D. Farrington, 68–85. Beverly Hills, Calif.: Sage.

Tolan, P. H., D. Gorman-Smith, and D. Henry. 2000. "The Developmental Ecology of Influences on Urban Youth Violence: Community, Neighborhoods, Parenting, and Deviant Peers." *Developmental Psychology* 16:169–97.

Tolan, P. H., D. Gorman-Smith, L. R. Huesmann, and A. Zelli. 1997. "Assessment of Family Relationship Characteristics: A Measure to Explain Risk for Antisocial Behavior and Depression in Youth." *Psychological Assessment* 9:212–23.

Tolan, P. H., and N. G. Guerra. 1994. *What Works in Reducing Adolescent Violence: An Empirical Review of the Field.* Monograph prepared for the Center for the Study and Prevention of Youth Violence. Boulder: University of Colorado.

———. 1996. "Progress and Prospects in Youth Violence Prevention Evaluation." *American Journal of Preventive Medicine* 12:129–31.

Tolan, P. H., N. G. Guerra, and P. Kendall. 1995. "A Developmental-Ecological Perspective on Antisocial Behavior in Children and Adolescents: Towards a Unified Risk and Intervention Framework." *Journal of Consulting and Clinical Psychology* 63:515–17.

Tolan, P. H., and R. P. Lorion. 1988. "Multivariate Approaches to the Identification of Delinquency-Proneness in Males." *American Journal of Community Psychology* 16:547–61.

Tolan, P. H., and M. McKay. 1996. "Preventing Serious Antisocial Behavior in Inner-City Children: An Empirically Based Family Prevention Program." *Family Relations* 45:148–55.

Tolan, P. H., and M. E. Mitchell. 1989. "Families and the Therapy of Antisocial and Delinquent Behavior." *Journal of Psychotherapy and the Family* 6:29–48.

Tolan, P. H., L. Sherrod, D. Gorman-Smith, and D. Henry. In press. "A Developmental-Ecological Approach to Positive Youth Development in the Inner City." In *Positive Youth Development: Research and Policy,* ed. K. Maton, B. Ledheather, and A. Solarz. Washington, D.C.: American Psychological Association.

Tonry, M., and D. P. Farrington. 1995. *Strategic Approaches to Crime Prevention: Building a Safer Society.* Chicago: University of Chicago Press.

Turnock, B. J. (1997). *Public Health: What it Is and How it Works.* Gaithersburg, MD: Aspen Publications

Wasserman G. and Miller. L. 1998. "The Prevention of Serious and Violent Juvenile Offending." In *Serious and Violent Juvenile Offenders: Risk Factors and Successful Interventions,* ed. R. Loeber and D. P. Farrington, 197–247. Thousand Oaks, Calif.: Sage.

Weissberg, R. P., and M. T. Greenberg. 1997. "School and Community Competence-Enhancement and Prevention Programs." In *Handbook of Child Psychology,* vol. 6, *Child Psychology in Practice,* ed. I. E. Sigel and K. A. Renninger, 1–85. New York: Wiley and Sons.

Weisz, J. R., B. R. Walter, B. Weiss, G. A. Fernandez, and V. A. Mikov. 1990. "Arrests among Emotionally Disturbed Violent and Assaultive Individuals following Minimal versus Lengthy Intervention through North Carolina's Willie M Program." *Journal of Consulting and Clinical Psychology* 58 (6):720–28.

Williams, D. T., R. Mehl, S. Yudofsky, D. Adams, and B. Roseman. 1982. "The Effect of Propanolol on Uncontrolled Rage Outbursts in Children and Adolescents with Organic Brain Dysfunction." *Journal of the American Academy of Child Psychiatry* 21 (2):129–35.

Wilson, W. J. 1987. *The Truly Disadvantaged: The Inner-City, the Underclass, and Public Policy.* Chicago: University of Chicago Press.

CHAPTER 6
David P. Farrington

FAMILIES AND CRIME

References

Baumrind, Diana. 1966. "Effects of Authoritative Parental Control on Child Behavior." *Child Development* 37:887–907.

Bor, William, J. M. Najman, M. J. Andersen, M. O'Callaghan, G. M. Williams, and B. C. Behrens. 1997. "The Relationship Between Low Family Income and Psychological Disturbance in Young Children: An Australian Longitudinal Study." *Australian and New Zealand Journal of Psychiatry* 31:664–75.

Bowlby, John. 1951. *Maternal Care and Mental Health.* Geneva: World Health Organization.

Brezina, Timothy. 1998. "Adolescent Maltreatment and Delinquency: The Question of Intervening Processes." *Journal of Research in Crime and Delinquency* 35:71–99.

Brownfield, David, and Ann M. Sorenson. 1994. "Sibship Size and Sibling Delinquency." *Deviant Behavior* 15:45–61.

Buehler, Cheryl, C. Anthony, A. Krishnakumar, G. Stone, J. Gerard, and S. Pemberton. 1997. "Interparental Conflict and Youth Problem Behaviors: A Meta-Analysis." *Journal of Child and Family Studies* 6:233–47.

Capaldi, Deborah M., and G. R. Patterson. 1991. "Relation of Parental Transitions to Boys' Adjustment Problems." *Developmental Psychology* 27:489–504.

Carlson, Elizabeth A., and L. A. Sroufe. 1995. "Contribution of Attachment Theory to Developmental Psychopathology." In *Developmental Psychopathology,* vol. 1: *Theory and Methods,* ed. Dante Cicchetti and Donald J. Cohen, 581–617. New York: Wiley.

Catalano, Richard F., and J. D. Hawkins. 1996. "The Social Development Model: A Theory of Antisocial Behavior." In *Delinquency and Crime: Current Theories,* ed. J. David Hawkins, 149–97. Cambridge: Cambridge University Press.

Cohen, Patricia, and Judith S. Brook. 1995. "The Reciprocal Influence of Punishment and Child Behavior Disorder." In *Coercion and Punishment in Long-Term Perspectives,* ed. Joan McCord, 154–64. Cambridge: Cambridge University Press.

Conger, Rand D., Gerald R. Patterson, and Xiaojia Ge. 1995. "It Takes Two to Replicate: A Mediational Model for the Impact of Parents' Stress on Adolescent Adjustment." *Child Development* 66:80–97.

Conseur, Amy, Frederick P. Rivara, Robert Barnoski, and Irvin Emanuel. 1997. "Maternal and Perinatal Risk Factors for Later Delinquency." *Pediatrics* 99:785–90.

Darling, Nancy, and Laurence Steinberg. 1993. "Parenting Style in Context: An Integrative Model." *Psychological Bulletin* 113:487–96.

Deater-Deckard, Kirby, Kenneth A. Dodge, John E. Bates, and Gregory S. Pettit. 1996. "Physical Discipline among African American and European American Mothers: Links to Children's Externalizing Behaviors." *Developmental Psychology* 32:1065–72.

DiLalla, Lisabeth F., and Irving I. Gottesman. 1991. "Biological and Genetic Contributions to Violence—Widom's Untold Tale." *Psychological Bulletin* 109:125–29.

Dishion, Thomas, J., Gerald R. Patterson, and Kathryn A. Kavanagh. 1992. "An Experimental Test of the Coercion Model: Linking Theory, Measurement, and Intervention." In *Preventing Antisocial Behavior: Interventions from Birth through Adolescence*, ed. Joan McCord and Richard E. Tremblay, 253–82. New York: Guilford Press.

Dodge, Kenneth A., Gregory S. Pettit, and John E. Bates. 1994. "Socialization Mediators of the Relation Between Socioeconomic Status and Child Conduct Problems. *Child Development* 65:649–65.

Ellis, Lee. 1988. "The Victimful-Victimless Crime Distinction, and Seven Universal Demographic Correlates of Victimful Criminal Behavior." *Personality and Individual Differences* 3:525–48.

Eron, Leonard D., L. Rowell Huesmann, and Arnaldo Zelli. 1991. "The Role of Parental Variables in the Learning of Aggression. In *The Development and Treatment of Childhood Aggression*, ed. Debra J. Pepler and Kenneth J. Rubin, 169–88. Hillsdale, N.J.: Lawrence Erlbaum.

Farrington, David P. 1992a. "Juvenile Delinquency." In *The School Years*, ed. John C. Coleman, 2nd ed., 123–63. London: Routledge.

———. 1992b. "The Need for Longitudinal-Experimental Research on Offending and Antisocial Behavior." In *Preventing Antisocial Behavior: Interventions from Birth through Adolescence*, ed. Joan McCord and Richard E. Tremblay, 353–76. New York: Guilford Press.

———. 1993. "Childhood Origins of Teenage Antisocial Behavior and Adult Social Dysfunction." *Journal of the Royal Society of Medicine* 86:13–17.

———. 1994. "Childhood Adolescent and Adult Features of Violent Males." In *Aggressive Behavior: Current Perspectives*, ed. L. Rowell Huesmann, 215–40. New York: Plenum Press.

———. 2000. "Explaining and Preventing Crime: The Globalization of Knowledge—The American Society of Criminology 1999 Presidential Address." *Criminology*, 38:1–24.

Farrington, David P., Geoffrey Barnes, and Sandra Lambert. 1996. "The Concentration of Offending in Families." *Legal and Criminological Psychology* 1:47–63.

Farrington, David P., and J. David Hawkins. 1991. "Predicting Participation, Early Onset, and Later Persistence in Officially Recorded Offending." *Criminal Behavior and Mental Health* 1:1–33.

Farrington, David P., Darrick Jolliffe, Rolf Loeber, Magda Stouthamer-Loeber, and Larry M. Kalb. 2001. "The Concentration of Offenders in Families, and Family Criminality in the Prediction of Boys' Delinquency." *Journal of Adolescence* 24 (in press).

Farrington, David P., and Rolf Loeber. 1999. "Transatlantic Replicability of Risk Factors in the Development of Delinquency." In *Historical and Geographical Influences on Psychopathology*, ed. Patricia Cohen, Cheryl Slomkowski, and Lee N. Robins, 299–329. Mahwah, N.J.: Lawrence Erlbaum.

———. 2001. "How Can The Relationship Between Race and Violence Be Explained?" In *Violent Crimes: The Nexus of Ethnicity, Race and Class*, ed. Darnell F. Hawkins. Cambridge: Cambridge University Press, in press.

Farrington, David P., and Brandon C. Welsh. 1999. "Delinquency Prevention using Family-Based Interventions." *Children and Society* 13:287–303.

Farrington, David P., and Donald J. West. 1995. "Effects of Marriage, Separation, and Children on Offending by Adult Males." In *Current Perspectives on Aging and the Life Cycle*, vol. 4: *Delinquency and Disrepute in the Life Course*, ed. John Hagan, 249–81. Greenwich, Conn.: JAI Press.

Fergusson, David M., and L. John Horwood. 1998. "Exposure to Interparental Violence in Childhood and Psychosocial Adjustment in Young Adulthood." *Child Abuse and Neglect* 22:339–57.

Fergusson, David M., L. John Horwood, and Michael T. Lynskey. 1992. "Family Change, Parental Discord, and Early Offending". *Journal of Child Psychology and Psychiatry* 33:1059–75.

Fischer, Dean G. 1984. "Family Size and Delinquency." *Perceptual and Motor Skills* 58:527–34.

Forehand, Rex, Heather Biggar, and Beth A. Kotchick. 1998. "Cumulative Risk across Family Stressors: Short and Long Term Effects for Adolescents." *Journal of Abnormal Child Psychology* 26:119–28.

Frick, Paul J., Rachel E. Christian, and Jane M. Wootton. 1999. "Age Trends in the Association Between Parenting Practices and Conduct Problems." *Behavior Modification* 23:106–28.

Gorman-Smith, Deborah, Patrick H. Tolan, Arnaldo Zelli, and L. Rowell Huesmann. 1996. "The Relation of Family Functioning to Violence among Inner-City Minority Youths." *Journal of Family Psychology* 10:115–29.

Grove, William M., Elke D. Eckert, Leonard Heston, Thomas J. Bouchard, Nancy Segal, and David T. Lykken. 1990. "Heritability of Substance Abuse and Antisocial Behavior: A Study of Monozygotic Twins Reared Apart." *Biological Psychiatry* 27:1293–304.

Haapasalo, Jaana, and Elina Pokela. 1999. "Child-Rearing and Child Abuse Antecedents of Criminality." *Aggression and Violent Behavior* 1:107–27.

Hawkins, J. David, Richard F. Catalano, Rick Kosterman, Robert Abbott, and Karl G. Hill. 1999. "Preventing Adolescent Health Risk Behaviors by Strengthening Protection During Childhood." *Archives of Pediatrics and Adolescent Medicine* 153:226–34.

Hawkins, J. David, Elizabeth von Cleve, and Richard F. Catalano. 1991. "Reducing Early Childhood Aggression: Results of a Primary Prevention Program." *Journal of the American Academy of Child and Adolescent Psychiatry* 30:208–17.

Henry, Bill, Terrie Moffitt, Lee Robins, Felton Earls, and Phil Silva. 1993. "Early Family Predictors of Child and Adolescent Antisocial Behavior: Who Are the Mothers of Delinquents?" *Criminal Behavior and Mental Health* 3:97–118.

Hunter, Andrea G., and Margaret E. Ensminger. 1992. "Diversity and Fluidity in Children's Living Arrangements: Family Transitions in an Urban Afro-American Community." *Journal of Marriage and the Family* 54:418–26.

Jang, Sung J., and Carolyn A. Smith. 1997. "A Test of Reciprocal Causal Relationships among Parental Supervision, Affective Ties, and Delinquency." *Journal of Research in Crime and Delinquency* 34:307–36.

Jones, Marshall B., David R. Offord, and N. Abrams. 1980. "Brothers, Sisters, and Antisocial Behavior." *British Journal of Psychiatry* 136:139–45.

Juby, Heather, and David P. Farrington. 2001. "Disentangling the Link between Disrupted Families and Delinquency." *British Journal of Criminology* 41:22–40.

Kellam, Sheppard G., Margaret E. Ensminger, and R. Jay Turner. 1977. "Family Structure and the Mental Health of Children." *Archives of General Psychiatry* 34:1012–22.

Kelley, Michelle L., Thomas G. Power, and Dawn D. Wimbush. 1992. "Determinants of Disciplinary Practices in Low-Income Black Mothers." *Child Development* 63:573–82.

Kolbo, Jerome R., Eleanor H. Blakely, and David Engleman. 1996. "Children Who Witness Domestic Violence: A Review of Empirical Literature." *Journal of Interpersonal Violence* 11:281–93.

Kolvin, Israel, F. J. W. Miller, M. Fleeting, and P. A. Kolvin. 1988a. "Risk/Protective Factors for Offending with Particular Reference to Deprivation." In *Studies of Psychosocial Risk: The Power of Longitudinal Data*, ed. Michael Rutter, 77–95. Cambridge: Cambridge University Press.

———. 1988b. "Social and Parenting Factors Affecting Criminal-Offence Rates: Findings from the Newcastle Thousand Family Study (1947–1980)." *British Journal of Psychiatry* 152:80–90.

Krueger, Robert F., Terrie E. Moffitt, Avshalom Caspi, April Bleske, and Phil A. Silva. 1998. "Assortative Mating for Antisocial Behavior: Developmental and Methodological Implications." *Behavior Genetics* 28:173–86.

Larzelere, Robert E., and Gerald R. Patterson. 1990. "Parental Management: Mediator of the Effect of Socioeconomic Status on Early Delinquency." *Criminology* 28:301–24.

Lauritsen, Janet L. 1993. "Sibling Resemblance in Juvenile Delinquency: Findings from the National Youth Survey." *Criminology* 31:387–409.

Lewis, C., Elizabeth Newson, and John Newson. 1982. "Father Participation through Childhood and Its Relationship with Career Aspirations and Delinquency." In *Fathers: Psychological Perspectives*, ed. N. Beail and J. McGuire, 174–93. London: Junction.

Lipsey, Mark W., and James H. Derzon. 1998. "Predictors of Violent or Serious Delinquency in Adolescence and Early Adulthood: A Synthesis of Longitudinal Research." In *Serious and Violent Juvenile Offenders: Risk Factors and Successful Interventions*, ed. Rolf Loeber and David P. Farrington, 86–105. Thousand Oaks, Calif.: Sage.

Loeber, Rolf, and Thomas Dishion. 1983. "Early Predictors of Male Delinquency: A Review." *Psychological Bulletin* 94:68–99.

Loeber, Rolf, Magda Stouthamer-Loeber, Welmoet van Kammen, and David P. Farrington. 1991. "Initiation, Escalation, and Desistance in Juvenile Offending and Their Correlates." *Journal of Criminal Law and Criminology* 82:36–82.

Loeber, Rolf, and David P. Farrington. 1997. "Strategies and Yields of Longitudinal Studies on Antisocial Behavior". In *Handbook of Antisocial Behavior*, ed. David M. Stoff, James Breiling, and Jack D. Maser, 125–39. New York: Wiley.

Loeber, Rolf, David P. Farrington, Magda Stouthamer-Loeber, and Welmoet van Kammen. 1998a. *Antisocial Behavior and Mental Health Problems: Explanatory Factors in Childhood and Adolescence*. Mahwah, N.J.: Lawrence Erlbaum.

———. 1998b. "Multiple Risk Factors for Multi-Problem Boys: Co-occurrence of Delinquency, Substance Use, Attention Deficit, Conduct Problems, Physical Aggression, Covert Behavior, Depressed Mood, and Shy/Withdrawn Behavior." In *New Perspectives on Adolescent Risk Behavior*, ed. Richard Jessor, 90–149. Cambridge: Cambridge University Press.

Loeber, Rolf, and Magda Stouthamer-Loeber. 1986. "Family Factors as Correlates and Predictors of Juvenile Conduct Problems and Delinquency. In *Crime and Justice*, ed. Michael Tonry, and Norval Morris, vol. 7, 29–149. Chicago: University of Chicago Press.

Lytton, Hugh. 1990. "Child and Parent Effects in Boys' Conduct Disorder: A Reinterpretation." *Developmental Psychology* 26:683–97.

Lytton, Hugh, and David M. Romney. 1991. "Parents' Differential Socialization of Boys and Girls: A Meta-Analysis." *Psychological Bulletin* 109:267–96.

McCord, Joan. 1977. "A Comparative Study of Two Generations of Native Americans." In *Theory in Criminology*, ed. Robert F. Meier, 83–92. Beverly Hills, Calif.: Sage.

———. 1979. "Some Child-Rearing Antecedents of Criminal Behavior in Adult Men." *Journal of Personality and Social Psychology* 37:1477–86.

———. 1982. "A Longitudinal View of the Relationship between Paternal Absence and Crime. In *Abnormal Offenders, Delinquency, and the Criminal Justice System,* ed. John Gunn and David P. Farrington, 113–28. Chichester, England: Wiley.

———. 1983. "A Forty Year Perspective on Effects of Child Abuse and Neglect." *Child Abuse and Neglect* 7:265–70.

———. 1997. "On Discipline." *Psychological Inquiry* 8:215–17.

Maxfield, Michael G., and Cathy S. Widom. 1996. "The Cycle of Violence Revisited Six Years Later." *Archives of Pediatrics and Adolescent Medicine* 150:390–95.

Mednick, Birgitte R., Robert L. Baker, and Linn E. Carothers. 1990. "Patterns of Family Instability and Crime: The Association of Timing of the Family's Disruption with Subsequent Adolescent and Young Adult Criminality." *Journal of Youth and Adolescence* 19:201–20.

Moffitt, Terrie E., Avshalom Caspi, Michael Rutter, and Phil A. Silva. 2001. *Sex Differences in Antisocial Behavior.* Cambridge: Cambridge University Press, in press.

Morash, Merry, and Lila Rucker. 1989. "An Exploratory Study of the Connection of Mother's Age at Childbearing to her Children's Delinquency in Four Data Sets." *Crime and Delinquency* 35:45–93.

Nagin, Daniel S., Greg Pogarsky, and David P. Farrington. 1997. "Adolescent Mothers and the Criminal Behavior of their Children." *Law and Society Review* 31:137–62.

Newson, John, and Elizabeth Newson. 1989. *The Extent of Parental Physical Punishment in the UK.* London: Approach.

Olds, David L., Charles R. Henderson, Robert Chamberlin, and Robert Tatelbaum. 1986. "Preventing Child Abuse and Neglect: A Randomized Trial of Nurse Home Visitation." *Pediatrics* 78:65–78.

Olds, David L., John Eckenrode, Charles R. Henderson, Harriet Kitzman, Jane Powers, Robert Cole, Kimberly Sidora, Pamela Morris, Lisa M. Pettitt, and Dennis Luckey. 1997. "Long-Term Effects of Home Visitation on Maternal Life Course and Child Abuse and Neglect: Fifteen-Year Follow-up of a Randomized Trial." *Journal of the American Medical Association* 278:637–43.

Olds, David L., Charles R. Henderson, Robert Cole, John Eckenrode, Harriet Kitzman, Dennis Luckey, Lisa Pettitt, Kimberly Sidora, Pamela Morris, and Jane Powers. 1998. "Long-Term Effects of Nurse Home Visitation on Children's Criminal and Antisocial Behavior: 15-Year Follow-up of a Randomized Controlled Trial." *Journal of the American Medical Association* 280:1238–44.

Pagani, Linda, Richard E. Tremblay, Frank Vitaro, Margaret Kerr, and Pierre McDuff. 1998. "The Impact of Family Transition on the Development of Delinquency in Adolescent Boys: A Nine-Year Longitudinal Study." *Journal of Child Psychology and Psychiatry* 39:489–99.

Paternoster, Raymond. 1988. "Examining Three Wave Deterrence Models: A Question of Temporal Order and Specification." *Journal of Criminal Law and Criminology* 79:135–79.

Patterson, Gerald R. 1982. *Coercive Family Process.* Eugene, Oregon: Castalia.

———. 1995. "Coercion as a Basis for Early Age of Onset for Arrest." In *Coercion and Punishment in Long-Term Perspectives,* ed. Joan McCord, 81–105. Cambridge: Cambridge University Press.

Patterson, Gerald, R., Patti Chamberlain, and John B. Reid. 1982. "A Comparative Evaluation of a Parent Training Program." *Behavior Therapy* 13:638–50.

Patterson, Gerald R., John B. Reid, and Thomas J. Dishion. 1992. *Antisocial Boys.* Eugene, Oregon: Castalia.

Raine, Adrian. 1993. *The Psychopathology of Crime: Criminal Behavior as a Clinical Disorder.* San Diego, Calif.: Academic Press.

Raine, Adrian, Patricia A. Brennan, and David P. Farrington. 1997. "Biosocial Bases of Violence: Conceptual and Theoretical Issues." In *Biosocial Bases of Violence,* ed. Adrian Raine, Patricia A. Brennan, David P. Farrington, and Sarnoff A. Mednick, 1–20. New York: Plenum.

Rasanen, Pirkko, Hilina Hakko, Matti Isohanni, Sheilagh Hodgins, Marjo-Riitta Jarvelin, and Jari Tiihonen. 1999. "Maternal Smoking during Pregnancy and Risk of Criminal Behavior among Adult Male Offspring in the Northern Finland 1966 Birth Cohort." *American Journal of Psychiatry* 156:857–62.

Reiss, Albert J., and David P. Farrington. 1991. "Advancing Knowledge about Co-offending: Results from a Prospective Longitudinal Survey of London Males." *Journal of Criminal Law and Criminology* 82:360–95.

Robins, Lee N. 1979. "Sturdy Childhood Predictors of Adult Outcomes: Replications from Longitudinal Studies." In *Stress and Mental Disorder,* ed. J. E. Barrett, R. M. Rose, and Gerald L. Klerman, 219–35. New York: Raven Press.

———. 1992. "The Role of Prevention Experiments in Discovering Causes of Children's Antisocial Behavior." In *Preventing Antisocial Behavior: Interventions from Birth through Adolescence,* ed. Joan McCord and Richard E. Tremblay, 3–18. New York: Guilford Press.

Rothbaum, Fred, and John R. Weisz. 1994. "Parental Caregiving and Child Externalizing Behavior in Nonclinical Samples: A Meta-Analysis." *Psychological Bulletin* 116:55–74.

Rowe, David C. 1994. *The Limits of Family Influence: Genes, Experience, and Behavior.* New York: Guilford Press.

Rowe, David C., and David P. Farrington. 1997. "The Familial Transmission of Criminal Convictions." *Criminology* 35:177–201.

Sampson, Robert J., and John H. Laub. 1993. *Crime in the Making: Pathways and Turning Points Through Life.* Cambridge, Mass.: Harvard University Press.

Smith. Carolyn A., Marvin D. Krohn, Alan J. Lizotte, Cynthia P. McCluskey, Magda Stouthamer-Loeber, and Anne Weiher. 2000. "The Effect of Early Delinquency and Substance Use on Precocious Transitions to Adulthood among Adolescent Males." In *Families, Crime, and Criminal Justice,* ed. Greer L. Fox and Michael L. Benson, vol. 2, 233–53. Amsterdam: JAI Press.

Smith, Carolyn A., and Susan B. Stern. 1997. "Delinquency and Antisocial Behavior: A Review of Family Processes and Intervention Research." *Social Service Review* 71:382–420.

Smith, Carolyn A., and Terence P. Thornberry. 1995. "The Relationship Between Childhood Maltreatment and Adolescent Involvement in Delinquency." *Criminology* 33:451–81.

Smith, Judith R., and Jeanne Brooks-Gunn. 1997. "Correlates and Consequences of Harsh

Discipline for Young Children." *Archives of Pediatrics and Adolescent Medicine* 151:777–86.

Steinberg, Laurence, Susie D. Lamborn, Sanford M. Dornbusch, and Nancy Darling. 1992. "Impact of Parenting Practices on Adolescent Achievement: Authoritative Parenting, School Involvement, and Encouragement to Succeed." *Child Development* 63:1266–81.

Stern, Susan B., and Carolyn A. Smith. 1995. "Family Processes and Delinquency in an Ecological Context." *Social Service Review* 69:705–31.

Stouthamer-Loeber, Magda, Rolf Loeber, David P. Farrington, Quanwu Zhang, Welmoet van Kammen, and Eugene Maguin. 1993. "The Double Edge of Protective and Risk Factors for Delinquency: Inter-Relations and Developmental Patterns." *Development and Psychopathology* 5:683–701.

Symons, Ronald L., Chyi-In Wu, Christine Johnson, and Rand D. Conger. 1995. "A Test of Various Perspectives on the Intergenerational Transmission of Domestic Violence." *Criminology* 33:141–71.

Tremblay, Richard E., Linda Pagani-Kurtz, Louise C. Masse, Frank Vitaro, and Robert O. Pihl. 1995. "A Bimodal Preventive Intervention for Disruptive Kindergarten Boys: Its Impact Through Mid-Adolescence." *Journal of Consulting and Clinical Psychology* 63:560–68.

Wadsworth, Michael. 1979. *Roots of Delinquency.* London: Martin Robertson.

Wasserman, Gail A., and Laurie S. Miller. 1998. "The Prevention of Serious and Violent Juvenile Offending". In *Serious and Violent Juvenile Offenders: Risk Factors and Successful Interventions*, ed. Rolf Loeber and David P. Farrington, 197–247. Thousand Oaks, Calif.: Sage.

Webster-Stratton, Carolyn. 1998. "Preventing Conduct Problems in Head Start Children: Strengthening Parenting Competencies." *Journal of Consulting and Clinical Psychology* 66:715–30.

Webster-Stratton, Carolyn, and Mary Hammond. 1997. "Treating Children with Early-Onset Conduct Problems: A Comparison of Child and Parent Training Interventions." *Journal of Consulting and Clinical Psychology* 65:93–109.

Webster-Stratton, Carolyn, Mary Kolpacoff, and Terri Hollinsworth. 1988. "Self-Administered Videotape Therapy for Families with Conduct-Problem Children: Comparison with Two Cost-Effective Treatments and a Control Group." *Journal of Consulting and Clinical Psychology* 56:558–66.

Wells, L. Edward, and Joseph H. Rankin. 1991. "Families and Delinquency: A Meta-Analysis of the Impact of Broken Homes." *Social Problems* 38:71–93.

Welsh, Brandon C., David P. Farrington, and Lawrence W. Sherman, eds. 2001. *Costs and Benefits of Preventing Crime.* Boulder, Colorado: Westview Press.

West, Donald J., and David P. Farrington. 1973. *Who Becomes Delinquent?* London: Heinemann.

———. 1977. *The Delinquent Way of Life.* London: Heinemann.

Widom, Cathy S. 1989. "The Cycle of Violence." *Science* 244:160–66.

Widom, Cathy S., and M. Ashley Ames. 1994. "Criminal Consequences of Childhood Sexual Victimization." *Child Abuse and Neglect* 18:303–18.

Wikström, Per-Olof, and Rolf Loeber. 2000. "Do Disadvantaged Neighborhoods Cause Well-Adjusted Children to Become Adolescent Delinquents? A Study of Male Juvenile Serious Offending, Individual Risk and Protective Factors, and Neighborhood Context." *Criminology* 38:1109–42.

CHAPTER 7
Denise C. Gottfredson, David B. Wilson,
and Stacy S. Najaka
THE SCHOOLS

Correspondence should be sent to the author at Institute for Juvenile Research, University of Illinois at Chicago, 840 S. Wood, Chicago, IL 60612.

Notes

1. In the SCS data, violent victimization included physical attacks or taking property from a student directly by force, weapons, or threats. Property victimization included theft of property from a student's desk, locker, or other locations.

2. The criteria used to select studies are discussed in the following section.

3. The overall method rating was informed by a series of items in the coding protocol addressing assignment to conditions, unit of assignment, unit of analysis, use of control variables in the analyses to adjust for initial group differences, rating of initial group similarity, variable measurement, and attrition.

4. Although not necessarily illegal, the behaviors included in the "antisocial" category are highly predictive of violent and serious delinquency in adolescence and early adulthood (Lipsey and Derzon 1998).

5. This differs slightly from the method used in an earlier publication (Gottfredson, Wilson, and Najaka 2000) that included separate estimates of effects on the same subject sample for pre- and post–booster session treatment-comparison contrasts. Only the post–booster session contrasts have been included below, and, as such, the mean effects may differ slightly from our previous publication.

6. The average effect sizes reported below were computed using the inverse variance weighted method under a statistical model that assumes that instability in an effect size stems from both subject-level sampling error and study-level sampling error. That is, the statistical model explicitly acknowledges that larger studies produce more precise estimates than smaller studies and that there are a host of differences across studies that may contribute to the size of an effect (Lipsey and Wilson 2001, Overton 1998).

7. Descriptions in the section are taken with only minor change from descriptions published earlier in Gottfredson 1997; Gottfredson 2000; and Gottfredson, Wilson, and Najaka 2000.

References

Adelman, H. S., and L. Taylor. 2000. "Moving Prevention from the Fringes into the Fabric of School Improvement." *Journal of Education and Psychological Consultation* 11 (1): 7–36.
Botvin, G. J. 1990. "Substance Abuse Prevention: Theory, Practice, and Effectiveness." In *Crime and Justice: A Review of the Research,* vol. 13, *Drugs and Crime,* ed. M. Tonry and J. Q. Wilson, 461–519). Chicago: University of Chicago Press.

Botvin, G. J., E. Baker, E. M. Botvin, A. D. Filazzola, and R. B. Millman. 1984. "Prevention of Alcohol Misuse through the Development of Personal and Social Competence: A Pilot Study." *Journal of Studies on Alcohol* 45:550–52.

Botvin, G. J., E. Baker, N. L. Renick, A. D. Filazzola, and E. M. Botvin. 1984. "A Cognitive-Behavioral Approach to Substance Abuse Prevention." *Addictive Behaviors* 9:137–47.

Botvin, G. J., S. Schinke, and M. A. Orlandi. 1995. "School-based Health Promotion: Substance Abuse and Sexual Behavior." *Applied and Preventive Psychology* 4:167–84.

Brooks, K., V. Schiraldi, and J. Ziedenberg. 2000. *School House Hype: Two Years Later.* Washington, D.C.: Justice Policy Institute, Children's Law Center, Inc.

Bryk, A. S., and M. E. Driscoll. 1988. *The School as Community: Theoretical Foundations, Contextual Influences, and Consequences for Students and Teachers.* Madison, Wis.: University of Wisconsin, National Center on Effective Secondary Schools.

Chandler, K. A., C. D. Chapman, M. R. Rand, and B. M. Taylor. 1998. *Student's Reports of School Crime: 1989 and 1995.* NCES 98-241/NCJ-169607. Washington, D.C.: U.S. Departments of Education and Justice.

Cohen, J. 1988. *Statistical Power Analysis for the Behavioral Sciences.* Hillsdale, N.J.: Erlbaum.

Devine, J. 1996. *Maximum Security: The Culture of Violence in Inner-city Schools.* Chicago: University of Chicago Press.

Dryfoos, J. G. 1990. *Adolescents at Risk: Prevalence and Prevention.* New York: Oxford University Press.

Durlak, J. A. 1995. *School-based Prevention Programs for Children and Adolescents.* Thousand Oaks, Calif.: Sage.

Elliott, D. S., D. Huizinga, and S. Menard. 1989. *Multiple Problem Youth: Delinquency, Substance Use, and Mental Health Problems.* New York: Springer-Verlag.

Federal Bureau of Investigation. 1999. *Crime in the United States—1998* (Online). http://www.fbi.gov/ucr.thm (Accessed Jan. 30, 2001).

Feindler, E. L., S. A. Marriott, and M. Iwata. 1984. "Group Anger Control Training for Junior High School Delinquents." *Cognitive Therapy and Research* 8 (3): 299–311.

Gallup Poll. 1999. *School Violence Still a Worry for American Parents* (Online]). 9/7/99. http://205.219.140.75/poll/releases/pr990907.asp (Accessed Jan. 30, 2001). Princeton, N.J.: Gallup Organization.

Gottfredson, D. C. 1986. "An Empirical Test of School-based Environmental and Individual Interventions to Reduce the Risk of Delinquent Behavior." *Criminology* 24 (4): 705–731.

———. 1990. "Changing School Structures to Benefit High-risk Youths." In *Understanding Troubled and Troubling Youth*, ed. P. E. Leone, 246–71. Newbury Park, Calif.: Sage.

———. 1997. "School-based Crime Prevention." In *Preventing Crime—What Works, What Doesn't, What's Promising: A Report to the United States Congress*, L. W. Sherman, D. C. Gottfredson, D. MacKenzie, J. Eck, P. Reuter, and S. Bushway. Washington, D.C.: U.S. Department of Justice, Office of Justice Programs.

———. 2001. *Schools and Delinquency.* New York: Cambridge University Press.

Gottfredson, D. C., G. D. Gottfredson, and L. G. Hybl. 1993. "Managing Adolescent Behavior: A Multiyear, Multischool Study." *American Educational Research Journal* 30 (1):179–215.

Gottfredson, D. C., D. B. Wilson, and S. S. Najaka. 2000. "School-based Crime Prevention." In *Evidenced-based Crime Prevention*, ed. D. P. Farrington, L. W. Sherman, and B. Welsh. United Kingdom: Harwood Academic Publishers.

Gottfredson, G. D. 1984. "A Theory-ridden Approach to Program Evaluation: A Method for Stimulating Researcher-Implementer Collaboration." *American Psychologist* 39 (10): 1101–112.

Gottfredson, G. D., and D. C. Gottfredson. 1985. *Victimization in Schools*. New York: Plenum Press.

Gottfredson, G. D., D. C. Gottfredson, E. R. Czeh, D. Cantor, S. Crosse, and I. Hantman. 2000. *A National Study of Delinquency Prevention in Schools*. Ellicott City, Md.: Gottfredson Associates, Inc.

Gottfredson, G. D., D. E. Rickert, D. C. Gottfredson, and N. Advani. 1984. "Standards for Program Development Evaluation Plans." *Psychological Documents* 14 (2):32 (ms. no. 2668).

Greenwood, P. W., K. E. Model, C. P. Rydell, and J. Chiesa. 1996. *Diverting Children from a Life of Cime: Measuring Costs and Benefits*. Santa Monica, Calif.: RAND.

Hansen, W. B. 1992. "School-based Substance Abuse Prevention: A Review of the State of the Art in Curriculum, 1980–1990." *Health Education Research* 7:403–430.

Hansen, W. B., and J. W. Graham. 1991. "Preventing Alcohol, Marijuana, and Cigarette Use among Adolescents: Peer Pressure Resistance Training versus Establishing Conservative Norms." *Preventive Medicine* 20:414–30.

Hawkins, J. D., M. W. Arthur, and R. F. Catalano. 1995. "Preventing Substance Abuse." In *Crime and Justice: A Review of the Research*, vol. 19, *Building a Safer Society: Strategic Approaches to Crime Prevention*, ed. M. Tonry and D. P. Farrington, 343–427. Chicago: University of Chicago Press.

Institute of Medicine. 1994. *Reducing Risks for Mental Disorders: Frontiers for Preventive Intervention Research*. Washington, D.C.: National Academy Press.

Johnson, G., and R. Hunter. 1985. *Law-related Education as a Delinquency Prevention Strategy: A Three-year Evaluation of the Impact of LRE on Students*. Boulder, Colo.: Center for Action Research.

Johnston, L. D., P. M. O'Malley, and J. G. Bachman. 1999. *Drug Trends in 1999 among American Teens Are Mixed* (Online). http://www.monitoringthefuture.org (Accessed Jan. 30, 2001). Ann Arbor: University of Michigan Institute for Social Research.

Kann, L., S. A. Kinchen, B. I. Williams, J. G. Ross, R. Lowry, C. V. Hill, J. A. Grunbaum, P. S. Blumson, J. L. Collins, and L. J. Kolbe. 1998. "Youth Risk Behavior Surveillance—United States, 1997." *Morbidity and Mortality Weekly Report Surveillance Summaries* (Online) 47, no. SS-03 (Aug. 14). http://www.cdc.gov/epo/mmwr/preview/ind98_ss.html (Accessed Jan. 30, 2001). Atlanta, Ga.: Centers for Disease Control and Prevention.

Kaufman, P., X. Chen, S. P. Choy, K. A. Chandler, C. D. Chapman, M. R. Rand, and C. Ringel. 1998. *Indicators of School Crime and Safety, 1998*. NCES 98-251/NCJ-172215. Washington, D.C.: U.S. Departments of Education and Justice.

Lipsey, M. W. 1992. "Juvenile Delinquency Treatment: A Meta-analytic Inquiry into the Variability of Effects." In *Meta-analysis for Explanation*, ed. T. D. Cook, H. Cooper, D. S. Cordray, H. Hartmann, L. V. Hedges, R. J. Light, T. A. Louis, and F. Mosteller, 83–127. New York: Russell Sage Foundation.

Lipsey, M. W., and J. H. Derzon. 1998. "Predictors of Violent or Serious Delinquency in Adolescence and Early Adulthood: A Synthesis of Longitudinal Research." In *Serious and Violent Juvenile Offenders: Risk Factors and Successful Interventions*, ed. R. Loeber, and D. P. Farrington, 86–105. Thousand Oaks, Calif.: Sage.

Lipsey, M. W., and D. B. Wilson. 2001. *Practical Meta-analysis*. Thousand Oaks, Calif.: Sage.

Lochman, J. E. 1992. "Cognitive-Behavioral Intervention with Aggressive Boys: Three-year Follow-up and Preventive Effects." *Journal of Consulting and Clinical Psychology* 60 (3):426–32.

Lochman, J. E., P. R. Burch, J. F. Curry, and L. B. Lampron. 1984. "Treatment and Generalization Effects of Cognitive-Behavioral and Goal-setting Interventions with Aggressive Boys." *Journal of Consulting and Clinical Psychology* 52 (5):915–16.

Morrison, G. M., M. J. Furlong, and R. L. Morrison. 1997. "The Safe School: Moving beyond Crime Prevention to School Empowerment." In *School Violence Intervention: A Practical Handbook*, ed. A. P. Goldstein and J. C. Conoley, 236–64. New York: Guilford Press.

Moskowitz, J. M., E. Schaps, and J. H. Malvin. 1982. "Process and Outcome Evaluation in Primary Prevention: The Magic Circle Program." *Evaluation Review* 6 (6):775–88.

Olweus, D. 1991. "Bully/Victim Problems among Schoolchildren: Basic Facts and Effects of a School Based Intervention Program." In *The Development and Treatment of Childhood Aggression*, ed. D. J. Pepler and K. H. Rubin, 411–48. Hillsdale, N.J.: Lawrence Erlbaum.

———. 1992. "Bullying among Schoolchildren: Intervention and Prevention." In *Aggression and Violence throughout the Life Span*, ed. R. DeV. Peters, R. J. McMahon, and V. L. Quinsey, 100–125). Newbury Park, Calif.: Sage.

Olweus, D., and F. D. Alsaker. 1991. "Assessing Change in a Cohort-longitudinal Study with Hierarchical Data." In *Problems and Methods in Longitudinal Research: Stability and Change*, ed. D. Magnusson, L. R. Bergman, G. Rudinger, and B. Torestad, 107–132. Cambridge: Cambridge University Press.

Overton, R. C. 1998. "A Comparison of Fixed-Effects and Mixed (Random-Effects) Models for Meta-analysis Tests of Moderator Variable Effects." *Psychological Methods* 3 (3):354–79.

Pentz, M. A., J. H. Dwyer, D. P. MacKinnon, B. R. Flay, W. B. Hansen, E. Y. I. Wang, and C. A. Johnson. 1989. "A Multicommunity Trial for Primary Prevention of Adolescent Drug Abuse: Effects on Drug Use Prevalence." *Journal of the American Medical Association* 261 (22):3259–66.

Rosenthal, R., and D. B. Rubin. 1983. "A Simple, General Purpose Display of Magnitude of Experimental Effect." *Journal of Educational Psychology* 74 (2):166–69.

Sheley, J. F., and J. D. Wright. 1998. *High School Youths, Weapons, and Violence: A National Survey.* National Institute of Justice Research in Brief. NCJ-172857. Washington, D.C.: U.S. Department of Justice.

Shure, M. B., and G. Spivak. 1979. "Interpersonal Cognitive Problem-Solving and Primary Prevention: Programming for Preschool and Kindergarten Children." *Journal of Clinical Child Psychology* 8:89–94.

———. 1980. "Interpersonal Problem-Solving as a Mediator of Behavioral Adjustment in Preschool and Kindergarten Children." *Journal of Applied Developmental Psychology* 1:29–44.

———. 1982. "Interpersonal Problem-Solving in Young Children: A Cognitive Approach to Prevention." *American Journal of Community Psychology* 10 (3):341–56.

Silvia, E. S., and J. Thorne. 1997. *School-Based Drug Prevention Programs: A Longitudinal Study in Selected School Districts.* Research Triangle Park, N.C.: Research Triangle Institute.

Stuart, R. B. 1974. "Teaching Facts about Drugs: Pushing or Preventing?" *Journal of Educational Psychology* 66 (2): 189–201.

Timmer, S. G., J. Eccles, and I. O'Brien. 1985. "How Children Use Time." In *Time, Goods, and Wellbeing*, ed. F. T. Juster and F. B. Stafford, 353–82. Ann Arbor: University of Michigan Institute for Social Research.

Tobler, N. S. 1986. "Meta-analysis of 143 Adolescent Drug Prevention Programs: Quantitative Outcome Results of Program Participants Compared to a Control or Comparison Group." *Journal of Drug Issues* 16:537–67.

————. 1992. "Drug Prevention Programs Can Work: Research Findings." *Journal of Addictive Diseases* 11:1–28.

Tremblay, R. E., and W. M. Craig. 1995. "Developmental Crime Prevention." In *Crime and Justice: A Review of the Research,* vol. 19, *Building a Safer Society: Strategic Approaches to Crime Prevention,* ed. M. Tonry and D. P. Farrington, 151–236. Chicago: University of Chicago Press.

U.S. Census Bureau. 2000. *Population Estimates* (Online). http://www.census.gov/ population/www/estimates/popest.html (Accessed Jan. 30, 2001). Washington, D.C.

U.S. Department of Education. 1998. *Violence and Discipline Problems in U.S. Public Schools: 1996–97.* NCES 98-030. Washington, D.C.

Walker, H., K. Kavanagh, B. Stiller, A. Golly, H. H. Severson, and E. Feil. 1998. "First Step to Success: An Early Intervention Approach for Preventing School Antisocial Behavior." *Journal of Emotional and Behavioral Disorders* 6 (2):66–80.

Wright, W. E., and M. C. Dixon. 1977. "Community Prevention and Treatment of Juvenile Delinquency: A Review of Evaluation Studies." *Journal of Research in Crime and Delinquency* 14:35-67.

CHAPTER 8
Shawn Bushway and Peter Reuter
LABOR MARKETS AND CRIME

Notes

1. To be clear, this means that this chapter will not directly access the empirical support for the economics and crime model. There are several excellent review articles that provide this service (Freeman 1999; Piehl 1998).

2. See Fagan and Freeman (1999) for an overview.

3. The degree of distinction between labor markets is somewhat arbitrary. For example, is there a separate labor market for retail clerks versus fast food employees? Ultimately, the distinction is a conceptual one made based on the question of interest. Most, although certainly not all, of the people who live in urban areas characterized by high crime and low employment will participate in low-skill labor markets.

4. This latter problem is sometimes referred to as the spatial mismatch hypothesis.

5. The federal evaluation was completed by Abt Associates in December 2000.

6. This result is especially interesting given that a before and after study by Rubin (1990) found substantial effects in New Jersey.

7. The lack of outcome evaluations is attributed to the flexibility of the programs, the lack of credible evidence about what would have occurred in the absence of the program, and the inability to conceptualize and measure clear outcomes at a neighborhood level.

8. A full 80 percent of recipients said that the loan was crucial to their activity, while enterprise zone incentives were typically important for 30 to 40 percent of all enterprise zone businesses (Wilder and Rubin 1996).

9. Although these numbers appear to suggest that higher CDBG funding generates improvements, this conclusion is not possible without some other comparison. For example,

there may be selection bias; better organized communities, which are more likely to be improving economically anyway, may do better in the grant application process.

10. One reason that the evaluation is weak is that the idea was so attractive to policy makers. Many Weed and Seed sites were funded before evaluations could be launched.

11. These are the most serious offenses recorded by the police for the Uniform Crime Reports.

12. This could reflect the difficulties associated with this part of the evaluation, which had substantial nonresponse rates. The problems led to the use of inperson interviews in the first wave and phone interviews in the second wave, which may not be comparable.

13. The sample is different for the children and the mothers. The children come from a sample originally composed in 1982. They were reinterviewed in 1989. Only 59 percent of the original sample could be located, and most of those located had not moved from the original location. The potential for bias exists because the harder-to-locate families might vary by suburban or urban location.

14. Of course, many of the same objectives met by housing dispersal programs could be achieved by encouraging gentrification of older, depressed neighborhoods, though gentrification often involves the exit of current residents.

15. Within this area, we noted the absence of any discussion of the role of crime in driving business to the suburbs, or the potential crime-prevention effects of new job connections in the suburbs.

16. Evidence as to whether or not more money matters will become available when the results of federal enterprise zones are released.

17. Participating in crime is sometimes referred to by economists as participating in the illegal labor market.

18. It is difficult to classify all job training programs in terms of our programmatic interest. For example, Job Training and Partnership Act (JTPA)-Title IIA ($955 million in FY 1999) is aimed at economically disadvantaged adults; some of those adults may be involved with the criminal justice system and others may still be young enough to be reasonably classified as "youths," but many may be at slight risk of serious criminal involvement. Given the large number of other JTPA Titles that were more directly targeted at disadvantaged youth, we did not include any of Title-IIA.

19. Strictly speaking, the provision of a job is not a job training or education program. However, many employment skills are learned on the job; employment increases future employability.

20. Self-reports from program participants about crime involve inquiring about sensitive behaviors. Official record checks of criminal histories require information from a different set of agencies, with different sensitivities, from those providing the other outcome data.

21. This result is consistent with the conclusion of Sampson and Laub (1990), who found that the critical variable is not the job but the social bonds of the workplace—bonds that probably are absent in a short-term subsidized work environment.

22. Of these applicants, 5,997 were assigned to a control group and not allowed to sign up for Job Corps for three years. They were allowed to participate in other training programs; and during the follow-up period, 64 percent participated in some type of education program, receiving on average one-half year of education including vocational training. The fact that

they can and do make use of other educational opportunities may lead to underestimates of the benefits of job training more generally.

23. In fact, the males who are in the nonresidential programs are no less likely to be arrested than the control group.

24. For example, researchers such as Laub, Sampson, and Nagin (1998) have demonstrated the power of marriage to lead to desistance. And the decline of marriage as an institution is one of the social problems identified by Wilson (1996) as something that leads to the decline of social capital. Yet, it is not clear that a societal consensus could be reached for a policy advocating marriage as a common good. Moreover, it is not clear what type of policy one would implement to increase marriage.

25. See Levitt (Forthcoming) for a review of this new literature.

References

Ahlstrom, W., and R. J. Havighurst. 1982. "The Kansas City Work / Study Experiment." In *School Programs for Disruptive Adolescents,* ed. D. J. Safer, 259–75. Baltimore: University Park Press.

Anderson, E. 1990. *Streetwise: Race, Class, and Change in an Urban Community.* Chicago: University of Chicago Press.

Bartik, T. J. 1991. *Who Benefits from State and Local Economic Development Policies?* Kalamazoo, Mich.: W. E. Upjohn Institute for Employment Research.

Bartik, T. J., and R. D. Bingham. 1997. "Can Economic Development Programs Be Evaluated?" In *Significant Issues in Urban Economic Development.* ed. R. Bingham and R. Mier, Newbury Park, Calif.: Sage.

Bernstein, J., and E. Houston. 2000. *Crime and Work: What We Can Learn from the Low-Wage Labor Market.* Washington, D.C.: Economic Policy Institute.

Berry, J. M., K. E. Portney, and K. Thomson. 1991. "The Political Behavior of Poor People." In *The Urban Underclass* ed. C. Jencks and P. E. Peterson, 357–72. Washington, D.C.: Brookings Institution.

Black, D., S. Levitt, and S. Sanders. 1998. "When Work Disappears: A Preliminary Investigation into the Relationship between Job Destruction and Crime." Unpublished manuscript. Research Initiation Fund.

Bloom, H., L. L. Orr, G. Cave, S. H. Bell, F. Doolittle, and W. Lin. 1994. *The National JTPA Study: Overview of Impacts, Benefits, and Costs of Title IIA.* Bethesda, Md.: Abt Associates.

Bluestone, B., and B. Harrison. 1982. *The Deindustrialization of America: Plant Closings, Community Abandonment, and the Dismantling of Basic Industry.* New York: Basic Books.

Boarnet, M. G., and W. T. Bogart. 1996. "Enterprise Zones and Employment: Evidence from New Jersey." *Journal of Urban Economics* 40:198–215.

Bondonio, D., and J. Engberg. 2000. "States' Enterprise Zone Policies and Local Employment: What Lessons Can Be Learned?" *Regional Science and Urban Economics* 30:519–49.

Bostic, R. W. 1996. *Enterprise Zones and the Attraction of Businesses and Investment: The Importance of Implementation Strategies and Program Incentives.* Washington, D.C.: Division of Research and Statistics, Board of Governors of the Federal Reserve System.

Bushway, S. D. 1996. "The Impact of a Criminal History Record on Access to Legitimate Employment." Unpublished Ph.D. dissertation. Pittsburgh, Pa.: Carnegie Mellon University.

Bushway, S., and P. Reuter. 1997. "Labor Markets and Crime Risk Factors." In *Preventing Crime: What Works, What Doesn't, What's Promising,* ed. L. W. Sherman, D., Cave, G., F.

Doolittle, H. Bos, and C. Toussaint. 1993. *JOBSTART: Final Report on a Program for High School Dropouts.* New York: Manpower Demonstration Research Corporation.

Cave, G., and J. Quint. 1990. *Career Beginnings Impact Evaluation: Findings from a Program for Disadvantaged High School Students.* New York: Manpower Demonstration Research Corporation.

Chiricos, T. 1987. "Rates of Crime and Unemployment: An Analysis of Aggregate Research Evidence." *Social Problems* 34:187–212.

Cook, P., and G. Zarkin. 1985. "Crime and the Business Cycle." *Journal of Legal Studies* 14:115–28.

Crane, J. 1991. "Effects of Neighborhood on Dropping Out of School and Teenage Child-bearing." In *The Urban Underclass,* ed. C. Jencks and P. E. Peterson, 299–320. Washington, D.C.: Brookings Institution.

Cullen, J. B., and S. D. Levitt. 1996. *Crime, Urban Flight, and the Consequences for Cities.* Working Paper no. 5737. Cambridge, Mass.: National Bureau of Economic Research.

Currie, E. 1993. *Reckoning: Drugs, the Cities, and the American Future.* NY: Hill and Wang.

Engberg, J., and R. Greenbaum. 1999. "State Enterprise Zones and Local Housing Markets." *Journal of Housing Research* 10:163–87.

Erickson, R. A., and S. W. Friedman. 1991. "Comparative Dimensions of State Enterprise Zone Policies." In *Enterprise Zones: New Dimensions in Economic Development,* ed. R. E. Green, 155–76. Newbury Park, Calif.: Sage.

European Committee on Crime Problems. 1985. *Economic Crisis and Crime.* Strasbourg, Germany: Council of Europe.

———. 1994. *Crime and Economy.* Strasbourg, Germany: Council of Europe.

Fagan, J. 1989. "Cessation of Family Violence: Deterrence and Dissuasion." In *Family Violence: Crime and Justice—An Annual Review of Research,* ed. L. Ohlin and M. Tonry, 377–425. Chicago: University of Chicago Press.

Fagan, J., and R. B. Freeman. 1999. "Crime and Work." In *Crime and Justice: A Review of Research,* ed. M. Tonry, 113–78. Chicago: University of Chicago Press.

Farkas, G., D. A. Smith., E. W. Stromsdorfer, G. Trask, and R. Jerrett. 1982. *Impacts from the Youth Incentive Entitlement Pilot Projects: Participation, Work, and Schooling over the Full Program Period.* New York: Manpower Demonstration Research Corporation.

Farrington, D. P., B. Gallagher, L. Morley, R. J. St. Ledger, and D. J. West. 1986. "Unemployment, School Leaving, and Crime." *British Journal of Criminology* 6:335–56.

Field and Freeman. 1998. 1999.

Finn, M. A., and K. G. Willoughby. 1996. "Employment Outcomes of Ex-Offender Job Training Partnership Act (JTPA) Trainees." *Evaluation Review* 20:67–83.

Fogg, N., and A. Sum. 1999. *The Employment Status and Job Characteristics of Out-of-School Youth in the Three Initial YOA Demonstration Sites: Key Findings of Wave Two Followup Surveys.* Boston: Northeastern University, Center for Labor Market Studies.

Freeman, R. B. 1999. "The Economics of Crime." In *Handbook of Labor Economics,* vol. 3, ed. O. Ashenfelter and D. Card, 3529–71. New York: Elsevier Science.

Freeman, R. B., and W. Rodgers. 1999. *Area Economic Conditions and the Labor Market Outcomes of Young Men in the 1990s Expansion.* Working Paper no. 7073. Chicago: National Bureau of Economic Research.

Gans, H. 1990. "Deconstructing the Underclass: The Term's Danger as a Planning Concept." *Journal of the American Planning Association* 56:271–77.

Gould, E. D., B. A. Weinberg, and D. B. Mustard. 1998. *Crime Rates and Local Labor*

Market Opportunities in the United States: 1979–1995. Discussion Paper. National Bureau of Economic Research.

Gottfredson, D. MacKenzie, J. Eck, P. Reuter, and S. Bushway, 6.1–6.59. Washington, D.C.: Office of Justice Programs, U.S. Department of Justice.

Greenbaum, R., and J. Engberg. 1999. "The Impact of State Enterprise Zones on Urban Business Outcomes." Manuscript under review.

Greenbaum, R., and J. Engberg. 2000. "An Evaluation of State Enterprise Zone Policies: Measuring the Impact on Urban Housing Market Outcomes." *Policy Studies Review* 17:29–46.

Grogger, J. 1995. "The Effect of Arrests on the Employment and Earnings of Young Men." *Quarterly Journal of Economics* 110:51–71.

Grossman, J. B., and C. L. Sipe. 1992. *Summer Training and Education Program (STEP): Report on Long-Term Impacts.* Philadelphia: Public / Private Ventures.

Hagan, J. 1993. "The Social Embeddedness of Crime and Unemployment." *Criminology* 31:465–92.

Hagedorn, J. N. 1988. *People and Folks: Gangs, Crime, and the Underclass in a Rustbelt City.* Chicago: Lakeview Press.

Hahn, A., T. Leavitt, and P. Aaron. 1994. *Evaluation of the Quantum Opportunities Program (QOP): Did the Program Work?* Waltham, Mass.: Brandeis University, Center for Human Resources.

Heckman, J. J. 1994. "Is Job Training Oversold?" *The Public Interest* Number 115, (Spring), 1994 91–115.

Hillsman, S. 1982. "Pretrial Diversion of Youthful Adults: A Decade of Reform and Research." *The Justice System Journal* 7:361–87.

Holzer, H. J. 1991. "The Spatial Mismatch Hypothesis: What Has the Evidence Shown?" *Urban Studies* 28:105–22.

———. 1996. *What Employers Want: Job Prospects for Less-Educated Workers.* New York: Russell Sage Foundation.

Hughes, M. A. 1993. *Over the Horizon: Jobs in the Suburbs of Major Metropolitan Areas.* Philadelphia: Public / Private Ventures.

Jencks, C. 1991. "Is the American Underclass Growing?" In *The Urban Underclass* ed. C. Jencks and P. E. Peterson, 28–100. Washington, D.C.: Brookings Institution.

Katz, L. F., J. R. Kling, and J. B. Liebman. 1999. "Moving to Opportunity in Boston: Early Impacts of a Housing Mobility Program." Unpublished manuscript. Washington, D.C.: National Bureau of Economic Research.

Kemple, J. J., and J. C. Snipes. 2000. *Career Academies: Impacts on Students' Engagement and Performance in High School.* New York: Manpower Demonstration Research Corporation.

Kennedy, D. M., A. M. Piehl, and A. A. Braga. 1996. "Youth Violence in Boston: Gun Markets, Serious Youth Offenders, and Use Reduction Strategy." *Law and Contemporary Problems* 59:147–96.

Kling, J. R. 2000. "The Effect of Prison Sentence Length on the Subsequent Employment and Earnings of Criminal Defendants." Unpublished manuscript. Princeton, N.J.: Princeton University.

Laub, J. H., R. J. Sampson, and D. S. Nagin. 1998. "Trajectories of Change in Criminal Offending: Good Marriages and the Desistance Process." *American Sociological Review* 63:225–38.

Leiber, M. J., and T. L. Mawhorr. 1995. "Evaluating the Use of Social Skills Training and Employment with Delinquent Youth." *Journal of Criminal Justice* 23:127–41.

Lemert, E. 1951. *Social Pathology.* New York: McGraw-Hill.

Lerman, R. I. 1989. "Employment Opportunities of Young Men and Family Formation." *American Economic Review* 19:62–66.

Levitt, S. D. Forthcoming. "Alternative Strategies for Identifying the Link between Unemployment and Crime." *Journal of Quantitative Criminology.*

Ludwig, J., G. J. Duncan, and P. Hirschfield. 1999. "Urban Poverty and Juvenile Crime: Evidence from a Randomized Housing-Mobility Experiment." Unpublished manuscript. Washington, D.C.: Georgetown Public Policy Institute.

Ludwig, J., G. J. Duncan, and J. C. Pinkston. 2000. "Neighborhood Effects on Economic Self-Sufficiency: Evidence from a Randomized Housing-Mobility Experiment." Unpublished manuscript. Washington, D.C.: Georgetown Public Policy Institute.

Mallar, C., S. Kerachsky, C. Thornton, and D. Long. 1982. *Evaluation of the Economic Impact of the Job Corps Program: Third Follow-Up Report.* Princeton, N.J.: Mathematica Policy Research.

Martinson, R. 1974. "What Works? Questions and Answers about Prison Reform." *Public Interest* 35:22–54.

Maruna, S. 2001. *Making Good: How Ex-Convicts Reform and Rebuild Their Lives.* Washington, D.C.: American Psychological Association.

Massey, D. S., and N. A. Denton. 1993. *American Apartheid: Segregation and the Making of the Underclass.* Cambridge, Mass.: Harvard University Press.

Mayer, S. E. 1991. "How Much Does a High School's Racial and Socioeconomic Mix Affect Graduation and Teenage Fertility Rates?" In *The Urban Underclass,* ed. C. Jencks and P. E. Peterson, 321–41. Washington, D.C.: Brookings Institution.

Maynard, R. 1980. *The Impact of Supported Work on Young School Dropouts.* New York: Manpower Demonstration Research Corporation.

Needels, K. 1996. "Go Directly to Jail and Do Not Collect? A Long-Term Study of Recidivism, Employment, and Earnings Patterns among Prison Releasees." *Journal of Research on Crime and Delinquency* 33:471–96.

Needels, K., M. Dynarski, and W. Corson. 1998. *Helping Young People in High-Poverty Communities: Lessons from Youth Fair Chance.* Princeton, N.J.: Mathematica Policy Research.

Office of Inspector General. 2000. *Audit Findings from First 18 Months of the Three Kulick Youth Opportunity Pilot Sites Suggest Additional Innovation Is Needed for Youth Training Undertaken with JTPA Demonstration Grant Funds.* Washington, D.C.: Office of Inspector General, U.S. Department of Labor.

Papke, L. E. 1993. "What Do We Know about Enterprise Zones?" In *Tax Policy and the Economy,* ed. J. M. Poterba. Cambridge, Mass.: MIT Press.

———. 1994. "Tax Policy and Urban Development: Evidence from the Indiana Enterprise Zone Program." *Journal of Public Economics* 54:37–49.

Peterson, P. E. 1991. "The Urban Underclass and the Poverty Paradox." In *The Urban Underclass,* ed. C. Jencks and P. E. Peterson, 3–27. Washington, D.C.: Brookings Institution.

Piehl, A. M. 1998. "Economic Conditions, Work, and Crime." In *The Handbook of Crime and Punishment,* ed. M. Tonry, 302–19. New York: Oxford University Press.

Piliavin, I., and S. Masters. 1981. *The Impact of Employment Programs on Offenders, Addicts, and Problem Youth: Implications from Supported Work.* Madison, Wis.: University of Wisconsin, Institute for Research and Poverty Discussion.

Raphael, S., and R. Winter-Ebmer. 1998. *Identifying the Effect of Unemployment on Crime.* Discussion Paper no. 98-19. San Diego: University of California at San Diego.

Reuter, P., R. J. MacCoun, and P. J. Murphy. 1990. *Money from Crime: The Economics of Drug Selling in Washington, D.C.* Santa Monica, Calif.: Rand Corporation.

Rosenbaum, J. E. 1992. "Black Pioneers—Do Their Moves to the Suburbs Increase Economic Opportunity for Mothers and Children." *Housing Policy Debate,* 2:1179–213.

Rosenbaum, J. E. 1996. *Institutional Networks and Informal Strategies for Improving Work-Entry for Disadvantaged Youth: New Directions for Research and Policy.* Evanston, Ill.: Northwestern University.

Rovner-Pieczenik, R. 1973. "A Review of Manpower R&D Projects in the Correctional Field (1963–1973)." *Manpower Research Monograph* no. 28. Washington, D.C.: U.S. Department of Labor.

Rubin, M. 1990. "Urban Enterprise Zones: Do They Work? Evidence from New Jersey." *Public Budgeting and Finance* 10:3–17.

Sampson, R. J., and J. H. Laub. 1990. "Crime and Deviance over the Life Course: The Salience of Adult Social Bonds." *American Sociological Review* 55:609–27.

———. 1993. *Crime in the Making: Pathways and Turning Points through Life.* Cambridge, Mass.: Harvard University Press.

Sampson, R. J., S. W. Raudenbush, and F. Earls. 1997. "Neighborhoods and Violent Crime: A Multilevel Study of Collective Efficacy." *Science* 277:918–24.

Sampson, R. J., and W. J. Wilson. 1995. "Toward a Theory of Race, Crime, and Urban Inequality." In *Crime and Inequality,* ed. J. Hagan and R. Peterson, 37–54. Stanford, Calif.: Stanford University Press.

Saylor, W. G., and G. G. Gaes. 1996. *PREP: Training Inmates through Industrial Work Participation, and Vocational and Apprenticeship Instruction.* Washington, D.C.: U.S. Federal Bureau of Prisons.

Schochet, P. Z., J. Burghardt, and S. Glazerman. 2000. *National Job Corps Study: The Short-Term Impacts of Job Corps on Participants' Employment and Related Outcomes.* Princeton, N.J.: Mathematica Policy Research.

Shover, N. 1996. *Great Pretenders: Pursuits and Careers of Persistent Thieves.* Boulder, Colo.: Westview Press.

Stewart, James K. 1986. "The Urban Strangler." *Policy Review* (Summer) 37:6–10.

Sullivan, M. L. 1989. *"Getting Paid": Youth Crime and Work in the Inner City.* Ithaca, N.Y.: Cornell University Press.

Thornberry, T. 1987. "Toward an Interactional Theory of Delinquency." *Criminology* 25:863–91.

Thornberry, T., and R. L. Christenson. 1984. "Unemployment and Criminal Involvement: An Investigation of Reciprocal Causal Structures." *American Sociological Review* 56:609–27.

Uggen, C. 2000. "Work as a Turning Point in the Life Course of Criminals: A Duration Model of Age, Employment, and Recidivism." *American Sociological Review* 65:529–46.

Uggen, C., and M. Thompson. 1999. "The Socioeconomic Determinants of Ill-Gotten Gains: Within-Person Changes in Drug Use and Illegal Earnings." Manuscript under review.

Urban Institute. 1995. *Federal Funds, Local Choices: An Evaluation of the Community Development Block Grant Program.* Washington, D.C.: Urban Institute, Center for Public Finance and Housing.

U.S. Department of Labor. 1995. *What's Working (and What's Not).* Washington, D.C.: Office of the Chief Economist, U.S. Department of Labor.

U.S. General Accounting Office, Human Resources Division. Job Training Partnership Act: *Summer Youth Programs Increase Emphasis on Education.* GAO Report No. HRD-87-101BR. Washington D.C.: U.S. Government Printing Office, June.

Vicusi, W. K. 1986. "Market Incentives for Criminal Behavior." In *The Black Youth Unemployment Crisis,* ed. R. B. Freeman and H. J. Holzer, 301–46. Chicago: University of Chicago Press and the National Bureau of Economic Research.

Warr, M. 1993. "Age Peers and Delinquency." *Criminology* 31:17–40.

White, G. 1999. "Crime and the Decline of Manufacturing, 1970–1990." *Justice Quarterly* 16:81–97.

Wilder, M. G., and B. M. Rubin. 1996. "Rhetoric vs. Reality: A Review of Studies on State Enterprise Zone Programs." *Journal of the American Planning Association* (Fall) 62 (4): 473–91.

Wilson, D. B., C. A. Gallagher, and D. L. MacKenzie. In press. "A Meta-Analysis of Corrections-Based Education, Vocation, and Work Programs for Adult Offenders." *Journal of Research in Crime and Delinquency.* 37 (4):347–368.

Wilson, J. Q., and A. Abrahamse. 1992. "Does Crime Pay?" *Justice Quarterly* 9:359–77.

Wilson, W. J. 1987. *The Truly Disadvantaged: The Inner City, The Underclass, and Public Policy.* Chicago: University of Chicago Press.

———. 1991. "Public Policy and *The Truly Disadvantaged.*" In *The Urban Underclass,* ed. C. Jencks and P. E. Peterson, 460–81. Washington, D.C.: Brookings Institution.

———. 1996. *When Work Disappears: The World of the New Urban Poor.* New York: Alfred A. Knopf.

Wolf, W., S. Leiderman, and R. Voith. 1987. *The California Conservation Corps: An Analysis of Short-Term Impacts on Participants.* Philadelphia: Public / Private Ventures.

Wolf, W., J. M. Kelley, J. Good, and R. Silkman. 1982. *The Impact of Pre-Employment Services on the Employment and Earnings of Disadvantaged Youth.* Philadelphia: Public / Private Ventures.

Wood, R. G. 1995. "Marriage Rates and Marriageable Men: A Test of the Wilson Hypothesis." *The Journal of Human Resources* 30:163–93.

CHAPTER 9
Robert J. Sampson
THE COMMUNITY

Notes

1. This chapter draws extensively from the more detailed review found in Sampson and Lauritsen (1994) and Sampson (1999). I focus primarily on studies that make inferences about "neighborhoods" or "local communities" within urban areas. Cities and metropolitan areas are large, highly aggregated, and heterogeneous units with politically-defined and hence artificial ecological boundaries. Although intraurban units of empirical analysis (e.g., census tracts, wards, block-groups) are imperfect substitutes for the concept of neighborhood or local community, they possess more ecological integrity (e.g., natural boundaries, social homogeneity) than cities or metropolitan areas and are more closely linked to the causal processes thought to generate variations in crime.

2. Unfortunately, most ecological research has been forced to rely on official statistics (e.g., police and court records) that may be biased because of nonreporting or discrimination by the criminal justice system. To address these problems, many studies limit the domain of inquiry to serious crimes such as homicide and robbery where police biases appear to be minimal. A wide-ranging body of research shows that, for serious crimes, police bias and underreporting are very small and/or unrelated to individual-level and community variables of interest. Moreover, self-reported offense behavior and victimization experiences have been brought to bear on the validity of official statistics. As shown in Sampson and Lauritsen (1994), a general convergence of community-level findings between official police statistics and "unofficial" rates of violence has been achieved. Coupled with the fact that they generate the most fear and calls for public action, this chapter focuses primarily on violent crimes.

3. For an excellent recent review of research in this area, see Vieraitis (2000), who also comes to the conclusion that the results are "mixed."

4. The systemic conceptualization of community addresses the early criticism that Chicago-school social ecologists over-emphasized disorganization and dysfunction. In Street Corner Society, W.F. Whyte (1943) argued that what looks like social disorganization from the outside is actually an intricate internal organization. That is, he maintained that the real problem of slums was simply that their social organization failed to mesh with the structure of the society around it. However, public and parochial dimensions of informal social control (e.g., collective supervision of youth; density and strength of local organizations) may be weak even when certain forms of internal social organization (e.g., dense primary group relations; kinship networks; organized crime) are present.

5. Note too that the research limitations just noted are no worse than those typically found in individual-level research. The difference is that the assumptions embodied in individual-level research are usually accepted at face value. Consider, as noted earlier, that many individual or group-level correlates of of crime (e.g., race, family supervision) may in fact stem from community-related processes.

References

Bandura, Albert. 1997. *Self Efficacy: The Exercise of Control.* New York: W. H. Freeman.

Bellair, Paul. 2000. "Informal Surveillance and Street Crime: A Complex Process." *Criminology* 38:137–70.

Block, C. 1991. "Early Warning System for Street Gang Violence Crisis Areas: Automated Hot Spot Identification in Law Enforcement." Chicago: Illinois Criminal Justice Information Authority.

Block, R. 1979. "Community, Environment, and Violent Crime." *Criminology* 17:46–57.

Briggs, Xavier de Souza, and Elizabeth Mueller with Mercer Sullivan. 1996. "From Neighborhood to Community: Evidence on the Social Effects of Community Development" (Executive Summary). New York: Community Development Research Center, New School for Social Research.

Bursik, R. 1986. "Delinquency Rates as Sources of Ecological Change." In *The Social Ecology of Crime*, ed. J. Byrne and R. Sampson. New York: Springer-Verlag, Inc.

———. 1988. "Social Disorganization and Theories of Crime and Delinquency: Problems and Prospects." *Criminology* 26:519–52.

———. 1989. "Political Decision-Making and Ecological Models of Delinquency: Conflict and Consensus." In *Theoretical Integration in the Study of Deviance and Crime,* ed. S. Messner, M. Krohn, and A. Liska. Albany: State University of New York Press.

Bursik, R.J., Jr., and H. Grasmick. 1993. *Neighborhoods and Crime: The Dimensions of Effective Community Control.* New York: Lexington.

———1988. "Social Capital in the Creation of Human Capital." *American Journal of Sociology* 94:S95–120.

Coleman, J. 1990. *Foundations of Social Theory.* Cambridge, MA: Harvard University Press.

Coulton, C., J. Korbin, M. Su, and J. Chow. 1995. "Community Level Factors and Child Maltreatment Rates." *Child Development* 66:1262–76.

Curry, G.D., and I. Spergel. 1988. "Gang Homicide, Delinquency, and Community." *Criminology* 26:381–406.

Daley, S., and R. Meislin. 1988. "New York City, the Landlord: A Decade of Housing Decay." *New York Times,* February 8, 1988.

Earls, Felton, and Maya Carlson. 1996. "Promoting Human Capability as an Alternative to Early Crime Prevention." In *Integrating Crime Prevention Strategies: Propensity and Opportunity,* ed. Ronald V. Clarke, Joan McCord, and Per-Olof Wikström. Stockholm, Sweden: National Council for Crime Prevention.

Elliott, Delbert, William J. Wilson, David Huizinga, Robert J. Sampson, Amanda Elliott, and Bruce Rankin. 1996. "The Effects of Neighborhood Disadvantage on Adolescent Development." *Journal of Research in Crime and Delinquency* 33:389–426.

Felson, M., and L. Cohen. 1980. "Human Ecology and Crime: A Routine Activity Approach." *Human Ecology* 8:389–406.

Frey, W. 1979. "Central City White Flight: Racial and Non Racial Causes." *American Sociological Review* 44:425–48.

Garbarino, J., and A. Crouter. 1978. "Defining the Community Context for Parent-Child Relations: The Correlates of Child Maltreatment." *Child Development* 49:604–16.

Glueck, S., and E. Glueck. 1950. *Unraveling Juvenile Delinquency.* New York: Commonwealth Fund.

Greenberg, S., W. Rohe, and J. Williams. 1985. "Informal Citizen Action and Crime Prevention at the Neighborhood Level." Washington, DC: National Institute of Justice.

Hirsch, A. 1983. *Making the Second Ghetto: Race and Housing in Chicago 1940–1960.* Chicago: University of Chicago Press.

Hope, Tim. 1995. "Community Crime Prevention." In *Building a Safer Society,* ed. Michael Tonry and David Farrington. Chicago: University of Chicago Press.

Hunter, Albert. 1985. "Private, Parochial and Public Social Orders: The Problem of Crime and Incivility in Urban Communities." In *The Challenge of Social Control,* ed. Gerald Suttles and Mayer Zald. Norwood, NJ: Ablex.

INTERFACE. 1985. "Crossing the Hudson: A Survey of New York Manufacturers Who Have Moved to New Jersey." New York, NY, Unpublished report.

Jargowsky, Paul. 1997. *Poverty and Place: Ghettos, Barrios, and the American City.* New York: Russell Sage Foundation.

Katzman, M. 1980. "The Contribution of Crime to Urban Decline." *Urban Studies* 17:277–86.

Kornhauser, R. 1978. *Social Sources of Delinquency.* Chicago: University of Chicago Press.

Logan, J., and H. Molotch. 1987. *Urban Fortunes: The Political Economy of Place.* Berkeley: University of California Press.

Ludwig, J., G. Duncan, and Hirschfield, P. 1998. "Urban Poverty and Juvenile Crime: Evidence From a Randomized Housing-Mobility Experiment." *Quarterly Journal of Economics, 2001.*

Maccoby, E., J. Johnson, and R. Church. 1958. "Community Integration and the Social Control of Juvenile Delinquency." *Journal of Social Issues* 14:38–51.

Massey, D., and N. Denton. 1993. *American Apartheid: Segregation and the Making of the Underclass.* Cambridge, MA: Harvard University Press.

Meares, Tracey, and Dan Kahan. 1998. "Law and (Norms of) Order in the Inner City." *Law and Society Review* 32:805–38.

Messner, S., and K. Tardiff. 1986. "Economic Inequality and Levels of Homicide: An Analysis of Urban Neighborhoods." *Criminology* 24:297–318.

Pattillo, Mary. 1998. "Church Culture as a Strategy of Action in the Black Community." *American Sociological Review* 63:767–84.

Reiss, A. J., 1986. "Co-offender Influences on Criminal Careers." In *Criminal Careers and Career Criminals,* ed. A. Blumstein, J. Cohen, J. Roth, and C. Visher. Washington, DC: National Academy Press.

Reiss, A.J. and J. Roth eds. 1993. *Understanding and Preventing Violence.* Washington, DC: National Academy Press.

Robins, L. 1966. *Deviant Children Grown Up.* Baltimore: Williams and Wilkins.

Roncek, D. 1981. "Dangerous Places: Crime and Residential Environment." *Social Forces* 60:74–96.

Rosenbaum, D., 1991. "Crime Prevention, Fear Reduction, and the Community." In *Local Government Police Management,* ed. D. Rosenbaum, E. Hernandez, and S. Daughtry, Washington, DC: International City Management Association.

Rosenbaum, J. and S. Popkin. 1991. "Employment and Earnings of Low-Income Blacks Who Move to the Suburbs." In *The Urban Underclass,* ed. C. Jencks and P. Peterson. Washington, DC: The Brookings Institution.

Rountree, Pamela Wilcox, and Barbara D. Warner 1999. "Social Ties and Crime: Is the Relationship Gendered?" *Criminology* 37(4): 789-812.

Sampson, R. J. 1985. "Neighborhood and Crime: The Structural Determinants of Personal Victimization." *Journal of Research in Crime and Delinquency* 22:7–40.

———. 1986. "Neighborhood Family Structure and the Risk of Criminal Victimization." In *The Social Ecology of Crime,* ed. J. Byrne and R. Sampson. New York: Springer-Verlag.

———. 1992. "Family Management and Child Development: Insights from Social Disorganization Theory." In *Advances in Criminological Theory* (Volume 3), ed. J. McCord. New Brunswick: Transaction.

———.1999. "What 'Community' Supplies." In *Urban Problems and Community Development,* ed. Ronald F. Ferguson and William T. Dickens. Washington, D.C: Brookings Institution Press.

Sampson, R. J., and W. B. Groves. 1989. "Community Structure and Crime: Testing Social-Disorganization Theory." *American Journal of Sociology* 94:774–802.

Sampson, Robert J., and Janet L. Lauritsen. 1994. "Violent Victimization and Offending: Individual-, Situational-, and Community-level Risk Factors." In *Understanding and Preventing Violence: Social Influences* (Volume 3), ed. Albert J. Reiss Jr., and Jeffrey Roth. (National Research Council.) Washington, DC: National Academy Press.

Sampson, R. J., and W. J. Wilson. 1995. "Toward a Theory of Race, Crime, and Urban Inequality." In *Crime and Inequality,* ed. John Hagan and Ruth Peterson. Stanford: Stanford University Press.

Sampson, R. J., and J. Wooldredge. 1986. "Evidence That High Crime Rates Encourage Migration Away from Central Cities." *Sociology and Social Research* 90:310–14.

Sampson, Robert J., and Steve Raudenbush. 1999. "Systematic Social Observation of Public Spaces: A New Look at Disorder in Urban Neighborhoods." *American Journal of Sociology* 105: 603–651.

Sampson, Robert J., Stephen Raudenbush, and Felton Earls. 1997. "Neighborhoods and Violent Crime: A Multilevel Study of Collective Efficacy." *Science* 277:918–24.

Schuerman, L., and S. Kobrin. 1986. "Community Careers in Crime." In *Communities and Crime,* ed. A. J. Reiss, Jr. and M. Tonry. Chicago: University of Chicago Press.

Shaw, C. and H. McKay. 1942 (1969, revised edition). *Juvenile Delinquency and Urban Areas.* Chicago: University of Chicago Press.

Sherman, L. 1995. "Patrol Strategies for Police." In *Crime,* ed. J.Q. Wilson and J. Petersilia. San Francisco, CA: ICS Press.

Sherman, L., P. Gartin, and M. Buerger. 1989. "Hot Spots of Predatory Crime: Routine Activities and the Criminology of Place." *Criminology* 27:27–56.

Simcha-Fagan, O. and J. Schwartz. 1986. "Neighborhood and Delinquency: An Assessment of Contextual Effects." *Criminology* 24:667–704.

Skogan, W. 1986. "Fear of Crime and Neighborhood Change." In *Communities and Crime,* ed. A.J. Reiss, Jr. and M. Tonry. Chicago: University of Chicago Press.

———. 1991. *Disorder and Decline.* New York: Free Press.

Smith, D. R. and G. R. Jarjoura. 1988. "Social Structure and Criminal Victimization." *Journal of Research in Crime and Delinquency* 25:27–52.

Sullivan, M. 1989. *Getting Paid: Youth Crime and Work in the Inner City.* Ithaca, NY: Cornell University Press.

Taylor, R., and J. Covington. 1988. "Neighborhood Changes in Ecology and Violence." *Criminology* 26:553–90.

Taylor, R., S. Gottfredson, and S. Brower. 1984. "Block Crime and Fear: Defensible Space, Local Social Ties, and Territorial Functioning." *Journal of Research in Crime and Delinquency* 21:303–31.

Thrasher, F. 1963. *The Gang: A Study of 1,313 Gangs in Chicago* (Revised Edition). Chicago: University of Chicago Press.

Tienda, M. 1991. "Poor People and Poor Places: Deciphering Neighborhood Effects on Poverty Outcomes." In *Macro-Micro Linkages in Sociology,* ed. J. Huber. Newbury, CA: Sage.

Vieraitis, Lynne M. 2000. "Income Inequality, Poverty, and Violent Crime: A Review of the Empirical Evidence." *Social Pathology* 6:24–45.

Wallace, R., and D. Wallace. 1990. "Origins of Public Health Collapse in New York City: The Dynamics of Planned Shrinkage, Contagious Urban Decay and Social Disintegration." *Bulletin of the New York Academy of Medicine* 66:391–434.

Warner, Barbara, and Pamela Wilcox Rountree. 1997. "Local Social Ties in a Community and Crime Model: Questioning the Systemic Nature of Informal Control." *Social Problems* 44:520-536.

Whyte, W. F. 1943. *Street Corner Society: The Social Structure of an Italian Slum.* Chicago: University of Chicago Press.

Widom, C. 1989. "The Cycle of Violence." *Science* 244:160–66.

Wilson, J. Q., and G. Kelling. 1982. "Broken Windows." *Atlantic Monthly* March: 29–38.

Wilson, W. J. 1987. *The Truly Disadvantaged: The Inner City, the Underclass, and Public Policy.* Chicago: University of Chicago Press.
———. 1996. *When Work Disappears.* New York: Knopf.

CHAPTER 10
Francis T. Cullen
REHABILITATION AND TREATMENT PROGRAMS

References

Adams, Kenneth, Katherine J. Bennett, Timothy J. Flanagan, James W. Marquart, Steven J. Cuvelier, Eric Fritsch, Jurg Gerber, Dennis R. Longmire, and Velmer S. Burton, Jr. 1994. "A Large-Scale Multidimensional Test of the Effect of Prison Education Programs on Offenders' Behavior." *The Prison Journal* 74:433–49.

Adams, Stuart. 1976. "Evaluation: A Way Out of Rhetoric. In *Rehabilitation, Recidivism, and Research*, ed. Robert Martinson, Ted Palmer, and Stuart Adams, 75–91. Hackensack, N.J.: National Council on Crime and Delinquency.

Allen, Francis A. 1981. *The Decline of the Rehabilitative Ideal: Penal Policy and Social Purpose.* New Haven, Conn.: Yale University Press.

Andrews, D. A. 1995. "The Psychology of Criminal Conduct and Effective Treatment." In *What Works: Reducing Reoffending*, ed. James McGuire, 35–62. West Sussex, U.K.: John Wiley.

Andrews, D. A., and James Bonta. 1998. *The Psychology of Criminal Conduct*, 2d ed. Cincinnati: Anderson.

Andrews, D. A., Craig Dowden, and Paul Gendreau. 1999. Clinically Relevant and Psychologically Informed Approaches to Reduced Reoffending: A Meta-Analytic Study of Human Service, Risk, Need, Responsivity, and Other Concerns in Justice Contexts. Unpublished manuscript, Carleton University, Ottawa, Ontario, Canada.

Andrews, D. A., Ivan Zinger, Robert D. Hoge, James Bonta, Paul Gendreau, and Francis T. Cullen. 1990. "Does Correctional Treatment Work? A Clinically Relevant and Psychologically Informed Meta-Analysis." *Criminology* 8:369–404.

Antonowicz, Daniel H., and Robert R. Ross. 1994. "Essential Components of Successful Rehabilitation Programs for Offenders." *International Journal of Offender and Comparative Criminology* 38:97–104.

Applegate, Brandon K., Francis T. Cullen, and Bonnie S. Fisher. 1997. "Public Support for Correctional Treatment: The Continuing Appeal of the Rehabilitative Ideal." *The Prison Journal* 77:237–58.

Backer, Thomas E., Susan L. David, and Gerald Soucy, eds. 1995. *Reviewing the Behavioral Science Knowledge Base on Technology Transfer.* Rockville, Md.: National Institute on Drug Abuse, U.S. Department of Health and Human Services.

Bailey, Walter C. 1966. "Correctional Outcome: An Evaluation of 100 Reports." *Journal of Criminal Law, Criminology and Police Science* 57:153–60.

Binder, Arnold, and Gilbert Geis. 1984. "*Ad Populum* Argumentation in Criminology: Juvenile Diversion as Rhetoric." *Crime and Delinquency* 30:624–47.

Blumstein, Alfred. 1997. "Interaction of Criminological Research and Public Policy." *Journal of Quantitative Criminology* 12:349–61.

Blumstein, Alfred, and Joan Petersilia. 1995. "Investing in Criminal Justice Research." In *Crime*, ed. James Q. Wilson and Joan Petersilia, 465–87. San Francisco: ICS Press.

Bonta, James. 1996. "Risk-Needs Assessment and Treatment." In *Choosing Correctional Interventions That Work: Defining the Demand and Evaluating the Supply*, ed. Alan T. Harland, 18–32. Thousand Oaks, Calif.: Sage.

Bonta, James, Suzanne Wallace-Capretta, and Jennifer Rooney. 2000. "A Quasi-Experimental Evaluation of an Intensive Supervision Rehabilitation Program." *Criminal Justice and Behavior* 27:312–29.

Bouffard, Jeffrey A., Doris Layton MacKenzie, and Laura J. Hickman. 2000. "Effectiveness of Vocational Education and Employment Programs for Adult Offenders: A Methodology-Based Analysis of the Literature." *Journal of Offender Rehabilitation* 31:1–41.

Bureau of Justice Statistics. 1992. *Drugs, Crime, and the Justice System: A National Report*. Washington, D.C.: Bureau of Justice Statistics, U.S. Department of Justice.

Bushway, Shawn, and Peter Reuter. 1997. "Labor Markets and Crime Risk Factors." Chapter 6 in *Preventing Crime: What Works, What Doesn't, What's Promising*, ed. Lawrence W. Sherman, Denise Gottfredson, Doris Layton MacKenzie, John Eck, Peter Reuter, and Shawn Bushway. Washington, D.C.: National Institute of Justice, U.S. Department of Justice.

Camp, Camille Graham, and George M. Camp. 1999. *The Corrections Yearbook 1999: Adult Corrections*. Middletown, Conn.: Criminal Justice Institute.

Clear, Todd R. 1994. *Harm in American Penology: Offenders, Victims, and Their Communities*. Albany: State University of New York Press.

Corrections Compendium. 1997. "Survey Summary: Education Opportunities in Correctional Settings." 22 (September):4–16.

Cose, Ellis. 2000. "The Prison Paradox." *Newsweek* November 13: 40–49.

Cullen, Francis T., and Robert Agnew. 1999. *Criminological Theory: Past to Present*. Los Angeles: Roxbury.

Cullen, Francis T., and Brandon Applegate, eds. 1997. *Offender Rehabilitation: Effective Correctional Intervention*. Aldershot, U.K.: Ashgate/Dartmouth.

Cullen, Francis T., Bonnie S. Fisher, and Brandon K. Applegate. 2000. "Public Opinion About Punishment and Corrections." In *Crime and Justice: A Review of Research*, vol. 27, ed. Michael Tonry, 1–79. Chicago: University of Chicago Press.

Cullen, Francis T., and Paul Gendreau. 1989. "The Effectiveness of Correctional Treatment: Reconsidering the 'Nothing Works' Debate." In *The American Prison: Issues in Research and Policy*, ed. Lynne Goodstein and Doris L. MacKenzie, 23–44. New York: Plenum.

———. 2000. "Assessing Correctional Rehabilitation: Policy, Practice, and Prospects." In *Criminal Justice 2000: Volume 3 – Policies, Processes, and Decisions of the Criminal Justice System*, ed. Julie Horney, 109-175. Washington, DC: U.S. Department of Justice, National Institute of Justice.

———. 2001. "From Nothing Works to What Works: Changing Professional Ideology in the 21st Century." *The Prison Journal*. 81:313–338.

Cullen, Francis T., and Karen E. Gilbert. 1982. *Reaffirming Rehabilitation*. Cincinnati: Anderson.

Cullen, Francis T., and Melissa M. Moon. Forthcoming. "Reaffirming Rehabilitation: Public Support for Correctional Treatment." In *What Works: Risk Reduction Interventions for Special Needs Offenders*, ed. Harry E. Allen. Lanham, Md.: American Correctional Association.

Cullen, Francis T., Travis C. Pratt, Sharon Levrant Micelli, and Melissa M. Moon. Forthcoming. "Dangerous Liaison? Rational Choice Theory as the Basis for Correctional Intervention." In *Rational Choice and Criminal Behavior*, edited by Alex R. Piquero and Stephen G. Tibbetts. New Brunswick, N.J.: Transaction Publishers.

Cullen, Francis T., John Paul Wright, and Brandon K. Applegate. 1996. "Control in the Community: The Limits of Reform?" In *Choosing Correctional Interventions That Work: Defining the Demand and Evaluating the Supply*, ed. Alan T. Harland, 69–116. Newbury Park, Calif.: Sage.

Cullen, Francis T., John Paul Wright, Shayna Brown, Melissa M. Moon, Michael B. Blankenship, and Brandon K. Applegate. 1998. "Public Support for Early Intervention Programs: Implications for a Progressive Policy Agenda." *Crime and Delinquency* 44:187–204.

Currie, Elliott. 1985. *Confronting Crime: An American Dilemma*. New York: Pantheon.

Davis, Su Perk. 1993. "Work and Educational Release, 1993." *Corrections Compendium* 18 (April): 5–18, 22.

Dowden, Craig, and D. A. Andrews. 1999. "What Works for Female Offenders: A Meta-Analysis." *Crime and Delinquency* 45:438–52.

Duguid, Stephen. 2000. *Can Prisons Work? The Prisoner as Object and Subject in Modern Corrections*. Toronto: University of Toronto Press.

Fagan, Jeffrey, and Richard B. Freeman. 1999. "Work and Crime." In *Crime and Justice: A Review of Research*, vol. 25, ed. Michael Tonry, 225–90. Chicago: University of Chicago Press.

Finckenauer, James O., and Patricia W. Gavin. 1999. *Scared Straight: The Panacea Phenomenon Revisited*. Prospect Heights, Ill.: Waveland.

Flanagan, Timothy J. 1989. "Prison Labor and Industry." In *The American Prison: Issues in Research and Policy*, ed. Lynne Goodstein and Doris Layton MacKenzie, 135–61. New York: Plenum.

———. 1994. *Prison Education Research Project: Final Report*. Huntsville, Tex.: Sam Houston State University.

Foucault, Michel. 1977. *Discipline and Punish: The Birth of the Prison*. New York: Pantheon.

Frankel, Marvin E. 1972. *Criminal Sentences: Law Without Order*. New York: Hill and Wang.

Fulton, Betsy, Edward J. Latessa, Amy Stichman, and Lawrence F. Travis III. 1997. "The State of ISP: Research and Policy Implications." *Federal Probation* 61 (December):65–75.

Gaes, Gerald G., Timothy J. Flanagan, Larry Motiuk, and Lynn Stewart. 1999. "Adult Correctional Treatment." In *Crime and Justice: A Review of Research*, vol. 26, ed. Michael Tonry, 85–150. Chicago: University of Chicago Press.

Gallagher, Catherine A., David B. Wilson, Paul Hirschfield, Mark B. Coggeshall, and Doris L. MacKenzie. 1999. "A Quantitative Review of the Effects of Sex Offender Treatment on Sexual Reoffending." *Corrections Management Quarterly* 3 (Fall):19–29.

Gallagher, Catherine A., David B. Wilson, and Doris L. MacKenzie. 2000. A Meta-Analysis of the Effectiveness of Sex Offender Treatment Programs. Unpublished paper, University of Maryland, College Park.

Garland, David. 1990. *Punishment and Modern Society: A Study in Social Theory*. Chicago: University of Chicago Press.

Gendreau, Paul. 1996. "The Principles of Effective Intervention with Offenders." In *Choosing Correctional Interventions That Work: Defining the Demand and Evaluating the Supply*, ed. Alan T. Harland, 117–30. Newbury Park, Calif.: Sage.

Gendreau, Paul, Francis T. Cullen, and James Bonta. 1994. "Intensive Rehabilitation Supervision: The Next Generation in Community Corrections?" *Federal Probation* 58 (March): 72–78.

Gendreau, Paul, and Claire Goggin. 1997. "Correctional Treatment: Accomplishments and Realities." In *Correctional Counseling and Rehabilitation*, 3d ed., ed. Patricia Van Voorhis, Michael Braswell, and David Lester, 271–79. Cincinnati: Anderson.

Gendreau, Paul, Claire Goggin, Francis T. Cullen, and D. A. Andrews. 2000. "The Effects of Community Sanctions and Incarceration on Recidivism." *Forum on Corrections Research* 12 (May):10–13.

Gendreau, Paul, Claire Goggin, and Mario Paparozzi. 1996. "Principles of Effective Assessment for Community Corrections." *Federal Probation*, 60 (September):64–70.

Gendreau, Paul, Claire Goggin, and Paula Smith. 2000. "Generating Rational Correctional Policies: An Introduction to Advances in Cumulating Knowledge." *Corrections Management Quarterly* 4 (Spring):52–60.

———. Forthcoming. "Implementation Guidelines for Correctional Programs in the 'Real World.'" In *Inside the "Black Box" in Corrections: Treatment Integrity and the Implementation of Effective Correctional Programs—Policy, Administrative, and Clinical Issues*, ed. Gary A. Bernfeld, Alan Leischied, and David P. Farrington. Scarborough, Ontario: Wiley.

Gendreau, Paul, Tracy Little, and Claire Goggin. 1996. "A Meta-Analysis of the Predictors of Adult Offender Recidivism: What Works!" *Criminology* 34:575–607.

Gendreau, Paul, and Robert R. Ross. 1979. "Effective Correctional Treatment: Bibliotherapy for Cynics." *Crime and Delinquency* 25:463–89.

———. 1987. "Revivification of Rehabilitation: Evidence from the 1980s." *Justice Quarterly* 4:349–407.

Gerber, Jurg, and Eric J. Fritsch. 1995. "Adult Academic and Vocational Correctional Education Programs: A Review of Recent Research." *Journal of Offender Rehabilitation* 22:119–42.

Gibbons, Don C. 1999. "Review Essay: Changing Lawbreakers—What Have We Learned Since the 1950s?" *Crime and Delinquency* 45 (April):272–93.

Gilliard, Darrell K., and Allen J. Beck. 1998. *Prisoners in 1997*. Washington, D.C.: Bureau of Justice Statistics, U.S. Department of Justice.

Glaser, Daniel. 1995. *Preparing Convicts for Law-Abiding Lives: The Pioneering Penology of Richard A. McGee*. Albany: State University of New York Press.

Glass, Gene V., Barry McGraw, and Mary Lee Smith. 1981. *Meta-Analysis in Social Research*. Beverly Hills, Calif.: Sage.

Gottfredson, Michael R. 1979. "Treatment Destruction Techniques." *Journal of Research in Crime and Delinquency* 16:39–54.

Greenberg, David F. 1977. "The Correctional Effects of Corrections: A Survey of Evaluations." In *Corrections and Punishment*, ed. David F. Greenberg, 111–48. Beverly Hills, Calif.: Sage.

Halleck, Seymour L., and Anne D. Witte. 1977. "Is Rehabilitation Dead?" *Crime and Delinquency* 23:372–82.

Hanson, R. Karl, Arthur Gordon, Andrew J. R. Harris, Janice K. Marques, William Murphy, Vernon L. Quinsey, and Michael C. Seto. 2000. The 2000 ATSA Report on the Effectiveness of Treatment for Sex Offenders. Paper presented at the annual meeting of the ATSA, November, San Diego, Calif.

Harland, Alan T., ed. 1996. *Choosing Correctional Options That Work: Defining the Demand and Evaluating the Supply*. Thousand Oaks, Calif.: Sage.

Hedges, Larry V. 1987. "How Hard Is Hard Science, How Soft Is Soft Science? The Empirical Cumulativeness of Research." *American Psychologist* 42:443–55.

Henggeler, Scott W., Sonja K. Schoenwald, Charles M. Borduin, Melisa D. Rowland, and Phillippe B. Cunningham. 1998. *Multisystemic Treatment of Antisocial Behavior in Children and Adolescents*. New York: Guilford Press.

Hester, Reid K., and William R. Miller, eds. 1995. *Handbook of Alcoholism Treatment Approaches: Effective Alternatives*, 2d ed. Boston: Allyn and Bacon.

Hirschi, Travis, and Michael R. Gottfredson. 1995. "Control Theory and the Life-Course Perspective." *Studies in Crime and Crime Prevention* 4:131–42.

Klockars, Carl B. 1975. "The True Limits of The Effectiveness of Correctional Treatment." *The Prison Journal* 55 (Spring–Summer): 53–64.

Kittrie, Nicholas N. 1971. *The Right To Be Different: Deviance and Enforced Therapy*. Baltimore: Penguin.

Kuhn, Thomas S. 1962. *The Structure of Scientific Revolutions*. Chicago: University of Chicago Press.

Latessa, Edward J., and Alexander Holsinger. 1998. "The Importance of Evaluating Correctional Programs: Assessing Outcome and Quality." *Corrections Management Quarterly* 2 (Fall): 22–29.

Latessa, Edward J., and Melissa M. Moon. 1992. "The Effectiveness of Acupuncture in an Outpatient Drug Treatment Program." *Journal of Contemporary Criminal Justice* 8:317–31.

Lester, David, and Patricia Van Voorhis. 1997. "Cognitive Therapies." In *Correctional Counseling and Rehabilitation*, 3d ed., ed. Patricia Van Voorhis, Michael Braswell, and David Lester, 163–85. Cincinnati: Anderson.

Lillis, Jamie. 1993. "Survey Summary: Youth Count Drops by 15%; Overcrowding Remains." *Corrections Compendium* 18 (December):7–14.

———. 1994. "Survey Summary: Education in U.S. Prisons—Part Two." *Corrections Compendium* 19 (April):10–16.

Lin, Ann Chih. 2000. *Reform in the Making: The Implementation of Social Policy in Prison*. Princeton, N.J.: Princeton University Press.

Lipset, Seymour Martin, and William Schneider. 1983. *The Confidence Gap: Business, Labor, and Government in the Public Mind*. New York: The Free Press.

Lipsey, Mark W. 1992. "Juvenile Delinquency Treatment: A Meta-Analytic Inquiry into the Variability of Effects." In *Meta-Analysis for Explanation: A Casebook*, ed. Thomas D. Cook, Harris Cooper, David S. Cordray, Heidi Hartmann, Larry V. Hedges, Richard J. Light, Thomas A. Lewis, and Frederick Mosteller, 83–127. New York: Russell Sage.

———. 1995. "What Do We Learn from 400 Research Studies on the Effectiveness of Treatment with Juvenile Delinquency?" In *What Works: Reducing Reoffending*, ed. James McGuire, 63–78. West Sussex, U.K.: John Wiley.

———. 1999a. "Can Rehabilitative Programs Reduce the Recidivism of Juvenile Offenders? An Inquiry into the Effectiveness of Practical Programs." *Virginia Journal of Social Policy and Law* 6:611–41.

———. 1999b. "Can Intervention Rehabilitate Serious Delinquents?" *Annals of the American Academy of Political and Social Science* 564:142–66.

Lipsey, Mark W., and James H. Derzon. 1998. "Predictors of Violent and Serious Delinquency in Adolescence and Early Adulthood." In *Serious and Violent Juvenile Offenders: Risk Factors and Successful Interventions*, ed. Rolf Loeber and David P. Farrington, 86–105. Thousand Oaks, Calif.: Sage.

Lipsey, Mark W., and David B. Wilson. 1993. "The Efficacy of Psychological, Educational, and Behavioral Treatment." *American Psychologist* 48:1181–209.

————. 1998. "Effective Intervention for Serious Juvenile Offenders: A Synthesis of Research." In *Serious and Violent Juvenile Offenders: Risk Factors and Successful Interventions*, ed. Rolf Loeber and David P. Farrington, 313–45. Thousand Oaks, Calif.: Sage.

Lipton, Douglas, Robert Martinson, and Judith Wilks. 1975. *The Effectiveness of Correctional Treatment: A Survey of Treatment Evaluation Studies*. New York: Praeger.

Loeber, Rolf, and David P. Farrington, eds. 1998. *Serious and Violent Juvenile Offenders: Risk Factors and Successful Interventions*. Thousand Oaks, Calif.: Sage.

Logan, Charles H. 1972. "Evaluation Research in Crime and Delinquency: A Reappraisal." *Journal of Criminal Law, Criminology and Police Science* 63:378–87.

Logan, Charles H., and Gerald Gaes. 1993. "Meta-Analysis and the Rehabilitation of Punishment." *Justice Quarterly* 10:245–63.

Losel, Friedrich. 1995. "The Efficacy of Correctional Treatment: A Review and Synthesis of Meta-evaluations." In *What Works: Reducing Reoffending*, ed. James McGuire, 79–111. West Sussex, U.K.: John Wiley.

————. Forthcoming. "Evaluating the Effectiveness of Correctional Programs: Bridging the Gap Between Research and Practice." In *Inside the "Black Box" in Corrections: Treatment Integrity and the Implementation of Effective Correctional Programs—Policy, Administrative, and Clinical Issues*, ed. Gary A. Bernfeld, Alan Leischied, and David P. Farrington. Scarborough, Ontario: Wiley.

Lurigio, Arthur J. 2000. "Drug Treatment Availability and Effectiveness; Studies of the General and Criminal Justice Populations." *Criminal Justice and Behavior* 27:495–528.

MacKenzie, Doris Layton. 1997. "Criminal Justice and Crime Prevention." Chapter 9 in *Preventing Crime: What Works, What Doesn't, What's Promising*, ed. Lawrence W. Sherman, Denise Gottfredson, Doris Layton MacKenzie, John Eck, Peter Reuter, and Shawn Bushway. Washington, D.C.: National Institute of Justice, U.S. Department of Justice.

————. 2000. "Evidence-Based Corrections: Identifying What Works." *Crime and Delinquency* 46:457–71.

MacKenzie, Doris Layton, and Laura J. Hickman. 1998. *What Works in Corrections? An Examination of the Effectiveness of the Type of Rehabilitation Programs Offered by Washington State Department of Corrections*. College Park: University of Maryland.

McLaren, Kaye. 1992. *Reducing Reoffending: What Works Now*. Wellington, New Zealand: Penal Division, Department of Justice.

Martinson, Robert. 1974a. "What Works?—Questions and Answers About Prison Reform." *The Public Interest*, 35 (Spring):22–54.

————. 1974b. "Viewpoint." *Criminal Justice Newsletter* 5 (November 18):4–5.

————. 1979. "New Findings, New Views: A Note of Caution Regarding Sentencing Reform." *Hofstra Law Review* 7:243–58.

Maruna, Shadd. 2001. *Making Good: How Ex-Convicts Reform and Rebuild Their Lives*. Washington, D.C.: American Psychological Association.

Merton, Robert K. 1973. *The Sociology of Science: Theoretical and Empirical Investigations*. Chicago: University of Chicago Press.

Moon, Melissa M., Jody L. Sundt, Francis T. Cullen, and John Paul Wright. 1999. "Is Child Saving Dead? Public Support for Rehabilitation." *Crime and Delinquency* 46:38–60.

Morris, Norval. 1974. *The Future of Imprisonment*. Chicago: University of Chicago Press.

Morris, Norval, and Michael Tonry. 1990. *Between Prison and Probation: Intermediate Punishments in a Rational Sentencing System*. New York: Oxford University Press.

Mumola, Christopher J. 1998. *Substance Abuse and Treatment: State and Federal Prisoners, 1997*. Washington, D.C.: Bureau of Justice Statistics, U.S. Department of Justice.

Mumola, Christopher, with the assistance of Thomas P. Bonczar. 1998. *Substance Abuse and Treatment of Adults on Probation, 1995*. Washington, D.C.: Bureau of Justice Statistics, U.S. Department of Justice.

Palmer, Ted. 1975. "Martinson Revisited." *Journal of Research in Crime and Delinquency* 12:133–52.

———. 1992. *The Re-Emergence of Correctional Intervention*. Newbury Park, Calif.: Sage.

Paternoster, Raymond, and Ronet Bachman, eds. 2001. *Explaining Criminals and Crime: Essays in Contemporary Criminological Theory*. Los Angeles: Roxbury.

Pearson, Frank S., and Douglas S. Lipton. 1999a. The Effectiveness of Educational and Vocational Programs: CDATE Meta-Analyses. Paper presented at the Annual Meeting of the American Society of Criminology, November, Toronto.

———. 1999b. "A Meta-Analytic Review of the Effectiveness of Corrections-Based Treatment for Drug Abuse." *The Prison Journal* 79:384–410.

Pearson, Frank S., Douglas S. Lipton, and Charles M. Cleland. 1996. Some Preliminary Findings from the CDATE Project. Paper presented at the annual meeting of the American Society of Criminology, November, Chicago.

Pearson, Frank, Douglas S. Lipton, Charles M. Cleland, and Dorline S. Yee. 2000. The Effects of Behavioral/Cognitive Behavioral Programs on Recidivism. Unpublished paper, National Development and Research Institutes, New York.

Petersilia, Joan. 1998. "A Decade of Experimenting with Intermediate Sanctions: What Have We Learned?" *Federal Probation* 62 (December):3–9.

Petersilia, Joan, and Susan Turner. 1993. "Intensive Probation and Parole." In *Crime and Justice: An Annual Review of Research*, vol. 17, ed. Michael Tonry, 281–335. Chicago: University of Chicago Press.

Phillips, Sarah, and Kent L. Sandstrom. 1990. "Parental Attitudes Toward Youth Work." *Youth and Society* 22:160–83.

Piehl, Anne Morrison. 1998. "Economic Conditions, Work, and Crime." In *The Handbook of Crime and Punishment*, ed. Michael Tonry, 302–19. New York: Oxford University Press.

Prendergast, Michael L., M. Douglas Anglin, and Jean Wellisch. 1995. "Treatment for Drug-Abusing Offenders Under Community Supervision." *Federal Probation* 59 (December): 66–75.

Redondo, Santiago, Julio Sanchez-Meca, and Vincente Garrido. 1999. "The Influence of Treatment Programmes on the Recidivism of Juvenile and Adult Offenders: An European Meta-Analytic Review." *Psychology, Crime and Law* 5 (no. 3):251–78.

Reynolds, Morgan O. 1996. *Crime and Punishment in Texas: An Update*. Dallas: National Center for Policy Analysis.

Rhine, Edward E., ed. 1998. *Best Practices: Excellence in Corrections*. Lanham, Md.: American Correctional Association.

Robison, James, and Gerald Smith. 1971. "The Effectiveness of Correctional Programs." *Crime and Delinquency* 17:67–80.

Ross, Robert R., Daniel H. Antonowicz, and Gurmeet K. Dhaliwal. 1995. "Something Works." In *Going Straight: Effective Delinquency Prevention and Offender Rehabilitation*, ed. Robert R. Ross, Daniel H. Antonowicz, and Gurmeet K. Dhaliwal, 3–28. Ottawa: Air Training and Publications.

Ross, Robert R., and Elizabeth A. Fabiano. 1985. *Time to Think: A Cognitive Model of Delinquency Prevention and Offender Rehabilitation*. Johnson City, Tenn.: Institute of Social Sciences and Arts.

Rothman, David J. 1980. *Conscience and Convenience: The Asylum and Its Alternatives in Progressive America*. Boston: Little, Brown.

Rotman, Edgardo. 1990. *Beyond Punishment: A New View on the Rehabilitation of Offenders*. New York: Greenwood.

Sampson, Robert J., and John H. Laub. 1993. *Crime in the Making: Pathways and Turning Points Through Life*. Cambridge, Mass.: Harvard University Press.

Schur, Edwin M. 1973. *Radical Non-Intervention: Rethinking the Delinquency Problem*. Englewood Cliffs, N.J.: Prentice-Hall.

Sechrest, Lee, Susan O. White, and Elizabeth D. Brown, eds. 1979. *The Rehabilitation of Criminal Offenders: Problems and Prospects*. Washington, D.C.: National Academy of Sciences.

Selcraig, Bruce. 2000. "Camp Fear." *Mother Jones* November–December:64–71.

Serrill, Michael S. 1975. "Is Rehabilitation Dead?" *Corrections Magazine* 1 (May–June): 21–32.

Silverman, Ira J., and Manuel Vega. 1996. *Corrections: A Comprehensive Review*. Minneapolis: West.

Spiegler, Michael D., and David C. Guevremont. 1998. *Contemporary Behavior Therapy*, 3d ed. Pacific Grove, Calif.: Brooks/Cole.

Stephan, James J. 1997. *Census of State and Federal Correctional Facilities, 1995*. Washington, D.C.: Bureau of Justice Statistics, U.S. Department of Justice.

Taxman, Faye S. 1999. "Unraveling 'What Works' for Offenders in Substance Abuse Treatment Services." *National Drug Court Institute Review* 2:93–134.

Tewksbury, Richard, David John Erickson, and Jon Marc Taylor. 2000. "Opportunities Lost: The Consequences of Eliminating Pell Grant Eligibility for Correctional Education Students." *Journal of Offender Rehabilitation* 31:43–56.

Toby, Jackson 1964. "Is Punishment Necessary?" *Journal of Criminal Law, Criminology, and Police Science* 55:332–37.

Turner, Susan, and Joan Petersilia. 1996. *Work Release: Recidivism and Corrections Costs in Washington State*. Washington, D.C.: National Institute of Justice, U.S. Department of Justice.

Uggen, Christopher. 1999. "Ex-Offenders and the Conformist Alternative: A Job Quality Model of Work and Crime." *Social Problems* 46:127–51.

Van Voorhis, Patricia. 1987. "Correctional Effectiveness: The High Cost of Ignoring Success." *Federal Probation* 51 (March):59–62.

Van Voorhis, Patricia, Michael Braswell, and David Lester, eds. 1997. *Correctional Counseling and Rehabilitation*, 3d ed. Cincinnati: Anderson.

Wees, Gregory. 1996. "Survey Summary: Sex Offenders in State and Federal Prisons Top 100,000 Mark." *Corrections Compendium* 21 (May):10–25.

———. 1997a. "Survey Summary: Work and Educational Release 1996." *Corrections Compendium* 22 (May): 8–23.

———. 1997b. "Survey Summary: Prison Industries 1997." *Corrections Compendium* 22 (June): 10–21.

Wexler, Harry K., Gregory P. Falkin, and Douglas P. Lipton. 1990. "Outcome Evaluation of a Prison Therapeutic Community for Substance Abuse Treatment." *Criminal Justice and Behavior* 17:71–92.

Whitehead, John T., and Steven P. Lab. 1989. "A Meta-Analysis of Juvenile Correctional Treatment." *Journal of Research in Crime and Delinquency* 26 (August):276–95.

Wilson, David B., Catherine A. Gallagher, Mark B. Coggeshall, and Doris L. MacKenzie. 1999. "A Quantitative Review and Description of Corrections-Based Education, Vocation, and Work Programs." *Corrections Management Quarterly* 3 (Fall):8–18.

Wilson, David B., Catherine A. Gallagher, and Doris L. MacKenzie. 2000. "A Meta-Analysis of Corrections-Based Education, Vocation, and Work Programs for Adult Offenders." *Journal of Research in Crime and Delinquency* 37:347–68.

Wilson, James Q. 1975. *Thinking About Crime*. New York: Vintage Books.

Wilson, James. 2000. *Drug Use, Testing, and Treatment in Jails*. Washington, D.C.: Bureau of Justice Statistics, U.S. Department of Justice.

Wines, E. C., ed. 1871. *Transactions of the National Congress on Penitentiary and Reformatory Discipline*. Albany, N.Y.: Weed Parsons.

Wright, John Paul, and Francis T. Cullen. 2000. "Juvenile Involvement in Occupational Delinquency." *Criminology* 38:863–92.

Wunder, Amanda. 1994. "Working for the Weekend: Prison Industries and Inmate-Employees." *Corrections Compendium* 19 (October):9–22.

CHAPTER 11
Philip J. Cook, Mark H. Moore, and Anthony A. Braga

GUN CONTROL

Acknowledgments: this chapter has been much improved by suggestions from a number of people, including Mark Duggan, Dennis Henigan, James Jacobs, Jens Lugwig, Eric Monkkonen, Jeremy Travis, and Franklin Zimring.

Notes

1. Kleck (1991: appendix 2) offers another explanation, that the true prevalence trended upward during the past couple of decades, but that survey respondents have become increasingly reluctant to admit to gun ownership during this period. We favor the explanation offered in the text because it is supported by the survey evidence on the number of guns per household, and it makes sense given the growth in household disposable income during this period.

2. It should be kept in mind that these patterns are based on surveys and are subject to potential biases induced by the sensitivity of the topic and the difficulty of contacting a representative sample of young urban males.

3. This survey is conducted annually by the Fish and Wildlife Service of the U.S. Department of the Interior.

4. Much has been made of the unintentional firearm deaths of children; but, tragic as such cases are, it should be noted they are quite rare. Between 1985 and 1990 the annual average number of deaths for children less than ten years old was ninety-four (Fingerhut 1993).

5. On the other hand, the demography of gun suicide looks much more like that of gun sports, with victims coming disproportionately from the ranks of older white males.

6. The NCVS may lead to a modest underestimate of the self-defense uses of guns. It only provides respondents an opportunity to say that they used a gun in self-defense if they first say that they were the victims of an assault, robbery, rape, or other. Respondents may fail to report instances in which they used a gun to scare off a person who intended to steal something from them or attack them, simply because they would not consider themselves as "victims" in that instance. For a further discussion, see Smith (1997).

7. It is, after all, a tautology.

8. Kleck, like Wright, Rossi, and Daly (1983), claims that Zimring and others have not succeeded in demonstrating that guns are more lethal than knives, but accept with confidence the claim that long guns are more lethal than handguns. See Cook (1991) for a discussion of this paradox.

9. It does appear that in jurisdictions that have banned or strictly limited private possession of handguns, such as Chicago, Washington, D.C., Massachusetts, and Canada, it remains true that most gun crimes are still committed with handguns.

10. The source is unpublished data provided by the Bureau of Justice Statistics. See Cook (1991) for details.

11. The authors of the case-control study of homicide discuss the possibility that their results are due in part to reverse causation, noting that in a limited number of cases, people may have acquired a gun in response to a specific threat which eventually led to their murder. They also note that both gun ownership and homicide may be influenced by a third, unidentified factor (Kellermann et al. 1993, p. 1089). From those characteristics that were observed in this study, it is clear that the victims differed from the controls in a number of ways that may have contributed to the likelihood that there was a gun in the house. In comparison with their controls, the cases or the people they lived with were more likely to have a criminal record, to use illicit drugs, and to have a drinking problem. Cummings et al. (1997) report a similar study with an arguably more reliable measure of whether there was a gun in the house (administrative-record data); their findings comport with Kellermann's.

12. Kleck and Patterson (1993) assert that the intercity differences in the prevalence of gun ownership are influenced by crime rates. While this may explain some small part of the variance, it could not reasonably be considered the dominant explanation. For one thing, the vast majority of gun owners in the United States are sportsmen, for whom self-defense is a secondary purpose at most.

13. A recent comparison of victim survey estimates found that the U.S. robbery rate was substantially higher than that of England, Germany, Hungary, Hong Kong, Scotland, and Switzerland. On the other hand, Canada's robbery rate was nearly twice as high as that of the United States (Block 1993).

14. They computed weighted least squares estimates, where the weights were proportionate to the population of the county.

15. Lott and Mustard do report the results of two-stage least squares estimates that are intended to accommodate the problem of endogeneity. The results are rather bizarre. See Ludwig (2000).

16. The notable exception is gender. Male victims predominate in both homicide and suicide.

17. For a highly critical review of the public health literature on firearms and homicide, see Blackman (1997).

18. This is true not just for law-abiding citizens but is felt even more keenly by drug dealers and other criminals who are frequently threatened by the bad company they keep (Wright and Rossi 1994).

19. Jefferson to Peter Carr, 19 August 1785, quoted in Kates (1992: 96).

20. Bellesiles (2000) argues that the arming of American households did not begin in earnest until 40 or 50 years after ratification of the U.S. Constitution. At the time the Second Amendment was being debated, guns were expensive, unreliable, and rare. See Monkkonen (2000) for further evidence on gun ownership in the nineteenth century.

21. William Van Alstyne (1994) argues that the Second Amendment has generated almost no useful body of law to date, substantially because of the Supreme Court's inertia on this subject. In his view, Second Amendment law is currently as undeveloped as First Amendment law was up until Holmes and Brandeis began taking it seriously in a series of opinions in the 1920s.

22. The idea that citizens have responsibility for their own self-defense is now widely embraced by police executives, and is central to the strategy known as "community policing," which seeks to establish a close working partnership between the police and the community. But the emphasis in this approach is on community-building activities such as the formation of block watches, groups, or neighborhood patrols, rather than on individual armaments.

23. The McClure-Volkmer Amendment of 1986 eased the restriction on out-of-state purchases of rifles and shotguns. Such purchases are now legal as long as they comply with the regulations of both the buyer's state of residence and the state in which the sale occurs.

24. An important loophole allowed the import of parts of handguns that could not meet the "sporting purposes" test of the Gun Control Act. This loophole was closed by the McClure-Volkmer Amendment of 1986.

25. There is good evidence on other unsafe behaviors by youth. In particular, youthful consumption of cigarettes and beer has been shown to be highly responsive to price. It should be noted that there is a possibility that higher prices of guns will stimulate gun theft somewhat; if so, that might have the good effect of encouraging owners to store their guns more securely.

26. While federal law does not prohibit gun possession by youth, a number of states have placed limits on when youth can carry guns in public.

27. An example of this restrictive approach was until quite recently embodied in the North Carolina pistol permit requirement: permit applicants were required to satisfy their sheriff that they were of "good moral character" and needed the gun to defend their homes.

28. One distinction may be deemed important here. Driver's licenses are required only for operating a vehicle on the public highways, and not on one's own land. By analogy, a licensing requirement for guns could be limited to those who wish to carry the gun in public.

29. The term "secondary market" was coined by Cook, Molliconi, and Cole (1995), and refers to transactions that do not involve a federally licensed dealer.

30. Marvell and Moody (1995) find that such policies have no discernible effect.

References

(ATF). Bureau of Alcohol, Tobacco, and Firearms. 1997. *Crime Gun Trace Analysis Reports: The Illegal Youth Firearms Market in 17 Communities.* Washington, D.C.: U.S. Department of the Treasury.

————. 2000a. *Commerce in Firearms in the United States.* Washington, D.C.: U.S. Department of the Treasury.

————. 2000b. *Following the Gun: Enforcing Federal Laws Against Firearms Traffickers.* Washington, D.C.: U.S. Department of the Treasury.

Ayres, Ian and John Donahue. 2000. *American Law and Economics Review.*

Bellesiles, Michael A. 2000. *Arming America: The Origins of a National Gun Culture.* New York: Knopf.

Black, Donald and Daniel Nagin. 1998. "Do 'Right-to-Carry' Laws Deter Violent Crime?" *Journal of Legal Studies* 26:209–20.

Blackman, Paul H. 1997. "A Critique of the Epidemiologic Study of Firearms and Homicide." *Homicide Studies* 1:169–89.

Block, Richard. 1993. "A Cross-Section Comparison of the Victims of Crime: Victim Surveys of Twelve Countries." *International Review of Criminology* 2:183–207.

Bonnie, Richard J., Carolyn E. Fulco, and Catharyn T. Liverman, eds. 1999. *Reducing the Burden of Injury.* Washington, D.C.: National Academy Press.

Braga, Anthony A., David M. Kennedy, Anne M. Piehl, and Elin J. Waring. 2001. *The Boston Gun Project: Impact Evaluation Findings.* Research Report. Washington, D.C.: National Institute of Justice, U.S. Department of Justice.

Bureau of Justice Statistics. 1999. *Presale Handgun Checks, the Brady Interim Period, 1994–1998.* Washington, D.C.: Bureau of Justice Statistics, U.S. Department of Justice.

————. 2000. *Criminal Victimization in the United States, 1998.* Washington, D.C.: Bureau of Justice Statistics, U.S. Department of Justice.

Clotfelter, Charles T. 1993. "The Private Life of Public Economics." *Southern Economic Journal* 59 (4):579–96.

Coleman, Veronica, Walter Holton, K. Olson, S. Robinson, and S. Stewart, 2000. "Using Knowledge and Teamwork to Reduce Crime." *National Institute of Justice Journal* October:16–23.

Conklin, John E. 1972. *Robbery and the Criminal Justice System.* Philadelphia: Lippincott.

Cook, Philip J. 1976. "A Strategic Choice Analysis of Robbery." In *Sample Surveys of the Victims of Crimes,* ed. Wesley Skogan. Cambridge, Mass.: Ballinger.

————. 1979. "The Effect of Gun Availability on Robbery and Robbery Murder: A Cross-Section Study of Fifty Cities." *Policy Studies Review Annual* 3. Beverly Hills: Sage.

————. 1980. "Reducing Injury and Death Rates in Robbery." *Policy Analysis* Winter:21–45.

————. 1981. "The Effect of Gun Availability on Violent Crime Patterns." *Annals of the American Academy of Political and Social Science* 455:63–79.

————. 1985. "The Case of the Missing Victims: Gunshot Woundings in the National Crime Survey." *Journal of Quantitative Criminology* 1:91–102.

————. 1986. "The Relationship between Victim Resistance and Injury in Noncommerical Robbery." *Journal of Legal Studies* 15 (1):405–16.

————. 1987. "Robbery Violence." *Journal of Criminal Law and Criminology* 78:357–76.

————. 1991. "The Technology of Personal Violence." In *Crime and Justice: A Review of Research*, ed. Michael Tonry, vol. 14. Chicago: University of Chicago Press.

Cook, Philip J. and Anthony Braga. 2000. "The Use and Abuse of Firearms Trace Data," Program in Criminal Justice Policy and Management working paper series; Cambridge, Mass.: Kennedy School of Government, Harvard University.

Cook, Philip J. and James Leitzel. 1996. "Perversity, Futility, Jeopardy: An Economic Analysis of the Attack on Gun Control." *Law and Contemporary Problems* 59:91-118.

Cook, Philip J. and Jens Ludwig. 1996. *Guns in America: Results of a Comprehensive National Survey on Firearms Ownership and Use.* Washington, D.C.: Police Foundation.

————. 2000. *Gun Violence: The Real Costs.* New York: Oxford University Press.

Cook, Philip J., Jens Ludwig, and David Hemenway. 1997. "The Gun Debate's New Mythical Number: How Many Defensive Gun Uses per Year?" *Journal of Policy Analysis and Management* 16:463–69.

Cook, Philip J., Stephanie Molliconi, and Thomas Cole. 1995. "Regulating Gun Markets." *Journal of Criminal Law and Criminology* 86:59–92.

Cummings, P., T. D. Koepsell, D.C. Grossman et al. 1997. "The Association between the Purchase of a Handgun and Homicide or Suicide." *American Journal of Public Health.* 87:974–78.

Decker, Scott H., Susan Pennell, and A. Caldwell. 1997. *Illegal Firearms: Access and Use by Arrestees.* Washington, D.C.: National Institute of Justice, U.S. Department of Justice.

Deutsch, Stuart Jay. 1979. "Lies, Damn Lies, and Statistics: A Rejoinder to the Comment by Hay and McCleary." *Evaluation Quarterly* 3:315–28.

Duggan, Mark. In press. "More Guns, More Crime." *Journal of Political Economy.*

Ehrman, Keith A., and Dennis A. Henigan. 1989. "The Second Amendment in the Twentieth Century: Have You Seen Your Militia Lately?" *University of Dayton Law Review* 15(1), 5–58.

Fagan, Jeffrey, Franklin Zimring, and J. Kim. 1998. "Declining Homicide in New York City: A Tale of Two Trends." *Journal of Criminal Law and Criminology* 88: 1277–323.

Federal Bureau of Investigation. 1971–1999. *Crime in the United States: Uniform Crime Reports.* Washington, D.C.: U.S. Department of Justice.

Fingerhut, Lois A. 1993. "Firearm Mortality among Children, Youth, and Young Adults 1–34 Years of Age, Trends, and Current Status: United States, 1985–90." *Advance Data from Vital and Health Statistics.* No 231. Hyattsville, Md: National Center for Health Statistics.

Halbrook, Stephen P. 1986. "What the Framers Intended: A Linguistic Analysis of the Right to 'Bear Arms.'" *Law and Contemporary Problems* 49:151–62.

Hemenway, David. 1997. "The Myth of Millions of Self-Defense Gun Uses: An Explanation of Extreme Overestimates." *Chance,* 10:6–10.

————. In press. *Private Guns, Public Health.*

Henigan, Dennis A. 1991. "Arms, Anarchy and the Second Amendment" *Valparaiso University Law Review* 26(1):107-29.

Hood, M.V. and Grant W. Neeley. 2000. "Packin' in the Hood?: Examining Assumptions of Concealed-Handgun Research." *Social Science Quarterly* 81:523–537.

Jacobs, James B., and Kimberly A. Potter. 1995. "Keeping Guns out of the Wrong Hands: The Brady Law and the Limits of Regulation." *Journal of Criminal Law and Criminology* 86(1):101–30.

————. 1998. "Comprehensive Handgun Licensing & Registration: An Analysis & Critique of Brady II, Gun Control's Next (and Last?) Step" *Journal of Criminal Law and Criminology* 89:81–110.

Kairys, David. 2000. "The Governmental Handgun Cases and the Elements and Underlying Policies of Public Nuisance Law." *Connecticut Law Review* 32(4):1175–87.

Karlson, T. A., and S. W. Hargarten. 1997. *Reducing Firearms Injury and Death: A Public Health Sourcebook on Guns*. New Brunswick, N.J.: Rutgers University Press.

Kates, Don B., Jr. 1983. "Handgun Prohibition and the Original Meaning of the Second Amendment." *Michigan Law Review* 82(2):204–73.

———. 1992. "The Second Amendment and the Ideology of Self-Protection." *Constitutional Commentary* 9(1):87–104.

Kellermann, Arthur L., and Philip J. Cook. 1999. "Armed and Dangerous: Guns in American Homes." In *Lethal Imagination: Violence and Brutality in American History*, ed. M. A. Bellesiles. New York: New York University Press.

Kellermann, Arthur L., F. P. Rivara, N.B. Rushforth, J. G. Banton, D. T. Reay, J. T. Francisco, A.B. Locci, J. Prodzinski, B. B. Hackman, and G. Somes. 1993. "Gun Ownership as a Risk Factor for Homicide in the Home." *New England Journal of Medicine* 329 (7 October):1084–91.

Kellermann, Arthur L., F. P. Rivara, G. Somes, D. T. Reay, J. Francisco, J. G. Banton, J. Prodzinski, C. Fligner, and B. B. Hackman. 1992. "Suicide in the Home in Relation to Gun Ownership." *New England Journal of Medicine* 327 (August 13):467–72.

Kennedy, David M. 1997. "Pulling Levers: Chronic Offenders, High-Crime Settings, and a Theory of Prevention." *Valparaiso University Law Review* 31:449–484.

———. 1998. "Pulling Levers: Getting Deterrence Right." *National Institute of Justice Journal* July: 3–8.

Kennedy, David. M., and Anthony A. Braga. 1998. "Homicide in Minneapolis: Research for Problem Solving." *Homicide Studies* 2: 263–90.

Kennedy, David M., Anthony A. Braga, and Anne M. Piehl. 1997. "The (Un)Known Universe: Mapping Gangs and Gang Violence in Boston." In *Crime Mapping and Crime Prevention*, ed. David Weisburd and J. Thomas McEwen. New York: Criminal Justice Press.

Kennedy, David. M., Anne M. Piehl, and Anthony A. Braga. 1996a. "Gun Buy-Backs: Where Do We Stand and Where Do We Go?" In *Under Fire: Gun Buy-back, Exchanges, and Amnesty Programs*, ed. Martha Plotkin. Washington, D.C.: Police Executive Research Forum.

———. 1996b. "Youth Violence in Boston: Gun Markets, Serious Youth Offenders, and a Use-Reduction Strategy." *Law and Contemporary Problems* 59:147–96.

Killias, Martin. 1993. "Gun Ownership, Suicide, and Homicide: An International Perspective." In *Understanding Crime: Experiences of Crime and Crime Control*, edited by A. Del-Frate, U. Zvekic, and J. J. van Djik. Rome: United Nations Interregional Crime and Justice Research Institute.

Kleck, Gary. 1984. "Handgun-only Control: A Policy Disaster in the Making." In *Firearms and Violence: Issues of Public Policy*, ed. Don B. Kates, Jr. Cambridge, MA: Ballinger.

———. 1988. "Crime Control through the Private Use of Armed Force." *Social Problems* 35:1–22.

———. 1991. *Point Blank: Guns and Violence in America*. New York: Aldine de Gruyter.

Kleck, Gary, and Marc Gertz. 1995. "Armed Resistance to Crime: The Prevalence and Nature of Self-Defense with a Gun." *Journal of Criminal Law and Criminology* 86:150–87.

Kleck, Gary, and Karen McElrath. 1991. "The Effects of Weaponry on Human Violence." *Social Forces* 69:669–92.

Kleck, Gary, and E. Britt Patterson. 1993. "The Impact of Gun Control and Gun Ownership Levels on Violence Rates." *Journal of Quantitative Criminology* 9(3):249–87.

Koper, Christoper S., and Peter Reuter. 1996. "Suppressing Illegal Gun Markets: Lessons from Drug Enforcement." *Law and Contemporary Problems* 59:119–43.

Levitt, Steven D., and Sudhir Alladi Venkatesh. 2000 "An Economic Analysis of a Drug-Selling Gang's Finances." *Quarterly Journal of Economics* CXV(3):755–90.

Lott, John. 2000. *More Guns, Less Crime,* 2nd ed. Chicago: University of Chicago Press.

Lott, John, and David Mustard. 1997. "Crime, Deterrence, and the Right-to-Carry Concealed Handguns." *Journal of Legal Studies* 26:1–68.

Ludwig, Jens. 1998. "Concealed-Gun-Carrying Laws and Violent Crime: Evidence from State Panel Data. *International Review of Law and Economics* 18:239–54.

———. 2000. "Gun Self-Defense and Deterrence." *Crime and Justice: An Annual Review of Research*, Volume 27, ed. Michael Tonry. Chicago: University of Chicago Press.

Ludwig, Jens, and Philip J. Cook. 2000. "Homicide and Suicide Rates Associated with Implementation of the Brady Handgun Violence Prevention Act." *Journal of the American Medical Assn* 284(5):585–91.

McDowall, David, Colin Loftin, and Brian Wiersema. 1992a. "The Incidence of Civilian Defensive Firearm Use." Institute of Criminology and Criminal Justice, University of Maryland, College Park.

———. 1992b. "A Comparative Study of the Preventive Effects of Mandatory Sentencing Laws for Gun Crimes." *Journal of Criminal Law and Criminology* 83(2):378–94.

Marvell, Thomas, and Carlisle Moody. 1995. "The Impact of Enhanced Prison Terms for Felonies Committed with Guns." *Criminology* 33:247–281.

Monkkonen, Eric H. 2000. *Homicide in New York City.* Berkeley, Calif.: University of California Press.

Moore, Mark H. 1980. "Police and Weapons Offenses." *Annals of the American Academy of Political and Social Science* 452:22–32.

———. 1981. "Keeping Handguns from Criminal Offenders." *Annals of the American Academy of Political and Social Science* 455:92–109.

———. 1983. "The Bird in Hand: A Feasible Strategy for Gun Control." *Journal of Policy Analysis and Management* 2(2):185–95.

Moore, Mark H., Deborah Prothrow-Stith, Bernard Guyer, and Howard Spivak. 1994. "Violence and Intentional Injuries: Criminal Justice and Public Health Perspectives on an Urgent National Problem." In *Understanding and Preventing Violence, Vol. 4: Consequences and Control,* ed. Albert J. Reiss, Jr. and Jeffrey A. Roth. Washington, D.C.: National Academy Press.

Mullin, Wallace P. 2001. "Will Gun Buyback Programs Increase the Quantity of Guns?" *International Review of Law & Economics*, In press.

Pierce, Glenn L., and William Bowers. 1981. "The Bartley-Fox Gun Law's Short-Term Impact on Crime in Boston." *Annals of the American Academy of Political and Social Science* 455:120–37.

Pierce, Glenn L., LeBaron Briggs, and David Carlson. 1998. *National Report on Firearms Trace Analysis for 1996–1997.* Boston, Mass.: Center for Criminal Justice Policy Research, Northeastern University.

Polsby, Daniel D. 1993. "Equal Protection." *Reason* October:35–38.

———. 1994. "The False Promise of Gun Control." *The Atlantic Monthly* March:57–60.

Robinson, Krista D., Stephen Teret, Jon Vernick, and Daniel Webster. 1998. *Personalized Guns: Reducing Gun Deaths Through Design Changes.* Second Edition. Baltimore, Md: The Johns Hopkins Center for Gun Policy Research.

Robuck-Mangum, Gail. 1997. "Concealed Weapon Permit Holders in North Carolina: A Descriptive Study of Handgun-Carrying Behavior." M.Sc. Thesis, School of Public Health, University of North Carolina.

Romero, M., G. Wintemute, and J. Vernick. 1998. "Characteristics of a Gun Exchange Program, and an Assessment of Potential Benefits." *Injury Prevention* 4:206–10.

Rosenfeld, Richard. 1996. "Gun Buy-Backs: Crime Control or Community Mobilization?" In *Under Fire: Gun Buy-Back, Exchanges, and Amnesty Programs*, ed. Martha Plotkin. Washington, D.C.: Police Executive Research Forum.

Roth, Jeffrey A., and Christopher S. Koper. 1997. *Impact Evaluation of the Public Safety and Recreational Firearms Use Protection Act of 1994*. Washington, D.C.: The Urban Institute.

Saltzman, L.E., J.A. Mercy, P.W. O'Carroll, M.L. Rosenberg, and P.H. Rhodes. 1992. "Weapon Involvement and Injury Outcomes in Family and Intimate Assaults." *Journal of the American Medical Association* 267 (22):3043–47.

Sheley, Joseph F. and James D. Wright. 1995. *In the Line of Fire: Youth, Guns, and Violence in Urban America*. New York: Aldine de Gruyter.

Sherman, Lawrence. 2000. "Gun Carrying and Homicide Prevention." *Journal of the American Medical Association* 283(9) March 1:1193–95.

Sherman, Lawrence, James W. Shaw, and Dennis P. Rogan. 1995. *The Kansas City Gun Experiment*. Washington, D.C.: National Institute of Justice, U.S. Department of Justice.

Siebel, Brian J. 1999. "City Lawsuits Against the Gun Industry: A Roadmap for Reforming Gun Industry Misconduct" *Saint Louis University Public Law Review* 18(1):247–90.

Skogan, Wesley. 1978. "Weapons Use in Robbery: Patterns and Policy Implications." Center for Urban Affairs, Northwestern University. Unpublished.

Smith, M. Dwayne. 1996. "Sources of Firearms Acquisition Among a Sample of Inner-City Youths: Research Results and Policy Implications." *Journal of Criminal Justice* 24:361–67.

Smith, Tom W. 1997. "A Call for a Truce in the DGU War." *Journal of Criminal Law and Criminology* 87:1462–69.

———. 2000. "1999 National Gun Policy Survey of the National Opinion Research Center: Research Findings." University of Chicago, NORC. Unpublished.

Snyder, Jeffrey R. 1993. "A Nation of Cowards." *The Public Interest* 113 (Fall):40–55.

Teret, Stephen P. 1986. "Litigating for the Public's Health." *American Journal of Public Health* 76(8):1027–29.

Teret, Stephen P., Susan DeFrancesco, Stephen W. Hargarten, and K. Robinson. 1998. "Making Guns Safer." *Issues in Science and Technology* Summer:37–40.

Teret, Stephen, Daniel Webster, J. Vernick, T. Smith, Deborah Leff, Garen Wintemute, Philip Cook, Darnell Hawkins, Arthur Kellerman, S. Sorenson, and S. DeFrancesco. 1998. "Support for New Policies to Regulate Firearms: Results of Two National Surveys. *New England Journal of Medicine* 339:813–18.

Teret, Stephen P. and Garen J. Wintemute. 1993. "Policies to Prevent Firearm Injuries." *Health Affairs* Winter:96–108.

U.S. Department of the Interior. 1991. *Survey of Fishing, Hunting, and Wild-life Associated Recreation*. Washington, D.C.: U.S. Government Printing Office.

Van Alstyne, William. 1994. "The Second Amendment and the Personal Right to Arms." *Duke Law Journal* 43:1236–55.

Vernick, Jon S., and Stephen P. Teret. 1999. "New Courtroom Strategies Regarding Firearms: Tort Litigation Against Firearm Manufacturers and Constitutional Challenges to Gun Laws." *Houston Law Review* 36(5):1713–54.

Vernick, Jon S., Daniel W. Webster, and Lisa M. Hepburn. 1999. "Effects of Maryland's Law Banning Saturday Night Special Handguns on Crime Guns." *Injury Prevention* 5:259–63.

Violence Policy Center. 1992. *More Gun Dealers Than Gas Stations.* Washington, D.C.

Wachtel, Julius. 1998. "Sources of Crime Guns in Los Angeles, California" *Policing: An International Journal of Police Strategies and Management* 21(2):220–39.

Weil, David, and R. Knox. 1996. "Effects of Limiting Handgun Purchases on Interstate Transfers of Firearms." *Journal of the American Medical Association* 275:1759–61.

Wills, Garry. 1995. "To Keep and Bear Arms." *New York Review of Books* September 21.

Wilson, James Q. 1994. "Just Take Their Guns Away: Forget About Gun Control." *New York Times Magazine* March 20:46–47.

Wintemute, Garen J. 1996. "The Relationship Between Firearm Design and Firearm Violence: Handguns in the 1990s." *Journal of the American Medical Assn.* 275:1749–53.

———. 2000a."Relationship between Illegal Use of Handguns and Handgun Sales Volume." *Journal of the American Medical Assn.* 284:566–67.

———. 2000b. "Guns and Gun Violence." In *The Crime Drop in America,* ed. Alfred Blumstein and Joel Wallman. New York: Cambridge University Press.

Wintemute, Garen J., Mona Wright, Carrie Parham, Christina Drake, and James Beaumont. 1999. "Denial of Handgun Purchase: A Description of the Affected Population and a Controlled Study of Their Handgun Preferences." *Journal of Criminal Justice* 27:21–31.

Wolfgang, Marvin E. 1958. *Patterns in Criminal Homicide.* Philadelphia: University of Pennsylvania.

Wright, James D. 1981. "Public Opinion and Gun Control: A Comparison of Results from Two Recent National Surveys." *Annals of the American Academy of Political and Social Science* 455:24–39.

———. 1995. "Ten Essential Observations on Guns in America." *Society* March/April:63–68.

Wright, James D., and Peter H. Rossi. 1994. *Armed and Considered Dangerous: A Survey of Felons and Their Firearms,* 2nd ed. Hawthorne, New York: Aldine de Gruyter.

Wright, James D., Peter H. Rossi, and Kathleen Daly. 1983. *Under the Gun: Weapons, Crime, and Violence in America.* Hawthorne, New York: Aldine de Gruyter.

Wright, James D., Joseph Sheley, and M. Dwayne Smith. 1992. "Kids, Guns, and Killing Fields." *Society* November/December:84–89.

Wright, M., G. Wintemute, and F. Rivara. 1999. "The Effectiveness of Denial of Handgun Purchase to Persons Believed to be at High Risk for Firearms Violence." *American Journal of Public Health* 89:88–90.

Zimring, Franklin E. 1968. "Is Gun Control Likely to Reduce Violent Killings?" *University of Chicago Law Review* 35:21–37.

———. 1972. "The Medium Is the Message: Firearm Caliber as a Determinant of Death from Assault." *Journal of Legal Studies* 35:21–37.

———. 1976. "Street Crime and New Guns: Some Implications for Firearms Control." *Journal of Criminal Justice* 4:95–107.

———. 1991. "Firearms, Violence, and Public Policy." *Scientific American* 265(5):48–54.

Zimring, Franklin E., and Gordon Hawkins. 1997. *Crime is Not the Problem: Lethal Violence in the United States.* New York and London: Oxford University Press.

CHAPTER 12
David A. Boyum and Mark A. R. Kleiman

SUBSTANCE ABUSE POLICY
FROM A CRIME-CONTROL PERSPECTIVE

Notes

1. "Predatory" in the analytic sense that victims of theft and assault flee from their victimizers, while victims of drug abuse seek out their dealers; no moral distinction is intended.

2. When a reporter approached Coolidge as he came out of church and asked him what the preacher had spoken about, "Sin," was Coolidge's answer. When the reporter asked what the preacher had said about sin, Silent Cal replied: "He was against it."

References

Anderson, Elijah. 1994. "The Code of the Streets." *The Atlantic Monthly* 273, no. 5 May: 80–94.

———. 1999. *Code of the Street: Decency, Violence, and the Moral Life of the Inner City.* New York: W. W. Norton.

Anglin, M. Douglas, and Yih-Ing Hser. 1990. "Treatment of Drug Abuse." In *Drugs and Crime*, ed. Michael H. Tonry and James Q. Wilson, 393–460. Vol. 13 of *Crime and Justice: A Review of Research*. Chicago: University of Chicago Press.

Anglin, M. Douglas, D. Longshore, and S. Turner. 1999. "Treatment Alternatives to Street Crime." *Criminal Justice and Behavior* 26, no. 2:168–95.

Anglin, M. Douglas, and George Speckart. 1986. "Narcotics Use, Property Crime, and Dealing: Structural Dynamics Across the Addiction Career." *Journal of Quantitative Criminology* 2:355–75.

———. 1988. "Narcotics Use and Crime: A Multisample, Multimethod Analysis." *Criminology* 26:197–233.

Ball, John C. 1986. "The Hyper-criminal Opiate Addict." In *Crime Rates and Drug Abusing Offenders*, ed. Bruce D. Johnson and Eric Wish. New York: Narcotic and Drug Research.

Ball, John C., Lawrence Rosen, John A. Flueck, and David N. Nurco. 1981. "The Criminality of Heroin Addicts: When Addicted and When Off Opiates." In *The Drugs-Crime Connection*, ed. James A. Inciardi, 39–65. Beverly Hills: Sage.

———. 1982. "Lifetime Criminality of Heroin Addicts in the United States." *Journal of Drug Issues* 12:225–39.

Ball, John C., John W. Shaffer, and David N. Nurco. 1983. "The Day-to-Day Criminality of Heroin Addicts in Baltimore: A Study in the Continuity of Offense Rates." *Drug and Alcohol Dependence* 12:119–42.

Behrens, Doris A., Jonathan P. Caulkins, Gernot Tragler, and Gustav Feichtinger. 2000. "Optimal Control of Drug Epidemics: Prevent and Treat—But Not at the Same Time." *Management Science* 46, no. 3:333–47.

Bejerot, Nils. 1970. "A Comparison of the Effects of Cocaine and Synthetic Central Stimulants." *British Journal of Addiction* 65:35–37.

Block, Carolyn Rebecca, and Richard Block. 1993. *Street Gang Crime in Chicago*. National Institute of Justice, Research in Brief. Washington, D.C.: United States Department of Justice, December.

Blumstein, Alfred. 1993. "Making Rationality Relevant: The American Society of Criminology 1992 Presidential Address." *Criminology* 31, no. 1:1–16.

BOTEC Analysis Corporation. 1990. *Program Evaluation: Santa Cruz Street Drug Reduction Program.* Cambridge, Mass.: BOTEC Analysis.

Boyum, David. 1992. Reflections on Economic Theory and Drug Enforcement. Ph.D. diss., Harvard University.

———. 1998. "The Distributive Politics of Drug Policy." *Drug Policy Analysis Bulletin* No. 4.

Brown, George F., and Lester P. Silverman. 1974. "The Retail Price of Heroin: Estimation and Applications." *Journal of the American Statistical Association* 69:595–606.

Brown, Joel H., and Ita G. G. Kreft. 1998. "Zero Effects of Drug Prevention Programs: Issues and Solutions." *Evaluation Review* 22, no. 1 (February):1–14.

Brownsberger, William N. 2000. "Race Matters: Disproportionality of Incarceration for Drug Dealing in Massachusetts." *Journal of Drug Issues* 30, no. 2:345–74.

———. 2001. "Limits on the Role of Testing and Sanctions: A Comment on Coerced Abstinence." In *Drug Addiction and Drug Policy*, ed. Philip B. Heymann and William N. Brownsberger. Cambridge, Mass.: Harvard University Press.

Brownsberger, William N., and Anne M. Piehl. 1997. "Profile of Anti-Drug Law Enforcement in Urban Poverty Areas in Massachusetts." Cambridge, Mass.: Harvard Medical School, Division on Addictions.

Caulkins, Jonathan P. 1996. "Estimating the Elasticities and Cross Elasticities of Demand for Cocaine and Heroin." Carnegie Mellon University, Heinz School Working Paper 95–113.

Caulkins, Jonathan, Peter Rydell, Susan Everingham, James Chiesa, and Shawn Bushway. 1998. *An Ounce of Prevention, a Pound of Uncertainty.* Santa Monica, Calif.: RAND.

Cavanagh, David P., and Mark A. R. Kleiman. 1990. *A Cost-Benefit Analysis of Prison Cell Construction and Alternative Sanctions.* Cambridge, Mass.: BOTEC Analysis.

Chaiken, Jan M., and Marcia R. Chaiken. 1990. "Drugs and Predatory Crime." In *Drugs and Crime*, vol. 13 of *Crime and Justice: A Review of Research*, ed. Michael H. Tonry and James Q. Wilson, 203–39. Chicago: University of Chicago Press.

Clayton, Richard R., and Harwin L. Voss. 1981. *Young Men and Drugs in Manhattan: A Causal Analysis.* NIDA Research Monograph No. 39. Rockville, Md.: Alcohol, Drug Abuse, and Mental Health Administration.

Cohen, Jacqueline, and Daniel S. Nagin. 1993. "Criminal Careers of Drug Offenders: A Comparison." Paper presented at the annual meeting of the American Society of Criminology, Phoenix, 29 October.

Collins, James J., Robert L. Hubbard, and J. Valley Rachal. 1985. "Expensive Drug Use and Illegal Income: A Test of Explanatory Hypotheses." *Criminology* 23:743–64.

Cook, Philip J. 1981. "Research in Criminal Deterrence: Laying the Groundwork for the Second Decade." In *Crime and Justice: A Review of Research*, vol. 2, ed. Michael H. Tonry and Norval Morris, 211–68. Chicago: University of Chicago Press.

———. 1986. "The Demand and Supply of Criminal Opportunities." In *Crime and Justice: A Review of Research*, vol. 7, ed. Michael H. Tonry and Norval Morris, 1–27. Chicago: University of Chicago Press.

Cook, Philip J., and George Tauchen. 1982. "The Effect of Liquor Taxes on Heavy Drinking." *Bell Journal of Economics* 13.

Cork, Daniel. 1999. "Examining Space-Time Interaction in City-Level Homicide Data: Crack Markets and the Diffusion of Guns Among Youth." *Journal of Quantitative Criminology* 15:379–406.

Dewey, W. L. 1986. "Cannabinoid Pharmacology." *Pharmacology Review* 38:151–78.

DiNardo, John. 1991. "Are Marijuana and Alcohol Substitutes? The Effect of State Drinking Age Laws on the Marijuana Consumption of High School Seniors." Santa Monica, Calif.: RAND.

Dukes, R. L., J. B. Ullman, J. A. Stein. 1996. "Three-Year Follow-up of Drug Abuse Resistance Education (D.A.R.E)." *Evaluation Review*, 20, no. 1 (February):49–66.

DuPont, Robert L., and Mark H. Greene. 1973. "The Dynamics of a Heroin Addiction Epidemic." *Science* 181:716–22.

DuPont, Robert L., and Eric D. Wish. 1992. "Operation Tripwire Revisited." *Annals of the American Academy of Political and Social Science* 521 (May):91–111.

Fagan, Jeffrey. 1990. "Intoxication and Aggression." In *Drugs and Crime*, vol. 13 of *Crime and Justice: A Review of Research*, ed. Michael Tonry and James Q. Wilson, 241–320. Chicago: University of Chicago Press.

———. 1992. "Drug Selling and Licit Income in Distressed Neighborhoods: The Economic Lives of Street-Level Drug Users and Dealers." In *Drugs, Crime, and Social Isolation*, ed. Adele V. Harrell and George E. Peterson, 99–146. Washington, D.C.: Urban Institute Press.

Ferguson, Ronald. 1993. Personal communication with the authors. 14 December.

Gallegher, J. J., 1996. "Project Sentry Final Program Report." Lansing, Mich.: Project Sentry.

Gallegher, J. J., 1997. "Project Sentry Quarterly Program Report." Lansing, Mich.: Project Sentry.

Gersh, Debra. 1988. "Some Newspapers Refuse to Run Anti-drug Ad, Object to Photo of a Man with a Gun Pointed Up His Nose." *Editor and Publisher* 23 January: 17.

Gerstein, Dean R., and Henrick J. Harwood, eds. 1990. *Treating Drug Problems*, vol. 1. Washington, D.C.: National Academy Press.

Gerstein, D. R., R. A. Johnson, H. J. Harwood, K. Fountain, N. Suter, and K. Malloy, 1994. *Evaluating Recovery Services: The California Drug and Alcohol Treatment Assessment (CALDATA) General Report*. Sacramento, Calif.: California Department of Alcohol and Drug Programs.

Goldman, Fred. 1976. "Drug Markets and Addict Consumption Behavior." In *Drug Use and Crime: Report of the Panel on Drug Use and Criminal Behavior*, ed. Robert Shellow, 273–96. Washington, D.C.: National Technical Information Service.

———. 1977. "Narcotics Users, Narcotics Prices, and Criminal Activity: An Economic Analysis." In *The Epidemiology of Heroin and Other Narcotics*, ed. J. Rittenhouse, 30–36. NIDA Research Monograph Series, No. 16. Rockville, Md.: National Institute on Drug Abuse.

———. 1981. "Drug Abuse, Crime and Economics: The Dismal Limits of Social Choice." In *The Drugs-Crime Connection*, ed. James A. Inciardi, 155–82. Beverly Hills: Sage.

Goldstein, Paul J. 1985. "The Drugs/Violence Nexus: A Tripartite Conceptual Framework." *Journal of Drug Issues* 15, no. 4):493–506.

Goldstein, Paul J., and Henry H. Brownstein. 1987. *Drug Related Crime Analysis: Homicide*. Report to the National Institute of Justice, Drugs, Alcohol, and Crime Program. Washington, D.C.: United States Department of Justice, July.

Goldstein, Paul J., Henry H. Brownstein, Patrick J. Ryan, and Patricia A. Bellucci. 1990. "Crack and Homicide in New York City, 1988: A Conceptually Based Event Analysis." *Contemporary Drug Problems* 16, no. 4: 651–87.

Golub, Andrew Lang, and Bruce D. Johnson. 1997. "Crack's Decline: Some Surprises Across U.S. Cities." *Research in Brief*. Washington, D.C.: National Institute of Justice.

Grinspoon, Lester, and James B. Bakalar. 1985. *Cocaine: A Drug and Its Social Evolution*, rev. ed. New York: Basic Books.

Haaga, John, and Peter Reuter. 1995. "Prevention: The (Lauded) Orphan of Drug Policy." In *Handbook on Drug Abuse Prevention*, ed. Robert Coombs and Douglas Ziedonis, 3–17. Englewood Cliffs, N.J.: Allyn and Bacon.

Harrell, A., S. Cavanagh, and J. Roman. 1999. *Findings from the Evaluation of the D.C. Superior Court Drug Intervention Program*. Washington, D.C.: The Urban Institute.

Harrell, A., A. Hirst, and O. Mitchell. 2000. *Implementing System-wide Interventions for Drug-Involved Offenders in Birmingham, Alabama: Evaluation of the Breaking the Cycle Demonstration*. Report submitted to the National Institute of Justice, Washington, D.C.: The Urban Institute.

Hamid, Ansley. 1990. "The Political Economy of Crack-Related Violence." *Contemporary Drug Problems* 17 (Spring):31–78.

Heyman, Eugene. 2001. "Is Substance Abuse a Chronic, Relapsing Condition?" In *Drug Addiction and Drug Policy*, ed. Philip B. Heymann and William N. Brownsberger. Cambridge, Mass.: Harvard University Press.

Heymann, Philip. 1994. Personal communication with Mark Kleiman.

Higgins, Stephen. 1997. "Applying Behavioral Economics to the Challenge of Reducing Cocaine Abuse." In *The Economic Analysis of Substance Use and Abuse: An Integration of Econometric and Behavioral Economic Research*, ed. Frank J. Chaloupka, Warren K. Bickel, Michael Grossman, and Henry Saffer. Cambridge, Mass.: National Bureau of Economic Research.

Higgins, S. T., A. J. Budney, W. K. Bickel, F. E. Foerg, R. Donham, and G. J. Badger. 1994. "Incentives Improve Outcome in Outpatient Behavioral Treatment of Cocaine Dependence." *Archives of General Psychiatry*, 51: 568–76.

Hser, Yih-Ing, Douglas Longshore, and M. Douglas Anglin. 1994. "Prevalence of Drug Use Among Criminal Offender Populations: Implications for Control, Treatment, and Policy." In *Drugs and Crime: Evaluating Public Policy Initiatives*, ed. Doris Layton McKenzie and Craig D. Uchida, 18–41. Thousand Oaks, Calif.: Sage.

Horgan, John. 1990. "An Antidrug Message Gets Its Facts Wrong." *Scientific American no. 262* (May):36.

Hubbard, Robert L., Mary Ellen Marsden, J. Valley Rachal, Hendrick J. Harwood, Elizabeth R. Cavanaugh, and Harold M. Ginzburg. 1989. *Drug Abuse Treatment: A National Study of Effectiveness*. Chapel Hill: University of North Carolina Press.

Hyatt, Raymond, and William Rhodes. 1992. *Price and Purity of Cocaine: The Relationship to Emergency Room Visits and Deaths, and to Drug Use Among Arrestees*. Report prepared for the Office of National Drug Control Policy, Washington, D.C.

Inciardi, James A. 1979. "Heroin Use and Street Crime." *Crime and Delinquency* 25 (July): 335–46.

———. 1980. "Youth, Drugs, and Street Crime." In *Drugs and the Youth Culture*, ed. Frank R. Scarpitti and Susan K. Datesman, 175–203. Beverly Hills: Sage.

Inciardi, James A., Ruth Horowitz, and Anne E. Pottieger. 1993. *Street Kids, Street Drugs, Street Crime: An Examination of Drug Use and Serious Delinquency in Miami*. Belmont, Calif.: Wadsworth.

Inciardi, James A., and Anne E. Pottieger. 1991. "Kids, Crack, and Crime." *Journal of Drug Issues* 21 (Spring):257–70.

Johnson, Bruce D., Kevin Anderson, and Eric D. Wish. 1988. "A Day in the Life of 105 Drug Addicts and Abusers: Crimes Committed and How the Money Was Spent." *Sociology and Social Research* 72, no. 3:185–91.

Johnson, Bruce D., Paul J. Goldstein, Edward Preble, James Schmeidler, Douglas S. Lipton, Barry Spunt, and Thomas Miller. 1985. *Taking Care of Business: The Economics of Crime by Heroin Users.* Lexington, Mass.: Lexington Books.

Kaplan, John. 1971. *Marijuana: The New Prohibition.* New York, NY: The World Publishing Company.

Kennedy, David M. 1993. "Closing the Market: Controlling the Drug Trade in Tampa, Florida." National Institute of Justice Program Focus, NCJ 139963. Washington, D.C.: U.S. Department of Justice, April.

———. 1994. "Can We Keep Guns Away From Kids?" *The American Prospect* 5 (Summer): 74–80.

———. 1997. "Pulling Levers: Chronic Offenders, High-Crime Settings, and a Theory of Prevention." *Valparaiso University Law Review* 31, no. 2 (May).

Kleiman, Mark A. R. 1992a. *Against Excess: Drug Policy for Results.* New York: Basic Books.

———. 1992b. "Neither Prohibition nor Legalization: Grudging Toleration in Drug Control Policy." *Dædalus* 12, no. 3 (Summer):53–83.

———. 1993. "Enforcement Swamping: A Positive-Feedback Mechanism in Rates of Illicit Activity." *Mathematical and Computer Modeling* 17, no. 2 (January):65–75.

———. 1997a. "The Problem of Replacement and the Logic of Drug Law Enforcement." *Drug Policy Analysis Bulletin* no. 3.

———. 1997b. "Reducing the Prevalence of Cocaine and Heroin Dealing Among Adolescents." *Valparaiso University Law Review,* 31, no. 2 (May).

———. 1997c. "Coerced Abstinence: A Neo-Paternalistic Drug Policy Initiative." In *The New Paternalism,* ed. Lawrence A. Mead. Washington, D.C.: Brookings Institution.

———. 1999a. "Getting Deterrence Right: Applying Tipping Models and Behavioral Economics to the Problems of Crime Control." In *Perspectives on Crime and Justice: 1998–1999.* Washington, D.C.: National Institute of Justice.

———. 2001. "Controlling Drug Use and Crime Among Drug-Involved Offenders: Testing, Sanctions, and Treatment." In *Drug Addiction and Drug Policy,* ed. Philip B. Heymann and William N. Brownsberger. Cambridge, Mass.: Harvard University Press.

Kleiman, Mark A. R., Christopher E. Putala, Rebecca M. Young, and David P. Cavanagh. 1988. "Heroin Crackdowns in Two Massachusetts Cities." Report prepared for the Office of the District Attorney for the Eastern District, Commonwealth of Massachusetts, Hon. Kevin M. Burke, under National Institute of Justice Grant no. 85-JJ-CX-0027.

Kleiman, Mark A.R., and Sally Satel, 1997. "Rebalancing the Drug Budget: A Shadow Play," Drug Policy Analysis Bulletin #1 (January).

Kushner, Jeffrey. 1993. "Salient and Consistent Sanctions: Oregon's Key to Reducing Drug Use." *Treatment Improvement Exchange Communiqué.* Washington, D.C.: Center for Substance Abuse Treatment, Spring.

Lipton, D. S. 1994. "The Correctional Opportunity: Pathways to Drug Treatment for Offenders." *Journal of Drug Issues* 24, no. 1–2:331–48.

MacCoun, Robert, and Peter Reuter. 2001. *Drug War Heresies: Learning from Other Vices, Times and Places.* Cambridge: Cambridge University Press.

MacIntyre, Alasdair. 1981. *After Virtue.* Notre Dame, Ind.: University of Notre Dame Press.

Manning, Willard G., Emmet B. Keeler, Joseph P. Newhouse, Elizabeth M. Sloss, and Jeffrey M. Wasserman. 1989. "The Taxes of Sin: Do Smokers and Drinkers Pay Their Way?" *Journal of the American Medical Association* 261:1604–09.

McBride, Duane C., and Clyde B. McCoy. 1982. "Crime and Drugs: The Issues and the Literature." *Journal of Drug Issues* 12 (Spring):137–52.

Martin, W. R. 1983. "Pharmacology of Opioids." *Pharmacology Review* 35:283–323.

Mill, John Stuart. [1859] 1989. *On Liberty.* Reprint, Cambridge: Cambridge University Press.

Model, Karyn. 1991. The Effect of Marijuana Decriminalization on Hospital Emergency Room Drug Episodes: 1975–1987. Department of Economics, Harvard University. Unpublished paper.

———. 1994. Personal communication with Mark Kleiman.

Moore, Mark H. 1973. "Policies to Achieve Discrimination on the Effective Price of Heroin." *American Economic Review* 63:270–77.

———. 1990. *An Analytic View of Drug Control Policies.* Program on Criminal Justice Policy and Management, John F. Kennedy School of Government, working paper no. 90-01-19. Cambridge, Mass.: Harvard University.

———. 1991. "Drugs, the Criminal Law, and the Administration of Justice." *The Milbank Quarterly* 69, no. 4:529–60.

Nadelman, Ethan A. 1988. "The Case for Legalization." *The Public Interest* 92 (Summer): 3–31.

National Institute of Justice. 2000. *1999 Annual Report on Drug Use Among Adult and Juvenile Arrestees.* Washington, D.C.: U.S. Department of Justice.

Nurco, David N., John C. Ball, John W. Shaffer, and Thomas F. Hanlon. 1985. "The Criminality of Narcotics Addicts." *Journal of Nervous and Mental Disease* 173:94–102.

Nurco, David N., Thomas E. Hanlon, Timothy W. Kinlock, and Karen R. Duszynski. 1988. "Differential Criminal Patterns of Narcotic Addicts Over an Addiction Career." *Criminology* 26:407–23.

Nurco, David N., Timothy Kinlock, and Mitchell B. Balter. 1993. "The Severity of Preaddiction Criminal Behavior Among Urban, Male Narcotic Addicts and Two Nonaddicted Control Groups." *Journal of Research in Crime and Delinquency* 30, no. 3:293–316.

Office of Justice Programs, U.S. Department of Justice. 1998. "Looking at a Decade of Drug Courts." Prepared by the Drug Court Clearinghouse and Technical Assistance Project. Washington, D.C.: American University.

Office of National Drug Control Policy. 1994. *National Drug Control Strategy.* Washington, D.C.: The White House.

Pacula, R. L. Forthcoming. "Does Increasing the Beer Tax Reduce Marijuana Consumption?" *Journal of Health Economics.*

Pacula, R. L., and F. J. Chaloupka. Forthcoming. "The Effects of Macro-level Interventions on Addictive Behavior." *Journal of Substance Use and Misuse.*

Piehl, Anne Morrison, and John J. DiIulio, Jr. 1995. "'Does Prison Pay?' Revisited." Brookings Review 13 (Winter):20–25.

Pindyck, Robert S. 1979. *The Structure of World Energy Demand.* Cambridge, Mass.: MIT Press.

Post, Robert M. 1975. "Cocaine Psychoses: A Continuum Model." *American Journal of Psychiatry* 132:225–31.

Prendergast, M., D. M. Anglin, and J. Wellisch. 1995. "Treatment for Drug-abusing Offenders under Community Supervision." *Federal Probation* 59:66–75.

Reinventing Probation Council. 1999. *"Broken Windows" Probation: The Next Step in Fighting Crime.* New York: The Manhattan Institute.

Reiss, Albert J., Jr., and Jeffrey A. Roth, eds. 1993. *Understanding and Preventing Violence.* Washington, D.C.: National Academy Press.

Reuter, Peter, and Mark A. R. Kleiman. 1986. "Risks and Prices." In *Crime and Justice: A Review of Research*, vol. 7, ed. Michael Tonry and Norval Morris, 289–340. Chicago: University of Chicago Press.

Reuter, Peter, Robert MacCoun, and Patrick Murphy. 1990. *Money from Crime: A Study of the Economics of Drug Dealing*. Santa Monica, Calif.: RAND.

Rhodes, William, Paul Scheiman, and Kenneth Carlson. 1993. *What America's Users Spend on Illegal Drugs, 1988–1991*. Washington, D.C.: Office of National Drug Control Policy.

Riley, Kevin Jack. 1997. *Crack, Powder Cocaine, and Heroin: Drug Purchase and Use Patterns in Six U.S. Cities*. Washington, D.C.: National Institute of Justice.

Rocheleau, Ann Marie, and Mark A. R. Kleiman. 1993. *Measuring Heroin Availability: A Demonstration*. Washington, D.C.: Office of National Drug Control Policy.

Roth, Jeffrey A. 1994. *Psychoactive Substances and Violence*. National Institute of Justice, Research in Brief. Washington, D.C.: U.S. Department of Justice, February.

Rydell, C. Peter, and Susan M. Sohler Everingham. 1994. *Controlling Cocaine: Supply Versus Demand Programs*. Santa Monica, Calif.: RAND.

Sheley, Joseph F., and James D. Wright. 1993. *Gun Acquisition and Possession in Selected Juvenile Samples*. National Institute of Justice, Office of Juvenile Justice and Delinquency Prevention, Research in Brief. Washington, D.C.: U.S. Department of Justice, December.

Silverman, Lester P., and Nancy L. Spruill. 1977. "Urban Crime and the Price of Heroin." *Journal of Urban Economics* 4:80–103.

Stephens, Richard C., and Duane C. McBride. 1976. "Becoming a Street Addict." *Human Organization* 35:87–93.

Tragler, Gernot, Jonathan P. Caulkins, and Gustav Feichtinger. 2001. "Optimal Dynamic Allocation of Treatment and Enforcement in Illicit Drug Control." In *Operations Research* 49, no. 3 (forthcoming).

Trebach, Arnold S., and James A. Inciardi. 1993. *Legalize It? Debating American Drug Policy*. Washington, D.C.: American University Press.

U.S. Department of Justice. 1992. *Drugs, Crime, and the Justice System*. Bureau of Justice Statistics. Washington, D.C.: U.S. Department of Justice.

———. 1999. *Substance Abuse and Treatment, State and Federal Prisoners*. Bureau of Justice Statistics. NCJ-172871. Washington, D.C.: U.S. Department of Justice, January.

———. 2000. *Correctional Populations in the United States, 1997*. Bureau of Justice Statistics. NCJ-177613. Washington, D.C.: U.S. Department of Justice.

Wasserman, Robert. 1993. Personal communication with the authors. 14 December.

Watters, John K., Craig Reinarman, and Jeffrey Fagan. 1985. "Causality, Context, and Contingency: Relationship between Drug Abuse and Delinquency." *Contemporary Drug Problems* 12, no. 3:351–73.

Weisman, J. C., S. W. Marr, and P. L. Katsampes. 1976. "Addiction and Criminal Behavior: A Continuing Examination of Criminal Addicts." *Journal of Drug Issues* 6:153–65.

Weiss, Roger D., and Steven M. Mirin. 1987. *Cocaine: The Human Danger, the Social Costs, the Treatment Alternatives*. New York: Ballantine Books.

Wilson, James Q. 1985. *Thinking About Crime*, rev. ed. New York: Vintage Books.

Wilson, James Q., and Richard J. Herrnstein. 1985. *Crime and Human Nature*. New York: Touchstone.

Wilson, James Q., and George Kelling. 1982. "Broken Windows: The Police and Neighborhood Safety," *The Atlantic Monthly*. 249, no. 3 (March):29–38.

CHAPTER 13
Lawrence W. Sherman
FAIR AND EFFECTIVE POLICING

References

Abrahamse, Allan F., Patricia A. Ebener, Peter W. Greenwood, Nora Fitzgerald, and Thomas E. Kosin. 1991. "An Experimental Evaluation of the Phoenix Repeat Offender Program." *Justice Quarterly* 8:141–68.

American Baptist Convention. 2000. *Christian Action.* November. Valley Forge, Penn.: American Baptist Churches U.S.A.

Berk, Richard, Alec Campbell, Ruth Klap, and Bruce Western. 1992. "The Deterrent Effects of Arrest in Incidents of Domestic Violence: A Bayesian Analysis of Four Field Experiments." *American Sociological Review* 57:698–708.

Black, Donald. 1980. *Manners and Customs of the Police.* New York: Academic.

Blumstein, Alfred, Jacqueline Cohen, Jeffrey A. Roth, and Christy A. Visher. 1986. *Criminal Careers and "Career Criminals."* Washington, D.C.: National Academy Press.

Blumstein, Alfred, and Joel Wallman, eds. 2000. *The Crime Drop in America.* New York: Cambridge University Press.

Boydstun, John. 1975. *The San Diego Field Interrogation Experiment.* Washington, D.C.: Police Foundation.

Bratton, William. 1998. *Turnaround: How America's Top Cop Reversed the Crime Epidemic.* New York: Random House.

Buerger, Michael E. 1993. Convincing the Recalcitrant: Re-examining the Minneapolis RECAP Experiment. Ph.D. diss., Rutgers University, Newark.

Clarke, Ronald V. 1997. *Situational Crime Prevention: Successful Case Studies,* 2d ed. Guilderland, N.Y.: Harrow and Heston.

Copson, G. 1995. *Coals to Newcastle? Police Use of Offender Profiling.* London: Home Office, Police Department.

Farrington, David, and Sandra Lambert. 2000. "Statistical Approaches to Offender Profiling." In *Profiling Property Crimes,* ed. David Canter and Laurence Alison, 235–73. Offender Profiling Series, vol. IV. Aldershot, U.K.: Ashgate.

FBI. *Crime in America: The Uniform Crime Reports, 1992–1999.* Washington, D.C.: FBI.

Fogel, Robert William. 2000. *The Fourth Great Awakening and the Future of Egalitarianism.* Chicago: University of Chicago Press.

Fosdick, Raymond B. [1915] 1969. *European Police Systems.* Reprint. Glen Ridge, N.J.: Patterson Smith.

Friederich, Robert. 1977. The Impact of Organizational, Individual, and Situational Factors on Police Behavior. Ph.D. diss., University of Michigan, Department of Political Science.

Flynn, Kevin. 2001. "Poll Reveals Higher Marks for the Police." *New York Times,* 3 February, B1.

Gladwell, Malcolm. 2000. *The Tipping Point.* Boston: Little, Brown.

Gonzalez, Raquel. 2001. Unpublished memorandum; The Crime Control Research Corporation. Philadelphia, Penn.: Crime Control Research.

Hazelwood, Roy, and Anne Burgess, eds. 1987. *Practical Aspects of Rape Investigation.* Amsterdam: Elsevier.

Hindelang, Michael. 1978. "Race and Involvement in Common Law Personal Crimes." *American Sociological Review* 43:93–109.

Inglehart, Ronald. 1997. "Postmaterialist Values and the Erosion of Institutional Authority." In *Why People Don't Trust Government,* ed. Joseph S. Nye, Jr., Philip D. Zelikow, and David C. King. Cambridge, Mass.: Harvard University Press.

Johnson, David R. 1979. *Policing the Urban Underworld: The Impact of Crime on the Development of the Urban Police, 1800–1885.* Philadelphia: Temple University Press.

Kelling, George, Antony M. Pate, Duane Dieckman, and Charles Brown. 1974. *The Kansas City Preventive Patrol Experiment: Summary.* Washington, D.C.: Police Foundation.

Kocieniewski, David, and Robert Hanley. 2000. "An Inside Story of Racial Bias and Denial." *New York Times,* 3 December, 53.

Koper, Christopher. 1995. "Just Enough Police Presence: Reducing Crime and Disorderly Behavior by Optimizing Patrol Time in Crime Hot Spots." *Justice Quarterly* 12:649–72.

Lardner, James, and Tomas Reppetto. 2000. *NYPD: A City and Its Police.* New York: Henry Holt.

Larson, Richard. 1975. "What Happened to Patrol Operations in Kansas City?" *Journal of Criminal Justice* 3:267–97.

McGarrell, Edward, 2000. Personal communication, November 16.

Marciniak, Elizabeth. 1994. Community Policing of Domestic Violence: Neighborhood Differences in the Effect of Arrest. Ph.D. diss., University of Maryland.

Martin, Susan E., and Lawrence W. Sherman. 1986. "Selective Apprehension: A Police Strategy for Repeat Offenders." *Criminology* 24, no. 1 (February):155–73.

Marvell, Thomas B., and Carlisle Moody. 1996. "Specification Problems. Police Levels and Crime Rates." *Criminology* 34:609–46.

Miller, Wilbur. 1977. *Cops and Bobbies: Police Authority in New York and London, 1830–1870.* Chicago: University of Chicago Press.

Miyazawa, Setsuo. 1992. *Policing in Japan: A Study in Making Crime.* Albany, N.Y.: SUNY Press.

Moore, Mark H. 1980. "The Police and Weapons Offenses." In *The Police and Violence,* ed. L. W. Sherman. Annals of the American Academy of Political and Social Science. Thousand Oaks, Calif., Sage, vol. 452.

Morin, Richard. 2001. "Nonprofit, Faith-Based Groups Near Top of Poll on Solving Social Woes." *Washington Post,* 1 February, A19.

National Conference of Catholic Bishops. 2000. "Responsibility, Rehabilitation, and Restoration: A Catholic Perspective on Crime and Criminal Justice. A Statement of the Catholic Bishops of the United States." New York: United States Catholic Conference.

Pate, Antony M., and Edwin E. Hamilton. 1992. "Formal and Informal Deterrents to Domestic Violence: The Dade County Spouse Assault Experiment." *American Sociological Review* 57:691–97.

Paternoster, Raymond, Robert Brame, Ronet Bachman, and Lawrence W. Sherman. 1997. "Do Fair Procedures Matter? The Effect of Procedural Justice on Spouse Assault." *Law and Society Review* 31:163–204.

Philadelphia Inquirer. 24 December, 2000.

Police Foundation. 1981. *The Newark Foot Patrol Experiment.* Washington, D.C.: Police Foundation.

Reiss, Albert J., Jr. 1971. *The Police and the Public.* New Haven, Conn.: Yale University Press.

Reiss, Albert J., Jr., and Jeffrey A. Roth. 1993. *Understanding and Preventing Violence.* Washington, D.C.: National Academy Press.

Ressler, Robert K., Anne Burgess, and J. E. Douglas. 1988. *Sexual Homicide: Patterns and Motives.* Lexington, Mass.: Lexington Books.

Rybczynski, Witold. 1995. *City Life*. New York: Touchstone.

Sampson, Robert. 1987. "Urban Black Violence: The Effect of Male Joblessness and Family Disruption." *American Journal of Sociology* 93:348–82.

Sampson, Robert, and Jacqueline Cohen. 1988. "Deterrent Effects of Police on Crime: A Replication and Theoretical Extension." *Law and Society Review* 22:163-189.

Shalev, Orit. 2001. Personal communication.

Shaw, James. 1995. "Community Policing Against Guns: Public Opinion of the Kansas City Gun Experiment." *Justice Quarterly* 12:695–710.

Sherman, Lawrence W. 1990. "Police Crackdowns: Initial and Residual Deterrence." In *Crime and Justice: A Review of Research*, ed. Michael Tonry and Norval Morris, 1–48. Crime and Justice: Annual Review of Research vol. 12. Chicago: University of Chicago Press.

———. 1992. *Policing Domestic Violence*. New York: Free Press.

———. 1997. "Policing for Crime Prevention." In *Preventing Crime: What Works, What Doesn't, What's Promising*, ed. L. W. Sherman, Denise Gottfredson, Doris MacKenzie, John Eck, Peter Reuter, and Shawn D. Bushway. www.preventingcrime.org.

———. 1998. *Evidence-Based Policing*. Washington, D.C.: Police Foundation.

———. 2000. "Gun Carrying and Homicide Prevention." *Journal of the American Medical Association* 283:1193–95.

———. 2001. *Trust and Confidence in Criminal Justice*. Washington, D.C.: National Institute of Justice.

Sherman, Lawrence W., and Richard A. Berk. 1984. "The Specific Deterrent Effects of Arrest for Domestic Assault." *American Sociological Review* 49:261–72.

Sherman, Lawrence W., and Ellen G. Cohn. 1989. "The Impact of Research on Legal Policy: The Minneapolis Domestic Violence Experiment." *Law & Society Review* 23 (1989): 117-144.

Sherman, Lawrence W., Patrick R. Gartin, and Michael E. Buerger. 1989 "Hot Spots of Predatory Crime: Routine Activities and the Criminology of Place." *Criminology* 27:27–55.

Sherman, Lawrence W., and Dennis P. Rogan. 1995a. "Effects of Gun Seizures on Gun Violence: 'Hot Spots' Patrol in Kansas City." *Justice Quarterly* 12:673–93.

———. 1995b. "Deterrent Effects of Police Raids on Crack Houses: A Randomized, Controlled Experiment." *Justice Quarterly* 12:755–81.

Sherman, Lawrence W., and Douglas A. Smith. 1992. "Crime, Punishment and Stake in Conformity: Legal and Informal Control of Domestic Violence." *American Sociological Review* 57:680–90.

Sherman, Lawrence, Heather Strang, and Daniel Woods. 2000. "Recidivism Patterns in the Canberra Reintegrative Shaming Experiments (RISE)." www.aic.gov.au/rjustice/rise/index.html.

Sherman, Lawrence, and David Weisburd. 1995. "General Deterrent Effects of Police Patrol in Crime 'Hot Spots': A Randomized, Controlled Trial." *Justice Quarterly* 12:625–48.

Smith, Douglas, and Christy Visher. 1981. "Street-Level Justice: Situational Determinants of Police Arrest Decisions." *Social Problems* 29:167–78.

Spitzer, Eliot. 1999. "The New York City Police Department's 'Stop and Frisk' Practices: A Report to the People of the State of New York from the Office of the Attorney General." New York: New York State Attorney General.

Strang, Heather. 2000. Victim Participation in a Restorative Justice Process: The Canberra Reintegrative Shaming Experiments. Ph.D. diss., Australian National University.

Tyler, Tom. 1990. *Why People Obey the Law*. New Haven, Conn.: Yale University Press.

—————. 1998. "Trust and Democratic Governance." In *Trust and Governance,* ed. Valerie Braithwaite and Margaret Levi. New York: Russell Sage Foundation.

Weisburd, David, and Lorraine Green. 1995. "Policing Drug Hot Spots: The Jersey City Drug Market Analysis Experiment." *Justice Quarterly* 12:711–35.

Wills, Garry. 1999. *A Necessary Evil: A History of American Distrust of Government.* New York: Simon & Schuster.

Wilson, James Q. 1980. "What Can Police Do About Violence?" In *The Police and Violence,* ed. L. W. Sherman. Annals of the American Academy of Political and Social Science, vol. 452.

—————. 1994. "Forget Gun Control: Just Take Away Their Guns." *New York Times Magazine,* 20 March, 46–47.

Wilson, James Q., and George L. Kelling. 1982. "Broken Windows: The Police and Neighborhood Safety." *Atlantic Monthly* March, 29–38.

Wolfgang, Marvin, Robert Figlio, and Thorsten Sellin. 1972. *Delinquency in a Birth Cohort.* Chicago: University of Chicago Press.

Zimbardo, Philip. 1969. "The Human Choice: Individuation, Reason and Order Versus Deindividuation, Impulse and Chaos." In *Nebraska Symposium on Motivation,* vol. 17, ed. W.J. Arnold and D. Levine, 237–307. Lincoln: University of Nebraska Press.

CHAPTER 14
Ralph B. Taylor

PHYSICAL ENVIRONMENT, CRIME, FEAR, AND RESIDENT-BASED CONTROL

Notes

1. This chapter relies partially on several earlier reviews (Taylor, Gottfredson, and Brower 1980; Taylor and Gottfredson 1984; Taylor and Harrell 1996; Taylor 1997b), but most heavily on the review with Adele Harrell. Her contributions to the 1996 piece were substantial and are reflected in several portions of the current chapter.

2. The contingent view described here does not usually apply to situational crime-prevention techniques applied at the site level, whose effectiveness is well demonstrated in the situational crime prevention literature.

3. The assumption of architectural determinism has been seriously questioned since the emergence of environment-behavior studies (Broady 1972), but that refutation does not mean design or physical environment or land use has no influence on individual or social behavior.

4. The streetblock comprises the two sides of the block that face each other and end at the cross streets. It is a viable physical and social organizational unit (Taylor 1997c).

5. Questions of what makes a guardian "capable," and in whose eyes, remain to be explored.

6. In essence, in an ANOVA framework, routine activities is largely a theory about three-way interactions.

7. This description of the incivilities thesis draws on Taylor (1999).

8. I am indebted to an anonymous reviewer of Taylor and Harrell (1996) for making this point.

References

Appleyard, D. 1981. *Livable Streets.* Berkeley: University of California Press.

Atlas, R., and W. LeBlanc. 1994. "Environmental Barriers to Crime." *Ergonomics in Design,* October: 9–16.

Barker, R. G. 1968. *Ecological Psychology.* Stanford, Calif.: Stanford University Press.

Baum, A., A. G. Davis, and J. R. Aiello. 1978. "Crowding and Neighborhood Mediation of Urban Density." *Journal of Population* 1:266–79.

Bevis, C., and J. B. Nutter. 1977. "Changing Street Layouts to Reduce Residential Burglary." Paper presented at the Annual Meeting of the American Society of Criminology, Atlanta, Georgia. Minneapolis: Minnesota Crime Prevention Center.

Bourgois, P. 1996. *In Search of Respect.* Cambridge: Cambridge University Press.

Brantingham, P., and P. Brantingham. 1981. "Notes on the Geometry of Crime." In *Environmental Criminology,* ed. P. Brantingham and P. Brantingham. Beverly Hills: Sage.

Broady, M. 1972. "Social Theory in Architectural Design." In *People and Buildings,* ed. R. Gutman, 170–85. New York: Basic Books.

Brower, S. 1988. *Design in Familiar Places: What Makes Home Environments Look Good.* New York: Praeger.

Brower, S., K. Dockett, and R. B. Taylor. 1983. "Resident's Perceptions of Site-Level Features." *Environment and Behavior* 15:419–37.

Brunson, L., F. E. Kuo, and W. C. Sullivan. 2000. Sowing the Seeds of Community: Greening and Gardening in Inner-city Neighborhoods. Unpublished manuscript. Human-Environment Research Lab, University of Illinois.

Bursik, R. J., Jr. 1989. "Political Decisionmaking and Ecological Models of Delinquency: Conflict and Consensus." In *Theoretical Integration in the Study of Deviance and Crime: Problems and Prospects,* ed. S. F. Messner and M. D. Krohn, 105–17. Albany, N.Y.: SUNY Press.

Bursik, R. J., Jr., and H. G. Grasmick. 1993. *Neighborhoods and Crime: The Dimensions of Effective Social Control.* New York: Lexington Books.

Clarke, R. V. 1983. "Situational Crime Prevention: Its Theoretical Basis and Practical Scope." In *Crime and Justice: An Annual Review of Research* 4, ed. M. Tonry and N. Morris, 225–56. Chicago: University of Chicago Press.

———. ed. 1992. *Situational Crime Prevention.* Albany, N.Y.: Harrow and Heston.

———. 1995. "Situational Crime Prevention." In *Building a Safer Society: Strategic Approaches to Crime Prevention,* ed. M. Tonry and D. Farrington, 91–150. Chicago: University of Chicago Press.

Clarke, R. V., and D. B. Cornish. 1985. "Modeling Offenders' Decisions: A Framework for Research and Policy." In *Crime and Justice: An Annual Review of Research* 6, ed. M. Tonry and N. Morris. Chicago: University of Chicago Press.

Coley, R. L., F. E. Kuo, and W. C. Sullivan. 1997. "Where Does Community Grow: The Social Context Created by Nature in Urban Public Housing." *Environment and Behavior* 29:468–94.

Cook, F. L., and W. G. Skogan. 1984. "Evaluating the Changing Definition of a Policy Issue in Congress: Crime Against the Elderly." In *Public Policy and Social Institutions,* ed. H. R. Rodgers Jr., 287–332. Greenwich, Conn.: JAI Press.

Cornish, D. 1994. "The Procedural Analysis of Offending and Its Relevance for Situational Prevention." In Crime Prevention Studies 3, ed. R. V. Clarke, 151–96. Monsey, N.Y.: Willow Tree Press.

Cornish, D. B., and R. V. G. Clarke. 1986. "Situational Prevention, Displacement of Crime, and Rational Choice Theory." In *Situational Crime Prevention,* ed. K. Heal and G. Laycock, 1–16. London: Her Majesty's Stationery Office.

Crowe, T. D. 1991. *Crime Prevention through Environmental Design: Applications of Architectural Design and Space Management Concepts.* London: Butterworth-Heinemann.

Donnelly, P G.., and T. Majka. 1996. "Change, Cohesion, and Commitment in a Diverse Urban Neighborhood." *Journal of Urban Affairs* 18:269–84.

———. 1998. "Residents' Efforts at Neighborhood Stabilization: Facing the Challenges of Inner-city Neighborhoods." *Sociological Forum* 13:189–214.

Eck, J. E. 1995. "Review Essay: Examining Routine Activity Theory." *Justice Quarterly* 12:783–97.

Eck, J. E., and D. Weisburd. 1995. "Crime Places in Crime Theory." In *Crime and Place* Crime Prevention Studies, 4, ed. J. E. Eck and D. Weisburd. Monsey, N.Y.: Criminal Justice Press.

Fagan, J., and G. Davies. 1997. Crime in Public Housing: Two-way Diffusion Effects in Surrounding Neighborhoods. Paper Presented at Workshop on Identification and Evaluation of Methods for Measuring and Analyzing Crime Patterns and Trends with GIS, February, CUNY Graduate School, New York.

Felson, M. 1994. *Crime in Everyday Life.* Thousand Oaks, Calif.: Pine Forge Press.

———. 1995. "Those Who Discourage Crime." In *Crime and Place* (Crime Prevention Studies, 4), ed. J. E. Eck and D. Weisburd, 53–66. Monsey, N.Y.: Criminal Justice Press.

Fisher, B., and J. L. Nasar. 1992. "Fear of Crime in Relation to Three Exterior Site Features: Prospect, Refuge and Escape." *Environment and Behavior* 24:35–65.

Fowler, F. J., and T. Mangione. 1986. "A Three-pronged Effort to Reduce Crime and Fear of Crime: The Hartford Experiment." In *Community Crime Prevention,* ed. D. Rosenbaum, 87–108. Newbury Park, Calif.: Sage.

Fowler, F. J., M. E. McCalla, and T. Mangione. 1979. *Reducing Residential Crime And Fear: The Hartford Neighborhood Crime Prevention Program.* Washington, D.C.: U.S. Government Printing Office.

Gardiner, R. A. 1976. "Crime and the Neighborhood Environment." HUD Challenge.

Garofalo, J., and J. Laub. 1978. "The Fear of Crime: Broadening Our Perspective." *Victimology* 3:242–53.

Gifford, R. 1997. "Meta-analysis for Environment-behavior and Design Research." In *Advances in Environment, Behavior, and Design* 4, ed. G. T. Moore and R. W. Marans. New York: Plenum.

Greenbaum, P. E., and S. D. Greenbaum. 1981. "Territorial Personalization: Group identity and Social Interaction in a Slavic-American Neighborhood." *Environment and Behavior* 13:574–89.

Greenberg, S., and W. Rohe. 1986. "Informal Social Control." In *Urban Neighborhoods: Research and Policy,* ed. R. B. Taylor. New York: Praeger.

Greenberg, S. W., J. R. Williams, and W. R. Rohe. 1982. "Safety in Urban Neighborhoods: A Comparison of Physical Characteristics and Informal Territorial Control in High and Low Crime Neighborhoods." *Population and Environment* 5:141–65.

Harcourt, B. E. 1998. "Reflecting on the Subject: A Critique of the Social Influence Conception of Deterrence, the Broken Windows Theory, and Order-maintenance Policing New York Style." *Michigan Law Review* 97:291–372.

Hindelang, M. J., M. R. Gottfredson, and J. Garofalo. 1978. *Victims of Personal Crime: An Empirical Foundation for a Theory of Personal Victimization.* Cambridge, Mass.: Ballinger.
——. 1979. *A Theory of Personal Victimization.* Cambridge, Mass.: Ballinger.
Hough, M. 1987. "Offenders' Choice of Targets: Findings from Victim Surveys." *Journal of Quantitative Criminology* 3:355–69.
Hunter, A., and T. L. Baumer. 1982. "Street Traffic, Social Integration, and Fear of Crime." *Sociological Inquiry* 52:122–31.
Jablonsky, T. J. 1993. *Pride in the Jungle: Community and Everyday Life in Back of the Yards Chicago.* Baltimore: Johns Hopkins University Press.
Jacobs, J. 1961. *The Death and Life of the American City.* New York: Vintage.
Jankowski, L. 1992. *Jail Inmates 1991.* Washington D.C.: Bureau of Justice Statistics.
Kuo, F. E., W. Sullivan, R. L. Coley, and L. Brunson. 1998. "Fertile Ground for Community: Inner-city Neighborhood Common Spaces." *American Journal of Community Psychology* 26:823–51.
Kuo, F. E., and W. Sullivan. 2000. Environment and Crime in the Inner City: Does Vegetation Reduce Crime? Unpublished Manuscript. Human-Environment Research Laboratory, University of Illinois.
Kurtz, E., B. Koons, and R. B. Taylor. 1998. "Land use, Physical Deterioration, Resident-based Control and Calls for Service on Urban Streetblocks." *Justice Quarterly* 15:121–49.
Maccoby, E. E., J. P. Johnson, and R. M. Church. 1958. "Community Integration and the Social Control of Juvenile Delinquency." *Journal of Social Issues* 14:38–51.
McPherson, M., G. Silloway, and D. L. Frey. 1983. *Crime, Fear, and Control in Neighborhood Commercial Centers.* Minneapolis: Minnesota Crime Prevention Center.
Merry, S. E. 1981. "Defensible Space Undefended: Social Factors in Crime Control Through Environmental Design." *Urban Affairs Quarterly* 16:397–422.
Miethe, Terance D. and Robert F. Meier. 1994. *Crime and its Social Context.* Albany, N.Y.: SUNY Press.
Murray, C. 1995. "The Physical Environment." In *Crime,* ed. J. Q. Wilson and J. Petersilia, 349–62. San Francisco: Institute for Contemporary Studies.
Murray, M. A. 1982. An Urban Area Analysis of Delinquency. M.A. thesis, Johns Hopkins University.
Newman, O. 1972. *Defensible Space.* New York: Macmillan.
——. 1976. *Design Guidelines for Creating Defensible Space.* Washington, D.C.: U.S. Government Printing Office.
Newman, O., and K. Franck. 1980. *Factors Influencing Crime and Instability in Urban Housing Developments.* Washington, D.C.: U.S. Government Printing Office.
——. 1982. "The Effects of Building Size on Personal Crime and Fear of Crime." *Population and Environment* 5:203–20.
Perkins, D. D., P. Florin, R. C. Rich, A. Wandersman, and D. M. Chavis. 1990. "Participation and the Social and Physical Environment of Residential Blocks: Crime and Community Context." *American Journal of Community Psychology* 18:83–115.
Perkins, D. D., J. W. Meeks, and R. B. Taylor. 1992. "The Physical Environment of Street Blocks and Resident Perceptions of Crime and Disorder: Implications for Theory and Measurement." *Journal of Environmental Psychology* 12:21–34.
Popkin, S. J., V. E. Gwiasda, L. M. Olson, D. P. Rosenbaum, and L. Buron. 2000. *The Hidden War: Crime and the Tragedy of Public Housing in Chicago.* New Brunswick: Rutgers University Press.

Poyner, B. 1983. *Design Against Crime: Beyond Defensible Space.* Stoneham, Mass.: Butterworth-Heineman.

Prestby, J. E., and A. Wandersman. 1985. "An Empirical Exploration of a Framework of Organizational Viability: Maintaining Block Organizations." *Journal of Applied Behavioral Science* 21:287–305.

Proshansky, H., W. Ittelson, and L. G. Rivlin, eds. 1970. *Environmental Psychology.* New York: Holt.

Rengert, G. 1996. *The Geography of Illegal Drugs.* Boulder, Colo.: Westview.

Rengert, G., and J. Wasilchick. 1985. *Suburban Burglary.* Springfield, Ill.: Charles C. Thomas.

Roncek, D. W. 1981. "Dangerous Places: Crime and Residential Environment." *Social Forces* 60:74–96.

Roncek, D. W., and R. Bell. 1981. "Bars, Blocks and Crime." *Journal of Environmental Systems* 11:35–47.

Roncek, D. W., and D. Faggiani. 1985. "High Schools and Crime: A Replication." *The Sociological Quarterly* 26:491–505.

Roncek, D. W., and A. Lobosco. 1983. "The Effect of High Schools on Crime in Their Neighborhoods." *Social Science Quarterly* 64:598–613.

Roncek, D., and P. A. Maier. 1991. "Bars, Blocks, and Crimes Revisited: Linking the Theory of Routine Activities to the Empiricism of 'Hot Spots'." *Criminology* 29:725–53.

Roncek, D. W., and M. A. Pravatiner. 1989. "Additional Evidence that Taverns Enhance Nearby Crime." *Sociology and Social Research* 73:185–88.

Rosenbaum, D. P. 1987. "The Theory and Research Behind Neighborhood Watch: Is it a Sound Fear and Crime Reduction Strategy?" *Crime & Delinquency* 33:103–34.

———. 1988. "A critical eye on neighborhood watch: Does it reduce crime and fear?" In *Communities and Crime Reduction,* ed. T. Hope and M. Shaw, 126–45. London: HMSO.

Sack, R. D. 1986. *Human Territoriality: Its Theory and History.* Cambridge: Cambridge University Press.

Sampson, R. J. 1993. "Linking Time and Place: Dynamic Contextualism and the Future of Criminological Inquiry." *Journal of Research in Crime and Delinquency* 30:426–44.

Sherman, L. W. 1995. "Hot Spots of Crime and Criminal Careers of Places." In *Crime and Place* (Crime Prevention Studies, 4), ed. J. E. Eck and D. Weisburd, 35–52. Monsey, N.Y.: Criminal Justice Press.

Simon, D., and E. Burns. 1997. *The Corner: A Year in the Life of an Inner-City Neighborhood.* New York: Broadway Books.

Simon, H. 1996. *Sciences of the Artificial,* 3d ed. Cambridge, Mass.: MIT Press.

Skogan, W. 1990. *Disorder and Decline: Crime and the Spiral of Decay in American Cities.* New York: Free Press.

Taylor, R. B. 1987. "Toward an Environmental Psychology of Disorder." In *Handbook of Environmental Psychology,* ed. D. Stokols and I. Altman, 951–86. New York: Wiley.

———. 1988. *Human Territorial Functioning.* Cambridge: Cambridge University Press.

———. 1997a. The Places Where Crime Happens. Plenary Address Presented at the Annual National Institute of Justice Research and Evaluation Conference, July, Washington, D.C.

———. 1997b. "Relative Impacts of Disorder, Structural Change, and Crime on Residents and Business Personnel in Minneapolis–St. Paul." In *Community Crime Prevention at the Crossroads,* ed. S. Lab, 63–75. Cincinnati: Anderson.

————. 1997c. "Social Order and Disorder of Streetblocks and Neighborhoods: Ecology, Microecology and the Systemic Model of Social Disorganization." *Journal of Research in Crime and Delinquency* 33:113–55.

————. 1999. "The Incivilities Thesis: Theory, Measurement and Policy." In *Measuring What Matters,* ed. R. L. Langworthy, 65–88. Washington, D.C.: National Institute of Justice, Office of Community Oriented Policing Services.

————. 2001. *Breaking Away from Broken Windows: Evidence from Baltimore Neighborhoods and the Nationwide Fight Against Crime, Grime, Fear and Decline.* New York: Westview Press.

————. Forthcoming. "Social Disorganization vs. Collective Efficacy." In *Theories of Crime and Deviance,* ed. R. Paternoster and R. Bachman. Los Angeles: Roxbury Publishing.

Taylor, R. B., S. D. Gottfredson, and S. N. Brower. 1980. "The Defensibility of Defensible space." In *Understanding Crime,* ed. T. Hirschi and M. Gottfredson. Beverly Hills: Sage.

————. 1984. "Understanding Block Crime and Fear." *Journal of Research in Crime and Delinquency* 21:303–31.

Taylor, R. B., and Harrell, A. (1996) Physical Environment and Crime. Washington: National Institute of Justice. NCJ157311 Reprinted in: R. Glensor, M. Correia, and K. Peak (eds.) (2000) *Policing Communities.* Los Angeles: Roxbury Publishing.

Taylor, R. B., B. Koons, E. Kurtz, J. Greene, and D. Perkins. 1995. "Streetblocks with More Nonresidential Landuse Have More Physical Deterioration: Evidence from Baltimore and Philadelphia." *Urban Affairs Review* (formerly *Urban Affairs Quarterly*) 30:120–36.

Titus, R. M. 1995. "Activity Theory and the Victim." *European Journal of Criminal Policy and Research* 3, no. 3 (Autumn).

Weber, M. 1950. *The City.* New York: Basic Books.

Weisburd, D. 1997. Reorienting Crime Prevention Research and Policy: From the Causes of Criminality to the Context of Crime. Research Report NCJ165041. Washington, D.C.: National Institute of Justice.

White, G. F. 1990. "Neighborhood Permeability and Burglary Rates." *Justice Quarterly* 7:57–68.

Wilson, J. Q. 1975. *Thinking about Crime.* New York: Basic.

Wilson, J. Q., and G. Kelling. 1982. "Broken Windows." *Atlantic Monthly* 211:29–38.

Ycaza, C. 1992. "Crime Rate Drops in Shores." *The Miami Herald,* May 17.

CHAPTER 15
Steven D. Levitt
DETERRENCE

Notes

1. For a discussion of policing strategy, see also Wilson (1983).

2. The classic example used to demonstrate the difference between true causality and Granger causality is Christmas cards. Christmas cards "Granger-cause" Christmas in the sense that before Christmas, cards begin to show up, then Christmas occurs. Clearly, however, in any true sense of causality, it is the existence of Christmas that causes Christmas cards to be sent. More generally, whenever people are forward-looking, Granger-causality and true causality need not coincide.

3.   Marvell and Moody (1996) also find that increases in crime lead, with a lag, to the hiring of more police. This is consistent with the argument above that correlational estimates will understate the true causal impact of police on crime.

4.   There is overwhelming evidence that most active criminals engage in a wide range of different criminal activities. See, for example, Beck (1989).

5.   Perhaps the most egregious case of this is Nagel (1977), which argues for a moratorium on prison building using the fallacious logic that since both the prison population and crime rates had been rising in the 1970s, if we just stopped building prisons, then the crime rate would stop rising also!

6.   See Cameron (1994) for a thorough survey of econometric studies of capital punishment.

7.   For some suggestive evidence regarding a deterrent effect of the death penalty in England and Wales, see Deadman and Pyle (1989).

References

Andreoni, James. 1991. "Reasonable Doubt and the Optimal Magnitude of Fines: Should the Penalty Fit the Crime." *RAND Journal of Economics* 22:385–95.

Ayres, Ian, and John Donohue. 1999. "Nondiscretionary Concealed Weapons Laws: A Case Study of Statistics, Standards of Proof, and Public Policy." *American Law and Economics Review* 1:436–70.

Ayres, Ian, and Steven Levitt. 1998. "Measuring the Positive Externalities from Unobservable Victim Precaution: An Empirical Analysis of Lojack." *Quarterly Journal of Economics* 113:43–77.

Bailey, William. 1982. "Capital Punishment and Lethal Assaults against Police." *Criminology* 19:608–25.

Beck, Allen. 1989. "Recidivism of Prisoners Released in 1983." Bureau of Justice Statistics Special Report No. NCJ 116261. Washington, D.C.: Bureau of Justice Statistics.

Becker, Gary. 1968. "Crime and Punishment: An Economic Approach." *Journal of Political Economy* 76:169–217.

Black, Dan, and Daniel Nagin. 1998. "Do 'Right-to-Carry' Laws Deter Violent Crime?" *Journal of Legal Studies* 27:209–19.

Blumstein, Alfred, Jacqueline Cohen, Jeffrey Roth, and Christy Visher, eds. 1986. *Criminal Careers and 'Career Criminals.'* Washington, D.C.: National Academy of Sciences.

Cameron, Samuel. 1988. "The Economics of Crime Deterrence: A Survey of Theory and Evidence." *Kyklos* 41:301–23.

———. 1994. "A Review of the Econometric Evidence on the Effects of Capital Punishment." *Journal of Socio-Economics* 23 (1):197–214.

Chaiken, Jan, and Marcia Chaiken. 1982. *Varieties of Criminal Behavior.* Santa Monica, Calif.: RAND.

Clotfelter, Charles. 1978. "Private Security and the Public Safety." *Journal of Urban Economics* V:388–402.

Corman, Hope, and Naci Mocan. 2000. "A Time-Series Analysis of Crime and Drug Use in New York City." *American Economic Review,* forthcoming.

Deadman, D., and Donald Pyle. 1989. "Homicide in England and Wales: A Time-Series Analysis." Discussion paper no. 102. Department of Economics, University of Leicester.

DiIulio, John, and Anne Piehl. 1991. "Does Prison Pay? The Stormy National Debate over the Cost-Effectiveness of Imprisonment." *The Brookings Review* (Fall), 28–35.

Duggan, Mark. 2000. "More Guns, More Crime." University of Chicago Department of Economics. Unpublished manuscript.

Ehrlich, Isaac. 1973. "Participation in Illegitimate Activities: A Theoretical and Empirical Investigation." *Journal of Political Economy* 81:531–67.

———. 1975. "The Deterrent Effect of Capital Punishment: A Question of Life and Death." *American Economic Review* 65:397–417.

———. 1977. "Capital Punishment and Deterrence: Some Further Thoughts and Evidence." *Journal of Political Economy* 85:741–88.

Ehrlich, Isaac, and Zhiqiang Liu. 1999. "Sensitivity Analyses of the Deterrence Hypothesis: Let's Keep the Econ in Econometrics." *Journal of Law and Economics* 42:455–87.

Fisher, Franklin, and D. Nagin. 1978. "On the Feasibility of Identifying the Crime Function in a Simultaneous Equations Model of Crime and Sanctions." In *Deterrence and Incapacitation: Estimating the Effects of Criminal Sanctions on Crime Rates,* ed. A. Blumstein, D. Nagin, and J. Cohen. Washington, D.C.: National Academy of Sciences.

Forst, Brian, Victor Filatov, and Lawrence Klein. 1978. "The Deterrent Effect of Capital Punishment: An Assessment of the Estimates." In *Deterrence and Incapacitation: Estimating the Effects of Criminal Sanctions on Crime Rates,* ed. A. Blumstein, D. Nagin, and J. Cohen. Washington, D.C.: National Academy of Sciences.

Freeman, Richard. 1995. "The Labor Market." In *Crime,* ed. James Q. Wilson and Joan Petersilia. San Francisco: ICS Press.

Glassner, Barry, Margret Ksander, Bruce Berg, and Bruce Johnson. 1983. "A Note on the Deterrent Effect of Juveniles vs. Adult Jurisdiction." *Social Problems* 31:219–21.

Glueck, Sheldon, and Eleanor Glueck. 1950. *Unraveling Juvenile Delinquency.* New York: Commonwealth Fund.

Greenwood, Peter, C. Peter Rydell, Allan Abrahamse, Jonathan Caulkins, James Chiesa, Karyn Model, and Stephen Klein. 1994. "Three Strikes and You're Out: Estimated Benefits and Costs of California's New Mandatory Sentencing Law." Santa Monica, Calif.: RAND.

Kaplow, Louis, and Steven Shavell. 1999. "Economic Analysis of Law." National Bureau of Economic Research working paper no. 6960.

Katz, Lawrence, Steven Levitt, and Ellen Shustorovich. 2000. "Prison Death Rates, Capital Punishment, and Deterrence." University of Chicago Department of Economics. Unpublished manuscript.

Kelling, George, Tony Pate, Duane Dieckman, and Charles Brown. 1974. *The Kansas City Preventative Patrol Experiment: A Summary Report, 1974.* Washington, D.C.: Olice Foundation.

Kennedy, David, Anne Piehl, and Anthony Braga. 1996. "Youth Violence in Boston: Gun Markets, Serious Youth Offenders, and a Use-Reduction Strategy." *Law and Contemporary Problems* LIX:147–83.

Kessler, Daniel, and Steven Levitt. 1999. "Using Sentence Enhancements to Distinguish between Deterrence and Incapacitation." *Journal of Law and Economics* 17 (1):343–63.

Larson. 1976.

Leamer, Edward. 1983. "Let's Take the Con out of Econometrics." *American Economic Review* 73:31–43.

Levitt, Steven. 1996. "The Effect of Prison Population Size on Crime Rates: Evidence from Prison Overcrowding Litigation." *Quarterly Journal of Economics* 111:319–52.

———. 1997a. "Using Electoral Cycles in Police Hiring to Estimate the Effect of Police on Crime." *American Economic Review. June, 1997.*

———. 1997b. "Private Information as an Explanation for the Use of Jail Sentences Instead of Fines." *International Review of Law and Economics* 17:179–92.

———. 1998a. "Why Do Increased Arrest Rates Appear to Reduce Crime: Deterrence, Incapacitation, or Measurement Error?" *Economic Inquiry* 36:353–72.

———. 1998b. "Juvenile Crime and Punishment." *Journal of Political Economy* 106:1156–85.

Levitt, Steven, and Sudhir Venkatesh. 2000. "An Economic Analysis of a Drug-Selling Gang's Finances." *Quarterly Journal of Economics,* forthcoming.

Lott, John. 1998. *More Guns, Less Crime,* Chicago: University of Chicago Press.

Lott, John, and William Landes. 1999. "Multiple Victim Public Shootings, Bombings, and Right-to-Carry Concealed Handgun Laws: Contrasting Private and Public Law Enforcement." University of Chicago Law School, John M. Olin Law and Economics working paper no. 73.

Lott, John, and David Mustard. 1997. "Crime, Deterrence, and Right-to-Carry Concealed Handguns." *Journal of Legal Studies,* XXVI(1):1–68.

Ludwig, Jens. 1998. "Concealed-Gun-Carrying Laws and Violent Crime: Evidence from State Panel Data." *International Review of Law and Economics* 18:239–54.

McCormick, Robert, and Robert Tollison. 1984. "Crime on the Court." *Journal of Political Economy,* XCII:223–35.

Marvell, Thomas, and Carlisle Moody. 1994. "Prison Population Growth and Crime Reduction." *Journal of Quantitative Criminology* 10:109–40.

———. 1996. "Specification Problems, Police Levels, and Crime Rates." *Criminology* 34:609–46.

Nagel, William. 1977. "On Behalf of a Moratorium on Prison Construction." *Crime and Delinquency* 23:152–74.

Nagin, Daniel. 1998. "Criminal Deterrence Research: A Review of the Evidence and a Research Agenda for the Outset of the 21st Century." *Crime and Justice* 23.

O'Brien, Robert. 1985. *Crime and Victimization Data.* Beverly Hills, Calif.: Sage.

Passell, Peter, and John Taylor. 1977. "The Deterrent Effect of Capital Punishment: Another View." *American Economic Review* 67:445–51.

Polinsky, A. Mitchell, and Steven Shavell. 1984. "The Optimal Use of Fines and Imprisonment." *Journal of Public Economics* 24:89–99.

Polinsky and Rubenfeild. 1991.

Posner, Richard. 1977. *Economic Analysis of Law.* Boston: Little, Brown, and Company.

Saltzman, Linda, Raymond Paternoster, Gordon Waldo, and Theodore Chiricos. 1982. Deterrent and Experiential Effects: The Problem of Causal Order in Perceptual Deterrence Research." *Journal of Research in Crime and Delinquency* 19:172–89.

Sampson, Robert, and John Laub. 1993. *Crime in the Making: Pathways and Turning Points through Life.* Cambridge, Mass.: Harvard University Press.

Shavell, Steven. 1991. "Individual Precautions to Prevent Theft: Private versus Socially Optimal Behavior." *International Review of Law and Economics* XI:123–32.

Sherman, Lawrence. 1992. "Attacking Crime: Policing and Crime Control." In *Modern Policing,* ed. Michael Tonry and Norval Morris. Chicago: University of Chicago Press.

Spelman, William. 1994. *Criminal Incapacitation.* New York: Plenum.

Stigler, George. 1970. "The Optimum Enforcement of Laws." *Journal of Political Economy* 78:526–36.

Tauchen, Helen, Anne Witte, and Harriet Griesinger. 1994. "Criminal Deterrence: Revisiting the Issue with a Birth Cohort." *Review of Economics and Statistics* 76:399–412.

Van Voorhis, Patricia, Sandra Browning, Marilyn Simon, and Jill Gordon. 1997. "The Meaning of Punishment: Inmates' Orientation to the Prison Experience." *The Prison Journal* 77:135–67.

Wilson, James Q. 1983. *Thinking about Crime.* New York: Random House.

Wilson, James Q., and Richard Herrnstein. 1985. *Crime and Human Nature.* New York: Simon and Schuster.

Wilson, William Julius. 1987. *The Truly Disadvantaged: The Inner City, the Underclass, and Public Policy.* Chicago: University of Chicago Press.

Witte, Ann. 1980. "Estimating the Economic Model of Crime with Individual Data." *Quarterly Journal of Economics* 94:57–84.

Wolfgang, Marvin, Robert F. Figlio, and Torstein Sellin. 1972. *Delinquency in a Birth Cohort.* Chicago: University of Chicago Press.

Zimring, Franklin, and Gordon Hawkins. 1991. *The Scale of Imprisonment.* Chicago: University of Chicago Press.

CHAPTER 16
Alfred Blumstein

PRISONS: A POLICY CHALLENGE

Notes

1. Alfred Blumstein (1983).

2. Blumstein and Cohen (1973). Subsequent work with Dr. Cohen and others led to further tests and development of that theory. These included Blumstein, Cohen, and Nagin (1977) and Blumstein and Moitra (1979).

3. Beck (2000).

4. The estimates here and in the following discussion of incarceration rate are based on inmates per 100,00 *adult* population. The use of adults (i.e., persons age 18 or older) as the denominator for the rates reflects the fact that almost all (99.6 percent) of state and federal inmates are of adult age.

5. The data reported here are drawn from Blumstein and Beck (1999). The data have been collected by the Bureau of Justice Statistics (BJS) of the U.S. Department of Justice from regular surveys of state and federal prisons.

6. The reports are published annually by the FBI as *Crime in the United States: Uniform Crime Reports,* U. S. Government Printing Office, Washington, D.C.

7. Estimated from table 15 of Beck (2000). Burglaries comprise 10.3 percent of prisoners and drug offenses another 20.7. These four are the only offense types other than drug offenses that account for more than 10 percent of inmates, and they collectively account for 56.8 percent of state prisoners.

8. Based on reports from hospital emergency departments reported in the DAWN survey, the number of drug-related episodes increased from 323,100 in 1978 to 425,900 in 1989, fell to 371,200 in 1990, and then rose steadily to 531,800 in 1995 (SAMHSA 1991, 1994).

9. See Blumstein (1998, pp. 951–53) for an indication of the role of domestic violence in the growth of aggravated assault rates. In 1985, the ratio between arrests for aggravated assault and for homicide were rather constant at about 15:1 from age 18 through the late 40s. By 1994, that same ratio prevailed until about age 21, but then increased to more than 35:1

by the 30s as the prevalence of domestic relationships increase and the associated potential for domestic assault develops.

10. Blumstein, Cohen, and Rosenfeld (1992) found that the UCR rates were lower than but increasing toward the NCVS rates. Also encouraging the speculation that the growth in the UCR rates may be a measurement artifact, is the observation that the NCVS estimates for both simple and aggravated assault, with very stable definitions in their questionnaires (until the measurement change in 1993), were both very flat at the time that aggravated assault rates in the UCR were increasing.

11. Langan (1991) has demonstrated the increase in probability of incarceration, but has claimed that there has been no increase in observed average sentence of those sent to prison. In the face of the increased incarceration risk, this observation of no change in average sentence could result even if all sentences were increased, because many of the sentences that were formerly zero (i.e., probation or suspended sentences and not counted in the average time served of those sent to prison) are converted to positive sentences; however, they are generally below the previous average, thereby compensating for the increase in sentences for all others. The expected sentence per crime is more properly calculated as $Q_i S_i$, where Q_i is the probability that a crime of type i will result in a prison sentence, and S_i is the average time served on such a sentence when imposed. If one is interested in calculating the average time served for a particular crime type, then it is important to include the zeroes in order to be sensitive to the effects of a shift in Q_i.

12. In this analysis, time served is measured as the stock/flow ratio—the prison population for each crime type divided by the number of new admissions for that crime type. In many other studies, time served is measured as the time served by a release cohort. This tends to bias the estimate downward because a release cohort is composed disproportionately of prisoners who serve a short time. Also, release cohorts don't contain any people serving true life sentences, whereas they are included in the stock/flow ratio.

13. The most influential synthesis of these studies was Martinson (1974). This study was based on Lipton, Martinson, and Wilks (1975). The results were reexamined in a study by the National Research Council's Panel on Research on Rehabilitative Techniques (Sechrest, White, and Brown 1979). This review confirmed the previous findings of no net rehabilitative effect. More recent reviews of the literature, including some of the careful meta-analyses by Paul Gendreau (see, for example, Paul Gendreau and D.A. Andrews [1990]) are generally more optimistic about the prospects of rehabilitative effectiveness under special conditions of inmate selection and focused treatment.

14. Mumola (1999).

15. The data for figures 16.7a and 16.7b were taken from the Federal Bureau of Investigation (1990). Data for 1989 and 1990 were provided by the FBI's Uniform Crime Reporting (UCR) Program; the assistance of Sharon Profiter in providing that information is much appreciated. Data after 1990 were estimated by the author from arrest data in the annual UCR and population estimates from the Census Bureau.

16. Beck (2000).

17. U.S. Department of Justice (1993).

18. Gender is even more salient than age in distinguishing criminal activity, but the gender composition is reasonably stable, and so is less relevant as a factor contributing to change.

19. The data come from Jennifer Cheeseman Day, "Population Projections of the United States, by Age, Sex, Race, and Hispanic Origin: 1993 to 2050." U.S. Bureau of the Census Series P25-1104 (Government Printing Office; Washington, D.C.) 1993. To smooth out the year-to-year fluctuations of the distribution, the figure presents at each age the average of the

number of people of that age and of the year before and the year after (i.e., for example, $N_{13sm} = [N_{12} + N_{13} + N_{14}]/3$).

20. See, for example, Easterlin (1980).

21. Blumstein, Cohen, and Miller (1980).

22. Of course, other factors, such as changing economic conditions or sanction policies, could influence the crime rate and make it higher or lower than that projected based on demographic considerations alone.

23. There are separate institutions for juvenile offenders. In 1997, there were 105,790 juveniles in those institutions on a single day (Snyder and Sickmund 1999).

24. The Statistical Abstract of the United States, 1996. Tables 333 and 235.

25. These states include Alaska, Arizona, California, Colorado, Maine, Nevada, Oregon, and Washington.

26. Morris and Tonry (1990).

27. Petersilia and Turner (1993).

28. Personal communication from Ralph Nolan, Colorado State Parole Supervisor.

29. "'Three Strikes' Laws: Five Years Later." The Sentencing Project, Washington, D.C.

30. For a review of the literature, see Nagin (1978).

31. See Alfred Blumstein, Jacqueline Cohen, and Paul Hsieh, 1982.

32. *Sourcebook of Criminal Justice Statistics, 1992*; U.S. Department of Justice, Bureau of Justice Statistics Report No. NCJ-143496, 1993 and "Prisoners in 1999", op cit.

33. Aspects of this approach are developed in Blumstein and Kadane (1983).

References

Baumer. 1998.

Beck, Allen J. 2000. *Prisoners in 1999.* Bureau of Justice Statistics Bulletin No. NCJ-183476 (August). Bureau of Justice Statistics, U.S. Department of Justice.

Beck, Allen, et al. 1993. *Survey of State Prison Inmates: 1991.* Report No. NCJ-136949 (March). Washington, D.C.: Federal Bureau of Investigation.

Blumstein, Alfred. 1995. "Prisons: Population, Capacity, and Alternatives." In *Crime and Public Policy,* ed. James Q. Wilson. San Francisco: ICS Press.

Blumstein, Alfred, and Allen J. Beck. 1999. "Population Growth in U.S. Prisons: 1980–1996." In *Crime and Justice: A Review of Research,* vol. 26, ed. M. Tonry and J. Petersilia. Chicago: University of Chicago Press.

Blumstein, Alfred, and Jacqueline Cohen. 1973. "A Theory of the Stability of Punishment." *Journal of Criminal Law and Criminology* 64(2):198–206.

Blumstein, Alfred, Jacqueline Cohen, and William Gooding. 1983. "The Influence of Capacity on Prison Population: A Critical Review of Some Recent Evidence." *Crime and Delinquency* 29(1):1–51.

Blumstein, Alfred, Jacqueline Cohen, and Paul Hsieh. 1982. "The Duration of Adult Criminal Careers." Final Report to the National Institute of Justice. Pittsburgh, Penn.: Urban Systems Institute, Carnegie Mellon University.

Blumstein, Alfred, Jacqueline Cohen, and Harold D. Miller. 1980. "Demographically Disaggregated Projections of Prison Populations." *Journal of Criminal Justice* 8(1):1–26.

Blumstein, Alfred, Jacqueline Cohen, and Daniel Nagin. 1977. "The Dynamics of Homeostatic Punishment Process." *Journal of Criminal Law and Criminology* 67(3): 317–34.

Blumstein, A., J. Cohen and Richard Rosenfeld. 1991. "Trend and Deviation in Crime Rates: A Comparison of the NCS and UCR Data for Burglary and Robbery." *Criminology* 29:(2):237-264.

Blumstein, Alfred, and Joseph Kadane. 1983. "An Approach to the Allocation of Scarce Imprisonment Resources." *Crime and Delinquency* 29(10):546–60.

Blumstein, Alfred, and Soumyo Moitra. 1979. "An Analysis of the Time Series of the Imprisonment Rate in the States of the United States: A Further Test of the Stability of Punishment Hypothesis." *Journal of Criminal Law and Criminology* 70(3):376–90.

Blumstein, Alfred, and Joel Wallman, eds. 2000. *The Crime Drop in America.* Cambridge: Cambridge University Press.

Cohen, Jacqueline, and Jose A. Canela-Cacho. 1994. "Incarceration and Violent Crime—1965–1988." In *Understanding and Preventing Violence,* ed. Albert J. Reiss, Jr. and Jeffrey A. Roth. Washington, D.C.: National Academy of Sciences.

Easterlin, Richard A. 1980. *Birth and Fortune.* New York: Basic Books, 1980.

Gendreau, Paul, and D. A. Andrews. 1990. "Tertiary Prevention: What the Meta-Analyses of the Offender Treatment Literature Tell Us About 'What Works'." *Canadian Journal of Criminology* 32: 173–84.

Golub, Andrew. 1992. "The Termination Rate of Adult Criminal Careers." Dissertation, Carnegie Mellon University.

Johnson, Bruce, Andrew Golub, and Eloise Dunlap. 2000. "The Rise and Decline of Hard Drugs, Drug Markets, and Violence in Inner-City New York." In *The Crime Drop in America,* ed. Alfred Blumstein and Joel Wallman. Cambridge: Cambridge University Press.

Langan, Patrick A. 1991. "America's Soaring Prison Population." *Science* 251 (March): 1568–73.

Lipton, Douglas, R. Martinson, and J. Wilks. 1975. *The Effectiveness of Correctional Treatment: A Survey of Treatment Evaluation Studies.* New York: Preager.

Martinson, Robert. 1974. "What Works?—Questions and Answers About Prison Reform." *The Public Interest* 35:22–54.

Morris, Norval, and Michael Tonry. 1990. *Between Prison and Probation: Intermediate Punishments in a Rational Sentencing System.* New York: Oxford University Press.

Mumola, Christopher J. 1999. "Substance Abuse and Treatment, State and Federal Prisoners, 1997." Bureau of Justice Statistics Special Report No. NCJ-172871 (January). Bureau of Justice Statistics, U.S. Department of Justice.

Nagin, Daniel. 1978. "General Deterrence: A Review of the Empirical Evidence," In *Deterrence and Incapacitation: Estimating the Effects of the Crime Rates,* ed. Alfred Blumstein et al. Washington, D.C.: National Academy of Sciences.

National Research Council. 1979. Panel on Research on Rehabilitative Techniques. "The Rehabilitation of Criminal Offenders: Problems and Prospects," ed. Lee B. Sechrest, Susan O. White, and Elizabeth Brown. Washington, D.C.: National Academy of Sciences.

Petersilia, Joan, and Susan Turner 1993. "Intensive Probation and Parole." In *Crime and Justice: A Review of Research,* ed. Michael Tonry. Chicago: University of Chicago Press.

Rosenfeld, Richard. 2000. "Patterns in Adult Homicide: 1980–1995." In *The Crime Drop in America,* ed. Alfred Blumstein and Joel Wallman. Cambridge: Cambridge University Press.

SAMHSA 1991, 1994.

Snyder, Howard N., and Melissa Sickmund. 1999. "Juvenile Offenders and Victims, 1999 National Report." National Center for Juvenile Justice; Office of Juvenile Justice and Delinquency Prevention, Washington, D.C.

Spelman William. 2000. "The Limited Importance of Prison Expansion." In *The Crime Drop in America*, ed. Alfred Blumstein and Joel Wallman. Cambridge: Cambridge University Press.

U. S. Bureau of the Census. 1993. *Population Projections of the United States, by Age, Sex, Race, and Hispanic Origin: 1993–2050*, Series P25-1104. Washington, D.C.: U.S. Govt. Printing Office.

U. S. Department of Justice. 1992. *Sourcebook of Criminal Justice Statistics: 1992*. Bureau of Justice Statistics Report No. NCJ-143496. Washington, D.C.: U.S. Govt. Printing Office.

———. 1993. *Prisoners in 1993*. Bureau of Justice Statistics Report No. NCJ-147036 (June). Washington, D.C.: U.S. Govt. Printing Office.

———. Federal Bureau of Investigation. 1993. *Age-Specific Arrest Rates and Race-Specific Arrest Rates for Selected Offenses, 1965–1992*. Uniform Crime Reporting Program (December). Washington, D.C.: U. S. Govt. Printing Office.

———. 1992. *National Juvenile Custody Trends: 1978–1989* (March). Washington, D.C.: Office of Juvenile Justice and Delinquency Prevention.

CHAPTER 17
Joan Petersilia
COMMUNITY CORRECTIONS

Notes

1. An interesting recent analysis by Zvekic (1996) shows that the United States and other Western European countries' preference for probation compared with prison is not shared by some other countries, most notably Japan, Israel, and Scotland. For example, the ratio of imprisonment to probation in Japan is 4:1.

2. In fact, a growing trend in probation supervision is "kiosk" reporting—where offenders complete the required "interview" at a kiosk machine (for example, indicating if they have moved, or are employed). They can even pay their fines and fees through the kiosk's bill acceptor (see www.automon.com/kioskdescription.htm, accessed Oct. 5, 2000).

3. Even in the national Intensive Supervision Probation/Parole demonstration project, run by the U.S. Department of Justice between 1986 and 1991, where caseloads were explicitly reduced to less than 40:1 for high-risk offenders, officers were only able to deliver an average of six face-to-face contacts per month, per offender (across the fourteen participating sites)—or one to two a week, each lasting about fifteen minutes (Petersilia and Turner 1993).

4. "Broken windows" probation draws from a metaphor first introduced by Wilson and Kelling in 1982 in an article titled "Broken Windows: The Police and Neighborhood Safety." The term explained how small disorders and breakdowns in civic norms, if left unattended, contribute in time to larger social disorders and serious crime. It called for the police to focus more of their attention on addressing disorderly behavior, especially in public spaces, and on attending to the standards and quality of neighborhood life in partnership with the community.

References

Anderson, Elijah. 1990. *Streetwise: Race, Class, and Change in an Urban Community.* Chicago: University of Chicago Press.

Austin, James. 2000. "Prisoner Reentry: Current Trends, Practices, and Issues." Washington, D.C.: Institute on Crime, Justice, and Corrections.

Beck, Allen, Darrell Gilliard, and Lawrence Greenfeld. 1993. "Survey of State Prison Inmates 1991." Washington, D.C.: Bureau of Justice Statistics.

Beck, Allen J. 2000a. "Prisoners in 1999." Washington, D.C.: Bureau of Justice Statistics.

———. 2000b. "State and Federal Prisoners Returning to the Community: Findings from the Bureau of Justice Statistics." Washington, D.C.: Bureau of Justice Statistics.

Beck, Allen, and Bernard Shipley. 1989. "Recidivism of Prisoners Released in 1983." Washington, D.C.: Bureau of Justice Statistics.

Blumstein, Alfred, and Allen J. Beck. 1999. "Population Growth in U.S. Prisons, 1980–1996." In *Prisons*, ed. Michael Tonry and Joan Petersilia, 17–62. Chicago: University of Chicago Press.

Bonczar, Thomas. 1997. "Characteristics of Adults on Probation, 1995." Washington, D.C.: Bureau of Justice Statistics.

Bonczar, Thomas, and Lauren Glaze. 1999. "Probation and Parole in the United States, 1998." Washington, D.C.: Bureau of Justice Statistics.

Bureau of Justice Statistics. 1993. "Justice Expenditure and Employment Extracts." Washington, D.C.: U.S. Department of Justice.

———. 2000a. "Incarcerated Parents and Their Children." Washington, D.C.: U.S. Department of Justice.

———. 2000b. "Probation and Parole in 1999—Press Release." Washington, D.C.: U.S. Department of Justice.

California Department of Corrections. 1997. "Preventing Parolee Failure Program: An Evaluation." Sacramento, California.

Camp, Camille, and George Camp. 1999. *The Corrections Yearbook 1998.* Middletown, Connecticut: Criminal Justice Institute, Inc.

Clear, Todd, and Ronald Corbett. 1999. "Community Corrections of Place." *Perspectives* 23:24–32.

Clear, Todd R., and Anthony Braga. 1995. "Community Corrections." In *Crime*, ed. J. Q. Wilson and J. Petersilia. San Francisco, Calif.: Institute for Contemporary Studies.

Clear, Todd R., and Harry R. Dammer. 2000. *The Offender in the Community.* Belmont, Calif.: Wadsworth.

Cullen, Francis, Bonnie Fisher, and Brandon Applegate. 2000. "Public Opinion about Punishment and Corrections." In *Crime and Justice: A Review of Research*, ed. Michael Tonry, 1–79. Chicago: University of Chicago Press.

Dickey, Walter J., and Michael Smith. 1998. "Rethinking Probation: Community Supervision, Community Safety." Washington, D.C.: U.S. Department of Justice.

Fabelo, Tony. 2000. "Technocorrections: The Promises, the Uncertain Threats." Washington, D.C.: National Institute of Justice.

Fellner, Jamie, and Marc Mauer. 1998. "Losing the Vote: The Impact of Felony Disenfranchisement Laws in the United States." Washington, D.C.: The Sentencing Project.

Finn, Peter. 1998a. "Chicago's Safer Foundation: A Road Back for Ex-Offenders." Washington, D.C.: National Institute of Justice.

————. 1998b. "Successful Job Placement for Ex-Offenders: The Center for Employment Opportunities." Washington, D.C.: National Institute of Justice.

————. 1998c. "Texas' Project RIO (Re-Integration of Offenders)." Washington, D.C.: National Institute of Justice.

Gendreau, P., and D. A. Andrews, 1990. Tertiary Prevention: What the Meta-analysis of the Offender Treatment Literature Tells Us About "What Works." *Canadian Journal of Criminology*, 32, 173-184.

Hagan, John, and Ronit Dinovitzer. 1999. "Collateral Consequences of Imprisonment for Children, Communities, and Prisoners." In *Prisons*, ed. Michael Tonry and Joan Petersilia, 121–62. Chicago: University of Chicago Press.

Hammett, Theodore M., Patricia Harmon, and Laura M. Maruschak. 1999. "1996–1997 Update: HIV/AIDS, STDs, and TB in Correctional Facilities." Washington, D.C.: Bureau of Justice Statistics.

Hurwitz, Jolynn E. 2000. "Mental Illness and Substance Abuse in the Criminal Justice System." Cincinnati, Ohio: The Health Foundation of Greater Cincinnati.

Institute of Medicine. 1990.

Kleiman, Mark. 1999. "Community Corrections as the Front Line in Crime Control." *UCLA Law Review* 46:1909–925.

Langan, Patrick. 1994. "Between Prison and Probation: Intermediate Sanctions." *Science* 264:791–94.

Langan, Patrick, and Mark Cunniff. 1992. "Recidivism of Felons on Probation, 1986–89." Washington, D.C.: Bureau of Justice Statistics.

Lehman, Joseph. 2000a. "Neighborhood Based Supervision." In *Correctional Best Practices: Directors' Perspectives*, ed. Reginald Wilkinson. Middletown, Conn.: Association of State Correctional Administrators.

————, ed. 2000b. *Offender Accountability Act in Washington*. Middleton, Conn.: Association of State Correctional Administrators.

Longmire, D.R., and Barbara Sims. 1995. "1995 Crime Poll: Texas and the Nation" (Executive Summary). Huntsville, TX: Sam Houston State University, Survey Research Program, Criminal Justice Center.

Los Angeles County Planning Committee. 1996. "Managing Offenders in Los Angeles County." Los Angeles, Calif.: Los Angeles Sheriff's Department.

McDonald, Douglas C. 1999. "Medical Care in Prisons." In *Prisons*, ed. Michael Tonry and Joan Petersilia, 427–78. Chicago: University of Chicago Press.

Morgan, Kathryn. 1993. "Factors Influencing Probation Outcome: A Review of the Literature." *Federal Probation* 57:23–29.

Parent, Dale, Dan Wentworth, Peggy Burke, and Becky Ney. 1994. "Responding to Probation and Parole Violations." Washington, D.C.: National Institute of Justice.

Petersilia, Joan. 1998. "Probation and Parole." In *The Oxford Handbook of Criminology*, ed. Michael Tonry. New York, N.Y.: Oxford University Press.

————. 1999. "A Decade of Experimenting with Intermediate Sanctions: What Have We Learned?" *Justice Research and Policy* 11:9–24.

————. 2000. "Challenges of Prisoner Reentry and Parole in California." Berkeley, Calif.: California Policy Research Center.

Petersilia, Joan, and Michael Tonry, eds. 1999. Prisons. Vol. 26, Crime and Justice: A Review of Research. Chicago: University of Chicago Press.

Petersilia, Joan, and Susan Turner. 1993. "Intensive Probation and Parole." In *Crime and Justice: An Annual Review of Research*, ed. Michael Tonry, 281–335. Chicago: University of Chicago Press.

Petersilia, Joan, Susan Turner, Joyce E. Peterson, National Institute of Justice (U.S.), and Rand Corporation. 1986. *Prison versus Probation in California: Implications for Crime and Offender Recidivism*. Santa Monica, Calif.: Rand Corporation.

Prendergast, Michael, Douglas Anglin, and Jean Wellisch. 1995. "Treatment for Drug-Abusing Offenders under Community Supervision." *Federal Probation* 66.

Reinventing Probation Council. 2000. "Transforming Probation through Leadership: The 'Broken Windows' Model." New York, N.Y.: Manhattan Institute for Policy Research.

Rhine, Edward, ed. 1998. *Best Practices: Excellence in Corrections*. Lanham, Md.: American Correctional Association.

Rhine, Edward, William Smith, Ronald Jackson, Peggy Burke, and Roger LaBelle. 1991. "Paroling Authorities: Recent History and Current Practice." Laurel, Md.: American Correctional Association.

Rose, Dina, Todd Clear, and Kristen Scully. 1999. "Coercive Mobility and Crime: Incarceration and Social Disorganization." Paper presented at the American Society of Criminology, Toronto, Canada.

Smith, Michael, and Walter Dickey. 1998. "What If Corrections Were Serious about Public Safety?" *Corrections Management Quarterly* 2:12–30.

Snyder, Howard, and Melissa Sickmund. 1999. "Juvenile Offenders and Victims: 1999 National Report." Washington, D.C.: Office of Juvenile Justice and Delinquency Prevention.

Taylor, Stan. 2000. "Violation of Probation Center and the 'Broken Windows' Theory." In *Correctional Best Practices: Directors' Perspectives*, ed. Reginald Wilkinson, 183–85. Middletown, Conn.: Association of State Correctional Administrators.

Tonry, Michael. 1999. "Executive Sessions on Sentencing and Corrections." Washington, D.C.: National Institute of Justice.

Tonry, Michael, and Mary Lynch. 1996. "Intermediate Sanctions" *Crime & Justice: A Review of Research*. Vol 20. Chicago: Chicago University Press.

Turner, Susan, and Joan Petersilia. 1996. "Work Release: Recidivism and Corrections Costs in Washington State." Washington, D.C.: National Institute of Justice.

Wilkinson, Reginald. 2000. "Correctional Best Practices: Directors' Perspectives." Middletown, Conn.: Association of State Correctional Administrators.

Wilson, James Q. and George Kelling 1982. "Broken Windows." *Atlantic Monthly*.

Zvekic, Ugljesa. 1996. "Probation in International Perspective." *Overcrowded Times* 7 (2).

CHAPTER 18
Brian Forst

PROSECUTION

The author wishes to thank Tom Brady, Joan Petersilia, Jim Lynch, Gerard Rainville, and James Q. Wilson for their helpful comments on earlier drafts of this chapter.

Notes

1. This is due largely to the effect of huge increases in imprisonments for felony drug offenses, typically reported only at the time of arrest. Total index crimes for 1970 and 1996 were 8,098,000 and 13,494,000, respectively (Federal Bureau of Investigation, *Uniform Crime Reports*, 1971, 1997). Total admissions to federal and state prisons for same years were 79,351 and 353,893 (Bureau of Justice Statistics, 1998, and *Statistical Abstract of the United States, 1998*, table 377).

2. The Bureau of Justice Statistics launched a series of reports on the outcomes of prosecution in the mid-1970s, conducted by the Institute for Law and Social Research until 1985, then by Abt Associates. The Bureau discontinued case-tracking statistics documenting the arrest-filing-conviction process after 1988, publishing instead numbers of convictions and incarcerations in selected years in its *Felony Defendants in Large Urban Counties* and *Felony Sentences in State Courts* series. The numbers in Figure 18.1 are derived from Boland, Mahanna, and Sones (1992); Hart and Reaves (1999); and Brown, Langan, and Levin (1999).

3. Some 690,000 were admitted to juvenile facilities in 1990 nationwide, over 80 percent to short-term confinement. Parent, et al., (1994), p. 1. See also Dougherty (1988); Snyder, et al. (1987); Forst and Blomquist (1992), p. 1; Barbara Allen-Hagen (1991); Bureau of Justice Statistics (1988).

4. The average case-processing time for felonies that go to trial is about one year (391 days for murder, 333 for rape and robbery, 259 for burglary, 248 for larceny); the numbers are somewhat higher in larger jurisdictions than in small ones. Solari (1992), p. 60.

5. Such findings were reported for Washington, D.C., by Forst, Lucianovic, and Cox (1977); similar findings were reported for New York by the Vera Institute (1977); for New Orleans, by Forst, et al. (1981).

6. For an in-depth analysis of the prosecutor's view of the witness problem, see Cannavale and Falcon (1976).

7. Forst, Lucianovic, and Cox (1977), p. 28. Similar findings were found for New York by the Vera Institute (1977) and for New Orleans by Forst, et al. (1981). Although recent data are less abundant, one can nonetheless speculate that public initiative on behalf of victims of domestic violence may have reduced these rates.

8. Some researchers have found that violent offenders in the family are also more likely to assault nonfamily members (Hotaling and Straus, 1989).

9. This is not to suggest that the practice of aborting or retarding prosecution is an appropriate response to questionable police procedures of obtaining evidence. The 30,000 or so felony cases that are rejected annually in the United States due to such violations of rights to due process may be 30,000 too many from the public's point of view; these episodes erode police legitimacy. We wish only to point out here that the problem is small from another perspective: for each case rejected due to an exclusionary rule violation, about twenty are rejected because the police failed to produce sufficient tangible or testimonial evidence.

10. This was found in Washington, D.C., by Forst, Lucianovic, and Cox (1977), and in seven jurisdictions by Forst, et al. (1981). In the latter study, arrests made by about 10,000 police officers during 1977-78 were examined; half of the convictions that followed those arrests were the product of a mere 12 percent of the officers. Nearly twice as many officers (22 percent) made arrests that failed to yield a single conviction. This pattern held up after the researchers accounted for the officer's assignment, the number of arrests made by the officer, the normal conviction rate associated with each officer's offense mix (e.g., the conviction rate for robbery is considerably higher than for assault), and randomness associated with the

small number of arrests made by most of the officers. Similar differences in conviction rates were found in a study of arrests for robbery and burglary by 25 different police departments operating in Los Angeles County in the 1980s—some departments produced arrests that resulted in conviction at twice the rate as others (Petersilia, Abrahamse, and Wilson, 1990b).

11. Consistent with this evidence is a summary statement by the National Academy of Sciences Panel on Sentencing Research: "Despite the number and diversity of factors investigated as determinants of sentences, two-thirds or more of the variance in sentence outcomes remains unexplained." Blumstein, et al. (1983), p. 10.

Judges were found to be responsible for several kinds of unwarranted sentence disparity. Some judges are inclined simply to give more severe (or lenient) sentences than others. Those who supported rehabilitation as the primary goal of sentencing, for example, were found to give more lenient sentences, while those who support the more strictly utilitarian goals of deterrence and incapacitation tend to give harsher sentences. More selective kinds of variation were also found; judges who were neither especially tough nor lenient on the whole were found to be tougher or more lenient than most judges for particular kinds of cases—for example, with defendants found guilty in trial or persons convicted of drug trafficking. Another source of variation was found to be the natural element of inconsistency among the sentencing decisions of an individual judge—some tended to be more inconsistent than others. Sentence disparity was, in short, found to be much more than just a matter of overall toughness or leniency.

12. These findings appeared later in a more extensive version (Lipton, Martinson, and Wilks, 1975). Similar findings had been obtained a decade earlier in a survey of 100 rehabilitation programs (Bailey, 1966).

13. Evidence on disparity in federal sentencing practices was presented to the U.S. Senate Subcommittee on Criminal Law (Senator Edward Kennedy presiding), prior to the enactment of federal sentencing guidelines under the 1984 Federal Sentencing Reform Act. See testimony of Brian Forst and William Rhodes, May 23, 1983, hearings before the U.S. Senate Subcommittee on Criminal Law of the Committee on the Judiciary, First Session on S.829 (Comprehensive Crime Control Act of 1983), Serial No. J-98-37, pp. 1000-04.

14. See, for example, Elsa Chen's dissertation at UCLA (2000).

15. Mandatory minimum statutes can be counterproductive in other ways as well, reducing defendants' incentives to plead guilty (a 1991 U.S. Sentencing Commission study found that trial rates were 2 times greater for offenses subject to mandatory penalties than for all offenses) and lengthening case-processing times, inducing prosecutors to dismiss cases and reduce charges excessively (thus depriving the community of potentially important deterrent effects), overturning thoughtfully crafted sentence guidelines, and creating dreadful prison overcrowding conditions. Moreover, in lengthening the sentences of some offenders while reducing others to zero, mandatory minimums actually *increase* the disparity in sanctions. The legislator's compulsion always to take a tough stand where the public's concern about crime is an issue, in spite of strong evidence against the effectiveness of mandatory minimum laws, makes other allegations of "political correctness" look trivial; it may accomplish little other than to give the public a false sense of security, while inflicting substantial costs and other harms on society. See Michael Tonry's accompanying chapter on sentencing.

16. In 1996 there were 2,343 chief prosecutors and some 22,000 assistant prosecutors serving the nation's counties and independent cities (DeFrances and Steadman) and another 94 federal prosecution offices. Nearly half of the United States population fell under the jurisdiction of just 127 local prosecution offices (Office of Victims of Crime, p. 2).

17. Differences within Los Angeles County have been reported by Petersilia, Abrahamse, and Wilson (1990a), and earlier by Greenwood, et al. (1976). Differences between United States Attorney's offices in adjacent federal districts were reported by Boland and Forst (1985), p. 11.

18. Nationwide, the ratio of pleas to trials, based on felony arrests, is slightly less than ten-to-one. Three jurisdictions with extremely low rates are Washington, D.C. (5:1), New Orleans (4:1), and Portland (4:1); two with extremely high rates are Geneva, Illinois (37:1), and Littleton, Colorado (19:1) (Forst and Boland, 1984), p. 2.

19. Boland and Forst (1985), pp. 11-13. In Manhattan, where the plea-to-trial ratio is 24:1, only 3 percent of all felony arrests are rejected; the local crime unit in the U.S. Attorney's Washington, D.C., office, with a plea-to-trial ratio of 5:1, rejects 15 percent. (Boland, Mahanna, and Sones, 1992).

20. Reductions in the case acceptance rate tend to increase the number of offenders set free at the screening stage and lower the ratio of pleas to trials and thus reduce the rate at which arrests end in conviction (Forst, 2000). At current conviction rates, the increases in these errors are likely to be substantially larger than increases in the number of innocents convicted.

21. Legislative attempts to ban plea bargaining have been studied extensively, with conclusions that, while varied, are consistent in their generally negative assessments. When such attempts fail to enlist the full support of the prosecutor, charge bargaining has been found to be replaced with sentence bargaining and increases in the rate at which cases are dropped by the prosecutor (Blumstein, et al. 1983; McCoy 1993). For analyses of the effects of attempts to ban plea bargaining under the 1973 New York drug law, see Joint Committee (1979). Rubinstein and White (1979) reported the findings of their study of the effects of a sweeping 1975 ban on plea bargaining. A 1977 plea bargaining ban in Michigan firearm cases was analyzed by Loftin, Heumann, and McDowall (1983), p. 287. The 1982 attempt to better serve victims with California's Proposition 8 referendum substantially accelerated the plea negotiation process in that state, but appears to have done so in a manner that undermines both the due process of defendants and the concerns of victims to have their views aired in court and receive appropriate levels of attention (McCoy 1993).

22. Kenneth Culp Davis has emphasized the ethical problem associated with prosecutorial discretion: "The question of what is justice in any particular case may not be determined by considering only the one case but must be determined in the light of what is done in comparable cases. If equality of treatment is one ingredient of justice, one cannot know whether penalizing B is just without looking at A's case—and C's and D's" (Davis, 1969), p. 170.

23. Here is a pointed observation made by the chief Democratic counsel to the House Judiciary Committee: "Since Watergate, the investigative apparatus has grown too unaccountable to the norms of prosecutorial judgment. Too often, prosecutors have been unleashed in pursuit of trivial, legally scant matters, and then seek to build a case on a single discrepancy in the hundreds of questions asked in the course of the investigation" (Epstein, 2000).

24. Prosecutors derive their authority from the voters only indirectly in five states: Alaska, Connecticut, Delaware, New Jersey, and Rhode Island. The heads of local prosecution offices in four of those states are appointed by the state attorney general ("chief state's attorney" in Connecticut); in New Jersey, the governor appoints the local prosecutors.

25. Forst (1995), pp. 372, 587 (Note 9).

26. In 1972, Marvin Wolfgang and his associates at the University of Pennsylvania reported that 18 percent of all boys born in Philadelphia in 1945 accounted for 52 percent

of all the offenses committed by the group (Wolfgang, et al., 1972, p. 88). A few years afterward Kristen Williams, analyzing PROMIS data from the District of Columbia for 1971-75, reported that 7 percent of the 46,000 different defendants arrested accounted for 24 percent of the 73,000 felony and serious misdemeanor cases handled by the prosecutor for that jurisdiction (Williams, 1979), pp. 5-6.

27. A few offices, such as Marion County (Indianapolis), Indiana, and Mecklenburg County (Charlotte), North Carolina, have used empirically derived prediction systems developed by researchers at Rand, the Institute for Law and Social Research, and elsewhere, but these were exceptional.

28. Ford and Regoli (1993) conducted two experiments in the Marion County District Attorney's office to test the effectiveness of eight alternative approaches to handling domestic violence cases. They found that arresting defendants by warrant and allowing victims to drop charges resulted in a rebattering rate (13 percent) less than half that of the overall rate (29 percent) for the other seven alternatives. Summoning defendants to court and pursuing noncounseling sentencing alternatives resulted in the highest rebattering rate (44 percent).

29. The Bureau of Justice Statistics has created data series that provide interesting and useful information about prosecution. One biennial BJS survey, *Prosecutors in State Courts*, reports characteristics and case outcomes of some 2,300 prosecutors' offices throughout the United States (budgets, staffing levels, and salaries by size of population served, types of computer applications, etc.). Another, the National Survey of Prosecutors, gives selected statistics on resources, policies and practices for a sample of some 300 offices biennially throughout the United States. Other reports present occasional statistics on such topics as juveniles prosecuted in adult courts and use of RICO statutes.

30. It is frequently argued that statistical prediction should not be used as a basis for criminal justice decision-making because of the false positives problem. In fact, nonstatistical assessment of dangerousness—the method preferred in most jurisdictions—has been found repeatedly to produce false positives at a *higher* rate than statistical assessments. See Monahan (1981); Steadman and Cocozza (1978); Meehl (1954).

The legitimacy of prediction as a basis for criminal justice decisions has been generally well established. Judges routinely base bail decisions on the perceived risk of defendant misbehavior prior to trial. The exercise of discretion by prosecutors in filing charges and in targeting cases involving dangerous offenders for special prosecution has not been subjected to challenge and reversal.

31. Interviews with 180 police officers who made arrests in New York City and Washington, D.C., revealed that none of the officers (nor their immediate supervisors) routinely received information about the court outcomes of their arrests. Forst, Leahy, et al. (1981).

Fortunately, there are signs of improvement on this front. A 1992 survey of prosecutors revealed that the rate at which prosecutors notify police and victims of the outcomes of their cases more than doubled from 1974 to 1990 (Bureau of Justice Statistics, 1992). Statutes aimed at improving prosecutors' treatment of victims have apparently had little impact. Here is the conclusion of a report of the Office of Victims of Crime (2000):

According to a study conducted by the Bureau of Justice Statistics in 1994, 86 percent of prosecutors offices nationwide were required by law to provide services to victims; 82 percent were required to notify victims of the disposition of felony cases concerning them; 60 percent were required to provide victim restitution assistance; and 58 percent were required to assist with victim compensation procedures. However, these legislative mandates have not been implemented by many prosecutors. For example, in a recent study sponsored by the

National Institute of Justice, nearly half of all violent crime victims were not informed of plea agreement negotiations, even where they had a legal right to be consulted.

32. Skogan has reported evidence of crime reduction effects of community policing in Chicago in more recent research. (Skogan and Hartnett).

33. Both counties are in the top ten in the United States in both income and wealth (Bredemeier).

34. In 1997, the homicide rate for Washington, D.C., was 57, and was 2.8 for Montgomery County and 1.8 for Fairfax County (*Uniform Crime Reports*).

35. Site visit with Mr. Gansler, April 10, 2000, and with Mr. Horan, July 6, 2000.

36. Cassell notes that the drafters of the Bill of Rights of the U.S. Constitution, schooled in English legal tradition, did not include rights for crime victims: "Special mention of victims' rights was unnecessary, because victims retained rights to act on their own as prosecutors" (Cassell, text at note 36).

37. See Rosen's interview with Susan Herman, director of the National Center for Victims of Crime, at p. 9.

References

Adams, Kenneth, and Charles Cutshall. 1987. "Refusing to Prosecute Minor Offenses: Relative Influence of Legal and Extralegal Factors." *Justice Quarterly* 4:595–607.

Adams, Lorraine. 2000. "$52 Million Starr Probe Costliest Ever." *Washington Post* (April 1), p. A2.

Allen-Hagen, Barbara. 1991. *Children in Custody, 1989*. Washington, D.C.: Office of Juvenile Justice and Delinquency Prevention.

Bailey, Walter C. 1966. "Correctional Outcome: An Evaluation of 100 Reports," *Journal of Criminal Law, Criminology, and Police Science* 57.

Bazemore, Gordon. 1998. "Restorative Justice and Earned Redemption: Communities, Victims, and Offender Reintegration." *The American Behavioral Scientist* 41:768–813.

Benson, Bruce L. 1998. *To Serve and Protect: Privatization and Community in Criminal Justice.* New York: New York University Press.

Blumstein, Alfred, Jacqueline Cohen, Susan E. Martin, and Michael H. Tonry, eds. 1983. *Research on Sentencing: The Search for Reform.* Washington, D.C.: National Academy Press.

Boland, Barbara. 1997. "Community Prosecution: The Manhattan Experiment," in *Crime and Place: Plenary Papers of the 1997 Conference on Criminal Justice Research and Evaluation.* Washington, D.C.: National Institute of Justice; also available in Bulletin NCJ-168618, pp. 51–67.

———. 1998. "Community Prosecution: The Portland Experiment," in *Community Justice*, ed. David Karp. Lanham, MD: Rowman and Littlefield, 1998.

———. 1999. *Community Prosecution in Washington, D.C.: The U.S. Attorney's Fifth District Pilot Project.* Washington, D.C.: National Institute of Justice; also available as Bulletin NCJ-181052 and at www.ncjrs.org/rr/vol12/13.html

Boland, Barbara, and Brian Forst. 1985. "Prosecutors Don't Always Aim to Please." *Federal Probation*, volume 49 (June): 11.

Boland, Barbara, Paul Mahanna, and Ronald Sones. 1992. *The Prosecution of Felony Arrests, 1988.* Washington, D.C.: Bureau of Justice Statistics.

Bredemeier, Kenneth. 2000. "Fairfax Grows More Affluent." *Washington Post* (June 10) pp. A1, A12.

Brosi, Kathleen. 1979. *A Cross-City Comparison of Felony Case Processing*. Washington, D.C.: Institute for Law and Social Research.

Brown, Jodi M., Patrick A. Langan, and David J. Levin. 1999. *Felony Sentences in State Courts, 1996*. Washington, D.C.: Bureau of Justice Statistics.

Bureau of Justice Statistics. 1988. *Survey of Youth in Custody, 1987*. Washington, D.C.: U.S. Department of Justice.

———. 1991. *Pretrial Release of Felony Defendants, 1988*. Washington, D.C.: U.S. Government Printing Office (February).

——— 1992. *Prosecutors in State Courts, 1990*. Washington, D.C.: U.S. Government Printing Office.

———. 2000. *Prisoners in State and Federal Institutions*. Washington, D.C.: U.S. Government Printing Office.

Cannavale, Jr., Frank J., and William D. Falcon. 1976 *Witness Cooperation*. Lexington, Mass.: D. C. Heath.

Cassell, Paul G. 1996. Statement on the Victims' Bill of Rights Amendment before the U.S. Senate Committee on the Judiciary (April 23).

Chaiken, Jan M., and Marcia R. Chaiken. 1982. *Varieties of Criminal Behavior*. Santa Monica, Calif.: Rand.

Chelimsky, Eleanor, and Judith Dahmann. 1981. *Career Criminal Program National Evaluation: Final Report*. Washington, D.C.: U.S. Department of Justice.

Chen, Elsa Y. 2000. *"Three Strikes and You're Out" and "Truth in Sentencing": Lessons in Policy Implementation and Inputs*, doctoral dissertation, UCLA.

Coles, Catherine M., and George L. Kelling. 1998. *Prosecution in the Community: A Study of Emergent Strategies—A Cross-Site Analysis*. Boston: Kennedy School of Government, Harvard University.

———. 1999 "Prevention Through Community Prosecution." *The Public Interest*, number 136 (Summer), pp. 69–84.

Davis, Kenneth Culp. 1969. *Discretionary Justice: A Preliminary Inquiry*. Baton Rouge: Louisiana State University Press.

DeFrances, Carol J., and Greg W. Steadman. 1998. *Prosecutors in State Courts, 1996*. Bureau of Justice Statistics, Department of Justice Bulletin NCJ-170092; www.ojp.usdoj.gov/bjs/pub/ascii/psc96.txt.

Department of Justice. 1996, 1999. *Youth Violence: A Community-Based Response—One City's Success Story*. Washington, D.C.; www.ncjrs.org/txtfiles/boston.txt.

Diamond, Shari S., and Hans Zeisel. 1975. "Sentencing Councils: A Study of Sentence Disparity and Its Reduction." *University of Chicago Law Review* 43.

Dougherty, Joyce. 1988. "A Comparison of Adult Plea Bargaining and Juvenile Intake." *Federal Probation* (June), pp. 72–79.

Epstein, Julian. 2000. "A Prosecution Too Far, Again." *Wall Street Journal* (July 14), p. A14.

Etzioni, Amitai. 1993. *The Spirit of Community: Rights, Responsibilities, and the Communitarian Agenda*. New York: Crown.

Federal Bureau of Investigation (FBI). 1971. *Uniform Crime Reports*. Washington, D.C.

———. 1993. *Uniform Crime Reports*. Washington, D.C.

———. 1997. *Uniform Crime Reports*. Washington, D.C.

Feeney, Floyd, Forrest Dill, and Adrianne Weir. 1983. *Arrests Without Conviction: How Often They Occur and Why*. Washington, D.C.: National Institute of Justice.

Ford, David A., and Mary Jean Regoli. 1993. *The Indianapolis Domestic Violence Prosecution Experiment*, final report to the National Institute of Justice, NCJ 157870 (October).

Forst, Brian. 1993. "The Prosecutor and the Public." In *The Socio-Economics of Crime and Justice.* Armonk, N.Y.: M. E. Sharpe.

――――. 1995. "Prosecution and Sentencing," In *Crime,* ed. James Q. Wilson and Joan Petersilia. San Francisco: ICS Press.

――――. 2001. "Toward an Understanding of the Effect of Changes in Standards of Proof on Errors in Justice," Forthcoming.

Forst, Martin L., and Martha-Elin Blomquist, 1992. "Punishment, Accountability, and the New Juvenile Justice," *Juvenile and Family Court Journal* 43.

Forst, Brian, and Barbara Boland. 1984. "The Prevalence of Guilty Pleas." *Bureau of Justice Statistics Special Report.* Washington, D.C. (December).

Forst, Brian, and Kathleen Brosi. 1977. "A Theoretical and Empirical Analysis of the Prosecutor." *Journal of Legal Studies* 6.

Forst, Brian, Frank Leahy, Jean Shirhall, Herbert Tyson, Eric Wish, and John Bartolomeo. 1981. *Arrest Convictability as a Measure of Police Performance.* Washington, D.C.: Institute for Law and Social Research.

Forst, Brian, and Judith Lucianovic. 1977. "The Prisoner's Dilemma: Theory and Reality." *Journal of Criminal Justice* 5 (Spring).

Forst, Brian, Judith Lucianovic, and Sarah Cox. 1977. *What Happens After Arrest?* Washington, D.C.: Institute for Law and Social Research.

Forst, Brian, and Peter K. Manning. 1999. *The Privatization of Policing: Two Views.* Washington, D.C.: Georgetown University Press.

Forst, Brian, William Rhodes, James Dimm, Arthur Gelman, and Barbara Mullin. 1982. *Targeting Federal Resources on Recidivists.* Washington, D.C.: INSLAW.

Forst, Brian, and Charles Wellford. 1981. "Punishment and Sentencing: Developing Sentencing Guidelines Empirically from Principles of Punishment," *Rutgers Law Review* 33.

Frankel, Marvin E. 1973. *Criminal Sentences: Law Without Order.* New York: Hill and Wang.

Greenwood, Peter W. 1982. *Selective Incapacitation.* Santa Monica, California: Rand.

Greenwood, Peter, Sorrel Wildhorn, E. Poggio, M. Strumsasser, and P. Deleon. 1976. *Prosecution of Adult Felony Defendants in Los Angeles County.* Santa Monica: Rand Corporation.

Hart, Timothy C., and Brian A. Reaves. 1999. *Felony Defendants in Large Urban Counties, 1996.* Washington, D.C.: Bureau of Justice Statistics.

Hillsman, Sally. 1982. "Pretrial Diversion of Youthful Adults: A Decade of Reform and Research." *The Justice System Journal* 7:361–87.

Hogarth, John. 1971. *Sentencing as a Human Process.* Toronto: University of Toronto Press.

Hotaling, Gerald T., and Murray A. Straus with Alan J. Lincoln. 1989. "Intrafamily Violence, and Crime and Violence Outside the Family." In *Family Violence,* ed. Lloyd Ohlin and Michael Tonry. Chicago: University of Chicago Press.

Jackson, Robert H. 1940. "The Federal Prosecutor." *Journal of the American Judicial Society* 24.

Jacoby, Joan E. 1981. *Prosecutorial Decisionmaking: A National Study.* Washington, D.C.: Bureau of Social Science Research.

Joint Committee on the New York Drug Laws. 1979. *The Nation's Toughest Drug Law: Evaluating the New York Experience.* Washington, D.C.: U.S. Government Printing Office.

Jost, Kenneth. 1999. "Plea Bargaining: Does the Widespread Practice Promote Justice?" *Congressional Quarterly Researcher* 9:113–36.

Kennedy, David M. 1999. "Boston Proves Something Can Be Done." *Washington Post Outlook* (May 23), p. B3.

Lipton, Douglas, Robert Martinson, and Judith Wilks. 1975. *The Effectiveness of Correctional Treatment.* New York: Praeger.

Loftin, Colin, Milton Heumann, and David McDowall. 1983. "Mandatory Sentencing and Firearm Violence." *Law and Society Review* 17.

McCoy, Candace 1993. *Politics and Plea Bargaining: Victims' Rights in California.* Philadelphia: University of Pennsylvania Press.

Macmillan, Ross. 2000. "Adolescent Victimization and Income Deficits in Adulthood: Rethinking the Costs of Criminal Violence from a Life-Course Perspective." *Criminology* 38 (May): 553–87.

Martinson, Robert. 1993. "What Works?—Questions and Answers About Prison Reform." *The Public Interest* 35 (Spring):22–54.

Meehl, Paul E. 1954. *Clinical vs. Statistical Prediction.* Minneapolis: University of Minnesota Press.

Monahan, John. 1981. *Predicting Violent Behavior: An Assessment of Clinical Techniques.* Beverly Hills, Calif.: Sage.

Nader, Ralph. 1965. *Unsafe at Any Speed.* New York: Grossman.

Office of Victims of Crime. 2000. *New Directions from the Field: Victims' Rights and Services for the 21st Century*, chapter 3, Prosecution. Washington, D.C.: U.S. Department of Justice; also available as Bulletin NCJ-172814,and at www.ojp.udoj.gov/ovc/new/directions/pdftxt /chap3.txt

Parent, Dale, V. Leiter, S. Kennedy, L. Livens, D. Wentworth, and S. Wilcox. 1994. *Conditions of Confinement: Juvenile Detention and Corrections Facilities.* Washington, D.C.: Office of Juvenile Justice and Delinquency Prevention.

Peters, Thomas J., and Robert H. Waterman. 1982. *In Search of Excellence: Lessons from America's Best-Run Companies.* New York: Harper and Row.

Petersilia, Joan, Allan Abrahamse, and James Q. Wilson. 1990a. "The Relationship Between Police Practice, Community Characteristics, and Case Attrition." *Policing and Society* 1:23–38.

Petersilia, Joan, Allan Abrahamse, and James Q. Wilson. 1990b. *Police Performance and Case Attrition.* Santa Monica: Rand Corporation.

Reiss, Jr., Albert J. 1974. "Discretionary Justice in the United States." *International Journal of Criminology and Penology* 2.

Rhodes, William. 1985. *Pretrial Release and Misconduct.* Washington, D.C.: Bureau of Justice Statistics.

Rosen, Marie Simonetti. 1999. "LEN Interview with Susan Herman," *Law Enforcement News*, vol. 25, No. 522 (November 30), pp. 8–11.

Rubinstein, Michael L., and Teresa J. White. 1979. "Alaska's Ban on Plea Bargaining." *Law and Society Review* 13.

Samuelson, Robert J. 2000 "The New Pork Barrel." *Washington Post* (June 28), p. A25.

Sherman, Lawrence W., Denise C. Gottfredson, Doris L. MacKenzie, John Eck, Peter Reuter, and Shawn D. Bushway. 1998. *Preventing Crime: What Works, What Doesn't, What's Promising.* Washington, D.C.: National Institute of Justice.

Skogan, Wesley. 1990. *Disorder and Decline: Crime and the Spiral of Decay in American Neighborhoods* New York: Free Press.

Skogan, Wesley, and Susan Hartnett, 1997. "Community Policing, Chicago Style." New York: Oxford University Press.

Snyder, Howard, Terrence A. Finnegan, Ellen Nimick, Melissa Sickmund, Dennis Sullivan, and Nancy Tierney. 1987. *Juvenile Court Statistics, 1984.* Pittsburgh: National Center of Juvenile Justice.

Solari, Richard. 1992. *National Judicial Reporting Program, 1988.* Washington, D.C.: Bureau of Justice Statistics.

Steadman, Henry J., and Joseph Cocozza. 1978. "Psychiatry, Dangerousness and the Repetitively Violent Offender." *Journal of Criminal Law and Criminology* Volume 69:226–31.

Stevens, Norma Mancini. 1994. "Defining Community Prosecution." *The Prosecutor* 28 (March/April):13–14.

Szanton, Peter L. 1972. *Public Policy, Public Good, and the Law.* Washington, D.C.: Rand Corporation.

Toborg, Mary. 1982. *Pretrial Release: A National Evaluation of Practices and Outcomes.* Washington, D.C.: National Institute of Justice.

United States Bureau of the Census. 1998. *Statistical Abstract of the United States.* Washington, D.C.

United States Department of Justice. 1977. *Justice Litigation Management.* Washington, D.C.: U.S. Government Printing Office.

United States Senate. 1983. Hearings before the Subcommittee on Criminal Law of the Committee on the Judiciary, First Session on S.829 (Comprehensive Crime Control Act of 1983), 23 May 1983. Serial No. J-98-37.

U.S. Sentencing Commission. 1991. *Special Report to the Congress: Mandatory Minimum Penalties in the Federal Criminal Justice System.* Washington, D.C.: U.S. Sentencing Commission.

Van Ness, Daniel W., and Karen H. Strong. 1997. *Restoring Justice.* Cincinnati, Ohio.

Vera Institute of Justice. Anderson. 1977. *Felony Arrests: Their Prosecution and Disposition in New York City's Courts.* New York: Vera Institute of Justice.

Williams, Kristen M. 1979. *The Scope and Prediction of Recidivism.* Washington, D.C.: Institute for Law and Social Research.

Will, George F. 1994. "Fangs of the Independent Counsel." *The Washington Post* (January 7), p. A19.

Wolfgang, Marvin E., Robert M. Figlio, and Thorstein Sellin. 1972. *Delinquency in a Birth Cohort.* Chicago: University of Chicago Press.

CHAPTER 19
James Q. Wilson
CRIME AND PUBLIC POLICY

References

Anglin, M. Douglas, and Yih-Ing Hser. 1990. "Treatment of Drug Abuse." In *Drugs and Crime*, ed. Michael Tonry and James Q. Wilson, 393–460. *Crime and Justice: A Review of Research*, vol. 13. Chicago: University of Chicago Press.

Ayres, Ian, and John Donohue. 1999. "Nondiscretionary Concealed Weapons Laws." *American Law and Economics Review* 1:436–70.

Braun. 2001.

Chaiken, Jan, and Marcia Chaiken. 1982. *Varieties of Criminal Behavior.* Santa Monica, Calif.: RAND.

Chen, Elsa Y. 1998. Estimating the Impacts of Three Strikes and You're Out and Truth in Sentencing on Crime and Corrections. Paper presented to Midwestern Political Science Association.

————. 2000. Three Strikes and Truth in Sentencing. Ph.D. diss., Department of Political Science, UCLA.

DiIulio, John J., and Anne Piehl. 1991. "Does Prison Pay?" *Brookings Review* 28–35.

Duggan, Mark. 2000. "More Guns, More Crime." NBER Working Paper 7967. Cambridge, Mass.: National Bureau of Economic Research.

Elliott. 1998.

Farrington, David P., and Patrick A. Langan. 1992. "Changes in Crime and Punishment in England and America in the 1980s." *Justice Quarterly* 9:5–46.

Farrington, David P., and Per-Olof Wikstrom. 1993. "Changes in Crime and Punishment in England and Sweden in the 1980s." In *Studies in Crime and Crime Prevention*, vol. 2, 142–70.

Greenwood, Peter, C. Peter Rydell, Allan F. Abrahamse, Nathan P. Caulkins, James Chiesa, Karyn E. Model, and S. P. Klein. 1994. "Three Strikes and You're Out: Estimated Benefits and Costs of California's New Mandatory Sentencing Law." Santa Monica, Calif.: RAND.

Lott, John R. 2000. *More Guns, Less Crime*, 2d ed. Chicago: University of Chicago Press.

Mehay, Stephen, and Rosalie Liccardo Pacula. 2000. "The Effectiveness of Workplace Drug Prevention Programs: Does 'Zero Tolerance' Work?" NBER Working Paper 7383. Cambridge, Mass.: National Bureau of Economic Research.

Monkkonen, Eric. 2001. *Murder in New York City*. Berkeley: University of California Press.

Satel, Sally. 1999. *Drug Treatment: The Case for Coercion*. Washington, D.C.: AEI Press.

Spelman, William. 1994. *Criminal Incapacitation*. New York: Plenum.

————. 2000. "The Limited Importance of Prison Expansion." In *The Crime Drop in America*, ed. Alfred Blumstein and Joel Wallman. New York: Cambridge University Press.

Wilson, James Q. 1983. *Thinking About Crime*, rev. ed. New York: Basic Books.

Wright, James, and Peter H. Rossi. 1986. *Armed and Dangerous: A Survey of Felons*. New York: Aldine de Gruyter.

Zimring, Franklin E., and Gordon Hawkins. 1997. *Crime Is Not the Problem: Lethal Violence in America*. New York: Oxford University Press.

Contributors

ALFRED BLUMSTEIN is the J. Erik Jonsson University Professor and former Dean at the H. John Heinz III School of Public Policy and Management of Carnegie Mellon University. He served the President's Crime Commission in 1966–67 as Director of its Task Force on Science and Technology. He has chaired NAS panels on deterrence and incapacitation, on sentencing, and on criminal careers. On the policy side, he served from 1979 to 1990 as Chairman of the Pennsylvania Commission on Crime and Delinquency, the state's criminal justice planning agency. He was the 1987 recipient of the ASC's Sutherland Award for "contributions to research," and was the president of the Society in 1991–92. His research has covered many aspects of criminal-justice phenomena and policy, including crime measurement, criminal careers, sentencing, deterrence and incapacitation, prison populations, demographic trends, juvenile violence, and drug-enforcement policy.

DAVID A. BOYUM is a policy and management consultant living and working in New York City. He has taught public policy analysis at Harvard's John F. Kennedy School of Government, where he received his Ph.D. in Public Policy.

ANTHONY A. BRAGA is a Senior Research Associate in the Program in Criminal Justice Policy and Management of the Malcolm Wiener Center for Social Policy at Harvard University's John F. Kennedy School of Government, and a Visiting Fellow at the National Institute of Justice, U.S. Department of Justice. His research focuses on developing crime prevention strategies to disrupt drug markets, control crime hot spots, and reduce firearms violence. He received his Ph.D. in Criminal Justice from Rutgers University.

SHAWN D. BUSHWAY is an Assistant Professor of Criminology in the Department of Criminology and Criminal Justice at the University of Maryland and a Fellow with the National Consortium of Violence Research. His primary research interests include studying the impact of arrest and criminal activity on labor market outcomes, the impact of work on the process of desistance, and racial discrimination in sentencing outcomes.

PHILIP J. COOK is the ITT/Terry Sanford Professor of Public Policy at Duke University. His recent books include *Gun Violence: The Real Costs* (Oxford University Press, 2000), coauthored with Jens Ludwig; *The Winner-Take-All Society* with Robert H. Frank (The Free Press, 1995); and *Selling Hope: State Lotteries in America* with Charles T. Clotfelter (Harvard University Press, 1989).

FRANCIS T. CULLEN is Distinguished Research Professor of Criminal Justice and Sociology at the University of Cincinnati. He has recently coauthored *Combating Corporate Crime: Local Prosecutors at Work* and *Criminological Theory: Context and Consequences*. His current research interests include the impact of social support on crime, the measurement of sexual victimization, and rehabilitation as a correctional policy.

661

DAVID P. FARRINGTON is Professor of Psychological Criminology at Cambridge University. He is a past President of the American Society of Criminology, the British Society of Criminology, and the European Association of Psychology and Law. His main research interest is in the development of offending and antisocial behavior from childhood to adulthood.

BRIAN FORST is Professor of Justice, Law & Society at the American University's School of Public Affairs. He was research director at the Institute for Law and Social Research (1974–85) and at the Police Foundation (1985–89). His research specialties include policing, prosecution, and sentencing. He coauthored "The Privatization of Policing" (Georgetown Press) with Peter Manning in 1999, and is currently writing a book on errors of justice.

DENISE C. GOTTFREDSON is a Professor at the University of Maryland Department of Criminology and Criminal Justice. Her research interests include delinquency and delinquency prevention, and particularly the effects of school environments on youth behavior. She is the author of *Schools and Delinquency* (2001) and co-author of *Victimization in Schools* (1985) and *Closing Institutions for Juvenile Offenders: The Maryland Experience* (1997).

PETER W. GREENWOOD is the President and CEO of Greenwood & Associates and the former Director of RAND's Criminal Justice Program. He has published widely in the areas of violence prevention, juvenile justice, criminal careers, sentencing, corrections, and law enforcement policy. He and his RAND colleagues have recently published several studies comparing the costs and benefits of alternative violence prevention strategies, and he is currently directing several evaluations of prevention programs for high-risk youth. In 1998 Dr. Greenwood was recognized by the American Society of Criminology for his contributions to the field of practice with the August Vollmer Award. He is also a member of the Homicide Research Working Group and is a past president of the California Association of Criminal Justice Research. He has served on the faculties of the University of Southern California, The RAND Graduate School, the Claremont Graduate School, and on the California Attorney General's Panel on Research and Statistics. He is a graduate of the U.S. Naval Academy and holds M.S. and Ph.D. degrees from Stanford University in Industrial Engineering.

MARK A. R. KLEIMAN is Professor of Policy Studies and Director of the Drug Policy Analysis Program at the UCLA School of Public Policy and Social Research. He is Chairman of BOTEC Analysis Corporation and co-chairs the drug policy project of the Federation of American Scientists. He edits the *Drug Policy Analysis Bulletin*. His books include *Against Excess: Drug Policy for Results*.

STEVEN D. LEVITT is Professor in the University of Chicago Department of Economics. He has published widely on the subject of crime and criminal justice.

JAMES P. LYNCH is a Professor in the Department of Justice, Law and Society at American University. He has co-authored *Understanding Crime Incidence Statistics* with Albert Biderman and written numerous articles on cross-national comparisons of crime and punishment. He is currently examining the role of incarceration in social control.

MARK H. MOORE is the Director of the Hauser Center for Nonprofit Organizations and the Faculty Chairman of the Kennedy School of Government's Program in Criminal Justice Policy and Management. He is also the Guggenheim Professor of Criminal Justice Policy and Management at the Kennedy School. He was the Founding Chairman of the School's Committee on Executive Programs, and served in that role for over a decade. His research interests are in public management and leadership; in civil society and community mobilization, in criminal justice policy and management; and in the intersection of the three domains. In the area of public management, he has recently published *Creating Public Value: Strategic Management in Government*. He has also written (with others) *Public Duties: The Moral Obligations of Public Officials*; *Ethics in Government: The Moral Challenges of Public Leadership*; and *Inspectors General: Junkyard Dogs or Man's Best Friend*. In the area of criminal justice policy, he has written *Buy and Bust: The Effective Regulation of an Illicit Market in Heroin* and *Dangerous Offenders: The Elusive Targets of Justice*. In the intersection of public management and criminal justice, he has written (with others) *From Children to Citizens: The Mandate for Juvenile Justice*; and *Beyond 911: A New Era for Policing*. His work in public management and criminal justice has focused on the ways in which leaders of public organizations can engage communities in supporting and legitimating the work of the public organizations; and in the role that value commitments play in enabling leadership in public sector enterprises. It is these strands that link his past work to his future challenge, learning about nonprofit enterprises.

STACY SKROBAN NAJAKA, Ph.D. is a Faculty Research Associate in the Department of Criminology and Criminal Justice at the University of Maryland, College Park. Her research interests include crime and delinquency prevention, program evaluation, and research methods. Currently, she is managing a three-year, follow-up study of the Baltimore City Drug Treatment Court.

JOAN PETERSILIA, Ph.D., is a Professor of Criminology, Law and Society in the School of Social Ecology, University of California, Irvine. Prior to joining UCI, she was the Director of the Criminal Justice Program at RAND. She has directed major studies in policing, sentencing, career criminals, parole, juvenile justice, corrections, and racial discrimination. Dr. Petersilia's current work focuses on probation, parole, intermediate sanctions, and prisoner re-entry. Dr. Petersilia has served as president of both the American Society of Criminology and of the Association of Criminal Justice Research in California. She is an elected fellow of the American Society of Criminology, and received its Vollmer Award for her contributions to the areas of crime and public policy. She is currently the Vice-Chair of the National Research Council's Law and Justice Committee. Her most recent books are *Reforming Probation and Parole* (2002), *Crime Victims with Developmental Disabilities* (2001), *Prisons: A Review of Research* (1999), *Criminal Justice Policy* (1998), *Community Corrections* (1998), and *Crime* (1995).

ADRIAN RAINE, D.Phil., is the Robert Grandford Wright Professor of Psychology at the University of Southern California. He previously spent four years as a prison psychologist in England and has spent the past 25 years researching the biosocial bases of antisocial and violent behavior. He is Director of the Mauritius Child Health Project, a biosocial longitudinal study of antisocial behavior.

PETER REUTER is a Professor in the School of Public Affairs and the Department of Criminology at the University of Maryland. Prior to joining the University of Maryland in 1993 he founded and directed RAND's Drug Policy Research Center. Since 1999 he has been editor of the *Journal of Policy Analysis and Management*. He is the co-author (with Robert MacCoun) of *Drug War Heresies: Learning from Other Vices, Times and Places* (Cambridge University Press, 2001).

ROBERT J. SAMPSON is the Lucy Flower Professor in Sociology at the University of Chicago, Senior Research Fellow at the American Bar Foundation, and Scientific Director of the

Project on Human Development in Chicago Neighborhoods. His major research interests include criminology, the life course, and urban sociology.

LAWRENCE W. SHERMAN is Greenfield Professor of Human Relations and Director of the Lee Center of Criminology at the University of Pennsylvania, where he is directing experiments in restorative justice and policing in England and Australia. He currently serves as President of the American Society of Criminology, of the International Society of Criminology, and of the American Academy of Political and Social Science.

RALPH B. TAYLOR received his Ph.D. in social psychology at Johns Hopkins University in 1977. He has held positions at Virginia Tech (1977–1979), Johns Hopkins University (1978–1985), and is currently professor of Criminal Justice at Temple University where he has been since 1984. He is the editor of *Urban Neighborhoods* (Praeger, 1986), and the author of *Human Territorial Functioning* (Cambridge, 1988), *Research Methods in Criminal Justice* (McGraw Hill, 1994), and the recently released *Breaking Away From Broken Windows: Evidence from Baltimore Neighborhoods and the Nationwide Fight Against Crime, Grime, Fear and Decline* (Westview).

PATRICK TOLAN, Ph.D., is Director, Institute for Juvenile Research, and Professor in Psychiatry, University of Illinois, Chicago. He is an internationally recognized authority on violence, families, and prevention research and policy. He is author/coauthor of more than 90 publications. He is a regular consultant to the several federal and state agencies and private foundations. He is Principal Investigator on three federal grants and co-investigator on three others. He is Chair, American Psychological Association's Committee on Children, Youth, and Families, and Board Member of the Blueprints for Youth Violence Prevention.

DAVID B. WILSON is a Jerry Lee Assistant Research Professor in the Department of Criminology and Criminal Justice at the University of Maryland, College Park. He received his Ph.D. in Applied Social Psychology from Claremont Graduate University. His research interests include program evaluation research methodology, meta-analysis, crime and general problem behavior prevention programs, and juvenile delinquency intervention effectiveness.

JAMES Q. WILSON was the Henry Lee Shattuck Professor of Government at Harvard until 1987 and the James Collins Professor of Management at UCLA from 1985 until 1997. He now lectures at Pepperdine University. He is the author of *Thinking About Crime*, and with Richard J. Herrnstein of *Crime and Human Nature*. His most recent books are *The Moral Sense, Moral Judgement*, and *The Marriage Problem*.

Index

ABOUT ICS

Founded in 1974, the Institute for Contemporary Studies (ICS) is a nonprofit, nonpartisan policy research institute.

To fulfill its mission to promote self-governing and entrepreneurial ways of life, ICS sponsors a variety of programs and publications on key issues including education, entrepreneurship, the environment, leadership, and social policy.

Through its imprint, ICS Press, the Institute publishes innovative and readable books that will further the understanding of these issues among scholars, policy makers, and the wider community of citizens. ICS Press books include the writing of eight Nobel laureates and influence the setting of the nation's policy agenda.

ICS programs seek to encourage the entrepreneurial spirit not only in this country but also around the world. They include the Institute for Self-Governance (ISG) and the International Center for Self-Governance (ICSG).